HANDBOOK OF PEDIATRIC NUTRITION

Edited by

Patricia M. Queen, MMSc, RD
Director
Department of Dietetics
Deaconess Hospital
Boston, Massachusetts

Carol E. Lang, MS, RD
Public Health Nutritionist
Washington, DC
Formerly, Director of Dietetics
Deaconess Hospital
Boston, Massachusetts

AN ASPEN PUBLICATION®
Aspen Publishers, Inc.
Gaithersburg, Maryland
1993

Library of Congress Cataloging-in-Publication Data

Handbook of pediatric nutrition / [edited by] Patricia M. Queen, Carol E. Lang.
p.   cm.
Includes bibliographical references and index.
ISBN 0-8342-0290-5
1. Children—Nutrition—Handbooks, manuals, etc. 2. Infants—
Nutrition—Handbooks, manuals, etc. 3. Children—Diseases—
Nutritional aspects—Handbooks, manuals, etc.
I. Queen, Patricia M. II. Lang, Carol E.
[DNLM: 1. Child Nutrition—handbooks. 2. Diet Therapy—in infancy
& childhood—handbooks. 3. Infant Nutrition—handbooks.
4. Nutrition Disorders—complications—handbooks. 5. Nutrition Disorders—in infancy &
childhood—handbooks. WS 39 H2363]
RJ206.H23   1992
618.92—dc20
DNLM/DLC
for Library of Congress
92-21928
CIP

Aspen Publishers, Inc., is not affiliated with the American Society of Parenteral and Enteral Nutrition

The editors have made every effort to ensure the accuracy of the information herein, particularly with regard to product selection, drug selection and dose. However, appropriate information sources should be consulted, especially for new or unfamiliar drugs or procedures. It is the responsibility of every practitioner to evaluate the appropriateness of a particular opinion in the context of actual clinical situations and with due consideration to new developments. The editors acknowledge the mention of specific products as examples of products in current clinical practice; however, this should not be construed as endorsements of the products. The editors and the publisher cannot be held responsible for any typographical or other errors found in this book.

Editorial Resources: Ruth Bloom

Library of Congress Catalog Card Number: 92-21928
ISBN: 0-8342-0290-5

Printed in the United States of America

1   2   3   4   5

This book,
with reverence,
is dedicated to all children.
May they never know hunger.
And this book is also dedicated
to the caregivers who nourish them.

Table of Contents

Contributors

Editors

Patricia M. Queen, MMSc, RD
Director
Department of Dietetics
Deaconess Hospital
Boston, Massachusetts

Carol E. Lang, MS, RD
Public Health Nutritionist
Washington, DC
Formerly, Director of Dietetics
Deaconess Hospital
Boston, Massachusetts

Contributors

Phyllis B. Acosta, PhD, RD
Director
Metabolic Diseases
Ross Laboratories
Columbus, Ohio

Diane M. Anderson, MS, RD
Assistant Professor of Pediatrics
Children's Hospital
Medical University of South Carolina
Charleston, South Carolina

Karen Antonelli, MPH, RD, LD
Clinical Manager, Dietary Services
The Mt. Sinai Medical Center
Cleveland, Ohio

Karen V. Barale, MS, RD, CD
Research Dietitian
Department of Clinical Nutrition
Fred Hutchinson Cancer Research Center
Seattle, Washington

Linda J. Boyne, MS, RD, LD
Assistant Professor
Division of Medical Dietetics
Department of Pediatrics
The Ohio State University
Columbus, Ohio

Andrea Bull-McDonough, MS, RD, LD
Nutrition Consultant
Private Practice
Baltimore, Maryland

Mariel Caldwell, MPH, MS, RD
Regional Nutrition Consultant
Department of Maternal and Child
  Health
U.S. Public Health Service
Region V
Chicago, Illinois

Wm. Cameron Chumlea, PhD
Fels Professor
Department of Community Health and
  Department of Pediatrics
Wright State University
School of Medicine
Dayton, Ohio

Harriet H. Cloud, MS, RD
Professor of Nutrition
Civitan International Research Center
Sparks Clinics
University of Alabama at Birmingham
Birmingham, Alabama

Susan W. Cooning, RN, MS
Director
Medical-Surgical Services
Primary Children's Hospital
Salt Lake City, Utah

Janice Hovasi Cox, MS, RD
Neonatal and Pediatric Nutritionist
Bronson Methodist Hospital
Kalamazoo, Michigan

Ruth W. Crocker, PhD, RD
Consultant Dietitian
Private Practice
Mystic, Connecticut

Johanna T. Dwyer, DSc, RD
Professor of Medicine and Community
  Health
Tufts University Medical School and
  School of Nutrition
Director
Frances Stern Nutrition Center
New England Medical Center Hospital
Boston, Massachusetts

Sylvia Evans, MS, RD
Clinical Dietitian Specialist
The Department of Nutrition and Food
  Service
Children's Hospital
Boston, Massachusetts

Linda M. Gallagher, RD
Quality Improvement/Education
  Coordinator
The Department of Nutrition and Food
  Service
Children's Hospital
Boston, Massachusetts

Michele M. Gottschlich, PhD, RD, CNSD
Director
Nutrition Services
Shriners Burns Institute
Cincinnati, Ohio
and
Assistant Professor
Department of Health and Nutrition
  Sciences
University of Cincinnati
Cincinnati, Ohio

Richard J. Grand, MD
Chief
Division of Pediatric Gastroenterology
  and Nutrition
New England Medical Center Hospitals
Professor of Pediatrics
Tufts University School of Medicine
Boston, Massachusetts

Sharon L. Groh-Wargo, RD, LD, MS
Senior Nutritionist
Department of Pediatrics
MetroHealth Medical Center
Cleveland, Ohio

Leo A. Heitlinger, MD
Assistant Professor
Division of Pediatrics
The Ohio State University
Columbus Children's Hospital
Columbus, Ohio

Susan Krug-Wispé, MS, RD, LD
Pediatric Nutritionist
Department of Pediatrics
University of Cincinnati Medical Center
Cincinnati, Ohio

Lyllis Ling, MS, RD, CDE
Director
Department of Nutrition Services
The Children's Mercy Hospital
Kansas City, Missouri

Catherine Detamore Lingard, MS, RD
Clinical Nutrition Specialist
Department of Nutrition
The Children's Mercy Hospital
Kansas City, Missouri

Betty Lucas, MPH, RD, CD
Nutritionist
Child Development Mental Retardation
   Center
University of Washington
Seattle, Washington

Joyce Mosiman, RD, CDE
Clinical Dietitian
Program Coordinator
Children's Diabetes Center
The Children's Mercy Hospital
Kansas City, Missouri

Nancy L. Nevin-Folino, MEd, RD
Clinical Pediatric Dietitian
The Children's Medical Center
Dayton, Ohio

Victoria L. Olejer, MS, RD
Enteral Nutritional Sales Representative
Mead-Johnson Enteral Nutritionals
San Antonio, Texas

Karen E. Peterson, DSc, RD
Assistant Professor of Nutrition
Department of Maternal and Child
   Health
Harvard School of Public Health
Boston, Massachusetts

Mary E. Smaha, MBA, RD
Clinical Nutrition Manager
The Department of Nutrition and Food
   Service
Children's Hospital
Boston, Massachusetts

Nancy S. Spinozzi, RD
Renal Dietitian
Children's Hospital
Boston, Massachusetts

Nancy H. Wooldridge, MS, RD
Clinical Nutrition Division
Department of Nutritional Science
University of Alabama at Birmingham
Birmingham, Alabama

Foreword

The field of pediatrics encompasses an ever expanding discipline whose scientific basis is growth and development. Indeed, no other branch of clinical medicine presents as many challenges as the care of the young, and no other specialty deals with such rapid changes in human biology. The successful progression from intrauterine to extrauterine life, and subsequent advances from infancy to childhood to adolescence and beyond, all depend upon optimal nutrition. Indeed, altered nutritional status is one of the greatest risks for the developing human organism.

Pediatric nutrition has come of age. The last two decades have witnessed an explosion in knowledge of pediatric nutrition. We have been able to define the clinical disorders associated with altered nutrition; methods have been developed which will allow more accurate measurement of nutritional status, body composition, and energy expenditure; therapeutic strategies have been established for many disorders of nutrition; and we have begun to apply our newly acquired knowledge to reverse the negative impact of chronic disease on nutritional status. Furthermore, we are beginning to elucidate the complex interactions between the nervous system, gastrointestinal hormones, the immune system, and food intake; and we are able to investigate the regulation of appetite—the central control mechanism for optimal nutrition. Some of the remaining challenges are to establish goals for the education of health care providers and consumers relating to optimal nutrition, to establish guidelines for coordinated care of patients with nutritional disorders, and to set standards for preventive measures aimed at reducing the prevalence of diseases such as diabetes, hypertension, and obesity.

This volume is focused on the clinical aspects of the nutritional care of the young. While directed mainly at nutritionists/dietitians, it is appropriate as well for the general pediatrician and other health care providers requiring detailed nutritional care plans. It will also serve well as an initial exposure to clinical pediatric nutrition for medical, nursing, and nutrition students. It is timely and appropriate, providing up to date information in easily used figures, tables, and text. At a time when the lay public is exposed to much misinformation about nutrition, it is vital for nutrition and other pediatric health care providers to have timely references at hand. This book provides such an excellent resource.

Richard J. Grand, MD
Chief
Division of Pediatric Gastroenterology
and Nutrition
New England Medical Center Hospitals
Professor of Pediatrics
Tufts University School of Medicine
Boston, Massachusetts

Preface

The purpose of the *Handbook of Pediatric Nutrition* is to provide a clinical reference manual on pediatric nutrition for the practitioner. The intent is to provide practical information required for optimal nutritional care to infants and children.

The handbook was designed to be used primarily by dietitians in pediatric practice but may also serve as a valuable resource for pediatricians, pediatric nurses, as well as other pediatric health care providers. It contains a detailed overview of normal growth and nutrition needs from birth to adolescence. It also addresses unique nutritional needs and management issues in a myriad of pediatric diseases and conditions.

The book is divided into two parts. The first part addresses pediatric nutrition issues of normal healthy infants and children. The second part addresses diseases or conditions and their nutritional implications. The authors for each chapter were selected because of their expertise in particular areas of pediatric nutrition practice.

Part one, on normal nutrition, provides core nutrition knowledge required for the dietitian or other health care provider working with infants and children. The first chapter contains an overview on normal growth and development. The second chapter on nutrition assessment contains information in tabular and chart form, along with practical suggestions, to facilitate completion of an in-depth pediatric nutritional assessment. Chapter 3 contains nutritional information about unique nutritional issues pertaining to the needs of premature infants, while Chapters 4 and 5 provide tips on dietary management for normal infants and children through adolescence. The next four chapters cover aspects of vegetarian diets, sports nutrition, food hypersensitivities, and community nutrition resources, as they pertain to the pediatric population.

The second part of the *Handbook of Pediatric Nutrition* serves as a resource on therapeutic pediatric nutrition. Chapters 10 and 11 include practical guidance on enteral and parenteral nutrition. This is followed by Chapter 12 focusing on the complexities of providing adequate nutrition to infants and children with inborn errors of metabolism and Chapter 13 involving the management of infants and children with failure to thrive. The needs of pediatric patients with AIDS are given detailed review in Chapter 14. Chapter 15 focuses on the challenge of meeting the nutrition needs of individuals with developmental disabilities. Meeting the nutritional requirements of infants and children with cystic fibrosis and bronchopulmonary dysplasia is highlighted in Chapter 16, while Chapter 17 deals with such gastrointestinal disorders as Crohn's disease, liver transplantation, and short bowel syndrome. Chapter 18 is devoted to renal disease, and Chapter 19 concerns the lifelong nutrition management of the child with diabetes mellitus. Nutritional needs of individuals with cancer and the nutritional impact of treatments, such as bone marrow transplant, are identified in Chapter 20. Nutritional management of the patient with major burns and the challenges of meeting fluid and nutritional needs during this stressed period is presented in a comprehensive manner in Chapter 21. Chapters 22 and 23 provide insight and assistance on the management of childhood obesity and eating disorders.

Expressed in these chapters are state-of-the-art principles of pediatric nutrition practice. These principles, the rationale on which they are based, and pragmatic suggestions for implementation, are the invaluable contribution of this book's contributors whose years of training and clinical experience have been the investment of these skilled professionals. They, and the editors, hope you will reap rich dividends from this book, their investment, and re-invest these riches by providing optimal nutrition support for every infant and child in your care.

Patricia M. Queen
Carol F. Lang

Acknowledgments

We wish to thank:

All of our authors for their dedication and patience, and our families for their encouragement and love. Patt would like to thank her husband, Charles E. Samour and her parents, Lillian and J. Emmett Queen, and Carol would like to thank her children, John Paul and Sara Catherine Elizabeth Lang.

We also want to remember the dynamic impact of Glenda Bible, RD, formerly of The Children's Hospital Medical Center, Dayton, Ohio on pediatric nutrition. Glenda served tirelessly as an advocate of optimal nourishment of infants and children.

Part I

Normal Pediatric Nutrition and Growth

Chapter 1

Growth and Development

Wm. Cameron Chumlea

PERIODS OF GROWTH

The growth and maturation of a child can be divided into four periods: infancy, from birth to 1 year of age; the preschool years, from 2 to 6 years of age; the middle childhood years, from 7 to 10 years of age; and adolescence, from about 11 to 18 years of age. During infancy there is a large amount of growth as a child changes from a helpless baby to a very active and real person. In the second two periods, most normal healthy children grow at a rather steady pace. With adolescence and the onset of puberty, there is a final growth spurt as a child's body matures into that of an adult. At any time, the size of a healthy child will reflect his or her own genetic growth potential, which is some combination of that of the parents. Stature has a strongly genetic component, and it is easily recognized that tall parents have tall children and short parents have short children. However, the size of a child at a given age is also related to his or her level of maturity. Early-maturing children are taller and heavier than slow-maturing children, but the latter generally finish as the taller adults.

Infancy

During the first few weeks after birth, an infant adjusts to life on the outside. Numerous physiologic changes occur at birth or shortly thereafter to sustain this new life. For example, the lungs start to function, and the stomach and intestines have to process and digest the external food the infant now receives. The very rapid growth that occurred in utero almost stops just before birth, and many full-term infants will lose some weight shortly after birth. If all goes well, by 8 to 10 days after birth these same infants have regained their birth weight and are growing again.

Note: This work was supported by the National Institutes of Health, Bethesda, Maryland, through grant HD-12252.

Infancy is a period of rapid growth in body size. Body dimensions increase at a greater rate than at any other time in postnatal life. In the first year of life weight increases 200%, body length 55%, and head circumference 40%. Similar changes occur in the length and breadth of the trunk and the arms and legs. At 2 months of age, an infant is growing at an average rate of between 36 to 40 cm per year. In 2 years, a child would be about 152 cm tall if this rate were maintained. By 11 months of age, however, the rate of growth has decreased to about 15 cm a year. Similar increases and changes occur in weight. Most normal infants double their birth weight by 5 months of age and triple it by the age of 1 year. In as short a time as a week the size and appearance of an infant can change noticeably, due to this rapid growth.

Compared to the size of the body, an infant's head is disproportionately large at birth. The diameter of the skull is greater than that of the chest, and the length of the head is about a quarter of the body's total length. At birth, head circumference is about 35 cm and increases about 12 cm during the first year to a value of about 47 cm on the average. The measurement of head circumference is important because it reflects brain growth, and the brain doubles its birth weight by 1 year of age. Obviously, faltering growth in head circumference could have serious implications for neural growth and maturation, or it could be diagnostic for possible problems of brain growth.

Preschool

A child's growth during the preschool years is characterized by a continued, steady increase in body size. The body's rate of growth slows from its high rate in infancy and stabilizes at a roughly constant rate by about 5 years of age. Between the ages of 1 and 2 years, an average child grows about 12 cm in stature and gains about 3.5 kg in weight. By the age of 4 years, the average annual increase in stature is down to about 6 to 8 cm per year and in weight, to an increase of about 2 to 4 kg per year. Sex differences in stature and weight during early childhood are slight, but the pattern of more adipose tissue in girls than boys appears in the values of mean skinfold measurements after the age of 2 years. These mean differences in adipose tissue thickness are distinct by 6 years of age.

Head circumference continues to be an important measure of growth during this period. From 1 to 2 years of age the head grows about 5 cm in circumference, but by age 3 the mean annual increase is down to less than a centimeter (Figure 1-1). The brain more than triples its birth weight by 6 years of age. Repeated measurements of head circumference are important during the first part of this period because a child with abnormal growth may have abnormal brain growth also. This is the period of the most rapid postnatal growth of the brain, and the occurrence of adverse conditions will have the greatest effect on brain growth.

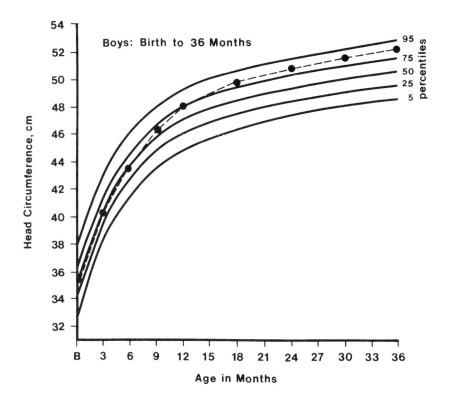

Figure 1-1 The head circumference of a boy from birth to 36 months of age plotted on NCHS percentiles. *Source:* Hamill PVV et al, *NCHS Growth Curves for Children Birth–18 Years*, USPHS, Pub No 165, 1977.

Middle Childhood

Middle childhood can be characterized as a period of continued steady growth in body size for most children. Boys and girls grow about 5 to 6 cm per year in stature. Growth in weight of boys and girls is about 2 kg at age 7 years but increases to an average rate of about 4 kg around age 10 years. For both stature and weight, the average girl grows slightly more per year than the average boy. This difference in growth rate contributes in part to the earlier appearance of significant sex differences in physical characteristics of girls at the onset of adolescence. At 7 years of age boys are, on the average, about 2 cm taller than girls the same age, but there is little difference in weight. By 10 years of age the average girl is about 1 cm taller than the average boy and about 1 kg heavier. These sex differences in overall body size become larger after 10 years of age because girls reach puberty before boys. Sex differences in other body areas also appear during this period. A particular difference is seen in the thickness of adipose tissue on the body. By 10 years of age the thickness of subcutaneous adipose tissue in girls is about 25% greater than that of boys the same age.

The shape and proportions of the body start to change during this period as a result of differential growth of the skeleton. For example, the legs have a greater rate of growth than the trunk during middle childhood. The trunk accounts for about 55% of total stature at age 7 years, but only about 45% at 10 years of age in white boys and girls. Black children have about the same amount of change in these body proportions as white children, but in black children the legs consistently account for about 2% more of the body's stature than in white children at the same ages. These racial and sexual group differences tend to persist throughout life.

Adolescence

Adolescence, the final frontier before becoming an adult, is not an easily defined period of life. Adolescence starts before puberty and spans the years until growth and maturation are completed, which is at about age 16 years in girls and age 18 years in boys. Puberty is an event, the age when the reproductive system matures and sexual reproduction becomes possible. Puberty is easily identified in girls by the onset of menstruation or menarche, but there is no similar marker in boys.

On the average, girls reach puberty about 2 years earlier than boys. Within each sex, however, there is a range of ages during which normal children may reach puberty. Normal girls may attain puberty as early as 7.5 years of age or as late as 13.5 years, with boys starting as early as 9.5 years or as late as 14 years of age. The time required for completion of physical and sexual maturity, i.e., attainment of adult status, varies also. In general, children who start their pubescent development early pass through the stages quickly; children starting at a later age may take a longer period of time to reach maturity.

The physical changes that transform a child's body into that of an adult are a final increase in body size and proportions, the development of secondary sex characteristics (pubic hair, growth of genitalia and the breasts), and development of the ability to reproduce sexually. Between 11 and 14 years of age, most girls have their pubescent growth spurts and are taller than boys the same age. These girls will also stop growing earlier than boys. Boys, on the average, do not enter their adolescent growth spurts until about 2 years after girls. As a result, boys have a 2-year advantage in prepubertal growth in stature. In addition, the adolescent growth spurt lasts for a longer time in boys than girls, and the amount of growth is greater. In boys, the average peak height velocity, the maximum rate of growth in stature during the adolescent growth spurt, ranges from 9.5 to 10.3 cm per year, and in girls the maximum velocity is 8.4 to 9.0 cm per year. These sex differences in growth help to produce the average greater body size in men than in women.

Body size and proportions change as a result of skeletal and muscular growth and differences in the amount and distribution of subcutaneous adipose tissue. During adolescence, boys develop more muscle tissue than girls, but girls add more total body fat than boys. Throughout adolescence, secondary sex characteristics (growth of the penis and testicles in boys, breast development in girls, and pubic hair for both) are developing coincident with sexual maturation. Concurrent with all this change is an increase in physical ability and performance, though again not as much for the average girl as for the average boy.

This physiologic progression of a child into an adult is controlled by the central nervous system, which integrates the activities of the endocrine glands. An increase in hormone production from the pituitary, gonads, and adrenal cortex, together with changes in the sensitivity of neuroreceptors, initiates and guides the differentiation of a child's body into its adult form.

GROWTH OF BODY TISSUES

The primary body tissues that change during growth are muscle, adipose tissue, and bone. These tissues can be quantified in children by various chemical and physical methods to provide an estimate of lean body mass and total body fat. Skeletal weight is very difficult to estimate accurately without exposure to ionizing radiation. Marked and significant changes and sex differences in all these tissues can be distinguished during growth.

Growth of Lean Body Mass

Lean body mass is the metabolically active protoplasm of the body, which is primarily muscle. Estimates of lean body mass include the weight of the internal organs and the skeleton and cannot avoid containing a small amount of structural fat. Growth in lean body mass is primarily due to an increase in muscle mass. Muscle is the largest single tissue component of the body. At birth, 25% of the body's weight is muscle, but at adulthood, muscle mass accounts for about 40% of the body's weight. Lean body mass increases at a similar rate in boys and girls during childhood and is roughly equal between them until about 13 years of age. The lean body mass of girls continues to grow into adolescence, but stops around 15 years of age (Figure 1-2). The lean body mass of boys starts to increase very rapidly after 13 years of age and reaches a maximum rate of increase late in ado-

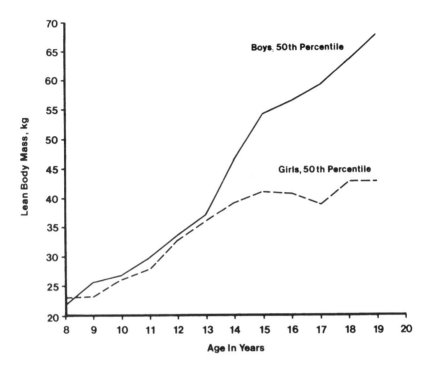

Figure 1-2 Changes in the 50th percentiles of lean body mass (LBM) in boys and girls. *Source:* Forbes GB, Body composition in adolescence, in *Human Growth*, Vol 2 by F Falkner and JM Tanner (eds), 1986, Plenum Press.

lescence. The total period of growth in the lean body mass of boys is about twice as long as the same period for girls, and as a result lean body mass in boys is several times greater than that of girls. The location of this greater muscle mass in boys is in the upper body.

Lean body mass is positively associated with stature; i.e., a tall child has a greater amount of lean body mass than a shorter child at the same level of maturity. After puberty, boys have greater absolute amounts of lean body mass than girls, irrespective of stature.

Growth of Total Body Fat

Body fat has two important functions: to store energy as adipose tissue and to act as a structural component in cell membranes. Storage fat is primarily subcutaneous adipose tissue, which contains the majority of the body's fat. The remaining adipose tissue is deposited around internal organs and visceral parts of the body. This internal adipose tissue cannot be separately measured in living subjects, but amounts of subcutaneous adipose tissue can be easily measured by skinfold calipers. A skinfold measurement is possible wherever a fold of skin and the underlying adipose tissue can be easily grasped, such as over the back of the arm or just below the shoulder blade.

There is significant growth in the adipose tissue of boys and girls. This growth occurs primarily in the subcutaneous or storage compartments of the body. The distribution and amount of subcutaneous adipose tissue are sex-specific. Girls have significantly more subcutaneous adipose tissue than boys, and this difference becomes considerable during adolescence. Differences in amounts of adipose tissue between boys and girls reflect actual differences in body composition and are not an artifact of the earlier maturation of girls. In addition to absolute differences in body fat, boys and girls also vary in the deposition and patterning of subcutaneous adipose tissue on the arms, legs, and trunk (Figure 1-3). Both sexes deposit adipose tissue on the torso during childhood and adolescence, but in adolescent girls additional adipose tissue is added to breasts, buttocks, thighs, and across the back of the arms (Figure 1-4). This additional adipose tissue accentuates the adult sex differences in body shape.

The adipose tissue thickness on the arms and legs of boys increases during childhood but decreases after about 13 years of age because the underlying muscle is growing at a greater rate. At this time, a boy's muscle and bone grow rapidly, causing the subcutaneous adipose tissue on the extremities to be stretched thinner. This differential growth accounts for the fall in the skinfold thickness of subcutaneous adipose tissue measured on the extremities. This may not indicate a loss of body fat, since the thickness of subcutaneous adipose tissue at the subscapular location continues to increase in boys during this time. Similar measures on girls show a continuous increase in adipose tissue thickness, with a marked increase after 12 years of age. For girls, adipose tissue grows about as rapidly as muscle and bone, and this allows an increase to occur in the subcutaneous adipose tissue on the arms and legs.

Skeletal Growth

There are three basic types of bones in the skeleton: long, round or irregular, and flat bones. Long bones are in the arms and legs, and round or irregular bones are the carpals in the wrist, tarsals in the ankle, and the vertebrae. Flat bones are found mainly in the vault of the skull and the pelvis.

The long bones of the legs and the vertebrae are a major location of growth in stature. Bone growth is rather steady until the adolescent growth spurt, but late in adolescence bone growth slows. After 18 years of age for girls and 20 years of age

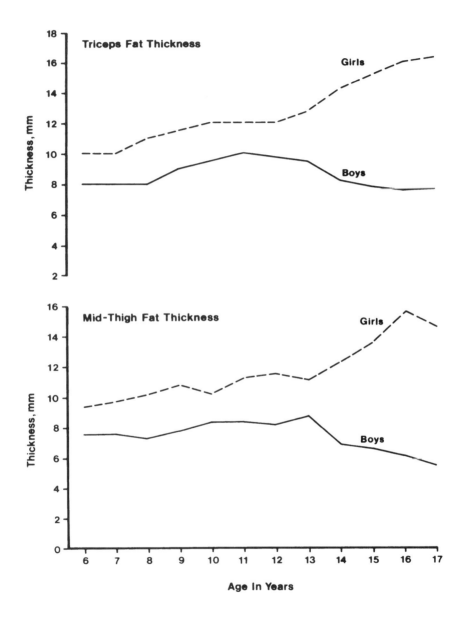

Figure 1-3 Skinfold thickness from the trunk of boys and girls. *Source:* Johnston FE, Hamill PVV and Lemeshow S, *Skinfold Thickness of Children 6–11 Years* and *Skinfold Thickness of Youths 12–17 Years*, USPHS Pub Nos 120 and 132, 1972, 1974.

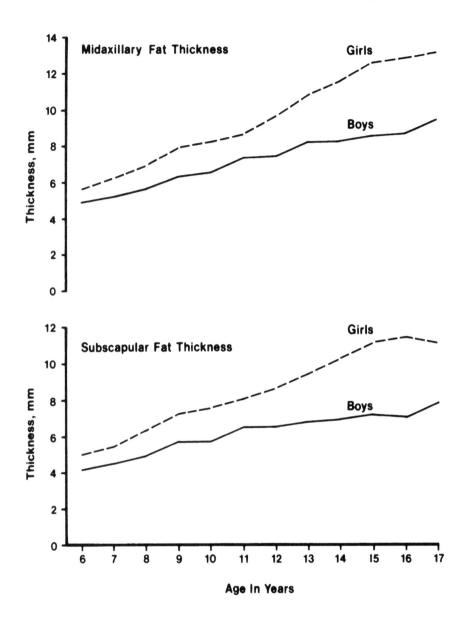

Figure 1-4 Skinfold and fat thicknesses (x-ray) on the arms and legs (respectively) of boys and girls. *Source:* Johnston FE, Hamill PVV and Lemeshow S, *Skinfold Thickness of Youths 12–17 Years*, USPHS Pub No 132, 1974.

for boys, the epiphyses or growth plates at the ends of most long bones have fused to the shaft or diaphysis. The cartilage of the growth plates, where growth in bone length occurs, has been replaced by bone, which prevents any further elongation.

Growth of the vault of the skull is, in part, a function of the growth of the nervous system. By about 7 years of age the skull, like the average brain, has completed approximately 95% of its growth. The bones of the vault of the skull do not experience a rapid period of growth during adolescence, but the base of the skull and the jaw, or lower face, have a growth spurt during adolescence.

Bones in the skeleton do not grow at the same uniform rate, but their growth is coordinated. Differential growth of bones in the skeleton contributes, in part, to changes in body proportions between the sexes, e.g., longer arms and broader shoulders in boys than in girls. Bones of the same type have different rates of growth, and they start or stop growing at different ages depending upon their location. For example, there is a distal-proximal difference in the rate of bone growth in the arms and legs, so that at a given age the hand is nearer its adult length than the upper arm.

MEASURING GROWTH

Accurate measures are needed for an assessment of the growth status of a child relative to his or her past growth and to provide some indication of future progress. Most normal children living in an adequate environment will maintain a level of growth from 1 year to the next relative to that of other children of the same chronologic age. For example, a child whose stature is at the 75th percentile at age 6 years will have a stature at approximately the same percentile at age 12 years and again at age 16 years (Figure 1-5). However, the growth of a child can be irregular and still considered normal due to differences in the rate of growth and maturation that can occur among children at the same chronologic age. Significant deviations in a child's growth, however, may be due to sickness or over- or undernutrition.

The most common measures of body size in children are recumbent length from birth to 3 years of age, stature after age 3 years, head circumference from birth to age 3 years, and weight at every age. Recumbent length and stature are indicators of the amount of linear growth, which is primarily due to bone growth of the skeleton. There is a variety of equipment for measuring growth and nutritional status, available from numerous suppliers and manufacturers.[1,2] Some of this equipment is more accurate, reliable, easier to use, and lower in cost than others. In making a selection of equipment, it is recommended that one consider all of these aspects in making a decision.

Recumbent length should be measured on an accurate device, and two people should be used. One person positions the child's head against the head board with the child looking straight up. The other person makes sure that the child is posi-

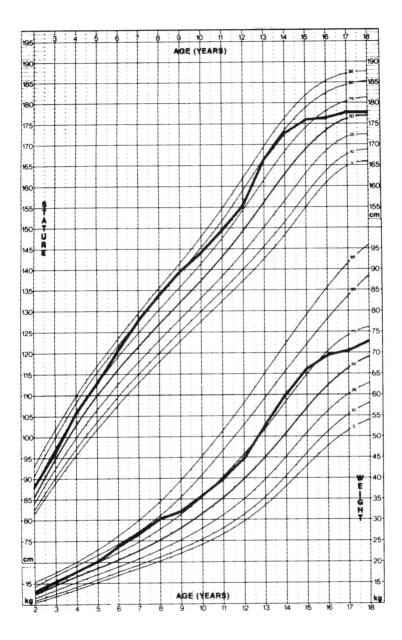

Figure 1-5 Stature and weight of a boy from 2 to 18 years of age plotted on NCHS growth charts. *Source:* Used with permission of Ross Laboratories, Columbus, OH 43216, from Ross Growth and Development Programs, © 1981 Ross Laboratories.

tioned down the length of the device with the shoulders and hips perpendicular to the trunk. The second person straightens the legs and brings the foot board up against the soles of the feet (Figure 1-6).

Stature should be measured on an accurate, stable device properly mounted to a wall, such as a measuring stick or a nonstretchable tape attached to a flat, vertical surface, or some form of a right-angle headboard. The measuring rod that is attached to many upright platform scales should not be used because it is not generally as accurate as more stable wall-mounted devices.[3] To measure stature, the child should be able to stand upright without assistance and with bare heels close together, legs straight, arms at the sides, and shoulders relaxed. The child looks straight ahead so that the line of vision is perpendicular to the body. The headboard is lowered onto the crown of the head (Figure 1-7). Stature is measured at maximum inspiration. The measurer's eyes should be level with the headboard to avoid reading errors due to parallax. Stature can be measured in children as young as 2 years of age, but most children cannot maintain a correct erect stature until about 3 years of age.

Weight is probably the most common measurement and is familiar to all of us. Weight measures growth in muscle, adipose tissue, and bone. Preferably, children

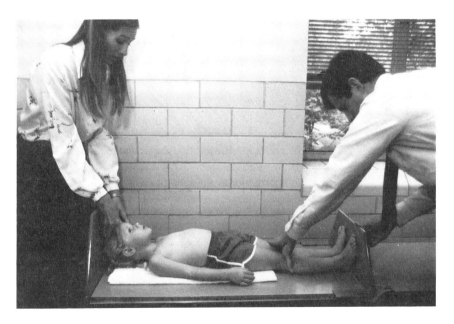

Figure 1-6 Measurement of recumbent length.

should be weighed nude after voiding with only a minimal amount of underclothing. If the child is clothed in undergarments, 0.1 kg or ¼ lb should be subtracted from the reading. Spring-type bathroom scales should never be used because they are not accurate enough for clinical purposes.

Head circumference should be measured with an inelastic tape between the ages of birth and 3 years of age. The technique will vary slightly between individuals, but certain points are important. The tape should be level across the front of the head with the child sitting. The greatest circumference of the head is located, and the tape is pulled tight (Figure 1-8).

Additional measures to consider in assessing the growth of children are arm circumference and the thickness of subcutaneous adipose tissue.[2] Subcutaneous adipose tissue can be measured at a variety of sites as the thickness of a skinfold. One of the most common sites for measuring a skinfold is on the back of the arm over the triceps muscle, and another possible location is just below the scapula. The triceps and subscapular skinfolds are highly correlated with total body fatness. Measuring skinfolds on an infant can be a problem because it is sometimes difficult to get a good separation of subcutaneous adipose tissue from the muscle tissue. Reference data are available for skinfold thickness of white, black, and

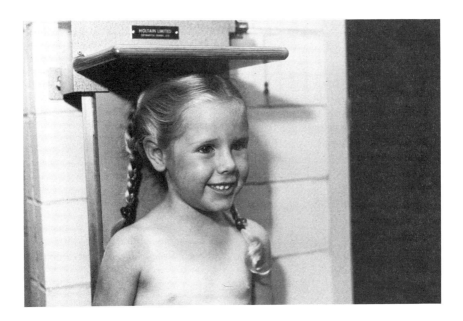

Figure 1-7 Measurement of stature.

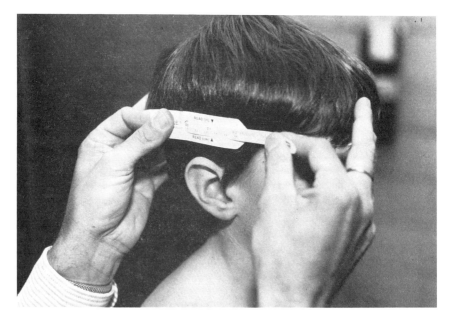

Figure 1-8 Measurement of head circumference.

Hispanic children older than 2 years of age from the National Center for Health Statistics.[4,5]

Measurement Error

For growth data to be of value, they must be collected in an accurate and reliable manner. This is especially true for infants and young children who cannot adequately cooperate. Also, because of the small size of the measurement values, the error is proportionally larger than in older children. Accuracy is how near a measurement is to its true value. The reliability of a measurement is the degree to which repeated trials of the same measurement differ from one another. A measurement that is repeated three times and has the same reading each time has perfect reliability. Measurements may be reliable but inaccurate because of inadequate equipment or the use of improper technique. Repeated measurements that differ from one another are less reliable but normal.

In most clinical settings there is usually a single observer, but he or she should always take two readings for each measurement, record both readings, and compute an average. A limit should also be placed on the allowable difference between the pair of readings for a measurement; for example, 0.2 kg for weight, 1.0 cm for stature, and 5.0 mm for skinfolds. If one of these limits is exceeded for a measurement, that pair of readings should be taken again. If the limit is still exceeded, an average of all four readings is recorded for a measurement and the average computed. The taking of at least a pair of readings for a measurement should provide an average value that is closer to the true value than a single measurement.

Knowledge of the proper use of equipment for collecting anthropometric growth data, including its maintenance and calibration, and the practice of correct procedures are also needed to help keep measurement errors to a minimum. For example, the accuracy of scales should be checked with a set of standard weights or by a dealer of weights and measures at least two or three times a year. Incorrect measurements may lead to wrong conclusions about a child's growth, nutritional status, or the effect of nutritional intervention. It is also important to make notes about the cooperation of a child when measurements are being taken. A very uncooperative child is difficult if not impossible to measure, and this can seriously affect the values of the measurements. The presence of a note about the child may aid in the interpretation of data collected for the same child at the next visit.

Growth Charts

Accurate records are necessary for assessing growth because they provide information on present status or any progress or response to treatment. Stature, recumbent length, and weight are representative of the general growth of the body. If they are measured annually and plotted against age, the curves are known as distance curves, like those found on the growth charts from the National Center for Health Statistics (NCHS) (Figure 1-9).[6] These charts indicate how the stature or length and weight of an infant or child compare to that of other American children at the same age. However, the use of stature, recumbent length, or weight alone in determining nutritional risk can be deceptive. A child may be of a certain length and at a certain weight, but is the child too light or too heavy for his or her length? Weight for length is an indicator of possible obesity or malnutrition and is plotted on weight-for-length charts.

There is only a single set of growth charts for children in the United States. At the time the NCHS charts were created, there were no significant group differences in the growth of black and white children except at the extremes. However, there may be some group differences in the growth of Mexican-American or Chinese- or Japanese-American children or American children of other racial or ethnic groups compared with that of white and black American children. It is recommended that the growth of children in the United States be plotted on the present growth charts. If the child is healthy, then he or she should track along the percentile lines on the charts. The child's position on the chart will be displaced as a function of the difference in his or her genetic background and that of the children

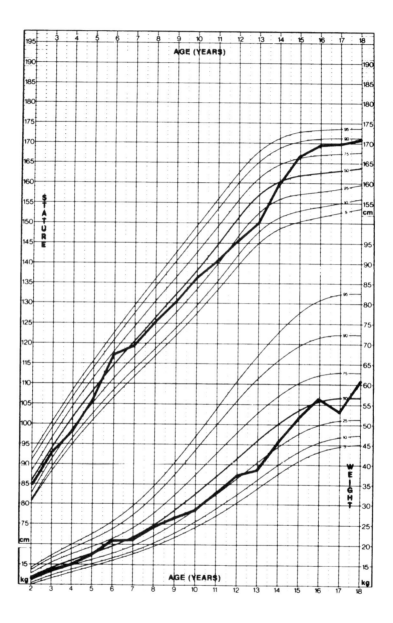

Figure 1-9 NCHS growth chart for girls 2 to 18 years. *Source:* Used with permission of Ross Laboratories, Columbus, OH 43216, from Ross Growth and Development Programs, © 1981 Ross Laboratories.

used to construct the charts. New growth charts for children in the United States will be available following the completion of the Third National Health and Nutrition Examination Survey in about 1995.

For premature infants or infants who are small at birth, it is important to account for their gestational age in plotting their growth data. This is done by subtracting the amount of prematurity from the infant's chronologic age. For a child with a gestational age of 28 weeks, this is a difference of 3 months. After about 2.5 years of age, it is generally no longer necessary to make an adjustment for gestational age for most premature children who are healthy. This is because the difference in body measurement values is less than the error for the measurements (see Chapter 3).

If growth assessments are made at repeated visits, the amount of change in a measurement or increments in stature, length, weight, and head circumference from one visit to the next can be quantified. This type of information provides an additional perspective on growth and can also be used to measure a child's response to nutritional intervention. Plots of annual increments are records of the velocity or the rate of growth per unit of time.

Increment growth charts are available for boys and girls (Figure 1-10).[2,7] For children aged 3 years and younger, there are increment charts for weight, recumbent length, and head circumference, and for older children there are charts for stature and weight. Use of the increment charts helps to determine whether a child's rate of growth is unusual by comparison with that of other normal American children at the same ages (see also Chapter 2).

The increment charts are distributions of growth increments from a group of healthy children, but there is no proof that children represented at the median (50th percentile) are healthier than other children at other percentiles at the same or other ages. These charts should be used to supplement the other growth charts in which attained size is plotted relative to chronologic age. The primary purpose of both these types of charts is to help identify children in need of further investigation or treatment and to monitor the results of such treatment.

There are also charts for plotting measures of triceps and subscapular skinfold thicknesses and midarm circumference.[2] These charts use data from the first National Health and Nutrition Examination Survey (NHANESI). These charts match the growth charts from 2 to 18 years of age with separate charts for boys and girls. There are race differences in the thickness of subcutaneous adipose tissue among whites, blacks, and Hispanics. These differences are most significant at extreme percentile values, so these charts can be used for white and black children.

Special Children

A difficult problem is collecting nutritional and growth information from children with "problems," e.g., gross obesity, contractures, braces, mental retardation,

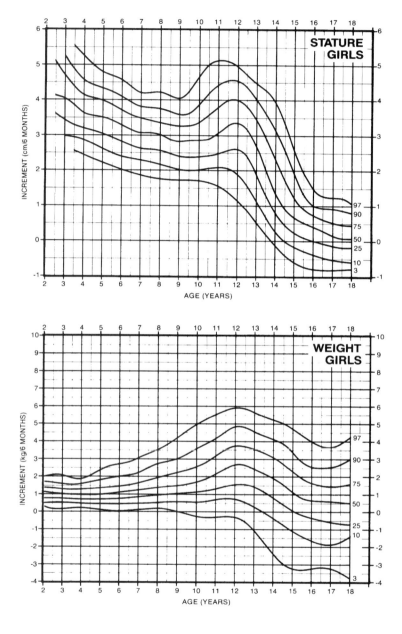

Figure 1-10 Increment charts for stature and weight of girls 2 to 18 years. *Source:* Used with permission of Ross Laboratories, Columbus, OH 43216, from Ross Growth and Development Programs, © 1981 Ross Laboratories.

etc. Because of the heterogeneity of these conditions among children, there are no recommended standard methods or sites of measurement and only limited or no specific reference data. If the child can stand, possibly standard methods can be applied. If the child is nonambulatory, then one can attempt to use recumbent methods. The reference data from the National Center for Health Statistics needs to be interpolated depending upon the condition of the child in question. However, there are growth charts for children with Trisomy 21.[8]

Two major problems to face in making a growth assessment of a handicapped child are how to make maximum use of the information collected and how to keep errors of measurement to a minimum. For example, one measurement is probably not going to be sufficient. It may be necessary to take several measurements, especially the more difficult the measurement or the more uncooperative the child. Accurate records are important, and the present growth charts can be used. A child may be at the 0.01th percentile, but the growth charts can still provide some information about his or her status, especially over time. Do not be concerned about going from one side of the body to the other to take a measurement, because in normal children lateral differences are minimal, but make a note of it if you do this.

For some children with growth problems, it is important to be able to predict their adult stature. Knowledge of the possible adult stature of a child can be useful in determining or in monitoring growth therapy. There are several methods available.[9] In general, each of the present methods requires a measure of the child's level of skeletal maturity, present stature, and the stature of both parents. It is important to remember that the stature value obtained by any method has a ± 3.0 to 5.0 cm error range.

PHYSICAL MATURATION

During the first 2 decades of life, children grow until they reach adult size, and their body tissues and systems progressively change until they reach adult levels or functions. This is the process of maturation, with maturity as its endpoint. In the body, maturation is a general but inter-related process. However, certain systems or tissues have been studied more closely than others because they provide more information about the level of maturity of a child relative to that of other children.

Skeletal Maturation

Skeletal growth is a continuous process, and repeated assessment of the levels of skeletal maturation can monitor this growth and provide investigators with an index of a child's biologic age. Two children of the same chronologic age may have different levels of skeletal maturation or skeletal ages, as they may also have different rates of muscle growth, weight gain, and sexual maturation. Skeletal age is highly correlated with aspects of physical and sexual maturation. For example, a child who is more mature sexually than another will generally have a more advanced skeletal age, although both children may have the same chronologic age.

Many parts of the skeleton can be used to estimate skeletal age, such as the foot–ankle, elbow, shoulder, and hip, but the most commonly used areas are the hand–wrist and knee. The hand–wrist has a long history in the study of skeletal maturation, even predating the use of radiography. However, the use of the knee in assessing skeletal maturity is important because it is a major site for growth in stature. Several of the techniques for assessing skeletal age are sample-specific and require training for accurate use. The newer methods need the assistance of a microcomputer.

Sexual Maturation

The onset and development of sexual maturation are under the control of the maturing neuroendocrine system. During childhood hormone levels are kept low by the active inhibition of the central nervous system. Toward the onset of puberty, there is a progressive decrease in the sensitivity of the inhibition of the nervous system to hormone levels, and the sex hormones appear in the blood in greater concentrations, reaching adult levels at puberty. Testosterone and estrogen influence sexual functions and general body growth and maturation. Boys and girls each produce testosterone and estrogen, but in significantly different amounts. Estrogen accelerates closure of epiphyseal growth plates in bones and deposition of fat, but more so in adolescence than childhood. Testosterone stimulates muscle growth, and due to its higher levels in boys, more muscle or lean body mass is deposited, particularly during adolescence. Estrogen, testosterone, and several androgenic hormones are also responsible for development of secondary sex characteristics. All hormones must operate together to ensure orderly, coordinated growth of the skeleton, muscles, and internal organs during childhood and adolescence. However, the ages of individual children at the onset of sexual maturation are highly variable.

In boys the first sign of puberty is enlargement of the testes and scrotum. About a year later, the penis starts to grow, just after the onset of the increased rate of growth in stature. Pubic hair appears shortly after the start of testicular growth. The adult male pattern of pubic hair distribution extends from the genitalia onto the thighs. About 2 years after the appearance of pubic hair, pigmented and coarse hair becomes visible on the face, and axillary hair develops in the armpits. The amount and distribution of hair on the rest of the male body is genetically determined.

Breast buds are the first hint of approaching puberty in young girls. With the beginning of breast development, the uterus and vagina also start to grow. A girl will generally start to menstruate about 2 years after her breasts and uterus start to grow. Pubic hair generally appears in girls with the onset of breast development, although pubic hair may develop before the breasts begin to mature. The distribution of pubic hair on a girl's body is more limited than in boys.

The rate of sexual maturation differs within and between the sexes. For example, two girls of the same chronologic age may have different rates of sexual maturation, and several similar rating systems have been developed in order to group children into levels of sexual maturity (refer to Chapter 2). Most adolescent events such as peak height velocity (age at most rapid growth in stature) or the appearance of pubic hair or its development occur in girls about a year or two before they occur in boys. However, the time difference between the sexes for mean ages of stages of maturity may be as short as $^4/_{10}$ of a year.

CONCLUSION

Childhood is a period of steady growth for the body, without significant changes. In adolescence, a child copes with his or her body as it grows, enlarges, changes shape, and matures from what he or she had grown accustomed to over the past 12 or so years. This new body is similar but with different and exciting capabilities and functions. Unfortunately, these changes may not be readily accepted as fact for several years. The emotional upheavals of puberty and adolescence for an individual, his or her family, and society might be avoided if growth and its changes were drawn out over a longer period of time. However, the ability to procreate necessitates the ability to carry a fetus to term and then to provide child care afterward. Thus the adult body must follow shortly on the heels of sexual maturity.

REFERENCES

1. Lohman TG, Roche AF, Martorell R, eds. *Anthropometric Standardization Reference Manual.* Champaign, Ill: Human Kinetics Books; 1988.

2. Moore WM, Roche AF. *Pediatric Anthropometry.* 3rd ed. Columbus, Ohio: Ross Laboratories; 1987.

3. Roche AF, Guo S, Baumgartner RN, Falls RA. The measurement of stature. *Am J Clin Nutr.* 1988;47:922.

4. Najjar MF, Rowland M. *Anthropometric Reference Data and Prevalence of Overweight. United States, 1976–1980.* Vital and Health Statistics no. 238. Washington, DC: US Government Printing Office; 1987.

5. Najjar MF, Kuczmarski RJ. *Anthropometric Data and Prevalence of Overweight for Hispanics: 1982–1984.* Vital and Health Statistics no. 239. Washington, DC: US Government Printing Office; 1989.

6. Hamill PVV, Drizd TA, Johnson CL, et al. Physical growth: National Center for Health Statistics percentiles. *Am J Clin Nutr.* 1979; 32:607–609.

7. Roche AF, Himes JH. Incremental growth charts. *Am J Clin Nutr.* 1980; 33:2041.

8. Cronk CE, Crocker AC, Pueschel SM, Shea AM, Zackai E, et al. Growth charts for children with Down syndrome: 1 month to 18 years of age. *Pediatrics.* 1988; 61:102–110.

9. Roche AF, Wainer H, Thissen D. The RWT method for the prediction of adult stature. *Pediatrics.* 1975; 56: 1026–1033.

SUGGESTED READING

Behnke AR, Wilmore JH. *Evaluation and Regulation of Body Build and Composition.* Englewood Cliffs, NJ: Prentice-Hall; 1974.

Chumlea WC, Knittle JL, Roche AF, Siervogel RM, Webb P. Size and number of adipocytes and measures of body fat in boys and girls 10 to 18 years of age. *Am J Clin Nutr.* 1981;34:1791.

Daughaday WH, Herington AC, Phillips LS. The regulation of growth of endocrines. *Annu Rev Physiol.* 1975;26:211.

Forbes GB. Body composition in adolescence. In: Falkner F, Tanner JM, eds. *Human Growth.* Vol. 2. New York, NY: Plenum Press; 1986:119–146.

Frisch RE, Revelle R. Height and weight at menarche and a hypothesis of critical body weight and adolescent events. *Science.* 1970;169:379.

Greulich W, Pyle SJ. *Radiologic Atlas of Skeletal Development of the Hand and Wrist.* 2nd ed. Stanford, CA: Stanford University Press; 1959.

Grumbach MM. The central nervous system and the onset of puberty. In: Falkner F, Tanner JM, eds. *Human Growth.* Vol. 2. New York, NY: Plenum Press; 1978:215–238.

Hamill PVV, Johnson CL, Reed RB, Drizd TA, Roche AF. *NCHS Growth Curves for Children Birth–18 Years.* Washington, DC: US Government Printing Office; 1977. US Public Health Service publication no. 165.

Johnston FE. Somatic growth of the infant and preschool child. In: Falkner F, Tanner JM, eds. *Human Growth.* Vol. 2. New York: Plenum Press; 1986:3–24.

Johnston FE, Hamill PVV, Lemeshow S. *Skinfold Thickness of Children 6–11 Years.* Washington, DC: US Government Printing Office; 1972. US Public Health Service publication no. 120.

Johnston FE, Hamill PVV, Lemeshow S. *Skinfold Thickness of Youths 12–17 Years.* Washington, DC: US Government Printing Office; 1974. US Public Health Service publication no. 132.

MacMahon B. *Age at Menarche.* Washington, DC: US Government Printing Office; 1973. US Public Health Service publication no. 133.

Malina RM. Adolescent changes in size, build, composition and performance. *Hum Biol.* 1974;46:117.

Malina RM. Growth of muscle tissue and muscle mass. In: Falkner F, Tanner JM, eds. *Human Growth.* Vol. 2. New York, NY: Plenum Press; 1986:77–100.

Malina RM, Hamill PVV, Lemeshow S. *Body Dimensions and Proportions White and Negro Children 6–11 Years.* Washington, DC: Government Printing Office; 1974. US Public Health Service publication no. 143.

Marshall WA. Puberty. In: Falkner F, Tanner JM, eds. *Human Growth.* Vol. 2. New York: Plenum Press; 1978:141–182.

McCammon RS. *Human Growth and Development.* Springfield, Ill: Charles C Thomas; 1970.

Reynolds EL. The distribution of subcutaneous fat in childhood and adolescence. *Monogr Soc Res Child Dev.* 1951;15.

Reynolds EL, Wines JF. Physical changes associated with adolescence in boys. *Am J Dis Child.* 1951;82:529.

Roche AF. Bone growth and maturation. In: Falkner F, Tanner JM, eds. *Human Growth.* Vol. 2. New York: Plenum Press; 1986:25–60.

Roche AF, Chumlea WC, Thissen D. *Assessing Skeletal Maturity of the Hand-Wrist: Fels Method.* Springfield, Ill: Charles C Thomas; 1988.

Roche AF, Wainer H, Thessen D. *Skeletal Maturity, the Knee Joint as a Biological Indicator.* New York: Plenum Press; 1975.

Sinclair D. *Human Growth after Birth.* London: Oxford University Press; 1978.

Tanner JM. *Growth at Adolescence.* Oxford: Blackwell Scientific Publications; 1962.

Tanner JM, Whitehouse RH, Marshall WA, Healy MJR, Goldstein H. *Assessment of Skeletal Maturity and Prediction of Adult Height: TW2 Method.* New York: Academic Press; 1975.

Winter JSD. Prepubertal and pubertal endocrinology. In: Falkner F, Tanner JM, eds. *Human Growth.* Vol. 2. New York: Plenum Press; 1978:183–214.

Chapter 2

Nutritional Assessment

Susan Krug-Wispé

Increased awareness of the role of nutrition in health maintenance, recognition of the existence of malnutrition among the United States population, and improved nutrition support technology have resulted in major changes in both the availability and the delivery of nutritional care. Today the assessment of nutritional status has become an integral component of pediatric health care, whether provided through a clinic, private physician's office, or other health care facility. The accurate collection and interpretation of nutritional assessment data are instrumental in providing quality care. The assessment identifies nutritionally depleted or at-risk infants and children, provides essential information for developing achievable nutritional care plans, and serves as a mechanism for evaluating the effectiveness of nutritional care.

SCREENING

The completion of in-depth nutritional assessments on all children served by a health care system is neither practical nor essential for providing quality nutrition care. Well-designed nutritional screening performed by trained personnel is effective in identifying children who require more comprehensive nutritional assessment.[1-5] The information gathered for screening includes indices of nutritional status routinely collected during scheduled health care appointments or upon admission to a health care facility.[6,7]

Nutritional screening protocols must be adapted to the needs of the population served as well as the staff and facility resources. The participation of administrative, medical, and nursing staffs is essential in developing a nutritional screening program since the measurement and documentation of many of the parameters involve nonnutrition personnel and equipment. The success of the program depends upon the coordinated efforts of the multidisciplinary team in completing assigned responsibilities.[1,8]

26

Key issues to be resolved when planning a nutritional screening program include designation of staff responsibilities, selection of nutritional parameters to be screened, and timing of the screening. A clinic or extended care facility may have nursing complete nutritional screening, whereas a hospital may assign it to dietetic technicians who collect data by interview and from nursing and laboratory documentation in the medical record. Age, weight, height (length), and head circumference (in children less than 3 years of age) are routinely included in most nutritional screenings. Other data collected vary depending on the types of nutritional problems commonly encountered and laboratory support available. Many programs include nutritional screening as a routine portion of a clinic or admission assessment. Extended care facilities and hospitals with long-term patients may also perform periodic screening to identify changes in nutritional risk status.[9] Exhibit 2-1 is an example of a hospital nutritional screening form.

Exhibit 2-1 Nutritional Screening Form for a Pediatric Hospital

---

NUTRITIONAL SCREENING

Diagnosis/Reason for Hospitalization: _____

Special Diet/Formula Ordered?	Y	N	Explain _____
Adm Wt or Ht <5th %tile	Y	N	Adm Wt ___ kg __%; Adm Ht ___ cm __%
Serum Albumin <3.5 g/dl?	Y	N	Lab Value & Date _____
Diet Order of NPO/Clears >3 days?	Y	N	Explain _____
Receiving Tube Feedings/ TPN?	Y	N	Explain _____
Oral Liquid Supplement?	Y	N	Explain _____
Chewing or Swallowing Problems?	Y	N	Explain _____
Persistent/Current Nausea or Vomiting?	Y	N	Explain _____
Persistent Fever >100°F for >3 days?	Y	N	Explain _____
Persistent/Current Diarrhea?	Y	N	Explain _____
Persistent/Current Constipation?	Y	N	Explain _____
Weight Change in Past Year?	Y	N	Explain _____
Recent Major Surgery (w/in 3 mon.)?	Y	N	Explain _____
Recent Hospitalization (w/in 3 mon.)?	Y	N	Explain _____
Special Diet Prior to This Admission?	Y	N	Explain _____
Poor Appetite/Food Refusal >3 days?	Y	N	Explain _____

COMMENTS:

Pref Card	Adm Date:	Screen Date:	
Given Rec'd	Food allergies/Intolerances:	Signature: _____	DT
		_____	RD
Name:	Diet:	Age: Sex: Room: Fl:	

Source: Courtesy of the Clinical Nutrition Services, Children's Hospital Medical Center, Cincinnati, Ohio.

If appropriate nutritional assessment referral is to be made, the criteria for identifying children at risk must be clearly defined. The weighing of "high" versus "moderate" risk criteria with specified guidelines for referral has been successful.[3,5] Other systems have all nutritional screening reviewed by registered dietitians for determination of nutritional risk.[2]

NUTRITIONAL ASSESSMENT

The assessment of a child's nutritional status is based on pertinent information collected from the medical history, physical examination, dietary interview, anthropometric measurements, and laboratory findings.[7] The specific data collected are individualized according to the child's age, diagnosis, and type of nutritional risk.

Medical History and Physical Examination

The medical history provides valuable information relating to a child's nutritional status. Specific areas of interest include the following:

- diagnosis (especially associated with malabsorption, altered nutrient metabolism, increased energy/nutrient requirements, or impaired appetite)
- history of acute or chronic illnesses
- surgical history
- growth—birthweight, gestational age at birth, deviation from previously established growth channel
- feeding difficulties—developmental delays, anorexia, vomiting, use of gavage feeding or other systems of nutritional support
- prescribed or self-imposed diets/unusual food intake patterns
- drug/medication history—nutritional supplements, prescribed medications, recreational drugs

At physical examination, the presence of clinical symptoms of a nutritional deficiency usually indicates an advanced state of depletion. However, milder, nonspecific signs of malnutrition are more commonly observed. These signs warrant laboratory evaluation to determine whether they are nutritional in etiology.[7,10] Table 2-1 includes a listing of clinical signs associated with nutrient deficiencies and specifies laboratory findings required to substantiate the diagnosis.

Table 2-1 Clinical Signs and Laboratory Findings in the Malnourished Child and Adult*

Clinical Sign	Suspect Nutrient	Supportive Objective Findings
Epithelial		
Skin		
Xerosis, dry scaling	Essential fatty acids	Triene/tetraene ratio >0.4
Hyperkeratosis, plaques around hair follicles	Vitamin A	↓ Plasma retinol
Ecchymoses, petechiae	Vitamin K	Prolonged prothrombin time
	Vitamin C	↓ Serum ascorbic acid
Hair		
Easily plucked, dyspigmented, lackluster	Protein-calorie	↓ Total protein ↓ Albumin ↓ Transferrin
Nails		
Thin, spoon-shaped	Iron	↓ Serum Fe ↑ TIBC
Mucosal		
Mouth, lips, and tongue	B vitamins	
Angular stomatitis (inflammation at corners of mouth)	B$_2$ (riboflavin)	↓ RBC glutathione reductase
Cheilosis (reddened lips with fissures at angles)	B$_2$ B$_6$ (pyridoxine)	See above ↓ Plasma pyridoxal phosphate†
Glossitis (inflammation of tongue)	B$_6$ B$_2$ B$_3$ (niacin)	See above See above ↓ Plasma tryptophan ↓ Urinary N-methyl nicotinamide†
Magenta tongue	B$_2$	See above
Edema of tongue, tongue fissures	B$_3$	See above
Gums		
Spongy, bleeding	Vitamin C	↓ Plasma ascorbic acid
Ocular		
Pale conjunctivae secondary to anemia	Iron Folic acid Vitamin B$_{12}$ Copper	↓ Serum Fe, ↑ TIBC, ↓ serum folic acid, or ↓ RBC folic acid ↓ Serum B$_{12}$ ↓ Serum copper
Bitot's spots (grayish, yellow, or white foamy spots on the whites of the eye)	Vitamin A	↓ Plasma retinol

continues

Table 2-1 continued

Clinical Sign	Suspect Nutrient	Supportive Objective Findings
Conjunctival or corneal xerosis, keratomalacia (softening of part or all of cornea)	Vitamin A	↓ Plasma retinol
Musculoskeletal		
Craniotabes (thinning of the inner table of the skull); palpable enlargement of costochondral junctions ("rachitic rosary"); thickening of wrists and ankles	Vitamin D	↓ 25 OH-vit D ↑ Alkaline phosphatase ± ↓ Ca, ↓ PO_4 Long bone films
Scurvy (tenderness of extremities, hemorrhages under periosteum of long bones; enlargement of costochondral junction; cessation of osteogenesis of long bones)	Vitamin C	↓ Serum ascorbic acid Long bone films
Skeletal lesions	Copper	↓ Serum copper X-ray film changes similar to scurvy since copper is also essential for normal collagen formation
Muscle wasting, prominence of body skeleton, poor muscle tone	Protein-calorie	↓ Serum proteins ↓ Arm muscle circumference
General		
Edema	Protein	↓ Serum proteins
Pallor 2° to anemia	Vitamin E (in premature infants)	↓ Serum vitamin E ↑ Peroxide hemolysis Evidence of hemolysis on blood smear
	Iron	↓ Serum Fe, ↑ TIBC
	Folic acid	↓ Serum folic acid Macrocytosis on RBC smear
	Vitamin B_{12}	↓ Serum B_{12} Macrocytosis on RBC smear
	Copper	↓ Serum copper
Internal systems		
Nervous		
Mental confusion	Protein	↓ Total protein, ↓ albumin, ↓ transferrin
	Vitamin B_1 (thiamine)	↓ RBC transketolase

continues

Table 2-1 continued

Clinical Sign	Suspect Nutrient	Supportive Objective Findings
Cardiovascular		
Beriberi (enlarged heart, congestive heart failure, tachycardia)	Vitamin B_1	Same as above
Tachycardia 2° to anemia	Iron Folic acid B_{12} Copper Vitamin E (in premature infants)	See above
Gastrointestinal		
Hepatomegaly	Protein-calorie	↓ Total protein, ↓ albumin, ↓ transferrin
Glandular		
Thyroid enlargement	Iodine	↓ Total serum iodine: inorganic, PBI[†]

* Fe, iron; PBI, protein-bound iodine; RBC, red blood cells; TIBC, total iron-binding capacity.
† Bio Science Laboratories, 7600 Tyrone Avenue, Van Nyes, CA 91405.

Source: Reprinted from *Manual of Pediatric Parenteral Nutrition* (pp 22–23) by A Kerner (ed) with permission of John Wiley and Sons, Inc, © 1983.

Dietary Evaluation

The dietary interview is adapted to collect information required for evaluating a child's food habits with respect to the nutritional problem or risk. The data gathered may include the following:[7,11–13]

- chronologic feeding history from birth or onset of nutritional problem
- current nutrient intake
- feeding skills development
- psychosocial factors that influence nutrient intake
- medication/recreational drug use and potential nutrient interactions
- history of prescribed or self-imposed diets and outcome
- activity patterns
- family history

Exhibit 2-2 shows an example of the diet interview summary from a nutrition clinic evaluation.

Exhibit 2-2 Dietary Interview Summary Portion of a Nutrition Clinic Evaluation

NUTRITION CLINIC EVALUATION

Date of Visit: _____ Age: _____

Diagnosis: _____ Onset: _____

Concomitant Conditions: _____

_____ Ref. Phys. _____

Problem: _____

_____

Concerns of Parents or Patient: _____   _____

_____

Nutrition History: _____

_____

Recent Nutrition History: _____

_____

Formula: Kind _____   Amount _____   Cal. Density _____

Food Intake: _____

_____

Food Summary (no. of servings/day):

Meat _____   Milk _____   Fr/Veg _____   Grains _____

_____

Fever/Vomiting: _____   Elimination: _____

Appetite: _____

Feeding Ability/Concerns: _____

_____

_____   _____

Vitamin Mineral Supp: _____

Activity level 1–8, 8 high _____

Social Setting in regard to meal prep: _____

_____

Social History: _____

_____

Pertinent family medical/weight history: _____

_____

_____

Source: Courtesy of the Clinical Nutrition Services, Children's Hospital Medical Center, Cincinnati, OH.

Collection of Current Intake Data

The method of inquiry selected for determining current nutrient intake depends on the degree of quantitation desired. In some cases the identification of the presence or absence of sources for specific nutrients may be sufficient to support a diagnosis. For example, identifying early introduction of cow's milk to a diet with few iron-containing solid foods may be sufficient to implicate a dietary basis for iron deficiency anemia in a 9-month-old infant. Several approaches are available when greater quantitation is desired. One or more of these techniques may be used in a nutritional assessment.

A *diet history* is designed to determine pattern of usual food intake. This type of history requires a detailed interview by a trained nutritionist.[14,15] From the collected data an estimate of nutrient intake is calculated. Studies indicate this method yields higher estimated values than the 24-hour recall and diet record.[16–18]

A *24-hour recall* provides an estimate of nutrient intake based on the individual's recollection of food consumed over the previous day. This method has been used successfully for groups of individuals. However, it is less valid in evaluating diet adequacy for an individual since the 24-hour period assessed may not be representative of the usual diet. Nutrient intakes calculated from 24-hour recalls are lower than those based on dietary histories or food records.[16–20]

Three-day to 7-day *food records* provide prospective food intake data. These are recorded by the parent, child, or other caregiver and are returned to the nutritionist for analysis. A detailed 7-day food record provides more accurate information than one of shorter duration due to the inclusion of both weekend and weekday meal patterns. However, accuracy of diet record keeping often deteriorates over time. When a 7-day food record is not possible, use of shorter time periods including selected days of the week is an adequate alternative.[21]

In inpatient facilities, *nutrient intake analyses* (calorie counts) are frequently ordered to assess a child's food intake. These are used to determine the ability of a child to consume a sufficient amount of food for growth or to verify the achievement and adequacy of a prescribed feeding regimen. These records, however, do not provide data representative of intake within the home environment.

Food frequencies estimate the frequency and amount of specific foods eaten. These often consist of questionnaires that can be self-administered and, therefore, reduce professional interview time. Over-reporting of food intake is common with this method.[16,17,22,23]

Dietary Intake Evaluation

Estimated intakes of specific nutrients are calculated using values derived from food composition tables or computerized nutrient analysis programs. The calculated intake is evaluated for adequacy by comparing it with a reference intake allowance. The Recommended Dietary Allowances (RDAs) are the most commonly used reference allowances in the United States.[24] These recommended levels for nutrient intake are estimated to meet the nutritional needs of practically all healthy persons. Therefore, they are designed to include a wide margin of safety above amounts required to prevent deficiency.[25] Tables 2-2 through 2-5 list the 1989 RDAs.

The RDAs were originally intended for use in assessing the adequacy of diet for groups of healthy persons. When used as a reference for an individual, validity of assessment is dependent on the accuracy of estimated intake and duration of time the intake has been maintained.[24,25] An estimated intake for a nutrient that falls below the RDA may not represent a nutritional deficiency or even a nutritional risk due to the margin of safety incorporated into the recommendations. However, intakes found to be substantially below the RDA for a sufficient length of time can be used as supportive evidence for a suspected diet-related nutritional deficiency or to identify areas that merit further evaluation.[24] When assessing the adequacy of diets for infants and children with acute or chronic disease, potential alterations in nutrient requirements should be considered.

Calculation of Energy Requirements

An individual's total energy expenditure (TEE) consists of the energy required to meet the basal metabolic rate (BMR) plus specific dynamic action of food (SDA) plus activity energy expenditure (AEE).[24,27] BMR is defined as the heat expenditure of an individual under the following basal conditions:[27]

1. fasting (at least 10 to 12 hours after the last meal)
2. awake and resting in a lying position (measurements are taken shortly after awakening)
3. normal body and ambient temperature
4. absence of psychologic or physical stress

Resting energy expenditure (REE) is the energy expenditure of an individual at rest and in conditions of thermal neutrality. REE may include the thermic effect of a previous meal and is commonly defined as BMR plus SDA. BMR and REE usually differ by less than 10%.[24,27]

Standard equations have been developed to estimate REE and BMR based on age, sex, and weight or surface area.[24,28–30] However, in using such equations the practitioner needs to remember that individual variation exists, and energy intake may require adjustment to achieve the desired outcome. The majority of variation in REE/BMR between individuals of the same age, weight, and sex is related to lean body mass. The person with the higher lean body mass will have the higher energy expenditure.[24] Table 2-6 lists equations for estimating REE based on age,

Table 2-2 Median Heights and Weights and Recommended Energy Intake*

Category	Age (years) or Condition	Weight (kg)	(lb)	Height (cm)	(in)	REE† (kcal/day)	Multiples of REE	Per kg	Per day§
Infants	0.0–0.5	6	13	60	24	320		108	650
	0.5–1.0	9	20	71	28	500		98	850
Children	1–3	13	29	90	35	740		102	1300
	4–6	20	44	112	44	950		90	1800
	7–10	28	62	132	52	1130		70	2000
Males	11–14	45	99	157	62	1440	1.70	55	2500
	15–18	66	145	176	69	1760	1.67	45	3000
	19–24	72	160	177	70	1780	1.67	40	2900
	25–50	79	174	176	70	1800	1.60	37	2900
	51+	77	170	173	68	1530	1.50	30	2300
Females	11–14	46	101	157	62	1310	1.67	47	2200
	15–18	55	120	163	64	1370	1.60	40	2200
	19–24	58	128	164	65	1350	1.60	38	2200
	25–50	63	138	163	64	1380	1.55	36	2200
	51+	65	143	160	63	1280	1.50	30	1900
Pregnant	1st trimester								+0
	2nd trimester								+300
	3rd trimester								+300
Lactating	1st 6 months								+500
	2nd 6 months								+500

* REE, resting energy expenditure.
† Calculations based on World Health Organization equations (1985), then rounded (see reference 26).
‡ In the range of light to moderate activity, the coefficient of variation is ±20%.
§ Figure is rounded.

Source: Reprinted with permission from *Recommended Dietary Allowances*, 10th ed, © 1989 by the National Academy of Sciences. Published by National Academy Press.

Table 2-3 Recommended Daily Dietary Allowances, Revised 1989*

Category	Age (years) or Condition	Weight† (kg)	Weight† (lb)	Height† (cm)	Height† (in)	Protein (g)	Fat-Soluble Vitamins Vitamin A (µg re)‡	Vitamin D (µg)§	Vitamin E (mg α-te)‖	Vitamin K (µg)
Infants	0.0–0.5	6	13	60	24	13	375	7.5	3	5
	0.5–1.0	9	20	71	28	14	375	10	4	10
Children	1–3	13	29	90	35	16	400	10	6	15
	4–6	20	44	112	44	24	500	10	7	20
	7–10	28	62	132	52	28	700	10	7	30
Males	11–14	45	99	157	62	45	1,000	10	10	45
	15–18	66	145	176	69	59	1,000	10	10	65
	19–24	72	160	177	70	58	1,000	10	10	70
	25–50	79	174	176	70	63	1,000	5	10	80
	51+	77	170	173	68	63	1,000	5	10	80
Females	11–14	46	101	157	62	46	800	10	8	45
	15–18	55	120	163	64	44	800	10	8	55
	19–24	58	128	164	65	46	800	10	8	60
	25–50	63	138	163	64	50	800	5	8	65
	51+	65	143	160	63	50	800	5	8	65
Pregnant						60	800	10	10	65
Lactating 1st 6 months						65	1,300	10	12	65
2nd 6 months						62	1,200	10	11	65

* The allowances, expressed as average daily intakes over time, are intended to provide for individual variations among most normal persons as they live in the United States under usual environmental stresses. Diets should be based on a variety of common foods in order to provide other nutrients for which human requirements have been less well defined.

† Weights and heights of Reference Adults are actual medians for the U.S. population of the designated age, as reported by NHANES II. The median weights and heights of those under 19 years of age were taken from Hamill et al. (1979). The use of these figures does not imply that the height-to-weight ratios are ideal.

Water-Soluble Vitamins							Minerals						
Vitamin C (mg)	Thiamine (mg)	Riboflavin (mg)	Niacin (mg NE)‡	Vitamin B6 (mg)	Folate (µg)	Vitamin B12 (µg)	Calcium (mg)	Phosphorus (mg)	Magnesium (mg)	Iron (mg)	Zinc (mg)	Iodine (µg)	Selenium (µg)
30	0.3	0.4	5	0.3	25	0.3	400	300	40	6	5	40	10
35	0.4	0.5	6	0.6	35	0.5	600	500	60	10	5	50	15
40	0.7	0.8	9	1.0	50	0.7	800	800	80	10	10	70	20
45	0.9	1.1	12	1.1	75	1.0	800	800	120	10	10	90	20
45	1.0	1.2	13	1.4	100	1.4	800	800	170	10	10	120	30
50	1.3	1.5	17	1.7	150	2.0	1,200	1,200	270	12	15	150	40
60	1.5	1.8	20	2.0	200	2.0	1,200	1,200	400	12	15	150	50
60	1.5	1.7	19	2.0	200	2.0	1,200	1,200	350	10	15	150	70
60	1.5	1.7	19	2.0	200	2.0	800	800	350	10	15	150	70
60	1.2	1.4	15	2.0	200	2.0	800	800	350	10	15	150	70
50	1.1	1.3	15	1.4	150	2.0	1,200	1,200	280	15	12	150	45
60	1.1	1.3	15	1.5	180	2.0	1,200	1,200	300	15	12	150	50
60	1.1	1.3	15	1.6	180	2.0	1,200	1,200	280	15	12	150	55
60	1.1	1.3	15	1.6	180	2.0	800	800	280	15	12	150	55
60	1.0	1.2	13	1.6	180	2.0	800	800	280	10	12	150	55
70	1.5	1.6	17	2.2	400	2.2	1,200	1,200	320	30	15	175	65
95	1.6	1.8	20	2.1	280	2.6	1,200	1,200	355	15	19	200	75
90	1.6	1.7	20	2.1	260	2.6	1,200	1,200	340	15	16	200	75

‡ Retinol equivalents. 1 retinol equivalent = 1 µg retinol or 6 µg β-carotene. See text for calculation of vitamin A activity of diets as retinol equivalents.

§ As cholecalciferol. 10 µg cholecalciferol = 400 IU of vitamin D.

‖ α-Tocopherol equivalents. 1 mg d-α tocopherol = 1 α-TE.

1 NE (niacin equivalent) is equal to 1 mg of niacin or 60 mg of dietary tryptophan.

Source: Reprinted with permission from *Recommended Dietary Allowances,* 10th edition, © 1989 by the National Academy of Sciences. Published by National Academy Press.

Table 2-4 Estimated Safe and Adequate Daily Dietary Intakes of Selected Vitamins and Minerals*

Category	Age (Years)	Vitamins		Trace Elements†				
		Biotin (µg)	Pantothenic Acid (mg)	Copper (mg)	Manganese (mg)	Fluoride (mg)	Chromium (µg)	Molybdenum (µg)
Infants	0–0.5	10	2	0.4–0.6	0.3–0.6	0.1–0.5	10–40	15–30
	0.5–1	15	3	0.6–0.7	0.6–1.0	0.2–1.0	20–60	20–40
Children and adolescents	1–3	20	3	0.7–1.0	1.0–1.5	0.5–1.5	20–80	25–50
	4–6	25	3–4	1.0–1.5	1.5–2.0	1.0–2.5	30–120	30–75
	7–10	30	4–5	1.0–2.0	2.0–3.0	1.5–2.5	50–200	50–150
	11+	30–100	4–7	1.5–2.5	2.0–5.0	1.5–2.5	50–200	75–250
Adults		30–100	4–7	1.5–3.0	2.0–5.0	1.5–4.0	50–200	75–250

* Because there is less information on which to base allowances, these figures are not given in the main table of RDA and are provided here in the form of ranges of recommended intakes.

† Since the toxic levels for many trace elements may be only several times usual intakes, the upper levels for the trace elements given in this table should not be habitually exceeded.

Source: Reprinted with permission from *Recommended Dietary Allowances*, 10th edition, © 1989 by the National Academy of Sciences. Published by National Academy Press.

Table 2-5 Estimated Sodium, Chloride, and Potassium Minimum Requirements of Healthy Persons

Age	Weight (kg)*	Sodium (mg)*,†	Chloride (mg)*,†	Potassium (mg)‡
Months				
0–5	4.5	120	180	500
6–11	8.9	200	300	700
Years				
1	11.0	225	350	1,000
2–5	16.0	300	500	1,400
6–9	25.0	400	600	1,600
10–18	50.0	500	750	2,000
>18§	70.0	500	750	2,000

* No allowance has been included for large, prolonged losses from the skin through sweat.

† There is no evidence that higher intakes confer any health benefit.

‡ Desirable intakes of potassium may considerably exceed these values (3,500 mg for adults).

§ No allowance included for growth. Values for those below 18 years assume a growth rate at the 50th percentile reported by the National Center for Health Sciences (see reference 36) and averaged for males and females. See reference 24 for information on pregnancy and lactation.

Source: Reprinted with permission from *Recommended Dietary Allowances*, 10th edition, © 1989 by the National Academy of Sciences. Published by National Academy Press.

sex, and body weight (kg). Table 2-7 lists a comparison of basal metabolic rates per square meter surface area per hour as measured at four different laboratories. Figure 2-1 is a nomogram for use in calculating surface area in children.

REE and BMR estimates determined using standard calculations are based on the assumption that the individual is free of pathology and fever that affect energy expenditure. Figure 2-2 summarizes the percent change in energy expenditure associated with various stress conditions.[31] These values can be used to estimate REE for various medical conditions. However, regular re-evaluation of energy needs should be completed as REE decreases toward normal during recovery.[32] An additional stress variable is fever. REE increases approximately 13% for each degree Centigrade of fever (7.2% for each degree Fahrenheit).[30]

The final factor to determine in calculating energy needs is AEE. This can be accomplished by determining the amounts of time spent performing various types of activities and calculating an activity factor based on a 24-hour time period. Activity factors of 1.3 are associated with sedentary lifestyles, whereas activity factors equal to or greater than 2.0 represent lifestyles high in physical activity. Children under normal, unconstrained conditions are considered to be active, with activity factors ranging from 1.7 to 2.0 × REE. Table 2-8 lists the approximate

Table 2-6 Equations for Predicting Resting Energy Expenditure from Body Weight*

Sex and Age Range (years)	Equation to Derive REE in kcal/day	R†	SD†
Males			
0–3	$(60.9 \times wt^{\ddagger}) - 54$	0.97	53
3–10	$(22.7 \times wt) + 495$	0.86	62
10–18	$(17.5 \times wt) + 651$	0.90	100
18–30	$(15.3 \times wt) + 679$	0.65	151
30–60	$(11.6 \times wt) + 879$	0.60	164
>60	$(13.5 \times wt) + 487$	0.79	148
Females			
0–3	$(61.0 \times wt) - 51$	0.97	61
3–10	$(22.5 \times wt) + 499$	0.85	63
10–18	$(12.2 \times wt) + 746$	0.75	117
18–30	$(14.7 \times wt) + 496$	0.72	121
30–60	$(8.7 \times wt) + 829$	0.70	108
>60	$(10.5 \times wt) + 596$	0.74	108

* From reference 26. These equations were derived from BMR data.
† Correlation coefficient (R) of reported BMRs and predicted values, and standard deviation (SD) of the differences between actual and computed values.
‡ Weight of person in kilograms.

Source: Reprinted with permission from *Recommended Dietary Allowances,* 10th edition, © 1989 by the National Academy of Sciences. Published by National Academy Press.

energy expenditure for various activities in relation to REE. Table 2-9 demonstrates the method of calculating an activity factor and the TEE for a child.

Indirect Calorimetry. Indirect calorimetry is now available for determining individual REE in many acute care facilities. These measurements require the establishment of a closed system for determination of oxygen (O_2) consumption, which may be accomplished with a ventilated canopy, face mask, or mouthpiece with noseclips. In pediatrics, the use of indirect calorimetry may be limited due to inability to scale equipment to small children, failure to achieve a closed system, or lack of patient cooperation. REE measurements are particularly useful when developing individualized nutritional support regimens for critically ill patients.[34] The measured REE may approximate TEE in immobilized patients. Ambulatory hospitalized individuals require an increase in energy of 25% to 30% to allow for activity (e.g., activity factor = 1.25 to 1.3).[27]

When expired carbon dioxide (CO_2) is also included in the indirect calorimetry measurement, the patient's respiratory quotient (RQ) can be calculated using the equation

$$RQ = VCO_2/VO_2$$

Table 2-7 Standards of Basal Metabolism[†]

Kcal per Square Meter per Hour

Age—Years	1	2	3	4	5	6	7	8	9	10	11	12	13	14	15	16
Boys																
Fleisch	53.0	52.4	51.3	50.3	49.3	48.3	47.3	46.3	45.2	44.0	43.0	42.5	42.3	42.1	41.8	41.4
Rob.	—	—	60.1*	57.9	56.3	54.2	52.1	50.1	48.2	46.6	45.1	43.8	42.7	41.8	41.0	40.3
B. B. & D.	—	—	—	—	—	53.0	52.4	51.5	49.9	48.0	47.2	46.8	46.5	46.4	46.1	45.5
Lewis	—	56.9	54.5	52.6	51.0	49.6	48.2	46.6	45.0	43.6	42.2	41.5	41.4	41.1	40.5	—
Girls																
Fleisch	53.0	52.4	51.2	49.8	48.4	47.0	45.4	43.8	42.8	42.5	42.0	41.3	40.3	39.2	37.9	36.9
Rob.	—	—	54.5*	53.9	53.0	51.8	50.2	48.4	46.4	44.3	42.4	40.6	39.1	37.8	36.8	36.0
B. B. & D.	—	—	—	—	—	50.5	48.5	46.7	46.1	45.7	45.1	43.9	42.5	41.1	39.7	38.6
Lewis	—	52.9	51.3	49.9	48.4	46.9	45.5	44.0	42.7	41.4	40.4	39.7	38.4	36.8	35.2	—

Age—Years	17	18	19	20	25	30	35	40	45	50	55	60	65	70	75	80
Men																
Fleisch	40.8	40.0	39.2	38.6	37.5	36.8	36.5	36.3	36.2	35.8	35.4	34.9	34.4	33.8	33.2	33.0
Rob.	39.7	39.2	38.8	38.4	37.1	36.4	35.9	35.5	34.1	33.8	33.4	33.1	32.7	32.4*	32.0*	—
B. B. & D.	44.4	42.9	42.2	41.6	40.3	39.6	38.9	38.3	37.6	37.0	36.3	35.7	35.1*	34.5*	33.4*	—
Women																
Fleisch	36.3	35.9	35.5	35.3	35.2	35.1	35.0	34.9	34.5	33.9	33.3	32.7	32.2	31.7	31.3	30.9
Rob.	35.3	34.9	34.5	34.3	34.0	34.1	33.5	32.6	32.2	31.9	31.6	31.3	31.0	30.7	—	—
B. B. & D.	37.6	37.0	36.6	36.3	36.0	35.8	35.7	35.5	35.3	34.4	33.4	32.8	32.4*	32.2*	32.0*	—

* Extrapolated or based on less than 7 subjects.
† The new standards of Fleisch and of Robertson and Reid compared with the older standards of Boothby, Berkson, and Dunn (Mayo Clinic); and of Lewis, Duval, and Iliff. See references 28, 29, 97, and 98.

Source: Reprinted with permission from the *Annual Review of Physiology*, Vol 16, © 1954 by Annual Reviews Inc.

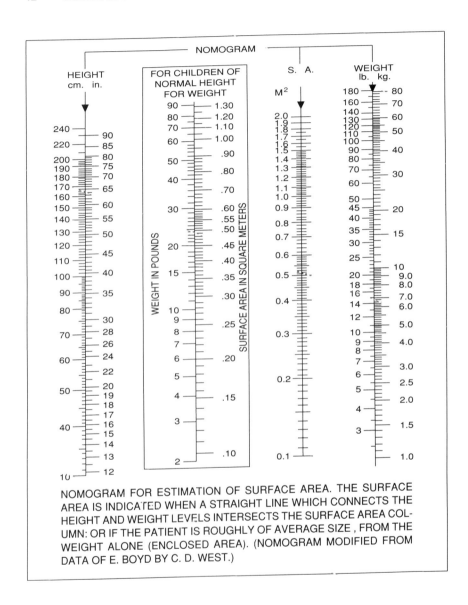

NOMOGRAM FOR ESTIMATION OF SURFACE AREA. THE SURFACE AREA IS INDICATED WHEN A STRAIGHT LINE WHICH CONNECTS THE HEIGHT AND WEIGHT LEVELS INTERSECTS THE SURFACE AREA COLUMN: OR IF THE PATIENT IS ROUGHLY OF AVERAGE SIZE , FROM THE WEIGHT ALONE (ENCLOSED AREA). (NOMOGRAM MODIFIED FROM DATA OF E. BOYD BY C. D. WEST.)

Figure 2-1 Nomogram for estimation of surface area. *Source:* Reprinted from *Nelson's Textbook of Medicine*, ed 13 (p 1521) by RE Behrman and VC Vaughan (eds) with permission of WB Saunders, © 1987.

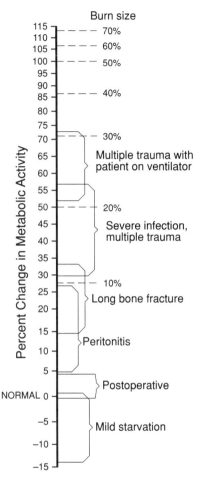

Figure 2-2 Increased energy needs with stress. *Source:* Adapted with permission from *The Metabolic Management of the Critically Ill* (p 36) by D Wilmore with permission of Plenum Press, © 1977.

The RQ reflects the source of metabolic fuel and its utilization. Oxidation of carbohydrate produces an RQ of 1, whereas oxidation of fat decreases the RQ toward 0.7. RQs greater than 1 indicate the synthesis of fat from carbohydrate and represent inefficient substrate utilization. Therefore, reducing RQ through alteration of energy substrates can be medically advantageous.[27,35]

Table 2-8 Approximate Energy Expenditure for Various Activities in Relation to Resting Needs for Males and Females of Average Size*

Activity Category†	Representative Value for Activity Factor per Unit Time of Activity
Resting	REE × 1.0
Sleeping, reclining	
Very light	REE × 1.5
Seated and standing activities, painting trades, driving, laboratory work, typing, sewing, ironing, cooking, playing cards, playing a musical instrument	
Light	REE × 2.5
Walking on a level surface at 2.5 to 3 mph, garage work, electrical trades, carpentry, restaurant trades, house-cleaning, child care, golf, sailing, table tennis	
Moderate	REE × 5.0
Walking 3.5 to 4 mph, weeding and hoeing, carrying a load, cycling, skiing, tennis, dancing	
Heavy	REE × 7.0
Walking with load uphill, tree felling, heavy manual digging, basketball, climbing, football, soccer	

* Data from references 26 and 33.
† When reported as multiples of basal needs, the expenditures of males and females are similar.

Source: Reprinted with permission from *Recommended Dietary Allowances*, 10th edition, © 1989 by the National Academy of Sciences. Published by National Academy Press.

Anthropometric Measurements

Monitoring growth through measurement of weight, length/height, and head circumference (in children 3 years of age or less) is a routine practice in most pediatric health care systems. These data are plotted on growth charts according to age for comparison with growth of a reference population of healthy, normal infants/children. (See Chapter 1.)

Weight-for-Stature Index

The weight-for-stature index is used to identify infants and children with obesity or acute protein-energy malnutrition (PEM). This index is calculated by dividing the child's actual weight by the 50% weight for length. Children with an index equal to or greater than 1.1 (110% of standard) require further evaluation for overweight/obesity; those falling below 0.9 (90% of standard) require assessment for acute PEM.[37–39]

Table 2-9 Example of Calculation for Total Energy Expenditure in an 11-Year-Old Boy*

Activity Type	REE Multiple	Duration (hr)	Weighted REE Factor
Resting	1.0	9	9
Very light	1.5	8	12
Light	2.5	4	10
Moderate	5.0	2	10
Heavy	7.0	1	7
TOTALS		24	48

Activity factor = weighted REE ÷ hours
  = 48 ÷ 24
  = 2.0

Total energy expenditure:

Gender	Age (yr)	Wt (kg)	REE† (kcal/d)	×	Activity Factor	=	TEE (kcal/d)
Male	11	35	1263.5	×	2.0	=	2527

* Hypothetical activity pattern.
† Calculated from equations in Table 2-6.

Charts[36] (see Figures 2-3 through 2-6) and detailed tables[40] for children greater than 12 are also available for evaluating the weight-for-stature index. These provide a percentile format of weight for stature in which infants and children greater than the 95% level are at risk for obesity and those less than the 5% level are at risk for acute PEM.

Incremental Growth

Incremental growth charts and tables have been developed for comparing short-term rates of growth to those of a reference population at specified age intervals.[41-44] Unlike conventional growth charts in which attained growth measurements are expected to follow a growth channel, growth increments usually show variability at successive age intervals within an individual. The prolonged maintenance of rates of gain for any growth parameter in excess of or below the 50th percentile may indicate abnormal growth and require further evaluation. In addition to identifying abnormal growth patterns, incremental growth assessments are helpful in evaluating individual response to nutritional intervention or other therapies that may alter growth rates (see Chapter 1).

When using incremental growth charts or tables, measurements need to be mathematically adjusted for the reference time increment. For example, if the time

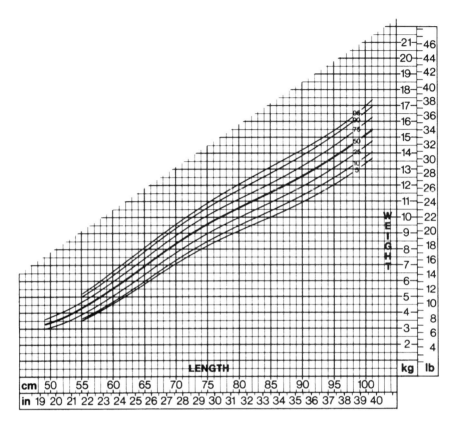

Figure 2-3 National Center for Health Statistics percentiles for weight for length, girls less than 4 years. *Source:* Used with permission of Ross Laboratories, Columbus, OH 43216, from Ross Growth and Development Programs, © 1981 Ross Laboratories.

between weight measurements is 200 days, adjustment for a 6-month weight increment is made by dividing the measured change in weight by 200 and then multiplying the result by 182 (number of days in 6 months). (Figures 2-A1 through 2-A10 in Appendix 2-A are 6-month incremental growth charts developed from the Fels Longitudinal Study of normal white American children from birth through 18 years.[41])

Skinfold Measurements

Skinfold measurements are useful in determining a depletion or excess of fat stores (see also Chapter 1). The triceps and subscapular skinfold thicknesses are the two measurements most commonly included as part of a nutritional assess-

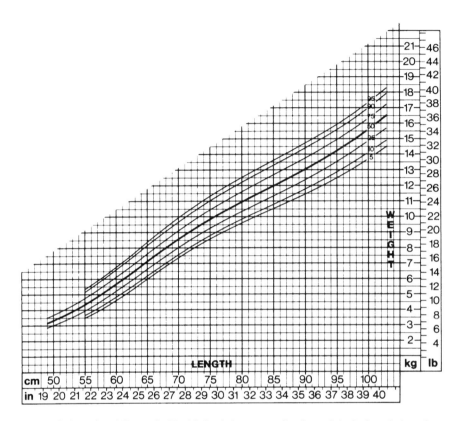

Figure 2-4 National Center for Health Statistics percentiles for weight for length, boys less than 4 years. *Source:* Used with permission of Ross Laboratories, Columbus, OH 43216, from Ross Growth and Development Programs, © 1981 Ross Laboratories.

ment.[45–47] When only one skinfold measurement is performed, the triceps skinfold thickness is recommended since it is the more valid indicator of percent body fat. Skinfold measurements are not currently recommended for routine nutritional screening but are useful in clarifying the nutritional status of children above the 90th or below the 10th percentile of weight for stature.[45] Figures 2-7 through 2-10 show triceps and subscapular percentiles for a reference United States population based on the National Health and Nutrition Examination Survey (NHANES) II and III and National Health and Nutrition Examination Survey (NHANES) I. Table 2-10 provides tabular percentile data for triceps skinfold of whites based on NHANES I data.[52] Variation found between graphs and this table most likely re-

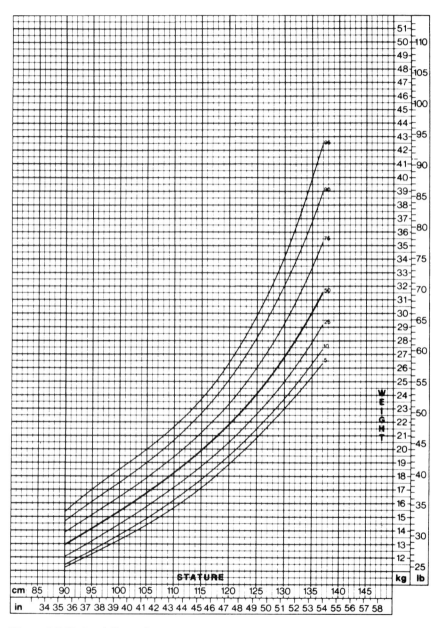

Figure 2-5 National Center for Health Statistics percentiles for weight for stature, prepubescent girls. *Source:* Used with permission of Ross Laboratories, Columbus, OH 43216, from Ross Growth and Development Programs, © 1981 Ross Laboratories.

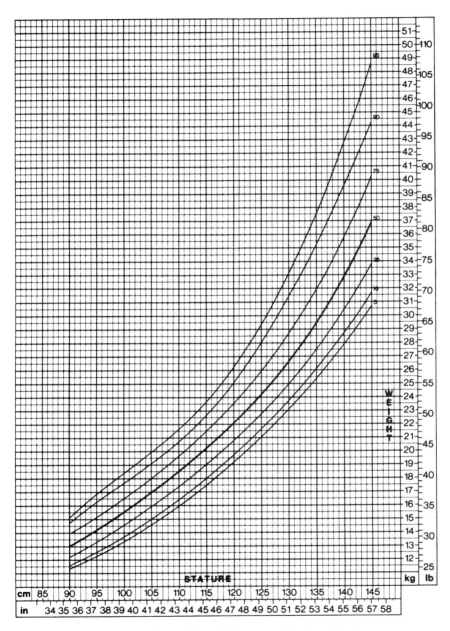

Figure 2-6 National Center for Health Statistics percentiles for weight for stature, prepubescent boys. *Source:* Used with permission of Ross Laboratories, Columbus, OH 43216, from Ross Growth and Development Programs, © 1981 Ross Laboratories.

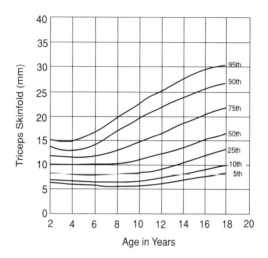

Figure 2-7 Smoothed percentiles of triceps skinfold for girls aged 2 to 18 years, by age: United States, 1963 to 1965, 1966 to 1970, 1971 to 1974. *Source:* Reprinted from Basic data on anthropometric measurements and angular measurements of the hip and knee joints for selected age groups 1–74 years of age, by CL Johnson, R Fulwood, S Abraham, and JD Bryner. DHHS Publication No. (PHS) 81-1669.

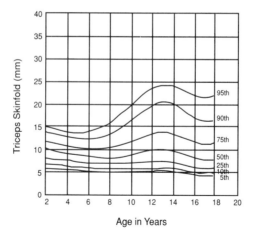

Figure 2-8 Smoothed percentiles of triceps skinfold for boys aged 2 to 18 years, by age: United States, 1963 to 1965, 1966 to 1970, 1971 to 1974. *Source:* Reprinted from Basic data on anthropometric measurements and angular measurements of the hip and knee joints for selected age groups 1–74 years of age, by CL Johnson, R Fulwood, S Abraham, and JD Bryner. DHHS Publication No. (PHS) 81-1669.

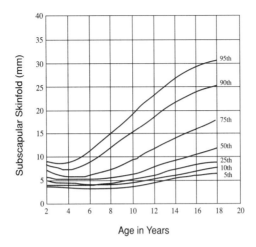

Figure 2-9 Smoothed percentiles of subscapular skinfold for girls aged 2 to 18 years, by age: United States, 1963 to 1965, 1966 to 1970, 1971 to 1974. *Source:* Reprinted from Basic data on anthropometric measurements and angular measurements of the hip and knee joints for selected age groups 1–74 years of age, by CL Johnson, R Fulwood, S Abraham, and JD Bryner. DHHS Publication No. (PHS) 81-1669.

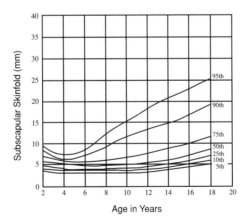

Figure 2-10 Smoothed percentiles of subscapular skinfold for boys aged 2 to 18 years, by age: United States, 1963 to 1965, 1966 to 1970, 1971 to 1974. *Source:* Reprinted from Basic data on anthropometric measurements and angular measurements of the hip and knee joints for selected age groups 1–74 years of age, by CL Johnson, R Fulwood, S Abraham, and JD Bryner. DHHS Publication No. (PHS) 81-1669.

lates to the racial composition of the two populations. Table 2-11 presents measurements for 7- to 13-month-old infants collected by Ross Laboratories.[46]

Triceps skinfold measurements are taken at the midpoint between the acromion and olecranon in the midline on the posterior aspect of the right upper arm. A double fold of the skin and underlying subcutaneous tissue parallel to the longitudinal axis of the arm is measured. The standard position has the child sitting or standing with the arm extended along the trunk. However, measurements performed on patients lying in bed have been reported to compare favorably with measurements taken in the standard position.[48] Subscapular skinfold measurements are taken just inferior to the inferior angle of the right scapula, with the shoulder and arm relaxed. The fold parallels the natural cleavage lines of the skin. Spring-type calipers that exert a force of 10 g/cm^2 are recommended. Measurements are read 2 to 3 seconds after application of the caliper, with repeat readings taken until duplicates agree within 1 mm. The skinfold is held throughout the measurement.[45,49]

Upper Arm Measurements

Upper arm measurements used in the assessment of nutritional status include mid-arm circumference (MAC), mid-arm area (MAA), mid-arm muscle circumference (MAMC), mid-arm muscle area (MAMA), and mid-arm fat area (MAFA). The mid-arm circumference measurement is taken at the midpoint between the acromion and olecranon of the right arm and recorded in centimeters to the nearest 0.1 cm.[49] The mid-arm area is calculated from the mid-arm circumference using the following equation:

$$\text{MAA (mm)}^2 = \quad /4 \times (\text{MAC (mm)}/ \quad ^2)$$
$$= 0.785 \times (\text{MAC (mm)}/3.14^2)$$

The remaining mid-arm measurements are calculated using these two indices plus the triceps skinfold (TSF) measurement.

$$\text{MAMC (cm)} = \text{MAC (cm)} - (\quad \times \text{TSF (cm)})$$
$$= \text{MAC (cm)} - (3.14 \, \text{TSF (cm)})$$
$$\text{MAMA (mm)}^2 = (\text{MAC (mm)} - \quad \times \text{TSF (mm)})^2/4$$
$$= (\text{MAC (mm)} - 3.14 \, \text{TSF (mm)})^2/12.56$$
$$\text{MAFA (mm)}^2 = \text{MAA (mm)}^2 - \text{MAMA (mm)}^2$$

The mid-arm circumference has been shown to be a sensitive index in predicting the risk for mortality among young children in developing countries that have a high incidence of malnutrition.[50] However, it has not proven to be as effective a predictor of morbidity or mortality among hospitalized North American children.[51]

The mid-arm muscle area and mid-arm fat area measurements are used to clarify other anthropometric findings.[47,52,53] For example, a child with a weight for height greater than the 95% due to a large muscle mass may erroneously be iden-

Table 2-10 Percentiles for Triceps Skinfold for Whites of the United States Health and Nutrition Examination Survey I of 1971 to 1974

Triceps Skinfold Percentiles (mm²)

Age Group	Males								Females							
	n	5	10	25	50	75	90	95	n	5	10	25	50	75	90	95
1–1.9	228	6	7	8	10	12	14	16	204	6	7	8	10	12	14	16
2–2.9	223	6	7	8	10	12	14	15	208	6	8	9	10	12	15	16
3–3.9	220	6	7	8	10	11	14	15	208	7	8	9	11	12	14	15
4–4.9	230	6	6	8	9	11	12	14	208	7	8	8	10	12	14	16
5–5.9	214	6	6	8	9	11	14	15	219	6	7	8	10	12	15	18
6–6.9	117	5	6	7	8	10	13	16	118	6	6	8	10	12	14	16
7–7.9	122	5	6	7	9	12	15	17	126	6	7	9	11	13	16	18
8–8.9	117	5	6	7	8	10	13	16	118	8	8	9	12	15	18	24
9–9.9	121	6	6	7	10	13	17	18	125	7	8	10	13	16	20	22
10–10.9	146	6	6	8	10	14	18	21	152	7	8	10	12	17	23	27
11–11.9	122	6	6	8	11	16	20	24	117	7	8	10	13	18	24	28
12–12.9	153	6	6	8	11	14	22	28	129	8	9	11	14	18	23	27
13–13.9	134	5	5	7	10	14	22	26	151	8	8	12	15	21	26	30
14–14.9	131	4	5	7	9	14	21	24	141	9	10	13	16	21	26	28
15–15.9	128	4	5	6	8	11	18	24	117	8	10	12	17	21	25	32
16–16.9	131	4	5	6	8	12	16	22	142	10	12	15	18	22	26	31
17–17.9	133	5	5	6	8	12	16	19	114	10	12	13	19	24	30	37
18–18.9	91	4	5	6	9	13	20	24	109	10	12	15	18	22	26	30
19–24.9	531	4	5	7	10	15	20	22	1060	10	11	14	18	24	30	34
25–34.9	971	5	6	8	12	16	20	24	1987	10	12	16	21	27	34	37
35–44.9	806	5	6	8	12	16	20	23	1614	12	14	18	23	29	35	38
45–54.9	898	6	6	8	12	15	20	25	1047	12	16	20	25	30	36	40
55–64.9	734	5	6	8	11	14	19	22	809	12	16	20	25	31	36	38
65–74.9	1503	4	6	8	11	15	19	22	1670	12	14	18	24	29	34	36

Source: Reprinted with permission from AR Frisancho, New norms of upper limb fat and muscle areas for assessment of nutritional status, in *American Journal of Clinical Nutrition* (1981;34:2540–2545), Copyright © 1981, American Society for Clinical Nutrition.

Table 2-11 Observed Means, Standard Deviations, and Smoothed Percentile Values of Triceps Skinfold (mm) by Sex and Age for Infants 7 to 13 Months Old

Age (months)	n	Mean	SD	Percentile						
				5th	10th	25th	50th	75th	90th	95th
Males										
7	45	9.2	3.1	—	5.9	7.1	7.5	8.0	11.0	—
8	80	8.8	2.2	5.0	5.9	7.2	8.4	9.2	11.1	11.8
9	95	8.8	2.1	5.2	5.8	7.2	8.6	9.6	11.1	12.1
10	124	9.3	2.3	5.4	6.2	7.4	8.6	9.7	10.8	12.6
11	103	9.3	3.1	5.6	6.8	7.6	8.8	10.3	13.3	15.0
12	68	10.0	3.5	5.6	7.0	7.6	9.3	10.3	13.1	15.9
13	30	9.5	2.5	—	—	—	9.5	—	—	—
Females										
7	46	8.2	2.5	—	3.0	5.2	7.5	9.0	11.0	—
8	88	8.6	2.7	3.0	3.5	5.5	7.5	9.3	10.8	12.0
9	109	8.4	2.5	3.7	4.2	5.6	7.5	9.2	10.8	12.0
10	120	8.7	2.3	3.9	4.6	5.8	7.7	9.5	11.1	13.3
11	95	9.4	3.5	4.4	5.0	6.0	8.3	9.7	11.1	13.8
12	70	9.2	2.7	5.2	5.4	6.4	8.9	10.2	11.1	12.3
13	27	9.5	1.9	—	—	—	9.2	—	—	—

Source: Reprinted with permission from AS Ryan and GA Martinez, Physical growth of infants 7 to 13 months of age: results from a national survey, in American Journal of Physical Anthropology (1987;73:449), Copyright © 1987, Alan R Liss, Inc.

tified as obese unless the mid-arm muscle area is measured. Figure 2-11 shows a nomogram for determining mid-arm muscle circumference and areas based on mid-arm circumference and triceps skinfold measurements. Tables 2-12 and 2-13 list mid-arm fat and muscle circumference and area percentiles with respect to age for whites as assessed within the NHANES I (1971 to 1974).[52]

Although the calculations of mid-arm anthropometric data are based on some assumptions that are not entirely accurate, these measurements continue to be useful in identifying the status of lean and fat body compartments. Computerized axial tomography (CAT) scans provide a more accurate area measurement and are of value for research.[54-56] However, the expense of these measurements and lack of reference data make these techniques less practical for the routine assessment of children at nutritional risk.

Other Considerations

The developmental maturity of the child needs to be considered when interpreting anthropometric data. Correction for gestational age at birth is essential in the assessment of infants born prematurely (refer to Chapter 3). Children evaluated for delayed or precocious growth often have bone age assessments based on radiographic studies, which should be considered. For the older child, data relating to the stage of sexual maturity can alter assessment findings.[44,57] Table 2-14 presents a summary of Tanner's staging of the progression of sexual development.[58] Acceleration in rates of incremental growth is directly related to the onset of puberty[41] (see Chapter 1). In boys, a prepubescent increase in fat stores is often reflected in triceps skinfold measurements.[48,59]

Racial and ethnic differences in body composition are evident in children. In general, newborn black infants are smaller than newborn white infants. Black and white children are of similar size by 1 year. Although black children are longer and heavier than white children by age 3, they are also leaner, as indicated by lower triceps skinfolds. This trend continues through age 17.[45,46,63,64] After about age 12, Mexican-American children tend to be shorter than either white or black children.[59] The median skinfold thicknesses and weight/stature^2 indexes are higher among Mexican-American children than white or black children throughout childhood.[65,66]

Laboratory Measurements

Some laboratory measurements of nutritional status are routinely collected as part of a normal health care evaluation. Others are performed when the diagnosis, medical history, or nutritional history indicates nutritional risk. Table 2-15 lists

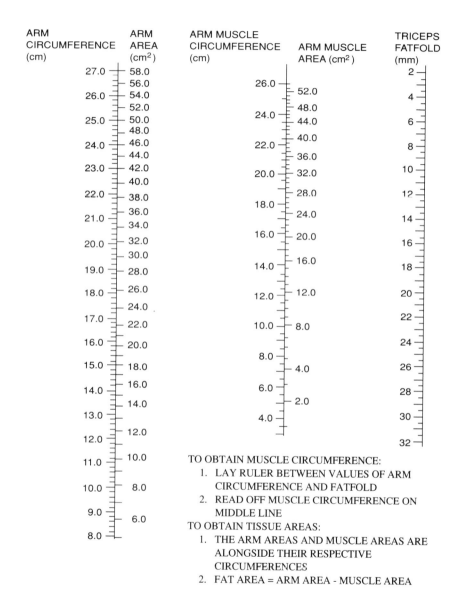

TO OBTAIN MUSCLE CIRCUMFERENCE:
1. LAY RULER BETWEEN VALUES OF ARM
    CIRCUMFERENCE AND FATFOLD
2. READ OFF MUSCLE CIRCUMFERENCE ON
    MIDDLE LINE
TO OBTAIN TISSUE AREAS:
1. THE ARM AREAS AND MUSCLE AREAS ARE
    ALONGSIDE THEIR RESPECTIVE
    CIRCUMFERENCES
2. FAT AREA = ARM AREA - MUSCLE AREA

Figure 2-11 Arm anthropometry nomogram for children. *Source:* Reprinted with permission from JM Gurney and DB Jeliffe, Arm anthropometry in nutritional assessment: nomogram for rapid calculation of muscle circumference and cross-sectional muscle and fat areas, in *American Journal of Clinical Nutrition* (1973;26:912–915). Copyright © 1973, American Society for Clinical Nutrition.

Table 2-12 Percentiles of Upper Arm Circumference (mm) and Estimated Upper Arm Muscle Circumference (mm) for Whites of the United States Health and Nutrition Examination Survey I of 1971 to 1974

Males

Age Group	Arm Circumference (mm)							Arm Muscle Circumference (mm)						
	5	10	25	50	75	90	95	5	10	25	50	75	90	95
1–1.9	142	146	150	159	170	176	183	110	113	119	127	135	144	147
2–2.9	141	145	153	162	170	178	185	111	114	122	130	140	146	150
3–3.9	150	153	160	167	175	184	190	117	123	131	137	143	148	153
4–4.9	149	154	162	171	180	186	192	123	126	133	141	148	156	159
5–5.9	153	160	167	175	185	195	204	128	133	140	147	154	162	169
6–6.9	155	159	167	179	188	209	228	131	135	142	151	161	170	177
7–7.9	162	167	177	187	201	223	230	137	139	151	160	168	177	190
8–8.9	162	170	177	190	202	220	245	140	145	154	162	170	182	187
9–9.9	175	178	187	200	217	249	257	151	154	161	170	183	196	202
10–10.9	181	184	196	210	231	262	274	156	160	166	180	191	209	221
11–11.9	186	190	202	223	244	261	280	159	165	173	183	195	205	230
12–12.9	193	200	214	232	254	282	303	167	171	182	195	210	223	241
13–13.9	194	211	228	247	263	286	301	172	179	196	211	226	238	245
14–14.9	220	226	237	253	283	303	322	189	199	212	223	240	260	264
15–15.9	222	229	244	264	284	311	320	199	204	218	237	254	266	272
16–16.9	244	248	262	278	303	324	343	213	225	234	249	269	287	296
17–17.9	246	253	267	285	308	336	347	224	231	245	258	273	294	312
18–18.9	245	260	276	297	321	353	379	226	237	252	264	283	298	324
19–24.9	262	272	288	308	331	355	372	238	245	257	273	289	309	321
25–34.9	271	282	300	319	342	362	375	243	250	264	279	298	314	326
35–44.9	278	287	305	326	345	363	374	247	255	269	286	302	318	327
45–54.9	267	281	301	322	342	362	376	239	249	265	281	300	315	326
55–64.9	258	273	296	317	336	355	369	236	245	260	278	295	310	320
65–74.9	248	263	285	307	325	344	355	223	235	251	268	284	298	306

continues

Table 2-12 continued

Females

Age Group	Arm Circumference (mm)							Arm Muscle Circumference (mm)						
	5	10	25	50	75	90	95	5	10	25	50	75	90	95
1–1.9	138	142	148	156	164	172	177	105	111	117	124	132	139	143
2–2.9	142	145	152	160	167	176	184	111	114	119	126	133	142	147
3–3.9	143	150	158	167	175	183	189	113	119	124	132	140	146	152
4–4.9	149	154	160	169	177	184	191	115	121	128	136	144	152	157
5–5.9	153	157	165	175	185	203	211	125	128	134	142	151	159	165
6–6.9	156	162	170	176	187	204	211	130	133	138	145	154	166	171
7–7.9	164	167	174	183	199	216	231	129	135	142	151	160	171	176
8–8.9	168	172	183	195	214	247	261	138	140	151	160	171	183	194
9–9.9	178	182	194	211	224	251	260	147	150	158	167	180	194	198
10–10.9	174	182	193	210	228	251	265	148	150	159	170	180	190	197
11–11.9	185	194	208	224	248	276	303	150	158	171	181	196	217	223
12–12.9	194	203	216	237	256	282	294	162	166	180	191	201	214	220
13–13.9	202	211	223	243	271	301	338	169	175	183	198	211	226	240
14–14.9	214	223	237	252	272	304	322	174	179	190	201	216	232	247
15–15.9	208	221	239	254	279	300	322	175	178	189	202	215	228	244
16–16.9	218	224	241	258	283	318	334	170	180	190	202	216	234	249
17–17.9	220	227	241	264	295	324	350	175	183	194	205	221	239	257
18–18.9	222	227	241	258	281	312	325	174	179	191	202	215	237	245
19–24.9	221	230	247	265	290	319	345	179	185	195	207	221	236	249
25–34.9	233	240	256	277	304	342	368	183	188	199	212	228	246	264
35–44.9	241	251	267	290	317	356	378	186	192	205	218	236	257	272
45–54.9	242	256	274	299	328	362	384	187	193	206	220	238	260	274
55–64.9	243	257	280	303	335	367	385	187	196	209	225	244	266	280
65–74.9	240	252	274	299	326	356	373	185	195	208	225	244	264	279

Source: Reprinted with permission from AR Frisancho, New norms of upper limb fat and muscle areas for assessment of nutritional status, in *American Journal of Clinical Nutrition* (1981;34:2540–2545), Copyright © 1981, American Society for Clinical Nutrition, Inc.

Table 2-13 Percentiles for Estimates of Upper Arm Fat Area (mm²) and Upper Arm Muscle Area (mm²) for Whites of the United States Health and Nutrition Examination Survey I of 1971 to 1974

Males

Age Group	Arm Muscle Area Percentiles (mm²)							Arm Fat Area Percentiles (mm²)						
	5	10	25	50	75	90	95	5	10	25	50	75	90	95
1–1.9	956	1014	1133	1278	1447	1644	1720	452	486	590	741	895	1036	1176
2–2.9	973	1040	1190	1345	1557	1690	1787	434	504	578	737	871	1044	1148
3–3.9	1095	1201	1357	1484	1618	1750	1853	464	519	590	736	868	1071	1151
4–4.9	1207	1264	1408	1579	1747	1926	2008	428	494	598	722	859	989	1085
5–5.9	1298	1411	1550	1720	1884	2089	2285	446	488	582	713	914	1176	1299
6–6.9	1360	1447	1605	1815	2056	2297	2493	371	446	539	678	896	1115	1519
7–7.9	1497	1548	1808	2027	2246	2494	2886	423	473	574	758	1011	1393	1511
8–8.9	1550	1664	1895	2089	2296	2628	2788	410	460	588	725	1003	1248	1558
9–9.9	1811	1884	2067	2288	2657	3053	3257	485	527	635	859	1252	1864	2081
10–10.9	1930	2027	2182	2575	2903	3486	3882	523	543	738	982	1376	1906	2609
11–11.9	2016	2156	2382	2670	3022	3359	4226	536	595	754	1148	1710	2348	2574
12–12.9	2216	2339	2649	3022	3496	3968	4640	554	650	874	1172	1558	2536	3580
13–13.9	2363	2546	3044	3553	4081	4502	4794	475	570	812	1096	1702	2744	3322
14–14.9	2830	3147	3586	3963	4575	5368	5530	453	563	786	1082	1608	2746	3508
15–15.9	3138	3317	3788	4481	5134	5631	5900	521	595	690	931	1423	2434	3100
16–16.9	3625	4044	4352	4951	5753	6576	6980	542	593	844	1078	1746	2280	3041
17–17.9	3998	4252	4777	5286	5950	6886	7726	598	698	827	1096	1636	2407	2888
18–18.9	4070	4481	5066	5552	6374	7067	8355	560	665	860	1264	1947	3302	3928
19–24.9	4508	4777	5274	5913	6660	7606	8200	594	743	963	1406	2231	3098	3652
25–34.9	4694	4963	5541	6214	7067	7847	8436	675	831	1174	1752	2459	3246	3786
35–44.9	4844	5181	5740	6490	7265	8034	8488	703	851	1310	1792	2463	3098	3624
45–54.9	4546	4946	5589	6297	7142	7918	8458	749	922	1254	1741	2359	3245	3928
55–64.9	4422	4783	5381	6144	6919	7670	8149	658	839	1166	1645	2236	2976	3466
65–74.9	3973	4411	5031	5716	6432	7074	7453	573	753	1122	1621	2199	2876	3327

continues

Table 2-13 continued

Females

Age Group	Arm Muscle Area Percentiles (mm²)							Arm Fat Area Percentiles (mm²)						
	5	10	25	50	75	90	95	5	10	25	50	75	90	95
1–1.9	885	973	1084	1221	1378	1535	1621	401	466	578	706	847	1022	1140
2–2.9	973	1029	1119	1269	1405	1595	1727	469	526	642	747	894	1061	1173
3–3.9	1014	1133	1227	1396	1563	1690	1846	473	529	656	822	967	1106	1158
4–4.9	1058	1171	1313	1475	1644	1832	1958	490	541	654	766	907	1109	1236
5–5.9	1238	1301	1432	1598	1825	2012	2159	470	529	647	812	991	1330	1536
6–6.9	1354	1414	1513	1683	1877	2182	2323	464	508	638	827	1009	1263	1436
7–7.9	1330	1441	1602	1815	2045	2332	2469	491	560	706	920	1135	1407	1644
8–8.9	1513	1566	1808	2034	2327	2657	2996	527	634	769	1042	1383	1872	2482
9–9.9	1723	1788	1976	2227	2571	2987	3112	642	690	933	1219	1584	2171	2524
10–10.9	1740	1784	2019	2296	2583	2873	3093	616	702	842	1141	1608	2500	3005
11–11.9	1784	1987	2316	2612	3071	3739	3953	707	802	1015	1301	1942	2730	3690
12–12.9	2092	2182	2579	2904	3225	3655	3847	782	854	1090	1511	2056	2666	3369
13–13.9	2269	2426	2657	3130	3529	4081	4568	726	838	1219	1625	2374	3272	4150
14–14.9	2418	2562	2874	3220	3704	4294	4850	981	1043	1423	1818	2403	3250	3765
15–15.9	2426	2518	2847	3248	3689	4123	4756	839	1126	1396	1886	2544	3093	4195
16–16.9	2308	2567	2865	3248	3718	4353	4946	1126	1351	1663	2006	2598	3374	4236
17–17.9	2442	2674	2996	3336	3883	4552	5251	1042	1267	1463	2104	2977	3864	5159
18–18.9	2398	2538	2917	3243	3694	4461	4767	1003	1230	1616	2104	2617	3508	3733
19–24.9	2538	2728	3026	3406	3877	4439	4940	1046	1198	1596	2166	2959	4050	4896
25–34.9	2661	2826	3148	3573	4138	4806	5541	1173	1399	1841	2548	3512	4690	5560
35–44.9	2750	2948	3359	3783	4428	5240	5877	1336	1619	2158	2898	3932	5093	5847
45–54.9	2784	2956	3378	3858	4520	5375	5964	1459	1803	2447	3244	4229	5416	6140
55–64.9	2784	3063	3477	4045	4750	5632	6247	1345	1879	2520	3369	4360	5276	6152
65–74.9	2737	3018	3444	4019	4739	5566	6214	1363	1681	2266	3063	3943	4914	5530

Source: Reprinted with permission from AR Frisancho, New norms of upper limb fat and muscle areas for assessment of nutritional status, in *American Journal of Clinical Nutrition* (1981;34:2540–2545), Copyright © 1981, American Society for Clinical Nutrition, Inc.

Table 2-14 Pubertal Events Profile—Sequence of Events in Adolescent Development

Pubertal Changes by Sex*	Tanner Stage†	Mean Age of Onset in Years
Females		
Breasts	2	11.2
Pubic hair	2	11.7
Peak velocity of height growth		12
Breasts	3	12.2
Pubic hair	3	12.4
Pubic hair	4	12.9
Breasts	4	13.1
Menarche		13
Pubic hair	5	14.4
Breasts	5	15.3
Males		
Genital	2	11.6
Genital	3	12.9
Pubic hair	2	13.4
Genital	4	13.8
Pubic hair	3	13.9
Peak velocity of height growth		14
Pubic hair	4	14.4
Genital	5	14.9
Pubic hair	5	15.2

* Data adapted from references 60 to 62.

† Tanner Stage, or sexual maturity rating: 1. Prepubertal; 2. First visible signs of pubertal change appear; 3. Pubic hair increases and becomes darker and coarser, breasts enlarge, and genitalia lengthen and enlarge; 4. Pubic hair becomes more abundant and coarse, genitalia and breasts increase in size; 5. Adult characteristics visible for breasts, pubic hair, and genitalia.

Source: Reprinted with permission from EJ Gong and BA Spear, Adolescent growth and development: implications for nutritional needs, in *Journal of Nutrition Education* (1988;20:274), copyright © 1988, Society for Nutrition Education.

laboratory norms based on age categories for selected tests of nutritional status.[7] The interpretation of laboratory findings must take into consideration the medical status of the infant or child. Many biochemical indexes of nutritional status for normal individuals are altered by acute or chronic disease.

Serum Proteins

Albumin is the serum protein most commonly measured for assessment of nutritional status. However, due to half-life of approximately 2 weeks and reduced degradation during periods of low protein intake, diagnosis of nutritional deple-

Table 2-15 Table of Guidelines for Criteria of Nutritional Status for Laboratory Evaluation

Nutrient and Units	Age of Subject (years)	Criteria of Status		
		Deficient	Marginal	Acceptable
†Hemoglobin (g/100 ml)	6–23 mos.	Up to 9.0	9.0–9.9	10.0+
	2–5	Up to 10.0	10.0–10.9	11.0+
	6–12	Up to 10.0	10.0–11.4	11.5+
	13–16M	Up to 12.0	12.0–12.9	13.0+
	13–16F	Up to 10.0	10.0–11.4	11.5+
	16+M	Up to 12.0	12.0–13.9	14.0+
	16+F	Up to 10.0	10.0–11.9	12.0+
	Pregnant (after 6+ mos.)	Up to 9.5	9.5–10.9	11.0+
†Hematocrit (Packed cell volume in percent)	Up to 2	Up to 28	28–30	31+
	2–5	Up to 30	30–33	34+
	6–12	Up to 30	30–35	36+
	13–16M	Up to 37	37–39	40+
	13–16F	Up to 31	31–35	36+
	16+M	Up to 37	37–43	44+
	16+F	Up to 31	31–37	33+
	Pregnant	Up to 30	30–32	33+
†Serum albumin (g/100 ml)	Up to 1	—	Up to 2.5	2.5+
	1–5	—	Up to 3.0	3.0+
	6–16	—	Up to 3.5	3.5+
	16+	Up to 2.8	2.8–3.4	3.5+
	Pregnant	Up to 3.0	3.0–3.4	3.5+
†Serum protein (g/100 ml)	Up to 1	—	Up to 5.0	5.0+
	1–5	—	Up to 5.5	5.5+
	6–16	—	Up to 6.0	6.0+
	16+	Up to 6.0	6.0–6.4	6.5+
	Pregnant	Up to 5.5	5.5–5.9	6.0+
†Serum ascorbic acid (mg/100 ml)	All ages	Up to 0.1	0.1–0.19	0.2+
†Plasma vitamin A (μg/100 ml)	All ages	Up to 10	10–19	20+
†Plasma carotene (μg/100 ml)	All ages	Up to 20	20–39	40+
	Pregnant	—	40–79	80+
†Serum iron (μg/100 ml)	Up to 2	Up to 30	—	30+
	2–5	Up to 40	—	40+
	6–12	Up to 50	—	50+
	12+M	Up to 60	—	60+
	12+F	Up to 40	—	40+
†Transferrin saturation (percent)	Up to 2	Up to 15.0	—	15.0+
	2–12	Up to 20.0	—	20.0+
	12+M	Up to 20.0	—	20.0+
	12+F	Up to 15.0	—	15.0+
‡Serum folacin (ng/ml)	All ages	Up to 2.0	2.1–5.9	6.0+
‡Serum vitamin B_{12} (pg/ml)	All ages	Up to 100	—	100+

Nutrient and Units	Age of Subject (years)	Criteria of Status		
		Deficient	Marginal	Acceptable
†Thiamine in urine (µg/g creatinine)	1–3	Up to 120	120–175	175+
	4–5	Up to 85	85–120	120+
	6–9	Up to 70	70–180	180+
	10–15	Up to 55	55–150	150+
	16+	Up to 27	27–65	65+
	Pregnant	Up to 21	21–49	50+
†Riboflavin in urine (µg/g creatinine)	1–3	Up to 150	150–499	500+
	4–5	Up to 100	100–299	300+
	6–9	Up to 85	85–269	270+
	10–16	Up to 70	70–199	200+
	16+	Up to 27	27–79	80+
	Pregnant	Up to 30	30–89	90+
‡RBC transketolase-TPP-effect (ratio)	All ages	25+	15–25	Up to 15
‡RBC glutathione reductase-FAD-effect (ratio)	All ages	1.2+	—	Up to 1.2
‡Tryptophan load (mg xanthurenic acid excreted)	Adults (Dose: 100 mg/kg body weight)	25+ (6 hrs) 75+ (24 hrs)	— —	Up to 25 Up to 75
‡Urinary pyridoxine (µg/g creatinine)	1–3	Up to 90	—	90+
	4–6	Up to 80	—	80+
	7–9	Up to 60	—	60+
	10–12	Up to 40	—	40+
	13–15	Up to 30	—	30+
	16+	Up to 20	—	20+
†Urinary N'methyl nicotinamide (mg/g creatinine)	All ages	Up to 0.5	0.5–1.59	1.6+
	Pregnant	Up to 0.8	0.8—2.49	2.5+
‡Urinary pantothenic acid (µg)	All ages	Up to 200	—	200+
‡Plasma vitamin E (mg/100 ml)	All ages	Up to 0.2	0.2—0.6	0.6+
‡Transaminase index (ratio)				
EGOT	Adult	2.0+	—	Up to 2.0
EGPT	Adult	1.25+	—	Up 20 1.25

Note: EGOT, erythrocyte glutamic oxalacetic transaminase; EGPT, erythrocyte glutamic pyruvic transaminase; FAD, flavine adenine dinucleotide; RBC, red blood cell; TPP, thiamin pyrophosphate.

† Adapted from the Ten State Nutrition Survey.

‡ Criteria may vary with different methodology.

tion can be missed or delayed if based solely on serum albumin level. Likewise, serum albumin level serves as a relatively late indicator of nutritional repletion. For these reasons serum proteins with shorter half-lives, including transferrin, retinol binding protein, and thyroxine-binding prealbumin, are often measured.[67–71] Two additional serum proteins with short half-lives, fibronectin and somatomedin C, have potential to be useful in assessing early response to nutritional therapy.[70,72,73] Levels of all these serum proteins may be reduced with inadequate energy intake as well as deficiencies of other nutrients in addition to protein. Therefore, decreased levels of any of these serum proteins cannot be considered specific for protein depletion. Infection, trauma, enteropathy, liver, or renal diseases can also result in altered serum protein values.[67,75] Table 2-16 lists half-life and normal reference values for serum proteins commonly used for nutritional assessment.

Creatinine Height Index

Creatinine height index is an indirect measure of somatic protein status.[76,77] However, the required 24-hour urine collection can be difficult to complete in

Table 2-16 Serum Proteins Used in Assessing Nutritional Status

Protein	Half-Life	Normal Value	Factors Known to Alter Concentration*
Albumin	18–20 days	Preterm: 2.5–4.5 g/dl Term: 2.5–5.0 g/dl 1–3 mo.: 3.0–4.2 g/dl 3–12 mo.: 2.7–5.0 > 1 year: 3.2–5.0	↓ inflammation, infection, trauma, liver disease, renal disease, protein-losing enteropathy; altered by fluid status
Transferrin†	8–9 days	180–260 mg/dl	↓ inflammation, liver disease; ↑ iron deficiency; altered by fluid status
Prealbumin	2–3 days	20–50 mg/dl	↓ liver disease, cystic fibrosis, hyperthyroidism, infection, trauma
Retinol binding protein	12 hours	30–40 µg/ml	↓ liver disease, zinc or vitamin A deficiency, infection; ↑ renal disease

* Any condition that can alter a protein's rate of synthesis, degradation, or excretion has potential to alter the serum concentration.
† Transferrin may be calculated from total iron binding capacity (TIBC): (0.8 × TIBC) − 43 (See reference 74).
Source: Data from references 67, 75, and 99.

some pediatric patients. The index is calculated as (24-hour excretion of creatinine [in mg]/creatinine excretion of normal individuals of same height and sex) × 100. Values of 80% and 60% of standard indicate moderate and severe depletion, respectively. Creatinine clearance is altered by sepsis, trauma, malignancy, and other conditions that increase protein breakdown. Table 2-17 lists normal values for 24-hour creatinine excretion.[78]

Iron Status

Hemoglobin and/or hematocrit measurements are commonly used to assess iron nutrition. These are late signs of iron deficiency but are easily monitored in both clinic and hospital settings.[79] Serum ferritin level is highly correlated with total body stores of iron and is the most sensitive index of iron status among healthy individuals. An elevated free erythrocyte protoporphyrin level and a decreased serum iron/total iron-binding capacity ratio and transferrin saturation occur when iron stores are depleted. These biochemical findings are present before changes in hemoglobin and red blood cell morphology. With the exception of serum ferritin level, which rises, laboratory indicators for iron deficiency decrease during infection and chronic inflammation.[80,81] Table 2-18 summarizes iron status and hematologic abnormalities in states of negative iron balance.

Immunologic Function

Protein-energy malnutrition, as well as subclinical deficiencies of one or more nutrients, can impair immune response and increase risk for infection. The measurement of functional parameters of the immune system is therefore useful in assessing nutritional status. Among the immunologic indexes that are associated with nutritional status are levels of T-lymphocytes and leukocyte terminal deoxynucleotidyl transferase, appearance of delayed cutaneous hypersensitivity, opsonic function, salivary IgA, and total lymphocyte count. These tests vary in sensitivity for detecting nutritional depletion.[83] Infection, trauma, chemotherapy, immunosuppressant drug therapy, and lack of previous exposure to antigen in the case of delayed cutaneous hypersensitivity can alter the results of these functional measures.[83]

The total lymphocyte count (TLC) is the index of immune function most readily available for hospitalized patients. This value can be calculated from white blood cell (WBC) counts as follows:

$$WBC/mm^3 \times \% \text{ lymphocytes} = TLC/mm^3$$

Values less than 1500 are associated with nutritional depletion. In infants less than 3 months of age, values of less than 2500 may be abnormal.[10]

Table 2-17 Normal Values for 24-Hour Creatinine Excretion

Height (cm)	Creatinine Values (mg/24 h)		
	Both Sexes*	Males[†]	Females[†]
55	50.0		
60	65.2		
65	80.5		
70	97.5		
75	118.0		
80	139.6		
85	167.6		
90	199.9		
95	239.8		
100	278.7		
105	305.4		
110	349.8		
115	394.5		
120	456.0		
125	535.1		
130		448.1	525.2
135		480.1	589.2
140		556.3	653.1
145		684.3	717.2
150		812.3	780.9
155		940.3	844.8
160		1,068.3	908.8
165		1,196.3	
170		1,324.3	
175		1,452.3	
180		1,580.3	

* Data from reference 77.
[†] Data from reference 76.

Source: Reprinted from R Merritt and G Blackburn, Nutritional assessment and metabolic response to illness of the hospitalized child, in *Textbook of Pediatric Nutrition* by R Suskind (ed) with permission of Raven Press, © 1981.

DATA EVALUATION AND PLAN

The assessment of nutritional status is based on the careful evaluation of all gathered information. Inter-relationships between the health status of the child, feeding abilities, eating habits, anthropometric data and laboratory findings need

Table 2-18 Iron Status and Hematologic Abnormalities in States of Negative Iron Balance*

| | Normal | Iron Depletion | Iron Deficiency | Iron Deficiency Anemia | |
				Early	Advanced
Storage iron	NL	DECR	DECR	DECR	DECR
Erythron iron	NL	NL	DECR	DECR	DECR
Hemoglobin, Hematocrit, RBC count	NL	NL	NL	DECR	DECR
RBC indices	NL	NL	NL	NL	DECR

* NL, normal; DECR, decrease; RBC, red blood cell.

Source: Adapted from AJ Cecalupo and HJ Cohen, Nutritional anemias, in *Pediatric Nutrition Theory and Practice* (p 491) by RJ Grand, JL Sutphen and WH Dietz (eds) with permission of Butterworth Heinemann, © 1987.

to be considered. Exhibit 2-3 is an example of a detailed nutritional assessment summary for hospitalized infants and young children.

Protein-Energy Malnutrition

The identification of the presence and severity of protein-energy malnutrition (PEM) among children in hospitals and clinics is a valuable function of nutritional assessment. Table 2-19 outlines anthropometric indices that have been developed to quantitate the severity of chronic and acute PEM.[37–39] Children may present with one or both forms of PEM. Acute but not chronic PEM has been associated with increased morbidity and increased length of hospital stay.[84] For more information on "standard" reference values, refer to Chapter 13, Failure To Thrive.

Marasmus and Kwashiorkor

Marasmus and kwashiorkor are two classifications of severe acute PEM. Marasmus develops over a period of weeks or months and is characterized by a

Exhibit 2-3 Nutritional Assessment Summary for Hospitalized Infant or Young Child

NUTRITIONAL ASSESSMENT
(Birth to 36 months)

Date of Birth _____ Admitting Diagnosis _____ % Weight change in _____

Significant Medical Problems _____

Growth History: Previous Weights _____ Previous Lengths _____ Previous Growth Velocity: _____

date   kg   %ile   date   cm   %ile

	NUTRITIONAL RISK CRITERIA
Date	
Age	
Length (cm)	< 5th %ile suggests growth retardation
%ile	
Weight (kg)	< 5th %ile
%ile	
Weight/Length Index (actual weight ÷ ideal weight for length)	80% to 90%: Mild PEM* 70% to 80%: Moderate PEM* < 70%: Severe PEM*
Ideal Weight for Length	
Head Circumference (cm)	< 5th %ile
%ile	
Arm Circumference/ Head Circumference Ratio	.28 to .31: Mild PEM* .25 to .28: Moderate PEM* < .25%: Severe PEM*
Arm Circumference (cm)	< 5th %ile
%ile	
Arm Muscle Circumference (mm)	< 5th %ile
%ile	
Arm Muscle Area (mm²)	< 5th %ile
%ile	
Tricep Skinfold (mm)	< 5th %ile
%ile	
Subscapular Skinfold (mm)	< 5th %ile
%ile	

*PEM: Protein Energy Malnutrition

	NUTRITIONAL RISK CRITERIA
Date	0–6 mo <2.9 gm/dl 6 mo–3yr <3.5 gm/dl
Albumin	
Transferrin	
Pre Albumin	<200 mg/dl
Retinol Binding Protein	
Total Lymphocyte Count	< 1500 mm³

Intake _____ Dates _____

Kcal/kg _____

gm pro/kg _____

Oxygen consumption: Date: _____ REE = _____

NUTRITIONAL NEEDS* _____ Kcal/kg _____ gm pro/kg

based on _____ (*energy needs increase 7% per degree F.)

Expected rate of weight gain for size: _____

Comments:

Source: Courtesy of the Clinical Nutrition Services, Children's Hospital Medical Center, Cincinnati, OH.

Table 2-19 Anthropometric Indexes Associated with Protein-Energy Malnutrition

Type PEM	Anthropometric Index	Normal	Mild	Moderate	Severe
			Degree of PEM		
Chronic (stunting)					
	Height for age as % standard*	95	90–94	85–89	<85
Acute (wasting)					
	Weight for age as % standard*	90	75–89	60–74	<60
	Weight for height as % standard*	90	80–89	70–79	<70
	Arm circumference/ head circumference ratio†	>0.31	0.28–0.31	0.25–0.28	<.25

* Original data for determining degree of PEM used the 50th percentile of Boston growth data as standard. The 50th percentile on NCHS growth charts is now commonly used as the standard with these assessments.

† Ratio has been found to correlate with weight for age in children 3 months to 4 years of age.

Source: Data from Gomez F, Galvan R, Frenks, Munoz JC, Chavez R, Vasquez J. Mortality in second and third degree malnutrition. *J Trop Pediatr.* 1956;2:77 and Waterlow J. Classification and definition of protein calorie malnutrition. In Beaton G, Bengoa X, eds. *Nutrition in Preventive Medicine.* WHO monograph series No. 62. Geneva: WHO; 1976.

wasted appearance due to diminished subcutaneous fat. Infants and children with marasmus have normal or low levels of serum albumin and other transport proteins and no evidence of edema. Liver size is normal.[37–39,85]

Conversely, kwashiorkor develops acutely, often in conjunction with an infection. Levels of serum albumin, other transport proteins, and lymphocytes are reduced. Edema is present over the trunk, extremities, and face. These infants and children often have subcutaneous fat stores that mask muscle wasting. Dermatitis and hair changes (flag sign) are usually present. In severe cases fatty infiltration of the liver occurs.[37–39,85]

Marasmic kwashiorkor is the classification used to describe the presence of symptoms of kwashiorkor in a child with a weight for height less than 70% of standard or weight for age less than 60% of standard. This condition often develops following acute stress and is associated with high mortality.[37–39,85]

Failure-To-Thrive

Failure-to-thrive (FTT) is a serious condition affecting the growth and nutritional status of infants and young children. FTT is characterized by growth delay and often accompanied by increased illness, decreased activity, delays in cognitive development, poor school performance, and behavior and social problems.[86–88] FTT is reported in 1 to 5% of children admitted to pediatric teaching hospitals and in 7 to 10% of low-income preschool children seen in community-based settings in the United States.[89–93] For additional information, please see Chapter 13, Failure To Thrive.

Overweight and Obesity

Overweight has been defined as a weight for height greater than 110% of standard[38] and obesity as 120% of standard.[94] However, these definitions simply reflect that an individual's weight is greater than expected. The weight-for-height index does not provide sufficient information to determine whether excess weight is due to increased muscle or fat stores. In children and adolescents the triceps skinfold measurement is often used to identify obesity. Individuals with triceps skinfold measurements greater than the 85th percentile for age are obese; those with measurements greater than the 95th percentile for age are classified as superobese.[94–96]

Obesity is increasing among children in the United States with a current incidence of approximately 25%.[95] The presence and severity of obesity in children beyond 10 years of age is correlated with continued obesity into adulthood.[87] Early identification and intervention may be a key component for establishing a successful weight management program. For additional information, please see Chapter 22, Obesity.

Care Plan

The nutritional care plan is developed to correct nutritional problems or reduce nutritional risks identified through the assessment. Basic information included in the medical and dietary histories provides a foundation for designing a plan that is reasonable and achievable within a given setting. The effectiveness of the nutritional intervention is determined through periodic nutritional reassessment. The care plan is modified as needed for changes in nutritional status/risk.

CONCLUSION

The provision of quality nutritional services to children is dependent on identifying those who are nutritionally depleted or at nutritional risk, through routine screening. In-depth nutritional assessments including a medical history and physical examination, dietary evaluation, anthropometric, and laboratory measurements, are completed on these children. Assessment data are used to identify specific nutritional problems and to develop workable nutrition care plans targeted to improve nutritional status.

REFERENCES

1. Shapiro LR. Streamlining and implementing nutritional assessment. The dietary approach. *J Am Diet Assoc.* 1979;75:230–237.

2. Hunt DR, Maslovitz A, Rowlands BJ, Brooks B. A simple nutrition screening procedure for hospital patients. *J Am Diet Assoc.* 1985;85:332–335.

3. Christensen KS, Gstundtner KM. Hospital-wide screening improves basis for nutrition intervention. *J Am Diet Assoc.* 1985;85:704–706.

4. DeHoog S. Identifying patients at nutritional risk and determining clinical productivity: essentials for an effective nutrition care program. *J Am Diet Assoc.* 1985;85:1620–1622.

5. Hedberg AM, Garcia N, Trejus IJ, Weinmann-Winkler S, Gabriel ML, Lutz AL. Nutrition risk screening: development of a standardized protocol using dietetic technicians. *J Am Diet Assoc.* 1988;88:1553–1556.

6. Fomon SJ. *Nutritional Disorders of Children.* Rockville, Md: US Department of Health and Human Services, Education and Welfare; 1976:1-610, PHS publication no. (HSA) 75-5612.

7. Christakis G. Nutritional assessment in health programs. *Am J Public Health.* 1973;63 (suppl):1–56.

8. Kamath SK, Lawler M, Smith AE, Kalat T, Olson R. Hospital malnutrition: a 33 hospital screening study. *J Am Diet Assoc.* 1986;86:203–206.

9. Noel MB, Wojnaroski SM. Nutrition screening for long-term care patients. *J Am Diet Assoc.* 1987;87:1557–1558.

10. Hattner JT, Kerner JA Jr. Nutritional assessment of the pediatric patient. In: Kerner JA Jr., ed. *Manual of Pediatric Parenteral Nutrition.* New York, NY: John Wiley & Sons; 1983:19–60.

11. Carruth BR. Nutritional assessment: a guide for nutrition education. *J Nutr Educ.* 1988;20:280–288.

12. Mason M, Wenberg BG, Welsch PK. The dietary history. In: *The Dynamics of Clinical Dietetics.* New York, NY: John Wiley & Sons; 1982:106–132.

13. Pipes PL, Bumbalo J, Glass RP. Collecting and assessing food intake information. In: Pipes P, ed. *Nutrition in Infancy and Childhood.* St. Louis, MO: Times Mirror Mosby; 1989:58–85.

14. Burke BS. The dietary history as a tool in research. *J Am Diet Assoc.* 1947;23:1041.

15. Frank GC, Hollatz AT, Webber LS, Berenson GS. Effect of interviewer recording practices on nutrient intake—Bogalusa Heart Study. *J Am Diet Assoc.* 1984;84:1432–1439.

16. Medlin C, Skinner JD. Individual dietary intake methodology: a 50-year review of progress. *J Am Diet Assoc.* 1988;88:1250–1257.

17. Block G. A review of validations of dietary assessment methods. *Am J Epidemiol.* 1982;115:492–504.

18. Persson LA, Carlgren G. Measuring children's diets: evaluation of dietary assessment techniques in infancy and childhood. *International J Epidemiol.* 1984;113:506–517.

19. Carter RL, Sharbaugh CO, Stapell CA. Reliability and validity of the 24-hour recall. *J Am Diet Assoc.* 1981;79:542–547.

20. Emmons L, Hayes M. Accuracy of 24-hr recalls of young children. *J Am Diet Assoc.* 1973;62:409–415.

21. St Jeor SR, Guthrie HA, Jones MB. Variability in nutrient intake in a 28-day period. *J Am Diet Assoc.* 1983;83:155–162.

22. Willett WC, Sampson L, Stampfer MJ, et al. Reproducibility and validity of a semiquantitative food frequency questionnaire. *Am J Epidemiol.* 1985;122:51–65.

23. Larkin FA, Metzner HL, Thompson FE, Flegal KM, Guire KE. Comparison of estimated nutrient intakes by food frequency and dietary records in adults. *J Am Diet Assoc.* 1989;89:215–223.

24. Subcommittee on the Tenth Edition of the RDAs, Food and Nutrition Board, National Research Council. *Recommended Dietary Allowances.* 10th ed. Washington, DC: National Academy Press; 1989.

25. Guthrie HA. The 1985 Recommended Dietary Allowance Committee: an overview. *J Am Diet Assoc.* 1985;85:1646–1648.

26. World Health Organization (WHO). *Energy and Protein Requirements.* Report of a joint FAO/WHO/UNU Expert Consultation. Geneva: World Health Organization; 1985. Technical report series 724.

27. Bursztein S, Elwyn DH, Askanazi J, Kinney JM. The theoretical framework of indirect calorimetry and energy balance. In: *Energy Metabolism, Indirect Calorimetry, and Nutrition.* Baltimore, Md: William & Wilkins; 1989:27–83.

28. Boothby WM, Berkson J, Dunn HL. Studies of the energy metabolism of normal individuals. *Am J Physiol.* 1936;116:468–484.

29. Fleish A. Le metabolisme basal standard et sa determination au moyen du "Metabocalculator." *Helv Med Acta.* 1951;81:23–44.

30. Dubois EF. Energy metabolism. *Ann Rev Physiol.* 1954;16:125–134.

31. Wilmore D. *The Metabolic Management of the Critically Ill.* New York, NY: Plenum Press; 1977.

32. Long CL. Energy balance and carbohydrate metabolism in infection and sepsis. *Am J Clin Nutr.* 1977;30:1301–1310.

33. Durnin JVGA, Passmore R. *Energy, Work and Leisure.* London: Heinemann Educational Books; 1967.

34. Segal KR. Comparison of indirect calorimetric measurements of resting energy expenditure with a ventilated hood, face mask, and mouthpiece. *Am J Clin Nutr.* 1987;45:1420–1423.

35. Ireton-Jones CS, Turner WW Jr. The use of respiratory quotient to determine the efficacy of nutrition support systems. *J Am Diet Assoc.* 1987;87:180–183.

36. Hamill PV, Drizd TA, Johnson CL, Reed RB, Roche AF, Moore WM. Physical growth: National Center for Health Statistics percentiles. *Am J Clin Nutr.* 1979;32:607–629.

37. Waterlow JC. Classification and definition of protein-calorie malnutrition. *Br Med J.* 1972;3:566–569.

38. McLaren DS, Read WWC. Classification of nutritional status in early childhood. *Lancet.* 1972;2:146–148.

39. Waterlow JC. Note on the assessment and classification of protein-energy malnutrition in children. *Lancet.* 1973;2:87–89.

40. Hamill PV, Drizd TA, Johnson CL, Reed RB, Roche AF. *NCHS Growth Curves for Children, Birth–18 Years, United States.* Hyattsville, Md: National Center for Health Statistics; 1977. Vital and Health Statistics, series 11, no. 165. DHEW publication, no. PHS 78-1650.

41. Roche AF, Himes JH. Incremental growth charts. *Am J Clin Nutr.* 1980;33:2041–2052.

42. Baumgartner RN, Roche AF, Himes JH. Incremental growth tables. *Am J Clin Nutr.* 1986;43:711–722.

43. Roche AF, Guo S, Moore WM. Weight and recumbent length from 1 to 12 mos. of age: reference data for 1-mo increments. *Am J Clin Nutr.* 1989;49:599–607.

44. Tanner JM, Davis PSW. Clinical longitudinal standards for North American children. *J Pediatr.* 1985;107:317–329.

45. Owen GM. Measurement, recording, and assessment of skinfold thickness in childhood and adolescence: report of a small meeting. *Am J Clin Nutr.* 1982;35:629–638.

46. Ryan AS, Martinez GA. Physical growth of infants 7 to 13 months of age: results from a national survey. *Am J Phys Anthropol.* 1987;73:449–457.

47. Frisancho AR. Triceps skinfold and upper arm muscle size norms for assessment of nutritional status. *Am J Clin Nutr.* 1974;27:1052–1058.

48. Jensen TG, Dudrick SJ, Johnston DA. A comparison of triceps skinfold and upper arm circumference measurements taken in standard and supine positions. *J Parenter Enter Nutr.* 1981;5:519–521.

49. Jelliffe DB. *The Assessment of the Nutritional Status of the Community.* Geneva: World Health Organization; 1966. WHO monograph series 53.

50. Alam N, Wojtyniak B, Rahaman MM. Anthropometric indicators and risk of death. *Am J Clin Nutr.* 1989;49:884–888.

51. Merritt RJ, Suskind RM. Nutritional survey of hospitalized pediatric patients. *Am J Clin Nutr.* 1979;32:1320–1325.

52. Frisancho AR. New norms of upper limb fat and muscle areas for assessment of nutritional status. *Am J Clin Nutr.* 1981;34:2540–2545.

53. Frisancho AR, Tracer DP. Standards of arm muscle by stature for the assessment of nutritional status of children. *Am J Phys Anthropol.* 1987;73:459–465.

54. Lerner A, Feld LG, Riddleberger MM, Rossi TM, Lebenthal E. Computed axial tomographic scanning of the thigh: an alternative method of nutritional assessment in pediatrics. *Pediatrics.* 1986;77:732–737.

55. Buckley DC, Kudsk KA, Rose BS, Fatzinger P, Koetting CA, Schlatter M. Anthropometric and computerized tomographic measurements of lower extremity lean body mass. *J Am Diet Assoc.* 1987;87:196–199.

56. Forbes GB, Brown MR, Griffiths HJL. Arm muscle plus bone area: anthropometry and CAT scan compared. *Am J Clin Nutr.* 1988;47:929–931.

57. Tanner JM. Issues and advances in adolescent growth and development. *J Adolesc Health Care.* 1987;8:470–478.

58. Gong EJ, Spear BA. Adolescent growth and development: implication for nutritional needs. *J Nutr Educ.* 1988;20:273–278.

59. Roche AF, Guo S, Baumgartner RN, Chumlea WC, Ryan AS, Kuczmarski RJ. Reference data for weight, stature and weight/stature² in Mexican-Americans from the Hispanic Health and Nutrition Examination Survey (HHANES 1982–1984). *Am J Clin Nutr.* 1990;51:917S–924S.

60. Katchadourian H. *The Biology of Adolescence.* San Francisco, CA: Freeman & Company; 1977:22–120.

61. Neinstein LS. *Adolescent Health Care. A Practical Guide.* Baltimore, Md: Urban & Schwarzenbert; 1984:3–33.

62. Slap GB. Normal physiological and psychosocial growth in the adolescent. *J Adolesc Health Care.* 1986;7:13S–23S.

63. Cronk CE, Roche AF. Race- and sex-specific reference data for triceps and subscapular skinfolds and weight/stature². *Am J Clin Nutr.* 1982;35:347–354.

64. Owen GM, Lubin AH. Anthropometric differences between black and white preschool children. *Am J Dis Child.* 1973;126:168–169.

65. Ryan AS, Martinez GA, Baumgartner RN, Roche AF, Guo S, Chumlea WC, Kuczumarski RJ. Median skinfold thickness distributions and fat-wave patterns in Mexican-American children from the Hispanic Health and Nutrition Examination Survey (HHANES 1982–1984). *Am J Clin Nutr.* 1990;51:925S–935S.

66. Ryan AS, Martinez GA, Roche AF. An evaluation of the associations between socioeconomic status and the growth of Mexican-American children data from the Hispanic Health and Nutrition Examination Survey (HHANES 1982–1984). *Am J Clin Nutr.* 1990;51:944S–952S.

67. Golden MHN. Transport proteins as indices of protein status. *Am J Clin Nutr.* 1982;35:1159–1165.

68. Fletcher JP, Little JM, Guest PK. A comparison of serum transferrin and serum prealbumin as nutritional parameters. *J Parenter Enter Nutr.* 1987;11:144–147.

69. Winkler MF, Gerrior SA, Pomp A, Albina JE. Use of retinol binding protein and prealbumin as indicators of response to nutrition therapy. *J Am Diet Assoc.* 1989;89:684–687.

70. Yoder MC, Anderson DC, Gopalakrishna GS, Douglas SD, Polin RA. Comparison of serum fibronectin, prealbumin and albumin concentrations during nutritional repletion in protein-calorie malnourished infants. *J Pediatr Gastroenterol Nutr.* 1987;6:84–88.

71. Smith FR, Goodman DS, Zaklama MS, Gabr MK, Maraghy SE, Patwardhan VN. Serum vitamin A, retinol-binding protein and prealbumin concentrations in protein-calorie malnutrition. 1. A functional defect in hepatic retinol release. *Am J Clin Nutr.* 1973;26:973–981.

72. Buonpane EA, Brown RO, Boucher BA, Fabian TC, Luther RW. Use of fibronectin and somatomedin C as nutritional markers in the enteral support of traumatized patients. *Crit Care Med.* 1989;17:126–132.

73. Clemmons DR, Underwood LE, Dickerson RN, et al. Use of plasma somatomedin C/insulin-like growth factor. 1. Measurements to monitor the response to nutritional repletion in malnourished patients. *Am J Clin Nutr.* 1985;41:191–198.

74. Crosley LO, Giandomenico A, Forster J, Mullen JL. Relationships between serum total iron binding capacity and transferrin. *J Parenter Enter Nutr.* 1984;8:274–278.

75. Williams CS. Laboratory values and their interpretation. In: Krey SH, Murray RL, eds. *Dynamics of Nutrition Support: Assessment, Implementation, Evaluation.* Norwalk, Ct: Appleton-Century-Crofts; 1986:83–97.

76. Graystone JE. Creatinine excretion during growth. In: Cheek DB, ed. *Human Growth.* Philadelphia, PA: Lea & Febiger; 1968:182–197.

77. Viteri FE, Alvarado J. The creatinine height index: its use and the estimation of the degree of preterm depletion and repletion in protein calorie malnutrition. *Pediatrics.* 1970;46:696–706.

78. Merritt RJ, Blackburn GL. Nutritional assessment and metabolic response to illness of the hospitalized child. In: Suskind R, ed. *Textbook of Pediatric Nutrition.* New York, NY: Raven Press; 1981:296.

79. Expert Scientific Working Group. Summary of a report on assessment of the iron nutritional status of the United States population. *Am J Clin Nutr.* 1985;42:1318–1330.

80. Yip R, Johnson C, Dallman PR. Age-related changes in laboratory values used in the diagnosis of anemia and iron deficiency. *Am J Clin Nutr.* 1984;39:427–436.

81. Yip R, Dallman PR. The roles of inflammation and iron deficiency as causes of anemia. *Am J Clin Nutr.* 1988;48:1295–1300.

82. Cecalupo AJ, Cohen HJ. Nutritional anemias. In: Grand RJ, Sutphen JL, Dietz WH Jr, eds. *Pediatric Nutrition: Theory and Practice.* Boston, Ma: Butterworth Publishing; 1987:491.

83. Puri S, Chandra RK. Nutritional regulation of host resistance and predictive value of immunologic tests in assessment of outcome. *Pediatr Clin North Am.* 1985;32:499–515.

84. Pollack MM, Ruttimann UE, Wiley JS. Nutritional depletions in critically ill children: associations with physiologic instability and increased quantity of care. *J Parenter Enter Nutr.* 1985;9:309–313.

85. Solomons NW. Rehabilitating the severely malnourished infant and child. *J Am Diet Assoc.* 1985;85:28–339.

86. Bithoney W, Rathbun J. Failure to thrive. In: Levine MD, Carey WB, Crocker AC, Rathbun J, eds. *Developmental Behavioral Pediatrics.* Philadelphia, Pa: WB Saunders Co; 1983.

87. Rathbun JM, Peterson KE. Nutrition in failure-to-thrive. In: Grand RJ, Sutphen JL, Dietz WH, eds. *Pediatric Nutrition: Theory and Practice.* Boston: Butterworth Publishers; 1987;627–643.

88. Frank DA, Ziesel SSH. Failure-to-thrive. *Pediatr Clin North Am.* 1988;35:1187–1206.

89. Berwick D. Nonorganic failure to thrive. *Pediatr Rev.* 1980;1:265.

90. English P. Failure to thrive without organic reason. *Pediatr Ann.* 1978;7:774.

91. Mitchell WG, Gorrell RW, Greenberg RA. Failure-to-thrive: a study in a primary case setting: epidemiology and follow-up. *Pediatr.* 1980;65:971–976.

92. Massachusetts Department of Public Health Office of Nutrition. Nutrition Counts. Boston: Massachusetts Dept. of Public Health; 1990.

93. Dietz, WH. Undernutrition of children in Massachusetts. *J Nutr.* 1990;120:948–954.

94. Rosenbaum M, Liebel RL. Obesity in childhood. *Pediatr Rev.* 1989;11:43–55.

95. Gortmaker SL, Dietz WH Jr, Sobol AM, Wehler MS. Increasing pediatric obesity in the United States. *Am J Dis Child.* 1987;141:535–540.

96. Garn SM, Clark DC. Trends in fatness and the origins of obesity. *Pediatrics.* 1976;56:443–456.

97. Robertson JD, Reid DD. Standards for the basal metabolism of normal people in Britain. *Lancet.* 1952;1:940–943.

98. Lewis RC, Duval AM, Iliff A. Standards for the basal metabolism of children from 2 to 15 years of age inclusive. *J Pediatr.* 1943;23:1–18.

99. Cole CH, ed. *The Harriet Lane Handbook. A Manual for Pediatric House Officers*, 10th ed. Chicago: Year Book Medical; 1984:354.

Appendix 2-A

Six-Month Incremental Growth Charts from Birth through 18 Years

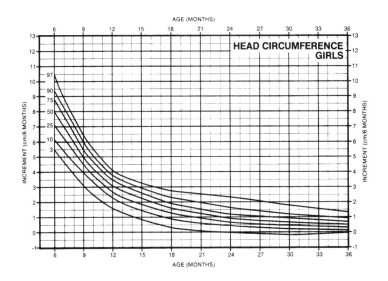

Figure 2-A1 Incremental growth for head circumference (centimeters per 6 months) in white girls aged 6 to 36 months. *Source:* Used with permission of Ross Laboratories, Columbus, OH 43216, from Ross Growth and Development Programs, © 1981 Ross Laboratories.

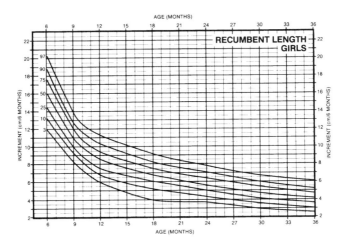

Figure 2-A2 Incremental growth for recumbent length (centimeters per 6 months) in white girls aged 6 to 36 months. *Source:* Used with permission of Ross Laboratories, Columbus, OH 43216, from Ross Growth and Development Programs, © 1981 Ross Laboratories.

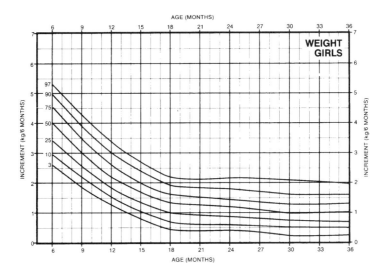

Figure 2-A3 Incremental growth for weight (kilograms per 6 months) in white girls aged 6 to 36 months. *Source:* Used with permission of Ross Laboratories, Columbus, OH 43216, from Ross Growth and Development Programs, © 1981 Ross Laboratories.

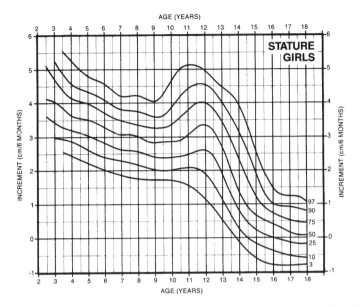

Figure 2-A4 Incremental growth for stature (centimeters per 6 months) in white girls aged 2 to 18 years. *Source:* Used with permission of Ross Laboratories, Columbus, OH 43216, from Ross Growth and Development Programs, © 1981 Ross Laboratories.

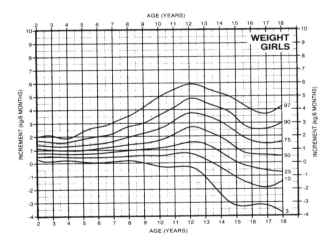

Figure 2-A5 Incremental growth for weight (kilograms per 6 months) in white girls aged 2 to 18 years. *Source:* Used with permission of Ross Laboratories, Columbus, OH 43216, from Ross Growth and Development Programs, © 1981 Ross Laboratories.

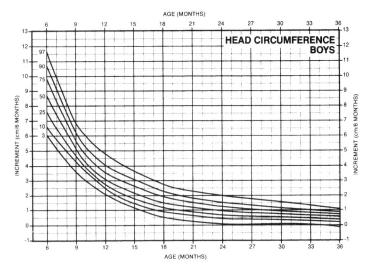

Figure 2-A6 Incremental growth for head circumference (centimeters per 6 months) in white boys aged 6 to 36 months. *Source:* Used with permission of Ross Laboratories, Columbus, OH 43216, from Ross Growth and Development Programs, © 1981 Ross Laboratories.

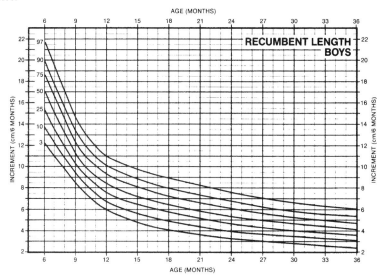

Figure 2-A7 Incremental growth for recumbent length (centimeters per 6 months) in white boys aged 6 to 36 months. *Source:* Used with permission of Ross Laboratories, Columbus, OH 43216, from Ross Growth and Development Programs, © 1981 Ross Laboratories.

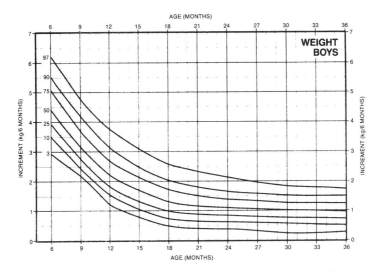

Figure 2-A8 Incremental growth for weight (kilograms per 6 months) in white boys aged 6 to 36 months. *Source:* Used with permission of Ross Laboratories, Columbus, OH 43216, from Ross Growth and Development Programs, © 1981 Ross Laboratories.

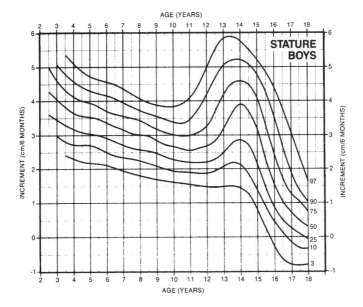

Figure 2-A9 Incremental growth for stature (centimeters per 6 months) in white boys aged 2 to 18 years. *Source:* Used with permission of Ross Laboratories, Columbus, OH 43216, from Ross Growth and Development Programs, © 1981 Ross Laboratories.

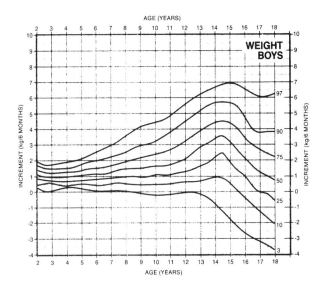

Figure 2-A10 Incremental growth for weight (kilograms per 6 months) in white boys aged 2 to 18 years. *Source:* Used with permission of Ross Laboratories, Columbus, OH 43216, from Ross Growth and Development Programs, © 1981 Ross Laboratories.

Chapter 3

Nutrition for Premature Infants

Diane M. Anderson

Premature infants are defined as infants born before 38 weeks gestation as compared to full-term infants born from 38 to 42 weeks.[1] The physiologic immaturity of premature infants renders them susceptible to a number of problems (see Table 3-1), many of which imperil their nutrition and growth (see Table 3-2). "Low birth weight" refers to infants with a birth weight of less than 2500 g; very low birth weight infants weigh less than 1500 g.[1] Infants can be low birth weight but yet be full-term due to poor intrauterine growth. Assessment of intrauterine growth is determined by plotting the infant's birth weight by gestational age on various charts. On the Lubchenco chart, small-for-gestational-age (SGA) infants have a birth weight at the 10th percentile or less.[2] Large-for-gestational-age (LGA) infants have a birth weight at the 90th percentile or greater.[2] Average-for-gestational-age infants are between the 10th and 90th percentiles (see Figure 3-1). On the Babson Growth Chart SGA and LGA age are defined as two standard deviations from the mean birth weight (see Figure 3-2).[3] Tables 3-3 and 3-4 list

---

Table 3-1 Problems of the Premature Infant

Hypotension	Patent ductus arteriosus
Anemia	Asphyxia
Retinopathy of prematurity	Respiratory distress syndrome
Poor temperature control	Uncoordinated suck and swallow
Apnea	Hyperbilirubinemia
Hypoglycemia	Hypocalcemia
Necrotizing enterocolitis	Intraventricular hemorrhage
Hydrocephaly	Infection
Undernutrition	Fat malabsorption
Decreased gastric motility	Limited renal function

Source: Data from references 26 and 29.

Table 3-2 Premature Infants' Risk Factors for Nutritional Deficiencies

1. Decreased nutrient stores
   - Premature infants are born before anticipated quantities of nutrients are deposited.
   - Low stores include glycogen, fat, protein, fat soluble vitamins, calcium, phosphorus, magnesium, and trace minerals.
2. Increased growth rate
   - Full-term infants triple their birthweight by 1 year of age; for the preterm infant a tenfold increase may be needed to achieve optimal catch-up growth.
   - With rapid growth, energy and nutrient needs will be increased.
3. Immature physiological systems
   - Digestion and absorption capabilities are decreased due to low concentrations of lactase, pancreatic lipase, and bile salts.
   - Gastrointestinal motility and stomach capacity are decreased, which limits gastric emptying and feeding volume.
   - A coordinated suck and swallow is not developed until 32 to 34 weeks' gestation.
   - Hepatic enzymes are decreased, which may make specific amino acids conditionally essential (cysteine) or toxic (phenylalanine) due to the inability to synthesize or degrade.
   - Renal concentrating ability is limited.
4. Illnesses
   - Respiratory distress syndrome delays the introduction of enteral feedings because of the increased risk of aspiration. Gastrointestinal motility will also be decreased, and feedings may not be tolerated.
   - Patent ductus arteriosus often requires fluid restriction, which limits caloric intake.
   - Necrotizing enterocolitis forces nutrition management to parenteral nutrition for bowel rest. With refeeding, an elemental infant formula is often indicated. Some infants may develop short-gut syndrome as a complication and require extensive nutritional management for malabsorption.
   - Bronchopulmonary dysplasia leads to an increased energy demand with fluid restriction. Calorically dense formulas are often utilized. Chronic diuretic use will create electrolyte and calcium depletion.
   - Hyperbilirubinemia may be treated by phototherapy, which increases the infant's insensible water loss and fluid requirement. If exchange transfusion is needed, introduction of enteral feedings will be delayed. Necrotizing enterocolitis has been reported as a complication of exchange transfusion therapy.
   - Sepsis and suspected sepsis will result in withholding all enteral fluids until it is established that the infant is stable. The affected infant may have an altered mesenteric blood flow, which can result in necrotizing enterocolitis, or may have apnea, which may cause aspiration of feedings.
   - Severe intraventricular hemorrhage may result in the infant's inability to feed orally or to tolerate feedings.

Source: Klaus MH and Fanaroff AA, *Care of the High-Risk Neonate,* ed 3, 1986, WB Saunders.

---

etiologies for SGA and LGA infants. The Babson chart can be used to follow the premature infant's growth through the first year of life. These assessments are used to anticipate medical and nutritional problems and management needs of the

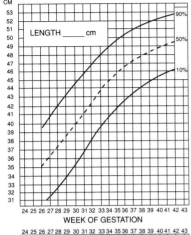

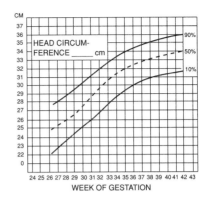

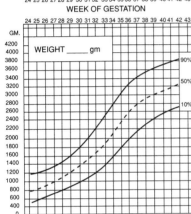

Figure 3-1 Intrauterine growth charts. *Source:* Mead Johnson and Co, Classification of newborns based on maturity and intrauterine growth, 1978; Lubchenco LC, Hansman C and Boyd E, *Pediatrics* (1966;37:403); Battaglia FC and Lubchenco LC, *Journal of Pediatrics* (1967;71:159).

infant (see Table 3-5). For example, consider an infant born at 34 weeks' gestation whose birth weight is 1200 grams. This infant is premature since the gestational age is less than 38 weeks. On both the Lubchenco and Babson growth grids, the infant is SGA because birth weight is less than the 10th percentile or less than two standard deviations from the mean birth weight.

SGA infants are further classified by their body length and head circumference as symmetrically or asymmetrically growth retarded.[4] The symmetrically SGA infant's birth weight, head circumference, and body length are all classified as

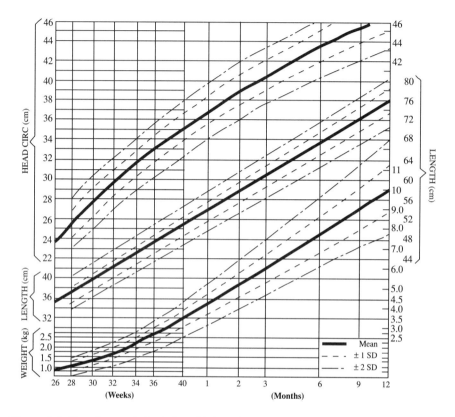

Figure 3-2 Growth records for infants birth to 1 year. *Source:* Adapted with permission from SG Babson and GI Benda, Growth graphs for the clinical assessment of infants of varying gestational age, in *Journal of Pediatrics* (1976;89:814–820), copyright © 1976, CV Mosby Co; courtesy of Ross Laboratories, Columbus, OH.

small, whereas the asymmetrically SGA infant has a small body weight but an appropriate head circumference and body length. The asymmetrically SGA infant stands the better chance for catch-up growth because poor growth has been of shorter duration. This period of poor growth usually only represents the last trimester of pregnancy. The symmetrically SGA infant has usually sustained an early insult to growth and development, such as infection, genetic abnormality, or maternal drug abuse.[4] Infants who experience this type of growth retardation usually do not obtain their full potential for physical growth and often have poor neurologic development. Hack et al. have reported that at 9 months of age SGA infants whose body weight is not within two standard deviations of the mean weight for age will generally not attain catch-up growth.[5]

Table 3-3 Etiologic Factors for SGA Births

Low socioeconomic status	High altitude
Pregnancy-induced hypertension	Elevated maternal hematocrit
Chronic hypertension	Multiple gestation
Chronic renal disease	Congenital malformations
Diabetes with vascular complications	Chromosomal abnormalities
Intrauterine infection	Placental insufficiency
Malnutrition	Twin-to-twin transfusion
Cigarette smoking	Single umbilical artery
Drug or alcohol abuse	

Source: Data from references 12, 25, and 29.

Another tool, the mid-arm circumference to head circumference ratio, has been suggested to assess intrauterine growth and to predict medical problems.[6,7] Since this standard was calculated from measurements made on the second and third days of life, this ratio requires further testing on day 1 of life to see if early interventions are possible. For example, hypoglycemia is a common problem for the SGA infant. By classifying the infant as SGA, early calories can be supplied and blood glucose monitoring can be done to prevent the development of hypoglycemia. This ratio might identify infants as SGA who were not so determined by birth weight alone.

Premature infants represent a heterogeneous population for nutrition management. Intrauterine growth establishes nutritional status at birth, and gestational age determines nutrient need and feeding modality employed. Postnatally, as the infant matures, nutrient need and feeding modality will vary. Finally, the infant's clinical condition can acutely change and alter nutrition care. Due to these factors, their nutrition management is a day-to-day decision-making process regarding what to feed, what volume and nutrient density to provide, and how to administer nourishment. The goal is to provide nutrition for optimal growth and development to take place. The intrauterine growth rate without metabolic complications has been advocated as the aim of premature infant nutrition, but others question if it is appropriate in an extrauterine environment.[8,–11]

Table 3-4 Etiologic Factors for LGA Births

Infant of diabetic mother	Genetic predisposition
Beckwith's syndrome	Rh isoimmunization
Transposition of the great vessels	High prepregnancy weight with
Miscalculation of expected day of confinement	large pregnancy weight gain

Source: Data from references 25 and 29.

Table 3-5 Anticipated Problems for SGA and LGA Infants

Problems	Issues
Small for gestational age	
Perinatal asphyxia	Introduction of enteral feeding may be delayed because of the risk of necrotizing enterocolitis
	Neurologic developmental problems may occur
Hypoglycemia	Caused by
	Low glycogen stores
	Low fat stores
	Decreased gluconeogenesis
	Increased metabolic rate
Increased energy need	Caused by
	Increased metabolic rate
	Increased growth rate
Heat loss	Due to large surface area and decreased subcutaneous fat
Polycythemia	Due to relative hypoxia in utero
Large for gestational age	
Low Apgars	Feeding difficulty
Birth trauma	Shoulder dystocia, fractured clavicle, depressed skull fracture, brachial plexus palsy, facial paralysis
Hypoglycemia	Caused by hyperinsulinism

Source: Data from references 8, 12, and 29.

PARENTERAL NUTRITION

Parenteral nutrition is indicated in the first few days of life to allow the premature infant to adapt to the extrauterine environment before enteral feedings are begun. It also may supplement enteral feedings, for premature infants have decreased enteral feeding tolerance and small gastric capacities, which limit volume intakes. Tables 3-6 and 3-7 give suggested guidelines for parenteral administration of specific nutrients, vitamins, and trace minerals. Table 3-8 briefly describes a protocol for parenteral nutrition management.

Central parenteral nutrition is employed for the infant who has limited venous access, is fluid restricted, or has an increased nutrient demand that cannot be met by peripheral nutrition support. Infants with gastrointestinal anomalies or illnesses will often require prolonged parenteral nutrition therapy, and central venous lines may be used in these cases.

Table 3-6 Parenteral Nutrition Guidelines

Energy, Energy Nutrients and Minerals per Day

Nutrient	Amount per Kilogram
Energy (kcal)	80
Glucose (mg/kg/min)	11–12
Lipids (g)	0.5–3.0
Protein (g)	2–3
Sodium (mEq)	2–3
Potassium (mEq)	2
Calcium (mg)	30–40
Phosphorus (mg)	30–40
Magnesium (mg)	15–25
Zinc (µg)	300
Copper (µg)	20
Chromium (µg)	0.14–0.2
Manganese (µg)	2–10

Vitamins per Day by Infant's Weight

Vitamin	<1 kg	1–3 kg
Vitamin A (µg)	210	455
Vitamin E (mg)	2.1	4.5
Vitamin K (µg)	60	130
Vitamin D (µg)	3	6.5
Vitamin C (mg)	24	52
Thiamin (mg)	0.36	0.78
Riboflavin (mg)	0.42	0.91
Niacin (mg)	5.1	11.05
Vitamin B$_6$ (mg)	0.3	0.65
Folate (µg)	42	91
Vitamin B$_{12}$ (µg)	0.3	0.65
Biotin (µg)	6.0	13
Pantothenic acid (mg)	1.5	3.25

Source: Data from references 8, 30, and 32.

Management Concerns and Medical Problems

Fluid management is very individualized for the preterm infant. Insensible water losses will be high, and the infant's renal function and neuroendocrine control will be immature.[12] Fluid overload should be avoided to prevent the development of necrotizing enterocolitis, bronchopulmonary dysplasia, and patent ductus

Table 3-7 Suggested Parenteral Vitamin and Trace Mineral Formulation for Preterm Infants

Lipid-Soluble Packet

Vitamin	Dose/kg
Vitamin A (μg)	500
Vitamin E (mg)	2.8
Vitamin K (μg)	80
Vitamin D (μg)	4

Water-Soluble Packet

Vitamin	Dose/kg
Ascorbic Acid (mg)	25
Thiamin (mg)	0.35
Riboflavin (mg)	0.15
Niacin (mg)	6.8
Vitamin B_6 (mg)	0.18
Folate (μg)	56
Vitamin B_{12} (μg)	0.3
Biotin (μg)	6.0
Pantothenic acid (mg)	2.0

Trace mineral	(μg/kg/d)*
Zinc	400
Copper	20[†]
Chromium	0.2[‡]
Manganese	1.0[†]
Selenium	2.0[‡]
Molybdenum	0.25[‡]
Iodide	1.0

* Only used for total parenteral nutrition of over 4 weeks except for zinc, which begins with the initiation of parenteral nutrition.
† Should be discontinued with obstructive jaundice.
‡ Should be discontinued with renal failure.

Source: Adapted with permission from HL Greene, KM Hambidge, R Schanler, et al. Guidelines for the use of vitamins, trace elements, calcium, magnesium, and phosphorus in infants and children receiving total parenteral nutrition: Report of the Subcommittee on Pediatric Parenteral Nutrition Requirements from the Committee on Clinical Practice Issues of the American Society for Clinical Nutrition in *American Journal of Clinical Nutrition* (1988;48:1324), copyright © 1988, American Society for Clinical Nutrition.

arteriosus. Table 3-9 gives laboratory parameters that should be observed in guiding parenteral therapy and nutrition.

Insensible fluid losses are high for many reasons.[12] First, the premature infant's skin offers little protection from evaporative losses. It has a high water content,

Table 3-8 Parenteral Nutrition Progression

1. Fluids
   - Begin at 80 to 120 ml/kg/d on day of life (DOL) 1.
   - Increase fluids gradually to meet fluid and energy needs.
2. Glucose
   - Prevent hypoglycemia by providing glucose at 4–6 mg/kg/min on DOL 1.
   - Build up to 11–12 mg/kg/min.
   - Decrease glucose load for hyperglycemia; insulin use not recommended.
3. Sodium chloride
   - Add to fluids on DOL 2.
   - Allow diuresis to occur the first few days of life to decrease extracellular blood volume.
   - Start sodium to prevent hyponatremia.
4. Potassium
   - Add potassium to fluids on DOL 3.
   - Excreting potassium is not obligatory on DOL I.
   - Add potassium after urine flow is established and serum potassium level is normal.
   - Check for hyperkalemia since the premature infant often has a decreased glomerular filtration rate, acidosis, and the release of nitrogen and potassium secondary to negative nitrogen balance.
5. Amino acids
   - Begin on DOL 3.
   - Start at 0.5 g/kg/d.
   - Increase by 0.5 g/kg/d.
   - Give maximum of 3.0 g/kg/d.
6. Lipids
   - Begin on DOL 3.
   - Start at 0.5 g/kg/d.
   - Increase by 0.5 g/kg/d.
   - Provide maximum dose of 3.0 g/kg/d.
   - Provide a rate no greater than 0.12 g/kg/h.
   - Provide lipids over an 18- to 24-hour period.
7. Vitamins and minerals
   - Begin on DOL 3.
8. Parenteral nutrition progression may be slowed due to the following:
   - Fluid and electrolyte imbalance.
   - Renal failure.
   - Enteral feedings anticipated.
   - Enteral feedings initiated and tolerated.

Source: Data from references 8, 30, and 33.

and the epidermis is thin and highly permeable. Second, environmental factors in the newborn intensive care unit increase insensible fluid losses, e.g., the use of radiant warmers or phototherapy, or high or low ambient temperature.[12] These losses can be decreased by the use of incubators, plastic shields, and plastic wraps or clothing.

Previously, intravenous lipid administration was contraindicated for the premature infant suffering from hyperbilirubinemia. It was believed that the free fatty

Table 3-9 Fluid and Electrolyte Monitoring Parameters

Fluid intake	80–150 ml/kg/d[†]
Urine output	1–3 ml/kg/h
Daily body weights	Allow 1%–3% daily weight loss or 8%–15% maximum total weight loss
Serum sodium	130–150 mEq/L
Blood urea nitrogen	3–30 mg/dL
Urine specific gravity	1.008–1.012
Urine osmolality	100–300 mOsm

[†] The premature infant in the newborn intensive care unit has highly variable fluid needs. This range represents the usual volume of fluid administered. To prevent over- or underhydration, fluids should be provided so as to keep the other monitoring parameters within normal levels.

Source: Data from references 12, 29, 30, and 34.

---

acids released from the lipids would compete with the indirect bilirubin for binding onto the albumin molecule. Without binding to albumin, bilirubin can cross the blood-brain barrier and cause kernicterus. Recent data have demonstrated that intravenous lipids at 0.5 to 1.0 g/kg/d are not harmful with hyperbilirubinemia.[13] At this dosage level, free fatty acids bind to albumin and alter its configurations, which facilitates more bilirubin binding. If exchange transfusion is indicated to treat the infant with hyperbilirubinemia, intravenous lipids are usually not given. Often with severe lung disease intravenous lipids are not administered because oxygen diffusion decreases, but a rate of less than 0.2 g/kg/h is generally safe.[13]

There are several amino acid solutions designed for the pediatric patient.[14] These solutions contain a larger percentage of total nitrogen as essential amino acids and branch chain amino acids. They have a balanced pattern of nonessential amino acids instead of a single amino acid concentration, and they contain taurine and N-acetyl-L-tyrosine. Improved weight gain and nitrogen balance have been reported for low-birth-weight neonates provided these solutions.[14,15] However, the study groups were examined at different time periods in the newborn intensive care unit, which means the total care in the nursery may not be similar during the study periods.[15] Plasma N-acetyl-L-tyrosine levels were elevated in infants receiving this formula.[14] Additional data are needed to determine the superiority of these solutions.

Weaning to enteral feedings is necessarily a slow process, to facilitate feeding tolerance. Enteral feedings are gradually increased in volume and strength as parenteral fluids are decreased at a similar volume. The two fluid types are coordinated to keep the total fluids provided stable. Intravenous lipids are often discontinued when the enteral feedings provide 3% of the total calories as linoleic acid. However, with increased energy demands, intravenous lipids may be continued to provide additional calories. Until enteral feedings provide adequate nutrition for growth, parenteral fluids providing glucose, protein, vitamins, and minerals are continued.

ENTERAL NUTRITION

Enteral feeding is initiated when the infant has become clinically stable. Table 3-10 outlines factors in deciding to initiate enteral feeding, and Table 3-11 describes some of the advantages and disadvantages of enteral feedings. The type of formula selected depends on individual factors and can sometimes involve complex decisions. Table 3-12 lists factors that must be considered. Whatever formula is chosen, it should provide appropriate amounts of energy, protein, minerals, and vitamins (see Table 3-13). The goal is to promote growth and to prepare the infant for discharge. Many problems inhibit the introduction of feedings. Daily evaluations of the appropriateness of enteral feedings should be made.

In Table 3-14 selected nutrients are compared (at 150 ml of milk or formula). This value represents the average volume intake for a premature infant on full

---

Table 3-10 Considerations in Initiating Enteral Feedings

1. Adaptation to extrauterine life
2. Vital signs stable
3. Bowel sounds present
4. Abdomen not distended
5. Medical risk factors
   • Absence of asphyxiation or low Apgar scores
   • Respiratory distress syndrome
   • Apnea and bradycardia
   • Acute sepsis
6. Equipment barriers or procedures
   • Ventilators (inhibit feeding by mouth)
   • Oxygen therapy
   • Intubation/extubation
   • Exchange transfusion
7. Experience of staff
   • Dictates when feeds will be started
   • Dictates which feeding methods can be employed
8. Physical development
   • Dictates method of feeding
   • Coordinated suck and swallow present at 32 to 34 weeks gestation
   • Small gastric size and slow emptying, which limit feed volume and rate

Source: Data from references 24 and 36.

Table 3-11 Risks and Benefits of Introducing Enteral Feedings

Risks	Benefits
Necrotizing enterocolitis	Improved nutrient intake
Aspiration	Shortened physiologic jaundice
Feeding intolerance	Prevents cholestatic jaundice
Intestinal perforation with transpyloric	Stimulates gastrointestinal tract development
feedings	Full-volume feeds earlier

Source: Data from references 24 and 35.

enteral feedings. There is a large range in nutrient density, but the premature infant formulas will more closely meet the nutritional needs of the premature infant.

A multiple-vitamin supplement is often indicated to supplement infant formulas once full enteral fluid volume has been achieved.[8] Each formula must be evaluated against the guidelines for premature infants,[8] for some formulas are fortified by the quart to meet the Recommended Dietary Allowances for full-term infants. Premature infants will not consume 1 quart of formula. Alternatively, formulas designed for premature infants are vitamin dense and do not always require supplementation. Since vitamin supplements have a high osmolality, which can lead to feeding intolerance, it is helpful to mix the supplement with formula to dilute its osmolality.[16] Often for infants less than 1000 g, the dosage is divided into two or four doses per day, to improve feeding tolerance. Iron supplementation is indicated to begin between 2 weeks to 2 months of life.[8] Formula with iron can easily meet the guideline of 2 to 3 mg/kg/d when the infant is consuming approximately 120 kcal/kg/d.

Pharmacologic dosage of vitamin E (50 to 100 mg/kg) is not recommended for the premature infant.[17] Previously, 50 to 100 IU/d were given to prevent retinopathy of prematurity and bronchopulmonary dysplasia by vitamin E's antioxidant properties. Recent investigations have not shown that this helped prevent these illnesses. Reported complications of administration include necrotizing enterocolitis, sepsis, intraventricular hemorrhage, and death.

Recently, a daily intake of 1500 to 2800 IU/kg/d of vitamin A has been suggested to prevent bronchopulmonary dysplasia by this vitamin's mediation of cell differentiation.[18] Although this study suggests positive results, further investigation is necessary before this supplementation becomes standard practice.[19]

There were several reports of zinc deficiency with premature infants receiving either total parenteral nutrition or human milk.[20,21] With the recent promulgation of guidelines for parenteral zinc, there should be little risk for zinc deficiency except for infants with ostomies. These infants have high fluid and zinc losses.

Table 3-12 Milk or Formula Selection—Indications and Concerns

1. Human milk
   - Nutrients are readily absorbed.
   - Anti-infective factors are present.
   - Maternal-infant attachment may be enhanced.
   - Nutrient composition is unique.
   - The concentration of protein, calcium, phosphorus, and sodium is too low to meet the needs of many premature infants. To increase nutrient density, human milk fortifiers can be added to the milk, or the milk can be mixed with premature infant formulas.
   - Milk from mothers who deliver prematurely will often have a higher protein concentration than that found in the milk from mothers who deliver at term. This elevated protein concentration decreases by 28 days of lactation and may not meet the protein needs of the rapidly growing premature infant.
   - Milk volume production may be inadequate to nourish the infant.
   - Maternal emotional support by the family and health care team is indicated to facilitate lactation.
2. Standard infant formulas
   - Formula may not be easily digested and absorbed. Lactose is the sole carbohydrate source, and vegetable oils without medium-chain triglycerides (MCTs) are incorporated into the formula.
   - Protein, calcium, phosphorus, and sodium may not be present in adequate concentrations for the small premature infant.
   - These formulas are appropriate when the infant is discharged home from the hospital.
   - Suggest changing formula to a standard one prior to the infant's discharge to document adequate weight gain.
3. Formulas for premature infants
   A. Compositional uniqueness
      - Glucose polymers comprise 50% to 60% of the carbohydrate calories, which decreases the lactose load presented to the premature infant for digestion. Glucose polymers also decrease the osmolality of the formula.
      - Lactose comprises 40% to 50% of the carbohydrate calories, which facilitates calcium absorption.
      - MCTs are 10% to 50% of the fat calories. MCTs do not require pancreatic lipase or bile salts for digestion and absorption. Use of MCTs enhances the absorption of fat, nitrogen, and calcium.
      - Protein is at a higher concentration than that incorporated into standard infant formulas, to meet the increased protein needs of the premature infant.
      - The protein is a 60:40 whey to casein ratio as compared to the 18:82 whey to casein ratio found in bovine milk. This whey predominance decreases the incidence of metabolic acidosis, and the development of lactobezoars and elevated plasma phenylalanine and tyrosine levels.
      - Calcium and phosphorus are two to four times the concentration found in standard infant formulas. These levels will maintain normal serum calcium and phosphorus levels, prevent osteopenia, and promote calcium and phosphorus accretion at the fetal rate.
      - Sodium, potassium, and chloride concentrations are greater than in standard infant formulas to meet the increase electrolyte needs of the premature infant.

continues

Table 3-12 continued

- Vitamins, trace minerals, and additional minerals are incorporated into these formulas at a high concentration to meet the infants' increased nutrient need while facilitating a limited volume intake.
- Iron-fortified formulas are available, which decrease the number of high-osmolar supplements that must be provided to the premature infant.
- Formula osmolality is within the physiologic range of 280 to 300 mOsm, which facilitates formula tolerance.
- These formulas can be mixed with human milk to increase the infants' nutrient intake.
- Infants with osteopenia may be discharged home with this formula.
- It is unknown when the best time is to discontinue the use of premature formulas.
  - B. Cautionary recommendations
    - This formula is designed for the healthy, growing premature infant.
    - Infant formula manufacturers recommend that initial feedings be provided at 10 or 12 kcal/oz.
    - Feeding volumes and strengths should be advanced slowly with the very low birth weight infant.
    - The bottle of formula must be shaken prior to use, for the minerals to be suspended.
    - With any signs of feeding intolerance, feedings should be discontinued, diluted, decreased, or not advanced.
    - For the infant with renal insufficiency, this formula may provide too much protein, phosphorus, and electrolytes.
    - For the older infant who suffers from bronchopulmonary dysplasia, this formula may contain excessive sodium.
- 4. Elemental infant formulas
  - Protein, calcium, phosphorus, and sodium are not present in adequate concentrations.
  - Premature infants who do not tolerate standard or premature formulas will often benefit from a formula containing glucose polymers, protein hydrolysate, and MCT oil.
  - Infants who are recovering or suffering from gastrointestinal disorders can benefit from elemental infant formulas.
  - The time to switch to a premature formula must always be considered, to improve nutrient intake. Depending on the infant's feeding history, the formulas can be just switched, or a stair step approach of mixing the two formulas with altering parts per solution can be used.
- 5. Soy formulas
  - These formulas are not indicated for premature infants.
  - Phosphorus absorption is hindered by phytates binding the phosphorus, which makes it unavailable for absorption.
  - The amino acid profile may be inadequate for the premature infant.

Source: Data from references 8, 37 to 44.

Zinc supplementation has not been advocated for the premature infant fed human milk, but if symptoms of zinc deficiency appear, they should be evaluated.

Osteopenia or poor bone mineralization is commonly reported with premature infants on prolonged parenteral nutrition, receiving human milk, and/or on chronic diuretic therapy. The disease may be the result of inadequate availability

Table 3–13 Enteral Nutrition Guidelines for Energy, Protein, Minerals and Vitamins per Day

Nutrient	Amount	Nutrient	Amount
Energy (kcal/kg)	120	Vitamin A (µg RE)	375
Protein (g/kg)	3.5–4.0	Vitamin D (µg)*	12.5
Sodium (mEq/kg)	2.5–3.5	Vitamin E (IU/100 kcal)†	0.7
Chloride (mEq/kg)	2.5–3.1	Vitamin K (µg)‡	5
Potassium (mEq/kg)	2.0–3.0	Vitamin C (mg)§	35
Calcium (mg/kg)	185–210	Thiamin (mg)	0.3
Phosphorus (mg/kg)	123–140	Riboflavin (mg)	0.4
Magnesium (mg/kg)	8.5–10.0	Niacin (mg)	5
Zinc (mg/100 kcal)	0.5	Vitamin B6 (mg)	0.3
Manganese (µg/100 kcal)	5	Folate (µg)‖	50
Copper (µg/100 kcal)	90	Vitamin B12 (µg)	0.3
Iron (mg/kg)	2.0–3.0	Biotin (µg)	10
Iodine (µg/100 kcal)	5	Pantothenic acid (mg)	2
Selenium (µg)	10		

* The American Academy of Pediatrics Committee on Nutrition (AAPCON) suggested 12.5 µg/d of vitamin D, but more recent recommendations have been made for 10.0 µg/d. See references 8 and 22.

† The AAPCON recommended a 5 to 25 IU supplement per day of vitamin E, and the most recent Recommended Dietary Allowances suggest a 17 mg/d supplement. See references 8 and 45.

‡ The AAPCON suggests that at birth the premature infant receive 1 mg of vitamin K intramuscularly to prevent hemorrhaging; see reference 8.

§ The AAPCON had recommended 35 mg/d of vitamin C as supplement to infant formula intake. The supplement was recommended to prevent the development of tyrosinemia. Today, in premature infant formulas whey predominates over protein, and the protein is provided at less than 5 g/kg/d, which places the infant at a decreased risk for tyrosinemia. An additional vitamin C supplement may not be indicated. See references 8 and 46.

‖ The AAPCON recommended 50 µg/d of folate. However, there have been no reports of improved growth or hematologic indexes for infants who have received this supplementation except for higher plasma and red blood cell folate levels. Folate supplementation remains controversial. See references 8 and 46.

Source: Adapted from Anderson DM, Nutrition care for the premature infant, *Topics in Clinical Nutrition* (1987;2:1).

Table 3-14 Selected Nutrient Comparison per 150 ml of Milk or Formula

Guidelines (per kg)	Human	Standard	Premature
120 kcal	101	101	121
3.5 g protein	1.67	2.25	3.0–3.6
3 mEq sodium	1.2	0.98–1.2	2.09–2.26
185 mg calcium	50	63–76	113–218
123 mg phosphorus	23.3	42–59	60–109

Source: Data from references 8, 41, and 43.

of calcium and phosphorus for bone mineralization.[23] Aluminum loading has been suggested as another factor in the development of osteopenia.[22] The exact mechanism of aluminum interference with bone mineralization is unclear. Aluminum is a contaminant of many nutrient products, but enterally fed infants are not at high risk for aluminum toxicity since aluminum is poorly absorbed.

The feeding method employed will depend on the infant's gestational age, clinical condition, and nursery staff experience. Table 3-15 describes four methods in use and Table 3-16 gives guidelines for amounts and rates of feedings. Due to the infant's constantly changing condition, several methods will be used. Numerous studies have been completed on feeding methodologies, but there is no consensus on which method is best nor whether there is a difference between continuous infusion or bolus feedings.[24]

Breastfeeding

Mothers who want to breastfeed their premature infant must usually express their milk. During the infant's prolonged hospitalization, it will be difficult for the mother to be available for 24-hour breastfeeding. Further, their infants are too little and/or sick to nurse. Family members, friends, and nursery staff must pro-

---

Table 3-15 Methods of Feeding

Type	Considerations
Bottle/breast	Most physiologic methods
	Infant at least 32 to 34 weeks' gestation
	Use bottle nipple of appropriate size
	Infant medically stable
	Infant's respiratory rate less than 60 breaths per minute
Gavage	Supplement to bottle/breast feedings
	Suggested for infants less than 32 weeks' gestation
	Use when respiratory rate less than 80 breaths per minute
	Use for intubated infant
	Use for the neurologically impaired neonate
Transpyloric	Employ when gavage feedings not tolerated
	Use when respiratory rate greater than 80 breaths per minute
	Infant intubated
	Use for the infant with decreased gut motility
	Must wait for passage of tube to begin feedings
	Requires radiographic assessment to check placement
	Complications include necrotizing enterocolitis, infection, nutrient malabsorption, perforation of intestine
Gastrostomy	Gastrointestinal malformations

Source: Data from references 12 and 24.

Table 3-16 Suggested Feeding Guidelines*

Weight (g)	Feeding Frequency	Initial Volume	Feeding Increments	Minimum Days to Full Feeds†
<1000	CIF	0.5 ml/h	0.5 ml/h	14
1000–1200	CIF	0.5–1.0 ml/h	0.5–1.0 ml/h	7–10
1201–1500	Bolus	2–5 ml/feed	1–3 ml/feed	7–10
1501–2000	Bolus	10–15 ml/feed	2–5 ml/feed	5–7
2001–2500	Bolus	15–30 ml/feed	5–10 ml/feed	2–4
>2500	Bolus	20–30 ml/feed	10–15 ml/feed	1–2

CIF, continuous infusion.

*Data obtained from guidelines used at The Children's Hospital Medical University of South Carolina. These are based on the use of only CIF or every-3-hour bolus feedings. Bolus feedings of every 1, 2, and 4 hours are also employed at different institutions. Feeding volume should be adjusted for the frequency of the feeding. Advancement of feedings should only occur as the infant demonstrates tolerance enteral feedings. Clinical signs of feeding intolerance or illness dictate discontinuing feedings or holding the advancement of feedings. Clinical signs are discussed in the nutritional assessment section of this chapter. Infants less than 1800 g are started on human milk or diluted-strength premature formula. Formula strength is increased as tolerated. Infants greater than 1800 g are begun on either standard infant formula or human milk.
†Full feeds are defined as 120 kcal/kg (150 ml of 24 cal/oz formula or 180 ml of 20 cal/oz formula).

vide support for these women to enable them to be successful in providing milk during this stressful period (see Table 3-17).

NUTRITIONAL ASSESSMENT

Dietary Considerations

Daily assessment is needed to determine need for changing feeding volume, solution strength, or feeding method. Intake is evaluated against nutrient guidelines. Finally, feeding technique needs to be advanced to the most physiological method possible for the infant. Bottle feedings are introduced after the infant's coordination of sucking and swallowing is established.

Anthropometric Measurements

Anthropometric measurements are difficult to perform on premature infants, principally due to the infants' small size. Clinical condition may prohibit measuring; for example, medical equipment can interfere with measurement or can add to the recorded weight. Also, the infant is at risk for cold stress during measurement.

Daily weights should be recorded on a premature infant growth grid (see Figure 3-3). Weights will be influenced by the medical equipment attached to the infant,

Table 3-17 Steps To Support Lactating Women

1. Instruction
    - Proper methods of milk expression
    - Sterilization of expression equipment
    - Storage and transport of milk
    - Diet for lactation
    - Tips for relaxation
2. Tips to help with let down prior to expression
    - Showering
    - Hand massaging of the breasts
    - Applying warm washcloths to the breasts
    - Consuming warm beverages
    - Visiting the infant
    - Talking to the infant's nurse by phone
    - Placing the infant's picture on the pump
3. Nursery staff and nursery support
    - Electric pump and breastfeeding room conveniently available to the nursery
    - Hand pumps available for purchase
    - Education of nursery staff on milk expression
    - Mother's milk used to feed the infant whenever it is available
    - Help mother with the initiation of nursing
4. Initiation of breastfeeding
    - Wake baby up
    - Express a little milk prior to nursing so nipple is easier to grasp by the small infant
    - Position infant so mother and infant are stomach to stomach
    - Allow mother to room in with baby prior to discharge to establish breastfeeding pattern

Source: Data from reference 47.

---

the use of different scales, and the infant's hydration status. Take weights at the same daily time to avoid recording normal diurnal variations. At the time of measurement, document on the infant's record the scale used and the equipment attached to the infant. The goal is 15 to 30 g/d weight gain.[12]

Head circumference should be measured weekly. Alterations in measurement will occur from birth to week 1 of life due to head molding or edema. Additional errors are introduced when scalp intravenous lines are employed or the head has been shaved. Record the measurement on a premature growth grid (see Figures 3-1, 3-2). Expect to see catch-up growth for the SGA infant or the infant who has been severely ill.[25]

Length measurements are difficult to obtain accurately. Generally they are not used in routine clinical practice in the nursery, but they are indicated for research purposes. To obtain accurate measurements, a length board and two trained health care providers are needed.

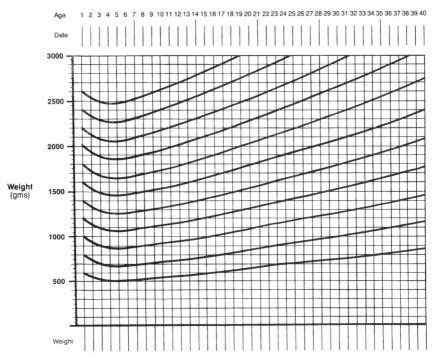

Figure 3-3 Premature infant growth grid. *Source:* Reprinted with permission from Shaffer SG, Quimiro CL, Anderson JV and Hall RT, Postnatal weight changes in low-birth-weight infants, *Pediatrics* (1987;79:702), copyright © 1987, Pediatrics.

Skinfolds and mid-arm circumference measurements do not change rapidly enough to be more helpful than weight measurements for diet changes. These measurements are generally not employed for routine clinical care but are indicated for growth studies. The measurement site must be determined, for there are limited standards or norms. Skinfold calipers are usually left in place until the reading becomes stable. The neonate's high body water composition can cause an elevated reading. Accessibility of a site to perform measurements can be limited due to intravenous lines and gel pads. It may be preferable to measure both the right and left sides, since one site may not be consistently available.

Assessing Inadequate Weight Gain

When a series of daily measurements indicate inadequate weight gain, a search must be made for the cause. Table 3-18 outlines areas to check.

Table 3-18 Possible Etiologies of Inadequate Weight Gain

1. Nutrient calculations are incorrect.
2. Infant is not receiving ordered diet.
   • Intravenous fluid administration has been interrupted to give blood or drugs, or the intravenous line has become infiltrated.
   • Infant is unable to consume what is ordered by bottle, and no gavage supplements were provided.
   • Feedings were held because the infant's respiratory rate increased or body temperature instability developed.
3. Infant does not tolerate given formula.
4. Calculated nutrient guidelines are inadequate for the infant due to growth retardation, illness, or high physical activity.
5. Infant is cold stressed.
6. Infant has outgrown previous diet order.
7. Nutrition solution was not prepared correctly.
8. Incorrect formula was provided to infant.

Assessment of Feeding Tolerance

Several parameters are used to assess feeding tolerance and early signs of NEC.[25] Depending on the findings, feedings may be held, decreased, diluted, or discontinued, or their frequency may be changed. Feeding intolerance is common for the premature infant, so constant surveillance is required. Feedings must be withheld at any sign of related illness, i.e., NEC. Gastric residuals are often present but what exactly constitutes an unacceptable volume is difficult to define. Some infants have small aspirates no matter what the feeding volume and yet are tolerating feedings.[26] The content of the residuals may determine the necessary action. Mucus residuals are not a concern and are often present in the infant recovering from lung disease. Undigested formula may dictate that the feeding volume is too large, that the infant does not tolerate this formula, or that the infant is constipated. Residuals containing bile are not uncommon when the infant is fed transpylorically.

Abdominal girth circumference increases will occur with growth, air swallowing, feeding intolerance, or NEC. The abdomen must be checked for tonicity. A very tight abdomen may suggest intestinal gas retention and NEC. Also, the abdomen must be observed for visible loops of bowel, which may indicate illness.

Reducing substances or blood in the stool is a concern and should be evaluated. Reducing substances can indicate overfeeding or be an early sign of NEC. Blood may be a sign of illness, feeding tube irritation of the intestine, anal fissure, or swallowed blood during delivery.

Assessment of Nutrient Adequacy and Tolerance

Both the specific clinical signs of nutrient deficiency/toxicity and the associated laboratory values should be regularly assessed. Acceptable standards for laboratory values are difficult to establish because premature infants differ by their physical maturity, clinical condition, and nutrient stores. For example, serum proteins will vary by the infant's hepatic maturity, energy and protein intake, vitamin and mineral nutritional status, and clinical condition.

Certain stabilization parameters are monitored in all premature infants: serum electrolyte levels, blood glucose level, serum creatinine levels, hematocrit, and blood urea nitrogen level. It is particularly important to watch electrolyte levels of infants receiving diuretics. Additional parameters monitored when parenteral nutrition is being administered are direct bilirubin and serum triglyceride levels.

Serum calcium, phosphorus, and alkaline phosphatase levels are monitored in infants at risk for osteopenia, who include those fed human milk, on long-term parenteral nutrition, or receiving chronic diuretics. Vitamin assays should be performed when pharmacological dosing of vitamins are being given to permit detection of vitamin toxicity.

DISCHARGE CONCERNS

The premature infant is ready for discharge from the hospital when body temperature can be maintained and bottle or breastfeeding supports growth. Most important, the caretaker must be ready to care for this high-risk infant. Rooming in with the infant will help to facilitate care and give confidence to the parent. Generally, discharge will occur on the infant's original due date.

The infant should be evaluated for participation in the Women, Infants, and Children (WIC) program, and enrollment into a developmental follow-up program for premature infants. The follow-up program should monitor the infant's growth and development, offer aid with chronic illness management, provide early detection of problems, make referrals to specialized services as indicated, and give the parents support and guidance in caring for their prematurely born infant.[12,27] These clinics not only aid with early detection of problems, but also evaluate the care that newborn intensive care units provide.

A clinic or private physician must be identified to provide well-baby and sick care, and an appointment should be established prior to discharge to home. Most infants will be discharged home on human milk or standard infant formula with iron and multiple vitamin supplements. Infants who have osteopenia may need to be discharged on premature infant formulas, and infants suffering from bronchopulmonary dysplasia may need a concentrated-calorie formula.

CONCLUSION

Although premature infants begin life in a compromised nutritional state, enteral and parenteral nutrition interventions have been altered over the last few years to provide optimal nutrient intake to overcome deficiencies and promote growth.[28] Daily evaluation of the nutrition care provided to the premature infant is necessary to meet the infant's nutrition needs during constant growth and development.

REFERENCES

1. American Academy of Pediatrics and American College of Obstetricians and Gynecologists. *Guidelines for Perinatal Care.* Elk Grove, Ill: American Academy of Pediatrics; 1988.

2. Battaglia FC, Lubchenco LO. A practical classification of newborn infants by weight and gestational age. *J Pediatr.* 1967;71:159.

3. Babson SG, Benda GI. Growth graphs for the clinical assessment of infants of varying gestational age. *J Pediatr.* 1976;89:814.

4. Vohr BR, Hack M. Developmental follow-up of low-birth-weight infants. *Pediatr Clin North Am.* 1982;29:1441.

5. Hack M, Merkatz IR, Gordon D, et al. The prognostic significance of postnatal growth in very low-birth weight infants. *Am J Obstet Gynecol.* 1982;143:693.

6. Sasanow SR, Georgieff MK, Pereira GR. Mid-arm circumference and mid-arm/head circumference ratios: standard curves for anthropometric assessment of neonatal nutritional status. *J Pediatr.* 1986;109:311.

7. Georgieff MK, Sasanow SR, Mammel MC, et al. Mid-arm circumference/head circumference ratios for identification of symptomatic LGA, AGA, and SGA newborn infants. *J Pediatr.* 1986;109:316.

8. American Academy of Pediatrics Committee on Nutrition. Nutritional needs of low-birth-weight infants. *Pediatrics.* 1985;75:976.

9. Pereira GR, Barbosa NMM. Controversies in neonatal nutrition. *Pediatr Clin North Am.* 1986;33:65.

10. Reichman B, Chessex P, Putet G, et al. Diet, fat accretion and growth in premature infants. *N Engl J Med.* 1981;305:1495.

11. Reichman B, Chessex P, Verellen G, et al. Dietary composition and macronutrient storage in preterm infants. *Pediatrics.* 1983;72:322.

12. Klaus MH, Fanaroff AA. *Care of the High-Risk Neonate.* 3rd ed. Philadelphia, Pa: WB Saunders; 1986.

13. Stahl G, Spear ML, Hamosh M. Intravenous administration of lipid emulsions to premature infants. *Clin Perinatol.* 1986;13:133.

14. Heird WC, Hay W, Helms RA, et al. Pediatric parenteral amino acid mixture in low birth weight infants. *Pediatrics.* 1988;81:41.

15. Helms RA, Christensen ML, Mauer EC, et al. Comparison of a pediatric versus standard amino acid formulation in preterm neonates requiring parenteral nutrition. *J Pediatr.* 1987;110:466.

16. Ernst JA, Williams JM, Glick MR, et al. Osmolality of substances used in the intensive care nursery. *Pediatrics*. 1983;72:347.

17. Slagle TA, Gross SJ, Vitamin E. In: Tsang RC, Nichols BL, eds. *Nutrition during Infancy*. St. Louis, Mo: CV Mosby; 1988:277–288.

18. Shenai JP, Kennedy KA, Chytil F, et al. Clinical trial of vitamin A supplementation in infants susceptible to bronchopulmonary dysplasia. *J Pediatr*. 1987;111:269.

19. Lawson EE, Stiles AD. Vitamin A therapy for prevention of chronic lung disease in infants. *J Pediatr*. 1987;111:247.

20. Herson VC, Philipps AF, Zimmerman A. Acute zinc deficiency in a premature infant after bowel resection and intravenous alimentation. *Am J Dis Child*. 1981;135:968.

21. Parker PH, Helinek GL, Meneely RL, et al. Zinc deficiency in a premature infant fed exclusively human milk. *Am J Dis Child*. 1982;136:76.

22. Koo WWK, Tsang TC. Calcium, magnesium and phosphorus. In: Tsang TC, Nichols BL, eds. *Nutrition during Infancy*. St. Louis, Mo: CV Mosby; 1988;175–190.

23. Koo WWK, Kaplan LA. Aluminum and bone disorders: with specific reference to aluminum contamination of infant nutrients. *J Am Coll Nutr*. 1988;7:199.

24. Schanler RJ. Special methods in feeding the preterm infant. In: Tsang RC, Nichols BL, eds. *Nutrition during Infancy*. St. Louis, Mo: CV Mosby; 1988:314–326.

25. Ohio Neonatal Nutritionists. *Nutritional Care for High Risk Newborns*. Philadelphia, Pa: George F. Stickley Co; 1985.

26. Rickard K, Gresham E. Nutritional considerations for the newborn requiring intensive care. *J Am Diet Assoc*. 1975;66:592.

27. Baucher H, Brown E, Peskin J. Premature graduates of the newborn intensive care unit: a guide to followup. *Pediatr Clin North Am*. 1988;35:1207.

28. Georgieff MK, Mills MM, Lindeke L, et al. Changes in nutritional management and outcome of very-low-birth-weight infants. *Am J Dis Child*. 1989;143:82.

29. Korones SB. *High-Risk Newborn Infants: The Basis for Intensive Nursing Care*. 4th ed. St Louis, Mo: CV Mosby; 1986.

30. Pittard WB, Levkoff AH. Parenteral nutrition for the neonate. In: Tsang RC, Nichols BL, eds. *Nutrition during Infancy*. St. Louis, Mo: CV Mosby; 1988:327–339.

31. Lemons JA, Neal P, Ernst J. Nitrogen sources for parenteral nutrition in the newborn infant. *Clin Perinatol*. 1986;13:91.

32. *M.V.I. Pediatric Package Insert*. Kankakee, Ill: Armour Pharmaceutical Co; 1985.

33. Brans YW, Andrew DS, Carrillo DW, et al. Tolerance of fat emulsions in very-low-birth-weight neonates. *Am J Dis Child*. 1988;142:145.

34. Lorenz JM, Kleinman LI, Kotagal UR, et al. Water balance in very low birth weight infants: relationship to water and sodium intake and effect on outcome. *J Pediatr*. 1982;101:423.

35. Dunn L, Hulman S, Weiner J, et al. Beneficial effects of early hypocaloric enteral feeding on neonatal gastrointestinal function: preliminary report of a randomized trial. *J Pediatr*. 1988;112:622.

36. O'Leary MJ. Nourishing the premature and low birth weight infant. In: Pipes PL, ed. *Nutrition in Infancy and Childhood*. St Louis, Mo: Times Mirror/Mosby College Publishing; 1989:301–360.

37. American Academy of Pediatrics Committee on Nutrition. Soy-protein formulas: recommendations for use in infant feeding. *Pediatrics*. 1983;72:359.

38. Shenai JP, Jhaveri BM, Reynolds JW, et al. Nutritional balance studies in very low-birth-weight infants: role of soy formula. *Pediatrics*. 1981;76:631.

39. Hall RT, Callenbach JC, Sheehan MB, et al. Comparison of calcium- and phosphorus-supplemented soy isolate formula with whey-predominant premature formula in very low birth weight infants. *J Pediatr Gastroenterol Nutr*. 1984;3:571.

40. Steichen JJ, Krug-Wispe SK, Tsang RC. Breastfeeding the low birth weight premature infant. *Clin Perinatol*. 1987;14:131.

41. Neonova^R Nutrition Optimizer. Columbus, Ohio: Ross Laboratories; 1988.

42. *Nutrient Levels of Mead Johnson Formulas Used in Hospitals*. Evansville, Ind: Mead Johnson & Co; 1989.

43. *Comparison of Infant Formulas*. Philadelphia, Pa: Wyeth Laboratories; 1986.

44. Schreiner RL, Brady MS, Ernst JA, Lemons JA. Lack of lactobezoars in infants given predominantly whey protein formulas. *Am J Dis Child*. 1982;136:437.

45. Food and Nutrition Board. *Recommended Dietary Allowances*. 10th ed. Washington, DC: National Academy Press; 1989.

46. Schanler RJ. Water-soluble vitamins. In: Lebenthal E, ed. *Textbook of Gastroenterology and Nutrition in Infancy*. New York, NY: Raven Press; 1989:377–392.

47. Anderson DM. Nutrition care for the premature infant. *Top Clin Nutr*. 1987;2:1.

Chapter 4

Normal Nutrition during Infancy

Sharon L. Groh-Wargo and Karen Antonelli

New discoveries in infant nutrition challenge feeding traditions and invite updated guidelines. The purpose of this chapter is to describe currently recommended feeding practices for healthy full-term infants and discuss common feeding problems encountered during the first year.

BREASTFEEDING

Breastfeeding is the recommended method of feeding for virtually all infants. Both the American Academy of Pediatrics[1] and the American Dietetic Association[2] published papers during the 1980s supporting breastfeeding as the preferred infant feeding choice. The number of women choosing to breastfeed their newborn infants increased steadily from a low of 25% in the early 1970s to about 60% by the mid-1980s.[3] Since that time, however, this number has gradually slipped to about 51% in 1990 (personal communication, Ross Laboratories, 1990).

Not all women choose breastfeeding in equal numbers. Statistically, blacks, the poor, the less educated, and those younger than 20 years of age choose to breastfeed less often.[3] In addition, a significant number of women, about 20%, stop breastfeeding by the time their babies are 2 months old.[3] This is often due to anxiety about feeding technique or the adequacy of the baby's intake.[4] Only about 20% of mothers are still breastfeeding at 5 to 6 months (personal communication, Ross Laboratories, 1990). Education and support can help these groups make informed choices. Health professionals must often fill this role and, therefore, need to be knowledgeable about both the science and art of breastfeeding.

Informed Choice

In order to make an informed decision, each mother, together with the baby's father or other significant family member, needs to weigh the implications of feeding choice. This process is ideally completed early in the pregnancy. Some of the advantages commonly listed for human milk and breastfeeding are

- superior nutritional composition[2,5]
- provision of immunologic and enzymatic components[5,6]
- health benefits for mothers[7]
- lower cost and increased convenience[7]
- enhanced maternal–infant bonding[8]
- decreased incidence of respiratory and gastrointestinal infections[9]

Evidence also exists that breastfed infants develop fewer allergies,[10] although this is controversial.[11]

Human Milk Composition

The composition of human milk varies from individual to individual and with the stage of lactation, time of day, time into the feeding, and maternal diet. Colostrum is the milk produced during the first several days following delivery. It is lower in fat and energy than mature milk but higher in protein, fat-soluble vitamins, minerals, and electrolytes.[12] It is also a rich source of antibodies.[12] A transitional milk is produced after about 7 days, followed by mature milk after approximately 2 weeks postpartum.[12] Milk production is higher during the day,[13] and fat content increases toward the end of the feeding.[14]

Table 4-1 summarizes the content of major nutrients in mature human milk. There is wide variation in the composition data reported in the literature, and older data may be inaccurate due to inferior analysis techniques that were commonly used. Extended lactation (7 months to 2 years) results in milk different from colostrum, transitional, and mature human milk. Its carbohydrate, protein, and fat content remains relatively stable, but concentrations of several vitamins and minerals decrease.[15,16]

Maternal Diet during Breastfeeding

The Subcommittee on the 10th Edition of the Recommended Dietary Allowances (RDAs) of the Food and Nutrition Board, National Research Council, National Academy of Sciences offers the most widely recognized standards for the lactating woman (see Tables 2-2 and 2-3).[17] The additional daily energy intake of 500 kcal/d suggested in the RDAs assumes an average daily milk production of 600 to 750 ml and a store of 2 to 3 kg of body fat from weight gain during pregnancy.[17] Energy requirements are greater if weight gain during the pregnancy was low, weight during lactation falls below standards for height and age, and/or more

Table 4-1 Composition of Mature Human Milk and Cow Milk

Nutrient	Human Milk (100 ml)	Cow Milk (100 ml)
Macronutrients		
Energy (kcal)	70	61
Protein (g)	0.9	3.3
Carbohydrate (g)	7.3	4.7
Fat (g)	4.1	3.3
Vitamins		
Vitamin A (IU)	133–177	126
β-Carotene (μg)	16–21	N/A
Vitamin D (IU)	2.5	41*
Vitamin E (IU)	0.48	0.06
Vitamin K (μg)	0.23	6.0
Vitamin C (mg)	5.2	0.94
Thiamine (μg)	18.3	38
Riboflavin (μg)	31.0	162
Vitamin B_6 (μg)	10.7	42
Vitamin B_{12} (μg)	0.02	0.36
Nicotinic acid (μg)	0.18	0.08
Folic acid (μg)	4.2	5.0
Pantothenic acid (μg)	261	314
Biotin (μg)	0.53	N/A
Minerals		
Calcium (mg)	29.4	119
Phosphorus (mg)	13.9	93
Magnesium (mg)	3.0	13
Iron (mg)	0.02	0.05
Zinc (mg)	0.15	0.38
Manganese (μg)	0.41	2–4
Copper (μg)	31	30
Chromium (μg)	0.03	0.8–1.3
Selenium (μg)	1.6	0.5–5.0
Fluoride (μg)	2.5	N/A
Sodium (mg)	11.2	49
Potassium (mg)	44.3	152
Chloride (mg)	37.3	N/A
Other composition data		
Protein source	Human; 80% whey; 20% casein	Cow; 18% whey; 82% casein
% Calories protein	6	21
Carbohydrate source	Lactose	Lactose

continues

Table 4-1 continued

Nutrient	Human Milk (100 ml)	Cow Milk (100 ml)
% Calories carbohydrate	39	31
Fat source	Human	Butterfat
% Calories fat	55	48
Osmolality (mOsm/kg H₂O)	300	288

*Vitamin D added.
NA, not available

Source: Data from references 49, 71, and 105 to 119.

than one infant is being nursed. There is some evidence that successful lactation can be maintained at energy intakes somewhat lower than the RDAs, allowing for gradual weight loss.[18] It must be emphasized, however, that although not the most common reason for inadequate milk production, substantially restricted energy intakes can reduce milk volume.

Increases in protein, vitamin, and mineral requirements can be met by consuming the appropriate number of servings from the basic four food groups (see Table 4-2) and choosing nutritious foods for the additional calories needed to support milk production. For those mothers not motivated to eat a well-balanced diet or for those intolerant to milk, continuation of prenatal vitamin and/or calcium supplementation, respectively, is recommended. It is suggested that iron supplementation of the mother be continued postpartum whether breastfeeding or not, in order to replenish iron stores depleted by pregnancy.[17]

Most breastfeeding women experience increased thirst. This should naturally result in additional intake of fluids. There are no data to support the idea that forcing fluids will increase, or restricting fluids will decrease, milk production.[19,20]

Table 4-2 Daily Food Guide during Breastfeeding

Food Group	Number of Servings
Milk (and milk substitutes)	4 cups (6 cups teens) or equivalent
Meat (and meat substitutes)	Two 2- to 3-oz servings or equivalent
Fruits and vegetables	Four 1/2-cup servings (vitamin C source daily; vitamin A source 3–4 times/week)
Breads and cereals	Four servings (serving equal to one slice of bread or 1/2–3/4 cup)

Source: Adapted with permission from *Guide to Good Eating*. Rosemont, IL: National Dairy Council; © 1989.

Although the quality of human milk is remarkably preserved even when the mother is poorly nourished, maternal diet can affect composition in the following ways:

- decreased milk volume from a diet low in energy, carbohydrate, and/or protein[12,20,21]

- altered fatty acid composition, which mirrors maternal intake[22]

- varied content of some vitamins and minerals (see Table 4-3)

- appearance of colic symptoms in babies whose mothers drink a lot of cow milk, due to transmission to allergens in the milk[23]

- passage of caffeine, nicotine, and alcohol into milk, possibly causing adverse affects in the baby when maternal consumption is high[24–26]

- passage of medications, drugs, and environmental contaminants[12,21]

Table 4-3 Effect of Changes in Maternal Diet on Vitamin and Mineral Composition of Human Milk

Yes *Maternal Diet Can* *Change Composition*	*No* *Maternal Diet Cannot* *Change Composition*	*Unknown* *Effect of Maternal* *Diet Not Known*
Vitamins		
Vitamin A	Vitamin K	Vitamin E
Vitamin D	Folate	Pyridoxine
Vitamin C		Biotin
Thiamine		
Riboflavin		
Niacin		
Pantothenic Acid		
Cyanocobalamin		
Minerals		
Manganese	Sodium	Selenium
Iodine	Calcium	
	Phosphorus	
	Magnesium	
	Iron	
	Zinc	
	Copper	
	Fluoride	

Source: Data from references 20, 120, and 121.

Management

Infant suckling stimulates release of the hormones prolactin, responsible for milk production, and oxytocin, responsible for milk release, from the pituitary. In order to establish and sustain lactation, therefore, it is necessary to allow the baby access to the breast on demand. The more a mother nurses, the more milk she will make. The following list offers some tips for ensuring breastfeeding success:

1. Initial breastfeeding: Ideally, this should take place as soon after delivery as possible.
2. Positioning: Find a comfortable position either lying down or sitting up. Use pillows to support the baby's body and the mother's back and arms. Change the position of the baby with every feeding during the first few weeks so that pressure and friction on the mother's nipple are rotated. The mother should use one hand to support and guide her breast and put the other around the baby and on the baby's bottom to support and move the baby.
3. Latching on: Stimulate the rooting reflex by touching the baby's closest cheek. When the mouth is open wide, pull the baby close. Be sure that most of the mother's areola is in the baby's mouth, the baby's lower lip is turned out, and the tongue is under the mother's nipple. Rapid sucking, followed by slower, rhythmic sucking and swallowing, will stimulate the let-down reflex, or the actual release of milk. Signs that let-down has occurred include tingling in the breast, tightening in the uterus, milk around the baby's mouth, or milk dripping from the other breast. Use the little finger to break the suction before moving the baby.
4. Timing: During the first few weeks nurse the baby 8 to 12 times a day, or about every 2 to 3 hours. The feedings will become less frequent after breastfeeding is established. Build up to at least 10 to 15 minutes per breast per feeding and offer both breasts at each feeding. It takes several minutes to elicit the let-down reflex. The majority of the milk volume is emptied after 5 to 7 minutes of sucking.
5. Assessing adequacy (or "How do I know if my baby is getting enough?"): A baby who is receiving adequate fluid and calories will (1) have at least 6 to 8 thoroughly wet diapers a day, (2) have regular bowel movements, (3) nurse 8 to 12 times a day, (4) seem satisfied after nursing, and (5) grow at a relatively predictable rate.[27–29]

A number of situations often arise during the early weeks of breastfeeding that, if unanticipated and poorly managed, can jeopardize a successful nursing experience. They include the following:

1. Sore nipples: These are most often the result of improper positioning. The treatment includes nursing on the least sore nipple first, using vitamin E sparingly on a dry nipple following breastfeeding, and changing the position of the baby's mouth on the mother's nipple.

2. Engorgement: This painful swelling of the breast can occur as mature milk production begins and is accompanied by an increase in blood flow and fluid accumulation. Frequent nursing may help to minimize the discomfort until the breast adjusts. Expressing more milk than is necessary to just relieve the pressure will only result in increased milk production and should be discouraged.

3. Jaundice: Jaundice in the newborn is associated with an elevated bilirubin level and is often the result of inadequate feeding.[30] Early and frequent feedings will facilitate a good milk supply and encourage stooling, the excretion route of bilirubin in the baby. Supplemental water has not been shown to be an effective treatment and may interfere with establishing breastfeeding skills in the baby and, therefore, a good milk supply in the mother.[31,32]

4. Poor milk supply: This is probably more a theoretical concern than an actual problem because many mothers are insecure with their ability to successfully provide adequate nutrition without tangible evidence of consumption. Information about assessing adequacy should be presented in a positive and supportive manner. Frequent feedings and adequate rest will do more to promote milk production than forcing fluids or increasing calories, unless the diet is severely restricted. Overuse of pacifiers, swings, and other calming devices may deter the mother from offering the breast as comfort.

Many new mothers return to work or school after their babies are born. They can continue to breastfeed by (1) arranging to go to the baby or having the baby brought to them, (2) pumping and saving the milk, or (3) discontinuing the feeding(s) when they are away but continuing to nurse at other times. There are several good sources that discuss these alternatives, as well as issues related to milk storage.[7,12]

Supplementation

Since the human race has evolved over the centuries on an infant diet of human milk, the argument can be made that no routine supplementation should be necessary. There are several nutrients, however, for which this may not be entirely true. They are vitamin K, vitamin D, iron, and fluoride (see Tables 4-4 and 4-5).

Table 4-4 Suggested Vitamin and Mineral Supplementation for Full-Term Infants (0–12 Months)

	Human Milk-Fed Infants	Commercial Infant Formula-Fed Infants
Vitamin K	Single dose at birth: IM 0.5–1.0 mg PO 1.0–2.0 mg	Single dose at birth: IM 0.5–1.0 mg PO 1.0–2.0 mg
Vitamin D	400 IU/d Especially at-risk infants*	
Iron	1 mg/kg/d to maximum 15 mg/d by 4–6 months; iron drops are best source	1 mg/kg/d to maximum 15 mg/d by 4 months; iron-fortified formula is best source†
Fluoride	0.25 mg/d by 2 weeks if local H_2O has < 0.3 ppm Fl	0.25 mg/d by 2 weeks if local H_2O has <0.3 ppm Fl or ready-to-feed formula is used

* See text for definition of at-risk infants.
† An iron-fortified formula (20 kcal/oz and 12 mg iron per quart) supplies approximately 2 mg/kg iron when fed at 120 kcal/kg.

Source: Data from references 33, 43, 44, and 68.

A one-time dose of vitamin K at birth is effective protection against hemorrhagic disease of the newborn.[33] This is recommended for both breastfed and bottle-fed infants.

The need for supplemental vitamin D in exclusively breastfed infants is controversial. While some do not believe it is necessary,[34] most support the practice.[33,35,36] Infants particularly at risk are those who

1. live in northern urban areas, especially during the winter
2. are dark skinned
3. are kept covered due to cultural practices or beliefs
4. have mothers with inadequate intakes of vitamin D or little exposure to sunlight[33,35]

Although the amount of iron in human milk is minimal, its bioavailability is quite high. About 50% of the iron is absorbed.[12] Some studies suggest that exclusively breastfed term infants remain iron sufficient for up to 9 to 12 months.[37,38] Most authorities, however, recommend another source of iron by 4 to 6 months of age.[33,39–41] Iron deficiency anemia is associated with cognitive and motor impairments that may be irreversible.[42] It seems prudent to supply generous iron during the first year before the vigorous infant "connoisseur" becomes the "picky" tod-

Table 4-5 Composition of Selected Infant Vitamin and Mineral Drops

Product and Suggested Dose	Vitamin D (IU)	Vitamin C (mg)	Vitamin A (IU)	Fe (mg)	Fl (mg)
ADC drops 1.0 ml e.g.: Tri-Vi-Sol (Mead Johnson); Vi-Daylin ADC (Ross)	400	35	1500	—	—
ADC drops with iron 1.0 ml e.g.: Tri-Vi-Sol with iron (Mead Johnson); Vi-Daylin ADC plus iron (Ross)	400	35	1500	10	—
ADC drops with fluoride 1.0 ml* e.g.: Tri-Vi-Flor 0.25 mg (Mead Johnson); Vi-Daylin/F ADC (Ross)	400	35	1500	—	0.25
ADC drops with fluoride and iron* 1.0 ml e.g.: Tri-Vi-Flor 0.25 mg with iron (Mead Johnson); Vi-Daylin/F ADC plus iron (Ross)	400	35	1500	10	0.25
Iron drops: Fer-In-Sol (Mead Johnson) 0.6 ml	—	—	—	15	—
Fluoride drops Pediaflor (Ross)* e.g., 0.5 ml	—	—	—	—	0.25

*Prescription required.

Source: Data from product handbooks by Mead Johnson Nutritional Division and Ross Laboratories, 1990.

---

dler. At 4 to 6 months infant cereal is probably the most convenient source of iron, but iron drops are a more reliably absorbed source.[43] After 6 months of age, the breastfed infant who receives cereal should have another source of iron added to the diet.

If the breastfed newborn lives in an area with fluoridated water, it may not be necessary to give a fluoride supplement.[44] Although fluoride does not appear to pass into the mother's milk,[45] infants fed only human milk and not receiving fluoride supplements have caries rates comparable to those of formula-fed infants.[46] When the water is not fluoridated (e.g., well water, bottled water), the American Academy of Pediatrics recommends a daily supplement.

BOTTLE FEEDING

When breastfeeding is not chosen, is unsuccessful, or is stopped before 1 year of age, bottle feeding with a commercially prepared infant formula is the recommended alternative. A wide variety of products are available.

Table 4-6 Composition of Selected Standard Formulas

	Enfamil with Iron		Similac with Iron		SMA		Gerber with Iron	
	per 100 kcal	per 100 ml	per 100 kcal	per 100 ml	per 100 kcal	per 100 ml	per 100 kcal	per 100 ml
Macronutrients								
Energy(kcal)	100	67	100	67	100	67	100	67
Protein (g)	2.2	1.5	2.2	1.5	2.2	1.5	2.2	1.5
Carbohydrate (g)	10.3	7.0	10.7	7.2	10.6	7.2	10.7	7.2
Fat (g)	5.6	3.8	5.4	3.6	5.3	3.6	5.4	3.6
Linoleic acid (g)	1.1	0.7	1.3	0.9	0.5	0.3	1.3	0.9
Vitamins								
Vitamin A (IU)	310	209	300	202	300	202	300	200
Vitamin D (IU)	62	42	60	40	60	40	60	40
Vitamin E (IU)	3.1	2.1	3.0	2.0	1.4	0.9	3.0	2.0
Vitamin K (µg)	8.6	5.8	8.0	5.4	8.0	5.4	8.0	5.3
Vitamin C (mg)	8.1	5.5	9.0	6.1	8.5	5.7	9.0	6.0
Thiamine (µg)	78	53	100	67	100	67	100	67
Riboflavin (µg)	156	105	150	101	150	101	150	100
Vitamin B$_6$ (µg)	62	42	60	40	63	43	60	40
Vitamin B$_{12}$ (µg)	0.2	0.2	0.2	0.2	0.2	0.1	0.2	0.2
Niacin (µg)	1250	844	1050	709	750	506	1050	698
Folic acid (µg)	16	10	15	10	7.5	5.1	15	10
Pantothenic acid (µg)	470	317	450	304	315	213	450	302
Biotin (µg)	2.3	1.6	4.4	3.0	2.2	1.5	4.4	2.9
Choline (mg)	16	10	16	11	15	10.1	16	11
Inositol (mg)	4.7	3.2	4.7	3.2	4.7	3.2	4.7	3.1

	1	2	3	4	5	6	7
Minerals							
Calcium (mg)	69	75	51	63	43	75	50
Phosphorus (mg)	47	58	39	42	28	58	39
Magnesium (mg)	7.8	6.0	4.0	7	4.7	6.0	4.0
Iron (mg)	1.9	1.8	1.2	1.8	1.2	1.8	1.2
Zinc (mg)	0.8	0.8	0.5	0.8	0.5	0.8	0.5
Manganese (µg)	16	5.0	3.4	22	15	5	3.3
Copper (µg)	94	90	61	70	47	90	60
Iodine (µg)	10	15	10	9	6	15	10
Sodium (mg)	27	28	19	22	15	33	22
Potassium (mg)	108	108	73	83	56	108	72
Chloride (mg)	62	66	44	55	38	70	47
Other composition data							
Protein source	Cow milk; 60% whey		Cow milk; 82% casein		Cow milk; 60% whey		Cow milk; 82% casein
% Calories protein	9		9		9		9
Carbohydrate source	Lactose		Lactose		Lactose		Lactose
% Calories carbohydrate	41		43		43		43
Fat source	Palm olein, soy, coconut, & high oleic sunflower oils		Soy & coconut oils		Coconut, safflower, soybean oils, & oleo		Palm olein, soy, coconut, & high oleic sunflower oils
% Calories fat	50		48		48		48
Osmolality (mOsm/kg H_2O)	300		300		300		N/A
Manufacturer/Distributor	Mead Johnson		Ross		Wyeth-Ayerst		Gerber

Table 4-7 Composition of Selected Soy Formulas

	Isomil		Prosobee		Nursoy	
	per 100 kcal	per 100 ml	per 100 kcal	per 100 ml	per 100 kcal	per 100 ml
Macronutrients						
Energy (kcal)	100	67	100	67	100	67
Protein (g)	2.7	1.8	3.0	2.0	3.1	2.1
Carbohydrate (g)	10.1	6.8	10.0	6.7	10.2	6.9
Fat (g)	5.5	3.7	5.3	3.6	5.3	3.6
Linoleic acid (g)	1.3	0.9	1.0	0.7	0.5	0.3
Vitamins						
Vitamin A (IU)	300	202	310	209	300	202
Vitamin D (IU)	60	40	62	42	60	40
Vitamin E (IU)	3.0	2.0	3.1	2.1	1.4	0.9
Vitamin K (µg)	15	10	16	10	15	10
Vitamin C (mg)	9.0	6.1	8.1	5.5	8.5	5.7
Thiamine (µg)	60	40	78	53	100	67
Riboflavin (µg)	90	61	94	63	150	101
Vitamin B_6 (µg)	60	40	62	42	63	43
Vitamin B_{12} (µg)	0.4	0.3	0.3	0.2	0.3	0.2
Niacin (µg)	1350	911	1250	844	750	506
Folic acid (µg)	15	10	16	10	7.5	5.1
Pantothenic acid (µg)	750	506	470	317	450	304
Biotin (µg)	4.5	3.0	7.8	5.3	5.5	3.7
Choline (mg)	8.0	5.4	7.8	5.3	13	8.8
Inositol (mg)	5.0	3.4	4.7	3.2	4.1	2.8
Minerals						
Calcium (mg)	105	71	94	63	90	61
Phosphorus (mg)	75	51	74	50	63	43
Magnesium (mg)	7.5	5.1	11	7.4	10	6.7
Iron (mg)	1.8	1.2	1.9	1.3	1.7	1.2
Zinc (mg)	0.8	0.5	0.8	0.5	0.8	0.5
Manganese (µg)	30	20	25	17	30	20
Copper (µg)	75	51	94	63	70	47
Iodine (µg)	15	10	10	6.9	9.0	6.1
Sodium (mg)	44	30	36	24	30	20
Potassium (mg)	108	73	122	82	105	71
Chloride (mg)	62	42	83	56	56	38
Other composition data						
Protein source	Soy isolate & L-methionine		Soy isolate & L-methionine		Soy isolate & L-methionine	
% Calories protein	11		12		12	
Carbohydrate source	Corn syrup & sucrose		Corn syrup solids		Sucrose	

Table 4-7 continued

	Isomil	Prosobee	Nursoy
% Calories carbohydrate	40	40	41
Fat source	Soy & coconut oils	Palm olein, soy, coconut, & high oleic sunflower oils	Oleo, coconut, safflower, & soy oils
% Calories fat	49	48	47
Osmolality (mOsm/kg H_2O)	240	200	296
Manufacturer	Ross	Mead Johnson	Wyeth-Ayerst

Infant Formula Composition

Both the American Academy of Pediatrics[47] and the Food and Drug Administration[48] have identified some nutrient requirements for infants. Tables 4-6 to 4-9 list the nutrient composition of many of the most common formulas; Table 4-10 gives the nutrient requirements for infant formulas. They are grouped by the following categories: standard, soy, protein hydrolysate, and follow-up.

Standard

The most common human milk substitutes are standard formulas. They are made from cow milk that is altered by removing the butterfat, adding vegetable oils and carbohydrate, and decreasing the protein. Some standard formulas contain demineralized whey. This produces a whey:casein ratio of 60:40. Human milk has a ratio of about 80:20.[49] Standard formulas without the demineralized whey have a ratio of 20:80. Although the addition of the demineralized whey appears to make those formulas closer to human milk, there are no clear scientific data to support superior performance when they are fed to babies.[50–52] There is some evidence that the amount of protein found in standard formulas is excessive and that, unless the quantity is lowered, the ideal protein quality will be difficult to precisely determine.[53] Taurine, a free amino acid present in human milk, is often added to standard formulas.

Standard formulas are marketed as iron fortified (12 mg/quart) and low iron (1 mg/quart). Only the iron-fortified variety meets the iron requirements of infancy. Although only about 4% of the iron in iron-fortified formula is absorbed,[54] its generous content makes it an adequate source of iron for the entire first year of life.

Soy

Soy formulas contain methionine-fortified soy protein isolate, vegetable oils, and a carbohydrate source other than lactose. The protein content of soy formulas

Table 4-8 Composition of Selected Protein Hydrolysate Formulas

	Nutramigen		Pregestimil		Alimentum		Good Start	
	per 100 kcal	per 100 ml	per 100 kcal	per 100 ml	per 100 kcal	per 100 ml	per 100 kcal	per 100 ml
Macronutrients								
Energy (kcal)	100	67	100	67	100	67	100	67
Protein (g)	2.8	1.9	2.8	1.9	2.8	1.9	2.4	1.6
Carbohydrate (g)	13.4	9.0	10.3	7.0	10.2	6.9	11.0	7.4
Fat (g)	3.9	2.6	5.6	3.8	5.5	3.7	5.1	3.4
Linoleic acid (g)	2.0	1.4	0.8	0.5	1.6	1.1	0.4	0.3
Vitamins								
Vitamin A (IU)	310	209	375	253	300	202	300	202
Vitamin D (IU)	62	42	75	51	60	40	60	40
Vitamin E (IU)	3.1	2.1	3.8	2.5	3.0	2.0	1.2	0.8
Vitamin K (µg)	16	10	19	13	15	10	8.2	5.5
Vitamin C (mg)	8.1	5.5	12	7.9	9.0	6.1	8.0	5.4
Thiamine (µg)	78	53	78	53	60	40	60	40
Riboflavin (µg)	94	63	94	63	90	61	135	91
Vitamin B$_6$ (µg)	62	42	62	42	60	40	75	51
Vitamin B$_{12}$ (µg)	0.3	0.2	0.3	0.2	0.4	0.3	0.2	0.2
Niacin (µg)	1250	844	1250	844	1350	911	750	506
Folic acid (µg)	16	10	16	10	15	10	9.0	6.1
Pantothenic acid (µg)	470	317	470	317	750	506	450	304
Biotin (µg)	7.8	5.3	7.8	5.3	4.5	3.0	2.2	1.5
Choline (mg)	13	9.0	13	9.0	8.0	5.4	12	8.1
Inositol (mg)	4.7	3.2	4.7	3.2	5.0	3.4	6.1	4.1

Minerals				
Calcium (mg)	94	94	105	64
Phosphorus (mg)	62	62	75	36
Magnesium (mg)	11	11	7.5	6.7
Iron (mg)	1.9	1.9	1.8	1.5
Zinc (mg)	0.8	0.9	0.8	0.8
Manganese (µg)	31	31	30	7.0
Copper (µg)	94	94	75	80
Iodine (µg)	7.0	7.0	15	8.0
Sodium (mg)	47	47	44	24
Potassium (mg)	109	109	118	98
Chloride (mg)	86	86	80	59
Other composition data				
Protein source	Casein hydrolysate	Casein hydrolysate	Casein hydrolysate	Whey hydrolysate
% Calories protein	11	11	11	10
Carbohydrate source	Corn syrup solids & corn starch	Corn syrup solids, glucose & starch	Sucrose & tapioca starch	Maltodextrin & lactose
% Calories carbohydrate	54	40	40	44
Fat source	Corn oil	MCT; corn & high oleic safflower oils	MCT; safflower & soy oils	Palm, high oleic safflower & coconut oils
% Calories fat	35	49	49	46
Osmolality (mOsm/kg H$_2$O)	320	320	370	265
Manufacturer	Mead Johnson	Mead Johnson	Ross	Carnation

Note: MCT, medium-chain triglycerides.

Table 4-9 Composition of Selected Follow-Up Formulas

	Follow-Up Formula		Advance	
	per 100 kcal	per 100 ml	per 100 kcal	per 100 ml
Macronutrients				
Energy (kcal)	100	67	100	54
Protein (g)	3.0	2.0	3.7	2.0
Carbohydrate (g)	13.2	8.9	10.2	5.5
Fat (g)	3.9	2.6	5.0	2.7
Linoleic acid (g)	0.7	0.5	2.3	1.2
Vitamins				
Vitamin A (IU)	250	169	300	162
Vitamin D (IU)	65	44	60	32
Vitamin E (IU)	0.8	0.5	3.0	1.6
Vitamin K (µg)	8.1	5.5	8	4.3
Vitamin C (mg)	8.0	5.4	10	5.4
Thiamine (µg)	80	54	120	65
Riboflavin (µg)	96	65	170	92
Vitamin B_6 (µg)	66	45	75	41
Vitamin B_{12} (µg)	0.3	0.2	0.3	0.2
Niacin (µg)	1280	864	1300	702
Folic acid (µg)	16	11	19	10
Pantothenic acid (µg)	480	324	560	302
Biotin (µg)	1.5	1.0	4.4	2.4
Choline (mg)	—	—	16	8.6
Inositol (mg)	—	—	4.7	2.5
Minerals				
Calcium (mg)	135	91	94	51
Phosphorus (mg)	90	61	72	39
Magnesium (mg)	8.4	5.7	7.6	4.1
Iron (mg)	1.9	1.3	1.8	1.0
Zinc (mg)	0.6	0.4	0.9	0.5
Manganese (µg)	7.0	4.7	6	3.2
Copper (µg)	76	51	110	59
Iodine (µg)	5.7	3.8	18	9.7
Sodium (mg)	39	26	35	19
Potassium (mg)	135	91	146	79
Chloride (mg)	90	61	88	48
Other composition data				
Protein source	Cow milk; 82% casein		Cow milk & soy protein isolate	
% Calories protein	12		15	

Table 4-9 continued

	Follow-Up Formula	*Advance*
Carbohydrate source	Lactose & corn syrup solids	Corn syrup & lactose
% Calories carbohydrate	53	40
Fat source	Palm, corn, & high-oleic safflower oils	Soy & corn oils
% Calories fat	35	45
Osmolality (mOsm/kg H$_2$O)	N/A	200
Manufacturer	Carnation	Ross

Note: N/A, not available.

is higher than standard formulas because the biologic value of soy protein is lower than cow milk protein. They have three major indications: intolerance to cow milk protein, galactosemia, and lactose intolerance. Infants who are allergic to cow milk formulas may also be allergic to soy formula.[55] Lactose intolerance can be due to either primary congenital lactase deficiency (rarely) or secondary lactase deficiency as a result of a diarrheal episode. In the latter case, the use of soy formula may be indicated for the short-term until the small intestine regenerates lactase. While all soy formulas are lactose-free, some are also sucrose-free or corn-free. Studies confirm that soy formulas promote normal growth and development when fed to full-term healthy infants.[56] Recent changes in some soy formulas include the addition of taurine, carnitine, and selenium and enhanced calcium and phosphorus availability.[57]

Protein Hydrolysates

When an infant is allergic to the intact protein of cow milk and/or soy protein, a casein hydrolysate may be appropriate. Casein hydrolysates contain nonantigenic peptides of <1200 molecular weight[58] and have been used successfully for over 40 years. Enzymatic hydrolysates of whey contain some peptides of >2000 molecular weight, have had limited clinical use, and may be an acceptable alternative only for those infants who are sensitive but not truly allergic to cow milk or soy.[59] Sources of carbohydrate and fat vary among the protein hydrolysates and should be considered when they are fed for indications other than protein allergy or sensitivity.

Follow-Up

Follow-up formulas are intended for older infants who are taking solid foods. There are two products on the market. Advance (Ross) has a lower fat content and

Table 4-10 Nutrient Requirements for Infant Formulas

	Per 100 kcal	
	Minimum	Maximum
Macronutrients		
Protein (g)	1.8	4.5
Carbohydrate (g)	—	—
Fat (g)	3.3	6.0
Linoleic acid (g)	0.3	—
Vitamins		
Vitamin A (IU)	250	750
Vitamin D (IU)	40	100
Vitamin E (IU)	0.7	—
Vitamin K (µg)	4	—
Vitamin C (mg)	8	—
Thiamine (µg)	40	—
Riboflavin (µg)	60	—
Vitamin B_6 (µg)	35	—
Vitamin B_{12} (µg)	0.15	—
Niacin (µg)	250*	—
Folic acid (µg)	4	—
Pantothenic acid (µg)	300	—
Biotin (µg)	1.5[†]	—
Choline (mg)	7[†]	—
Inositol (mg)	4[†]	—
Minerals		
Calcium (mg)	60	—
Phosphorus (mg)	30	—
Magnesium (mg)	6	—
Iron (mg)	0.15	3
Zinc (mg)	0.5	—
Manganese (µg)	5	—
Copper (µg)	60	—
Iodine (µg)	5	75
Sodium (mg)	20	60
Potassium (mg)	80	200
Chloride (mg)	55	150

* Includes nicotinic acid and niacinamide.
† Required only for nonmilk-based formulas.

Source: Data from reference 48.

has limited usefulness when lower caloric density is desired. Follow-up Formula (Carnation) was more recently introduced to the market. It has a higher percentage of calories from protein and carbohydrates and a lower percentage of calories from fat. This seems inappropriate since protein requirements go down during the second half of the first year,[17] while typical solid foods fed to infants, e.g., cereals, fruits, and vegetables, are low in fat and high in carbohydrate. It does offer a good source of vitamins and iron, if those are lacking in the solid foods the infant likes. The American Academy of Pediatrics stated that "while nutritionally adequate," this type of follow-up formula offers "no clearly established superiority over currently used feedings for infants at this age."[60] This opinion has been recently restated by Zeigler.[61]

Evaporated Milk Formulas

While not recommended, a home-prepared formula from evaporated milk is probably superior to using unmodified cow milk and may be acceptable if breastfeeding is not possible or the cost of a commercial formula is prohibitive. The usual recipe is one can of evaporated whole milk (13 oz), $19^1/_2$ oz of water, and 3 tablespoons of sugar or corn syrup.[39] The evaporation process denatures the protein, rendering it softer and more digestible, and adding the sugar or corn syrup improves the ratio of protein/fat/carbohydrate. Other than these two factors, however, evaporated milk formula has all the disadvantages for infants as unmodified cow milk: poorly digested fat, low concentration of iron and vitamin C, and excessive amounts of sodium and phosphorus. A vitamin A and D supplement is needed unless the evaporated milk is fortified, additional vitamin C and iron are needed unless the infant takes sufficient quantities of the appropriate solid foods, and supplemental fluoride is needed unless the water used in formula preparation is fluoridated.[33,39] A vitamin A+D+C supplement drop plain or with iron and/or fluoride is appropriate (see Tables 4-5 and 4-11).

Management

Bottle-feeding parents need information about how infant formulas are packaged, prepared, and stored. They may also need advice on bottles and nipples and on feeding techniques.

Preparation of Infant Formulas

Infant formulas usually come packaged in three ways:

1. ready-to-feed (32-oz cans)
2. concentrated liquid (13-oz cans)
3. powder (12- to 16-oz cans)

Table 4-11 Products *Not* Recommended for Infant Feeding

Nutrient Distribution	Ideal*	Goat's Milk†	Evaporated Milk‡	Whole Cow Milk†	Skim Milk	Low-Fat Milk†
Kcal/100 ml	67	67	66	62	35	43
% Pro	7–16	20	16	21	38	31
% CHO	35–65	26	42	30	57	45
% Fat	30–55	54	45	49	5	24
Nutrient excesses		Protein	Butterfat	Protein	Protein	Protein
Nutrient deficiencies		Folic acid	Vitamin C	Vitamin C	Vitamin C	Vitamin C
		Iron	Iron	Iron	Iron	Iron
					Fat	Fat
Daily supplementation required§						
Vitamin C‖		+	+	+	+	+
Folic acid¶		+	–	–	–	–
Iron¶		+	+	+	+	+
Comments		High renal solute load with mineral composition similar to cow milk*#	Cost is similar to powdered commercial infant formulas*#	High renal solute load. Guaiac-positive stools may develop, precipitating iron deficiency anemia#	Unacceptable feeding alternative during infancy#	Unacceptable feeding alternative during infancy#

* Data from reference 68.
† Data from reference 119.
‡ One can (13 oz) evaporated milk with 2 T. corn syrup and 18 oz water.
§ Fluoride supplement 0.25 mg/d if local water has <0.3 ppm Fl or water not consumed (see Table 4-4).
‖ May be given as fruit juice (3.5 oz/d infant juice or 2 oz/d regular orange juice).
¶ See RDA for age (Table 2-3).
# See text.

Source: Adapted from *Pediatric Nutrition Theory and Practice* (p 334) by RJ Grand, JL Sutphen and WH Dietz (eds) with permission of Butterworth Publishers, © 1987.

Concentrated liquid is cheaper than ready-to-feed, is readily available, mixes easily, and can be the vehicle for fluoridated water. Powder is convenient if only a small amount of formula is desired. This form is popular among breastfeeding mothers who need to miss a feeding. Manufacturers recommend boiling the water for 5 minutes and cooling it before mixing. The prepared formulas can be kept in the refrigerator for 24 to 48 hours after opening. Powders have a 30-day shelf life after opening. Although often recommended at the time of discharge, sterilization of equipment is probably not carried out and is unnecessary if

1. The formula source is a sterile, commercially prepared formula.
2. The water source is from a supervised city filtration plant.
3. Hand are washed during preparation and before feeding.
4. Equipment is washed well in warm, soapy water and rinsed thoroughly.
5. Formula is promptly refrigerated after preparation.[62,63]

Although there is no evidence that babies prefer warmed milk, most caregivers do not feed cold bottles from the refrigerator. Warming is best done quickly in a pan of hot water. Microwave heating is not recommended as it is difficult to monitor and predict. Formula heated in a microwave has been associated with facial and palatal burns.[64,65]

Feeding Techniques and Schedules

Good bottle-feeding technique includes holding the infant so that face-to-face contact is maximized and tilting the bottle so that the nipple is filled with milk. The bottle should never be propped since this practice can lead to dental caries.[66] The addition of sugar to the milk or sucrose-containing fluids to the bottle increases the risk for this disease.[67] Adding solids, such as cereal, is also not recommended.

Most infants can finish a bottle in 15 to 20 minutes. Possible reasons for slow feeding include a nipple with a hole that is too small or clogged or a collapsed nipple. Burping is usually done midway through the feeding and at the end of the feeding. Partially used bottles should be discarded after the feeding, not saved for the next feeding time. Table 4-12 gives a suggested bottle-feeding schedule for infants.

Supplementation

Table 4-4 summarizes vitamin and mineral supplementation recommendations. Healthy full-term infants fed commercially prepared formula do not need daily vitamin supplementation. It is recommended they receive a one-time dose of vitamin K at birth as prophylaxis against hemorrhagic disease of the newborn.[33] Com-

Table 4-12 Suggested Number and Volume of Bottle Feedings for a Normal Infant

Age	Number	Volume
Birth–1 week	6–10	30– 90 ml
1 week–1 month	7–8	60–120 ml
1 month–3 months	5–7	120–180 ml
3 months–6 months	4–5	180–210 ml
6 months–9 months	3–4	210–240 ml
10 months–12 months	3	210–240 ml

Source: Reprinted from *Manual of Pediatric Nutrition* (p 38) by DG Kelts and EG Jones with permission of Little, Brown and Company, © 1984.

mercial formulas do not contain fluoride. If they are mixed with fluoridated water, no supplement is needed. If the infant is regularly fed ready-to-feed formulas or is living in an area without fluoridated water, the American Academy of Pediatrics recommends a daily supplement.[44] Iron supplementation should begin no later than 4 months in formula-fed term infants.[68] There are no data to support the opinion that iron-fortified formulas are not as well tolerated as low-iron formulas. With the exception of stool color, no differences in stool frequency or behavior (fussiness, cramps, regurgitation, flatus) have been documented in blinded, crossover studies.[69,70] Based on this research, it seems prudent to start bottle-fed newborns on iron-fortified formula rather than waiting until, and possibly forgetting at, 4 months.

WEANING AND FEEDING PROGRESSION

The introduction of solids into an infant's diet is ideally conducted in a way that balances nutrient needs with a variety of foods and textures and that encourages feeding skills development. The goal of weaning is the transition from a liquid diet to a well-balanced table food diet. Readiness generally occurs during the first 6 months of life, but observations of physical and psychologic developments are more superior determinants of readiness than age alone.

Nutrient Needs

In the absence of physical or developmental hindrance, a neonate can usually obtain the necessary calorie requirement from human milk or infant formula alone. As the infant grows, nutrient needs become greater than human milk or formula can provide. Supplemental foods become necessary for adequate satiety.

The distribution of calories is generally recommended to be 40% to 50% fat[71] and 7% to 11% protein,[17] with the remainder from carbohydrate. The recommended water-to-energy ratio is 1.5 ml/kcal.[17] Both human milk and infant formulas, as seen in Tables 4-1 and 4-6 to 4-9, resemble these distributions. Adding supplemental foods to the diet may alter the distribution of nutrients. This is a significant factor when deciding the type and amount of solids to add to the diet.

Vitamin and mineral intake is also affected by the introduction of solid foods, especially as the solids begin to replace the volume of milk taken daily. At this point in the changing infant's diet, the solids are relied upon to provide adequate vitamins and minerals. For this reason, any solids fed should be nutrient-dense items.

Physical Readiness for Solids

Before 4 or 5 months of age, an infant possesses an extrusion reflex that enables him or her to swallow only liquid foods.[72] By 4 to 6 months of age, an infant learns oral and gross motor skills that aid in accepting solid foods. Oral motor skills have evolved from the reflexive suck to the ability to swallow nonliquid foods and to transfer food from the front of the tongue to the back. Gross motor advancement includes sitting independently and maintaining balance while using hands to reach and grasp objects.[73] At this stage, the infant is ready to sit in a highchair and grasp pieces of food; however, the infant still lacks the hand-to-mouth coordination necessary to feed himself or herself.

Psychologic Readiness for Solids

Independent eating behaviors are encouraged as the infant advances from reflexive and imitative behaviors to more independent and exploratory behaviors. This transitional milestone occurs sometime during the fourth month of life.[73] After 6 months, an infant is able to indicate a desire for food by opening his or her mouth and leaning forward to indicate hunger, and disinterest or satiety by leaning back and turning away. Until an infant can express these feelings, feeding of solids will probably represent a type of forced feeding,[39] potentially leading to overfeeding and obesity.

In addition to determining the quantity of feeds, the infant should be encouraged to hold the bottle or cup, attempt to feed himself or herself, and demand the timing of feeds, in an effort to promote self-regulation of food-getting and ingestive behaviors.[74]

Later in infancy, a variety of foods are introduced into the diet. These introductions of unfamiliar foods are noteworthy as they allow the infant to gain experi-

Table 4-13 Guidelines for Progression of Solid Foods

Years in Months	Feeding Skills	Oral Motor Skills	Types of Food	Suggested Activities
B–4		Rooting reflex Sucking reflex Swallowing reflex Extrusion reflex	Breast milk Infant formula	Breastfeed or bottle feed
5	Able to grasp objects voluntarily Learning to reach mouth with hands	Disappearance of extrusion reflex		Possible introduction of thinned cereal
6	Sits with balance while using hands	Transfers food from front of tongue to back	Infant cereal Strained fruit Strained vegetables	Prepare cereal with formula or breast milk to a semiliquid texture Use spoon Feed from a dish Advance to 1/3– 1/2 cup cereal before adding fruits or vegetables
7	Improved grasp	Mashes food with lateral movements of jaw Learns side-to-side or "rotary" chewing	Infant cereal Strained to junior texture of fruits, vegetables, and meats	Thicken cereal to lumpier texture Sit in highchair with feet supported Introduce cup
8–10	Holds bottle without help Drinks from cup without spilling Decreases fluid intake and increases solids Coordinates hand-to-mouth movement		Juices Soft, mashed, or minced table foods	Begin finger foods Do not add salt, sugar, or fats to food Present soft foods in chunks ready for finger feeding
10–12	Feeds self Holds cup without help	Tooth eruption Improved ability to bite and chew	Soft, chopped table foods	Provide meals in pattern similar to rest of family Use cup at meals

Source: Data from references 39, 73, and 122.

ence with various tastes and textures, promoting successful weaning to the family diet. The importance of diversifying the diet at specific intervals during the infant's psychologic development can be observed in deprived environments in which the eating pattern is unvaried and monotonous or where weaning is delayed, both failing to stimulate interest in solid foods.[75]

First Foods

Commercial infant rice cereal thinned to a semiliquid consistency with breastmilk or infant formula is generally recommended as an infant's first food, as it is an unlikely allergen.[76] The cereal is traditionally introduced on a small spoon. Resistance to the initial spoon feeding is common as the infant is unaccustomed to the spoon as a dispenser of food. Holding the infant in one's arms rather than sitting him or her in a highchair may relieve some of the apprehension the infant may experience. Choking or gagging, however, indicates that despite the infant's chronologic age, he or she is not ready for the transition to solid foods.

Rice cereal is fed for 2 to 3 days while examining the infant for symptoms of intolerance such as skin rashes, diarrhea, or wheezing. In the absence of such symptoms, the quantity, frequency, and consistency of cereal feedings are increased, and a second food such as oatmeal or barley cereal is presented. Refer to Table 4-13 for further recommendations regarding the progression of solid foods.

Market Choices

Many commercial baby food products are available in markets today. Virtually all are prepared without added sodium and many without added sugar. Juices are generally enriched with vitamin C, while cereals are enriched with iron, thiamine, riboflavin, niacin, calcium, and phosphorus.

Those advertised as "first foods" are single-ingredient foods, in contrast to "dinners," baked goods, desserts, "junior foods," and some cereals, which contain a combination of ingredients. Textures from strained to chunky are available, along with foods designed for teething.

Commercial baby foods are a time-efficient means of providing an infant with solids and, if chosen wisely, can supply a nutrient-dense diet. Certain items will provide more nutrients than seemingly comparable choices. For example, plain meats contain from 220% to 250% of the protein and up to 200% of the iron of "meat dinners." While strained fruit is usually sugar-free, infant desserts may contain approximately 30% sucrose calories (personal communication, Gerber Products Company, May 1989). The nutrient content of selected commercial baby foods are listed in Table 4-14.

Table 4-14 Nutrient Content of Selected Commercial Baby Food Products

Food	Amount (g)	Calories	Protein (g)	Carbohydrate (g)	Fat (g)	Iron (g)	Sodium (g)
Infant cereal	100	389	11.8	73.0	5.4	47.5	8.8
Strained juices	100	48	0.2	11.5	0.2	0.3	3.7
Strained fruits "first foods"	100	69	0.6	15.9	0.2	0.3	3.4
Strained vegetables "first foods"	100	44	2.9	8.6	0.3	0.7	10.0
Strained meat	100	111	14.0	0.2	6.0	1.0	48.0
Strained meat dinner	100	70.7	5.7	7.0	1.7	0.6	23.0
Strained dinner	100	61	2.4	8.6	1.7	0.5	23.5

Note: Mean values derived from data provided by Gerber Products Company, Fremont, MI 49412.

Table 4-15 Steps in the Home Preparation of Baby Foods

1. Choosing appropriate foods
   - Use fresh or unsalted frozen foods. Do not use canned foods as they may contribute excessive sodium to the infant diet.
   - Spinach, carrots, broccoli, and beets should not be pureed at home because they may contain sufficient nitrite to cause methemoglobinemia in young infants.
2. Preparing fruits and vegetables
   - Thaw frozen vegetables/wash fresh produce.
   - Remove peels, cores, and seeds.
   - Steam or boil.
   - Puree in blender to desired consistency. Use liquid from cooking in order to preserve nutrients otherwise lost in cooking. Do not overblend as this may cause excessive oxidation of nutrients.
3. Preparing meats
   - Bake, broil, or stew.
   - Remove all skins.
   - Chop into small pieces.
   - Puree in blender to desired consistency.
4. Storing prepared foods
   - Keep refrigerated in a covered container. Use refrigerated foods within 48 hours.
   - Freeze in 2-T portions by pouring pureed food into an ice cube tray. Thaw desired portions in refrigeration before using.

Source: Data from references122, and 124 to 126.

Home Preparation of Baby Foods

Home prepared baby foods are an alternative to commercially prepared foods. They are more economical and allow greater flexibility in altering food consistency, but preparation can be time consuming. Low-income families should not be encouraged to prepare baby foods from their own meals if they lack variety in their diet, lack refrigeration and freezing, or have poor sanitation in their homes.[75] Also, home-grown foods should not be prepared for infants as the lead concentration of soil in residential areas may be excessive, leading to excessive levels of lead in the food grown.[77] These measures are to ensure a varied diet and food safety and prevent nutrient deficiencies, food-borne illness, and lead toxicity. Table 4-15 provides detailed instructions for the home preparation of baby foods.

Nursing Bottle Caries

Baby bottle tooth decay (BBTD) is an oral health disorder characterized by rampant dental caries that is associated with infant feeding practices. The disorder affects the primary teeth of infants and young children, particularly those who are

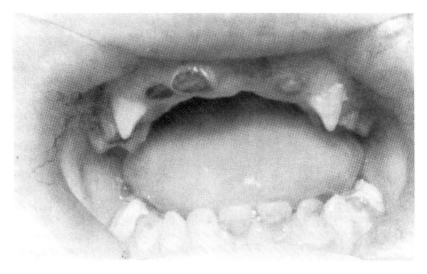

Figure 4-1 Baby bottle tooth decay.

permitted to fall asleep with a bottle filled with juice or other fermentable liquid.[71,78] Certain feeding practices can be altered to prevent BBTD.

Providing liquids concentrated in mono- and disaccharides, such as juice and sweetened beverages, is a leading cause of BBTD.[78] When an infant sleeps with a bottle in his or her mouth, swallowing and salivary flow decrease. This creates a pooling of liquid around the teeth. Sweet fluid contacting the teeth for a prolonged period of time provides plaque-forming bacteria, particularly *Streptococcus mutans*, with energy.[79] The outcome is otherwise known as dental plaque (see Figure 4-1).

Infants who refuse cold foods or grimace when chewing should be examined for BBTD. Those afflicted will have tooth discoloration varying from yellow to black. Preventive measures include the following:

- feeding only infant formula or water from a bottle
- cleaning the infant's teeth and gums with a damp washcloth or gauze pad after each feeding
- giving juices with a cup rather than a bottle
- filling bedtime bottles with water

Whole Cow Milk

Introduction of cow milk before 6 months is generally not recommended due to the risk of milk protein allergy, gastrointestinal blood loss, and poor iron nutriture.

Recent studies suggest that cow milk is not a suitable feeding for 6- to 12-month-old infants either.[61] When the infant is changed to cow milk, it should be whole cow milk, as opposed to 2% or skim (see Table 4-11).

Incidence of cow milk protein allergy is 1% to 2% during the first 2 years of life.[80] Early exposure to cow milk increases the risk of developing the allergy to milk protein and possibly to other foods as well. Resistance to allergy increases with gastrointestinal maturity,[81] so that at 6 months cow milk can be introduced into the diet with somewhat less risk of allergy.

Occult loss of blood from the gastrointestinal tract is associated with the introduction of cow milk in both early and later infancy. Blood loss, along with the lower concentration and bioavailability of iron in cow milk, predisposes the infant to iron deficiency anemia.[82–84] Neonatal iron stores become depleted by about 4 to 6 months in a term infant.[68] Iron-fortified infant cereal is traditionally introduced into the diet at this time or shortly thereafter, being depended upon as an excellent source of iron. However, the bioavailability of the electrolytic iron powders presently fortifying the cereal is currently being scrutinized.[85,86] Heme iron in meat is a reliable source of iron.[87] Until meat can be incorporated into the infant diet, those fed cow milk or unfortified formula should be provided with an iron supplement.

Cow milk is also a poor source of vitamin C, vitamin E, and essential fatty acids (EFAs). When an infant is changed to cow milk, either fruits, fruit juices, or vegetables should be a regular part of the diet, or a vitamin C–containing supplement should be prescribed. The American Academy of Pediatrics recommends 2.7% of calories as EFAs in infancy.[47] Meeting this requirement and the RDAs for vitamin E may be difficult for the infant on cow milk until a fairly wide variety of table foods are introduced into the diet.

Lastly, the additional protein and electrolytes in cow milk increases the renal solute load and places the infant at risk for dehydration during periods of vomiting, diarrhea, or exposure to dry heat in winter or to the sun in the summer. For all of the above reasons, it is best to delay the introduction of cow milk until the infant is 1 year old.

Common Feeding Problems

Formula intolerance, constipation, acute diarrhea, and food refusal are common feeding problems encountered during infancy. These problems can usually be resolved through simple measures. If ignored, they can have detrimental effects upon an infant's nutritional status.

Milk Allergy

Intolerance to lactose must not be confused with milk protein allergy. Lactose intolerance has an enzymatic etiology, while milk allergy is based upon immunologic mechanisms. Gastrointestinal disturbance is common to both disorders. Diarrhea is frequently observed in both but vomiting is exclusive to milk allergy. In addition to gastrointestinal symptoms, dermatologic, respiratory, and possibly systemic reactions such as anaphylactic shock (although this is rare) may occur in milk allergy.[88]

The usual onset of milk allergy occurs in the first 4 months of infancy. This onset is due to the immaturity of both the gastrointestinal tract and the immune system. In early infancy, the gastrointestinal tract adapts to the extrauterine environment against the penetration of harmful substances such as bacteria, toxins, and antigens within the intestinal lumen.[89] Mechanisms act to control and maintain the epithelium as an impermeable barrier to the uptake of such antigens as β-lactoglobulin and α-lactalbumin found in cow milk.

Treatment of milk allergy involves the elimination of suspected foods from the diet until 1 or 2 years of age, at which time a challenge with cow milk is done to determine whether the allergy persists. Goat milk has been used in the past for the treatment of cow milk allergy. It contains, however, inadequate folic acid and excessive protein and electrolytes and is not reliably hypoallergenic (see Table 4-11). Casein hydrolysate formulas are the feeding of choice in true cow milk allergy.

Food Allergy

Presence of milk protein allergy may correlate with allergies to other foods. Withholding the more allergenic foods from the diet for the first 6 to 12 months of life can be a prophylactic measure. Withholding these allergenic foods until the milk allergy has resolved may be indicated for more severe cases. Allergenic foods include the following: eggs, nuts, peas, fish, chocolate, citrus fruit, corn products, wheat, chicken, and fish. (See Chapter 8 for further information on food sensitivities.)

Constipation

Constipation is defined as infrequent stooling or as overly dry, hard, or small stools. Normal stooling patterns vary from infant to infant and with differences in dietary intake. Constipation is rare in the breastfed infant but more common in the bottlefed infant.[72] Refer to Table 4-16 for normal stooling patterns.

Treating nonanatomic constipation requires dietary intervention. Five measures can be taken, in the following sequence:

1. Verify constipation through family interview.
2. Ensure the proper diet.
3. Ensure accurate preparation of formula if infant is bottle fed.
4. Feed two additional ounces of water after each feed.
5. Recommend Maltsupex, a laxative consisting of malt-barley extract.[90]

Table 4-16 Stool Frequency and Weight in Normal Infants

	1 Week	8–28 Days	1–12 Months	13–24 Months
No. stools/24 hr.	4	2.2	1.8	1.7
Weight (g)	4.3	11	17	35
Water content (%)	72	73	75	73.5

Source: Reprinted from *Gastrointestinal Problems in the Infant* by J Grybowski and WA Walker with permission of WB Saunders, © 1983.

Acute Diarrhea

Acute infantile diarrhea is defined as the sudden onset of increased stool frequency, volume, and water content. The cause can be bacterial, viral, parasitic, or a result of large-dose antibiotics.[91,92] Dietary treatment varies with its duration and severity.

Diarrhea lasting more than 4 days or resulting in greater than 10% dehydration may require intravenous fluid therapy. However, bottle-fed infants suffering from mild to moderate diarrhea can be rehydrated with an oral electrolyte solution. Available commercial solutions include Pedialyte, Rehydralyte, and Ricelyte. Some investigators support refeeding mildly or moderately depleted bottle-fed infants with soy-based, lactose-free formula after only 4 hours of oral rehydration therapy, especially infants who are frequently afflicted by diarrhea.[93] This regimen may reduce the duration of diarrhea and the stool output[94] while preventing protein or energy deficits.[95] Juice, broth, carbonated beverages, or Gatorade should not be fed as their high osmolalities may induce osmotic diarrhea, exacerbating the initial problem.[92] Refer to Table 4-17 for the nutrient comparison

Table 4-17 Nutrient Comparison of Clear Liquids and Rehydration Solutions

Product	Na (mEq/L)	K (mEq/L)	Cl (mEq/L)	Sugar (g/L)	Starch (g/L)	Osmolality (mOsm/L)
Cola	1.7	0.1–0.6	—	53–58.5	—	750
Apple juice	4.6	26	1.1	39.5	—	747
Gatorade	20–23	2.5–3	23	25–28	—	330–365
Chicken broth	250	8	—	—	—	500
Rehydralyte	75	20	65	25	—	305
Pedialyte	45	20	35	25	—	250
Ricelyte	50	25	45	—	30	200

Source: Data from references 92 and 123 and from product information provided by Ross Laboratories and Mead Johnson Nutritionals.

of clear liquids and rehydration solutions. Most breastfed infants can be continued on their regular schedules if the diarrhea is mild and not long lasting. Solid food may be fed if the infant expresses hunger for it; however, if the stool output continues to rise, solids may be held up to 48 hours.

Gastroesophageal Reflux

Gastroesophageal reflux (GER) or chalasia affects many infants. GER is otherwise referred to as regurgitation, or "spitting up." While most infants will respond to eructation of swallowed air during and after feeds, others are significantly affected by it.[96] GER may induce failure to thrive, anemia, or pulmonary aspiration with pneumonia, and can potentially cause asthma or apnea.[96] Mild GER may be treated with modifications in feeding positions and dietary regimens. More severe GER may require pharmaceutical or surgical interventions.

An upright position during feeding may prevent GER. In this position, gravity may aid in gastric emptying. When an infant is placed in the semi-upright position of an infant seat, however, reduced truncal tone, common in early infancy, may result in slumping.[96] Slumping submerges the infants' posterior gastroesophageal junction into the stomach, increasing abdominal pressure, and therefore, increasing GER. A truly upright position is most reliable in preventing GER. If this is not possible, a prone position with the head elevated to a 30-degree angle may also be effective.[97,98]

Thickening feeds with cereal has been routine practice in preventing GER. There has been documentation of positive clinical response to this treatment, including decreased emesis and crying time and increased sleeping time in the postprandial period. However, there has been no proof of its efficacy in laboratory studies, and it may even increase the frequency of unsymptomatic reflux.[99–101] The clinician must also be aware that cereal increases the caloric concentration of formula, interferes with breastfeeding, and may delay gastric emptying.

Food Refusal

Food refusal can occur in infancy because of physical or emotional stress. Illness and unfavorable atmospheres for feeding are typical contributors to food refusal. The consequence of this problem is failure to thrive.

During illness, infants become irritable due to fever, congestion, or lack of sleep. At these times, food refusal is inevitable. The encouragement of fluids and possibly administration of parenteral fluids are necessary to prevent/treat dehydration.

Food refusal originating in excessive or deficient stimulation is more difficult to discern. Noise and commotion disturb feeding, while a quiet, relaxed atmosphere improves intake.[102] Similarly, a mother may move excessively or arrange her infant too often, disrupting the feeding pace. Her misinterpretation of the infant's cues to remain steady may foster this disruption. Concerned that her infant is feeding poorly, she becomes tense. This tension only exacerbates the reluctance to feed.

Deficient stimulation during feeding also inhibits the infant's appetite.[103,104] Neglecting to touch or communicate with the infant during meals may depress his or her appetite. Harmony in feeding demands an attentive feeder in a calm environment.

CONCLUSION

Issues related to breastfeeding, bottle feeding, the introduction and progression of solids, and common feeding problems have all been discussed in this chapter. Translating this scientific information into practical suggestions for parents is a necessity in order to ensure good nutrition for adequate growth and development.

REFERENCES

1. American Academy of Pediatrics. The promotion of breastfeeding. *Pediatrics.* 1982;69:654.

2. Position of the American Dietetic Association. Promotion of breastfeeding. *J Am Diet Assoc.* 1986;86:1580.

3. Martinez G, Krieger FW. 1984 Milk feeding patterns in the United States. *Pediatrics.* 1985;76:1004.

4. Loughlin HH, Clapp-Channing NE, Gehlbach SH, et al. Early termination of breastfeeding: identifying those at risk. *Pediatrics.* 1985;75:508.

5. Anderson GH. Human milk feeding. *Pediatr Clin North Am.* 1985;32:335.

6. Kovar MG, Serdula MG, Marks JS, et al. Review of the epidemiologic evidence for an association between infant feeding and infant health. *Pediatrics.* 1984;74:615.

7. Worthington-Roberts BS. Guidance for lactating mothers. In: Worthington-Roberts BS, Williams SR, eds. *Nutrition in Pregnancy and Lactation.* 4th ed. St Louis, Mo: Times Mirror/Mosby; 1989:323–397.

8. Newton N, Newton M. Psychologic aspects of lactation. *N Engl J Med.* 1967;277:1179.

9. Cunningham AS, Jelliffe DB, and Jelliffe EFP. Breast-feeding and health in the 1980s: A global epidemiologic review. *J Pediatr.* 1991;118:659.

10. Gruskay FL. Comparison of breast, cow and soy feedings in the prevention of onset of allergic disease. *Clin Pediatr.* 1982;21:486.

11. Kramer MS. Does breast feeding help protect against atopic disease? Biology, methodology, and a golden jubilee of controversy. *J Pediatr.* 1988;112:181.

12. Lawrence RA. *Breastfeeding—A Guide for the Medical Profession.* 3rd ed. St Louis, Mo: CV Mosby Co; 1989.

13. Brown KH. Clinical and field studies of human lactation: methodological considerations. *Am J Clin Nutr.* 1982;35:745.

14. Hall B. Changing composition of human milk and early development of appetite control. *Lancet.* 1975;1:779.

15. Dewey KG, Finley DA, Lonnerdal B. Breast milk volume and composition during late lactation (7–20 months). *J Pediatr Gastroenterol Nutr.* 1984;3:713–720.

16. Karra MV, Udipi SA, Kirksey A, Roepke JLB. Changes in specific nutrients in breast milk during extended lactation. *Am J Clin Nutr.* 1986;43:495–503.

17. Food and Nutrition Board, National Research Council, National Academy of Sciences. *Recommended Dietary Allowances.* 10th ed. Washington, DC: Government Printing Office; 1989.

18. Butte NF, Garza C, Smith EO, Nichols BL. Maternal energy balance during lactation. *Fed Proc.* 1983;42:922A.

19. Dusdieker LB, Booth BM, Stumbo PJ, Eichenberger JM. Effect of supplemental fluids on human milk production. *J Pediatr.* 1985;106:207–211.

20. Committee on Nutrition, American Academy of Pediatrics. Nutrition and lactation. *Pediatrics.* 1981;68:435–443.

21. Worthington-Roberts BS. Lactation and human milk: nutritional considerations. In: Worthington-Roberts BS, Williams SR, eds. *Nutrition in Pregnancy and Lactation.* 4th ed. St Louis, Mo: Times Mirror/Mosby; 1989:244–322.

22. Mellies MJ, Ishikawa TT, Gartside PS, et al. Effects of varying maternal dietary fatty acids in lactating women and their infants. *Am J Clin Nutr.* 1979;32:299.

23. Jakobsson I, Lindberg T. Cow's milk proteins cause infantile colic in breast-fed infants: a double-blind crossover study. *Pediatrics.* 1983;71:268.

24. Berlin CM, Denson HM, Daniel CH, Ward RM. Deposition of dietary caffeine in milk, saliva, and plasma of lactating women. *Pediatrics.* 1984;73:59.

25. Luck W, Nau H. Nicotine and cotinine concentrations in serum and urine of infants exposed via passive smoking or milk from smoking mothers. *J Pediatr.* 1985;107:816.

26. Binkiewicz A, Robinson MJ, Senior B. Pseudo-Cushing syndrome caused by alcohol in breast milk. *J Pediatr.* 1978;93:965.

27. Ahn CH, MacLean WC. Growth of the exclusively breast-fed infant. *Am J Clin Nutr.* 1980;33:183.

28. Chandra RK. Physical growth of exclusively breast-fed infants. *Nutr Rev.* 1982;2:275.

29. Matheny R, Picciano MF. Feeding and growth characteristics of human milk fed infants. *J Am Diet Assoc.* 1986;86:327.

30. Poland RL. Breast-milk jaundice. *J Pediatr.* 1981;99:86.

31. DeCarvalho M, Hall M, Harvey D. Effects of water supplementation on physiological jaundice in breast-fed babies. *Arch Dis Child.* 1981;56:568.

32. Kuhr M, Paneth N. Feeding practices and early neonatal jaundice. *J Pediatr Gastroenterol Nutr.* 1982;1:485.

33. Committee on Nutrition, American Academy of Pediatrics. Vitamin and mineral supplement needs in normal children in the United States. *Pediatrics.* 1980;66:1015.

34. Roberts CC, Chan GM, Folland D, et al. Adequate bone mineralization in breast-fed infants. *J Pediatr.* 1981;99:192.

35. Fomon SJ. Breast-feeding and evolution. *J Am Diet Assoc.* 1986;86:317.

36. Greer FR, Searcy JE, Levin RS, et al. Bone mineral content and serum 25-hydroxyvitamin D concentrations in breast-fed infants with and without supplemental vitamin D: one year follow-up. *J Pediatr.* 1982;100:919.

37. Pastel RA, Howanitz PJ, Oski FA. Iron sufficiency with prolonged exclusive breast-feeding in Peruvian infants. *Clin Pediatr*. 1981;20:625.

38. Siimes MA, Salmenpera L, Perheentopa J. Exclusive breast-feeding for 9 months: rise of iron deficiency. *J Pediatr*. 1984;104:196.

39. Fomon, SJ, Filer LJ, Anderson TA, Ziegler EE. Recommendations for feeding normal infants. *Pediatrics*. 1979;63:52.

40. Owen GM, Garry PJ, Hooper EM, et al. Iron nutriture of infants exclusively breast-fed the first five months. *J Pediatr*. 1981;99:237.

41. Saarinen UM. Need for iron supplementation in infants on prolonged breast feeding. *J Pediatr*. 1978;93:177.

42. Walter T, DeAndraca I, Chadud P, et al. Iron deficiency anemia: adverse effects on infant psychomotor development. *Pediatrics*. 1989;84:7.

43. Fomon SJ. Reflections on infant feeding in the 1970's and 1980's. *Am J Clin Nutr*. 1987;46:171.

44. Committee on Nutrition, American Academy of Pediatrics. Fluoride supplementation. *Pediatrics*. 1986;77:758.

45. Ekstrand J. No evidence of transfer of fluoride from plasma to breast milk. *Br Med J*. 1981;283:761.

46. Walton JL, Messer LB. Dental caries and fluorosis in breast-fed and bottle-fed children. *Caries Res*. 1981;15:124.

47. Forbes GB, Woodruff CW, eds. *Pediatric Nutrition Handbook*. 2nd ed. Elk Grove Village, Ill: American Academy of Pediatrics, 1985.

48. Food and Drug Administration. Rules and regulations. Nutrient requirements for infant formulas. *Fed Register*. 1985;50:45106–8. 21 CFR Sec 107.100.

49. Lonnerdal B, Forsum E. The casein:whey ratio of human milk. *Fed Proc*. 1984;43:468.

50. Jarvenpaa A-L, Raiha NCR, Rassin DK, et al. Milk protein quantity in the term infant, I: metabolic responses and effects on growth. *Pediatrics*. 1982;70:214.

51. Jarvenpaa A-L, Rassin DK, Raiha NCR. Milk protein quantity and quality in the term infant, II: effects on acidic and neutral amino acids. *Pediatrics*. 1982;70:221.

52. Voltz VR, Book LS, Churella HR. Growth and plasma amino acid concentrations in term infants fed either whey predominant formula or human milk. *J Pediatr*. 1983;102:27.

53. Janas LM, Picciano MF, Hatch TF. Indices of protein metabolism in term infants fed human milk, whey predominant formula, or cow's milk formula. *Pediatrics*. 1985;75:775.

54. Dallman PR, Siimes MA, Stekel A. Iron deficiency in infancy and childhood. *Am J Clin Nutr*. 1980;33:86.

55. Powell GK. Milk and soy induced enterocolitis of infancy: clinical features and standardization of challenge. *J Pediatr*. 1978;93:553.

56. Committee on Nutrition. Soy-protein formulas: recommendations for use in infant feeding. *Pediatrics*. 1983;72:359.

57. Hillman LS, Chow W, Salmons SS, et al. Vitamin D metabolism, mineral homeostasis, and bone mineralization in term infants fed human milk, cow milk-based formula or soy-based formula. *J Pediatr*. 1988;112:864.

58. Knights RJ. Processing and evaluation of the antigenicity of protein hydrolysates. In: Lifshitz F, ed. *Nutrition for Special Needs in Infancy*. New York, NY: Marcel Dekker; 1985:105–115.

59. Committee on Nutrition, American Academy of Pediatrics. Hypoallergenic infant formulas. *Pediatr*. 1989;83:1068.

60. Committe on Nutrition, American Academy of Pediatrics. Follow-up or weaning formulas. *Pediatr.* 1989; 83:1067.

61. Ziegler EE. Milk and formulas for older infants. *J Pediatr.* 1990;117:S76.

62. Hargrove CB, Temple AR, Chinn P. Formula preparation and infant illness. *Clin Pediatr.* 1974;13:1057.

63. Gerber MA, Berliner BC, Karolus JJ. Sterilization of infant formulas. *Clin Pediatr.* 1983;22:344.

64. Hibbard RA, Blevins R. Palatal burn due to bottle warming in a microwave oven. *Pediatrics.* 1988;82:382.

65. Puczynski M, Rademaker D, Gatson RL. Burn injury related to the improper use of a microwave oven. *Pediatrics.* 1983;72:714.

66. Shelton PG, Berkowitz RJ, Forrester DJ. Nursing bottle caries. *Pediatrics.* 1977;59:777.

67. Loesche WJ. Nutrition and dental decay in infants. *Am J Clin Nutr.* 1985;41:423.

68. Committee on Nutrition, American Academy of Pediatrics. Iron supplementation for infants. *Pediatrics.* 1976;58:765.

69. Oski FA. Iron-fortified formulas and gastrointestinal symptoms in infants: a controlled study. *Pediatrics.* 1980;66:168.

70. Nelson SE, Ziegler EE, Copeland AM, et al. Lack of adverse reactions to iron-fortified formula. *Pediatrics.* 1988;81:360.

71. Fomon S. *Infant Nutrition.* 2nd ed. Philadelphia, Pa: WB Saunders; 1974.

72. Lipsitt L, Crook C, Booth C. The transitional infant: behavioral development and feeding. *Am J Clin Nutr.* 1985;41:485.

73. Marlow D. *Textbook of Pediatric Nursing.* 6th ed. Philadelphia, Pa: WB Saunders; 1988.

74. Restak R. *The Infant Mind.* Garden City, NY: Doubleday, 1986.

75. Underwood B. Weaning practices in deprived environments: the weaning dilemma. *Pediatrics.* 1985;75(suppl):194.

76. Queen P, Wilson S. Growth and nutrient requirements of infants. In: Grand RJ, Sutphen JL, Dietz WH, eds. *Pediatric Nutrition Theory and Practice.* Stoneham, Mass: Butterworth Publishers; 1987:341–349.

77. Oskarsson A. *Exposure of Infants and Children to Lead.* Rome, Italy: Food and Agriculture Organization of the United Nations; 1989.

78. Shaw J, Sweeney E. Nutrition in relation to dental medicine. In: Goodhart R, Shills M, eds. *Modern Nutrition in Health and Disease.* 6th ed. Philadelphia, Pa: Lea and Febiger; 1980:855.

79. Alvarez J, Navia J. Nutritional status, tooth eruption, and dental caries: a review. *Am J Clin Nutr.* 1989;49:417.

80. Foucard T. Development of food allergies with special reference to cow's milk allergy. *Pediatrics.* 1985;75(suppl):177.

81. Committee on Nutrition, American Academy of Pediatrics. The use of whole cow's milk in infancy. *Pediatrics.* 1983;72:253.

82. Fomon S, Ziegler E, Nelson S, Edwards B. Cow milk feeding in infancy: gastrointestinal blood loss and iron nutritional status. *J Pediatr.* 1981;98:540.

83. Tunnessen WW, Oski FA. Consequences of starting whole cow milk at 6 months of age. *J Pediatr.* 1987;111:813.

84. Ziegler EE, Fomon SJ, Nelson SE, et al. Cow milk feeding in infancy: further observations on blood loss from the gastrointestinal tract. *J Pediatr.* 1990;116:11.

85. Fomon S. Bioavailability of supplemental iron in commercially prepared dry infant cereals. *J Pediatr*. 1987;110:660.

86. Rios E, Hunter R, Cook J, et al. The absorption of iron as supplements in infant cereal and infant formulas. *Pediatrics*. 1975;55:686.

87. Monsen E. Iron nutrition and absorption: dietary factors which impact iron bioavailability. *J Am Diet Assoc*. 1988;88:786.

88. Savilahti E, Kuitunen P, Visakorpi J. Cow's milk allergy. In: *Textbook of Gastroenterology and Nutrition in Infancy*. Vol. 2. New York, NY: Raven Press; 1981:689–708.

89. Walker A. Absorption of protein and protein fragments in the developing intestine: role in immunologic/allergic reactions. *Pediatrics*. 1985;75(suppl):167.

90. Silverman A, Roy C. Gastrointestinal tract. In: Kempe H, O'Brien K, eds. *Current Pediatric Diagnosis and Treatment*. 9th ed. East Norwalk, Conn: Appleton and Lange; 1987:522.

91. Moffet H, Shulenberger BH, Burkholder BE. Epidemiology and etiology of severe infantile diarrhea. *J Pediatr*. 1968;72:1–14.

92. Snyder J. Oral rehydration therapy for acute diarrhea. *Semin Pediatr Gastroenterol Nutr*. 1990;1:8.

93. Leake R, et al. Soy-based formula in the treatment of infantile diarrhea. *Am J Dis Child*. 1974;127:374.

94. Santosham M, Foster S, Reid R, et al. Role of soy-based, lactose-free formula during treatment of acute diarrhea. *Pediatrics*. 1985;76:292.

95. Brown K, MacLean W. Nutritional management of acute diarrhea: an appraisal of the alternatives. *Pediatrics*. 1984;73:119.

96. Orenstein S, Whitington P, Orenstein D. The infant seat as treatment for gastroesophageal reflux. *N Engl J Med*. 1983;309:760.

97. Herbst J. Gastroesophageal reflux. *J Pediatr*. 1981;98:859.

98. Orenstein S, Whitington P. Positioning for prevention of infant gastroesophageal reflux. *J Pediatr*. 1983;103:534.

99. Bailey D, Andres J, Danek G, Pineiro-Carrero V. Lack of efficacy of thickened feeding as treatment for gastroesophageal reflux. *J Pediatr*. 1987;110:187.

100. Orenstein S, Magill H, Brooks P. Thickening of infant feedings for therapy of gastroesophageal reflux. *J Pediatr*. 1987;110:181.

101. Ulshen M. Treatment of gastroesophageal reflux: is nothing sacred? *J Pediatr*. 1987;254.

102. Thomas A, Chess S. Genesis and evolution of behavioral disorders: from infancy to early adult life. *Am J Psychiatry*. 1984;141:1.

103. Whitten C, Pettit M, Fischhoff J. Evidence that growth failure from maternal deprivation is secondary to undereating. *JAMA*. 1969;209:1675.

104. Gardner L. The nosology of failure to thrive. *Am J Dis Child*. 1978;132:961.

105. Casey CE, Hambidge KM. Nutritional aspects of human lactation. In: *Lactation: Physiology, Nutrition and Breastfeeding*. New York, NY: Plenum Press; 1983.

106. Lammi-Keefe CJ, Jensen RG. Lipids in human milk: a review, II: Composition and fat-soluble vitamins. *J Pediatr Gastroenterol Nutr*. 1984;3:172.

107. Gebre-Medhin M, Vahlquist A, Hofvander Y, et al. Breast milk composition in Ethiopian and Swedish mothers, I: vitamin A and B-carotene. *Am J Clin Nutr*. 1976;29:441.

108. Hollis BW, Ross BA, Draper HH, Lambert PW. Occurrence of vitamin D sulfate in human milk whey. *J Nutr*. 1981;111:384.

109. Jansson L, Akesson B, Holmberg L. Vitamin E and fatty acid composition of human milk. *Am J Clin Nutr.* 1981;34:8.

110. Haroon Y, Shearer MJ, Rahim S, Gunn WG, McEnergy G, Barkhan P. The content of phylloquinone (vitamin K_1) in human milk, cow's milk and infant formula food determined by high-performance liquid chromatography. *J Nutr.* 1982;112:1102.

111. Moran JR, Vaughan R, Stroop S, et al. Concentrations and total daily output of micronutrients in breast milk of mothers delivering preterm: a longitudinal study. *J Pediatr Gastroenterol Nutr.* 1983;2:629.

112. Ford JE, Zechalko A, Murphy J, Brooke OG. Comparison of the B vitamin composition of milk from mothers of preterm and term babies. *Arch Dis Child.* 1983;58:367.

113. Butte NF, Garza C, Smith EO, et al. Macro- and trace-mineral intakes of exclusively breast-fed infants. *Am J Clin Nutr.* 1987;45:42.

114. Lemons JA, Moye L, Hall D, Simmons M. Differences in the composition of preterm and term human milk during early lactation. *Pediatr Res.* 1982;16:113.

115. Casey CE, Hambidge KM, Neville MC. Studies in human lactation: zinc, copper, manganese and chromium in human milk in the first month of lactation. *Am J Clin Nutr.* 1985;41:1193.

116. Smith AM, Picciano MF, Milner JA. Selenium intakes and status of human milk and formula fed infants. *Am J Clin Nutr.* 1982;35:521.

117. Ericsson Y, Hellstrom I, Hofvander Y. Pilot studies on the fluoride metabolism in infants on different feedings. *Acta Paediatr Scand.* 1972;61:459.

118. Tomarelli RM. Osmolality, osmolarity, and renal solute load of infant formulas. *J Pediatr.* 1976;88:454.

119. United States Department of Agriculture. *Composition of Foods: Dairy and Egg Products, Raw, Processed, Prepared.* Washington, DC: Agricultural Research Service; 1976. Handbook 8-1, item no. 01-078.

120. Specker BL, Tsang RC, Hollis BW. Effect of race and diet on human-milk vitamin D and 25-hydroxyvitamin D. *Am J Dis Child.* 1985;139:1134.

121. Greer FR, Tsang RC, Levin RS, et al. Increasing serum calcium and magnesium concentrations in breast-fed infants: longitudinal studies of minerals in human milk and in sera of nursing mothers and their infants. *J Pediatr.* 1982;100:59.

122. Hinton S, Kerwin D. *Maternal and Child Nutrition.* Chapel Hill, NC: Health Sciences Consortium Corporation; 1981.

123. Swedberg J, Steiner J. Oral rehydration therapy in diarrhea: not just for Third World children. *Postgrad Med.* 1983;74:336.

124. American Academy of Pediatrics. *Pediatric Nutrition Handbook.* Evanston, Ill: American Academy of Pediatrics; 1979.

125. American Academy of Pediatrics, Committee on Nutrition. Infant methemoglobinemia: the role of dietary nitrate. *Pediatrics.* 1970;46:475.

126. Kerr C, Reisinger K, Plankey F. Sodium concentration of homemade baby foods. *Pediatrics.* 1978;62:331.

Chapter 5

Normal Nutrition from Infancy through Adolescence

Betty Lucas

The ages 1 through adolescence incorporate most of the growing years. This includes physical, cognitive, and social-emotional growth. The 1-year-old toddler is taking his or her first steps into the bigger world, becoming more independent in self-help skills, and rapidly learning to communicate. At the other end of the spectrum, the 18-year-old is also taking steps into the wide world, becoming more independent and self-sufficient in many areas, and planning for the future. This chapter will focus on the nutritional needs and issues of normal, healthy children during these growing years.

PROGRESS IN GROWTH AND DEVELOPMENT

After the rapid growth of infancy, there is a considerable slowing in physical growth during the preschool and school years. The elementary school years are often referred to as the "latent period" prior to the pubertal growth spurt of adolescence. Individual children will have their own growth patterns, which may be erratic at times, with spurts in height and weight followed by periods of little or no growth. These patterns usually correspond to similar changes in appetite and food intake in healthy children and teenagers. Parents and other caregivers need to hear that these changes are normal so that they can avoid struggles over food and eating.

Developmental progress during the growing years influences many aspects of food and eating. The very young child prefers food that can be picked up or doesn't have to be chased across the plate. Food jags may be more an expression of independence than of actual likes and dislikes. In older children the influence of peers and the media will affect snack choices. Teenagers want foods that fit into their lifestyles—quick, easy to fix, and inexpensive. Understanding the developmental characteristics and milestones at any particular age will help parents and

145

professionals set realistic expectations, support eating behavior and food decisions that are developmentally appropriate, and avoid unnecessary conflicts. Satter has described well "the feeding relationship" between parents and children of all ages, which incorporates these developmental aspects.[1]

NUTRIENT NEEDS

A child's rate and stage of growth usually parallel nutrient needs and are primary factors in determining needs. Other factors include physical activity, body size, basal energy expenditure, and state of illness. There is a wide range of actual needs based on individual characteristics. The Recommended Dietary Allowances (RDAs) serve as a guide, but many of the data for children and adolescence are extrapolated values.[2] Since the RDAs provide a margin of safety greater than the physiologic requirements for most children in the United States and are meant to be applied to groups, they cannot be appropriately applied to individuals.

Energy

Energy needs are the most variable, due to individual differences in basal metabolism, growth, physical activity, onset of puberty, and body size. The RDAs provide an average energy allowance based on a reference weight for each age group.[2] Up to age 10 there is no distinction between sexes but at age 11 and above, allowances are based on sex and puberty. These allowances are not meant to be applied to individual children.

Age alone is not a good criterion for determining energy needs, especially in the pubertal years, when the growth spurt occurs at varying times. Weight is also a limited standard because of overweight or underweight status. Height, however, is a useful reference in determining appropriate energy intakes for individual children. Using kilocalories per centimeter of height, as shown in Table 5-1, is a good clinical tool for both assessing and estimating energy needs. This is applicable in situations of failure-to-thrive and catch-up growth as well as planning for weight loss or weight maintenance.

Protein

Adequate protein intake is needed to provide for optimal growth in children and adolescents. National surveys have reported actual protein intakes to be in the range of 10% to 15% of kilocalories for these ages.[3,4] This level assumes that enough energy is provided so that protein is spared for growth. Protein needs decrease as the growth rate slows after infancy. There is an increase again at puberty, with total protein intakes increasing steadily until about 12 years of age in girls and 16 years of age in boys.

Table 5-1 Energy Intake per Centimeter of Height*

	Males (Percentiles)			Females (Percentiles)		
Age	10th	50th	90th	10th	50th	90th
1	10.3	14.1	18.8	10.6	13.6	17.6
2–3	11.6	15.0	20.2	10.5	13.5	17.9
4–6	12.3	15.2	20.4	10.7	13.8	18.6
7–10	12.8	16.7	22.3	10.4	14.1	18.4
11–14	12.4	16.8	22.2	9.0	13.0	18.2
15–16	11.4	15.9	21.1	7.4	11.8	17.3

* These energy intakes are means of the age groups listed. The data were collected on normal, healthy children involved in a prospective study.

Source: Adapted from VA Beal, Nutritional intake, in *Human Growth and Development* (p 63) by RW McCammon (ed) with permission of Charles C Thomas Publishers, © 1970.

In the United States, protein intakes usually exceed recommended allowances. Some children and adolescents, however, may be at risk for protein malnutrition, i.e., those not receiving adequate kilocalories so that protein is used for energy (extreme use of low-fat diets, limited access to food, dieting to lose weight, athletes in training who limit food), those who are strict vegetarians, and some with food allergies. Dietary evaluation of protein intake should include the growth rate, energy intake, and quality of the protein sources.

Minerals and Vitamins

Although clinical signs of vitamin or mineral deficiency are rare in the United States, dietary intake studies have reported that the nutrients most likely to be low or deficient in the diets of children and adolescents are calcium, iron, ascorbic acid, vitamin A, folic acid, and vitamin B_6.[5,6] Certain populations of children, such as low-income, Native American, and other groups with limited food and health resources (i.e., the homeless), are more at risk for nutrient deficiencies.

Calcium

Primarily needed for bone mineralization, calcium needs are determined by growth velocity, rates of absorption, and other nutrients such as phosphorus, vitamin D, and protein. Because of individual variability, a child receiving less than the recommended allowance of calcium is not necessarily at risk. Approximately 100 mg of calcium per day is retained as bone in the preschool years. This doubles or triples for adolescents during peak growth periods.[7] Adolescence is a critical period for optimal calcium retention to achieve peak bone mass, especially for females who are at risk for osteoporosis in later years. Calcium intake, however, often decreases during the teen years. Balance studies indicate that young adolescent girls (less than 16 years of age) may need to consume more than the RDA level of 1200 mg/d to achieve maximum calcium intake and calcium balance.[7]

Since dairy products are the major sources of calcium, those who consume no or limited amounts of these foods are at risk for calcium deficiency. Some adolescents may also receive less calcium than needed because of rapid growth, dieting practices, and substituting carbonated beverage for milk. In assessing calcium status, vitamin D intake needs to be considered because of its major role in calcium metabolism. For children with limited sunshine exposure, dietary intake is critical. Vitamin D-fortified milk is the primary food source of this nutrient; other dairy products are not usually made with fortified milk. A child may be receiving adequate calcium from cheeses and yogurt but taking very little fluid milk and thus receiving minimal dietary vitamin D. Table 5-2 is a list of calcium food sources.

Iron

Requirements for iron are determined by the rate of growth, iron stores, increasing blood volumes, and rate of absorption from food sources. Menstrual losses, as well as rapid growth, increase the need in adolescent females. In order to reach adulthood with adequate storage iron, daily recommended intakes are 10 mg for children, 12 mg for pubertal males, and 15 mg for pubertal females.[2,8]

Table 5-2 Calcium Equivalents

1 cup whole milk =	1 cup skim milk* 1 cup 1% or 2% milk 1 cup buttermilk 1 cup (8 oz) yogurt ⎤ = 300 mg calcium (approximately)
3/4 cup milk =	1 oz cheddar, jack, or Swiss cheese
2/3 cup milk =	1 oz mozzarella or American cheese 2 oz canned sardines (with bones)
1/2 cup milk =	2 oz canned salmon (with bones) 1/2 cup custard or milk pudding 1/2 cup cooked greens (mustard, collards, kale)
1/4 cup milk =	1/2 cup cottage cheese 1/2 cup ice cream 3/4 cup dried beans, cooked or canned

* Some low-fat or skim milks and some low-fat yogurts have additional nonfat dry milk (NFDM) solids added. Some labels will read "fortified." These products will contain more calcium than indicated here.

Vitamins

Vitamins function in numerous metabolic processes. Vitamin needs are often dependent on energy intake or other nutrient levels. Most of the recommended allowances for children and adolescents have been extrapolated from studies on infants and adults.

Vitamin-Mineral Supplements

After infancy the use of supplements decreases but is still a common practice in the United States. About 37% of preschool children, 23% of school-age children, and 10% to 16% of adolescents take a vitamin and/or mineral preparation.[9] Children taking supplements do not necessarily represent those who need them most. The supplements may not be providing the marginal or deficient nutrients either; i.e., a child may be taking a vitamin but may actually need extra calcium or iron, not always provided in a supplement.

Except for fluoride supplementation in unfluoridated areas, the American Academy of Pediatrics does not support routine supplementation for normal, healthy children.[10] It does, however, identify four groups at nutritional risk who might benefit from supplementation. These include: (1) children from deprived families, especially those abused or neglected; (2) children with anorexia, poor appetites, and poor eating habits; (3) children consuming vegetarian diets without dairy products; and (4) pregnant teenagers. Both the American Medical Association and the American Dietetic Association have also recommended that nutrients for healthy children should come from food, not supplements.[11,12]

Dietary evaluation will determine the need for supplements. Children with food allergies, those who omit entire food groups, and those with limited food acceptances will be likely candidates for supplementation. No risk is involved if parents wish to give their children a standard pediatric multivitamin. Megadose levels of nutrients should be discouraged and parents counseled regarding the dangers of toxicity, especially of fat-soluble vitamins. Since many children's vitamins look and taste like candy, parents should be educated to keep them out of reach of children.

FOOD INTAKE PATTERNS AND GUIDELINES

Since appetite usually follows the rate of growth, food intake is not always smooth and consistent. After a good appetite in infancy, parents frequently describe their preschool children as having fair to poor appetites, a response to a slower growth rate. There is a wide variability in nutrient intake in healthy children. Daily energy intake of preschool children is surprisingly constant, despite a high variability from meal to meal. One longitudinal study found that the maximum intake of energy, carbohydrate, fat, and protein was two to three times the minimum intake. For ascorbic acid and carotene, the maximum:minimum ratios were 10:1 and 20:1, all in healthy children.[13]

Factors Influencing Food Intake

Food intake and habits are determined by numerous factors. Major influences for children include the family, peers, media, and body image.

Family

Eating habits and food likes/dislikes are formed in the early years and often continue into adulthood. Parents and siblings are primary models for young children when it comes to imitating behavior. Mealtime atmosphere, both positive and negative, can influence how a child approaches and handles family meals. As children move into adolescence, they eat fewer meals at home.

With more women employed outside the home, there may be less time available for food preparation and more use of fast food, eating out, and prepared foods. There is also a larger percentage of single-parent families, usually headed by women. This usually translates into lower income, with less money available for food.

Media

Television is the primary media influence on children of all ages. It has been estimated that by the time the average American child graduates from high school, he or she will have watched about 15,000 hours of television, compared to spending 11,000 hours in the classroom. Almost half of all commercials are for food, with an even higher percentage found in children's programs.[14] The items generally aimed for a young audience are sweetened cereals, fast food, snack foods, and candy—foods high in sugar, fat, and salt.

The commercial messages are not based on nutrition but on an emotional/psychologic appeal, i.e., "fun," "gives you energy," "yummy taste." Younger children cannot generally discriminate between the regular program and commercial messages, frequently giving more attention to the latter because of their fast attention-getting pace. Some consumer groups monitor children's television and work for positive legislative and governmental action.

Peers

As children move into the world, their food choices are influenced by others. In preschool the group snack time may encourage a child to try a new food. During school years, participation in the school lunch program may be decided by friends rather than the menu. Peer influence is particularly strong in adolescence as teenagers strive for more independence and eating becomes a more social activity outside the home. A chronic illness or disorder that requires diet modification, such as diabetes, phenylketonuria, or food allergies, can be a problem for children and teenagers when they want to be part of the group. These individuals need education regarding diet rationale appropriate to their developmental level, as well as problem-solving methods to explain it to their peers.

Body Image

Adolescence is the period when there is the most awareness of body image. It is normal for teens to be uncomfortable and dissatisfied with their changing bodies. The media and popular idols offer a standard that the adolescents compare themselves to, no matter how unrealistic it may be. In order to change their body image, they may try restrictive diets, purchase weight loss products, or in the case of males, try supplements or diets in the hope of increasing their muscles. Some of these dietary measures may put them at risk for poor nutritional status.

Feeding the Toddler and Preschool Child

Parents often become concerned when their toddler refuses some favorite foods and appears to be disinterested in eating. These periods ("food jags") vary in intensity from child to child and may last a few days or years. At the same time, the child is practicing self-feeding skills, with frequent spills, and often resorting to the use of fingers. These changes and behaviors during the preschool years are a normal part of the development and maturation of young children. When parents understand this, they are more likely to avoid struggles, issues of control, and negative feedback around food and eating.

Portion sizes for young children are small by adult standards. Table 5-3 provides a guide for foods and portion sizes. A long-standing rule of thumb is to initially offer 1 tablespoon of each food for every year of age for preschool children, with more provided according to appetite.

Because of smaller capacities and fluctuating appetites, most children eat four to six times a day. Snacks contribute significantly to the total day's nutrient intake and should be planned accordingly. Foods that make nutritious snacks are listed in Table 5-4. Foods chosen for snacks should be those the least likely to promote dental caries.

Parents of young children frequently become concerned about the adequacy of their child's intake—plain meats are often refused because they are more difficult to chew, very little or too much milk may be consumed, cooked vegetables are pushed away. Table 5-5 offers nutrition solutions to these common, normal variations in eating behaviors.

Just as important as providing adequate nutrients to young children is to support a positive feeding environment, both physically and emotionally, so that as they grow they acquire skills, develop positive attitudes, and have control over food

Table 5-3 Feeding Guide for Children

The following is a guide to a basic diet. Fats, sauces, desserts, and snack foods will provide additional energy to meet the growing child's needs. Foods can be selected from this pattern for both meals and snacks.

Food	2- to 3-Year Olds Portion Size/Servings	4- to 6-Year Olds Portion Size/Servings	7- to 12-Year Olds Portion Size/Servings	Comments
Milk and dairy products	1/2 cup (4 oz.) 4–5	1/2–3/4 cup (4–6 oz.) 3–4	1/2–1 cup (4–8 oz.) 3–4	The following may be substituted for 1/2 cup liquid milk: 1/2–3/4 oz. cheese, 1/2 cup yogurt, 2½ T. nonfat dry milk
Meat, fish, poultry or equivalent	1–2 oz. 2	1–2 oz. 2	2 oz. 3–4	The following may be substituted for 1 oz. meat, fish or poultry: 1 egg, 2 T. peanut butter, 4–5 T. cooked legumes
Fruits and vegetables	4–5	4–5	4–5	Include one green leafy or yellow vegetable for vitamin A, such as carrots, spinach, broccoli, winter squash
Vegetables				Include one vitamin C-rich fruit, vegetable or juice, such as citrus juices, orange, grapefruit, strawberries, melon, tomato, broccoli
Cooked	2–3 T.	3–4 T.	1/4–1/2 cup	
Raw*	Few pieces	Few pieces	Several pieces	
Fruit				
Raw	1/2–1 small	1/2–1 small	1 medium	
Canned	2–4 T.	4–6 T.	1/4–1/2 cup	
Juice	3–4 oz.	4 oz.	4 oz.	
Bread and grain products	3–4	3–4	4–5	The following may be substituted for 1 slice of bread: 1/2 cup spaghetti, macaroni, noodles, or rice; 5 saltines; 1/2 English muffin or bagel; 1 tortilla
Whole grain or enriched bread	1/2–1 slice	1 slice	1 slice	
Cooked cereal	1/4–1/2 cup	1/2 cup	1/2–1 cup	
Dry cereal	1/2–1 cup	1 cup	1 cup	

* Do not give to young children until they can chew well.

Source: Adapted from Lowenberg ME, Development of food patterns in young children, in *Nutrition Infancy and Childhood*, ed 4 (pp 146–147) by PL Pipes (ed) with permission of Times Mirror/Mosby College Publishing, © 1989.

Table 5-4 Foods That Make Nutritious Snacks

Protein Foods
  Natural cheese
  Milk
  Plain yogurt
  Cooked turkey or beef
  Unsalted nuts and seeds*
  Peanut butter*
  Hard-cooked eggs
  Cottage cheese
  Tuna

Breads and Cereals†
  Whole-grain breads
  Whole-grain, low-fat crackers
  Rice crackers
  English muffins
  Bagels
  Tortillas
  Pita bread
  Popcorn*

Fruits†
  Apple wedges*
  Bananas
  Pears
  Berries
  Melon
  Oranges and other citrus fruits
  Grapes*
  Unsweetened canned fruit
  Unsweetened fruit juices

Vegetables
  Carrot sticks*
  Celery*
  Green pepper strips*
  Cucumber slices*
  Cabbage wedges*
  Tomatoes
  Jicama*
  Vegetable juices
  Cooked green beans
  Broccoli and cauliflower flowerettes*

* Foods that are hard, round, and do not easily dissolve can cause choking. Do not give to children under 3 years of age. (Peanut butter is more dangerous when eaten in chunks or spread thickly rather than thinly spread on crackers or bread).

† Fruits, juices, and most cereal/bread products contain fermentable carbohydrate, which is a factor in the development of dental caries. Try to limit these foods to one serving in a snack.

---

decisions as is appropriate for their developmental level. General guidance in this area is listed in Table 5-6.

Children under age 4 are at greatest risk for choking on food. In some cases this can lead to death from asphyxiation.[15] Foods most likely to cause choking are those that are round, hard, and do not readily dissolve in saliva, such as hot dogs, grapes, raw vegetables, popcorn, peanut butter, nuts, and hard candy. Other foods can also cause choking problems if too much is stuffed in the mouth, if the child is running while eating, or if the child is unsupervised. Choking episodes can be prevented by common-sense management of foods and eating environment. Table 5-7 outlines the preventive approaches.

Feeding the School-Age Child

The years from 6 to 12 are a period of slow but steady growth with increases in food intake as a result of appetite (see Table 5-3). Most food behavior problems

Table 5-5 Common Feeding Concerns in Young Children

Common Concern	Possible Solutions
Refuses meats	• Offer small, bite-size pieces of moist, tender meat or poultry
	• Incorporate into meatloaf, spaghetti sauce, stews, casseroles, burritos, pizza
	• Include legumes, eggs, cheese
	• Offer boneless fish (including canned tuna and salmon)
Drinks too little milk	• Offer cheeses and yogurt, including cheese in cooking, e.g., macaroni and cheese, cheese sauce, pizza
	• Use milk to cook hot cereals; offer cream soups, milk-based puddings and custards
	• Allow child to pour milk from a pitcher and use a straw
	• Include powdered milk in cooking and baking, e.g., biscuits, muffins, pancakes, meatloaf, casseroles
Drinks too much milk	• Offer water if thirsty between meals
	• Limit milk to one serving with meals or offer at end of meal; offer water for seconds
	• If bottle is still used, wean to cup
Refuses vegetables and fruits	• If child refuses vegetables, offer more fruits, and vice-versa
	• Prepare vegetables that are tender but not overcooked
	• Steam vegetable strips (or offer raw if appropriate) and allow child to eat with fingers
	• Offer sauces and dips, e.g., cheese sauce for cooked vegetables, dip for raw vegetables, yogurt to dip fruit
	• Include vegetables in soups and casseroles
	• Add fresh or dried fruit to cereals
	• Prepare fruit in a variety of ways, e.g., fresh, cooked, juice, in gelatin, as a salad
	• Continue to offer a variety of fruits and vegetables
Eats too many sweets	• Limit purchase and preparation of sweet foods in the home
	• Avoid using as a bribe or reward
	• Incorporate into meals instead of snacks for better dental health
	• Reduce sugar by half in recipes for cookies, muffins, quick breads, etc.
	• Work with staff of day care, preschools, etc., to reduce use of sweets

Table 5-6 Tips for a Happy Mealtime

Physical Setting
• Schedule meals at regular times.
• Avoid having a child get too hungry or too tired before mealtime.
• Snacks should be at least 1$^1/_2$ to 2 hours before meals.
• Child should be able to sit up to the table comfortably without reaching.
• Provide support for the legs and feet, such as a booster seat, stool, etc.
• Use nonbreakable, sturdy dishes with sides to push food against.
• Spoons and forks should be blunt with broad, short handles.
• Use cups that are nonbreakable, broad based, and small.

Social-Emotional
• Serve a new food with familiar ones—don't be surprised by an initial rejection.
• Offer at least one food at a meal that you know your child will eat, but do not cater to his or her likes and dislikes.
• Avoid coaxing, nagging, bribing, or any other pressure to get your child to eat.
• Serve dessert (if any) with the meal—it becomes less important and cannot be used as a reward.
• Let children determine when they are full; amounts eaten will vary from child to child and day to day.
• Use the child's developmental stage to determine expectations for neatness and manners, but set limits on inappropriate behaviors, e.g., throwing food, playing.
• Attempt to have family meals be as pleasant as possible; avoid arguments and criticism.
• Allow children to help set the table or do part of the meal preparation.

---

from early childhood have been resolved except for extreme cases, but food dislikes may persist, especially if attention is given to them.

Since children are in school, they may eat fewer times in the day, but after-school snacks usually are a routine. Breakfast-skipping may begin in these years, with contributing factors such as time constraints, children left to get themselves off to school, and school starting early. With participation in organized sports, music lessons, and other activities, having a family meal may be less frequent.

An emerging trend in the United States is the increased responsibility for family shopping and cooking of children not yet in their teens. Surveys suggest that some of these children are frequently responsible for their own breakfasts, lunches, snacks, and even the dinner meal.[16] They also do food shopping on a regular basis and influence the family food purchases. Several factors contribute to this trend, including working parents, increased use of microwave ovens, more money available to spend on convenience and prepared foods, and less emphasis on family meals. Along with this trend, increasingly sophisticated advertising is being aimed at these children.

Children usually participate in the school lunch program or bring a packed lunch from home. The National School Lunch Program is administered by the

Table 5-7 Guidelines for Feeding Safety—Preschool Children

1. Insist that children eat sitting down. It lets them concentrate on chewing and swallowing.
2. An adult should supervise children while they eat.
3. Food on which preschoolers often choke, such as hot dogs, peanut butter, hard pieces of fruit and vegetables, should be avoided for children under 3 years of age.
4. Well-cooked foods, modified so that the child can chew and swallow without difficulty, should be offered.
5. Eating in the car should be avoided. If the child starts choking, it is hard to get to the side of the road safely.
6. Rub-on teething medications can cause problems with chewing and swallowing because the muscles in the throat may also become numb. Children who receive such medications should be carefully observed during feeding.

Source: Reprinted from *Nutrition in Infancy and Childhood*, ed 4 (p 126) by PL Pipes (ed) with permission of Times Mirror/Mosby College Publishing, © 1989.

United States Department of Agriculture (USDA) and supported by means of reimbursements and supplemental commodity foods. Federal guidelines are established for food groups and portion sizes so that the lunch provides approximately one third of the RDAs for students. Schools also have the opportunity to participate in the School Breakfast Program. Free and reduced-price meals are available for low-income children. Problems with the school lunch program have included plate waste, poor menu acceptance by students, competition from vending machines, and concerns regarding the amount of fat, sugar, and salt in the food. Recent changes have addressed these problems by including students in menu planning, offering popular items more frequently (i.e., pizza, tacos, hamburgers, salad bars), reducing the number of baked desserts, and allowing students to refuse one or two items from the menu. Guidance from USDA has also encouraged menus with a lower fat content. A sack lunch prepared at home will likely provide fewer nutrients than the school lunch meal.[17] The same favorite foods tend to be packed with less variety, and foods are limited to those that don't require heating or refrigeration.

Feeding the Adolescent

As adolescents go through their rapid-growth period, they seem to eat all the time. Their appetite usually guides their intake. As teenagers achieve more independence and spend more time away from home, they have a more variable intake and irregular eating patterns. Meal-skipping is greatest in this age group, particularly for breakfast and lunch. On the other hand, snacking tends to be a common characteristic. Whether they are called snacks or meals, adolescents who eat less than three times a day have poorer diets than those eating more often.[18]

Although fast foods are popular with all segments of the population, they have great appeal for teenagers. The food is inexpensive, well accepted, and can be eaten informally without utensils or plates. Fast food restaurants are also socially acceptable and a common employer of adolescents. Generally the menu items tend to be calorically dense, high in fat (some items have more than 50% of their calories as fat), high in sodium, and low in fiber, vitamin A, ascorbic acid, calcium, and folate. Recently these establishments have begun to offer more salads and lower-fat sandwiches. Any negative impact of fast foods on the diets of adolescents will depend on how frequently they are eaten and the choices they make.

NUTRITION ISSUES

As children grow and develop, various nutrition-related issues or problems arise. These are not uncommon in otherwise healthy children, and they can be prevented or managed with minimal intervention. Other specific problems, e.g., obesity, allergies, and chronic diseases, are discussed in other chapters.

Diet and Dental Health

Despite successful efforts in the past few decades, dental caries remain a common oral health disease in the pediatric population. In the years 1986 to 1987 the average number of decayed, filled, or missing permanent tooth surfaces (DMFS) in United States school children was 3.07. The caries level increased with age, with an average DMFS of 8.04 by 17 years of age.[19]

For dental caries to develop, there must be present carbohydrate, bacteria, and a susceptible tooth. The process of decay begins with the interaction of bacteria (*Streptococcus mutans*) and fermentable carbohydrate on the tooth surface. When the bacteria within the dental plaque (the gelatinous substance on the tooth surface) metabolizes the carbohydrate, organic acids are produced. When the acid reduces the pH to 5.5 or less, demineralization of the tooth enamel occurs.[20] Some individuals seem to be more susceptible to caries than others, suggesting a hereditary influence.

Sucrose is the most common carbohydrate recognized in the caries process. Although starch is considered less cariogenic than sucrose, it can easily be broken down into fermentable carbohydrate by salivary amylase. Also, many foods high in starch often contain sucrose or other sugars, which may make the food more cariogenic than sugar alone because starch is retained longer in the mouth. Honey is just as cariogenic as sucrose.

The cariogenicity of specific foods depends not only on the type and amount of fermentable carbohydrate but also on the retentiveness of foods to the tooth surface and the frequency of eating. Dental researchers believe that all of these factors influence the length of time the teeth are exposed to an acidic environment, which leads to tooth decay.[20]

Some protein foods, e.g., nuts, hard cheeses, eggs, and meats, do not decrease plaque pH and are thought to have a protective effect against caries.[21] Eating these foods at the same time as high-sugar foods prevents a reduction in plaque pH. Why these foods are protective is not known, but theories include the presence of protein and lipids in these foods, the presence of calcium and phosphorus, and the stimulation of alkaline saliva. Chewing sorbitol-sweetened (sugarless) gum after a sugar-containing snack may also counteract the decrease in pH, but this remains controversial.[22]

Prevention of Caries

Since children of all ages eat frequently, snacks should emphasize foods that are low in sucrose, are not sticky, and that stimulate saliva flow, thereby limiting acid production in the mouth (see Table 5-4). Including protein foods such as cheese and nuts may provide nutritional as well as dental benefits. Desserts, when consumed, should be eaten with meals. School-age children and adolescents may benefit from chewing sugarless gum after snacks containing fermentable carbohydrate.

Good oral hygiene complements the efforts of dietary control. In infancy parents can clean the gums and teeth with a clean cloth. The toothbrush should be introduced in the toddler period. The key is to incorporate brushing and flossing as a regular, consistent routine, with parental supervision in the early years. If the water supply is not fluoridated, a fluoride supplement is recommended into the teen years. See Table 5-8 for recommended fluoride dosages.

Baby Bottle Tooth Decay

Children under 3 years of age are most likely to have baby bottle tooth decay (BBTD). In some nonfluoridated communities the prevalence is about 20%; in

---

Table 5-8 Recommended Fluoride Supplement/Day[27]

Age	Fluoride Conc. <.3 ppm	Fluoride Conc. 0.3–0.7 ppm
2 wks–2 yrs	.25	0
2–3 yrs	.5	.25
3–16 yrs	1.0	.5

Source: Reprinted with permission from *Pediatrics* (1986; 77:758), Copyright © 1986, American Academy of Pediatrics.

Native American and Native Alaskan preschool children, the rate is more than 50%.[23] Rampant caries develop on the primary upper front teeth (incisors) and often on the cheek surface of primary upper first molars. Children from poor families are at highest risk for BBTD. A history of BBTD seems to increase the risk for future caries.

The primary cause of BBTD is prolonged exposure of the teeth to a sweetened liquid (formula, milk, juice, soda pop, sweetened drinks). This occurs most often when the child is routinely given a nursing bottle at bedtime or during naps. During sleep the liquid pools around the teeth, saliva flow decreases, and the child may continue to suck liquid over an extended period of time. Although BBTD has been documented in ad libitum breastfeeding, the occurrence is believed to be less than with bottle feeding.[23] Toddlers who hold their own bottle and have access to it anytime throughout the day are also at high risk. Dental treatment of BBTD is expensive, often requires a general anesthetic, and may be traumatic for the child and family.

Education is the primary strategy to prevent BBTD. Parents should be counseled about the disorder early in infancy and encouraged to avoid putting a baby to sleep with a bottle, as previously addressed in Chapter 4. Juices and liquids other than milk or formula should be offered in a cup. In normally developing infants, weaning from the bottle should begin at about 1 year of age. Day care providers and other caregivers should also be informed of the threat to oral health posed by use of the nursing bottle as a pacifier. For this educational approach to be successful, families often need help with positive parenting strategies and behavioral counseling.

Iron Deficiency Anemia

Iron deficiency anemia is most common in children between 1 and 3 years of age, with a prevalence of about 9%.[8] Other high-risk groups are young adolescent males and females of childbearing age. Reported trends have shown an overall decrease in the prevalence of iron deficiency anemia, both in low-income and middle-class pediatric populations.[24] Factors influencing this positive trend include increased and prolonged use of iron-fortified infant formulas, increased iron intake from other food sources, and the Women, Infants, and Children (WIC) food program.

Despite the encouraging trends, some young children, especially low income, are at high risk for iron deficiency. Although the relationship between iron deficiency and cognitive/behavioral function has been debated for a long time, poorer cognitive performance and delayed psychomotor development have been reported in infants and preschool children with iron deficiency compared to children without iron deficiency.[25,26] Iron deficiency in infancy may have long-term consequences, as demonstrated by poorer performance on a developmental test at age 5.[27]

Dietary factors as well as growth and physiologic needs play a role in development of anemia. Some toddlers consume a large volume of milk to the exclusion of solids; plain meats are often not well accepted by preschool children because they require more chewing. For many of these children, most dietary iron comes from nonheme sources such as vegetables, grains, and cereals. Since the typical American mixed diet contains approximately 6 mg iron per 1000 calories, adolescents dieting to lose weight will have minimal iron intake, especially if animal protein is limited.

Absorption of iron from food depends on several factors. One is the iron status of the individual; those with low iron stores will have a higher absorption rate. There is a higher rate of absorption from heme iron (in meat, fish, and poultry) than from nonheme iron (in vegetables, grains, and animal tissue). Absorption of nonheme iron can be increased by two enhancing factors, (1) ascorbic acid and (2) meat, fish, or poultry (MFP).[28] The presence of an ascorbic-acid-rich food and/or MFP in a meal will increase the rate of nonheme iron absorption. Other food or compounds inhibit iron absorption. Table 5-9 identifies good iron sources as well as absorption enhancers and inhibitors. Simple but conscientious menu planning can help improve iron availability to children and teenagers.

Effect of Diet on Learning and Behavior

What impact does a child's diet have on his or her school performance and behavior? For decades people have debated whether skipping breakfast affects classroom learning. Food additives, sugar, and allergies have been suggested as causes of hyperactivity in children. Although these are controversial issues, some scientific studies have examined them.

Diet and Learning

Although severe malnutrition early in life is known to negatively affect intellectual development, the impact of marginal malnutrition, skipping meals, or hunger has been more difficult to document. Past studies have indicated that children who go to school without breakfast are more likely to be lethargic, inattentive, and irritable, but a direct cause-effect relationship was not established.[29]

More recent studies have used standardized tests to measure cognitive functions (i.e., problem solving, attention, memory) in healthy school-age children in a laboratory setting. In one study, children were given either breakfast or no breakfast, and the fasted children generally, but not always, performed less well.[30] Another report, done under similar conditions, compared healthy children to those stunted, those who suffered severe malnutrition early in life, and those currently

Table 5-9 Food Sources of Iron

	Iron (mg)
Meat, Fish and Poultry* (1 oz)	
Chicken liver	2.8
Beef liver	2.2
Turkey, roasted	1.7
Beef pot roast	1.3
Hamburger	1.1
Fresh pork, roasted	1.1
Ham	0.7
Chicken	0.6
Tuna, canned	0.5
Hot dog	0.3
Salmon	0.3
Fish stick	0.1
Cereals, Grains, Vegetables, Fruits†	
Cooked cereals (1/2 cup)	0.7–1.3
Ready-to-eat cereals (3/4 cup)	0.3–9.0
Whole-wheat bread, enriched bread (1 slice)	0.6–0.8
Legumes, cooked (1/2 cup)	1.3–3.0
Greens (spinach, mustard, beet), cooked (1/2 cup)	1.5–2.0
Green peas, cooked (1/2 cup)	1.3
Dried fruit (1/4 cup)	1.0–1.5
Nuts, most kinds (2 T)	1.0
Wheat germ (1 T)	0.5
Molasses, light (1 T)	0.9

Dietary Enhancers of Nonheme Iron Absorption	**Dietary Inhibitors of Nonheme Iron Absorption**
Meat, fish, poultry	Tea (tannic acid)
Ascorbic acid	Antacids
	Sequestering additives (such as EDTA used in fats and soft drinks to clarify and prevent rancidity)

* Heme iron sources (approximately 40% of the iron in these foods); well-absorbed.

† Nonheme sources; lower level of absorption; enhancers eaten at the same time will increase absorption.

wasted (low weight for height). There was variation among groups in the response to the cognitive tests, but all the malnourished/undernourished children were adversely affected in their performance when they missed breakfast.[31]

In a recent report, standardized achievement test scores were compared before and after implementation of the School Breakfast Program in six schools in a predominantly low-income community.[32] Children participating in the breakfast program demonstrated improved academic performance compared to those qualified but not participating. The findings also noted decreased tardiness and absenteeism among the children in the breakfast program. These results indicate that efforts of nutrition education and feeding programs should be targeted to children at risk so that they might be better able to achieve in school.

Attention Deficit Hyperactivity Disorder

Commonly known as hyperactivity, attention deficit hyperactivity disorder (ADHD) is a clinical diagnosis with specific criteria, i.e., inattention, impulsivity, hyperactivity, onset before 7 years of age, and duration of at least 6 months. The etiology of ADHD is not clear, and some dietary factors have been proposed as causes, such as food additives, sugar, and food allergies. Although treatment usually includes behavioral management, medication, and/or special education, various dietary treatments have been proposed.

The Feingold diet, popularized in the 1970s, theorized that hyperactivity was caused by artificial colorings and flavorings in the food supply. Treatment was to remove from the child's diet those substances, natural salicylates (found mostly in fruits), and some preservatives (BHA, BHT). Although initial reports were positive, no controlled studies were done, and the response was believed to be a placebo effect. Controlled double-blind challenge studies have not supported the Feingold hypothesis.[33] Although it is accepted that a small percentage (no more than 5% to 10%) of hyperactive children (usually preschoolers) may benefit from the diet, one recent report suggests a greater diet impact. The study of preschool hyperactive boys used a total diet replacement design with crossover between experimental and control diets.[34] The experimental diet was the usual Feingold diet plus elimination of foods that the family thought were bothersome to their child, e.g., chocolate, sugar, or caffeine. Almost 50% of the boys showed some improvement in behavior using accepted rating scales. The modified Feingold diet, including fruits, has been evaluated favorably according to nutrient content and thus poses little risk for the child.[35] Families using the diet should receive nutritional counseling and should not disregard other helpful treatment for their child's ADHD.

Sugar (sucrose) is popularly believed to cause hyperactivity in children or behavior problems and delinquency in adolescents. Controlled challenge studies, however, have failed to show any negative behavioral effects from sucrose.[36,37] In one of the studies, children receiving the sugar were less active and quieter afterward than those receiving the placebo.[38] A double-blind challenge study with juvenile delinquents did not show impaired behavioral performance after a sucrose load.[39] There are many good reasons for reducing sugar consumption, including improved dental health and diets that are more nutrient dense. This can be reinforced with families, while helping them remain objective about a sugar-behavior relationship. There is always the rare possibility that a child may have an individual intolerance to sugar.

Stimulant medications such as methylphenidate (Ritalin) or dextroamphetamine (Dexedrine) are commonly used to treat ADHD. They usually result in improvement of motor restlessness, short attention span, and irritability. Anorexia is a side effect that has been shown to cause suppression of physical growth.[40] Over time there seems to be more tolerance for a medication's negative effect on growth, but the response is individual. Data suggest that there is a direct relationship between dosage of the medication and the degree of reduced growth.[41] Although the mechanisms involved are not clear, decreased energy intake is a factor. Children receiving these medications should have regular monitoring of growth, and the efficacy of the drug effect should be reassessed routinely. Since the effect of the medication will be noted about half an hour after being ingested and is usually absent after 4 to 6 hours, food should be offered to take advantage of the child's optimal appetite; i.e., the medication should be given with or after meals.[42]

Megavitamin therapy has been promoted for many disorders, including ADHD and behavior problems. Of the controlled studies done, none have supported the use of megavitamins, and there is the potential for vitamin toxicity or other negative effects.[43]

Food allergies as a factor in ADHD or behavioral difficulties in children are unclear. Many reports are subjective, and the validity and interpretation of allergy tests can be controversial. It is certainly possible that children suffering from allergies may manifest behaviors (irritability, poor attention) seen in children with ADHD, but whether elimination diets alleviate these symptoms is not clear. Children suspected of having food allergies should be seen by an allergist for diagnosis. Periodic nutrition evaluations are warranted for any child using an atypical dietary regimen.

Adolescent Pregnancy

Although pregnancy is a normal physiologic state, there are more risks and complications for pregnant teens. Compared to any other age group, they have higher rates of low-birth-weight infants, especially among those less than 15 years old. Birth rates have been consistently declining for all females of reproductive age, except those under 15 year of age.[44]

The nutritional status of the pregnant adolescent is influenced by both physiologic and environmental/social factors. Some evidence suggests that young pregnant teenage girls are still growing, theoretically creating a maternal-fetal competition for nutrients, and thus indicating increased nutrient needs in addition to pregnancy.[45] Other risk factors include a low prepregnancy weight and minimal nutrient stores at the time of conception. Many social factors can also affect the health and nutritional status of the teen, including late or no prenatal care, little financial support, limited food resources, poor eating habits, family difficulties, and various other emotional stresses.

Dietary guides for pregnant teens have usually added the pregnancy RDAs to the RDAs for 15- to 18-year-old females[46] (see Tables 2-2 and 2-3). Energy needs can vary greatly, depending on pubertal maturation and physical activity. An adequate weight gain is the best indicator of an appropriate energy intake. The pregnancy RDA for protein is 60 g, which is 14 to 16 g more than the RDA for teenage females.[2] Higher protein intakes may be needed, depending on body build and growth needs. A sufficient energy intake will protect the protein to be used for growth. Individualized nutrition assessments will help identify the nutrition and diet concerns to be prioritized for ongoing nutrition counseling and education.[46] Although an iron supplement of 30 mg is the only standard prenatal supplement routinely recommended,[47] a multivitamin-mineral supplement containing folic acid may be indicated in the presence of dietary and social-environmental risk factors.

For a positive outcome of pregnancy, weight gain for the pregnant adolescent needs to be more than the usual 25 to 35 pounds. The Committee on Nutritional Status during Pregnancy and Lactation of the Food and Nutrition Board recommends that pregnant teens should gain at the upper end of the recommended range for their prepregnancy weight.[47] Gains of 35 pounds or more have been shown to be appropriate.[48] The pattern of weight gain is important, with weight gain in the first and early second trimesters being related to improved birth weights.[49] This early weight gain is thought to be related to the adolescent's own growth plus the needed maternal reserves. Education and counseling are needed for the teen to accept the needed weight gain as part of a healthy pregnancy, plus the likelihood of a higher postpartum weight.[48]

Pregnant teenagers are best served by an interdisciplinary health care team to deal with their multiple health, psychosocial, and economic issues. Since most of them keep their babies, education and resource referrals are needed regarding infant care and feeding, continued schooling of the mother, parenting, and financial services.

Substance Abuse

Alcohol, tobacco, and marijuana are the most widely used substances among teenagers. Other street drugs are used by a small percentage of adolescents, but there is evidence of increased use of regular and crack cocaine in this age group in recent years.[50]

Alcoholism in adolescence is a significant public health problem. More than 90% of teenagers have had some experience with alcohol by the 12th grade, with many having their first exposure as early as 12 years of age.[51] Any negative effect on nutritional status will depend on the frequency and amount of drinking as well as usual food habits. A survey of teenage males who were alcohol and marijuana abusers did not show significant differences in biochemical measures, but decreased intakes of milk, fruits, and vegetables were reported, as well as more snack food consumption and more symptoms of poor nutrition (tiredness, bleeding gums, muscle weakness).[52] For the female who consumes alcohol and becomes pregnant, there is the risk of fetal alcohol syndrome in her infant.

Despite a decrease in cigarette smoking among adults in recent years, smoking remains relatively popular among teenagers. One national survey reported that 30% of high school seniors are regular smokers.[51] There may be increased need for some nutrients such as ascorbic acid, and smoking during pregnancy can reduce infant birth weight. Smokeless (chewing) tobacco has become popular with both school-age children and adolescents. Not a benign substance, regular use is related to periodontal disease, oral cancer, dependence, and hypertension.[53]

The negative nutritional consequences of a substance user's habit will depend on factors such as lifestyle, available food, and money to buy food. During a nutrition evaluation, the areas of alcohol consumption, tobacco use, and illegal drug use should not be ignored. Information will most likely be shared if a matter-of-fact, nonthreatening approach is used. Depending on the individual's situation, nutrition education and counseling can focus on improving health and nutrition. Other teenagers will need comprehensive treatment programs, which include a nutrition component.

HEALTH PROMOTION

Americans have been gradually altering their eating habits as a result of increased interest in their health and their concern about preventing heart disease, cancer, obesity, and hypertension. The federal government and nonprofit organizations have provided recommendations, such as the Dietary Guidelines, to promote healthy eating. To what degree, if any, should this advice be applied to growing children and adolescents?

The federally sponsored National Cholesterol Education Program (NCEP) recommends that everyone over 2 years of age follow a diet that includes no more than 30% of calories as fat (10% or less from saturated fat, up to 10% from unsaturated fat, 10% to 15% from monounsaturated fat) and no more than 300 mg cholesterol per day.[54] The panel also recommends cholesterol screening for children at risk: those with parents or grandparents diagnosed with coronary heart disease or a cardiac event before age 55, and those with one or both parents having a serum cholesterol of 240 mg or more. Although controversy exists regarding universal versus selective cholesterol screening,[55] screening in childhood appears to be a sensitive predictor of adult lipid levels.[56]

The NCEP intervention for children identified is dependent on low-density lipoprotein (LDL) cholesterol categories.[54] For those with an acceptable level (<110 mg/dL), the recommended dietary pattern (step-one diet) is suggested, with a repeat lipoprotein analysis in 5 years. Children with a borderline level of LDL cholesterol (110 to 129 mg/dL) would be provided with a step-one diet prescribed and individualized for them and a reevaluation in 1 year. Those with high LDL cholesterol levels (>130 mg/dL) would initially be given the step-one diet, and if necessary the step-two diet (further reduction to <7% saturated fat and <200 mg cholesterol per day).

Some pediatric experts have felt that these recommendations are not appropriate, especially for the young child.[57] Failure to thrive has been seen in some infants and toddlers whose parents, well intentioned but misguided, restricted their children's diet to prevent atherosclerosis, obesity, and poor eating habits.[58] (See Chapter 13, Failure To Thrive, for further information.) School-age children and adolescents, however, appear to be able to consume low-fat diets (<30% of calories as fat, <300 mg cholesterol) without negatively influencing the level of micronutrients consumed.[59] There remains a good deal of controversy over the questions of whether dietary intervention in the growing years will decrease serum cholesterol levels or modify other risk factors later in life.

For overall health promotion, moderation and common sense continue to be the best policy. Although prevention of obesity and other chronic conditions is a worthy goal, there are no conclusive data to support a massive change in the diets of growing children. For healthy, growing children the use of low fat dairy products and fewer high-fat foods is appropriate for those over 2 years of age. Limiting the intake of fermentable carbohydrate will enhance dental health. Increasing the intake of fruits, vegetables, whole-grain products, and legumes above the usual reported levels can have several benefits: reducing the percentage of fat in the diet, increasing the fiber content, increasing the amount of β-carotene and other dietary factors that may help prevent cancer, and making the total diet more nutrient dense. The more varied the diet, the more likely the child's nutrient needs will be met.

NUTRITION EDUCATION

Children first learn about food and nutrition from their families in their own homes. This begins in an informal manner with parental attitudes, foods commonly served (e.g., potatoes or tortillas are served daily; okra or bok choy is never served), and family opinions about what foods are "good for us." Later, more formal nutrition education occurs in preschools, Head Start programs, day care schools, and clubs such as 4-H. Information is also assimilated from the media, advertising, written materials, and peers.

Table 5-10 Piaget's Theory of Cognitive Development in Relation to Feeding and Nutrition

Developmental Period	Cognitive Characteristics	Relationships to Feeding and Nutrition
Sensorimotor (Birth–2 years)	—progression from newborn with automatic reflexes to intentional interaction with the environment and the beginning use of symbols	—progression is made from sucking and rooting reflexes to the acquisition of self-feeding skills —food is used primarily to satisfy hunger, as a medium to explore the environment, and to practice fine motor skills
Preoperations (2–7 years)	—thought processes become internalized; they are unsystematic and intuitive —use of symbols increases —reasoning is based on appearances and happenstance —approach to classification is functional and unsystematic —child's world is viewed egocentrically	—eating becomes less the center of attention than social, language, and cognitive growth —food is described by color, shape, and quantity but there is limited ability to classify food into "groups" —foods tend to be classed as "like" and "don't like" —foods can be identified as "good for you" but reasons are unknown or mistaken
Concrete operations (7–11 years)	—child can focus on several aspects of a situation simultaneously —cause/effect reasoning becomes more rational and systematic —ability to classify, reclassify and generalize emerges —decrease in egocentricism permits child to take another's view	—beginning realization that nutritious food has a positive effect on growth and health, but limited understanding of how or why this occurs —mealtimes take on a social significance —the expanding environment increases the opportunities for, and influences on, food selection (peer influence rises)
Formal operations (11 years and beyond)	—hypothetical and abstract thought expand —understanding of scientific and theoretical processes deepens	—the concept of nutrients from food functioning at physiological and biochemical levels can be understood —conflicts in making food choices may be realized (knowledge of nutritious food vs. preferences and non-nutritive influences)

Source: Reprinted from Lucas B, Nutrition in childhood, in *Food, Nutrition, and Diet Therapy*, ed 7 (p 295) by MU Krause and LK Mahan (eds) with permission of WB Saunders, © 1984.

A child's developmental level should be taken into account when teaching nutrition concepts. Table 5-10 correlates Piaget's learning theory with progress in feeding and nutrition. Younger children definitely do best with hands-on personal experience with food, not abstract nutrition concepts. A personal approach also works well with adolescents with the use of computer-assisted programs and using their own dietary profiles to determine areas of education and improvement.[60] Lastly, nutrition education efforts for children should not overlook parents and the family as a whole.

REFERENCES

1. Satter E. *How to Get Your Kid to Eat . . . But Not Too Much.* Palo Alto, Calif: Bull Publishing Co; 1987.

2. Food and Nutrition Board. *Recommended Dietary Allowances.* 10th ed. Washington, DC: National Academy of Sciences, National Research Council; 1989.

3. National Center for Health Statistics. *Dietary Intake Source Data: United States, 1976-1980.* Vital and Health Statistics series 11, no. 231. DHHS publication no. (PHS) 83-1681. Hyattsville, MD: 1983.

4. Farris RP, Hyg MS, Cresanta JL, et al. Macronutrient intakes of 10-year-old children, 1973 to 1982. *J Am Diet Assoc.* 1986; 86:765.

5. Science and Education Administration. *Nationwide Food Consumption Survey, 1977-78, Preliminary Report No. 2, Food and Nutrient Intakes of Individuals in 1 Day in the U.S., Spring, 1977.* Hyattsville, Md:1980; US Department of Agriculture.

6. Mahan LK, Rosebrough RH. Nutritional requirements and nutritional status assessment in adolescence. In: Mahan LK, Rees JM, eds. *Nutrition in Adolescence.* St. Louis, Mo: CV Mosby; 1984.

7 Matkovic V, Fontana D, Tominac C. Factors that influence peak bone mass formation: a study of calcium balance and the inheritance of bone mass in adolescent females. *Am J. Clin Nutr.* 1990;52:878.

8. Herbert V. Recommended dietary intakes (RDI) of iron in humans. *Am J Clin Nutr.* 1987;45:679.

9. Bowering J, Clancy KL. Nutritional status of children and teenagers in relation to vitamin and mineral use. *J Am Diet Assoc.* 1986;86:1033.

10. American Academy of Pediatrics. Committee on Nutrition. Vitamin and mineral supplementation needs in normal children in the United States. *Pediatrics* 1980; 66:1015.

11. American Dietetic Association. Recommendations concerning supplement usage: ADA statement. *J Am Diet Assoc.* 1987;87:1342.

12. American Medical Association, Council on Scientific Affairs. Vitamin preparations as dietary supplements and as therapeutic agents. *JAMA.* 1987;257:1929.

13. Beal VA. Dietary intake of individuals followed through infancy and childhood. *Am J Public Health.* 1961;51:1107.

14. Cotugna N. TV ads on Saturday morning children's programming—what's new? *J Nutr Educ.* 1988;20:125.

15. Harris CS, Baker SP, Smith GA. Childhood asphyxiation by food: a national analysis and overlook. *JAMA.* 1984;251:2231.

16. Guber S. Marketing to kids: it's elementary. *Prepared Foods.* 1989;158:48.

17. Ho CS, Gould RA, Jensen LN, et al. Evaluation of the nutrient content of school, sack and vending lunch of junior high students. *Sch Food Serv Res Rev.* 1991;15:85.

18. Hampton MC, Huenemann RL, Shapiro LR, et al. Caloric and nutrient intake of teenagers. *J Am Diet Assoc.* 1967;50:385.

19. US Department of Health and Human Services. *Oral Health of United States Children: The National Survey of Dental Caries in U.S. School Children (1986-87).* NIH publication no. 89-2247. Bethesda, MD: 1989.

20. White-Graves MV, Schiller MR. History of foods in the caries process. *J Am Diet Assoc.* 1986;86:241.

21. The role of diet and nutrition in oral health. *Dairy Council Digest.* 1986;57(3).

22. Jensen ME. Responses of interproximal plaque pH to snack foods and effect of chewing sorbitol-containing gum. *J Am Dent Assoc.* 1986;113:262.

23. Johnsen D, Nowjack-Raymer R. Baby bottle tooth decay (BBTD): issues, assessment, and an opportunity for the nutritionist. *J Am Diet Assoc.* 1989;89:112.

24. Yip R, Walsh KM, Goldfarb MG, et al. Declining prevalence of anemia in childhood in a middle-class setting: a pediatric success story? *Pediatrics.* 1987;80:330.

25. Pollitt E, Saco-Pollitt C, Leibel R, et al. Iron deficiency and behavioral development in infants and preschool children. *Am J Clin Nutr.* 1986;43:555.

26. Walter T, De Andraca I, Chadud P, et al. Iron deficiency anemia: adverse effects on infant psycho-motor development. *Pediatrics.* 1989;84:7.

27. Lozoff B, Jimenez E, Wolf AU. Long-term development outcome of infants with iron deficiency. *N Engl J Med.* 1991;325:687.

28. Monsen ER, Hallberg L, Layrisse M, et al. Estimation of available dietary iron. *Am J Clin Nutr.* 1978;31:134.

29. Pollitt E, Gersovitz M, Gargiulo M. Educational benefits of the United States school feeding program: a critical review of the literature. *Am J Public Health.* 1978;68:477.

30. Pollitt E, Leibel RL, Greenfield D. Brief fasting, stress, and cognition in children. *Am J Clin Nutr.* 1981;34:1526.

31. Simeon DT, Grantham-McGregor S. Effects of missing breakfast on the cognitive functions of school children of differing nutritional status. *Am J Clin Nutr.* 1989;49:646.

32. Meyers AF, Sampson A, Weitzman M, et. al. School breakfast program and school performance. *Am J Dis Child.* 1989;143:1234.

33. Lipton MA, Mayo JP. Diet and hyperkinesis—an update. *J Am Diet Assoc.* 1983;83:132.

34. Kaplan BJ, McNicol J, Conte RA, et al. Dietary replacement in preschool-aged hyperactive boys. *Pediatrics.* 1989;83:7.

35. Harper PH, Goyette CH, Conners CK. Nutrient intakes of children on the hyperkinesis diet. *J Am Diet Assoc.* 1978;73:515.

36. Wolraich M, Milich R, Stumbo P, et al. Effects of sucrose ingestion on the behavior of hyperactive boys. *J Pediatr.* 1985;106:675.

37. Ferguson HB, Stoddart C, Simeon JG. Double-blind challenge studies of behavioral and cognitive effects on sucrose-aspartame ingestion in normal children. *Nutr Rev.* 1986;44(suppl):144.

38. Behar D, Rapoport JL, Adams AJ, et al. Sugar challenge testing with children considered behaviorally "sugar reactive. *Nutr Behav.* 1984;1:277.

39. Bachorowski J, Newman JP, Nichols SL, et al. Sucrose and delinquency: behavioral assessment. *Pediatrics.* 1990;86:244.

40. Mattes JA, Gittelman R. Growth of hyperactive children on maintenance regimen of methylphenidate. *Arch Gen Psychiatry.* 1983;40:317.

41. Lucas B, Sells CJ. Nutrient intake and stimulant drugs in hyperactive children. *J Am Diet Assoc.* 1977;70:373.

42. Lucas B. Diet and behavior. In Pipes P, ed. *Nutrition in Infancy and Childhood.* St. Louis, Mo: Times Mirror/Mosby College Publishing; 1989.

43. Haslam RHA, Dalby JT, Rademaker AW. Effects of megavitamin therapy on children with attention deficit disorders. *Pediatrics.* 1984;74:103.

44. Committee on Adolescence, American Academy of Pediatrics. Adolescent pregnancy. *Pediatrics.* 1989;83:132.

45. Scholl TO, Hediger ML, Ances IG, et al. Growth during early teenage pregnancies. *Lancet.* 1988;1:701.

46. American Dietetic Association. Nutrition management of adolescent pregnancy: technical support paper. *J Am Diet Assoc.* 1989;89:104.

47. National Academy of Sciences. *Nutrition during Pregnancy.* Washington, DC: National Academy Press; 1990.

48. Meserole LP, Worthington-Roberts BS, Rees J, et al. Prenatal weight gain and postpartum weight loss patterns in adolescents. *J Adolesc Health Care.* 1984;5:21.

49. Hediger ML, Schall TO, Belsky DH. Patterns of weight gain in adolescent pregnancy: effect on birth weight and preterm delivery. *Obstet Gynecol.* 1989;74:6.

50. Smith DE, Schwartz RH, Martin DM. Heavy cocaine use by adolescents. *Pediatrics.* 1989;83:539.

51. Macdonald DI. Patterns of alcohol and drug use among adolescents. *Pediatr Clin North Am.* 1987;34:275.

52. Farrow JA, Rees JM, Worthington-Roberts B. Health, developmental and nutritional status of adolescent alcohol and marijuana abusers. *Pediatrics.* 1987;79:218.

53. Connolly GN, Winn DM, Hecht SS, et al. The reemergence of smokeless tobacco. *N Engl J Med.* 1986;314:1020.

54. National Heart, Lung and Blood Institute, National Cholesterol Education Program. *Report of the Expert Panel on Blood Cholesterol Levels in Children and Adolescents.* Bethesda, Md: National Heart, Lung, and Blood Institute; 1991.

55. Steiner NJ, Neinstein LS, Pennbridge J. Hypercholesterolemia in adolescents: effectiveness of screening strategies based on selected risk factors. *Pediatrics.* 1991;88:269.

56. Stuhldreher WL, Orchard TJ, Donahue RP, et al. Cholesterol screening in childhood: sixteen-year Beaver County Lipid Study experience. *J Pediatr.* 1991;119:551.

57. American Academy of Pediatrics, Committee on Nutrition. Prudent life style for children: dietary fat and cholesterol. *Pediatrics.* 1986;78:521.

58. Pugliese MT, Weyman-Daum M, Moses N, et al. Parental health beliefs as a cause of nonorganic failure to thrive. *Pediatrics.* 1987;80:175.

59. McPherson RS, Nichaman MZ, Kohl HW, et al. Intake and food sources of dietary fat among schoolchildren in The Woodlands, Texas. *Pediatrics.* 1990;86:520.

60. Contento I, Roberts S, Gussow JD. Using adolescents' dietary self-reports to tailor school-based nutrition education. *J Nutr Educ.* 1986;18:175.

Chapter 6

Vegetarianism in Children

Johanna T. Dwyer

This chapter summarizes our current knowledge of nutrition as it applies to vegetarianism during childhood in the United States today. It begins first with the reasons for concern about vegetarian diets in childhood. Second, the history of vegetarianism is briefly reviewed, to derive some lessons relevant to pediatric vegetarian diets. Third, some working definitions and estimates of the prevalence of vegetarian eating habits are presented. Fourth, the risks and benefits associated with vegetarian eating and lifestyles in the pediatric period are examined. Finally, some practical principles for counseling and diet planning are mentioned.

Vegetarianism in children deserves special attention because diets that sustain adults in good health are not necessarily appropriate for infants, young children, or adolescents. There are several reasons why this is so. The culture is omnivorous, and thus healthy vegan and vegetarian feeding patterns for young infants are unknown to most parents. In the absence of appropriate instruction, it is difficult to improvise appropriate vegetarian diets for children. The nutrient density of protein, vitamins, and minerals must be higher per calorie in pediatric diets than in adult diets, since nutrient needs per calorie are correspondingly higher during growth. In early infancy, diets low in caloric density and high in bulk may lead to inadequate energy intakes, since stomach capacity is limited and infants are unable to consume enough food to meet energy needs unless they are fed more frequently than is usual. Finally, sometimes the parents of vegetarian children have views that are at variance with conventional medical recommendations for age-appropriate diet and other health practices.

Note: Partial support for preparation of this chapter was provided from Training Grant MCJ 9120 to Dr. Dwyer from the U.S. Department of Health and Human Services.

171

HISTORY

A few years ago it was fashionable to assume that the first human beings consumed a largely vegetarian diet that was high in dietary fiber, low in fat, and in conformity with modern notions of healthful diets.[1] In fact, the situation is more complicated than this. There is little doubt that all human beings breastfed their young for many months, since no other sources of food suitable for infants were available. But once they were weaned from the breast, the diets of early human beings are not so easy to describe. Our earliest ancestors, the Australopithecines, were actually neither vegetarians, fruitarians, nor the hunters of ancient myth, but scavengers of kills made by other animals who ate a mixed diet of carrion and plant foods. These early human beings were followed by other hominids who ate various diets, including but by no means limited to game that they killed. With the advent of grain gathering and cereal agriculture, diets based on a single staple plant crop became more common.[2] At the same time the amount of animal protein in the diet decreased, single cereals became dietary staples, and body size decreased. The prehistoric human beings who were carnivores also suffered from various forms of malnutrition, and their adult size was smaller than it is today. The overall quality and variety of the diet and other environmental factors were the major factors influencing growth and health.[2]

Thus there is little archaeologic evidence to support the notion that either vegetarian or omnivorous diets are somehow especially well suited to human beings from the evolutionary standpoint. Human beings can subsist on a wide variety of different diets once they have been weaned from the breast. Diets adequate to support adults may not be so for infants and children, and so special care is needed in formulating diets for feeding infants and young children. However, there is abundant evidence to suggest that vegetable protein mixtures made from several plant foods can support excellent growth after weaning.[3] Thus there is no inherent reason why well-planned vegetarian as well as omnivorous diets cannot be appropriate for feeding children today.

History also teaches us that what human beings eat depends on many factors, including not only environmental realities and constraints but also culture. Although the word "vegetarian" was first used in the 19th century, the notion that eating a diet composed only of vegetables, fruits, and grains even when other foods were available originated in ancient times and was based on philosophic rather than on economic or practical concerns. Pythagoras, the ancient Greek philosopher and mathematician, urged his followers to consume vegetarian diets. And many of the world's great religions, including Hinduism, Buddhism, Jainism, and some Christian sects such as Seventh Day Adventists, have advocated vegetarian diets for different reasons, ranging from a belief in reincarnation to self-denial and concerns that animal foods might be harmful to the body. Although there is no scientific evidence that animal foods in moderation are unhealthful, there is good evidence that both vegetarian and nonvegetarian diets, if they are carefully planned, can be healthful.

If children are to be fed well-planned vegetarian diets, their parents must themselves eat well. Table 6-1 provided some rules of thumb for counseling vegetarian adults about their diets.

The first prerequisite of vegetarian diets is that they be adequate in energy, protein, vitamins and minerals. Good vegetarian diets for children are also balanced in the energy-yielding nutrients they provide, moderate in constituents posing health problems if present in excess (such as saturated fat and cholesterol), not excessively bulky, age and developmental level appropriate, and hygienic. Examples are described in recent publications.[4-6] Today we are able to describe the composition of such diets better than ever before, to observe their health effects, and to assess the likelihood that diets fed to children will meet or fail to meet child nutrition standards. Our state of knowledge today is such that no child, vegetarian or nonvegetarian, should be fed an inadequate diet.

DEFINITIONS AND PREVALENCE OF VEGETARIANISM

The major types of vegetarian diets are defined by whether and what type of animal foods are eaten. There are vegans, lacto-vegetarians, lacto-ovo-vegetarians, and semivegetarians. Each type is susceptible to certain dietary deficiencies if the diet is not well planned; these are described in Table 6-2.

Table 6-1 Practical Principles in Counseling Adult Vegetarians on an Adequate Diet

1. Reduce "empty calorie" foods and substitute fruits, especially fresh fruits, vegetables, and nonsweet bakery products made from whole-grain cereals.
2. Include two or more glasses of low or nonfat milk to ensure intake of vitamin B_{12} is sufficient (three or more glasses in small children), and obtain additional vitamin B_{12} from moderate use of eggs (three a week).
3. Substitute whole-grain for refined breads and cereals.
4. Include a variety of fresh fruits and vegetables.
5. Take additional special steps if a vegan diet is eaten:
   • Maintain adequate energy intakes by inclusion of legumes, breads and cereals, and nuts and nutlike seeds, which are relatively high in energy and fat (such as peanuts, sunflower seeds, soybeans, sesame seeds).
   • Include a vitamin D source (vitamin D fortified soy milk, dietary supplement providing vitamin D).
   • Include a vitamin B_{12} source (vitamin pill, vitamin B_{12} fortified soy milk, meat analogues, cereals, and other foods to which the vitamin has been added).
6. Make additional adjustments if needed for special physiological states and/or for disease so as to meet Recommended Dietary Allowances, including calories.

Table 6-2 Types of Vegetarian Diets and Common Dietary Deficiencies

Diet Type and Examples of Groups	Likely Common Deficiencies and Problems
Semivegetarian	Possibly lower intakes of iron
Vegetarian	Possibly lower intakes of iron
Lacto-vegetarian	Lower iron, zinc, and vitamin B_6 intakes, rarely giving rise to clinical problems
Lacto-ovo-vegetarian	Lower iron, zinc, and vitamin B_6 intakes, rarely giving rise to clinical problems
Vegan	Lower iron, zinc, vitamin B_6, vitamin B_{12}, and vitamin D intakes, sometimes reaching levels of clinical deficiency. Also bioavailability of protein and energy intakes may be inadequate. Dietary deficiencies include iron deficiency anemia, rickets, failure to thrive.

Vegans, or total vegetarians, consume no animal products. This is the rarest form of vegetarianism. As a result of vegans' total avoidance of animal foods (and often of certain other foods as well), unless vitamin and mineral supplements are used intakes of some nutrients may fall short. Special dietary planning, preferably including dietetic advice, is necessary to ensure that nutrient intakes are satisfactory, especially for vegan infants and children. If vegan parents can be convinced to use vitamin and mineral supplements, a vitamin supplement with iron is advisable. It is important to make sure that the supplement contains the Recommended Dietary Allowance (RDA) of vitamin B_{12}, or if it does not, to provide the child with vitamin B_{12} tablets and vitamin B_{12}, D, and calcium-fortified soy milk, or soy formula for the infant. Neither brewer's yeast by itself (yeast grown on a vitamin B_{12}-enriched medium), seaweed, tempeh (a fermented soy product), nor spirulina provide a form of vitamin B_{12} that can be utilized by the human body, although frequent claims are made that they do.[7] Calcium supplements should also be considered if calcium-fortified soy products are unacceptable (see Table 5-2 for a list of calcium equivalents). Vitamin D can be provided from supplements, from cod liver oil (if acceptable), or from vitamin D-fortified soy milk or formula. Sunshine alone cannot be relied upon throughout the year to supply sufficient ultraviolet rays to permit synthesis of vitamin D from the provitamin in the skin. Table 6-3 lists some special foods and supplements that may be helpful in meeting the needs of vegans (and certain other vegetarians).

Lacto-vegetarian diets include plant foods, milk, and dairy products, but they exclude all meat, fish, poultry, and eggs. This type of vegetarianism is relatively rare. Although improperly planned lactovegetarian diets can cause deficiencies in iron, zinc, vitamin D (if milk products unfortified in vitamin D are used), and vitamin B_{12}, deficiencies are somewhat rarer than they are on vegan diets.

Table 6-3 Supplements Available for Vegan and Other Types of Vegetarian Diets

Supplement	Comments
Soy formulas	Commercial soy-based infant formulas are complete foods for infants under 1 year of age and as such are good feeds for vegetarian infants.
Soy milk	May or may not be fortified with vitamins D and B$_{12}$ and calcium; check labels. In itself, soy protein is devoid of vitamins C, D, E, K, and B$_{12}$, so protein must be fortified.
Cod liver oil	Contains substantial but variable amounts of vitamins A and D. If acceptable, water-soluble vitamin D supplements are preferable, because dose is standardized and lipoid pneumonia risk is decreased if supplement is aspirated.
Meat analogues	Made from edible plant proteins such as proteins of soybean, peanut, wheat, and other less common sources. Usually contain less fat than the meat they replace, but otherwise nutritional quality is similar to the products they replace.
Textured vegetable proteins	These are soy-spun or soy-based products that are flavored and used in a variety of foods as meat substitutes and for other purposes.

Breast and formula-fed infants are effectively lacto-vegetarians for the first few months of life. Breast milk or hygienic (heat-treated) cow milk formulas fortified with vitamins and minerals support good growth for several months of life. After 4 to 6 months, breast milk usually becomes limited in energy and in other nutrients, such as vitamin D, ascorbic acid, and iron, so that supplementary feedings including other sources of these nutrients are also necessary.

Semivegetarian diets include plant foods, milk and dairy products, eggs, and some fish and poultry. They are increasingly common, probably more so than any other form of vegetarianism, especially among young adults. Although many vegetarians do not believe that semivegetarian diets are truly vegetarian, those who eat them regard themselves as vegetarians. Red meat is avoided or eaten only occasionally, and other forms of flesh may also be limited or eaten only in small amounts. Semivegetarian diets usually pose little or no nutritional risk. Dietary nutrient intakes are likely to be adequate, and in some cases they are laudable. Most Americans would benefit from diets lower in total fat, saturated fat, and cholesterol than they eat now, and so for many, semivegetarianism is a healthful step.

BENEFITS AND RISKS OF VEGETARIAN EATING STYLES

Vegetarian diets have benefits as well as risks. The possible benefits are listed in Table 6-4.

There is little definitive evidence that vegetarians live longer than nonvegetarians.[8] There is some evidence that risks for some diseases and conditions are lessened. However, the beneficial effects of vegetarian diets on the incidence of certain diseases are mixed up with simultaneous alterations in lifestyles that affect health and that are often present as well, such as abstinence from smoking and alcohol and avoidance of sedentary lifestyles. Nevertheless, it does appear that vegetarian adults are at lesser risk for obesity, atonic constipation, lung cancer, and alcoholism than omnivorous groups. In part, the lower risk is due to diet, but it also is related to a physically active lifestyle, not smoking, and nonuse or nonabuse of alcohol. The risks of hypertension, coronary artery disease, type II (adult-onset) diabetes mellitus, and gallstone are considerably lower among vegetarians. However, risks for breast cancer, diverticular disease of the colon, colon cancer, calcium kidney stones, osteoporosis, dental caries, dental erosion, and kidney disease do not seem to be lower among vegetarians.[8]

Risks of dietary insufficiency of energy, protein, vitamins, and minerals are generally somewhat higher than on omnivore diets. These risks vary somewhat from age to age and therefore are separately discussed for each major division of the pediatric period, below. It should be borne in mind that especially elevated physiologic needs increase risks from vegetarian diets.

RISKS OF VEGETARIAN DIETS AT VARIOUS AGES DURING CHILDHOOD

Table 6-5 briefly summarizes some of the problems that may arise at various ages among vegetarian infants and children. Many other factors also influence the adequacy of vegetarian diets, including type of diet, period of the life cycle, presence or absence of disease, and use or nonuse of vitamin and mineral supplements, to mention only a few. These are summarized and discussed in Table 6-6. However, it is important to remember that the effects of vegetarian diets will differ by age as nutrient needs vary.

Infants

Infants and children who consume a well-planned vegetarian diet and breast milk for much of the first 6 months of life usually thrive. However, after 4 to 6 months of life, particularly if the mother is a vegan, levels of vitamins D and B_{12} may be marginal in the mother's milk, and supplements are in order. In addition,

Table 6-4 Possible Benefits of Vegetarian Diets and Lifestyle Practices

Benefits	Comments
Well-established benefits and decreased risks	
Cancers related to smoking	Decreased risk depends on the cancer: Risks sharply lower for lung cancer and for smoking-related cancers, especially when tobacco is eschewed.
Other cancers	Possibly lower for colon and breast cancer, but unclear if due to meat, fat, saturated fat, or some other factor.
Atonic constipation	Definitely decreased risk of constipation.
Diverticular disease	Good evidence that vegetarian diets, due to their high fiber content, decrease constipation.
Obesity	Vegans are leaner, other vegetarians more variable, possibly due to low caloric density of diet, physically active lives, or conscious control over intakes.
Alcoholism and drug abuse	Low risk due to abstinence from alcohol and drugs.
Osteoporosis	Lacto- and lacto-ovo-vegetarians have very high intakes of calcium and also attain high bone masses during growth. Also, risk is decreased by physically active lives, not smoking.
Possible benefits with decreased risks	
Hypertension	Probably due to control of body weight, physically active life.
Type II diabetes mellitus	Probably due to lack of obesity, high complex carbohydrate and dietary fiber intakes.
Gallstones	Probably due to control of body weight.
Coronary artery disease	Vegans and some lacto-vegetarians have lower serum cholesterol levels, especially of low-density lipoprotein cholesterol, than nonvegetarians. Also high soluble fiber intakes, low saturated fat intakes, not smoking, regular exercise, and weight control contribute to low-risk profiles.
Weak evidence of benefit and decreased risk	
Breast cancer risk	If present, effects may be due to weight control, dietary fat, avoidance of alcohol, plant constituents, or physical activity.
Colon cancer risk	Dietary fiber, fat, saturated fat, constituents of fruits and vegetables, vitamins E and A, carotene, and calcium are all under investigation as possibly exerting protective effect against colon cancer.
Kidney stones	
Dental caries	
Mental illness	

Table 6-5 Problems of Vegetarian Diets in Children

| | Type of Vegetarians | |
Age	Vegan (No or Virtually No Animal Foods)	Other (Lacto-ovo-, Lacto-, or Semivegetarian Patterns)
Early infancy (0–6 months)	Failure to thrive and multiple deficiencies including rickets, iron deficiency anemia, and low vitamin B_{12} levels if no breast milk is fed.	Few or no problems occur if infant is fed at the breast or with commercial infant soy- or milk-based formula fortified with vitamins and minerals, or with home-prepared formula made from heat-treated milk such as evaporated milk fortified with iron, vitamin D, and ascorbic acid.
Later infancy (6–18 months)	Risks are less if breast feeding is extended and supplementary feeds high in iron, vitamin D, energy, calcium, vitamin B_{12}, and zinc are introduced early. Otherwise, failure to thrive, iron deficiency anemia, rickets, and megaloblastic anemia due to vitamin B_{12} deficiency are common. Also, low serum zinc, calcium, phosphorus, and vitamin K levels have been reported.	Risks are less if breast feeding is extended and supplementary feedings are introduced after 4 to 6 months. Multivitamin supplements with iron further decrease risks.
Early childhood (18 months to 5 years)	Slow growth, rickets, and iron deficiency anemia common, as are low levels of vitamin B_{12} in serum.	Iron deficiency anemia is common if iron-fortified foods and supplements are not used.
School children (5–11 years)	Same as above, but severity is decreased because growth has slowed and nutrient needs are lower. Also, child is more easily able to obtain food himself or herself.	Same as above, but severity is decreased because growth has slowed and nutrient needs are lower. Also, child is more easily able to obtain food himself or herself.
Adolescents	Dietary intakes may not be adequate to meet needs for calcium, iron, zinc, vitamins B_{12} and D. Iron deficiency and delay of growth spurt are the most common clinical signs.	Few or no problems are seen except for iron deficiency and insufficiency of zinc. Iron deficiency anemia may occur if supplemental iron or foods rich in iron are not eaten.

Table 6-6 Factors Affecting Nutrient Adequacy of Vegetarian Diets

Factor	Comments
Type of diet	The risks to vegans are higher than to lacto-ovo- or lacto-vegetarians, who in turn have more risks than semivegetarians. Since animal protein foods rich in vitamins B_{12}, D, B_6, and B_2, iron, zinc, and calcium are excluded to varying degrees by these diets, alternative nutrient sources must be found. Also, risks increase if many other foods are restricted. Further restrictions of choice may include processed or cooked foods and considerations of which foods are harmonious to eat together.
Period of life cycle	Risk is higher during infancy, childhood, adolescence, pregnancy, and lactation than at other times of life because nutrient needs are elevated.
Presence of disease	Secondary malnutrition due to disease increases health risks.
Use of vitamin-mineral supplements	Use may decrease risks of malnutrition.

Source: Jacobs K and Dwyer JJ. Vegetarian children: appropriate and inappropriate diets. *Am J Clin Nutr.* 1985;48:811–818.

supplementary sources of energy and iron are needed for growth to continue. It is important to distinguish between soy infant formulas, which are complete foods for small infants, and the various soy milks and other products, which may or may not be nutritionally adequate. Counselors should be alert to the fact that parents are sometimes confused about the differences. Needless to say, diluted nondairy creamer, crushed sesame seeds and water, and tea are inappropriate feeds for small infants. Occasionally, misguided parents have used them in the past, with disastrous results for their child's health. Aside from special considerations surrounding feedings to meet the parents' preferences, usual pediatric nutritional guidelines apply to these infants.[5]

Later infancy, from 6 to 18 months, is a period of high vulnerability for vegan infants due to the advent of weaning from the breast. Vegans are at special risk because the weanling has no readily available source of animal foods high in vitamin D, vitamin B_{12}, calcium, and iron. Indeed, the vegan diet presents special problems whenever biologic needs for nutrients are high, as they are in pregnancy, lactation, infancy, childhood, and adolescence. Thus feeding vegan diets to individuals in these groups greatly increases risks of inadequate intakes, especially of the vitamins B_{12} and D, which are found only in animal foods. The mineral elements calcium, zinc, and iron, found in highly bioavailable forms only in animal foods, may also be in short supply. Dietary fiber, oxalates, and phytates, levels of which are usually all quite high in vegan diets, further reduce the bioavailability of such minerals as iron, calcium, and zinc. Very high dietary fiber levels may also increase vitamin B_{12} excretion.

The bulk of the vegan diet is usually very high, so that it may be difficult to obtain adequate energy intakes, especially when ad libitum intakes are not possible or the individual must rely on someone else to feed him or her. Also, on vegan diets, especially when only a single plant food constitutes most of the calories, the biologic value of protein intakes may be poor. When various vegetable proteins are carefully mixed and matched, these difficulties can be overcome. Plant foods that are low in or lack certain amino acids may be eaten in combination with plant foods high in those amino acids to create a complete, or complementary, protein mixture, which satisfies the body's needs for protein. For example, by combining legumes with grains, nuts, or seeds containing the amino acids that are lacking in legumes, satisfactory levels of total protein can be developed. Vegetarians who eat some animal foods have fewer worries in this regard because even small amounts of these foods provide enough essential amino acids to satisfy the body's needs for protein.

In addition to dietary restrictions involving animal foods, many vegans also restrict or avoid other foods in their diets. These avoidances often involve processed or refined foods, with the result that the variety of the diets may be further restricted, sometimes having adverse effects on nutrient intakes.

Finally, vegan parents often have views on proper medical care that are at variance with conventional Western medical thinking, such as on the utility of immunizations for vaccine-preventable diseases, and the need for regular visits to the pediatrician. They often eschew the use of vitamin and mineral supplements, as well as of enriched or fortified foods and infant formulas, making it more difficult to obtain adequate intakes of certain nutrients such as vitamins B_{12}, D and iron.

Vegans usually breastfeed their infants, which provides adequate nutrition for the first 4 to 6 months. Plant food paps and other weaning foods fed to vegan infants and children are sometimes inadequate, putting the weanling vegan infant at special risk of malnutrition. This has been extensively documented among several groups, including adherents of macrobiotic diets and Rastafarians living both in this country and abroad.

The consequences of inadequate vegan diets fed to infants and young children are severe (see Table 6-5), including failure to thrive, iron deficiency anemia, megaloblastic anemia due to lack of vitamin B_{12} (which is often masked by high folic acid levels but which may still lead to eventual neurologic problems), and vitamin D deficiency rickets.[5] Although these effects have long been known, unfortunately some groups continue to feed their children inadequate diets resulting in such deficiencies.[9–12] These risks can all be avoided or minimized by ensuring that energy needs are met, that the bulk of the diet is not excessive, that comple-

Exhibit 6-1 Sample Menu for a 2- to 3-Year-Old Vegetarian Child

Breakfast	**Lunch**
Egg	Vegetarian bean patty
Cereal	Potato
Orange juice	Yellow vegetable
Bread, whole grain with margarine	Tomato and lettuce
Milk	Bread with margarine ($1/4$ to $1/2$ slice)
	Fruit
	Milk

Dinner
Vegetable soup
Peanut butter sandwich, $1/2$ to 1
Fruit
Milk

mentary sources of vegetable or animal proteins are consumed, and that diets meet RDAs for nutrients for infants and weanlings.

Exhibit 6-1 provides a sample menu suitable for a vegetarian child of 1 to 3 years of age, illustrating that with careful planning it is possible to meet recommended levels of nutrients.

Preschoolers

The diets of vegan and vegetarian preschoolers from 18 months to 5 years of age are less likely to be inadequate for their needs than those of weanlings.[5] Vegan preschool children continue to experience growth lags in height, weight, and fatness to a greater extent than do omnivore children, but these are usually less severe than in the weaning period since growth is slower and the child is somewhat more able to forage for himself or herself. Iron deficiency anemia usually continues to be a problem for vegans. Lacto-vegetarian, lacto-ovo-vegetarian, and semi-vegetarian children occasionally experience problems with iron deficiency anemia, but to much lesser degree.[5]

Grade Schoolers

By grade school, from approximately ages 5 to 11 years of age, growth rates decline, and the risks of vegetarian diets for children somewhat lessen. The diets of vegetarian children tend to be low in saturated and total fat, and cholesterol, high in dietary fiber, and high in complex carbohydrate, all characteristics considered desirable in diets of children of this age, as well as in the diets of their parents.[13] Wise dietary planning can minimize risks of dietary deficiencies.

Teenagers

The pubertal growth spurt again brings a period of rapid growth and of increased nutrient needs. Vegan adolescents, whose diets are especially limited, are at particular risk. Growth is so rapid that dietary intakes may be insufficient to prevent rickets, iron deficiency anemia, and slowing of growth velocity so that the pubertal spurt is delayed, sometimes by several months. Other concerns are that mineralization of bone may be poor since calcium needs are very high and difficult to meet even if green leafy vegetables, nuts and seeds, and calcium-fortified soy milk are supplied. Also, zinc intakes of vegan adolescents rarely meet the RDA.[14] Bioavailability of zinc is especially low in plant foods because of the presence of large amounts of dietary fiber and phytates; high phytate: zinc molar ratios make absorption difficult. Supplements providing calcium, iron, vitamin B_{12}, vitamin D, and zinc may be helpful.

Lacto-ovo-vegetarian and other types of vegetarian diets pose lesser problems but may also increase risks of malnutrition. Iron status is a problem for all teenagers due to rapid growth and the onset of menses in females. Since iron bioavailability is low in plant foods, it is especially difficult to meet iron needs. Special care needs to be taken to provide iron-fortified or whole-grain cereals and to keep ascorbic acid intakes, which enhance iron bioavailability, high.

ADVICE TO VEGETARIAN PARENTS

Good growth and reduced risks for chronic degenerative diseases as well as deficiency diseases can be achieved by following the eating pattern recommended by the recent Diet and Health Report of the National Academy of Sciences for the age and sex of the child and ensuring that nutrient intakes are at levels suggested in the RDAs.[13,14] Within these general guidelines there is room for a wide variety of ethnic diets, including all the major vegetarian cuisines in the world.

For some vegetarians, a simple list of alternative sources of nutrients and a few cookbooks are sufficient to help them achieve nutritionally well-balanced diets. Such a list is provided in Table 6-7 for reference purposes. However, many parents find it easier to use a food guide and an exchange system, which permits rapid checking of the diet to make sure that all needs are being met. Several good guides exist.[6,15] One such guide for vegetarian children of a variety of ages is presented in Table 6-8.

Vegan, lacto, lacto-ovo-vegetarian, and semivegetarian diets can promote excellent growth if they are well planned. While relatively straightforward dietary

Table 6-7 Alternative Sources of Nutrients on Lacto-Vegetarian and Vegan Diets

Nutrients	*Means of Achieving Nutritional Adequacy*
Protein	If acceptable, include some animal protein to help increase vitamin B_{12} intakes and to provide essential amino acids. Plan diets to ensure intake of complementary plant proteins to provide adequate intake of total protein. For example, legumes, low in methionine but adequate in lysine, complement cereals such as wheat, rice, and corn that are adequate in methionine but low in lysine. Multiple plant protein sources should be used. Include plenty of legumes (beans, soy, lentils, chickpeas), which are 20% protein, and cereal grains (wheat, rice, corn), which are 10% protein.
Calcium	Sources include milk; fortified soy milk like Soyalac (500–600 mg per quart); dark green leafy vegetables like mustard, kale, dandelion, parsley, spinach, collard greens; almonds, filberts.
Iron	Sources include iron fortified infant formula, iron-fortified cereals, legumes, green leafy and other vegetables, whole or enriched grains, nuts, dried fruits, iron-fortified milk. All should be consumed with ascorbic acid-rich foods and small amounts of animal food, if possible.
Riboflavin	Milk is the best source; also legumes, whole grains, vegetables.
Vitamin B_{12}	Sources include milk and eggs, if acceptable. Other possibilities are a vitamin B_{12} supplement, vitamin B_{12}-fortified soy milk, vitamin B_{12}-fortified soya meats.
Vitamin D	Sources include fortified cow milk or soy milk, cod liver oil, vitamin D supplement.
Zinc	Sources include nuts, beans, wheat germ, cheese.

advice usually suffices for the latter three types, vegans require detailed counseling, preferably by a registered dietitian, because food sources of nutrients in such diets are few and other constraints on eating and lifestyles may further limit what is acceptable. For example, it is highly unlikely that most vegan parents could easily plan a sample menu that was adequate in all nutrients for a 13-year-old with very high needs. (Exhibit 6-2 provides an example of an acceptable sample menu for such a child.) The dietitian needs to have a detailed knowledge of food sources of nutrients for vegans and the rudiments of vegan diet planning. These are provided in several readily available references.[4,6,16–19] Tables of food composition from Southeast Asia or supplementary tables of food composition from journal articles and publications of the American Dietetic Association or the Seventh Day Adventist Dietetic Association and from manufacturers of soy products and meat

Table 6-8 Food Guide for Vegetarian Children

		Servings per Age		
Food Group	Standard Serving	1– 3 yr	4–6 yr	7–12 yr
Milk and milk products	1 cup	2–3	2–3	3–4
Vegetable protein foods				
Legumes	1 cup	1/4	1/2	1/2
Textured vegetable protein	20–30 gm			
Nuts, seeds	1/2 T	1/4	1/2	3/4
Peanut butter	4T			
Fruits and vegetables				
Total per day	1/2 c cooked 1 cup raw	2–3	3–4	4–5
Green leafy	daily	1	1 or more	1 or more
Ascorbic acid rich	daily	1	1 or more	1 or more
Breads and cereals (whole grain and enriched or fortified)	1 slice	3	3–4	4–5
Other				
Eggs	1	1	1	1
Fats	1 tsp	1–3	2–3	2–3

Source: Vyhmeister I, Register UD, and Sonnenberg LM. Safe vegetarian diets for children. *Pediatr Clin North Am.* 1977;24:203–210.

Exhibit 6-2 Sample Menu of an Adequate Vegan Diet for a 13-Year-Old

Breakfast
Orange, 1 medium
Oatmeal, 3/4 cup
Soymilk, 6 oz
Bread, whole wheat, 1 slice
Jam, 2 tsp

Lunch
Tofu-miso soup with 1 tsp miso, 4 oz tofu
Sandwich of hummus (1 medium pita bread, 2 tsp hummus, 1/2 cup spinach, 2 slices tomato)
Carrot juice, 6 oz
Figs, dried, 3

Dinner
Casserole of beans (3/4 cup brown rice, 1/2 cup navy beans, 1 tsp safflower oil, 1 cup broccoli, 1/2 cup yellow squash, 1/4 cup onion)
Kale, cooked 3/4 cup

Snack
Watermelon, 1 slice
Strawberries, 1 cup
Gorp (1/4 cup almonds, 1/2 oz pumpkin seeds, 1/4 cup sunflower seeds, 1/4 cup raisins)

Source: Jacobs C, and Dwyer J. Vegetarian children: appropriate and inappropriate diets. *Am J Clin Nutr.* 1988;48:811–818.

analogues can also be helpful. Finally, for those who live near there, Seventh-Day Adventist hospitals employ dietitians who are highly knowledgeable about vegetarian eating practices of all sorts, and they are usually willing to share their expertise with other health professionals if asked.

In addition to lack of information about alternative sources of nutrients on vegetarian diets, vegetarian parents' notions about appropriate health care are sometimes out of synchrony with conventional pediatric surveillance schedules. In such situations, it is important to concentrate on the issues relating to food and health that are the most likely to be harmful, and to let other, less pressing issues, even if they are somewhat problematic, alone for the time being. The assistance of a social worker is helpful if problems persist.

In counseling vegetarian patients and clients, patience and forbearance are also in order. Remember that the dietary preferences of clients always deserve first priority in planning. The counseling process with reference to vegetarians is well summarized in a recent article by Johnston.[20]

REFERENCES

1. Eaton SB, Konner M. Paleolithic nutrition: a consideration of its nature and current implications. *New Engl J Med.* 1985;312:283–289.

2. Garn SM, Leonard WR. What did our ancestors eat? *Nutr Rev.* 1989;47:337–345.

3. Scrimshaw NS, Behar M, Wilson D, Viteri F, Arroyave G, Bressani R. All vegetable protein mixtures for human feeding V. Clinical trials with INCAP mixtures 8 and 9 and with corn and beans. *Am J Clin Nutr.* 1961;9:196–205.

4. Truesdell DD, Acosta PB. Feeding the vegan infant and child. *J Am Diet Assoc.* 1985;85:837–840.

5. Jacobs C, Dwyer JT. Vegetarian children: appropriate and inappropriate diets. *Am J Clin Nutr.* 1988;48:811–818.

6. Vyhmeiser IB, Register UD, Sonnenberg IM. Safe vegetarian diets for children. *Pediatr Clin North Am.* 1977;24:203–210.

7. Herbert V. Vitamin B_{12}: plant sources, requirements and assay. *Am J Clin Nutr.* 1988;48:852–858.

8. Dwyer JT. Health aspects of vegetarian diets. *Am J Clin Nutr.* 1988;48:712–738.

9. Specker B, Ellis K, Ho M, et al. Effect of macrobiotic diet on serum 1,25 di hydroxy vitamin D during lactation. *Pediatr Res.* 1986;20(4, part 2):22A. Abstract.

10. Specker BL, Miller D, Norman EJ, Greene H, Hayes KC. Increased urinary methylmalonic acid excretion in breast fed infants of vegetarian mothers and identification of an acceptable dietary source of vitamin B_{12}. *Am J Clin Nutr.* 1988;47:89–92. Abstract.

11. Dagnelie PC, Van Staveren WA, Vergote F, et al. Nutritional status of infants aged 4 to 18 months on macrobiotic diets and matched omnivorous control infants: a population based, mixed longitudinal study. II: Growth and psychomotor development. *Eur J Clin Nutr.* 1989;43:325–338.

12. Dagnelie PC, Van Staveren WA, Verschuren SAJM, Hautvast, JGAJ. Nutritional status of infants aged 4 to 18 months on macrobiotic diets and matched omnivorous control infants: a population

based, mixed longitudinal study. 1: Weaning pattern, energy, and nutrient intake. *Eur J Clin Nutr.* 1989;43:311–324.

13. Institute of Medicine, National Academy of Sciences, Committee on Diet and Health. *Diet and Health: Implications for Reducing Chronic Disease Risk.* Washington, DC: National Academy Press; 1989.

14. Institute of Medicine, National Academy of Sciences, Committee on Dietary Allowances, Food and Nutrition Board. *National Research Council Recommended Dietary Allowances.* 10th ed. Washington, DC: National Academy Press; 1989.

15. Fanelli MT, Kuczmarski R. Guidelines for lacto-ovo-vegetarian and vegan diets. In : Anderson JB, ed. *Nutrition and Vegetarianism: Proceedings of Public Health Nutrition Update.* Chapel Hill, NC: Health Sciences Corsortium; 1982:199–206.

16. Acosta, PB. Availability of essential amino acids and nitrogen in vegan diets. *Am J Clin Nutr.* 1988;48(suppl. 3):868–874.

17. Truesdell DD, Whitney EN, Acosta PB. Nutrients in vegetarian foods. *J Am Diet Assoc.* 1984;84:28–35.

18. Sonnenberg L, Zolber K, Register UD. *The Vegetarian Diet: Food for Us All Study Kit.* Chicago, Ill: American Dietetic Association; 1981.

19. American Dietetic Association. Position of the American Dietetic Association: vegetarian diets. *J Am Diet Assoc.* 1988;88:351–355.

20. Johnston P. Counseling the pregnant vegetarian. *Am J Clin Nutr.* 1988;48:901–905.

Chapter 7

Sports Nutrition for Children and Adolescents

Nancy L. Nevin-Folino

PHYSICAL ACTIVITY IN YOUTH

Activity should be encouraged for every youth, to initiate lifetime habits of physical exercise.[1–3] This physical involvement could determine the long-term health of the population to come. Benefits directly associated with physical activity include reduced incidence of coronary heart disease and other degenerative diseases, maintenance of desired weight for height, and lessened symptoms of anxiety and depression.[4–6] Exercise also provides children opportunities for developing basic communication skills, and social interaction and improves self-esteem and confidence.[2] Outlined in Table 7-1 are definitions of a variety of different levels of activity for children and adolescents with age recommendations, associated dietary comments, fluid needs, and appropriate health assessments.

Attitudes about physical activity are often patterned by events that happen to children before age 10.[6] Children's health fitness is associated with certain physical behaviors of the children and of their parents.[6]

PHYSIOLOGIC EFFECTS OF EXERCISE

If the child is healthy, follows recommended dietary guidelines, is matched to the exercise in maturation skill, and does not abuse the intensity of the sport, then the physiologic benefits of sports activity or training are many.[3,7,8] Goals stated for the 1990 Objectives for Physical Fitness and Exercise for 10- to 17-year-old youth include a health objective that 90% of this age group will participate in physical activities that are appropriate for maintenance of an effective cardiorespiratory system, because of the associated lifelong benefits.[1]

Some of the effects of cardiorespiratory exercise on the child are as follows:[6,9,10]

- improves strength and flexibility
- conditions the cardiorespiratory system

Table 7-1 Exercise Levels with Age, Nutrition, Fluid, and Health Assessment Guidelines*

Definitions	Examples (Not Inclusive)	Recommended Age	Nutrition Comments	Fluid Intake	Recommended Health Assessment
1. ROUTINE: The duration of the activity is less than 20 min, and it may or may not reach 60% of maximum heart beat rate.	Recess play, casual walking, recreational noncontinual sport (i.e., T-ball, volleyball)	Minimum activity level for any age	Normal nutrition for age from the basic food groups	Normal for age	Yearly routine exam from a pediatrician or physician for all age children.
2. HEALTH FITNESS: 60% to 80% of maximum heart beat rate is achieved for greater than 20 min at least three times per week for a minimum of 6 months. The activity should involve muscular strength and flexibility.	Brisk walking, jogging, running, cycling, hiking, swimming, dancing	Preferred level for any age	Normal nutrition for age from the basic food groups. If desired weight for height, possibly more calories.	Good hydration, especially in adverse weather. Normal requirements for age plus replacement of lost fluid from activity.	Yearly routine exam from a pediatrician or physician for all age children. Education from a physician or health professional on healthy practices (diet, fluid, injury prevention, warm-up and cool-down techniques, etc.). Immediate attention from an appropriate health professional for an injury or insult.
3. COMPETITIVE SPORTS: An activity less than or equal to 6 months that consists of team involvement, preseason training, and competing either as a	Swimming, gymnastics, diving, volleyball, wrestling, sprinting,	Junior high age and above	Nutrition assessment, recommendations, and education, preferably from a registered dietitian	Pre-event, event, and post-event (or prepractice and postpractice)	Preparticipation assessment by a health team consisting of a physician, dietitian, nurse or nurse practitioner, and

Classification	Sports	Age	Nutrition	Hydration	Notes
team member or individually at an intramural or interschool level.	relay, football, soccer, basketball, tennis, field hockey, cross country		for an individual's season intake to achieve weight and body composition for the sport. Recommendations will be dependent on type of activity, duration, and intensity.	hydration. Good hydration at other times. Electrolyte replacement may be needed if heavy sweating occurs or in adverse weather conditions.	possibly a physical therapist. Examination as well as education should be given to students at this time. Immediate attention from an appropriate health professional for any injury or insult during the sports season.
3a. Competitive < 6 months: Short Endurance—Intense activity that lasts for 20 min or less.	As above	Junior high age and above	2 g pro/kg for growing athletes 1 g pro/kg for mature athletes		
3b. Competitive <6 months: Long Endurance—Activity, intense or nonintense, that lasts for longer than 20 min.	As above	High school age and above	May need carbohydrate during the event if long in duration (> 4 h). Modified carbohydrate loading (normal diet, intense exercise 7–4 days before, high carbohydrate diet 3–1 days before event) no more than 2–3 times per year.	Electrolyte replacement needs assessed and replacement given if necessary.	

continues

Table 7-1 continued

Definitions	Examples (Not Inclusive)	Recommended Age	Nutrition Comments	Fluid Intake	Recommended Health Assessment
4. COMPETITIVE SPORTS: Longer than 6 months. Same as above Competitive, but usually involved at a personal level other than school.	Same as 3 above, but may include state or national competition	High school age and above	Same as 3 above	Same as 3 above	As above. It is very important that a physician determine that the maturation age of the participant is appropriate for the sport.
4a. Competitive 6 months: Short endurance—Same as above.	As above				
4b. Competitive 6 months: Long endurance—Same as above.	As above				
5. PERFORMING: An activity that requires dedicated practice (several times a week) to perform with a group or individually a routine lasting anywhere from 5 min to 1 h (or longer) in competition or performance.	Ballet, dance, or gymnastics	Junior high age and above as determined by a physician	Nutrition assessment, recommendations, and education provided, preferably by a registered dietitian due to the usually restricted intake to achieve desired weight for performance.	Normal hydration and replacement of lost fluids from practice or performance	Preparticipation assessment by a physician, dietitian, and possibly an orthopedist or physical therapist. Injury attention as in competitive sports.

| 6. MARCHING BAND: Involvement with a band that competes or performs in marching or choreographed performance. Includes preseason training as well as competition or performance. | High school marching or competing bands | Junior high age and above | Nutrition assessment, recommendations, and education, preferably from a registered dietitian in a group setting, or individually if necessary. | As above in 3a, 3b | Same as above in 2 or 3a, 3b. Nutrition attention by a registered dietitian if the participant is less than 85% or greater than 120% of desired weight for height. |
| 7. SEASONAL: Intramural involvement with a team or individual activity not based heavily on winning but just participation. Practice required. May or may not last longer than 20 min three or more times a week, but activity is not sustained longer than 2 or 3 months. | Soccer, softball, swimming lessons | All ages | As in 2 above. | As above in 3a, 3b | Preparticipation assessment by a pediatrician or physician, as in 2 above. Nutrition attention by a registered dietitian if the participant is less than 85% or greater than 120% of desired weight for height. |

*Data from references 6, 7, 9, 12, 16, 18, 20, 21, 29, 32, and 34.

- increases endurance
- develops power, agility, and speed
- aids in development of muscles
- exercises neuromuscular skill
- controls percentage of body fat
- provides mental well-being

To achieve cardiorespiratory effects, the exercise should be at least 20 minutes in duration, use large muscles, produce mild perspiration, and cause the heart to beat at 60% to 80% of maximum rate.[5,10,11] See Table 7-2 for heart beat rates for different ages.

Deleterious consequences of exercise can and should be prevented. Having contact with and assessment from health professionals before exercise or sport involvement is essential.[12–14] For training and participation in competitive sports, determination of the match of maturation age with the sport, injury risk, and general health status should be done preparticipation, by a pediatrician or a physician

Table 7-2 Suggested Training Heart Rates*

Age (yr)	Heart Rate (beats/min)		
	Maximum	80%	60%
5–8	220	176	132
10	210	168	126
11	209	167	125
12	208	166	125
13	207	165	124
14	206	165	123
15	205	164	123
16	204	163	122
17	203	162	122
18	202	162	121

* These numbers are taken from a variety of sources and are suggested guidelines initially developed for training athletes. Individuals will vary. If target heart rate seems too hard to maintain, then accept a lower one, and conversely, if the target rate does not seem high enough to make one perspire, then work harder.

Source: Adapted with permission from Jopling RJ, Health-related fitness as preventative medicine, in *Pediatrics in Review* (1988;10[5]:141–148), copyright © 1988, American Academy of Pediatrics.

knowledgeable about sports medicine.[7,8,12,13] Education on proper training, diet, and injury prevention should also be given prior to participation.[3,12] Coaches and trainers need to be conscious of the health consequences of sports and refer team members who develop risks during the season to the appropriate health professional (physician, dietitian, orthopedist, physical therapist, etc.). See Table 7-1 for preparticipation health assessment recommendations.

NUTRITIONAL CONCERNS

Nutritional needs of youths involved in exercise or sports are for adequate energy supplies that come from a normal recommended dietary intake for age.[3,15] If extra calories are needed, they should come from the four food groups.[3] Fluid needs are normal hydration for age and weight plus extra for training, participation, and cool-down activity.[3] There is no indication that there are increased needs for any other nutrient beyond the Recommended Dietary Allowances (RDAs). A normal diet with appropriate calories will be adequate. Independent and arbitrary use of vitamins and minerals is discouraged in youth. Megadoses of specific nutrients can be deleterious to health and should not be promoted by coaches or professional athletes to school-age sports participants. Guidelines for base calorie needs are outlined in the RDAs[16] (see Chapter 2). The need to increase calorie allotments for an activity will depend on the child's age, sex, present weight, desired weight, particular sport, and level of involvement. There is a lack of information in the literature on actual calorie expenditure for particular activities for children. This is partially due to the many factors that vary with each child. Achieving desired weight and maintaining the weight will be the indicators of adequate calories (see Table 7-3). Percent of fat content of the body should be determined to make sure the participant meets body weight expectations but does not have an excess of fat for body weight.[17] (See Table 7-4 for body fat composition recommendations for sex and sport. Age is not listed for the figures given; therefore, discretion should be used in a final body fat level recommendation.) Instructors and students need guidance in altering weight and body fat composition to ensure safe practices are followed.[17] Frequent monitoring is recommended if weight change is desired to prevent too rapid weight gain or loss.[17,18] Fluid requirements need to be emphasized to the growing athlete so that performance is not compromised by dehydration[19] (see Table 7-5). Table 7-6 compares beverages frequently consumed and available to youths. This chart also includes data on sports nutritional supplements. The need for so much instruction provides an excellent opportunity for the registered dietitian to be involved prior to training season as a consultant to groups sponsoring organized sports or dancing and to the participating youth.[20–25]

Table 7-3 Calorie Requirements*

	Recommended Daily Allowances (calories per pound per day)				Competitive‡			Long Endurance§		
Age	Low Calorie	Median Calorie	High Calorie	Health Fitness†	Weight Loss	Weight Stable	Weight Gain	Weight Loss	Weight Stable	Weight Gain
4–6	30	41	52	+3	—	—	—	—	—	—
7–10	27	39	54	+3	—	+8	+16	—	—	—
Males										
11–14	20	27	37	+2	+2	+7	+12	+19	+24	+29
15–18	14	19	27	+2	+1	+5	+8	+13	+16	+20
Females										
11–14	15	22	30	+2	+0	+5	+10	+14	+19	+24
15–18	10	17	25	+1½	+0	+4	+8	+12	+16	+20

*Note: The amounts listed are given in ranges to account for variability of body build and maturational level within an age group. For additional calorie needs for sports to achieve weight maintenance, add figures listed to the daily calorie needs per pound per day. Weight loss or gain is based on 1–lb change per week, with the object of losing body fat or gaining lean muscle mass. These figures are estimates and may need to be adjusted for the individual. Competitive and long endurance sports are not recommended for 4- to 10- year-olds. (see Table 7-1)

† Based on an average amount of calories expended for four 30-minute periods of exercise per wk.

‡ Based on an average amount of calories expended for six 2-hour practices per week.

§ Based on an average amount of calories expended for seven 3.5-hour practices per week plus three 4-hour competitive events per month.

Table 7-4 Relative Body Fat Values for Males and Females in Various Sports*

Sports	Males fat %	Females fat %
Baseball/softball	12–14	16–26
Basketball	7–10	16–27
Football	8–18	–
Gymnastics	4–6	9–15
Ice hockey	13–15	–
Jockeys	12–15	–
Skiing	7–14	18–20
Soccer	9–12	–
Speed skating	10–12	–
Swimming	5–10	14–26
Track and field		
Sprinters	6–9	8–20
Middle distance runners	6–12	8–16
Distance runners	4–8	6–12
Discus	14–18	16–24
Shot put	14–18	20–30
Jumpers and hurdlers	6–9	8–16
Tennis	14–16	18–22
Volleyball	8–14	15–26
Weightlifting	8–16	–
Wrestling	4–12	–

*The values represent the range of means reported in various published and unpublished studies.

Source: Reprinted with permission of Ross Laboratories, Columbus, OH 43216, from *Report of the Tenth Ross Roundtable on Critical Approaches to Common Pediatric Problems*, p 68, © 1979 Ross Laboratories.

EXERCISE RECOMMENDATIONS IN SPECIFIC GROUPS

Newborns to Age 3

Starting out with a stimulating environment for infant activity sets the stage for regular exercise as the child grows. Unstructured safe play without special exercise equipment can provide all the infant needs for healthy development.[26] Playpens and walkers restrict babies from exploring and from fully using their muscles and are not recommended for play time.

Ages 3 to 8 Years

Exercise interest should be piqued during these years to develop habits of routine participation in enjoyable physical activity.[6] Parental habits will be mimicked,

Table 7-5 Fluid Needs*

Age	Fluid per Day†	Fluid Needs to Replace for Activity	Pre-event	Competitive Event	Post-event	Preferred Fluid for Exercise Hydration	Electrolyte Replacement Above Normal Diet
4–6	26–50 oz	Normal hydrations. Drinking preferred before and after an activity.				Cold water or diluted beverage	Not necessary
7–10	40–56 oz	As above	12–15 oz 2 hours before; 4–8 oz 15 min before	2–4 oz per 15 min	Weight before minus weight after times 16 oz	Cold water or diluted beverage	Not necessary unless long endurance activity or profuse sweating. Individual assessment needs to be done, with salt, potassium and/or chloride to be contained in the diet or a diluted fluid.§
Males 11–15	52–70 oz	As above	15–20 oz 2 hours before; 8–12 oz 15 min before	4 oz per every 15 min	As above	Cold water. Sport beverage if needed for long endurance activity.	As above
16–18	60–80 oz	As above	As above	As above	As above	As above, for males 11–15	
Females 11–15	48–64 oz	As above	As above, males	As above, males	As above, males	As above, males	As above
16–18	52–69 oz	As above	As above, males	As above, males	As above, males	As above, males	

* Guidelines for normal hydration, activity needs, and competitive requirements are given in minimum amounts, and individual needs may vary.
† Data in this column from references 18 and 41.
§ The American College of Sports Medicine recommends 10 mEq sodium and 5 mEq potassium for adults.

Source: Data from references 10, 17, 18, 19, 22, 30, 32, 33, and 42.

Table 7-6 Fluid Comparison

Beverage	Serving Size	Cal	CHO	Na⁺	Minerals mg		Osmolality (mOsm/kg H2O)	Recommended Dilution*
					K^+	Cl^-		
Municipal water	8 oz	0	—	7	1	NA	2	None
Apple juice	8 oz	116	29 g	7	296	NA	718†	1 oz juice, 7 oz water
Kool-aid	8 oz	98	20 g	8	1	NA	243†	1 oz Kool-aid, 7 oz water
Gatorade	8 oz	39	14 g	110	25	NA	NA	1½ oz Gatorade, 6½ oz water
Cola	8 oz	100	27 g	6	0	NA	709†	1 oz cola, 7 oz water
Noncola	8 oz	95	24 g	31	1	NA	691†	1 oz noncola, 7 oz water
Sports beverages								To be used as intended by manufacturer for long endurance events
Exceed Fluid replacement and energy drink Manufacturer: Ross Labs	8 oz	70	17 g	50	45	80	250	None
Exceed Sports nutrition supplement Manufacturer: Ross Labs	8 oz	360	54 g	280 mg	430 mg	NA	650	None
Exceed High-carbohydrate source	16 oz	470	118 g	235 mg	NA	NA	560	None
Pripps Plus Manufacturer: Pripps, Inc.	8 oz	70	17 g	65	19	98	255	None

NA, not available.
* Dilute to provide 2.5 g carbohydrate per 100 ml.
† Measured in the Children's Medical Center Laboratory, Dayton, Ohio, by the Advanced Digimatic Osmomter, model 3DII Freezing Point.

Source: Data from reference 43 and product label information.

so ideally the entire family should be committed to physical activity.[6,11] Group as well as unorganized play also fosters normal physical and social development of children.[2,3] At this age it is vital that the activities offered focus on participation and not the end-all goal of winning.[2] Caution should be used so that organized sports at this age are for the children, not extended zealousness of the parents.

Ages 8 to 12 Years

The foundations of health and a lifelong pattern of regular exercise of the cardiorespiratory system need to be established at this formative age.[11] Fitness programs should consist of exercise that can be carried into adulthood.[6] Whether it be casual unorganized activity, school-sponsored competitive sport, or community programs, school-age children from third grade to sixth grade should be encouraged to participate.[10] School-age children accrue the same psychosocial and physical benefits of sports that younger children do.

If a child is considering serious sports involvement and/or competition, his or her maturation level should be determined by a physician.[7,8,12,13] The vast range of pubertal development is remarkable at this age, and the early maturer will excel in a sport because of his or her maturity-associated skill and muscular level. This advantage does not always continue as the child gets older.[8] Matching an early maturer with a late maturer could cause the latter to lose interest in sports permanently.[3]

Ages 13 to 18 Years

At this age physical activity should be incorporated into the lifestyle to yield enjoyment either from participation or accomplishments in a sport. This pleasure will be the motivating force in a child's continued participation in exercise.[27] Exercise should be a year-round activity, not just a sports season one. Problems with this may be encountered in the many children of this age who are immersed in competitive sports or performing arts, to the exclusion of other interests. These children should be helped to develop other, complementary interests, so that sports or dance is not the only arena for not only exercise but also social interaction.

Eating habits of teens usually consist of meal-skipping or erratic eating, snacking, reliance on fast foods, and often unfounded rituals (see Chapter 5). It is important that normal nutrition education be given and emphasized with this group, either in school classes or in conjunction with a sport.[2,21] Often students are willing to change their eating behaviors for the outcome of better performance and appearance.[28]

Competitive or Performing Sports

Many of today's youth are getting involved with competitive sports, dance, or gymnastics, often at the grade-school age. It is important to provide them assessment by appropriate health care professionals.[3,12–14] One efficient way to accomplish this is to assess all the aspiring competitors at once, setting up in some suitably large room stations for each type of assessment needed and staffing them with the appropriate professionals. Table 7-1 gives recommendations for the type of health professional that should be included in check-ups for various types of activities. The diet of a participant often gives medical information as well as predicting health status and potential, so a registered dietitian should be included in the assessment team. Exhibit 7-1 shows a sample preparticipation nutrition assessment form, which could be completed by the participant prior to the check-up session so that individual instruction would be possible during the session.

Adequate nutrition is of major importance for the budding athlete, and education on nutrition needs and safe nutrition practices should begin early.[27,29] The registered dietitian is the appropriate person to instruct coaches, dance teachers, parents, and students on normal diet needs for age, healthful diet practices for competition, and normal body changes, if necessary. This should help to combat the food fads and quackery often practiced by school-age athletes. Measuring body fat or composition is best performed by registered dietitians, who can obtain accurate results by virtue of their extensive training. Skinfold measurements, mid-arm circumference measurements, or body mass index should be used to assess body fat.[17,30] (See Chapters 1 and 2 for additional information). Calcium and iron nutriture should definitely be checked in all females participating and males of low socioeconomic status because of frequent deficiencies in these groups.[14,31] Protein for a young growing athlete should be at least 2 g/kg of body weight.[32] This can easily be met in the normal diet that contains milk products and meat/protein servings.

Carbohydrate loading is only effective for long endurance events. The complete 7-day ritual is definitely not recommended for prepubescent athletes.[18,33] A modified form using physical exertion on days 7 through 4 prior to the event with a normal diet and then a high-carbohydrate diet (350 to 500 g/d) for days 3 through 1 with little to no activity may be used by postpubertal youth. This will provide some of the benefits of full carbohydrate loading without the detrimental side effects.[15,24] Modified loading should only be used for long endurance events two to three times a year.[29,33]

Electrolyte losses in sweat can be easily recovered in a postevent meal.[30] If a participant sweats profusely, is involved with a very long endurance event, or participates in adverse weather, individual assessment for electrolyte replacement is recommended.

Exhibit 7-1 Preparticipation Nutrition Assessment Questionnaire Form

1. Have you ever been on a diet before? _____ If yes, why and for how long? _____

   Has anyone in your immediate family ever been on a diet for (circle appropriate answer/s)

   Blood Pressure   Cholesterol   Diabetes   If so, who?_____

2. Do you take a vitamin/mineral supplement? If yes, what and how often? _____

3. Have you ever tried to (circle the appropriate answer) gain or lose weight before? If yes,

   how much? _____ lbs

---

1. Do you drink milk?   Yes   No   If yes, how often (circle appropriate answer)

   4 glasses/day   1–3 glasses/day   4–6 glasses/week   1–3 glasses/week

2. Do you eat (circle foods eaten) cheese, yogurt, or cottage cheese? How often?

   1 or more times/day   4–6 times/week   1–3 times/week

3. Do you eat meat or protein foods?   Yes   No   How often?

   2 or more times/day   1 time/day   4–6 times/week   1–3 times/week

   List the types of meat or protein foods you eat:_____

4. Do you eat vegetables?   Yes   No   How often?

   2 or more times/day   1 time/day   4–6 times/week   1–3 times/week

   List the types of vegetables you eat: _____

5. Do you eat fruits or drink 100% fruit juice?   Yes   No   How often?

   2 or more times/day   1 time/day   4–6 times/week   1–3 times/week

   List the types of fruits you eat or juice you drink: _____

6. Do you eat (circle foods eaten) bread, cereal, pasta, potatoes, or crackers? How often? (total

   for foods circled)

   6 or more times/day   1–4 times/day   4–6 times/week   1–3 times/week

7. Do you drink water? Yes No   How many glasses per day? _____Size glass? _____

8. Check the foods or beverages you eat or drink and fill in how often in the space provided.

   __ Chips ____   __ Diet pop _____   __ Candy _____

   __ Pop ____   __ Cakes, pies _____   __ Cookies _____

---

1. Are you satisfied with your current weight? Yes No   If no, what would you like to

   weigh? _____ lbs

2. Are you satisfied with your present body composition?   Yes   No   If no, how

   would you like to change it?_____

3. Have you ever not eaten or drunk anything for up to a day before weigh in to make weight?

   Yes   No   If yes, how often?_____

Exhibit 7-1 continued

4. Do you ever get so hungry that you eat two to five times more than you usually do and then
   regret it?   Yes   No   If yes, have you ever not eaten the next day or taken laxatives
   because you felt guilty or did not want to gain weight? _____

Dietitian's Information

Student's: Name _____   Age _____Sex _____ Intended sport _____

Height: _____ %tile _____ Weight: _____ %tile _____ Comments: _____

If indicated: Hct/Hgb _____ Cholesterol _____Blood Pressure _____/_____ Other _____

% Desired weight for height _____% % Fat _____% Means of measurement _____

Weight change needed _____ % Body fat change needed _____

Calorie level _____/day ± _____ Milk Products ± _____ Meat/protein servings

Recommended fluid amounts _____ oz.   ± _____ Fruit/vegetable   ± _____ Grain group

Exercise time/day needed for weight change _____

Other diet needs: _____

Comments: _____

Recommended body measurement: _____   How often? _____

Often parents or trainers need information about pre-event meals. Meals should be timed to occur 3 to 4 hours before the event. Easily digested food high in carbohydrate but low in protein and fat can be eaten. Adequate fluid should be provided, as suggested in Table 7-5. If scheduling of events precludes time for a meal, or nervousness makes eating unpleasant, a liquid medical supplement may be used.[19,29] Table 7-6 gives an example of sports nutrition supplements, or products like Ensure (Ross Laboratories) or Sustacal (Mead Johnson) may be used. Both of the latter supplements can be purchased at drug or grocery stores.

Female athletes may need individual counseling because of their tendency to restrict caloric intakes.[20,34] Poor nutrition could affect their performance and their iron and calcium nutriture, as mentioned before.[35] A very low body fat status may interfere with normal menstrual cycles.[3] Amenorrhea needs to be assessed by a physician to determine its cause.[23]

It is beyond the scope of this chapter to provide nutrition guidance for those who have chosen to dedicate their time to long endurance or in-depth training for competition at a national or worldwide level. These children need instruction on physical conditioning, nutrition, and training practices similar to what is given to college-age or adult athletes.

Obese Children

Calorie intake of this group is not significantly different from that of normal-weight children, but their activity level is very low. Obese children should be encouraged to participate in any form of physical activity.[36] Most often, the obese child comes from a family with obese adults who engage in little activity themselves, so recommendations for family activity would be helpful for all. With its incidence rising for school-age children, all health professionals seeing school-age children should address the obesity problem.[37] Exercise should be included in any treatment plan.[32] Physical activity can serve as a cure for boredom and slowed metabolism and improve feelings of self-esteem and accomplishment, as it does for other children.[37] Exercise for obese children needs to be cardiorespiratory in nature as well as calorie burning. This can be accomplished by walking or biking three to five times a week for 30 minutes or longer. If the child is morbidly obese, approval from a physician is warranted.

Handicapped Children

For the child with a developmental disorder resulting in a physical handicap, physical activity at whatever level possible should be encouraged, to help the child develop self-esteem as well as obtain the benefits of exercise. Regular physical exercise will also combat the obesity that often comes in later years for these children. The handicapped child should be prescribed an appropriate physical activity that can be carried out at accessible facilities with professional guidance.

RECOGNITION AND TREATMENT OF NUTRITION DISORDERS RELATED TO SPORTS

The identification of eating disorders manifesting themselves in relation to sports involvement is a responsibility of all professionals involved with sports programs.[33] Preparticipation assessments may single out some students who have eating disorder symptoms or who are at risk for them because of bizarre eating rituals. In students with anorexia nervosa or bulimia nervosa, it is difficult to tell which came first, the eating disorder or the compulsive involvement in physical activity. Anyone noticed to have problems associated with food control should be referred to an appropriate professional.[38] Some of the unhealthful practices associated with efforts to influence weight and body composition changes can be eliminated if a protocol for safe body changes is established by a registered dietitian at the beginning of the weight training season, with an appropriate time frame to achieve the changes.[21,23,32]

Drugs abused by athletes range from steroids and amphetamines to street drugs. These drugs have detrimental health effects on the adolescent athlete, particularly steroids, whose use is condemned by the American Academy of Pediatrics.[39,40] The physician screening athletes as well as the coach should be asking in depth about drug usage. Giving preventive education at early ages and imposing severe consequences upon users can work to alleviate this problem. As with eating disorders, referral to appropriate professionals is required.

The use among school-age children of high intakes of caffeine prior to sports events, to hype up the body, is to be discouraged because of its side effects and the illegality of the practice in international competition.[22] Caffeine is widely available, and coaches or sponsors may not be aware of this abuse. The sports participant should be educated about caffeine's effects and the dangers or side effects of high doses.[22]

EXERCISE PROGRAM RECOMMENDATIONS

All sectors of society should be involved in exercise the year round.[6] Efforts should be made to provide education opportunities to the public through either the school systems or community resources about exercise safety, nutrition requirements, and the importance of achieving cardiorespiratory benefits.

REFERENCES

1. Powell KE, Spain KG, et al. The status of the 1990 objectives for physical fitness and exercise. *Public Health Rep.* 1986;101:15–21.

2. Shaffer TE. The physician and sports medicine. In: *Sports Medicine for Children and Youth. Report of the Tenth Ross Roundtable on Critical Approaches to Common Pediatric Problems.* Columbus, Ohio: Ross Laboratories; 1979.

3. Smith NJ. Some health care needs of the young athletes. *Adv Pediatr.* 1981;28:187–228.

4. Caspersen CJ, Christenson GM, Pollard RA. Status of the 1990 physical fitness and exercise objectives—evidence from NHIS 1985. *Public Health Rep.* 1986;101:587–592.

5. Jopling RJ. Health-related fitness as preventative medicine. *Pediatr Rev.* 1988;10:141–148.

6. Ross JG, Gilbert GG. A summary of findings. (The National Children and Youth Fitness Study). *J Phys Educ Recreation Dance.* 1985;56:1–48.

7. Rogoi AD. Effects of endurance training on maturation. *Consultant.* 1985;25:68–83.

8. Rarick GL. The significance of normal patterns of behavior and motor development as important determinants of participation in sports programs. In: *Sports Medicine for Children and Youth, Report of the Tenth Ross Roundtable on Critical Approaches to Common Pediatric Problems.* Columbus, Ohio: Ross Laboratories; 1979.

9. Birrer RB, Levine R. Performance parameters in children and adolescent athletes. *Sports Med.* 1987;4:211–227.

10. Mckeag DB. Adolescents and exercise. *J Adolesc Health Care.* 1986;7:121S–129S.

11. Sady SP. Cardiorespiratory exercise training in children. *Clin Sports Med.* 1986;5:493–514.

12. Goldberg B, Saraniti A, Witman P, Gavin M, Nicholas JA. Pre-participation sports assessment—an objective evaluation. *Pediatrics.* 1980;66:736–745.

13. Blum RW. Preparticipation evaluation of the adolescent athlete. *Adolesc Athlete.* 1985;78:52–69.

14. Garrick JG, Smith NJ. Pre-participation sports assessment. *Pediatrics.* 1980;66:803–806.

15. Vitale JJ. Nutrition in sports medicine. *Clinic Orthop.* 1985;198:158–168.

16. Food and Nutrition Board. Recommended Dietary Allowances. 9th ed. Washington, DC: National Academy of Sciences; 1980.

17. Smith NJ. Nutrition and athletic performance. *Med Times.* 1981;109:92–107.

18. Ziegler MM. Nutritional care of the pediatric athlete. *Sports Med.* 1982;1:371–381.

19. Hecker AL. Nutritional conditioning for athletic competition. *Clin Sports Med.* 1984;3:567–582.

20. Benson J, Gillien DM, Bourdet K, Luosli AR. Inadequate nutrition and chronic calorie restriction in adolescent ballerinas. *Phys Sports Med.* 1985;13:79–90.

21. Harvey JS. Nutritional management of the adolescent athlete. *Clin Sports Med.* 1984;3:671–678.

22. O'Neil FT, Hynak-Hankinson MT, Gorman J. Research and application of current topics in sports nutrition. *Am Diet Assoc.* 1986;86:1007–1015.

23. Calabrese LH. Nutritional and medical aspects of gymnastics. *Clin Sports Med.* 1985;4:23–30.

24. Masland RP. The adolescent. *J Adolesc Health Care.* 1983;3:237–240.

25. Parr RB, Porter MA, Hodgeson SC. Nutrition knowledge and practice of coaches, trainers and athletes. *Phys Sports Med.* 1984;12:127–138.

26. Committee on Sports Medicine 1986–1988. Infant exercise programs. *Pediatrics.* Vol 82 No. 5 November. 1988.

27. Douglas PD, Douglas JG. Nutrition knowledge and food practices of high school athletes. *J Am Diet Assoc.* 1984;84:1198–1202.

28. Lewis M, Brun J, Talmage H, Rashev S. Teenagers and food choices: the impact of nutrition education. *J Nutr Educ.* 1988;20:336–340.

29. Smith NJ. Nutrition and the young athlete. *Pediatr Ann.* 1978;7:49–63.

30. Manjarrez C, Birrer R. Nutrition and athletic performance. *Am Fam Phys.* 1983;28:105–115.

31. Benson JE, Geiger CJ, Eiserman PA, Wardlaw GM. Relationship between nutrient intake, body mass index, menstrual function, and ballet injury. *J Am Diet Assoc.* 1989;89:58–63.

32. Marino DD, King JC. Nutritional concerns during adolescence. *Pediatr Clin North Am.* 1980;27:125–139.

33. Cheung S. Issues in nutrition for the school-age athlete. *J School Health.* 1985;55:35–37.

34. Benardot D, Schwarz M, Heller DW. Nutrient intake in young, highly competitive gymnasts. *J Am Diet Assoc.* 1989;89:401–403.

35. Teitz CC. Sports medicine concerns in dance and gymnastics. *Pediatr Clin North Am.* 1982;29:1399–1421.

36. Huttunen NP, Knip M, Paavilainen T. Physical activity in obese children. *Int J Obesity.* 1986;10:519–525.

37. International Food Information Council. Food Insight. The Fight for Fit and Trim Kids. Washington, DC: International Food Information Council; 1989.

38. Marston AR, Jacobs DF, Singer RD, Widaman KE, Little TD. Characteristics of adolescents at risk for compulsive overeating on a brief screening test. *Adolescence.* 1988;23:59–65.

39. Committee on Sports Medicine 1986–1988. Anabolic steroids and the adolescent athlete. *Pediatrics.* 1989;83:127–128.

40. Duda M. Steroid use in high-school athletes. *Physician Sports Med.* 1988;16:16–17.

41. Nelson WE, Behrman RE, Vaughan VC. *Nelson Textbook of Pediatrics.* 13th ed. Philadelphia, Pa: WB Saunders; 1987:200.

42. Narins DM, Belkengren RP, Sapala S. Nutrition and the growing athlete. *Pediatr Nurs.* 1983;9:163–168.

43. Pennington JAT. *Bowes and Church Food Values of Portions Commonly Used.* 15th ed. Philadelphia, Pa: JB Lippincott, 1989.

SUGGESTED READINGS

National Dairy Council. *Food Power, a Coach's Guide to Improving Performance.* Rosemont, Ill: National Dairy Council.

National Dairy Council. *You, a Guide to Food, Exercise, and Nutrition.* Rosemont, Ill: National Dairy Council.

Smith NJ, Worthington-Roberts B. *Food for Sport.* Palo Alto, Calif: Bull Publishing, 1989.

Chapter 8

Food Hypersensitivities

Victoria L. Olejer

Traditionally, physicians and dietitians practicing in the area of adverse reactions to foods have been plagued by a host of perplexing problems capable of discouraging all but the most tenacious of clinicians. They include but are not limited to (1) a confusing set of terms used to describe the many categories of adverse food reactions, (2) an extensive differential diagnosis of food-related illnesses, (3) a general lack of definitive diagnostic procedures, and (4) few satisfactory prophylactic or treatment options.[1] Significant efforts have been made in recent years to address each of these issues, with varying success. In accordance with joint efforts of the American Academy of Allergy and Immunology and the National Institute of Allergy and Infectious Diseases to standardize the terminology used to classify adverse food reactions[1] the definitions introduced in Table 8-1 have been adopted in this text.

The terms "adverse food reaction" and "food sensitivity" may be used synonymously to describe any clinically abnormal response related to the ingestion of a food or food additive. In like manner, the terms "food hypersensitivity" and "food allergy" may be used interchangeably to more specifically indicate that an altered immune response is at the root of the reaction. Both food intolerance and food hypersensitivity reactions exist as subsets under the broader heading of adverse food reactions; these terms are reserved for reactions whose causative mechanisms have been identified. Care should therefore be exercised when describing these reactions, to avoid prematurely labeling an adverse food reaction before the underlying mechanism has been determined.

Due to the enormity of the task, little is known of the overall incidence of adverse food reactions in the general population. The incidence of food intolerance is believed to far outweigh that of true allergy, but proof of this awaits confirmation. Instead, attention has focused on the prevalence of food allergy in the general pediatric population, with particular emphasis on the incidence of cow's milk al-

Table 8-1 Categories of Adverse Food Reactions

Term	Definition
Adverse food reaction (food sensitivity)	General term applied to any clinically abnormal response resulting from ingestion of food/food additive. Term of choice when underlying causative mechanism(s) is unknown.
Food hypersensitivity (food allergy)	Immunologic hypersensitivity reaction resulting from ingestion of food/food additive.
Food intolerance	General term applied to any abnormal physiologic response resulting from ingestion of food/food additive that is proven not to be immunologically mediated.
Food toxicity (poisoning)	Adverse effect resulting from direct action of food/food additive on host recipient. May involve nonimmune release of chemical mediators. Toxins may be contained in food or released into food by microorganisms present in food.
Food idiosyncrasy	Quantitatively abnormal response to food/food additive. Includes reactions occurring in specific groups of individuals who may be genetically predisposed. May resemble hypersensitivity reaction but does not involve immune mechanisms.
Metabolic food reaction	Result of food/food additive on metabolism of host recipient. Majority of reactions caused by ingestion of average amounts of usually safe food/food additives by individuals who are susceptible because of medications taken, concurrent disease states, malnutrition, inborn errors of metabolism, etc.
Pharmacologic food reaction	Result of naturally occurring or added chemicals that produce a druglike effect in host.

Source: Reprinted from *Adverse Reactions to Foods* (pp 4–6) by JA Anderson and DD Sogn (eds), American Academy of Allergy and Immunology Committee on Adverse Reactions to Foods and National Institutes of Allergies and Infectious Diseases, USDHHS Pub No 84-2442.

lergy (CMA). Based on studies in the United States, Canada, Great Britain, and the Scandinavian countries, the estimated incidence of CMA is thought to fall in the range of 0.3 % to 7.5%, with the incidence decreasing with increasing age.[2–9] Not surprisingly, the incidence for CMA is much higher in allergic children, approaching, for example, 30% to 59% in children with atopic dermatitis referred to tertiary health care centers.[10–12] Allergy to hen's egg is estimated to occur in approximately 0.5% of the general pediatric population, increasing to approximately 5% in atopic children.[13]

In an impressive effort to examine the incidence of adverse food reactions in a normal pediatric population, 480 previously unselected, consecutively born infants were followed prospectively from birth to age 3 years.[14] Of the 133/480 (28%) children suspected by either parents or physicians of experiencing adverse food reactions, only 8% could be confirmed by elimination and oral provocative food challenge, pointing to the relatively high frequency with which foods are thought to result in symptoms in this age group. More conservative estimates place the incidence of adverse food reactions between 4% and 6% in infants and 1% and 2% in children.[15]

While experts disagree concerning the exact incidence of adverse food reactions in general and food allergies in particular, few contest the difficulty of diagnosing and managing these maladies. Until accurate laboratory tests possessing reliable clinical correlations are developed, clinicians must continue to rely upon repeated trials of elimination and challenge, with the obvious exception of systemic anaphylaxis, to substantiate the removal of individual foods from the diet.

Clinical expression of food allergy is typically the end result of a series of poorly defined interactions between ingested food antigens, the digestive tract, tissue mast cells and circulating basophils, and food-antigen-specific IgE.[2] While considerable research has been directed toward identifying contributing factors, the exact mechanisms responsible for these complex interactions continue to remain locked away in both the intricacies of the immune system and the complexities of the food antigens themselves.

The diagnostic process in food allergy, regardless of the age of the patient, always begins with a careful medical history and physical exam, aimed, first, at removing from consideration serious medical conditions or disease processes that may mimic a food allergy and, second, at distinguishing immunologically mediated reactions (i.e., food allergy or food hypersensitivity) from nonimmunologically mediated reactions (i.e., food intolerance). Due to the vast number of clinical settings in which a food allergy may initially appear suspect, utilizing a pertinent differential diagnosis to systematically rule out situations and conditions that may mimic an altered immune response to an ingested food is essential in arriving at a correct and timely diagnosis. Table 8-2 lists various compounds capable of causing an adverse reaction that are added to foods/drugs during their processing to achieve a desired effect or are present either as naturally occurring constituents or unintentional contaminants. Also listed are disease states or conditions whose early symptoms may suggest the presence of a food allergy. The reader is referred elsewhere for detailed descriptions of differential diagnoses.[16–18]

When possible, detailed information should be obtained from the primary caregiver(s), which may include grandparents, aunts, older siblings, etc., including (1) a description of symptoms, including the time of onset following ingestion and the duration; (2) the quantity of food required to elicit symptoms; (3) the form of the food or method of preparation most often associated with symptoms; (4) the number of times the reaction has been observed to occur, including the date of the most recent reaction; (5) the complexity of the diet with respect to individual food patterns; and (6) medications taken on a daily basis or to relieve symptoms. Despite the critical nature of this information in designing both the elimination and

Table 8-2 Differential Diagnosis for Adverse Food Reactions

I. Food additives
    A. Food colors
        1. Synthetic food colors
            a. Azo dyes: F.D.&C. yellow no. 5 (tartrazine), F.D.&C. yellow no. 6 (sunset yellow), etc.
            b. Non-azo dyes: F.D.&C. blue no. 1 (brilliant blue), F.D.&C. red no. 3 (erythrosine), etc.
        2. Naturally occurring food colors: grape skin color extract, caramel coloring, annotto, etc.
    B. Preservatives
        1. Sulfiting agents
        2. Parabens: benzoic acid, sodium benzoate
        3. Nitrate/nitrite
        4. BHA/BHT
    C. Flavor enhancers: L-Monosodium glutamate (MSG)
    D. Sweeteners
        1. Aspartame
        2. Sorbitol
        3. Sucrose
    E. Miscellaneous
        1. Salicylates
II. Unintentional food contaminants
    A. Plant toxins
        1. Cyanogenic compounds (glycosides)
        2. Oxalates
        3. Solanine alkaloids
        4. Goitrogenic compounds
        5. Psychotropic compounds: wild mushrooms, etc.
        6. Antimetabolites
    B. Animal toxins
        1. Scromboid poisoning
        2. Ciguatera poisoning
        3. Saxitoxin
    C. Microbial toxins
        1. Bacterial: *Staphylococcus aureus*, *Clostridium botulinum*, etc.
        2. Fungal (mycotoxins): aflatoxins, ergot, etc.
        3. Algal (dinoflagellates): ciguatoxin, saxitoxin, etc.
    D. Food-born infectious agents
        1. Bacterial: salmonellosis, *Campylobacter jejuni*, *Clostridium perfringens*, etc.
        2. Parasitics: *Giardia lambia*, *Trichinella spiralis*, flukes, etc.
        3. Viral: hepatitis, poliomyelitis, etc.
    E. Mold/fungal fragments/spores
    F. Insect/rodent parts/excrement
    G. Antibiotics: penicillin, etc.
    H. Pesticides
    I. Heavy metals

continues

Table 8-2 continued

III. Naturally occurring pharmacologic agents
   A. Methyl xanthines: caffeine, theobromine, theophylline
   B. Biologically active amines
      1. Psychoactive (neural transmitters): dopamine, norepinephrine
      2. Vasoactive amines (pressor amines): tyramine, isoamylamine, phenylethylamine, serotonin (5-hydroxytryptamine), histamine
   C. Hallucinogenic alkaloids: wild mushrooms, nutmeg, etc.
IV. Gastrointestinal diseases
   A. Structural abnormalities
      1. Gastroesophageal reflux
      2. Hiatal hernia
      3. Pyloric stenosis
      4. Intestinal obstruction
   B. Carbohydrate intolerance
      1. Primary ontogenetic lactase deficiency
      2. Congenital carbohydrate deficiency: lactase, sucrase-isomaltase
      3. Glucose-galactose malabsorption
      4. Acquired carbohydrate intolerance: lactase, sucrase-isomaltase
   C. Malignancy
   D. Other conditions
      1. Gastroenteritis
      2. Gastric/duodenal ulcer disease
      3. Cholelithiasis
      4. Diverticulitis
      5. Irritable bowel syndrome
      6. Inflammatory bowel disease
      7. Gluten-sensitive enteropathy
      8. Vascular insufficiency
      9. Mucosal damage secondary to drug therapy
V. Other conditions
   A. Malnutrition
   B. Inappropriate vitamin dosing
   C. Endocrine disorders
   D. Gustatory rhinitis
   E. Cystic fibrosis
   F. Psychopathology
      1. Somatization disorder
      2. Hypochondriasis
      3. Eating disorders
   G. Primary immunodeficiency
   H. Collagen vascular disease

challenge schemes, the reader is cautioned regarding the notoriously poor predictive capacity of the clinical history in diagnosing food allergy. Reports of even relatively recent and convincing adverse reactions following the consumption of specific foods are confirmed in less than half of the cases.[19–22]

The physical exam should be directed toward identifying objective signs that support the description of symptoms, particularly as they apply to the gastrointestinal, cutaneous, and respiratory systems. The sheer diversity of signs and symptoms attributed to adverse food reactions in general and to CMA in particular is quite impressive. Table 8-3 lists symptoms of CMA confirmed by double-blind, placebo-controlled food challenges. Any history of rapidly worsening serial reactions or life-threatening reactions to foods involving angioedema, laryngeal edema, wheezing, or hypotension should be duly noted in the medical record. These families should additionally be instructed in the proper procedures to be taken in an emergency.

Epicutaneous skin testing (i.e., prick, puncture, scratch) remains the most accessible diagnostic tool for evaluating the presence of food-specific IgE despite the lack of standardized commercially available food extracts. The popularity and utility of the use of skin testing as an aid in identifying potentially sensitizing foods rests largely in the strength of its negative predictive indexes.[23-25] Nonetheless, negative skin test results do not rule out the presence of an IgE-mediated food reaction.[25] Likewise, positive skin test results do not confirm the presence of a clinically relevant allergic response to the food in question[25] but merely provide a basis for additional investigation. Intradermal skin testing, as compared to epicutaneous skin testing, does not improve on the sensitivity of the test procedure, results in a higher frequency of false-positives, and risks the occurrence of systemic anaphylaxis in exquisitely sensitive individuals.[23] Radioallergosorbent tests (RAST) utilizing a patient's serum also do not add to the predictive accuracy of the test, contribute substantially to the cost, and are best reserved for the occa-

---

Table 8-3 Clinical Manifestations of Food Hypersensitivities Documented by Double-Blind Food Challenge

Organ System	Symptoms
Cardiovascular	Arrhythmia, tachycardia, hypotension, anaphylactic shock
Dermatologic	Pruritis, erythema, edema, urticaria, angioedema, atopic dermatitis, contact dermatitis
Gastrointestinal	Oral and pharyngeal pruritis, nausea, vomiting, diarrhea, distention, flatus, abdominal pain, colic, colitis, malabsorption, eosinophilic gastroenteritis, protein-losing enteropathy, iron deficiency anemia associated with occult fecal blood loss
Respiratory	Conjunctivitis, occular injection, rhinorrhea, nasal congestion, postnasal drip, cough, wheeze, Heiner's syndrome
Miscellaneous	Migraine, systemic anaphylaxis

sional patient with pronounced dermatographism, extensive eczematous or urticarial skin lesions, or a history of suspected or confirmed anaphylaxis to foods.[15]

As a convenient starting place in the absence of identified food-specific IgE, elimination diets have traditionally eliminated foods or families of foods that have repeatedly been observed to produce adverse reactions in sensitized individuals. In infants, cow's milk, soy, and wheat immediately come to mind due to their high level of allergenicity and frequent presence in infants' diets in the form of proprietary formulas and teething aids. Potato, English/green peas, string/green beans, sweet potato, apple, banana, peach, beef, pork, chicken, and rice are less frequently implicated in this age group but can also be troublesome due to the frequency with which they appear in infant diets. Clinically relevant sensitivities to such potent food allergens as egg, peanut, the true nuts (almond, pecan, walnut, cashew, etc.), citrus fruits (lemon, lime, orange, grapefruit, tangerine, etc.), cocoa, crustaceans (crab, crayfish, lobster, prawn, shrimp), and the bony fish are not often encountered in the first year of life due to their relative absence from the diet but represent particularly potent allergens for the older child. Indeed, milk, egg, peanut, and soy account for approximately 80% to 90% of the food allergy reactions diagnosed in the first few years of life.[11,13,23,26] There is no universally safe food.

The prospect for widespread cross-reactivity occurring among individual members of the many taxonomic food families represented by foods[27] appears to be less of a reality than originally suspected,[12,28-30] making generalizations regarding their utility in the diagnosis and management of food allergy somewhat questionable. In vitro studies identifying common allergenic determinants among members of individual food families, in particular legumes, the true nuts, bony fish, crustacea, and mollusks, should not automatically be interpreted as reflecting in vivo sensitivity.[30] Food allergy reactions appear to be highly specific, even among members of the same species,[31] despite the fairly common occurrence of in vitro cross-reactivity among foods with a shared taxonomic relationship. While these findings are encouraging, a continued cautious approach with respect to the potential for cross-reactivity (albeit it a rare event) appears prudent and is best assessed on a case-by-case basis employing appropriately administered food challenges to once again substantiate the removal of a food from the diet.

Very helpful in the initial work-up of children with suspected food allergies is the completion of 1- to 2-week baseline diet and symptom diaries. On these diaries, caregivers are instructed to record (1) the times of all feedings/meals/snacks; (2) the amount of formula and/or actual foods consumed; (3) the dosage and types of medications taken, including vitamin and mineral supplements; and (4) a description of symptoms, noting the time of their occurrence, their duration, and their severity. A scoring system may additionally be employed to more objectively grade the severity of reported symptoms. Due to their lack of maturity and poor communication skills, very young children present a more challenging assessment picture than older children and adolescents who are better able to vocalize and communicate pain and discomfort. Clinicians must instead rely on the very visual symptoms of rhinorrhea, nasal congestion, wheezing, coughing, chest congestion, vomiting, diarrhea, constipation, eczema, xerosis, erythema, and scratching as an indicator of pruritis. Subjective complaints of irritability, sleeplessness, etc., often occur with the former symptoms but are more difficult to grade objectively.

By indicating the amounts of formula and/or foods consumed, the diet may be assessed for nutritional adequacy. Many of the signs and symptoms of malnutrition have mistakenly been ascribed to a food allergy. Baseline diet diaries have the added advantage of forcing parents to more carefully examine the diet of their infant or child. These records may provide the practitioner with sufficient information to recommend only minor dietary changes as opposed to complicated elimination regimens. For example, certain foods will occasionally result in symptoms suggestive of food allergy based on an inherent irritant or pharmacologic activity. Prunes, most legumes, and the cruciferous vegetables (i.e., broccoli, cabbage, cauliflower, mustard, turnips, etc.) are notorious for producing gastroenteric complaints. Additionally, infants and small children especially fond of fruit and fruit juices who present with a history of frequent loose stools accompanied by bloating and abdominal pain may be consuming excessive amounts of sorbitol, a naturally occurring sugar alcohol that is poorly absorbed in the intestinal tract of small children. Sorbitol is present in large amounts in pears, in small amounts in apples, and is a frequent ingredient in sugar-free candies and chewing gums.

Methyl xanthines (i.e., caffeine, theobromine, theophylline) present in coffee, cocoa, colas, tea, and many soft drinks can result in nervousness, excitability, tremor, tachycardia, insomnia, abdominal pain, diarrhea, and nausea when consumed in excessive amounts.[17] It is not unusual for older infants and small children to consume pharmacologic amounts of these compounds in the form of iced tea and carbonated beverages given even in the form of frequent sips of a parent's or older sibling's drink.

Lactose intolerance presents a clinical picture amazingly similar to CMA and may, in fact, occur as a complication of CMA. As with other disaccharidase deficiencies, if disaccharide hydrolysis at the small bowel mucosal brush border is deficient or absent, the sugar accumulates in the distal ileum and colon where it is fermented by bacteria into organic acids, carbon dioxide, and hydrogen gas. The excess intraluminal sugar and organic acids osmotically draw water into the lumen, resulting in watery, frothy stools of low pH (pH less than 6.0) that contain excess sugar and tend to excoriate the buttocks. Bloating, flatulence, abdominal cramping, and borborygmi are often present, but steatorrhea is rare.[32] The presence of reducing substances in the stool (1+ or greater following Clinitest examination) distinguishes lactose intolerance from other disaccharidase deficiencies.

Infants with the rare congenital form of the deficiency become symptomatic following the first lactose-containing feeding, while the majority of the world's population present with the acquired form of the deficiency in increasing numbers following the ages of 3–5 years.[33] It has been estimated that approximately 80% of all black and Asian peoples and 5% to 20% of North American whites are deficient in lactase.[33] Lactose intolerance may additionally occur secondarily as a result of damage to the lining of the small bowel mucosa, irrespective of the cause. Secondary lactose intolerance may be transient or permanent, depending on the degree of damage inflicted on the bowel. In both the acquired and the secondary forms of the deficiency, gas production rather than diarrhea appears to be the most common manifestation, resulting in complaints of recurrent, vague, crampy abdominal pain.[32] Treatment consists of removal of all lactose-containing foods and drugs from the diet. Over-the-counter replacement enzymes are readily available and may be added directly to fluid milk or taken in pill form or chewable tablet with a meal. Considerable variation exists in patient-to-patient ability to tolerate small amounts of lactose in all but those with the congenital form of the deficiency.

Occasionally parents will innocently assert that their infant is consuming no other food by mouth but breast milk or formula. Following careful questioning, though, mention will be made that in addition to the breast milk or formula, the infant is also receiving small amounts of numerous other foods, usually in the form of small handouts or snacks, particularly if multiple caregivers are involved. Even small amounts of such complex food mixtures as cookies, ice cream, or macaroni and cheese may be sufficient to sensitize susceptible infants.

If sufficient information exists in the medical/dietary history to justify the use of an elimination diet, the degree of elimination to be exercised must next be determined. This can vary from the simple elimination of one or two key foods, such as cow's milk or soy in the formula-fed infant, to the complete removal of all native foods through the feeding of a hypoallergenic cow's milk casein hydrolysate-based infant formula or, possibly, in vary rare situations, a chemically defined elemental diet. Important criteria to consider when assessing the necessary degree of elimination include: (1) the child's age, (2) the severity of the child's symptoms, (3) the number of potentially unsafe foods suggested by the medical and dietary histories, (4) the availability of affordable alternative infant formulas and/or foods, and (5) the family's level of commitment and ability to comply to a potentially rigorous elimination diet (a cursory examination of the baseline diet and symptom diaries frequently provides some insight into the latter).

The goal of the elimination diet should be to achieve as asymptomatic a state as possible while also providing optimal nutrition. Gross malnutrition in very young children, often in the form of protein-calorie malnutrition, is not uncommon.[34–36] The length of time required to become symptom-free will vary from child to child depending on the type and severity of symptoms. Ideally, elimination diets should be of sufficient duration to cover the range of variability reported in the baseline symptom diary. Seven to 14 days are generally sufficient, but longer periods may occasionally be required. In highly atopic children, possible coexisting inhalant sensitivities may further complicate the diagnosis.

Infants are quite possibly the most rewarding population of food allergy patients to work with due to the simplicity of their diets and the relative immaturity of their senses of smell and taste. This lack of sophistication permits the clinician to make rather drastic dietary changes with relatively little fuss from the infant. Breast milk remains the ideal feeding choice for infants but is not always a viable alternative and may, indeed, be a source of antigenic stimulation in a subset of infants at high risk for allergies. Such infants include those born with a combination of an elevated level of cord blood IgE,[37–44] a low T cell count,[45–47] and a positive history of allergy in two or more immediate family members (i.e., mother, father, all siblings). High-risk infants are felt to represent an important target population toward which aggressive preventive measures should be directed.

It is well established that exquisitely sensitive, exclusively breastfed infants may become sensitized to foods the mother is consuming and passively transferring to the infant via her breast milk.[48–51] As a result, it may be necessary for mothers of these infants to adhere to individualized elimination diets (with appropriate supplementation) before maximum symptom relief may be achieved in an infant. Low levels of breast milk IgG[52] and IgA[53] in some nursing mothers coupled with the fairly common occurrence in breast milk of prominent food allergens are suspected of playing a permissive role in these infants. Nursing mothers with low or undetectable levels of breast milk IgG and IgA may represent an additional high-risk target group for whom dietary intervention and appropriate environmental manipulation directed at reducing allergen exposure may be especially helpful in preventing or delaying the onset of allergic disease in their infants.

The immunoprotective aspects of breastfeeding over formula feeding have long been the subject of much investigation in the medical community. It is widely accepted and promoted that breastfeeding protects against the development of atopic diseases in general and food allergies in particular.[41–43,54–60]

Despite these prevailing sentiments, considerable contradiction exists in the research literature regarding the strength of these claims. Comparisons between studies are difficult to make due to fundamental differences in experimental design, definitions of atopy and the high-risk infant, duration of breastfeeding, maternal diet permitted during breastfeeding, age of the infant when solid foods were first introduced, and the length of the follow-up period during which infants were observed for signs of atopy. Numerous studies have observed a preventive effect of breastfeeding, particularly when the diet of the breastfeeding mother has been restricted with respect to the consumption of sensitizing foods, while other studies that have not employed maternal dietary restrictions have failed to confirm these observations.[61,62]

In exclusively formula fed infants, a simple formula change using a different protein, carbohydrate, or fat source may be all that is necessary to either rule out or confirm a food allergy. A natural progression of formula changes might include cow's milk —> soy protein —> cow's milk casein hydrolysate (Nutramigen, Mead Johnson Nutritional Division, Evansville, IN; Alimentum, Ross Laboratories, Columbus, OH) —> chemically-defined elemental diet (Criticare HN, Mead Johnson Nutritional Division; Tolerex [formerly Standard Vivonex], Sandoz Nutrition, Minneapolis, MN).

Much discussion has surrounded the role of soy-based formulas in the diagnosis and management of CMA.[7,63–68] Soy-based formulas are not without their advocates and represent a first line of defense for infants with presumed CMA in many institutions.[66] They are readily available, convenient, and comparable in cost to standard milk-based formulas. In high-risk or seriously ill infants, it may be expeditious to proceed directly from a milk-based formula to one containing casein hydrolysates in light of the documented 15% to 50% incidence of soy protein allergy in cow's milk allergic infants[7,63,64] and the greater likelihood of inducing soy sensitivity in infants in whom gut damage has occurred. In mild to moderate cases of suspected CMA, the expense of using casein hydrolysates must be weighed against the presumed benefits of skipping over the more moderately priced soy-based formulas, as the cost can be prohibitive for even moderate-income families. A possible coexisting or newly developed soy protein allergy should be entertained when an infant's allergic symptoms are not significantly improved within 3 to 5 days of initiating a formula change from cow's milk to soy. Alternatively, temporary use of a casein hydrolysate formula to promote symptom relief and recovery of the gastrointestinal tract followed by the careful introduction of a soy-based formula may well be the most cost-effective approach. Fortunately, casein hydrolysates are available through the USDA Supplemental Food Program for Women, Infants, and Children (WIC) to qualifying infants of low-income families who are at nutritional risk, when the need is substantiated by a physician.

Milk contains two major classes of protein: caseins, which are precipitated by acid and form the basis of most cheeses, and whey proteins, which result in a small curd following acid hydrolysis. The whey proteins in breast milk differ greatly from the whey proteins of cow's milk.[67] Breast milk whey consists predominantly of α-lactalbumin, while β-lactoglobulin is the major whey protein of cow's milk. Goat's milk is occasionally considered an alternative to cow's milk but is unsuitable on two counts: It contains β-lactoglobulin that is cross-reactive with cow's milk, and it is reported to cause allergic symptoms in up to 80% of infants previously diagnosed with CMA.[69] Goat's milk is also deficient in folic acid,[70] further rendering it unsuitable for infants without appropriate supplementation.

Table 8–4 describes many of the hypoallergenic formulas commercially available for pediatric use. Not surprisingly, they vary considerably in their cost, availability, palatability, osmolality, and efficacy. There have been numerous additions in recent years to the "hypoallergenic" marketplace (i.e., Alimentum, Carnation Good Start, and Peptamen), presenting the clinician with what is often a confusing array of choices. Nutramigen has been the protein hydrolysate formula of choice due to approximately 50 years of accumulated experience in infants with sensitivities to intact proteins, but the utility of the remaining formulas should not be overlooked. The moderately high carbohydrate content of both Nutramigen and Pregestimil, which may aggravate underlying acquired carbohydrate malabsorption secondary to severe diarrhea, is counterbalanced by the fact that these formulas are both sucrose- and lactose-free. Both Pregestimil and Alimentum contain medium-chain triglycerides (MCTs) in a blend with other oils to prevent an essential fatty acid deficiency. MCTs are more readily hydrolyzed and absorbed than triglycerides from long-chain fatty acids and are indicated in conditions of impaired fat absorption. Ingestion of large amounts of MCTs, though, may produce abdominal distention, cramping, nausea, or diarrhea due to the hypertonic load resulting from the rapid hydrolysis of MCTs to free fatty acids and glycerol.[71]

Carnation Good Start, a whey protein hydrolysate, represents a break from the long-standing casein hydrolysate tradition due to the presumed increased allergenic potential of whey protein over caseins. Chandra and colleagues reported a significantly decreased incidence of atopic manifestations (i.e., eczema, wheeze, rhinitis, otitis, gastrointestinal, colic) in high allergic risk infants followed prospectively from birth to age 6 months on Carnation Good Start as compared to infants consuming either a cow's milk or a soy-based formula, or breastfed infants whose mothers were consuming unrestricted diets.[68] While there may be a specific population of infants who would benefit from the reduced allergic capacity, cost, and improved taste of this formula over the more tried casein hydrolysates, it would be premature at this time, in the author's opinion, to make any broad-based recommendations regarding the utility of Carnation Good Start in the diagnosis and management of infants with allergies to intact protein, based on the very limited amount of research conducted thus far.

Very rarely, infants may be encountered who do not tolerate casein hydrolysates but recover on a chemically defined elemental diet, presumably due to the further reduced allergenic load of simple amino acids or differences in carbohydrate content. When considering using elemental diets, an understanding of the limitations associated with their use in a pediatric population is essential.[66] Most adult-oriented enteral feedings are formulated to provide 30 kcal/oz (1 kcal/ml).

Table 8-4 Hypoallergenic Formulas—General Characteristics

Formula	Caloric Distribution (%)			Nutrient Sources			Kcal/oz	Osmolality mOs/kg H₂O
	Protein	CHO	Fat	Protein	CHO	Fat		
Breast milk	7.0	38.0	55.0	Whey, casein	Lactose	Human fat	22	300
Protein hydrolysates								
Nutramigen†	11.0	54.0	35.0	Casein hydrolysate	Glucose polymers, and modified food starch	Corn oil	20	320
Pregestimil†	11.0	41.0	48.0	Casein hydrolysate	Glucose polymers, and modified food starch	MCT oil (60%) Corn oil (20%), High oleic saffl. oil (20%)	20	320
Alimentum‡	11.0	41.0	48.0	Casein hydrolysate	Sucrose, Tapioca starch	MCT oil (50%), Saffl. oil (40%), Soy oil (10%)	20	370
Carnation Good Start§	9.8	44.2	46.0	Whey hydrolysate, Whey protein isolate	Lactose (70%), Maltodextrin	Palm oil (60%), Saffl. oil (22%), Coconut oil (18%)	20	265
Elemental formulas								
Criticare HN†	14.2	83.1	2.7	Casein hydrolysate	Maltodextrin, cornstarch	Saffl. oil	30	650
Tolerex¶	8.2	90.5	1.3	Crystalline amino acids	Glucose polymers	Saffl. oil	30	550
Peptamen§	16.0	51.0	33.0	Whey hydrolysate	Maltodextrin, starch	MCT oil (70%), Sunfl. oil (30%)	30	260

Note: MCT, medium-chain triglyceride.
† Mead Johnson Nutritional Division, Evansville, IN.
‡ Ross Laboratories, Columbus, OH.
§ Clintec Nutrition Company, Deerfield, IL.
¶ Sandoz Nutrition, Minneapolis, MN.

Infant formulas, on the other hand, are formulated to provide 20 kcal/oz (0.67 kcal/ml). Infant formulas providing up to 24 kcal/oz (0.8 kcal/ml) are generally well tolerated by most infants.[71] When the caloric density exceeds 24 kcal/oz, the resulting high osmolality and renal solute load may present added stresses for infants with excessive water losses, malabsorption, or restricted fluid intake.[71] These infants should be closely monitored for signs of dehydration and other complications.

The essential fatty acid content of Tolerex (formerly Standard Vivonex) is inadequate for infants and very young children, because linoleic acid provides only approximately 1% of the total calories versus the minimum of 2.7% recommended by the Committee on Nutrition of the American Academy of Pediatrics[72] and the nutrient requirements for infant formula published in federal regulations developed as a result of the Infant Formula Act of 1980.[73] Neocate (Scientific Hospital Supplies, Inc., Gaithersburg, MD 20877) represents the first elemental formula designed specifically with infants in mind. It has not been introduced into interstate commerce in the U.S. from Great Britain and experience with it is therefore quite limited. Peptamen represents the only isotonic elemental formula currently available. Due to the hypertonic nature (osmolality greater than 400 mOsm/kg of water) of the remaining elemental formulas, and their high carbohydrate content and frequently very low fat content, these diets should be viewed only as temporary diets of last resort. Infants consuming a chemically defined elemental diet should be weaned to a more nutritionally complete casein hydrolysate formula as soon as they are stabilized. Interaction with a registered dietitian or health care worker trained in the use of elemental diets for the diagnosis of adverse food reactions is very helpful in avoiding complications and in improving compliance.

Abrupt formula changes in older infants are occasionally met with some resistance. This may be greatly lessened by gradually titrating the new formula into the old formula in ever-increasing amounts over a period of several days to a week or until a 100% solution of the new formula is being consumed. The addition of a vanilla flavor packet to each 8-oz feeding of the new formula may facilitate the switch but will increase the osmolality.

Infants with a long-term history of suspected food sensitivities who are consuming a mixed diet of breast milk/formula plus solid foods and infants in whom symptoms suggestive of food allergies did not appear until after solid foods were introduced into the diet may be managed in a similar fashion. The goal in both situations is to remove from the diet as many potential food allergens as possible while also providing optimal nutrition. This is best accomplished by removing all solid foods from the diet and returning the infants, when possible, exclusively to either breast milk or a casein hydrolysate formula. Discretion should be used with infants who are older than 6 months of age, who are consuming more than 1 quart of formula per day, who have doubled their birth weight, or who are anemic. Due to their increased nutrient needs, these infants are best managed on a case-by-case basis, with attention given to both developmental and nutritional implications.

As infants mature, so do their palates. They tire very quickly of diets consisting solely of breast milk or formula. It becomes increasingly difficult, if not inappropriate, to return them to breast milk or casein hydrolysates exclusively. These infants, particularly those 9 months of age and older, are best managed, in the author's experience, by using a rotary elimination diet supplemented with appropriate amounts of breast milk or casein hydrolysates. Foods reputed to be highly sensitizing (i.e., cow's milk, egg, legumes, wheat, citrus fruits, cocoa, etc.) are temporarily removed from the diet. Any food that results in a positive RAST or prick-puncture skin test (i.e., wheal size 3 mm greater than the negative control) is also eliminated from the diet, in addition to foods suspected by the child's family or physician of causing an adverse response. In order to carry out these directives correctly, families must be educated regarding the fairly ubiquitous presence of derivatives of such foods as milk, egg, soy, corn, and wheat in commercially prepared foods and staple items and cautioned repeatedly to read all food and drug labels.

It is important not to exceed the capacity of a family to carry out an elimination diet by requiring the elimination of vast numbers of foods when, for example, there may be limited access to alternative foods or significant time constraints imposed on working parents. Foods to be eliminated and challenged in these situations are best prioritized and then eliminated in stages, addressing the most likely food offenders first. The remaining presumed safe foods are then arranged in a rotary pattern of varying length, with 3 to 4 days being the average.

While rotary elimination diets are considered controversial and of little or no benefit during the management phase, they have a twofold purpose in the brief diagnostic phase: (1) providing (although necessarily) a degree of variety necessary for optimal nutrition and patient compliance; and (2) providing a means of possibly recognizing the presence of any remaining sensitizing foods in the elimination pattern. Diet diaries kept during the elimination period serve as an important tool not only for assessing compliance but also for identifying the possible presence of any additional food triggers.

Partial or complete symptom relief occurring during the elimination phase strongly suggests that the child's symptoms were triggered by one or more of the eliminated foods. The diagnosis becomes definitive when challenge with adequate amounts of suspect food reproduces some or all of the child's symptoms.

If the infant or child does not achieve a measurable degree of improvement within 1 to 2 weeks on an elimination diet, several explanations are possible. Most obvious is the possibility that no food sensitivities exist. Other important considerations include (1) the possibility of poor dietary compliance, either willful or unintentional; (2) the continued presence of unrecognized offending foods in the elimination pattern; or (3) the presence of symptoms resulting from intercurrent infections or other disease processes occurring during the elimination period. Lengthening the elimination period is much preferred over incorrectly making a diagnosis that food sensitivities do not exist in children whose elimination diets have been interfered with by external circumstances.

Eliminated foods may be reintroduced into the diet of children in either an open or blinded format depending on the number of incriminated foods, the age of the patient, and the perceived level of physician and family bias. In open, oral provocative food challenges, both the observer (i.e., physician, nurse, dietitian, etc.) and the patient/patient's family are aware of the food's identity. Blinded food challenges, on the other hand, interject an element of mystery into the proceedings that many patients/patient's families find interesting. Blinded food challenges may be single-blind, where only the patient is unaware of the food's identity, or double-blind, where both the patient and the observer are left unaware. Placebo foods may additionally be randomly included in the challenge sequence to further remove bias and are considered necessary when a patient's symptoms are largely subjective in nature (i.e., hyperactivity, irritability, headache, etc.).

Double-blind, placebo-controlled food challenges (DBPCFCs) are universally considered the gold standard for the accurate diagnosis of an adverse food reaction. In DBPCFCs, a staff member other than the uninformed observer is responsible for randomizing, preparing, and administering the challenge foods. Individual DBPCFCs are best separated, in the author's experience, by a minimum of 24 hours or more, depending on the outcome of the previous challenge. DBPCTC participants are informed of the identity of the specific foods in the challenge sequence following the completion of all challenges. Bock et al.[74] provides excellent guidelines for the execution of DBPCFCs, in addition to many useful forms for the recording of pertinent data.

With infants and very small children, it is arguably unnecessary to "blind" the challenge food, except possibly with precocious youngsters. With this population of patients, it is occasionally more important to hide the food's identity from the patient's family. Challenge vehicles used to mask a food's identity in very young children include applesauce, pureed baby food apricots, milkshakes in the milk-tolerant patient, orange juice in the orange-tolerant patient, and on occasion, an elemental diet because of its superior capacity to mask strong flavors. All carrier foods should be documented safe foods. Opaque capsules, a frequently used challenge vehicle in older children and adults, are contraindicated in infants and small children, who are too young to swallow them. Capsules made from beef and/or pork gelatin should only be used in patients tolerant of these foods. Noseclamps, a blindfold, and repeated ice water chasers to rinse the mouth complete the blinding process. Carrier foods, as opposed to capsules, are preferred by many as a more appropriate challenge vehicle, irrespective of the logistical problems associated with capsules, because they permit contact of the challenge food with the oral mucosa.

It is important to give some thought to the potentially diverse tastes and textures of the particular food(s) a patient is scheduled to be challenged to when selecting the identity of the carrier food(s) and placebo(s). Some foods are better at masking certain flavors and textures than others. For example, a young child who is to be challenged to egg and wheat will invariably be able to detect the textural differences between the two foods if similarly textured placebos are not also included in the challenge scheme. It is therefore not surprising that dessicated foodstuffs are the preferred form of challenge food for blinded challenges, in light of the decreased volume displacement and textural characteristics inherent in them. Dessicated foods are widely available in many grocery stores and from camping supply stores.

Open challenges are not without their place in the reintroduction period and may be suitable for challenging foods that the history suggests result in only mild reactions but to which the patient skin-tested negatively, assuming the skin tests were a reliable indicator of IgE sensitization in these particular patients.[19,74] Open challenges may be carried out in the home of responsible families but are preferably conducted in an office setting if there is even a remote chance of a severe reaction's occurring.[19,74]

Regardless of the type of challenge format selected or the number of foods to be challenged, some general guidelines apply. The purest possible form of the food should be used for challenging purposes. It should contain as few other ingredients as possible and be only minimally processed. It should not contain derivatives of foods not yet challenged or previously shown to be poorly tolerated. Sample size is an extremely important consideration when challenging with potentially sensitizing foods. Until proven otherwise, it must be assumed that every child is exquisitely sensitive to each food eliminated from the diet. To avoid causing a severe reaction, always initiate the challenge with a very small portion size, gradually titrating up the amount of challenge food consumed until a serving size equal to or exceeding a meal-sized portion is consumed. If a reaction occurs at any time during the challenging of a food, no further testing of that food should be permitted, and the patient's symptoms should be treated accordingly. Symptoms resulting from a previous positive food challenge must have completely resolved before proceeding to the next food in the challenge sequence. No food that resulted in a severe or life-threatening reaction should be rechallenged without careful consideration of the risks involved and without immediate access to properly equipped treatment rooms staffed with personnel skilled in performing cardiopulmonary resuscitation.[75] If qualified emergency care is not available, challenges of this nature are best avoided. No food challenge is without risks. Patients and patients' families should be educated regarding the possible consequences of a severe reaction before proceeding with this phase of the work-up.

A challenge format employed by the author for infants and children is summarized below:

1. Since optimal nutrition is based on maximum variety in the diet, no food should be eliminated unless it is absolutely necessary.

2. Each challenge food is returned to the diet for a period of 3 consecutive days in the following manner:

Day 1:	Breakfast:	1/16 of a portion
	10:00 AM:	1/8 of a portion
	Noon:	1/4 of a portion
	2:00 PM:	1/2 of a portion
	4:00 PM:	1 whole portion
	Dinner:	1 whole portion
	Bedtime:	2 whole portions
	Total amt.	= 5 whole portions (approximately)

   Days 2 and 3: Consume at least 2 to 3 portions of challenge food each day.

3. "Portions" represent serving sizes considered to be meal-sized portions and have largely been taken from diabetic exchange lists so that the amount of protein, carbohydrate, and fat contributed by various members of individual food groupings is approximately the same.

4. The reintroduction scheme may be expanded to 54 days, or as necessary, to facilitate consumption of adequate amounts of challenge food for infants and very small children who are unable to consume large amounts of food.

5. Open oral challenges resulting in a positive reaction should be repeated to confirm the reaction. DBPCFCs should be employed in equivocal challenges or when bias is suspected.

6. Open oral challenges conducted in a home environment are to be carried out only on Mondays through Fridays, when medical office personnel are available for rapid consult. Positive open oral food challenges are to be reported to the office immediately.

7. If a reaction occurs anytime during the challenging of a food, discontinue any further feeding of that food, and treat symptomatically.

8. Symptoms resulting from a previous positive challenge must have completely resolved before proceeding to the next food in the challenge sequence.

The preceding format is condensed into a 4-hour block when utilized for either an open or blinded challenge performed in an office setting. Sufficient time should be permitted for observation following the completion of the challenge.

The primary objective in the treatment of individuals diagnosed with food allergies, regardless of the age of the patient, remains the complete removal of the offending food(s) from the diet. While simple in premise, this directive can be quite difficult in practice, depending on the number and identity of foods to be avoided. It is based on the assumption that the diagnosis was made by a qualified physician employing appropriate elimination diets followed by supervised provocation tests—ideally, DBPCFCs. A secondary objective is the appropriate medical management of symptoms resulting from poor dietary compliance, inadvertent exposures to an offending food (i.e., cooking vapors, topical exposures, etc.), and the possible incomplete recognition of all potentially sensitizing foods. While reputed to be of only limited benefit in preventing symptoms resulting from dietary indiscretions,[76] the judicious use of drugs and topical agents may reduce some of the discomfort and certainly much of the mortality associated with food allergies.

For patients with a history of particularly severe or anaphylactic reactions, instruction directed toward key family members and caretakers (i.e., teachers, sitters, day care workers, etc.) regarding the proper procedures to be taken in an emergency is paramount.[77] Two frequently used emergency devices, available by prescription only, include the EpiPen Jr./EpiPen-Autoinjector (Center Laboratories, Port Washington, NY) and the Ana-Kit Insect Sting Treatment Kit (Hillister-Stier Laboratories, Spokane, WA). These devices are not designed to permit dietary infractions but instead, when used as directed, may provide valuable time for the transport of the child to a site where appropriate emergency care may be given. Identification bracelets and necklaces (Body Guard, Brigantine, NJ) and clothing tags (Lifesaver Charities, Garden Grove, CA) listing the patient's name, address, responsible parties, and specific food allergies may also be indicated. There is no evidence at present to support either classic immunotherapy with food antigens[78] or oral desensitization/neutralization with gradually increasing amounts of food antigen[79] as valid treatment options.

The prognosis for food hypersensitivity reactions is, fortunately, an optimistic one, particularly in the very young. Spontaneous symptom remission rates ranging from 38% to 67% have been reported.[8,14,28,75,80–83] Factors thought to influence the rate of remission include the age of the patient when symptoms were first diagnosed and the identity of the sensitizing food(s). Tolerance to an offending food is more rapid very early in life, while symptoms that linger into childhood are less likely to resolve. Of the 20 newborn infants observed by Jakobsson and Lindberg to be allergic to cow's milk, 50% achieved tolerance by 1 year of age and 60% by 2 years of age.[8] Similarly, Ford and Taylor reported a remission rate of 60% in infants diagnosed in the first year of life compared to 33% in older children.[80] Of the children under 3 years of age in Bock's study, an amazing 73% achieved tolerance, while only 26% of the children older than 3 years of age experienced symptom resolution.[81]

The identity of the sensitizing food appears to exert an effect on the eventual outcome. Sampson and McCaskell observed a 42% remission rate in atopic dermatitis patients over a 1- to 2-year period, depending on the food antigen involved.[28] Sensitivities to peanut, fish, egg, and wheat appeared to be more persistent in this population of patients.[28] In reviewing numerous studies examining the natural history of food allergy, Eggleston calculated a 68% and 41% remission rate associated with cow's milk and egg allergy, respectively.[26] For the majority of patients in these studies, symptoms resulting from food allergies largely resolved, only to be replaced by symptoms resulting from inhalant sensitivities,[80,82] confirming the atopic nature of these patients.

The prospect for gradual resolution of symptoms strongly points to the need for the periodic reassessment of continuing sensitization. Indeed, physicians caring for children with a history of even severe adverse food reactions are encouraged to perform periodic supervised food challenges.[75] The challenges should be conducted in a setting where emergency medical care is readily available (i.e., emergency rooms, outpatient clinics, etc.) with properly equipped treatment rooms staffed by personnel skilled in performing cardiopulmonary resuscitation.[75] If qualified emergency care is not available, challenges in these children are, once again, best avoided.

Some controversy exists regarding the length of time a sensitizing food should be avoided before reintroducing it into the diet in the carefully orchestrated challenge format described in the diagnostic phase. Periods of 1 to 3 months, 6 months, and longer have been suggested, depending on the identity of the allergen involved, the severity of symptoms, and the degree of difficulty experienced with dietary avoidance.[74] A conservative approach employed by the author is summarized below:

1. Avoid at all costs any food that results in anaphylaxis. These foods should not be rechallenged.

2. Infants in whom food sensitivities were diagnosed prior to 6 months of age should not be rechallenged with an offending food until they are at least 12 months old.

3. Wait at least 6 months before rechallenging an offending food in children older than 6 months of age diagnosed with food sensitivities.

4. Always use single-ingredient foods when introducing a new food into the diet or when challenging with a previously sensitizing food.

5. When introducing a new food into an infant's diet, allow 1 to 2 small feedings per day for a period of 5 to 7 days, permitting the introduction of no more than one new food per week.

6. Challenges conducted during the management phase are performed identically to those conducted during the diagnostic phase.

Elimination diets used in managing patients with food sensitivities generally mirror diets employed in the diagnostic phase, with the exception that in the management phase only those foods documented to result in symptoms are eliminated from the diet. Parents of children with mild to moderate food sensitivities should be encouraged to experiment with various forms of an offending food (i.e., cooked versus raw; refined versus unrefined; individual fractions of a food) to determine if certain forms of a food are more tolerable than others. For example, both peanut oil and sunflower oil have been reported to be tolerated by individuals who experience anaphylaxis to whole peanut[84] and sunflower,[85] respectively, presumably due to the degree of refinement of the oils. Since the purity of an oil is difficult for the consumer to predict, caution is still the best advice. Additionally, parents should be counseled that periods of heightened sensitivity to a food may occur during times of illness, excessive fatigue, increased antigen load related to concomitant inhalant sensitivities, emotional stress, etc. Reassessment of continuing sensitization is best avoided during these times.

For many families, the prospect of long-term elimination of what may be favorite foods is viewed with great apprehension, particularly if milk, egg, or wheat is among the foods to be avoided. Including a registered dietitian on the treatment team not only improves compliance by ensuring strict dietary avoidance through education and appropriate substitution but also is essential for ensuring the nutritional adequacy of the diet. Implementation of the following suggestions in a patient's treatment plan should facilitate dietary compliance:

1. Provision of individualized patient education materials regarding
   - derivatives of food whose names on food labels bear little or no resemblance to the name of the parent food from which they were derived
   - frequently encountered "hidden sources" of foods the patient must avoid
   - alternative food sources, product suggestions, recipes, sample menus, etc.
   - proper measures to be taken in an emergency
2. Encourage
   - thorough label reading at all times
   - an adventurous approach in experimenting with alternative foods
   - appropriate coping behaviors
   - participation in a support group
   - semiannual nutritional assessment visits for all patients eliminating two or more major foods (milk, egg, soy, wheat) from the diet

As evidence accumulates regarding the benefits of early antigen avoidance, particularly in high allergic risk populations, future management approaches may have their greatest impact in preventing or delaying the appearance of food allergies rather than simply treating an existing allergy. In a comprehensive review of factors believed to influence both the onset and severity of allergic symptoms, Zeiger and coworkers [86] have formulated the following strategies for the prevention of allergic disease in high allergic risk infants:

1. encourage exclusive breastfeeding, when possible, for a period of at least 6 months
2. encourage the complete avoidance of cow's milk-, egg-, fish-, and peanut-containing foods from the mother's diet for the duration of the breast-feeding period
3. encourage the mother to reduce consumption of soy, wheat, citrus fruits, and cocoa for the duration of the breastfeeding period
4. supplement the infant's diet, when necessary, with casein hydrolysate-based formulas, completely avoiding cow's milk or soy-based formulas for the first year of life
5. withhold solid foods until the infant is at least 6 months old
   a. delay the introduction of cow's milk, wheat, corn, and citrus fruits until 1 year of age
   b. delay the introduction of egg and the true nuts until 2 years of age
   c. delay the introduction of fish and peanut until 3 years of age

These prophylactic measures are endorsed with slight modifications by numerous other research camps[42,43,55,57–60,87,88] and appear to be most effective in postponing the advent of allergic diseases rather than preventing them altogether. Postponing is perceived to be nearly synonymous with prevention owing to the often increased frequency and severity of allergic symptoms seen in infancy and early childhood and the difficulties in medicating this age group. Nonetheless, the hardships imposed by these dietary restrictions must be weighed against possible prophylactic benefits on a case-by-case basis.

REFERENCES

1. Anderson JA. Introduction. In: Anderson JA, Sogn DD, eds. *Adverse Reactions to Foods.* American Academy of Allergy and Immunology Committee on Adverse Reactions to Foods and National Institutes of Allergy and Infectious Diseases, US Department of Health and Human Services; 1984:4–6. Public Health Service publication no. 84-2442.

2. Metcalfe DD. Food allergens. *Clin Rev Allergy.* 1985;3:331.

3. Collins-Williams C. The incidence of milk allergy in pediatric practice. *J Pediatr.* 1956;48:39.

4. Bachmann KD, Dees SC. Milk allergy. II. Observations on incidence and symptoms of allergy to milk in allergic infants. *Pediatrics.* 1957;20:400.

5. Goldman AS, Anderson DW, Sellers WA, Saperstein S, Kniker WT, Halpern SR. Milk allergy. I. Oral challenge with milk and isolated milk proteins in allergic children. *Pediatrics.* 1963;32:425.

6. Freier S, Kletter B. Milk allergy in infants and young children. *Clin Pediatr.* 1970;9:449.

7. Gerrard JW, MacKenzie JWA, Goluboff N, Garson JZ, Maningas CS. Cow's milk allergy: prevalence and manifestations in an unselected series of newborns. *Acta Paediatr Scand.* 1973;234(suppl):1.

8. Jakobbson I, Lindberg T. A prospective study of cow's milk protein intolerance in Swedish infants. *Acta Paediatr Scand.* 1979;68:853.

9. Stintzing G, Zetterstrom R. Cow's milk allergy, incidence and pathogenetic role of early exposure to cow's milk formula. *Acta Paediatr Scand.* 1979;68:383.

10. Bachman KD, Dees SC. Milk allergy. I. Observations on incidence and symptoms in "well" babies. *Pediatrics.* 1957;20:393.

11. Sampson HA. The role of "allergy" in atopic dermatitis. *Clin Rev Allergy.* 1986;4:125.

12. Burks AW, Mallory SB, Williams LW, Sherrill MA. Atopic dermatitis: clinical relevance of food hypersensitivity reactions. *J Pediatr.* 1988;113:447.

13. Ratner B, Untracht S. Egg allergy in children. *Am J Dis Child.* 1952;83:309.

14. Bock SA. Prospective appraisal of complaints of adverse reactions to foods in children during the first three years of life. *Pediatrics.* 1987;79:683.

15. Sampson HA. Food hypersensitivity. In: Grant JA, ed. *Insights in Allergy.* St. Louis, Mo: CV Mosby, 1986.

16. Metcalfe DD. Food hypersensitivity. *J Allergy Clin Immunol.* 1984;73:749.

17. Sampson HA. Differential diagnosis in adverse reactions to foods. *J Allergy Clin Immunol.* 1986;78:213.

18. Lessof MH, Challacombe S. Gastrointestinal allergy. In: Lessof MH, Lee TH, Kemeny DM, eds. *Allergy: An International Textbook.* Baltimore, Md: Williams & Wilkins; 1987:455–480.

19. Sampson HA, Albergo R. Comparison of results of prick skin tests, RAST and double-blind, placebo-controlled food challenges in children with atopic dermatitis. *J Allergy Clin Immunol.* 1984;74:26.

20. May CD. Objective clinical and laboratory studies of immediate reactions to foods in infants and children. *J Allergy Clin Immunol.* 1976;58:500.

21. Bock SA, Lee W-Y, Remigio LK, May CD. Studies of hypersensitivity reactions to foods in infants and children. *J Allergy Clin Immunol.* 1978;62:327.

22. Sampson HA. Role of immediate food hypersensitivity in the pathogenesis of atopic dermatitis. *J Allergy Clin Immunol.* 1983;71:473.

23. Bock SA, Lee W-Y, Remigio L, Holst A, May CD. Appraisal of skin tests with food extracts for diagnosis of food hypersensitivity. *Clin Allergy.* 1978;8:559.

24. Sampson HA. Comparative study of commercial food antigen extracts for the diagnosis of food hypersensitivity. *J Allergy Clin Immunol.* 1988;82:718.

25. Foucard T. Development of food allergies with special reference to cow's milk allergy. *Pediatrics.* 1985;75(suppl):177.

26. Eggleston PA. Prospective studies in the natural history of food allergy. *Ann Allergy.* 1987;59:179.

27. US Department of Health and Human Services. *National Institute of Allergy and Infectious Diseases Task Force Report. Adverse Reactions to Foods.* 1984:17–25. Public Health Service publication no. 84-2442.

28. Sampson HA, McCaskill CM. Food hypersensitivity in atopic dermatitis: evaluation of 113 patients. *J Pediatr.* 1985;107:669.

29. Sach MI, O'Connel EJ. Cross-reactivity of foods—mechanisms and clinical significance. *Ann Allergy.* 1988;61:36.

30. Broadbent JB, Sampson HA. Cross-allergenicity in the legume botanical family in children with food hypersensitivity. *J Allergy Clin Immunol.* 1989;83:435.

31. Morgan JE, O'Neil CE, Daul CB, Lehrer SB. Species-specific shrimp allergens: RAST and RAST-inhibition studies. *J Allergy Clin Immunol.* 1989;83:1112.

32. Hamilton JR. Defects of specific enzymes or transport processes involved in digestion or absorption. In: Nelson WE, ed. *Textbook of Pediatrics.* Philadelphia, Pa: WB Saunders; 1987:807–809.

33. Gray GM. Absorption and malabsorption of dietary carbohydrate. In: Winick M, ed. *Nutrition and Gastroenterology.* New York, NY: John Wiley & Sons; 1980:50.

34. Lloyd-Still JD. Chronic diarrhea of childhood and the misuse of elimination diets. *J Pediatr.* 1979;95:10.

35. Sinatra FR, Merritt RJ. Iatrogenic kwashiorkor in infants. *Am J Dis Child.* 1981;135:21.

36. David TJ, Waddington E, Stanton RHJ. Nutritional hazards of elimination diets in children with atopic eczema. *Arch Dis Child.* 1984;59:323.

37. Kjellman N-IM, Johansson SGO. IgE and atopic allergy in newborns and infants with a family history of atopic disease. *Acta Paediatr Scand.* 1976;65:601.

38. Dannaeus A, Johansson SGO, Foucard T. Clinical and immunological aspects of food allergy in childhood. *Acta Paediatr Scand.* 1978;67:497.

39. Michel FB, Bousquet J, Greillier P, Coulomb Y, Robinet LM. Comparison of cord blood IgE concentrations and maternal allergy for the prediction of atopic disease in infancy. *J Allergy Clin Immunol.* 1980;65:422.

40. Croner S Kjellman N-IM, Eriksson B, Roth A. IgE screening in 1701 newborn infants and the development of atopic disease during infancy. *Arch Dis Child.* 1982;57:364.

41. Kjellman N-IM, Croner S. Cord blood IgE determination for allergy prediction—a follow-up to seven years of age in 1651 children. *Ann Allergy.* 1984;53:167.

42. Businco L, Marchetti F, Pellegrini G, Perlini R. Predictive value of cord serum IgE levels in "at risk" newborn babies and influence on type of feeding. *Clin Allergy.* 1983;13:503.

43. Chandra RK, Puri S, Cheema PS. Predictive value of cord blood IgE in the development of atopic disease and role of breast-feeding in its prevention. *Clin Allergy.* 1985;15:517.

44. Strimas JH, Chi DS. Significance of IgE level in amniotic fluid and cord blood for the prediction of allergy. *Ann Allergy.* 1988;61:133.

45. Juto P, Moller C, Engberg S, Bjorksten B. Influence of type of feeding on lymphocyte function and development of infantile atopy. *Clin Allergy.* 1982;12:409.

46. Bjorksten B, Juto P. Immunoglobulin E and T cells in infants. In: Kern JW, Ganderson MA, ed. *Proceedings of the XI International Congress of Allergy and Immunology.* London: Macmillan Press;10:144–148.

47. Bjorksten B. Immune responses to ingested antigens in relation to feeding pattern in childhood. *Ann Allergy.* 1986;57:143.

48. Matsumura T, Kuroume T, Oguri M, Iwasaki I, Kanbe Y, Yamada T, Kawabe S, Negishi K. Egg sensitivity and eczematous manifestations in breast-fed newborns with particular reference to intrauterine sensitization. *Ann Allergy.* 1975;35:221.

49. Kilshaw PJ, Cant AJ. Passage of maternal dietary proteins into human breast milk. *Int Arch Allergy Appl Immunol.* 1984;75:8.

50. Cant A, Marsden RA, Kilshaw PH. Egg and cow's milk hypersensitivity in exclusively breast fed infants with eczema and detection of egg protein in breast milk. *Br Med J.* 1985;291:932.

51. Cavagni G, Paganelli R, Caffarelli C, et al. Passage of food antigens into circulation of breast-fed infants with atopic dermatitis. *Ann Allergy.* 1988;61:361.

52. Casimir G, Gossart B, Vis HL. Antibody against beta-lactoglobulin (IgG) and cow's milk allergy. *J Allergy Clin Immunol.* 1985;75:206.

53. Machtinger S, Moss R. Cow's milk allergy in breast-fed infants: the role of allergen and maternal secretory IgA antibody. *J Allergy Clin Immunol.* 1986;77:341.

54. Kjellman N-IM. Atopic disease in seven-year-old children: incidence in relation to family history. *Acta Paediatr Scand.* 1977;66:465.

55. Businco L, Cantani A. Prevention of atopy—current concepts and personal experience. *Clin Rev Allergy.* 1984;2:107.

56. Zeiger RS, Heller S, Mellon M, O'Connor R, Hamburger RN. Effectiveness of dietary manipulation in the prevention of food allergy in infants. *J Allergy Clin Immunol.* 1986;78:224.

57. Businco L, Marchetti F, Pelligrini G, Cantani A, Perlini R. Prevention of atopic disease in "at-risk newborns" by prolonged breastfeeding. *Ann Allergy.* 1983;51:296.

58. Saarinen U. Prophylaxis for atopic disease: role of infant feeding. *Clin Rev Allergy.* 1984;2:151.

59. Miskelly FG, Burr ML, Vaughan-Williams E, Fehily AM, Butland BK, Merrett TG. Infant feeding and allergy. *Arch Dis Child.* 1988;63:388.

60. Hattevig G, Kjellman B, Sigurs N, Bjorksten B, Kjellman N-IM. Effect of maternal avoidance of eggs, cow's milk and fish during lactation upon allergic manifestations in infants. *Clin Exp Allergy.* 1989;19:27.

61. Van Asperen PP, Kemp AS, Mellis CM. Relationship of diet in development of atopy in infancy. *Clin Allergy.* 1984;14:525.

62. Savilahti E, Tainio VM, Salmenpera L, Siimes MA, Perheentupa J. Prolonged exclusive breast feeding and heredity as determinants in infantile atopy. *Arch Dis Child.* 1987;62:269.

63. Kjellman N-IM, Johansson SGO. Soy versus cow's milk in infants with a biparental history of atopic disease: development of atopic disease and immunoglobulins from birth to 4 years of age. *Clin Allergy.* 1979;9:347.

64. Perkkio M, Savilahti E, Kuitunen P. Morphometric and immunohistochemical study of jejunal biopsies from children with intestinal soy allergy. *Eur J Pediatr.* 1981;137:63.

65. Savilahti E, Verkasolo M. Intestinal cow's milk allergy: pathogenesis and clinical presentation. *Clin Rev Allergy.* 1984;2:7.

66. Brady MS, Rickard KA, Fitzgerald JF, Lemons JA. Specialized formulas and feedings for infants with malabsorption or formula intolerance. *J Am Diet Assoc.* 1986;86:191.

67. Benkov KJ, Leleiko NS. A rational approach to infant formulas. *Pediatr Ann.* 1987;16:225.

68. Chandra RK, Singh G, Shridhara B. Effect of feeding whey hydrolysate, soy and conventional cow milk formulas on incidence of atopic disease in high risk infants. *Ann Allergy.* 1989;63:102.

69. Juntunen K, Backman A. Goat's milk—a substitute for cow's milk? In: *Proceedings of the 2nd International Symposium on Immunological Clinical Problems of Food Allergy.* Milan, Italy: 1982.

70. Maksimak M, Winter HS. The infant at nutritional risk: cow's milk sensitivity and lactose intolerance. In: Howard RB, Winter RS, eds. *Nutrition and Feeding of Infants and Toddlers.* Boston, Mass: Little, Brown & Co; 1984:245–250.

71. Wilson SE, Dietz WH, Grand RJ. An algorithm for pediatric enteral alimentation. *Pediatr Ann.* 1987;16:233.

72. Committee on Nutrition. Commentary on breast-feeding and infant formulas, including proposed standards for formulas. *Pediatrics.* 1976;57:278.

73. United States Congress. Infant Formula Act of 1980. Public Law 96-359. September 26, 1980.

74. Bock SA, Sampson HA, Atkins FM, et al. Double-blind, placebo-controlled food challenge (DBPCFC) as an office procedure: a manual. *J Allergy Clin Immunol.* 1988;82:986.

75. Bock SA. Natural history of severe reactions to foods in young children. *J Pediatr.* 1985;107:676.

76. Sogn DD. Medications and their use in the treatment of adverse reactions to foods. *J Allergy Clin Immunol.* 1986;78:238.

77. Yunginger JW, Sweeney KG, Sturner WQ, et al. Fatal food-induced anaphylaxis. *JAMA.* 1988;260:1450.

78. Johnstone DE. Uses and abuses of hyposensitization in children. *Am J Dis Child.* 1972;123:78.

79. Golbert TM. A review of controversial diagnostic and therapeutic techniques employed in allergy. *J Allergy Clin Immunol.* 1975;56:170.

80. Ford RPK, Taylor B. Natural history of egg hypersensitivity. *Arch Dis Child.* 1982;57:649.

81. Bock SA. The natural history of food sensitivity. *J Allergy Clin Immunol.* 1982;69:173.

82. Businco L, Benincori N, Cantani A, Tacconi L, Picarazzi A. Chronic diarrhea due to cow's milk allergy. A 4- to 10-year follow-up study. *Ann Allergy.* 1985;55:844.

83. Kjellman N-IM, Bjorksten B, Hattevig G, Falth-Magnusson K. Natural history of food allergy. *Ann Allergy.* 1988;61:83.

84. Taylor SL, Busse WW, Sachs MI, Parker JL, Yunginger JW. Peanut oil is not allergenic to peanut sensitive individuals. *J Allergy Clin Immunol.* 1981;68:372.

85. Halsey AB, Martin ME, Ruff ME, Jacobs FO, Jacobs RL. Sunflower oil is not allergenic to sunflower seed-sensitive patients. *J Allergy Clin Immunol.* 1986;78:408.

86. Bjorksten B, Kjellman N-IM. Perinatal factors influencing the development of allergy. *Clin Rev Allergy.* 1987;5:339.

87. Kajosaari M, Saarinen UM. Prophylaxis of atopic disease by six months total solid food elimination. *Acta Paediatr Scand.* 1983;72:411.

88. Kjellman N-IM. Food allergy—treatment and prevention. *Ann Allergy.* 1987;59:168.

Chapter 9

Community Nutrition

Mariel Caldwell

Public health agencies have a mandate to promote and protect the health of the public. The goal of public health nutrition is to improve the nutritional status of the population served by the public health agency. The public health nutritionist is responsible for identifying the nutrition problems and needs in the community and developing solutions to the problems.[1,2] This requires a thorough understanding of the effect of economic, social, and political issues on health as well as on the community as a whole and their effect on community resources.

The entry level nutritionist

- counsels consumers/clients
- educates the public
- coordinates nutrition services within the agency

The experienced nutritionist

- sets standards
- plans, develops, and manages services
- implements and evaluates services and ensures quality
- locates and maximizes resources and financing
- provides expert consultation and educates health professional colleagues
- advocates for nutrition services
- informs decision and policy makers of service needs
- coordinates nutrition services with other agencies

The nutritionist at advanced level of practice

- participates in agency strategic and operational planning
- establishes policy

- supervises staff
- manages personnel and financing
- may conduct applied research[3]

DEVELOPMENT OF PROGRAM PLAN OR GRANT APPLICATION

Program planning is a critical activity in all health care settings. Establishing a program plan for the nutrition service encompasses many of the activities involved in developing a grant application. Grant funds are often used to develop, expand, or retain services to meet the nutritional needs of the population. Both tasks involve the functions described below.

Assessing the Community for Nutrition Problems or Needs

Assessing the community involves[3,4]

- identifying health problems that have implications for nutrition
- identifying resources available to solve or prevent the nutrition problems
- identifying gaps in needed services
- characterizing the population by culture, ethnicity, religion, education, socioeconomic status, age, sex, marital status, housing, schools, hospitals, group care settings and other institutions, health care providers, values, disease patterns, food supply, and marketplaces

Sources of data related to nutritional problems or needs are shown in Table 9-1.[5]

Identifying resources available to meet the needs of the population involves contacting health, nutrition, social service, and education agencies, organizations, and institutions to identify available nutrition and food programs and financial resources that can pay for nutrition services. See Appendix 9-A for a list of food and nutrition programs and resources found in many communities.

Establishing Goals and Objectives and Setting Priorities

Goals are statements of the long-range mission or purpose of a program[6] or broad ideals derived from values.[3] Objectives, on the other hand,

- are specific, measurable statements of what is to be accomplished by a given point in time
- should emphasize results or outcomes
- must be feasible within the available resources
- must be clearly related to the program goals

Table 9-1 Some Sources of Information on Nutrition Problems and Needs

The Community Profile	
Population	Census Bureau (most recent data)
	Health departments
	Social service departments
	Universities and colleges—programs in nutrition, medicine, urban health, allied health, community health, nursing
	Offices of congressional, state, and local representatives
	Federal, state, and local bureaus of labor, statistics, or commerce
	Department of Aging
	Board of Education
	City/county government offices
Housing	Same as above, and in addition: Departments of housing, Department of Housing and Urban Development
Food marketing facilities	Local offices for supermarket chains
	Local office of consumer affairs or markets
	Local association of food stores or farmers' markets
	Local newspapers and advertisements
Health statistics	Regional, state, and municipal health/hospital departments
	State and local health agencies
	State health and local universities and colleges, community medicine, population studies, health planning
	Health systems agencies
	Data from the National Center for Health Statistics and the Health and Nutrition Examination Survey
Community and mental health care programs	Local hospitals, nursing homes, home health care agencies
	Local health and social services departments
	Local prepaid health care groups
	Local programs for the elderly, handicapped, and special groups
	Community health centers
	Migrant health centers
	Indian health clinics
	School health services for data on pregnant teenagers
Community agencies	Local United Fund or equivalent
	Local telephone directory
	Local health, social services department, and education agencies
	Local March of Dimes
	Local community action and/or legal services organizations
	Local Agricultural Extension Service
	Local community colleges, universities, and professional schools
	Local home health care agencies
	Local heart, cancer, and similar associations
	Local court house

continues

Table 9-1 continued

Food and nutrition programs	State and local health departments, social services
	State or local board of education
	Local community action groups
Nutrition education programs	County, city health departments
	Board of education
	Social services departments
	Local extension or Farm Bureau office
	Local office of the Dairy Council and similar interest groups
Educational facilities	Local board of education
	State commissioner of education
Nutrition training programs	Local educational institutions, universities, and colleges
	Community colleges and vocational (trade) schools
	National, state, and local organizations of dietitians and nutritionists
	Local school food service office

Source: Adapted from *Nutrition Assessment: A Comprehensive Guide for Manning Intervention* (pp. 52–53) by MD Simko, C Cowell, and JA Gilbride, copyright © 1984, Aspen Publishers, Inc.

Objectives can often be stated by using the following formula: By (a specified date), (some condition) will be reduced by (a specific percent or amount).

Priorities must be established among objectives since resources are finite. They should consider the

- impact and severity of the problem
- size and nature of the problem (i.e., number affected)
- effect of intervention (great or small, certain or uncertain)
- feasibility of accomplishment (i.e., politically or economically feasible)

Establishing Course of Action or Methodology

This involves identifying and stating the activities that will be used to reach the objectives. Steps in defining the methodology include[3]

- determining the activities that must be carried out and their order of accomplishment
- determining a schedule or time line for completing the activities
- specifying the tasks in each activity

- determining the resources needed to carry out activities and tasks, including the amount and type of personnel and other resources needed and related costs
- assigning responsibility for each activity and task

Establishing Monitoring and Evaluation Methods

Evaluation determines whether program objectives are met and whether program resources are used in a cost-effective manner.[7] Monitoring determines success in carrying out the identified activities.

Evaluation and monitoring

- should be considered and methods determined at the time each objective and activity is written
- involves determining data items, including cost data, to be used in evaluation
- identifies mechanisms to obtain, compile, and summarize the data in a timely fashion
- places responsibility for obtaining data and establishes time frames for this activity
- are used for program control
- requires a feedback mechanism so that an ineffective or inefficient activity can be identified and changed while the program continues

Cost/benefit analysis, which involves converting all costs of and benefits from the program into monetary terms, and cost-effectiveness analysis, which measures the cost involved in attaining some desirable health-related outcome, are often used in program evaluation. Cost/benefit analysis allows for comparison of different types of projects, while cost-effectiveness analysis allows for comparison only of those projects sharing similar outcomes.[3,4,8]

Determining Needed Financial Resources

Financial resources needed to carry out the program plan include direct and indirect costs. Direct costs include personnel salaries and benefits, equipment, office and clinic supplies, counseling and educational materials, reference materials, and travel, phone and correspondence costs. Indirect costs include administrative overhead, clinic and office space, maintenance, depreciation, central supplies, bookkeeping, and data processing.[9] If the personnel needed to carry out the activities and tasks were identified while establishing the course of action, direct personnel costs can be readily determined. Time involved by each type of worker should be translated into man-days or full- or part-time employee equivalents. Employee benefit costs, which are often substantial, can usually be obtained from the business office.

Other material resource needs should similarly have been identified while planning the activities. Data collection and analysis costs may involve personnel costs and use of equipment or administrative charges or fees for data processing. If subcontracts are used, costs of administering these contracts must be included along with the costs of the contract itself.

Reviewing the budgets of similar programs is useful in identifying costs that might be overlooked. It is often wise to draft the budget and then have it reviewed by experienced administrators and fiscal managers.

ADVOCATING FOR PROGRAMS AND SERVICES

Meeting the needs of a community often involves obtaining more resources than are presently available and advocating for additional resources. The advocacy target may be an agency supervisor or policy maker; another public or private agency, organization, or foundation; or the city, state, or federal legislature.

Advocacy involves[3]

- being well informed about the need for the program by having sound statistics on the severity of the problem, the numbers of people affected, and the disadvantages of not having the program
- understanding views of opponents and being prepared to address them
- knowing alternate funding sources, ways of making the program self-supporting, or other financing mechanisms if financing is a major issue
- obtaining support for the program from appropriate sources such as other program directors, other agencies, professional organizations or civic groups, influential citizens, or "constituents"
- building a coalition with those with similar interests, particularly those with a track record of successful advocacy
- communicating effectively with the potential resource on a substantial basis, providing written documentation for your position, and being available to answer questions or problem solve
- understanding the legislative process if the advocacy target is a legislature, so that verbal and written comment can be appropriate, timely, and adequately prepared
- knowing when hearings are to be held on related regulations or guidelines so that testimony can be presented to include appropriate nutrition services

FINANCING NUTRITION SERVICES

Potential sources for financing nutrition services include

- federal, state, and local governmental agencies' formula, block, or project grants or contracts
- private sector funding sources such as foundation or corporate grants or contracts, civic organizations, not-for-profit health-related organizations, or associations
- fees for services
- income from sale of products such as educational materials

Major sources of information on funding resources include

- federal health, education, and agriculture agencies, especially the United States Public Health Service and the Department of Agriculture. Nutrition personnel of the federal agencies can provide information on specific federal support applicable to nutrition services (also see reference 10 and Appendix 9-A)
- *The Federal Register,* which contains requests for applications (RFAs) on programs funded by the federal government
- the Federal Office of Management and Budget, which disseminates information through the *Catalog of Federal Domestic Assistance*
- the Maternal and Child Health Clearinghouse, which can provide information on projects that have been funded through Maternal and Child Health grants
- state health, mental health, education, and social service agencies, whose employees can identify potential sources of financial support, including reimbursement for services
- corporations or foundations, which often have a department to deal with corporate giving
- the Foundation Center, with libraries in New York City, Cleveland, Washington, DC, and San Francisco and a nationwide network of reference collections with information on foundation grants and workshops for individuals seeking grants
- private and public insurers, which can provide information on coverage of specific nutrition services

PROVIDING CLIENT NUTRITION SERVICES

Direct provision of nutrition services to clients served by public agencies is sometimes a responsibility of local public health nutritionists. These services include the traditional clinical nutrition services of

- performing a nutrition assessment (see Chapter 2)
- providing nutrition counseling and education
- developing and monitoring the nutrition care plan
- utilizing all available resources needed by the client
- ensuring quality care and evaluation services
- providing case management when nutrition problems are a major concern of the client

Nutrition Assessment

For additional guidance on nutrition assessment of children see Chapter 2. Since nutrition resources are always in short supply, appropriate triaging of clients is essential to allow the nutritionist to spend more time counseling high-risk clients. This can be accomplished by

- utilizing non-nutrition personnel or nutrition technicians to screen clients for referral to the nutritionist
- using appropriate screening criteria
- determining during the initial interview which clients need more assistance
- developing care plans that meet the needs of the individual client but utilize the nutritionist's time efficiently

Some clients will need counseling by the nutritionist at each clinic visit if necessary changes in dietary habits are to take place; others may need to see the nutritionist only as nutrition problems are detected; some may need only basic nutrition counseling by another health professional such as a nurse, nutrition technician, health educator, or trained paraprofessional.

Interviewing and Counseling

Since clients of community health settings are often in the system for relatively long periods of time and may have many health, social, and economic problems, health education and counseling are major services. If the setting is conducive to effective group education and the education is well planned and executed, some clients can benefit from group education. However, many clients need individual counseling to improve dietary habits. Effective nutrition counseling is essential if the results are to be lifestyle changes needed to improve the nutritional health of the client and his or her family or caregiver.[11]

To bring about behavioral change, nutritionists must understand human behavior and how people learn.[3] Steps in the counseling process include[12–14]

- reviewing all available data, including the medical record, laboratory results, and socioeconomic information, prior to the interview
- explaining the counseling relationship to the client
- evaluating the client's nutritional state and relating food intake data to behavioral indicators
- assisting the client in setting realistic, achievable nutrition goals
- providing specific information as needed and indicated
- monitoring the client's performance
- ending the counseling and allowing for periodic follow-up
- evaluating the counselor's own performance

The following tips will help the nutritionist to achieve the foregoing objectives:

- develop mutual respect and rapport with the client
- determine through careful listening how the client feels about the nutrition problem/s, obstacles that need to be overcome if dietary changes are to occur, and specific actions that might be helpful for improving the diet
- encourage the client to provide information by comments that do not lead him or her to give "desirable" answers and by showing interest in what is being said and empathy for the client
- allow opportunity for clarifying or restating the situation
- assist the client in taking responsibility for action that will lead to improved dietary intake
- involve the client/caregiver in all decision making
- identify potential stumbling blocks to compliance
- assist the client in identification of reachable nutrition goals
- assist the client in understanding how to remove obstacles that make behavioral change difficult
- provide only the amount of information the client can utilize, and no more, during any one counseling session
- base counseling on the client's need to know
- if non-nutrition health or socioeconomic problems are of higher priority for the client, assist him or her in finding relevant resources before proceeding with nutrition counseling

- provide frequent brief counseling sessions, which may be more useful than longer but less frequent ones
- utilize standard behavior modification techniques as appropriate and allow clients to practice their dietary changes under supervision
- monitor the client's progress in reaching objectives and compliment his or her successes
- revise the care plan as indicated by progress or lack of it

Some deterrents to dietary adherence include[12]

- restrictiveness of dietary recommendations
- required changes in lifestyle and behavior
- lack of meaningful relief once changes are made
- increased cost of foods
- unavailability of foods
- change in food preparation techniques

COMMUNITY RESOURCES

Clients of community nutrition services may have many nutrition-related needs that must be met if nutritional status is to be improved. Knowing and using all available community food resources and nutrition services is an important part of community nutrition services.

Typical community food and nutrition resources are shown in Appendix 9-A. These resources are not available in all communities. Information on their availability can be obtained from the local health department or public health nursing service.

GROUP CHILD CARE (DAY CARE)

Day care is defined as the care, supervision, and guidance of children, unaccompanied by parents or guardians, on a regular basis, for periods of less than 24 hours per day, outside the children's own home.[15] The food and nutrition services provided by the day care program play a major role in the health and well-being of children in group care.[16] The goal of the nutrition service is to ensure that the child attains or maintains the best possible nutritional state.[17] To reach this goal the nutrition service should

- help meet the total nutritional needs of the children by providing meals and snacks that supply a proportional amount of nutrients and calories based on the length of time in the day care setting

- provide food with consideration for the cultural and ethnic patterns, food practices, and socialization needs of the child and his or her family
- provide food in a clean, safe, and pleasant environment
- encourage the development of good food habits as part of a healthful lifestyle
- help the child grow and develop appropriately
- provide a continuing nutrition education program for children, parents, and day care staff
- identify nutrition problems in the child and act to remedy the problems (see Chapter 15 and "Providing Client Nutrition Services," above).

Food service personnel must have a sound understanding of food sanitation and safety principles and practices and apply them in their daily activities.[18] They must also be knowledgeable about the nutritional needs of young children and ways to meet them through food, and understand the importance of helping children develop good food habits that will last a lifetime.

The nutrition education component of the program includes education of the children through the food service as well as through carefully planned nutrition education in the classroom. There are many excellent resources for preschool nutrition education.[19,20] Parents and staff should be included in this educational effort.

As increasing numbers of children with special health care needs are mainstreamed into local communities, larger numbers of children with handicaps and chronic diseases are participating in day care.[21] Day care nutrition services must be able to provide for the modified diets and atypical feeding methods these children will need.

To ensure safe and high-quality food and nutrition services in day care, the programs should employ or contract with a registered dietitian, well trained and experienced in child nutrition services, to direct, manage, and monitor the food and nutrition services; to provide nutrition training for personnel; to oversee the food service, nutrition education, and parent counseling; to assure nutrition assessment and care; and to help meet the special needs of some children.

National Health and Safety Performance Standards, which have recently been developed by a joint committee of the American Academy of Pediatrics and the American Public Health Association, include nutrition and food service standards that should be observed.[22]

REFERENCES

1. *Guide for Developing Nutrition Services in Community Health Programs.* Rockville, Md: US Department of Health, Education, and Welfare Public Health Service; 1978. DHEW publication no. (HSA) 78-5103.

2. Dodds JW, Kaufman M, eds. *Personnel in Public Health Nutrition for the 1990s.* Washington, DC: US Department of Health and Human Services; 1991. Officials Foundation; 1982.

3. Owen AY, Frankle RT. *Nutrition in the Community. The Art of Delivering Services.* St Louis, Mo: Times Mirror/Mosby College Publishing; 1986.

4. Simko MD, Cowell C, Gilbridge JA. *Assessing Nutritional Needs of Groups. A Handbook for the Health Care Team.* New York, NY: Department of Human Economics and Nutrition, New York University; 1980.

5. Simko MD, Cowell C, Gilbride JA. *Nutrition Assessment: A Comprehensive Guide for Planning Intervention.* Gaithersburg, Md: Aspen Publishers; 1984.

6. Kaufman M, ed. *Quality Assurance in Ambulatory Nutrition Care.* Chicago, Ill: American Dietetic Association; 1983.

7. Baer MT, ed. *Nutrition Services for Children with Handicaps. A Manual for State Title V Programs.* Los Angeles, Calif: University Affiliated Training, Center for Child Development and Developmental Disorders; 1982.

8. Disbrow D, Bertram K. *Cost Benefit Cost Effectiveness Analysis. A Practical Step-by-Step Guide for Nutrition Professionals.* Modesto, Calif: Bertram Nutrition Associates; 1984.

9. Splett P, Caldwell M. *Costing Nutrition Services. A Workbook.* Chicago, Ill: Region V Public Health Service, US Department of Health and Human Services; 1985.

10. Office of Disease Prevention and Health Promotion. *Locating Funds for Health Promotion Projects.* Washington, DC: US Department of Health and Human Services, Public Health Service.

11. Hodges PA, Vickery CE. *Effective Counseling Strategies for Dietary Management.* Gaithersburg, Md: Aspen Publishers; 1989.

12. Snetselaar LC. *Nutrition Counseling Skills: Assessment, Treatment, Evaluation.* Gaithersburg, Md: Aspen Publishers; 1983.

13. Raab C, Tillotson JL, eds. *Heart to Heart. A Manual on Nutrition Counseling for Reduction of Cardiovascular Disease Risk Factors.* Washington, DC: US Department of Health and Human Services, Public Health Service; 1983. NIH publication no. 83-1528.

14. Glanz K. Strategies for nutrition counseling. *J Am Diet Assoc.* 1979 (April); 74:431–437.

15. *Guides for Day Care Licensing.* Washington, DC: DHEW publication no. (OCD) 73-1053.

16. *Head Start Performance Standards*, 45 CFR 1304, US Department of Health and Human Services, 1984.

17. *Handbook for Local Head Start Nutrition Specialists.* Washington, DC: US Department of Health, Education and Welfare; 1975.

18. *Training Guide for Foodservice Personnel in Programs for Young Children.* Washington, DC: US Department of Health and Human Services; 1987. DHHS publication no. (OHDS) 87-31152.

19. *Head Start Nutrition Education Curriculum.* Washington, DC: US Department of Health and Human Services, Head Start Bureau; 1987.

20. Goodwin M, Pollen G. *Creative Food Experiences for Children.* Washington, DC: Center for Science in the Public Interest; 1980.

21. Public Law 99-457, Oct. 8, 1986, 99th Congress, 100 Stat. 1146 Education of the Handicapped Act Amendments of 1986.

22. American Academy of Pediatrics/American Public Health Association Collaborative Project. *Development of National Health and Safety Performance Standards for Out-of-Home Child Care Programs.* Washington, DC: American Public Health Association; in press.

Appendix 9-A

Food and Nutrition Resources

Program/Service	Assistance Provided	Sponsor
Food Resources		
Supplemental Food Program for Women, Infants and Children (WIC)	Vouchers to purchase or provide specific foods for low-income pregnant, postpartum, or lactating women, infants, and children 0 to 5 years at nutritional risk; limited nutrition education	USDA Food and Nutrition Service (FNS), state health, and tribal agencies
Commodity Supplemental Food Program	Commodity foods for populations similar to those eligible for WIC (see above)	FNS, state health, and tribal agencies
Food Stamp Program	Food stamps to purchase foods for low-income households	FNS, state welfare agencies
School Lunch and Breakfast Program	Lunch or breakfast free or at reduced price to eligible children in participating schools; encourages nutrition education	FNS, state education agency
Child Care and Adult Food Program	Free meals and snacks to children in participating child care centers and adults in group settings	FNS, state education agency, public or private nonprofit child care centers and adult group settings
Summer Food Program	Free meals and snacks to children during summer vacations in recreation centers, summer camps	FNS, state education agency, public or private nonprofits, or summer camps
Food depositories and pantries	Food for needy families and individuals	Churches, community organizations
Soup kitchens	Meals for needy families and individuals	Churches, community organizations

244

Program/Service	Assistance Provided	Sponsor
Home-delivered meals	Meals delivered to the homebound sick, handicapped, or elderly; free or reduced price	Official or voluntary welfare or health agencies, churches, hospitals

Nutrition Services

Program/Service	Assistance Provided	Sponsor
Public health nursing services	Home visiting, prenatal and child health clinics, pre- and postnatal educational classes for parents	State, local health departments; visiting nurse associations
Public health nutrition services	Nutrition assessments and counseling, nutrition education on general topics such as health promotion and weight control and on specific topics for audiences such as pregnant women, parents of young children, individuals with chronic diseases	State, local health departments; community health and migrant health centers
School health and nursing services	Assists school food services to meet student's special needs; may provide nutrition counseling	Local school systems
School occupational/physical therapy	Assists children with special health care needs with feeding problems: food modifications, adaptive feeding equipment, feeding techniques	Local school systems
Early intervention programs	Health services necessary to enable handicapped newborns to 5-year-olds to benefit from education and to prevent or minimize developmental delay	US Department of Education-designated state agency
Medicaid	Health care for low-income pregnant women and children; may include nutrition assessment and counseling	US Department of Health and Human Services (USDHHS); state welfare agency
Early and Periodic Screening, Diagnosis, and Treatment (EPSDT)	Health screening, diagnosis, and treatment, including nutrition, for low-income children	US Department of Health and Human Services (USDHHS); state welfare agency
State Program for Children with Special Health Care Needs (CSHCN)	Case management, diagnosis, and treatment for eligible children	USDHHS, designated state agency
University-Affiliated Programs (UAP)	Assessment and development of treatment plan, management, and care of the mentally handicapped/chronically ill as needed to support training of health professionals	USDHHS, institutions of higher learning

continues

Appendix 9-A continued

Program/Service	Assistance Provided	Sponsor
Head Start	Meals and snacks, nutrition education, parent counseling and education, nutrition screening for preschool children in low-income areas	USDHHS, not-for-profit community agencies, schools
Hospital outreach programs	Nutrition education, weight control, diet therapy classes, patient counseling	Medical centers, hospitals
Nutrition counseling services	Nutrition assessment and counseling of private patients, nutrition education, weight control, diet therapy classes	Dietitians in private practice

Nutrition Education Resources

Cooperative extension home economics services	Education in home economics, food and nutrition, child care, food preservation, food purchasing, menu planning, weight control	US Department of Agriculture (USDA), land grant colleges
Expanded Food and Nutrition Education Program (EFNEP)	Education by supervised paraprofessionals in nutrition, food preparation, money management, shopping, housekeeping, sanitation, child rearing, family relations; for low-income families	USDA, Cooperative Extension Service
Nutrition Education and Training (NET)	Teaches fundamentals of nutrition to children, parents, educators, and food service personnel	USDA, state agency
Dairy Council	Nutrition education materials for individuals, teachers, health professionals; nutrition education for preschool and school-age children, pregnant women	National Dairy Council and local affiliates
Heart Association	Educational materials and classes on prevention and control of heart disease for the public, individuals, and health professionals	American Heart Association and state and local affiliates
Cancer societies	Education materials on prevention and control of cancer for the public, individuals, and health professionals	American Cancer Society and state and area affiliates
Diabetes Association	Educational materials and classes on control of diabetes for the public, individuals, and health professionals	American Diabetes Association and affiliates and chapters
Red Cross	Educational materials and classes on nutrition, child care, prenatal care, menu planning, food service	American Red Cross and local chapters
March of Dimes	Educational materials, and classes on maternal and infant nutrition	March of Dimes Birth Defects Foundation national headquarters and local chapters

Part II

Therapeutic Pediatric Nutrition

Chapter 10

Enteral Nutrition

Catherine Detamore Lingard

Healthy infants and children possess the capacity to orally consume a diet that provides adequate nutrients. Unfortunately, this may not be possible for a number of pediatric patients with a variety of acute and/or chronic conditions. Infants and children who are unwilling or unable to ingest, digest, or absorb an adequate amount of nutrients orally are candidates for an alternate route of nutritional support. If the patient's gastrointestinal tract is functioning, enteral nutrition is indicated.

Enteral nutrition refers to the nonvolitional delivery of nutrients by a tube to the gastrointestinal tract. Enteral nutrition is preferred over the parenteral route because it is more physiologic,[1,2] is associated with fewer technical and infectious complications,[3] and is also less expensive.[4,5] Additionally, enteral feedings may be nutritionally superior to parenteral feedings since more is known about enteral nutrient requirements and utilization.[4] Advances in commercial formulas and equipment for their delivery have made enteral feeding safe and efficacious to administer to pediatric patients in either the hospital or home setting.

This chapter provides practical guidelines for: (1) selecting appropriate candidates for enteral nutrition, ranging in age from birth to 18 years; (2) selecting specific products; (3) administering and monitoring enteral feedings; and (4) considering age-related factors for the pediatric population. Note that enteral feeding of the premature infant is addressed in Chapter 3 of this text.

PATIENT SELECTION

Protein-energy malnutrition (PEM) has been well documented in pediatric hospital settings and is most frequently observed in critically ill infants and children who are diagnosed with various acute and chronic diseases.[6–11] PEM in infants and children is often associated with growth failure,[12] impaired immune function,[13] alterations in major organ function,[14] psychologic disturbances,[15] and a prolonged hospital stay.[8] Early identification of patients who are at nutritional risk and subsequent intervention may prevent PEM and its associated complications.

Candidates for enteral nutrition can be identified through a hospital screening program.[16] A screening program at Children's Mercy Hospital in Kansas City, Missouri, utilizes the joint expertise of both diet technicians and clinical dietitians. Essential information required for nutritional screening of pediatric patients was delineated by the clinical dietitians. Correspondingly, the diet technicians complete a form utilizing computerized admission data and associated medical records and questioning the patient and various family members.

The screening device is typically completed within 72 hours of admission. After completion, the dietitian reviews this information on a daily basis and formulates an appropriate nutritional care plan, which may include enteral nutrition support. (See Chapter 2 for additional information on nutritional screening.)

To summarize, pediatric patients with a variety of diseases are at nutritional risk and have been shown to benefit from enteral nutrition support (Table 10-1). However, when enteral nutrition is contraindicated due to severe intestinal dysfunction, parenteral nutrition constitutes the appropriate route for specific nutritional support (Table 10-2).

SELECTION OF SPECIFIC FEEDING ROUTES

Common routes for enteral nutrition in pediatric patients include nasogastric, nasoduodenal, nasojejunal, gastrostomy, and jejunostomy feedings. The risk of aspiration becomes a major consideration when determining whether the tube should be placed in the stomach or small intestine. The expected duration of the enteral feeding also is a factor when determining whether a nasoenteral or a surgically placed tube will be used.

Gastric Feeding

A direct gastric feeding is preferable to an intestinal feeding since it allows for a more normal digestive process. This is generally true since the stomach serves as a reservoir and provides for a gradual release of nutrients into the small bowel. Gastric feedings are associated with a larger osmotic and volume tolerance, a more flexible feeding schedule, easier tube insertions, and a lower frequency of diarrhea and dumping syndrome. In addition, gastric acid has a bactericidal effect that may be an important factor in decreasing the patient's susceptibility to various infections.

Nasogastric feeding is generally indicated when tube feedings are expected to continue for a short period of time or for patients who only require supplemental

Table 10-1 Indications for Enteral Nutrition in Pediatric Patients

Diminished Ability To Ingest Nutrients
1. Neurologic disorders
   • Coma
   • Guillain Barré syndrome
   • Head injury
   • Severe mental retardation
   • Cerebral palsy that affects oral motor skills
2. Wired jaw
3. Rhabdomyosarcoma of the nasopharynx
4. Injury to mouth or esophagus
5. Congenital anomalies
   • Tracheoesophageal fistula
   • Pierre Robin syndrome
   • Esophageal atresia
   • Severe cleft palate
Failure to Meet Full Nutrient Needs Orally
1. Increased metabolic needs
   • Burns
   • Sepsis
   • Trauma
   • Congenital heart disease
2. Anorexia due to chronic disease
   • Cancer
   • Chronic liver disease
   • Cystic fibrosis
   • Chronic renal disease
   • Sickle cell disease
3. Psychologic disorders
   • Anorexia nervosa
   • Nonorganic failure to thrive
Altered Absorption or Metabolism of Nutrients
1. Chronic diarrhea
2. Short bowel syndrome
3. Inflammatory bowel disease
4. Glycogen storage disease types I and III
5. Gastroesophageal reflux

Source: Data from references 17, 75 to 102.

---

nocturnal feedings. Practitioners have noted that many pediatric patients who receive home enteral nutrition often use nasogastric tubes for years.[17] These patients frequently insert the tube at night and remove it in the morning in order to attend school or other activities without feeling self-conscious about having a tube.

Nasogastric feeding is contraindicated in patients with severe esophagitis or who have an obstruction between the nose and stomach. In addition, nasogastric

Table 10-2 Potential Contraindications for Enteral Nutrition in Pediatric Patients

Necrotizing enterocolitis
Gastrointestinal obstruction
Intestinal atresia
Severe inflammatory bowel disease
Severe gastrointestinal side effects of cancer therapy
Severe acute pancreatitis

---

tubes may not be tolerated in neonates, who are obligate nose breathers. To prevent airway occlusion in this instance, orogastric tubes are often used when tube feeding is indicated.

A variety of small-bore soft nasogastric tubes are available for use in pediatric patients.[18,19] Desirable features of pediatric nasogastric tubes are outlined in Table 10-3. When selecting a feeding tube, considerations should be given to the child's age and size, the viscosity of the formula, and whether an infusion device will be used.[20] By selecting the tube with the smallest bore possible, the child's comfort will be increased and associated trauma will be minimized (Table 10-4). Note that longer tubes may be required for nasoduodenal or nasojejunal intubation.

Specific guidelines referring to tube insertion and placement verification have been published elsewhere.[20–22] Improper tube insertion or placement can lead to a number of potentially serious complications. For example, the soft small-bore tube may be inadvertently inserted into the trachea.[23] Practitioners should verify the correct placement of the nasogastric tube by utilizing both auscultation and aspiration techniques. If a gastric aspirate is not obtained, tube placement confirmation by radiography is mandatory in many institutions before feedings are initiated.

Table 10-3 Desirable Features of a Pediatric Nasogastric Tube

1. Made of silastic or polyurethane
2. Available in small diameters (size 10 French or less)
3. Available in variety of lengths with markings to facilitate measuring depth of tube insertion
4. Has a weighted tip to prevent dislodgement
5. Has a smooth bolus to facilitate easy insertion and removal
6. Has a stylet that remains in place during insertion, is prelubricated for easy removal, and is flow-through to determine proper tube placement with stylet still in place
7. Is radiopaque for placement verification
8. Is compatible with administration sets and with feeding containers in a variety of sizes to accommodate use in neonates and older children

Source: Reprinted from Cooning SW, Unique aspects in pediatric care, in *Nutritional Support in Critical Care* (p 399) by CE Lang (ed), Aspen Publishers, Inc, © 1987.

Table 10-4 Nasoenteric Tube Selection Guide for Infants and Children

Tube Length

	Length in Inches	
Age	*Nasogastric*	*Transpyloric*
<1 year	22 inch	22–36 inch
1–18 years	36 inch	36–43 inch

*Tube Diameter**

Formula Categories	*Tube Size (French) Gravity*	*Tube Size (French) Pump*
Infant formula	5–6	5–6
Blenderized	12–18	8–10
Milk-based	8–10	6–8
Lactose-free	8	6–8
Fiber-enriched	10	6–8
Elemental	6	6
High-density	8–10	6–10

**Source:* Adapted from *Handbook of Enteral Nutrition: A Practical Guide to Tube Feeding* (p 71) by D Del Rio, K Williams and B Esvelt, Medical Specifics Publishing, © 1982.

Gastrostomy feedings are indicated when a patient is incapable of obtaining adequate nutrition by eating over a prolonged period of time. However, gastrostomy tubes require surgical placement. They are frequently used with patients who have various congenital anomalies and neurologic disorders. Surgical techniques for gastrostomy tube placement and associated potential complications, as well as nursing care, are described elsewhere.[24,25]

Transpyloric Feedings

Nasoduodenal or nasojejunal feeding is desirable for patients who are at risk of aspiration. Typically, this includes patients who have a diminished gag reflex, delayed gastric emptying, frequent vomiting, or severe gastroesophageal reflux.

Nasojejunal feeding may be more efficacious than duodenal feeding in preventing aspiration. Gastric reflux of duodenally administered solutions has been reported.[26] Additionally, nasoduodenal tubes may fail to enter or stay in the duodenum, resulting in aspiration.[27] Thus aspiration precautions should be used during nasoduodenal feedings. Nasojejunal tubes may also be less likely than nasoduodenal tubes to become dislodged in children with cystic fibrosis, who may experience severe coughing episodes. This is also true for children with cancer, who may have vomiting associated with chemotherapy. Specific procedures for nasoduodenal or nasojejunal intubation have been outlined by Wesley.[24] The enteric position of the tube requires radiographic verification before feeding is initiated. A potential complication of transpyloric feeding is intestinal perforation with use of stiff, large-bore tubes.[23] Use of small-bore tubes made of polyurethane or silicone should decrease the incidence of this complication.

Jejunostomy Feeding

A surgically placed jejunostomy tube may be indicated for patients who require either an extended course of jejunal feeding or early postoperative feedings of a defined formula diet.[28] Some practitioners have reported placing a jejunal tube via a gastrostomy catheter or stoma to provide jejunal feeding.[29,30]

PRODUCT SELECTION

There is a wide variety of commercial infant and adult enteral formulas that can be utilized for pediatric patients. However, proper product selection is contingent upon a number of factors related to the specific medical and nutritional status of the patient.

Patient-specific factors include age, gastrointestinal function, history of feeding tolerance, nutrient requirements, and feeding route. Other important factors to take into consideration are formula-specific. These factors include osmolality, renal solute load, nutrient complexity, product availability and cost, and caloric density. Select patient- and formula-specific factors will be explored in greater detail below.

Infants Less Than 1 Year of Age

Human milk and/or commercial infant formulas constitute the most appropriate feedings for infants who are less than 1 year of age. Proposed standards specifying the nutrient content of infant formulas have been established by both the American Academy of Pediatrics[31] and the Infant Formula Act of 1980.[32] These standards are based upon estimated requirements, which will promote optimal growth in infants from birth to 12 months.

General categories of commercial infant formulas include standard cow's milk-based, soy formulas (lactose-free), casein hydrolysates (semi-elemental), and those modified in fat (Table 10-5). The available formula choices contain macro-

Table 10-5 Characteristics of Selected Enteral Formulas

Formula Classification	Product Characteristics	Possible Indications for Use	Infant Formula (Manufacturer)	Adult Formula (Manufacturer)
Standard milk-based	Intact protein Lactose containing Long-chain triglycerides Moderate residue Low to moderate osmolality	Normally functioning gastrointestinal tract Lactose tolerant	Human milk Similac (Ross) Enfamil (Mead Johnson) SMA (Wyeth) PM 60:40† (Ross)	Compleat* (Sandoz)
Standard lactose-free	Intact protein Low to moderate residue Low to moderate osmolality	Primary lactase deficiency Secondary lactase deficiency (intestinal injury or PEM) Galactosemia	Isomil (Ross) Prosobee (Mead Johnson) Nursoy (Wyeth)	Ensure (Ross) Osmolite§ (Ross) Isocal§ (Mead Johnson) Pediasure‖ (Ross)
Standard fiber-containing ¶	Intact protein Lactose-free 4.3 to 14 g fiber per 1000 ml Low to moderate osmolality	Constipation Diarrhea Normal digestive and absorptive capacity		Jevity§ (Ross) Sustacal with fiber (Mead Johnson) Compleat-Modified* (Sandoz)
Lactose-free/modified fat	Intact protein Fat content is 88% medium-chain triglycerides and 12% long-chain triglycerides	Chylothorax Intestinal lymphangiectasia Severe steatorrhea	Portagen§# (Mead Johnson)	Portagen§# (Mead Johnson)
Semi-elemental	Hydrolyzed protein** (peptides and amino acids) Lactose-free Low to moderate osmolality	Steatorrhea Intestinal resection Cystic fibrosis Chronic liver disease Inflammatory bowel disease	Pregestimil§ (Mead Johnson) Alimentum§ (Ross) Nutramigen†† (Mead Johnson)	Vital HN§ (Ross) Reabilan§ (O'Brien)

continues

Table 10-5 continued

Formula Classification	Product Characteristics	Possible Indications for Use	Infant Formula (Manufacturer)	Adult Formula (Manufacturer)
Semi-elemental (cont.)	Partial medium-chain triglyceride content	Diarrhea associated with hypoalbuminemia Allergy to cow's milk and soy proteins Not needed for jejunal feedings in patients with normal gastrointestinal function		
Elemental	Protein in form of free amino acids Lactose-free High osmolality Low fat Carbohydrate in form of glucose oligosaccharides	Intestinal fistula[tt] Glycogen storage disease Chylothorax or intestinal lymphangiectasia not responsive to Portagen		Tolerex[ss] (Sandoz)[tt]
Calorically dense	Intact protein Lactose-free High renal solute load High osmolality 1.5–2.0 kcal/ml	Fluid restriction Increased metabolic needs Not recommended for transpyloric feedings		Ensure Plus (Ross) Magnacal (Sherwood Medical)

* Blenderized feedings, contain 4.3 g dietary fiber per 1000 kcal.
† Low in phosphorus.
§ Contains medium-chain triglycerides as part of its total fat.
‖ Designed for children from ages 1 to 6.
¶ Average fiber intake of children aged 1 to 5 is 6.6 g per 1000 kcal. See reference 106.
# Standardly prepared from powder at a 20 cal/oz dilution for infants and a 30 cal/oz dilution for children and adults. Essential fatty acid deficiency may occur with long-term use in infants with chronic liver disease. See reference 107.
** Clinical trials are lacking that compare the use of protein hydrolysates to intact protein in gastrointestinal disease. See reference 108.
†† Does not contain medium-chain triglycerides.
‡‡ Use of elemental formulas decreases intestinal secretions. See reference 109.
§§ Essential fatty acid deficiency has been reported with use in children with cystic fibrosis. See reference 110.

Source: Data from references 46, 103 to 105.

nutrients in either complex or semi-elemental forms, which are suited for a variety of medical problems typically found in infants (Table 10-6). Guidelines for the use of the various infant formulas have been published by Brady et al.[33] The use of highly specialized formulas for infants and children with inborn errors of metabolism is addressed in Chapter 12.

Table 10-6 Macronutrient Content of Infant and Adult Formulas

	Carbohydrate	Protein	Fat
Caloric Distribution (standard products)			
Infant formulas	40%–54%	9%–14%	35%–50%
Adult formulas	45%–60%	12%–20%	30%–40%
Intact sources	Modified food starch* Vegetables Corn syrup solids Tapioca starch Hydrolyzed cereal solids	Milk[†] Casein isolate[†] Soy isolate[†] Lactalbumin[†] Beef[†] Sodium caseinate[†] Calcium caseinate[†] Egg white solids[†]	Long-chain triglycerides:[‡] corn oil, soy oil, sunflower oil, safflower oil, butterfat
Semi-elemental sources	Glucose oligosaccharides[§] Maltodextrins Lactose[‖] Sucrose[‖]	Partially hydrolyzed casein, whey, lactalbumin, meat, soy, fish[¶]	Medium-chain triglycerides: fractionated coconut oil[#]
Elemental forms**	Glucose	Crystalline amino acids[††]	Short-chain triglycerides[‡‡]

* Starch is well tolerated in most disease states.
[†] Pancreatic enzymes are required for digestion.
[‡] Long-chain triglycerides contain essential fatty acids (EFAs). The EFA requirement for infants is 2.7% of calories. Bile acids and pancreatic lipase are required for digestion and absorption. A trophic effect on bowel mucosa has been observed following intestinal resection. See references 31 and 111.
[§] Glucose polymers from 2–10 units, which are rapidly hydrolyzed by the brush border enzyme maltase.
[‖] Require disaccharidases in the brush border for hydrolysis prior to absorption.
[¶] Enzymatically hydrolyzed to oligopeptides, dipeptides, tripeptides, and free amino acids. There is a reduced allergenic response following mucosal injury; see reference 112.
[#] Fatty acid chains of 8 to 12 carbon atoms, which require less bile salts and pancreatic lipase than long-chain triglycerides for digestion and absorption. They are absorbed directly into the portal vein without micelle or chylomicron formation and do not contain essential fatty acids. See references 108 and 113.
**Contribute significantly to osmolality due to their small particle size.
[††] Short peptide chains have a more efficient absorption system than free amino acids; see references 114 and 115.
[‡‡] Less practical for use because of chemical instability; see reference 116.

The standard dilution for infant formulas is 20 cal/oz. However, infants who have increased metabolic needs and/or a decreased fluid tolerance may not be able to consume an adequate volume of standard formulas in order to promote growth. In this instance, a more concentrated formula may be needed. Formulas with a caloric density greater than 20 cal/oz are most commonly provided to infants with chronic lung disease and congenital heart disease, or to those infants with chronic renal failure who require continuous ambulatory peritoneal dialysis. Concentrated infant formulas may also be useful for infants with nonorganic failure to thrive during periods of catch-up growth.

Infant formulas can be safely concentrated to a maximum of 30 cal/oz (without modular additives) by adding less water to a concentrated liquid or powdered formula base.[34] If human milk is used in lieu of infant formulas, it can be concentrated with the addition of powdered infant formula. When this formula base (or human milk) is concentrated, the infant's water balance in relation to renal solute load should also be monitored (see Table 10-7).

If insensible water losses are increased (see Table 10-8), it would be advisable to only concentrate the base formula (or human milk) to 24 cal/oz. The caloric density can be further increased by utilizing modular additives of carbohydrate (glucose polymers) or fat (vegetable oil or medium-chain triglycerides).

Carbohydrate and fat additives do not increase the renal solute load. However, carbohydrate additives can cause a moderate increase in osmolality. With the addition of a long-chain triglyceride, the gastric emptying time may also be decreased.[35] This effect may only be clinically significant for those infants who are at risk for aspiration and already have delayed gastric emptying.

Increases in caloric density are best tolerated by the patient when advanced gradually in increments of 2 to 4 cal/oz/d. Formulas that consist of a base concentration of 24 to 26 cal/oz and also contain modular additives of fat (e.g., 0.25 to 0.50 g corn oil per ounce) and/or carbohydrates (e.g., 0.5 to 1 g glucose polymer per ounce), which equal 30 to 32 cal/oz, are generally well tolerated by infants.

When carbohydrate and fat modulars are added to a formula, caution is required

---

Table 10-7 Physical Signs and Symptoms of Dehydration

Weight loss > 1% per day
Increased thirst
Decreased skin turgor
Dry oral membranes
Increased urine specific gravity (>1.030)
Decreased urine output (<1–2 ml/kg/h)
Increased hematocrit and serum sodium, and blood urea nitrogen levels
Fever
Depressed anterior fontanel in an infant

Table 10-8 Fluid Requirements of Pediatric Patients

Weight of Patient (kg)	Baseline Fluid Requirement*
1–10	100 ml/kg
11–20	1000 ml plus 50 ml/kg for each kg >10 kg
>20	1500 ml plus 20 ml/kg for each kg > 20 kg
or	or
>10	1500–1800 ml/m²/d

*Insensible water losses are increased in the following conditions: (1) 13% per degree Centigrade elevation in body temperature; (2) 50%–100% in elevated environmental temperatures; and (3) 5–25 ml per 100 kcal/d with visible sweating. See references 34 and 117.

Source: Adapted from *Manual of Pediatric Parenteral Nutrition* (p 71) by JA Kerner (ed) with permission of Churchill Livingstone, © 1983.

to ensure that an appropriate distribution of calories is provided. Foman recommends the following caloric distribution for infants: 7% to 16% of calories from protein, 30% to 55% of calories from fat, and 35% to 65% of calories from carbohydrate.[36] It is important to note that when the protein intake provides for less than 6% of the caloric intake, protein deficiency may result.[36] Protein intakes accounting for more than 16% of calories could contribute to azotemia and negative water balance if associated fluid intakes are low. Additionally, high carbohydrate intakes may contribute to osmotic diarrhea, and fat intakes that exceed 60% of the formula calories could lead to ketosis.

Children Greater Than 1 Year

Feedings typically provided to children who are greater than 1 year of age include concentrated infant formulas, Pediasure (Ross Laboratories), various homemade blenderized feedings, and a number of commercial adult formulas. The caloric density of feedings typically utilized for children in this age group is approximately 30 cal/oz. Once again, the caloric density may need to be increased further if the patients have increased metabolic needs and/or decreased fluid tolerance.

Pediasure is the only commercially manufactured formula specifically designed for children from 1 to 6 years of age. Approximately 1100 ml of this product provides the daily Recommended Dietary Allowances (RDAs) for children who fall within this age group. Pediasure is isotonic and lactose-free, with a partial medium-chain triglyceride content to facilitate absorption.

Under specific conditions, infant formulas can be continued through age 4. These formulas can be concentrated to provide higher levels of nutrients. Additional vitamin or mineral supplementation may also be needed, depending upon the specific volume provided. Infant formulas have a lower renal solute load than products designed for patients who are older than 1 year of age. These formulas may be more appropriate for malnourished toddlers who may actually be infant size.

Blenderized Feedings

Blenderized feedings consist of a mixture of various meats, fruits, vegetables, milk (or formula), carbohydrates, fats, water, vitamins, and minerals. Although commercially manufactured blenderized feedings are available, a more common practice is to utilize a homemade version prepared either in the institution's kitchen or at home. Blenderized feedings are moderate in residue and moderate to high in osmolality and viscosity. Since their high viscosity hinders flow through small feeding tubes, these feedings are most often administered as gastrostomy tube feedings. Other disadvantages of blenderized feedings include a potentially high bacteria count[37] and the additional labor required for preparation. In addition, homemade blenderized feedings also provide a more variable nutrient content than commercially manufactured products.

On the other hand, blenderized feedings generally prove to be more economical in the home setting. Economics becomes particularly important to families of children with chronic diseases, and blenderized feedings will continue to represent a viable feeding alternative.

Since inappropriate homemade tube feedings can result in hypernatremic dehydration[38] and a number of nutrient deficiencies, it is of paramount importance to perform a periodic analysis of the recipe. This will allow the dietitian to determine the adequacy of the nutrients as well as the associated fluids. It is equally important to monitor the intake of protein and electrolytes since an excess may lead to a negative water balance in the patient. Guidelines for the safe use of homemade blenderized feedings for children with gastrostomy tubes are available.[39]

Commercial Adult Formulas

A large variety of adult enteral products are commercially available. These products contain macronutrients in various forms (Table 10-6) and can be divided into several general categories: standard milk-based, lactose-free, elemental, fiber-containing, and calorically dense. Table 10-5 describes the general characteristics of selected adult enteral products and provides possible indications for use. This list is not inclusive of all products that are commercially available but is intended to provide examples of products that are available in each general category. Information regarding the complete nutrient composition of commercial adult and infant formulas is readily available from various manufacturers. The utilization of highly specialized adult formulas designed for use in various states of organ failure is beyond the scope of this article and is reviewed elsewhere.[40]

It should be noted that adult enteral products have not been designed for use in children, nor have they been extensively tested in the pediatric population. Specific concerns regarding the use of these products in children are addressed in the upcoming discussions of renal solute load and nutrient requirements.

Renal Solute Load and Fluid Balance

The renal solute load of a formula consists primarily of electrolytes and metabolic end products of protein metabolism that must be excreted in the urine.[34] These solutes require water for urinary excretion. Infants have an immature renal system with limited concentrating ability and therefore require more free water to excrete solutes than do older children and adults. Therefore, infants are at particular risk for negative water balance and subsequent dehydration.

The renal solute load and fluid balance should be closely monitored when infants have a low fluid intake, are receiving calorically dense feedings, and have increased extrarenal fluid losses (i.e., fever, diarrhea, sweating) or impaired renal concentrating ability.[34] Additionally, neurologically impaired infants and children who are unable to indicate thirst may also be at risk for dehydration.

Baseline fluid requirements for pediatric patients and conditions that increase needs are outlined in Table 10-8. Note that infant formulas at standard dilution contain approximately 95% water[34] (preformed water plus water of oxidation). In contrast, standard adult enteral formulas contain approximately 85% water. Since adult formulas are also higher in protein and electrolytes, this contributes to a higher renal solute load. Therefore, when administering adult products to infants and toddlers, proper precautions should be taken. For example, additional water may be required and can usually be given while flushing the feeding tube.

Osmolality

Osmolality refers to the number of particles in a kilogram of solution. The osmolality of a formula may affect the tolerance. Feeding intolerances associated with delivering a hyperosmolar formula may include delayed gastric emptying, abdominal distention, vomiting, or diarrhea.

Carbohydrates, electrolytes, and amino acids are the major factors that determine the gastrointestinal osmotic load of a formula. Smaller particles, such as glucose and free amino acids, contribute more to a higher osmolality than do larger particles such as polysaccharides or intact protein molecules. Thus formulas that contain hydrolyzed protein and monosaccharides will tend to have a higher osmolality than formulas with intact protein and glucose polymers.

The American Academy of Pediatrics suggests that infant formulas should have osmolalities less than 460 mOsm/kg.[31] The osmolality of infant formulas at a caloric density of 20 cal/oz generally falls below this suggested limit (range of 150 to

380 mOsm/kg). However, several of the adult enteral products exceed this limit at a caloric density of 30 cal/oz and may require a dilution to two-thirds' strength prior to use in infants.

Nutrient Requirements

The RDAs published by the National Academy of Sciences (Food and Nutrition Board) are the standards most frequently used for the assessment of enteral intakes of children. It should be noted that the RDAs were intended to be recommendations for a healthy population and may not reflect the needs imposed by specific disease states or medications. In addition, the RDAs (with the exception of energy) include a safety factor that exceeds the requirements of most people in order to ensure that the specific needs of the majority of the population will be met.

Fomon and associates have published advisable intakes (AIs) for many major nutrients for infants and children who range in age from birth to 3 years. These AIs are based upon the apparent retention of nutrients during growth, with an added safety factor. The AI for protein is reported in relation to energy intake rather than actual body weight. In most cases, the AIs are lower than the RDAs and may be more appropriate for use in evaluating the individual intakes of infants and toddlers. The AI and the RDA may both be lower than potential therapeutic needs dictated by specific disease or deficiency states. In specific circumstances, both infant and adult formulas may require vitamin and/or mineral supplementation. Infant formulas that contain iron generally provide adequate amounts of vitamins and minerals with a volume of 1 quart. However, infants who have restricted fluid intakes may require vitamin and mineral supplementation (e.g., infants with congenital heart disease).

Adult enteral formulas are designed to provide the adult RDAs for vitamins and minerals when a volume of 1500 to 2000 ml/day is administered. But when these adult enteral products are administered to children at lower volumes, some nutrients may not be adequate. In this instance, the specific supplementation of vitamin D, calcium, phosphorus, iron, and zinc is frequently required.

Product Availability and Cost

The cost of commercial enteral formulas may exceed the financial resources of some families. Therefore, whenever medically possible, the least specialized enteral product should be considered. Generally, the more specialized the feedings are (i.e., hydrolyzed protein and medium-chain triglyceride oil), the higher the cost.

Formula costs do not necessarily constitute a socioeconomic barrier. Infants and children who range in age from birth through age 5 may be enrolled in the

Women, Infant, and Children (WIC) nutrition program if their family income falls below a certain threshold. A variety of infant formulas are available through this program. The Medicaid program and private insurance companies sometimes provide financial support for enteral formulas, but product and patient eligibility vary.

ADMINISTRATION OF FEEDING

Methods of Delivery

The specific method utilized for feeding delivery is contingent upon the clinical condition of the patient and the anatomic location of the tube (gastric or transpyloric). Continuous drip and intermittent bolus administration are the two methods most often used for delivery of enteral feedings to infants and children. Intermittent bolus feedings are generally delivered to the stomach by gravity over 15 to 30 minutes on a schedule of every 2 to 4 hours. In contrast, the continuous drip method provides an infusion of nutrients at a constant rate over several hours. Continuous drip feedings are beneficial for patients with altered gastrointestinal function and are essential for those receiving transpyloric or nocturnal feedings. Each method of delivery provides a number of specific advantages and disadvantages (see Table 10-9). In practice, the individual patient's tolerance ultimately dictates the method of delivery.

Pumps

Enteral feeding pumps are typically utilized to control the rate of delivery of continuous drip feedings. A number of enteral feeding pumps are available for use in pediatric patients.[18,19] Portable enteral pumps have also recently been developed, which allow for greater patient mobility.

Important features of enteral pumps for use in the pediatric population include the ability to provide low delivery rates (5 ml/h) and to advance in small increments (1 to 5 ml/h). Other desirable features of pediatric pumps include tamperproof controls, an occlusion alarm, and a low battery indicator.[41] These features all contribute to the safe and efficient delivery of continuous tube feedings for the pediatric population.

Initiation and Advancement of Feedings

A number of clinicians have published recommendations for advancing enteral nutrition in pediatric patients.[42–45] These recommendations are based upon institutional practices and modification of adult regimens. Generally, the rate of advancement of a feeding regimen (Table 10-10) is contingent upon the structure

Table 10-9 Methods of Delivering Enteral Feedings

Advantages	Disadvantages
Continuous Drip	
Ability to increase volume of formula more rapidly	More expensive feeding method because a pump is required for delivery
Improved absorption of major nutrients in infants with intestinal diseases	Restricts patient ambulation
Reduced stool output in hypermetabolic patients	Less physiologic
Associated with a reduced incidence of vomiting in infants with gastroesophageal reflux	
Greater caloric intake when volume tolerance may be a problem	
Intermittent	
More physiologic because a normal feeding schedule is mimicked	Associated with a longer time to reach nutritional goals
Less expensive because an enteral pump is not required	Reduced weight gain and nutrient absorption in infants with malabsorption
Greater flexibility in feeding schedule	Larger bore tube may be required for gravity administration (see Table 10-4)
Freedom from infusion equipment	More nursing time required for administration than for pump-delivered feedings

Source: Data from references 81, 94, 102, and 118.

and function of the patient's gastrointestinal tract. Parenteral nutrition support or malnutrition produce a number of physiologic alterations of the gastrointestinal tract that may affect a child's ability to digest and absorb nutrients. The various functional and histologic changes generally associated with malnutrition include: (1) shortened microvilli;[46] (2) decreased production of a number of pancreatic enzymes, including lipase, trypsin, and amylase;[47] and (3) decreased brush border enzyme activities of maltase, sucrase, and lactase.[46]

Parenteral nutrition support without concomitant enteral feeding also has been shown to lead to a decrease in enteric mucosal mass and associated brush border enzymes.[2] Therefore, children who are being weaned from parenteral nutrition and/or who are malnourished generally require a more conservative feeding progression than what is typically administered to children who have normal gastrointestinal function.

Table 10-10 Initiation and Advancement of Feedings

General Considerations
1. Plan for a 2- to 5-day period to meet nutritional goals.
2. Use isotonic feedings initially.
3. Avoid making a simultaneous change in volume and concentration.
4. Consider initial use of dilute feedings in patients with altered gastrointestinal function or when beginning transitional feeding following parenteral nutrition.
5. Advance more cautiously in patients who are critically ill and malnourished and those with histories of feeding intolerances.
6. Increase volume before concentration when administering transpyloric feedings.
7. Advance concentration before volume when administering gastric feedings.
8. If a feeding intolerance develops, return to the previously tolerated concentration and volume and progress more slowly.

Continuous Drip Feeding
1. Begin at a rate of 1–2 ml/kg/h.
2. Advance in increments of 0.5–1 ml/kg/h every 8–24 hours as tolerated, until nutritional goal is achieved.
3. Typical feeding rates for various age groups:

Age	Weight (kg)	Initial Rate (ml/h)	Maximum Rate (ml/h)
Infant	3–10	3–10	25–50
Toddler/preschool	10–20	10–20	60–70
School age	20–40	20–40	80–100
Teenage	>40	40–50	100–150

Intermittent Feeding
1. Determine the total volume of formula needed to provide nutritional goal.
2. Begin delivery at 25% of the volume goal on the first day.
3. Divide the formula volume equally between 5–8 feedings.
4. Increase formula volume by 25% per day as tolerated, with total volume equally divided between number of feedings.
5. Administer by gravity over 15 to 30 minutes.

Breast Milk Tube Feedings

Human milk provides the optimal feeding for infants and offers many immunologic and nutritional benefits. Infants who are unable to nurse at the breast can receive pumped breast milk through a feeding tube. However, the delivery of breast milk by tube requires some unique considerations. First of all, the mother must be taught safe methods for the collection and storage of her milk.[48] Breast milk administration techniques also need to be devised and implemented.

Continuous drip feedings of human milk have been associated with appreciable fat losses, which result in a significant reduction of energy delivered to the infant.[49–51] These losses occur because the fat in human milk separates and collects in the infusion system. A caloric loss of approximately 20% is typical. The delivery of essential fatty acids, phospholipids, cholesterol, and associated fat-soluble vitamins may also be diminished.[49]

It should be noted that when residual milk is flushed from the tubing, a large fat bolus may be delivered to the patient. This fat bolus may not be tolerated in patients with impaired gastrointestinal function.

Short-term refrigeration of human milk has been shown to increase the delivery of fat during continuous feedings.[49] Unfortunately, significant fat losses still occur. Therefore, when delivering a continuous feeding of breast milk, the use of refrigerated milk may be advantageous.

Intermittent bolus feeding of human milk, in contrast, does not result in a significant loss of fat in the tubing or the terminal delivery of a large fat bolus.[50,52] Therefore, intermittent bolus feeding is the preferred method of delivery for the tube feeding of human milk, whenever possible.

WEANING

When the patient's medical condition allows for normal oral feedings, weaning from tube feedings can be initiated. This process should not begin until the patient has achieved a satisfactory nutritional status, because the patient may stop gaining weight for a time during the transition.

The weaning time may vary from a few days to several months. Records of the patient's oral intake should be kept during this time since it is important to maintain an adequate intake. Tube feedings should be continued until the patient can demonstrate that maintenance requirements can be met by the oral route.

PREVENTION AND TREATMENT OF COMPLICATIONS

Complications associated with enteral nutrition support can be minimized by properly monitoring the patient.[23,53] Potential complications are generally classified into gastrointestinal, mechanical (tube related), metabolic, and psychologic categories. The frequency of enteral feeding complications that occur in pediatric patients has not been extensively documented in the literature. However, a large prospective study of 253 adult patients found that there are relatively few associated complications (11.7%). This study listed the three most frequent complications as gastrointestinal (6.2%), mechanical (3.5%), and metabolic (2%).[54]

Associated pediatric studies have not been as comprehensive. However, frequently reported complications include various mechanical problems related to gastrostomy[54–58] and nasogastric tubes,[59,60] metabolic disturbances,[38] and feeding disorders that are related to the delayed introduction of oral feedings.[61,62] Additionally, gastrointestinal complications have been associated with low serum albumin levels in pediatric surgical patients,[63] delayed enteral support in pediatric burn patients,[64] and with contaminated feedings.[65] A summary of the most common complications and associated management suggestions is presented in Table 10-11.

Enteral Feeding Contamination

Gastrointestinal complications can potentially result from the bacterial contamination of continuous drip enteral feedings. Contamination from gram-negative bacilli has been found to cause abdominal distention in both pediatric and adult patients who were receiving continuous drip feedings.[65]

A contaminated elemental diet administered to adult postoperative patients has also been found to produce septic-like symptoms, which include nausea, vomiting, diarrhea, fever, leukocytosis, hypotension, and tachycardia.[66] Various practitioners have reported an incidence of feeding contamination ranging from 5%[67] to 90%.[65] Nurses' hands have been found to be the most likely source of the contaminant.[68]

Feeding contamination generally occurs during the preparation, delivery, handling, or storage of the product. Formulas that require reconstitution or manipulation (dilution or additives) are at the greatest risk for bacterial contamination.[65] In contrast, the use of sterile, undiluted "ready-to-feed" products minimizes the risk of contamination.

Precautions that should be taken to guard against the contamination of enteral feedings include the daily changing of the feeding bag and tubing, careful attention to clean technique during handling of the feedings, and limiting the hang time of the formulas. Specific recommendations for preparation, administration, and monitoring of enteral feedings to maximize bacteriologic safety have been published.[69]

A hang time of 8 to 12 hours should be safe for commercially manufactured products provided that both a closed delivery system and clean technique are used in the transfer process.[70,71] In contrast, blenderized feedings[69] and breast milk should not remain in the feeding container for more than 4 hours. Guidelines for storage and administration of feedings are outlined in Table 10-12.

It is important to note that disposable enteral feeding bags should not be reused in the hospital setting.[69,72] However, for stable patients in the home setting where nosocomial pathogens are less common, it may be safe to wash feeding containers and reuse them.[69] In this instance, containers intended for reuse at home should be carefully washed with warm water and soap and thoroughly rinsed and hung to dry.[72]

Table 10-11 Management of Potential Complications

Potential Complication	Possible Cause	Management/Prevention Suggestions
Psychologic		
Fear of tube insertion	Psychologic trauma associated with insertion of nasogastric tube	Consult with a child psychologist Teach relaxation techniques to caretaker and child for use prior to tube insertion Allow child to handle the tube and administer feedings to doll Plan for two adults when placing tubes in infants and toddlers Cuddle child after tube insertion Involve family in nutritional care planning Teach older children and teenagers to insert their own tubes Provide home nursing support
Altered body image	Visible presence of nasogastric tube	Provide nocturnal feedings and remove tube during the day Consider use of surgically placed feeding tube for long-term use
Food refusal	Deprivation of normal oral feeding experiences	Initiate oral feedings when medically possible Provide positive oral experiences during tube feedings (see Table 10-13)
Gastrointestinal		
Vomiting	Too rapid advancement of formula volume and/or concentration	Return to previously tolerated strength and volume and advance more slowly
	Delayed gastric emptying	Consider utilizing metoclopramide Consider transpyloric route for feeding Consider a continuous infusion Consider decreasing osmolality and long-chain triglyceride content of formula Elevate head of bed 45 degrees during feeding administration
	Hyperosmolar formula	Consider changing formula to an isotonic product
	Hyperosmolar electrolyte supplements	Dilute electrolyte additives with enteral formula Consider parenteral route for electrolyte supplementation
Diarrhea	Lactose intolerance	Monitor stools for reducing substances. If positive, consider changing formula to a product that is lactose-free
	Hyperosmolar formula or additive	See vomiting entry, above
	Contaminated formula	Refer to Table 10-12 for safe feeding administration techniques

Potential Complication	Possible Cause	Management/Prevention Suggestions
Diarrhea (continued)	Hypoalbuminemia with inadequate oncotic pressure for absorption	Consider replacing albumin deficit in conjunction with delivery of adequate nutrients Consider use of a peptide-based semi-elemental formula
	Too rapid advancement of formula volume and/or concentration	See vomiting entry, above
	Low fiber intake	Consider use of fiber-containing product
	Fat malabsorption	Consider changing formula to a product with partial medium-chain triglyceride content
Constipation	Low fluid intake	Increase fluid intake
	Low fiber intake	Consider use of a fiber-containing formula
Metabolic/ nutritional		
Dehydration	Inadequate fluid intake in relation to needs	Monitor adequacy of fluid intake, especially when extrarenal water losses are increased (see Table 10-8) Monitor intake and output Assess renal solute load of formula Monitor hydration status of patient routinely (see Table 10-7)
Overhydration	Too-rapid refeeding of patients who have moderate to severe PEM	Advance feedings slowly Allow a 5- to 7-day period to meet nutritional goals
Electrolyte imbalances	Inadequate or excess electrolyte intake in relation to specific patient needs	Monitor electrolytes, phosphorus, and glucose levels for first 3 days; complete blood count and blood urea nitrogen, creatinine, electrolyte, phosphorus, and glucose levels weekly until stable, then monthly Evaluate electrolyte adequacy of specific formula and appropriateness of formula dilution
Failure to achieve appropriate weight gain	Inadequate nutrient intake	Evaluate adequacy of nutrient intake Perform routine nutritional assessments
Mechanical		
Obstruction of feeding tube	Precipitation of formula in feeding tube	Flush tube before and after aspirating for gastric residuals. Flush tube with 20 ml water after each bolus feeding and every 4 to 8 hours during continuous feedings

continues

Table 10-11 continued

Potential Complication	Possible Cause	Management/Prevention Suggestions
	Administration of medications through feeding tube	Assess physical compatibility of drug/ formula combination before mixing drug with enteral feeding
		Avoid mixing enteral products with pharmaceutical syrups having a pH <5
		Use elixir form of drug instead of a crushed tablet
		Attempt to clear obstruction with a mixture of warm water and meat tenderizer or 1/4 tsp pancreatic enzyme powder mixed with 15 ml water
Poor healing of surgically placed feeding tubes	Impaired wound healing associated with PEM	Provide postoperative parenteral nutrition to malnourished patients to enhance wound healing
Aspiration of formula into lung	Displacement of feeding tube	Confirm placement of tube prior to administering feeding

Source: Data from references 35, 53, 63, 104, 119 to 123.

Feeding Disorders

Infant and toddler feeding disorders constitute a tube-feeding complication that is unique to the pediatric population. Many times, when a chronically ill infant is medically ready to begin oral feedings, the infant may display no interest in eating. When offered feedings, the child typically refuses, cries, gags, or vomits.

Occasionally these children may perceive any form of oral stimulation as both unpleasant and frightening and may begin to cry when touched on the cheek or lips. This fear may be reinforced by anxious parents who attempt to force-feed. This chain of events frequently leads to frustration for the parents, the child, and all members of the health care team.

Illingsworth suggests that this resistant feeding behavior may be due to missing a "critical period" in the development of the child's feeding skills.[62] He indicates that the critical period for the development of chewing skills is 6 to 7 months of age; if solids are not introduced during this time, the child typically will have difficulty accepting them later.

Table 10-12 Guidelines for Storage and Administration of Feedings

Storage	Recommendation
Sterile* canned/bottled liquid products	Store at temperatures <30.5°C (85°F). Cover and refrigerate opened, unused product labeled with date and time opened.
	Use/discard within 24 to 48 hours or in accordance with manufacturer's recommendation and/or hospital policy.
Powdered products†	Store in cool, dry area. Cover opened, unused product labeled with date, time, and nature of preparation.
	Use/discard according to hospital policy.

Administration	Recommendation
Container and pump set	Change every 24 hours or in accordance with gavage or pump-set manufacturer's recommendations and/or hospital policy. Consider more frequent changes when nonsterile feedings are given.
	Rinse with water between feedings.
	Do not add new formula to that already in container.
Hang time	Sterile feedings* may be hung for 8 to 12 hours or in accordance with manufacturer's recommendations and/or hospital policy.
	Nonsterile feedings† should not remain in feeding container for >6 to 8 hours (or for >2 to 4 hours, if blenderized).
Feeding-tube irrigation	Rinse with water (eg, 20 to 30 ml) before and after each intermittent feeding or every 3 to 4 hours during continuous feeding.

* Sterile feedings include industrially produced prepacked liquid formulas that are "commercially sterile."
† Nonsterile feedings are those that may contain live bacteria and include hospital- or home-prepared (blenderized) formulas, reconstituted powdered feedings, and commercial liquid formulas to which nutrients and/or other supplements have been added in the kitchen, pharmacy, home, or ward.

Source: Reprinted with permission of Ross Laboratories, Columbus, Ohio 43216, from Enteral Nutrition Support of Children, p. 19, © 1988 Ross Laboratories.

Other important oral experiences during the first year of life include the development of the rooting and sucking reflexes, the oral exploration of objects, and the association of hunger with feeding.[73] When a child is deprived of these normal oral feeding experiences during the first year of life, he or she may subsequently experience feeding difficulties that last throughout the toddler and preschool years. These children may also demonstrate significant delays in gross motor and personality development.[61]

Table 10-13 Oral Motor Stimulation Exercises for Infants

1. Stroke side of infant's mouth with washcloth, terry cloth toy, etc.
2. Insert finger or blunt object into infant's mouth and allow infant to suck a few times per day.
3. Stimulate gums with finger and/or Q-tip—may be dipped in juice (no honey should be used under 1 year of age).
4. Allow infant to suck or bite on terry cloth soaked in formula or water.
5. If suck reflex is weak, assist infant by manually sealing lips around nipple or finger, etc.
6. Experiment with nipples of different shapes, lengths and hole sizes.
7. Encourage child to make sucking, kissing noises with mouth.
8. Stimulate oral area of infant with finger or other material listed above while laughing, smiling, etc. This will cause the infant to associate the mouth with pleasant experiences.
9. During family mealtime, have infant at table facing you or other family member. Let infant watch while you put food in your mouth and chew—and be sure you look like you are enjoying yourself.
10. Play games with infant, pointing to mouth, tongue, teeth, etc.
11. Have infant/child move his tongue to touch his lips, chin, cheek.
12. Encourage child to play with toys which require holding, squeezing, picking up, bringing objects to face and putting into appropriate containers.
13. Pushing and pulling toys also facilitates coordination.

Caution: Do not perform any of these exercises if the infant finds them aversive.

Source: Reprinted from: Nutrition and the High Risk Infant after Hospital Discharge. (eds) RE Wheeler, A Anderson, RT Hall, Missouri Dept of Health (In press). Material adapted from Hayasuka R, Georgeson KE, Cha CC. The neonatal intensive care dietitian and dietetic technician. *Nutr Supp Serv* 4(2):54, 1987. Used with permission.

Feeding disorders can be potentially minimized by initiating oral feedings as soon as medically possible. Additional strategies include other positive oral stimulation experiences such as non-nutritive sucking during the tube feedings (Table 10-13). Pediatric occupational therapists or speech pathologists are the health professionals most qualified to assess an infant's feeding potential and design an appropriate oral motor stimulation program. Lastly, textured foods should be ideally offered, if medically feasible, when the infant is at a developmental age of 6 to 7 months.

PLANNING FOR HOME ENTERAL SUPPORT

Whenever possible, enteral nutrition support should be provided in the home rather than in the hospital. Advantages of home enteral support include a number of psychosocial benefits for the child and the family, and an economic benefit is also provided since the costly hospital stay is minimized. A patient who is a candidate for home enteral feedings needs to be evaluated on the following criteria:[17,74]

1. The patient must be medically stable and have demonstrated a tolerance to the feeding regimen in the hospital.
2. A safe home environment is required, with available running water, electricity, refrigeration, and adequate storage space.
3. The family (or patient) must be willing and capable of administering the feedings at home.
4. A payment source is needed for the formula and associated tube-feeding equipment.
5. A physician must be willing to assume responsibility for following the patient after discharge from the hospital.

When the above criteria are met, discharge teaching is also required. The instructional plan needs to focus on the preparation, administration, and monitoring of the feeding. Feeding tube care and problem-solving techniques should also be addressed. Lastly, arrangements need to be made for outpatient follow-up.

REFERENCES

1. Alverdy J, Chi HS, Sheldon GF. The effect of parenteral nutrition on gastrointestinal immunity. The importance of enteral stimulation. *Ann Surg*. 1985;202:681.
2. Levine GM, Deren JJ, Steiger E, et al. Role of oral intake in maintenance of gut mass and disaccharidase activity. *Gastroenterology*. 1974;67:975.
3. Glass EJ, Hume R, Lang MA, et al. Parenteral nutrition compared with transpyloric feeding. *Arch Dis Child*. 1984;59:131.
4. Heymsfield SB, Bethel RA, Ansley JD, et al. Enteral hyperalimentation: an alternative to central venous hyperalimentation. *Ann Intern Med*. 1979;90:63.
5. Chrysomilides SA, Kaminski MV. Home enteral and parenteral nutrition support: a comparison. *Am J Clin Nutr*. 1981;34:2271.
6. Cooper A, Jakobowski D, Spiker J, et al. Nutritional assessment: an integral part of the preoperative pediatric surgical evaluation. *J Pediatr Surg*. 1981;16:554.
7. Parsons HG, Francoeur TE, Howland P, et al. The nutritional status of hospitalized children. *Am J Clin Nutr*. 1980;33:1140.
8. Merritt RJ, Suskind RM. Nutritional survey of hospitalized pediatric patients. *Am J Clin Nutr*. 1979;32:1320.
9. Mize CE, Cunningham C, Teitell BC, et al. Undernutrition of pediatric inpatients: repeated nutritional status evaluation. *Nutr Supp Serv*. 1984;4:27.
10. Pollack MM, Wiley JS, Kanter R, et al. Malnutrition in critically ill infants and children. *J Parenter Enter Nutr*. 1982;6:20.
11. Leleiko NS, Luder E, Fridman M, et al. Nutritional assessment of pediatric patients admitted to an acute care pediatric service utilizing anthropometric measurements. *J Parenter Enter Nutr*. 1986;10:166.

12. Fomon SJ, ed. Normal growth, failure to thrive and obesity. In: *Infant Nutrition*. 2nd ed. Philadelphia, Pa: WB Saunders; 1974:34–94.

13. Chandra RK. Nutrition, immunity, and infection: present knowledge and future directions. *Lancet*. 1983;1:688.

14. Rickard KA, Baehner RL, Coates TD. Supportive nutritional intervention. *Cancer Res Supp*. 1982;42:766.

15. Viteri F. Primary protein-calorie malnutrition—clinical, biochemical and metabolic changes. In: Suskind RM, ed. *Textbook of Pediatric Nutrition*. New York, NY: Raven Press; 1981:189–215.

16. Powers CA. A system for nutritional screening of hospitalized children. *Top Clin Nutr*. 1987;2:11.

17. Greene HL, Helinek GL, Folk CC. Nasogastric feeding at home: a method for adjunctive nutritional support of malnourished patients. *Am J Clin Nutr*. 1981;34:1131.

18. Moore MC, Green HL. Tube feeding of infants and children. *Pediatr Clin North Am*. 1985;32:401.

19. Walker WA, Hendricks KM, eds. Enteral nutrition: support of the pediatric patient. In: *Manual of Pediatric Nutrition*. Philadelphia, Pa: WB Saunders; 1985.

20. Paine JS. Practical aspects of nasogastric feeding in pediatric patients from a ward nursing perspective. *Nutr Supp Serv*. 1986;6:11.

21. Ziemer M, Carroll JS. Infant gavage reconsidered. *J Nurs*. 1978;78:1543.

22. Guest JE, Murray ND, Antonson DL. Continuous nasogastric feeding in pediatric patients. *Nutr Supp Serv*. 1982;2:34.

23. Bernard M, Forlaw L. Complications and their prevention. In: Rombeau RL, Caldwell MD, eds. *Enteral and Tube Feeding*. Philadelphia, Pa: WB Saunders; 1984:542–569.

24. Wesley JR. Special access to the intestinal tract. In: Balistreri WF, Farrell MK, eds. *Enteral Feeding: Scientific Basis and Clinical Applications, Report of the Ninety-Fourth Ross Conference on Pediatric Research*. Columbus, Ohio: Ross Laboratories; 1988:57–62.

25. Wink DM. The physical and emotional care of infants with gastrostomy tubes. *Issues Compr Pediatr Nurs*. 1983;6:195.

26. Gustke RF, Varma RR, Soergel KH. Gastric reflux during perfusion of the proximal small bowel. *Gastroenterology*. 1970;59:890.

27. Kiver KF, Hays DP, Fortin DF, et al. Pre- and post-pyloric enteral feeding: analysis of safety and complications. *J Pediatr Enter Nutr*. 1984;8:95. Abstract 87.

28. Andrassy RJ, Mahour GH, Harrison MR, et al. The role and safety of early postoperative feeding in the pediatric surgical patient. *J Pediatr Surg*. 1979;14:381.

29. Strife JL, Dunbar JS, Rice S. Jejunal intubation via gastrostomy catheters in pediatric patients. *Radiology*. 1985;154:249.

30. Mukherjee D, Emmens RW, Putham TC. Nonoperative conversion of gastrostomy to feeding jejunostomy in children and adults. *Surg Gynecol Obstet*. 1982;154:881.

31. Committee on Nutrition, American Academy of Pediatrics. Commentary on breast-feeding and infant formulas, including proposed standards for formulas. *Pediatrics*. 1979;63:52.

32. United States Congress, Infant Formula Act of 1980. Public Law 96-359, Sept. 26, 1980.

33. Brady MS, Rickard KA, Fitzgerald JF, et al. Specialized formulas and feedings for infants with malabsorption or formula intolerance. *J Am Diet Assoc*. 1986;86:191.

34. Bergmann KE, Ziegler EE, and Fomon SJ. Water and renal solute load. In: Fomon SJ, ed. *Infant Nutrition*. 2nd ed. Philadelphia, Pa: WB Saunders; 1974:245–266.

35. Cooke AR. Control of gastric emptying and motility. *Gastroenterology*. 1975;68:804.

36. Fomon SJ, Ziegler EE, O'Donnell, AM. Infant feeding in health and disease. In: Fomon SJ, ed. *Infant Nutrition.* 2nd ed. Philadelphia, Pa: WB Saunders; 1974;472–519.

37. Gallagher-Allred CR. Comparison of institutionally and commercially prepared formulas. *Nutr Supp Serv.* 1983;3:32.

38. Listernick R, Sidransky E. Hypernatremic dehydration in children with severe psychomotor retardation. *Clin Pediatr.* 1985;24:440.

39. Cowen SL. Feeding gastrostomy: nutritional management of the infant or young child. *J Pediatr Perinat Nutr.* 1987;1:51.

40. Skipper A. Specialized formulas for enteral nutrition support. *J Am Diet Assoc.* 1986;86:654.

41. Cooning SW. Unique aspects in pediatric care. In: Lang C, ed. *Nutrition Support in Critical Care.* Gaithersburg, Md: Aspen Publishers; 1987:395–404.

42. Robbins S, Thorp JW, Wadsworth C. Tube feeding of infants and children. ASPEN; 1982. Monograph.

43. Braunschweig CL, Wesley JR, Clark SF, et al. Rationale and guidelines for parenteral and enteral transition feeding of the 3- to 30-kg child. *J Am Diet Assoc.* 1988;88:479.

44. Wilson SE, Dietz WH, Jr, Grand RJ. An algorithm for pediatric enteral alimentation. *Pediatr Ann.* 1987;16:233.

45. Hohenbrink K, Oddleifson N. Pediatric nutrition support. In: Shronts EP, ed. *Nutrition Support Dietetics, Core Curriculum.* Silver Spring, MD: ASPEN; 1989:231–272.

46. Romer H, Urbach R, Gomez MA, et al. Moderate and severe protein energy malnutrition in childhood: effects on jejunal mucosal morphology and disaccharidase activities. *J Pediatr Gastroenterol Nutr.* 1983;2:459.

47. Barbezat GD, Hansen JDL. The exocrine pancreas and protein-caloric malnutrition. *Pediatrics.* 1968;42:77.

48. Ruth Lawrence. The storage of human milk and cross-nursing. In: Lawrence RA, ed. *Breastfeeding, a Guide for the Medical Profession.* 3rd ed. St Louis, Mo: CV Mosby Co; 1989.

49. Lavine M, Clark RM. The effect of short-term refrigeration of milk and addition of breast milk fortifier on the delivery of lipids during tube feeding. *J Pediatr Gastroenterol Nutr.* 1989;8:496.

50. Narayanan I, Singh B, Harvey D. Fat loss during feeding of human milk. *Arch Dis Child.* 1984;59:475.

51. Stocks RJ, Davies DP, Allen F, et al. Loss of breast milk nutrients during tube feeding. *Arch Dis Child.* 1985;60:164.

52. Greer FR, McCormick A, Loker J. Changes in fat concentration of human milk during delivery by intermittent bolus and continuous mechanical pump infusion. *J Pediatr.* 1984;105:745.

53. Krey S, Porcelli K, Lockett G, et al. Enteral nutrition. In: Shronts EP, ed. *Nutrition Support Dietetics, Core Curriculum.* Silver Spring, MD: ASPEN; 1989:63–81.

54. Cataldi-Betcher EL, Seltzer MH, Slocum BA, et al. Complications occurring during enteral nutrition support: a prospective study. *J Parenter Enter Nutr.* 1983;7:546.

55. Gallagher MW, Tyson KR, Ashcraft KW. Gastrostomy in pediatric patients: an analysis of complications and techniques. *Surgery.* 1973;74:536.

56. Haws EB, Sieber WK, Kiesewetter WB. Complications of tube gastrostomy in infants and children, 15-year review of 240 cases. *Ann Surg.* 1966;164:284.

57. Grunow JE, Al-Hafidh AS, Tunell WP. Gastroesophageal reflux following percutaneous endoscopic gastrostomy in children. *J Pediatr Surg.* 1989;24:42.

58. Canal DF, Vane DW, Goto S, et al. Reduction of lower esophageal sphincter pressure with Stamm gastrostomy. *J Pediatr Surg.* 1987;22:54.

59. Kellie SJ, Fitch SJ, Kovnar EH, et al. A hazard of using adult-sized weighted-tip enteral feeding catheters in infants. *Am J Dis Child.* 1988;142:916.

60. Allen DB. Postprandial hypoglycemia resulting from nasogastric tube malposition. *Pediatrics.* 1988;81:582.

61. Beratis M, Kolb R, Sperling E, et al. Development of a child with long lasting deprivation of oral feeding. *J Am Acad Child Psychiatry.* 1984;20:53.

62. Illingworth RS, Lister J. The critical or sensitive period, with special reference to certain feeding problems in infants and children. *J Pediatr.* 1964;65:8.

63. Ford EG, Jennings M, Andrassy RJ. Serum albumin (oncotic pressure) correlates with enteral feeding tolerance in the pediatric surgical patient. *J Pediatr Surg.* 1987;22:597.

64. Gottschlich MM, Warden GD, Michel M, et al. Diarrhea in tube-fed burn patients: incidence, etiology, nutritional impact, and prevention. *Parenter Enter Nutr.* 1988;12:388.

65. Freedland CP, Roller RD, Wolfe BM. Microbial contamination of continuous drip feedings. *J Parenter Enter Nutr.* 1989;13:18.

66. Baldwin BA, Allen JZ, Rose N. Bacterial contamination of continuously infused enteral alimentation with needle catheter jejunostomy—clinical implications. *J Parenter Enter Nutr.* 1984; 30.

67. Mandal JM, Hamilton BW, Hamilton TR, et al. A study of microbial contamination of enteral nutrient solutions. *Nutr Supp Serv.* 1985;5:58.

68. Schreiner RL, Eitzen H, Gfell MA, et al. Environmental contamination of continuous drip feedings. *Pediatrics.* 1979;63:232.

69. Guidelines for preventing contamination of enteric feedings. In: Cameron A, Redfern DE, eds. *Report of the Ross Workshop on Contamination of Enteral Feeding Products During Clinical Usage.* Columbus, Ohio: Ross Laboratories; 1983:40–42.

70. White WT, Acuff TE, Sykes TR, et al. Bacterial contamination of enteral nutrient solution: a preliminary report. *J Parenter Enter Nutr.* 1979;3:459.

71. Hostetler C, Lipman TO, Geraghty M, et al. Bacterial safety of reconstituted continuous drip tube feedings. *J Parenter Enter Nutr.* 1982;6:232.

72. Groschel DHM. Disposable enteral feeding bags should not be reused. *JAMA.* 1982;248:2536.

73. Dowling S. Seven infants with esophageal atresia. *Psychoanal Study Child.* 1977;32:215.

74. McCrae JD, Hall NH. Current practices for home enteral nutrition. *J Am Diet Assoc.* 1989;89:233.

75. Stool SE, Miner ME. Nutritional management after severe head injury in children. *Nutr Supp Serv.* 1983;3:21.

76. Patrick J, Boland M, Stoski D, et al. Rapid correction of wasting in children with cerebral palsy. *Dev Med Child Neurol.* 1986;28:734.

77. Bell SJ, Molnar JA, Carey M, et al. Adequacy of a modular tube feeding diet for burned patients. *J Am Diet Assoc.* 1986;86:1386.

78. Dominioni L, Trocki O, Mochizuki H, et al. Prevention of severe postburn hypermetabolism and catabolism by immediate intragastric feeding. *J Burn Care Rehabil.* 1984;5:106.

79. Andrassy RJ, Page CP, Feldtman RW, et al. Continual catheter administration of an elemental diet in infants and children. *Surgery.* 1977;82:205.

80. Bougle D, Iselin M, Kahyat A, et al. Nutritional treatment of congenital heart disease. *Arch Dis Child.* 1986;61:799.

81. Vanderhoof JA, Hofschire PJ, Baluff MA, et al. Continuous enteral feedings: an important adjunct to the management of complex congenital heart disease. *Am J Dis Child.* 1982;136:825.

82. Yahav J, Avigad S, Frand M, et al. Assessment of intestinal and cardiorespiratory function in children with congenital heart disease on high-caloric formulas. *J Pediatr Gastroenterol Nutr.* 1985;4:778.

83. Kaufman SS, Murray NM, Wood RP, et al. Nutritional support for the infant with extrahepatic biliary atresia. *J Pediatr.* 1987;110:679.

84. Levy LD, Durie PR, Pencharz PB, et al. Effects of long-term nutritional rehabilitation on body composition and clinical status in malnourished children and adolescents with cystic fibrosis. *J Pediatr.* 1985;107:225.

85. Boland MP, Stoski DS, MacDonald NE, et al. Chronic jejunostomy feeding with a nonelemental formula in undernourished patients with cystic fibrosis. *Lancet.* 1986;1:232.

86. Shepherd RW, Holt TL, Thomas BJ, et al. Nutritional rehabilitation in cystic fibrosis: controlled studies of effects of nutritional growth retardation, body protein turnover, and course of pulmonary disease. *J Pediatr.* 1986;109:788.

87. Strife CF, Quinlan M, Mears K, et al. Improved growth of three uremic children by nocturnal nasogastric feedings. *Am J Dis Child.* 1986;140:438.

88. Takala J. Growth failure due to uremia and congenital nephrosis: growth enhancement by aggressive nutritional therapy. *J Parenter Enter Nutr.* 1982;6:388.

89. Heyman MB, Katz R, Hurst D, et al. Growth retardation in sickle-cell disease treated by nutritional support. *Lancet.* 1985;1:903.

90. Winston DH. Treatment of severe anorexia nervosa with enteral tube feedings. *Nutr Supp Serv.* 1987;7:24.

91. Ramsay M, Zelazo P. Food refusal in failure-to-thrive infants: nasogastric feeding combined with interactive-behavioral treatment. *J Pediatr Psychol.* 1988;13:329.

92. Orenstein SR. Enteral versus parenteral therapy for intractable diarrhea of infancy: a prospective, randomized trial. *J Pediatr.* 1986;109:277.

93. Weizman Z, Schmueli A, Deckelbaum R. Continuous nasogastric drip elemental feeding. Alternative for prolonged parenteral nutrition in severe prolonged diarrhea. *Am J Dis Child.* 1983;137:253.

94. Parker P, Stroop S, Greene H. A controlled comparison of continuous versus intermittent feeding in treatment of infants with intestinal disease. *J Pediatr.* 1981;99:360.

95. Christie DL, Ament ME. Dilute elemental diet and continuous infusion technique for management of short bowel syndrome. *J Pediatr.* 1975;87:704.

96. Belli DC, Seidman E, Bouthillier L, et al. Chronic intermittent elemental diet improves growth failure in children with Crohn's disease. *Gastroenterology.* 1988;94:603.

97. Morin CL, Roulet M, Roy CC, et al. Continuous elemental enteral alimentation in children with Crohn's disease and growth failure. *Gastroenterology.* 1980;79:1205.

98. Navarro J, Vargas J, Cezard JP, et al. Prolonged constant rate enteral nutrition in Crohn's disease. *J Pediatr Gastroenterol Nutr.* 1982;1:541.

99. O'Morain C, Segal AM, Levi AJ, et al. Elemental diet in acute Crohn's disease. *Arch Dis Child.* 1983;53:44.

100. Daeschel IE, Janick LS, Kramish MJ, et al. Diet and growth of children with glycogen storage disease types I and III. *J Am Diet Assoc.* 1983;83:135.

101. Green HL, Slonim AF, O'Neill JA, et al. Type I glycogen storage disease: five years of management with nocturnal intragastric feeding. *J Pediatr.* 1980;96:590.

102. Ferry GD, Selby M, Pietro T. Clinical response to short-term nasogastric feeding in infants with gastroesophageal reflux and growth failure. *J Pediatr Gastroenter Nutr.* 1983;2:57.

103. Green HL. Response of the bowel to injury and the transition from parenteral to enteral feedings. *Acta Chir Scand Suppl.* 1983;517:21.

104. Brinson R, Kolts BE. Diarrhea associated with severe hypoalbuminemia: a comparison of a peptide-based chemically defined diet and standard enteral alimentation. *Crit Care Med.* 1988;16:130.

105. Heymsfield SB, Bleier J, Whitmire L, et al. Nutrient bioavailability from nasojejunally administered formulas: comparison to solid food. *Am J Clin Nutr.* 1984;39:243.

106. Craig LD, Ryan AS. Dietary fiber intakes of women, 19–50 years of age, and their children, 1–5 years of age, according to sociodemographic characteristics. *J Am Diet Assoc.* 1989;89(suppl):A12.

107. Gourley GR, Farrell PM, Odell GB. Essential fatty acid deficiency after portoenterostomy for biliary atresia. *Am J Clin Nutr.* 1982;36:1194.

108. Koretz RL, Meyer JH. Elemental diets—facts and fantasies. *Gastroenterology.* 1980;78:393.

109. Wolfe BM, Keltner RM, Willman VL. Intestinal fistula output in regular, elemental and intravenous alimentation. *Am J Surg.* 1972;124:803.

110. Parsons HG, Shillabeer G, Rodemaker AW. Early onset of essential fatty acid deficiency in patients with cystic fibrosis receiving a semisynthetic diet. *J Pediatr.* 1984;105:758.

111. Vanderhoff JA, Grandjean CJ, Kaufman SS, et al. Effect of high percentage medium-chain triglyceride diet on mucosal adaptation following massive bowel resection in rats. *J Parenter Enter Nutr.* 1984;8:685.

112. Lifschitz C. Intestinal permeability. *J Pediatr Gastroenteral Nutr.* 1985;4:520.

113. Isselbacher KJ. Metabolism and transport of lipid by intestinal mucosa. *Fed Proc.* 1965;24:16.

114. Adibi SA, Morse EL. Intestinal transport of dipeptides in man: relative importance of hydrolysis and intact absorption. *J Clin Invest.* 1971;50:2266.

115. Silk DBA, Fairclough PD, Clark ML, et al. Use of a peptide rather than free amino acid nitrogen source in chemically defined elemental diets. *J Parenter Enter Nutr.* 1980;4:548.

116. Foman SJ, ed. *Infant Nutrition.* 2nd ed. Philadelphia, Pa: WB Saunders; 1974.

117. Kerner JA Jr. Fluid requirements. In: Kerner JA Jr, ed. *Manual of Pediatric Parenteral Nutrition.* New York, NY: John Wiley and Sons; 1983:69–77.

118. Heibert JM, Brown A, Anderson RG, et al. Comparison of continuous vs intermittent tube feeding in adult burn patients. *J Parenter Enter Nutr.* 1981;5:73.

119. Niemiec PW, Vanderveen TW, Morrison JI, et al. Gastrointestinal disorders caused by medication and electrolyte solution osmolality during enteral nutrition. *J Parenter Enter Nutr.* 1983;7:387.

120. Patrick J. Death during recovery from severe malnutrition and its possible relationship to sodium pump activity in the leucocyte. *Br Med J.* 1977;1:1051.

121. Picou DM. Evaluation and treatment of the malnourished child. In: Suskind RM, ed. *Textbook of Pediatric Nutrition.* New York, NY: Raven Press; 1981:217–228.

122. Marcvard SP, Perkins AM. Clogging of feeding tubes. *J Parenter Enter Nutr.* 1988;12:403.

123. Cutie AJ, Altman E, Lenkel L. Compatibility of enteral products with commonly employed drug additives. *J Parenter Enter Nutr.* 1983;7:186.

Chapter 11

Parenteral Nutrition

Janice Hovasi Cox and Susan W. Cooning

Twenty-five years ago medical treatment of the hospitalized patient did not include parenteral nutrition. In 1964 Dudrick's experiments with the administration of intravenous amino acid and dextrose solutions to demonstrate positive nitrogen balance and to promote growth in beagle puppies led to the use of parenteral nutrition in humans. In the United States today, parenteral nutrition is viewed as an almost routine, but certainly essential, aspect in the treatment of a wide variety of conditions.

The technological advances and refinements in delivery systems that have made parenteral nutrition so commonplace in the hospital setting have now propelled this complex form of nutritional support into the home setting. Many of the improvements and advancements made in the formulation and delivery of parenteral nutrition have made it much more suitable for use with the pediatric population, both in and out of the acute care setting. This chapter will summarize the complexities of pediatric parenteral nutrition as it is utilized in the hospital and in the home.

This sophisticated form of intravenous therapy or parenteral nutrition (PN) provides nutrients to the patient whose nutritional needs cannot be met solely through the enteral route. Total parenteral nutrition (TPN) is the intravenous delivery of nutrients in the form of carbohydrates, fat, and protein to the patient unable to sufficiently tolerate or absorb any form of enteral nutrition. Other essential ingredients of the TPN solution include water, electrolytes, vitamins, minerals, and trace elements. The proportions of these key nutrients are individualized based on an assessment of the child's clinical and nutritional status in order to provide all of the essential nutrients that will promote weight gain or weight maintenance, wound healing, anabolism, and growth.

CLINICAL INDICATIONS

General indicators for parenteral nutrition include a weight loss of 10% of the actual body weight coupled with an inability to ingest enough enteral calories to reverse the weight loss. When the nutritional needs of the child cannot be met solely through the enteral route or when the gastrointestinal tract is dysfunctional due to disease, injury, or surgery and enteral feeding cannot be initiated for 3 or more days, parenteral nutrition is indicated. The limited nutritional reserves of the premature infant require initiation of TPN if enteral feedings are not begun by the third day of life.[1]

In conditions that interfere with the absorption of nutrients (see Table 11-1), PN may be indicated alone or as a combined regimen with enteral feeding. In bowel conditions requiring surgical resection, the extent of malabsorption depends on the amount of bowel resected, the presence or absence of the ileocecal valve, and

---

Table 11-1 Indications for Parenteral Nutrition in the Pediatric Population

1. Low-birth-weight neonate (< 1500 g)
2. Severe pulmonary disease
   - Bronchopulmonary dysplasia
   - Respiratory distress syndrome
3. Respiratory failure
4. Altered gastrointestinal function
   - Congenital anomalies: volvulus, meconium ileus, intussusception, atresia, gastroschisis, omphalocele, severe Hirschsprung's disease, enteric fistulas, diaphragmatic hernia
   - Inflammatory bowel disease: necrotizing enterocolitis, Crohn's disease, intractable diarrhea, radiation enteritis, ulcerative colitis
   - Chronic idiopathic pseudo-obstruction syndrome
   - Cystic fibrosis
   - Pancreatitis
   - Hepatic failure
5. Hypercatabolic states
   - Severe thermal injury
   - Trauma
   - Sepsis
   - Cancer
6. Chylothorax
7. Renal disease
8. Cardiac disease
   - Cardiac cachexia
9. Neurologic disorders
   - Absence of gag reflex
   - Drug-induced coma
10. Anorexia nervosa

the function of the remaining bowel. If the ileocecal valve is not intact, the rapid transit time of enteral formulas through the bowel may necessitate the initiation of parenteral nutrition. When a child is malnourished and a prolonged period of starvation is anticipated (postoperatively), parenteral nutrition may be necessary.[2]

Parenteral nutrition is indicated in malabsorption disorders related to inflammatory bowel processes. TPN will allow bowel rest for periods of time, alleviating symptoms such as diarrhea and cramping so that the bowel can heal. TPN and bowel rest may result in the remission of a chronic inflammatory process, but it may only be temporary, and surgical intervention may eventually be indicated. Gastrointestinal disorders requiring nutritional support are discussed in detail in Chapter 17.

Malnutrition in the child with cancer is another indicator for parenteral nutrition. Whether enteral feeding has been made impossible by the side effects of radiation and chemotherapy or by surgical procedures, the child with cancer may have an improved quality of life with parenteral nutrition.[3-6] Most clinicians believe that children receiving aggressive treatment for cancer should also receive aggressive nutritional support.

Children with severe neurologic disorders may also be candidates for TPN, particularly in the early stages after a head injury when enteral feeding must be delayed due to drug-induced paralysis, an absent gag reflex, or severe gastroesophageal reflux. The child with a severe seizure disorder or progressive, degenerative neurologic disease in which surgical intervention is contraindicated may also require TPN when the gag reflex is impaired to the point that the risk of aspirating enteral tube feedings becomes a concern.

In anorexia nervosa, TPN may be used early in the refeeding process simply because it has less resemblance to food than the enteral feeding. The use of TPN in these patients depends on the severity of malnutrition and on the patient's tendency to interfere with the infusion apparatus.[7,8]

VASCULAR ACCESS

Peripheral Venous Access

Parenteral nutrition needs may be met via a peripheral or central venous route, depending on the anticipated length of therapy, the glucose concentration, and the volume of the solution. Because a final concentration of no more than 10% dextrose solution is recommended for the administration of peripheral parenteral nutrition (PPN), sufficient calories cannot be delivered to meet the long-term nutritional needs of most children using this route. Compared to the central venous catheter (CVC) route of administration, PPN may be considered by some an easier, safer method of nutrient delivery because peripheral insertion is not a surgical procedure. However, the peripheral route cannot be assumed to be a safer route, as demonstrated in a study by Ziegler and co-workers where the complication rate per therapy day was slightly greater with the peripheral route versus the central route.[9] Peripheral parenteral nutrition is preferred when the anticipated length of therapy will be less than 5 days. The major complications associated with PPN are soft tissue sloughs and phlebitis. The peripheral delivery route also may be more restrictive to normal activity, depending on the site and stability of venous access.

Central Venous Access

Placement of a long-term CVC is indicated when the child will require more than 5 days of nutritional therapy or will be a candidate for home parenteral nutrition. Hypertonic nutritional solutions are more safely infused into the superior vena cava via the CVC, since the high blood flow rapidly dilutes the TPN solution, thereby reducing the risks of phlebitis, venous thrombosis, and sclerosis. Major complications associated with CVC insertion and use are highlighted in Table 11-2.

Central venous access for parenteral nutrition is traditionally held inviolate because of the higher infection risk associated with entering the CVC for purposes other than nutrition.[10–12] Other reasons to avoid interruption of the nutritional CVC are to reduce the risk of solution and drug incompatibility and to avoid hypoglycemia and a decreased caloric delivery over a 24-hour period.

A relatively new type of central venous access is now available for use in children. The peripherally inserted central catheter, also known as the PICC, long arm, or long line catheter, provides reliable central venous access and may be inserted at the bedside by a registered nurse.[13–16] Many of the insertion-related complications inherent in the surgically placed CVC, such as pneumothorax and hemothorax, are eliminated with the PICC line. The risks and costs associated with a surgical procedure are also eliminated. Insertion of the traditional CVC requires ligation of the vessel, so the vein can be used only once, which is not necessarily the case with the PICC line. The catheters come in a variety of sizes and are available through several manufacturers.

The surgically placed right atrial catheter (e.g., Broviac, Hickman) is the most suitable CVC for the pediatric long-term or home patient. The cutdown method can be used to place the catheter in the external jugular or the facial vein and thread it into the internal jugular and down into the superior vena cava. The distal end of the catheter is tunneled subcutaneously and exits midchest. The Dacron cuff affixed to the tunneled portion of the catheter helps secure the catheter because subcutaneous fibrous tissue adheres to the cuff.

Table 11-2 Potential Complications in Pediatric Parenteral Nutrition

CVC Insertion Complications	CVC Postinsertion Complications	Septic Complications
Pneumothorax	Venous thrombosis	Catheter-related sepsis (site infection, bacteremia, fungemia)
Hemothorax	Superior vena cava syndrome	Solution-related sepsis
Hydrothorax	Thrombophlebitis	Septic thrombosis
Brachial nerve plexus injury	Catheter erosion through vein	
Phrenic nerve injury	Aseptic phlebitis (PICC lines)	
Horner's syndrome	Catheter embolism	
Carotid artery injury	Air embolism	
Arteriovenous fistula	Catheter occlusion	
Arterial cannulation	Extravasation	
Subclavian artery injury	Exsanguination	
Subclavian or innominate vein laceration		
Thoracic duct laceration		
Cardiac perforation and tamponade		
Arrhythmias		
Tracheal puncture		
Catheter embolism		
Air embolism		
Catheter malposition		

Although a single-lumen CVC is the venous access device of choice for the pediatric TPN patient, two- and three-lumen CVCs have been developed to serve the high-tech pediatric population who require frequent infusions of blood products and medications in addition to the nutrition solution. Any lumens not in use must be heparinized and capped. Multiple-lumen catheters, particularly useful for the oncology patient who requires frequent blood sampling, chemotherapy, analgesics, and nutrition via the CVC, may be more suitable for the larger child rather than the neonate because of total catheter size. Strict aseptic technique is critical when the multilumen CVC is in place.[17,18]

The material of choice for the CVC is silicone, a material considered less irritating and less thrombocytic. Because of its softness and flexibility, the silicone catheter has a potential to kink or rupture when clamped repeatedly. Manufacturers have now begun to increase the density of silicone used in the CVC, and some manufacturers have built in a denser segment of the external portion of the catheter that is a designated area for clamping. Another new development is the attachable collagen cuff saturated with an antimicrobial solution that provides a 4- to 6-week chemical barrier as well as a physical barrier to bacterial migration.[19]

All externalized CVCs must have some type of dressing over the exit site. Controversy exists as to whether gauze and tape or a transparent dressing is the best material to use.[20,21] Some debate also exists as to the frequency of dressing change. Any type of dressing must be changed when it becomes nonocclusive.

In order to avoid some of the problems associated with the externalized CVC, the totally implantable vascular device consisting of a catheter connected to a chamber or port was developed.[22] The port, available in a variety of sizes with single or multiple access ports and made of a variety of materials, can be accessed percutaneously through a top or side entry septum on the port (depending on the model) using a Huber needle. The advantages of the implantable port are that it requires less care than the externalized CVC by eliminating the daily dressing change when not in use, it is not as disruptive to the body image, and it may minimize the risk of infection. When not in use, the implanted device allows a much freer lifestyle, such as swimming and bathing, and is more cosmetically appealing, but for the child on home parenteral nutrition the implanted CVC must be accessed daily or the Huber needle must be left in place with a dressing for days at a time, which may negate the overall benefits of the implanted device. Skin irritation and breakdown have been associated with frequent port access, and other CVC-related complications such as occlusion, infection, and extravasation are still risks with use of the implanted CVC. Also, children or adolescents who have decreased manual dexterity or who fear the percutaneous puncture necessary to access the port may find self-care and management of the implantable port very difficult. As long as the Huber needle is in place and the nutritional solution is infusing, an external site cleansing and dressing regimen must be implemented, as is required with the externalized CVC.

A new feature now available in both the implantable and the externalized CVC is the catheter pressure-sensitive valve. The Groshong catheter has a slit valve near the tip that prevents blood backflow while allowing solution infusion. The slit valve requires only a saline flush to maintain catheter patency, which is safer and more cost-effective than heparin flushing. The Groshong catheter tip allows blood to be drawn by slow, gentle aspiration with a syringe and minimizes the risk of air emboli and exsanguination.

SOLUTION ADMINISTRATION METHODS AND EQUIPMENT

Total parenteral nutrition solutions are initiated slowly and are gradually advanced as the child's fluid and glucose tolerance permits. Infusion pumps should be used to maintain the constant flow rate, thereby avoiding the blood glucose fluctuation that can occur with an irregular flow rate (see Table 11-3). If a TPN infusion flow rate falls behind schedule, the infusion should not be accelerated to catch up. If the TPN infusion should be interrupted or discontinued abruptly, a 5% dextrose solution should be infused until the TPN solution can be replaced.

Traditionally, combined dextrose and amino acid solution is infused via one arm of a Y-connector, and lipids are infused in the other. The initial dose of lipids should be infused slowly to test for adverse reactions. If a bacteria-retentive filter is used, the lipids should be piggy-backed proximal to filter because these filter pores are too small to allow the passage of lipid emulsions.

The use of filters in TPN is still controversial.[23-25] A 0.22-μm filter can be used to screen out bacteria and particulate matter and to reduce the risk of air embolism. However, there are concerns that use of a filter may cause some drugs to be adsorbed and become sources of endotoxin production. The added cost of the filter used in TPN is also a consideration. There are larger filters for use with lipids that filter out only particulate matter but would allow passage of bacteria.

Total Nutrient Admixture

Recently, a new delivery system known as the Total Nutrient Admixture (TNA), which combines the lipid emulsion, amino acid, and dextrose solution in the same container, has become available for use in the United States. The advantage of this system is the reduction in pharmacist and nurse time spent preparing the infusion solutions, since only a single container is prepared for the patient and hung at the bedside on a daily basis. The need for Y-tubing and other line manipu-

Table 11-3 Pediatric Parenteral Infusion Device—Desirable Features

1. Inexpensive
2. Suitable for use with clear and opaque solutions
3. Equipped with tamper-proof controls
4. Small and lightweight for ambulatory patients
5. Equipped with sturdy, wheeled stand or pole with a wide base of support to prevent overturning
6. Has audible and visual alarms for
   • Low battery
   • Occlusion
   • Infusion complete
   • Air in line
7. Easy to operate and set up
8. Pump pressure compatible for use with in-line filter devices
9. Delivers known fluid volume via peristaltic or volumetric syringe pump methods
10. Has flow rate that is accurate with delivery rates as low as 1 ml/h, which can be increased in 0.1 ml increments
11. Can be programmed to taper infusion rate for patient on cyclic infusion
12. Can operate accurately on long-life battery (12 to 24 hours)

---

lations necessary in hanging a two-bottle system is avoided with the TNA.[26–27] More data needs to be collected to document the potential for reduced infection rates and to document solution stability with this system. Some technical disadvantages of long-term TNA infusion include catheter occlusion and the potential release of the plasticizer di-2-ethylhexyl-phthalate (DEHP) from the polyvinylchloride administration sets into lipid emulsions.[28–30]

Cycling

This administration method provides for planned interruption of the nutrient infusion to allow for periods of time when the child is unencumbered by the nutritional solution and equipment. Cycling can also more closely simulate normal patterns of food ingestion and fasting.[31,32] Whether at home or in the hospital, cyclic TPN infused at night can allow the child a more normal daytime routine, enhancing mobility and activity patterns and also leaving a "window" of time for lipid clearance. Infants may not be able to receive their total required caloric and fluid load condensed in a 10- or 12-hour cycle, but older children who are more tolerant of the necessary fluid load can have their 24-hour caloric needs met over a shorter period of time. Weaning down the infusion rate over a period of time, rather than abruptly discontinuing it, may lessen the likelihood of hypoglycemia.

FLUID AND ELECTROLYTES

Guidelines for the administration of parenteral fluids to infants and children are based on normal maintenance estimates, with adjustments for increased or decreased losses due to disease or environmental conditions. Maintenance fluid and electrolyte requirements are directly related to metabolic rate.[33] Changes in metabolic rate and caloric intake will change the solute load and water required for renal excretion, losses through respiratory tract and skin, and endogenous water production from the oxidation of protein, carbohydrate, and fat (see Table 11-4).

Losses of fluid and electrolytes through the gastrointestinal tract in disease states may be measured directly for replacement or estimated by monitoring changes in body weight every 8 or 24 hours. Gastrointestinal losses may be due to vomiting, nasogastric suctioning, diarrhea, or ostomy drainage. Due to the wide range in electrolyte composition of various gastrointestinal fluids, direct measurement may be required to provide adequate replacement.

Urinary losses of fluid and electrolytes depend largely on intake and renal maturity. Infants less than 1 year of age can dilute urine to 50 mOsm/kg of water. Concentrating ability at birth is about 600 mOsm/kg of water and gradually increases to 1000 to 1200 mOsm/kg of water during the first year. During periods of growth, the renal solute load will be lower as nitrogen, phosphorus, sodium, potassium, and chloride are retained as constituents of body tissues. During periods of stress and tissue catabolism, the renal solute load will be higher.

Various conditions may alter urinary losses of fluid and electrolytes. Preterm infants have an immature capacity to either excrete or retain electrolytes.[34] This may be compounded by excessive antidiuretic hormone (ADH) secretion, which

Table 11-4 Daily Maintenance Fluid Requirements

Clinical Condition	Fluids Required per Day	
Sick newborn, day 1	40–80	ml/kg
Sick newborn, week 1	100–150	ml/kg
Anuria, extreme oliguria	45	ml/kg
Diabetes insipidus	up to 400	ml/100 kcal
1–10 kg body weight	100	ml/kg
11–20 kg body weight	1000 ml + 50	ml/kg above 10 kg
Body weight above 20 kg	1500 ml + 20	ml/kg above 20 kg
Body surface area	1500–1800	ml/m²

Source: Data from references 37 and 118.

is associated with hypoxia, hemorrhage, central nervous system insult, hypotension, anesthesia, pneumothorax, or pain. Inappropriate or excessive ADH secretion requires fluid restriction and sodium supplementation.[35] Fluid and electrolyte restriction may be necessary in some disease states such as congestive heart failure, head trauma, and renal insufficiency. Medications may be a significant source or may cause increased excretion or retention of some electrolytes. Saline flushes used in routine care of intravenous lines may be a significant source of sodium and chloride.[36] Direct measurement of urine volume and electrolytes may be necessary to provide adequate replacement.

While losses through urine and the gastrointestinal tract may be relatively easy to measure, insensible water loss (IWL) is more elusive and may be affected by environmental conditions. Prematurely born infants may lose 10% to 25% of their body weight during the first week of life, primarily from IWL. This is due to their greater percentage of total body water as extracellular water, their large body surface area relative to body mass, and their more permeable epidermis.[37] Radiant heat warmers and ultraviolet light therapy may increase IWL by 20% to 25%.[38,39] Use of double-walled isolettes may prevent this increase in water loss.[40] Use of mist tents and humidified air may decrease IWL.[41] Low-birth-weight infants may require up to 200 ml/kg/d due to their renal immaturity and increased insensible water losses. They may also be intolerant of excessive fluid intake. Patent ductus arteriosus, bronchopulmonary dysplasia, intraventricular hemorrhage, and necrotizing enterocolitis have each been linked with excessive fluid administration.[42–45]

Older infants and children may initially require fluids and electrolytes in excess of maintenance requirements to establish normal hydration. Hyperventilation and visible sweating often associated with fever may increase IWL in older infants and children by 20% to 25%. If peripherally administered, fluids will often exceed maintenance levels to provide adequate caloric intake.

ENERGY

Parenteral caloric needs are probably about 10% to 15% lower than estimated enteral needs for most infants and children due to reduced fecal losses and energy required for digestion and absorption (see Table 11-5).

The percentage contribution of protein, carbohydrate, and fat to total caloric intake will vary with individual tolerance to fluid, carbohydrate, and lipid infusion and the route of delivery. General guidelines for caloric distribution are 8% to 15% protein, 45% to 60% carbohydrate, and 25% to 40% fat.[37] Positive nitrogen balance is best achieved when the nonprotein calorie:nitrogen ratio is 150 to 300:1.[46,47]

Table 11-5 Daily Recommendations for Parenteral Administration of Nutrient

		Premature Infants	Term Infants	Age 1–3 Years	4–6 Years	7–10 Years	11–18 Years
Basal energy	(kcal/kg)[†]	46–55	55	40–55	38–40	25–38	23–25
Total energy	(kcal/kg)[‡]	80–120	105	75–90	65–75	55–75	40–55
Carbohydrate	(g/kg)	4–18	8–23	8–23	8–23	8–23	8–23
Protein[§]	(g/kg)	2.0–3.0	2.5–3.0	1.5–2.5	1.5–2.5	1.5–2.5	1.5–2.5
Fat	(g/kg)	0.5–3.0	0.5–4.0	0.5–2.5	0.5–2.5	0.5–2.5	0.5–2.0
Vitamins‖	(dose)	65%	100%	100%	100%	100%	100%
Sodium	(mEq/kg)	2–4	2–4	2–4	2–4	2–4	2–4
Potassium	(mEq/kg)	2–4	2–4	2–4	2–4	2–4	2–4
Chloride	(mEq/kg)	2–3	2–3	2–3	2–3	2–3	2–3
Magnesium¶	(mEq/kg)	0.3–0.5	0.25–1.0	0.25–1.0	0.25–1.0	0.25–0.5	0.25–0.5
Calcium#	(mEq/kg)	1.0–3.0	0.6–0.75	0.6–0.75	0.4–0.5	0.3–0.4	0.2–0.3
Phosphorus*	(mmol/kg)	1.3–1.5	1.3–1.5	0.5–2.0	0.5–2.0	0.5–2.0	0.5–2.0
Zinc	(µg/kg)	<3 kg 300; >3 kg 100	100	100	100	2.5–4.0[††]	2.5–4.0[††]
Copper[‡‡]	(µg/kg)	20	20	20	20	20	0.5–1.5[††]
Chromium	(µg/kg)	0.14–0.2	0.14–0.2	0.14–0.2	0.14–0.2	0.14–0.2	10–15[§§]
Manganese[‡‡]	(µg/kg)	2–10	2–10	2–10	2–10	2–10	0.15–0.8[††]
Selenium	(µg/kg)	3	3	3 or <40[§§]	3 or <40[§§]	3 or <40[§§]	3 or <40[§§]
Iron‖‖	(mg/kg)	1–1.5	1–1.5	1	1	1	1

[†] Basal calories up 12% for every degree of fever; up 15% to 25% in cardiac failure; up 20% to 30% in traumatic injury or major surgery; up 25% to 30% in severe respiratory distress or bronchopulmonary dysplasia; up 40% to 50% in severe sepsis; up 6 kcal/g weight gain for catch-up growth.

[‡] Total energy does not include calories normally required for digestion or stool losses.

[§] Protein needs are 0.8 to 2.0 g/kg/d in renal failure; 3 g/kg/d for necrotizing enterocolitis, major surgery, traumatic injury, sepsis; and 4 to 8 g/kg/d for thermal injury. Most efficient protein utilization occurs when nonprotein:calorie ratio is 150 to 250:1 (100 to 150:1 in burns, multiple trauma).

‖ Pediatric MVI, Armour Pharmaceutical Company. See Table 11-12.

¶ Magnesium sulfate 50% contains 500 mg magnesium sulfate heptahydrate or 4.1 mEq magnesium per milliliter.

Calcium gluconate 10% contains 100 mg calcium gluconate or 10 mg (0.5 mEq) of calcium per milliliter.

* Potassium phosphate contains 93 mg (3 mmol) phosphorus and 4.4 mEq potassium per milliliter; sodium phosphate contains 93 mg (3 mmol) phosphorus and 4 mEq sodium per milliliter.

[††] Milligrams per day.

[‡‡] As copper and manganese are excreted primarily through bile, decrease or temporarily omit these metals in patients with obstructive jaundice.

[§§] Micrograms per day.

‖‖ Iron is not routinely included in parenteral admixtures. See text. Do not give to prematurely born infants less than 2 months of age.

Source: Data from references 37, 47, 80, 102, 119, and 120.

CARBOHYDRATE

Nearly all centers use glucose (dextrose monohydrate, 3.4 kcal/g) as the primary source of parenterally administered carbohydrate. Glycerol, found in parenterally administered fat emulsions, is also a source of carbohydrate. Dose recommendations for infants and children are found in Table 11-6. Glucose in excess of 16 mg/kg/min (24 g/kg/d) is not recommended.[47]

Insulin is not generally added to parenteral nutrient admixtures as dose response varies widely, particularly in the low-birth-weight infant. Insulin, when needed, may be given in a separate infusion starting at 0.1 U/kg/h and increased or decreased as needed to maintain euglycemia.[48,49] Small glucose stores in the low-birth-weight infant and undernourished infants and children place them at a greater risk of developing hypoglycemia following abrupt cessation of parenteral glucose. Gradual weaning from parenteral glucose and adequate enteral feeding can help prevent the development of hypoglycemia.

The recommended dose of carbohydrate may be delivered while meeting normal fluid requirements by using a 10% to 12.5% dextrose solution. This concentration is compatible with peripheral intravenous infusion. Greater concentrations of carbohydrate are given by central venous infusion, generally up to a maximum concentration of 25%.[50] These may be needed when caloric needs are greater than 100 kcal/kg/d, when parenterally administered fat is poorly tolerated, or when fluid restriction is necessary.

PROTEIN

Several studies have undertaken to identify the optimal protein intake for infants,[51–54] though recommendations beyond infancy are more empirical or disease related.[47,54] General recommendations for protein administration for infants and

Table 11-6 Parenteral Glucose Dose Recommendations

	mg/kg/min	g/kg/d
Very low birth weight infants		
Initial dose	3–4	4–6
Dose during first few days	6–8	8.5–11.5
Dose after first week	8–12	12–18
Term infant or child		
Initial dose	6–8	8.5–11.5
Dose after first week	12–14	19–23

Source: Data from references 37, 47, and 48.

children are given in Table 11-5. Individual protein needs can be determined from nitrogen balance studies, though protein status is generally evaluated by monitoring serum total protein and albumin levels. Changes in serum prealbumin, transferrin, or retinol binding protein levels may identify changes in protein status more quickly. Recommendations concerning monitoring and complications of protein administration are found in Tables 11-7 and 11-8.

Recently, the focus of research has been crystalline amino acid (CAA) solution composition. CAA products have been developed for infants reflecting the amino acid composition of human milk or plasma aminograms of healthy term infants fed mature human milk (see Tables 11-9 and 11-10). The metabolic immaturity of the neonate has also been considered, as cystine, taurine, tyrosine, and histidine may be essential amino acids. Methionine, phenylalanine, and glycine concentrations have been decreased in these solutions, while histidine, tyrosine, taurine, glutamic acid, and aspartic acid may be added or their concentrations increased.

The addition of cystine to CAA solutions is controversial. Cystine is unstable in solution for prolonged periods of time but is available as L-cystine hydrochloride to be added separately at the time of administration. However, cystathionase activ-

Table 11-7 Suggested Laboratory Monitoring during Pediatric Parenteral Nutrition

Test	Initial Period (Week 1)	Later Period (When Stable)
Blood glucose	Daily until stable	3×/week
Serum electrolytes (Na, K, Cl, CO₂)	Daily until stable	Weekly
Creatinine, BUN	3×/week	Weekly
Ammonia	2×/week	Weekly
Chemistry profile (total protein, albumin, bilirubin, SGOT, SGPT, LDH, alkaline phosphatase, calcium, phosphorus, magnesium)	2×/week	Weekly
Acid-base status	2×/week	Weekly
Triglyceride, cholesterol	2×/week	Weekly (if fat emulsions used)
Serum turbidity	Daily	Daily
Complete blood count	2×/week	Weekly
Blood culture	—	When infection suspected
Serum folate, B₁₂	Monthly	Monthly
Hematology studies (iron, TIBC, ferritin)	—	When imbalance suspected
Trace elements	Baseline	When imbalance suspected

Note: BUN, blood urea nitrogen; LDH, lactic dehydrogenase; SGOT, serum glutamic-oxaloacetic transaminase; SGPT, serum glutamate pyruvate transaminase; TIBC, total iron-binding capacity.

Table 11-8 Metabolic Complications of Pediatric Parenteral Nutrition

Complication	Cause	Treatment
Hyperglycemia, glycosuria, osmotic diuresis, hyperosmolar nonketotic dehydration, coma	Excessive dose or rate of glucose infusion	Decrease rate, concentration of glucose; use insulin with caution, results are often erratic in the very low birth weight infant
Hypoglycemia	Abrupt discontinuation of glucose infusion; excess insulin	Maintain constant glucose infusion; decrease glucose infusion rates slowly; decrease insulin
Metabolic acidosis, hyperammonemia, prerenal azotemia	Excessive amino acid infusion, inappropriate protein/calorie ratio	Decrease amino acids, increase nonprotein calories
Hyperchloremic metabolic acidosis	Excessive chloride administration causing cation gap	Provide equal amount of sodium and chloride in infusate; neutralize cation gap with lactate or acetate if respiratory status allows*
Hypokalemia	Inadequate potassium infusion relative to increased requirements for protein anabolism	If potassium needs are greater than the potassium provided by potassium phosphate, potassium acetate is generally recommended*
Hyperkalemia	Excessive potassium administration; especially in metabolic acidosis	Decrease potassium in infusate
Volume overload, congestive heart failure	Excessive rate of fluid administration	Monitor weight daily, monitor intake and output daily to prevent volume overload; do not attempt to "catch up" by increasing rate of infusion; to treat, decrease rate of infusion
Hypocalcemia	Inadequate calcium administration or phosphorus administration without simultaneous calcium infusion; hypomagnesemia or hypoalbuminemia	Increase calcium infusion, maintaining appropriate phosphorus and magnesium infusion
Hypophosphatemia	Inadequate phosphorus administration especially relative to increased needs of protein anabolism	Increase phosphorus infusion,* maintaining appropriate calcium/phosphorus precipitation

Complication	Cause	Treatment
Hypomagnesemia	Inadequate magnesium infusion relative to increased gastrointestinal losses in chronic diarrhea or increased needs for protein anabolism	Increase magnesium infusion*
Essential fatty acid deficiency	Inadequate linoleic acid infusion	Provide at least 4%–8% of total calories as intravenous fat emulsion to provide 1%–4% of total calories as linoleic acid
Hypertriglyceridemia, hypercholesterolemia	Lipids infused at a rate greater than the capacity to metabolize	Decrease or interrupt lipid infusion; add heparin to infusate†
Anemia	Deficiency of iron, folic acid, vitamin B_{12}, or copper	Administer appropriate nutrient
Cholestatic jaundice	Sepsis, prematurity, starvation, essential fatty acid deficiency, lipid infusion, amino acid deficiency, amino acid excess, carbohydrate excess, decreased bile flow, bowel obstruction, lack of enteral feedings	Begin enteral feedings as soon as possible, maintain adequate but not excessive intake; liver function generally returns to normal within 6 to 9 months after cessation of therapy, but may progress to chronic liver disease

* Data from reference 121.
† Data from reference 37, chapter 7.

Source: Adapted from *Nutritional Care for High Risk Newborns* (pp 66–68) by the Ohio Neonatal Nutritionists, with permission of the Ohio Neonatal Nutritionists, © 1985.

ity matures to 70% of adult activity by 9 days of age in preterm infants and by 3 days of age in term infants.[55,56] Cystine supplementation does not increase overall nitrogen retention or improve growth in neonates when 120 mg methionine per kilogram per day is provided. If the total sulfur amino acid (methionine plus cystine) requirement for neonates is 40 mg/g of protein, cystine supplementation is needed for either of the two pediatric CAA products presently available but is not needed for standard solutions.[57–59]

Most of the studies evaluating the efficacy or comparing pediatric and standard CAA products have been done in only a small number of patients over 5 to 21 days.[48,60–62] While greater weight gain and nitrogen balance with pediatric products may be statistically significant, these differences may not be clinically significant. Other significant differences reported are the normalization of plasma

Table 11-9 Amino Acid Content of Parenteral Products (mg/dl of 2% Amino Acid Solution)

Amino Acid	Aminosyn	Freamine III	Travasol	Aminosyn PF	Trophamine
Isoleucine	146	138	96	153	163
Leucine	189	182	124	237	280
Lysine	146	146	116	135	163
Methionine	80	106	116	36	67
Phenylalanine	89	112	124	86	97
Threonine	106	80	84	103	83
Tryptophan	34	30	36	36	40
Valine	161	132	92	129	157
Alanine	258	142	415	140	106
Arginine	198	190	207	246	243
Histidine	60	56	88	63	97
Proline	175	224	84	163	137
Serine	86	118	—	99	77
Tyrosine	11	—	8	13	47
Glycine	258	280	415	77	73
Cystine	—	<5	—	—	<7
Glutamine	—	—	—	165	100
Asparagine	—	—	—	106	64
Taurine	—	—	—	14	5

Note: Aminosyn and Aminosyn PF: Abbott Laboratories, North Chicago, IL; Freamine III and Trophamine: Kendall-McGaw Laboratories, Irvine, CA; Travasol: Travenol, Baxter Healthcare Corporation, North Chicago, IL.

---

aminograms, specifically for methionine, phenylalanine, threonine, and glycine (and cystine if it is added as recommended). Plasma taurine levels are normal with all CAA products, but it must be noted that the duration of these studies has been relatively short term. Although the data are inconclusive, there may be a decreased incidence of cholestatic liver disease during pediatric CAA product administration.[59,63]

Several issues regarding the use of pediatric amino acid solutions remain unresolved. The greatest advantage seems to be that plasma amino acid patterns are similar to those of healthy breastfed neonates. What implications this has for use with older infants or children has not been clearly identified. As liver function studies show no significant differences between standard and pediatric CAA product administration over 5 to 21 days, standard CAA solutions may be sufficient for short-term use.

Practically, based on current literature, pediatric CAA products may be of benefit to the prematurely born infant or the infant who requires long-term parenteral nutrition. Pediatric CAA products may require cystine supplementation for infants less than 4 months of age (55 to 77 mg/kg/d) due to inadequate cystathionase

Table 11-10 Plasma Aminograms of Pediatric Patients on Parenteral Nutrition Compared to Plasma Aminograms of Healthy Breastfed Infants (mmol/dl)

Amino Acid	Breast Milk	Aminosyn Mean	SD	Freamine III Mean	SD	Travasol Mean	SD	Aminosyn PF Mean	SD	Trophamine Mean	SD
Isoleucine	24–100	97	20	62	5	70	16	39	2	67	6
Leucine	53–169	125	24	78	18	71	18	59	2	113	10
Lysine	80–231	299	54	140	15	103	39	83	4	161	15
Methionine	19–50	64	17	58	5	114	49	12	1	44	4
Phenylalanine	22–71	84	29	76	5	92	19	28	1	71	3
Threonine	70–197	288	78	138	18	279	67	137	7	190	14
Tryptophan	18–101			43	3			20	1	30	2
Valine	88–222	288	53	155	11	130	26	83	4	177	15
Alanine	125–647	376	81	218	18	359	84	173	10	195	19
Arginine	42–148	140	50	79	5	124	46	44	3	86	8
Histidine	34–119	98	16	73	5	83	36	42	3	72	5
Proline	82–319	284	66	238	21	165	30	136	7	177	15
Serine	43–326	271	84	183	23	196	41	116	5	162	11
Tyrosine	38–119	27	9	21	4	71	33	9	1	75	8
Glycine	60–376	699	142	532	40	993	266	188	7	311	23
Cystine	35–69	5	5	35	5	34	11	5	1	44	3
Glutamic Acid	24–243	282	98	70	9	} 509	133	189	16	63	6
Glutamine	142–850	304	138	366	34			129	9	386	43
Aspartic Acid	21–132	43	11	42	4	59	14	30	2	48	6
Taurine	1–167	97	57	50	11	82	44			73	6

Note: Mean protein intake range: 2.59–2.75 grams protein/per kilogram per day; mean caloric intake range 80–100 kcal/kg/d. SD = +/– 1 standard deviation. Bold print values indicate plasma amino acid levels outside target range.

Aminosyn and Aminosyn PF: Abbott Laboratories, North Chicago, IL; Freamine III and Trophamine: Kendall-McGaw Laboratories, Irvine, CA; Travasol: Travenol, Baxter Healthcare Corporation, North Chicago, IL.

Source: Data from references 48, 60–62, and 122.

activity and for all other infants and children (3 to 22 mg cystine per gram of total amino acids content) due to reduced methionine concentrations.[48,55,57–59]

Special solutions of L-isomer CAA formulated for adults with severe hepatic or renal failure appear to also be efficacious in children with severe hepatic or renal failure, though standard CAA solutions may better meet the amino acid needs of children with acute renal failure.[64–68] Older children with sepsis or traumatic injury may benefit from using formulations with increased amounts of branched-chain amino acids.[69]

FAT

Fat is included in parenteral nutrition regimens for infants and children as a source of essential fatty acids and calories. Linoleic acid deficiency is clinically manifested as dry, flaky skin, dry hair, poor growth, decreased platelets, and impaired wound healing. Biochemical deficiency of linoleic acid precedes these clinical manifestations. Plasma levels of linoleic, arachidonic, and eicosatrienoic acids are low; the ratio of plasma eicosatrienoic acid (triene:tetraene) is elevated. Linolenic acid deficiency has been reported in a child with symptoms including episodes of numbness, paresthesia, weakness, inability to walk, and blurring of vision.[70] Very low birth weight infants or infants and children with depleted body stores of fat or with a chronic history of fat malabsorption are at greatest risk of developing essential fatty acid deficiency.

Providing as little as 1% to 2% of the total daily caloric intake as linoleic acid and 0.54% of the total daily caloric intake as linolenic acid can prevent deficiency.[37] The fatty acid content of parenteral lipid emulsion products is given in Table 11-11. Providing 4% of total calories as lipid (0.5 or 5 ml of 10% lipid emulsion per kilogram per day) prevents essential fatty acid deficiency in most infants and children.

Limitations of glucose or fluid tolerance often dictate a greater intake of lipid than that which prevents deficiency. Fat may be needed as a source of calories, given in doses up to 4 g/kg/d, though doses of 2.5 to 3.0 g/kg/d may be better tolerated in prematurely born or small for gestational age infants.[37,47,71,72] In children over 2 years of age, it may be advisable to limit fat to 30% of total calories (generally 1.5 to 2.5 g/kg/d), as recommended by the American Academy of Pediatrics.[73] Fat should not provide more than 60% of total calories in any patient, as ketotic acidosis may occur.[74]

Preterm or malnourished infants and children may be at greater risk for impaired fat tolerance due to decreased adipose tissue mass, reduced lipoprotein lipase activity, hepatic immaturity, or carnitine deficiency. While heparin stimulates the release of lipoprotein lipase, it may not significantly affect lipid clearance over time and is not routinely recommended for that purpose.

Table 11-11 Composition of Intravenous Fat Emulsions

	Intralipid* 10% (Intralipid 20%)	Liposyn† II 10% (Liposyn II 20%)	Liposyn† III 10% (Liposyn III 20%)	Soyacal‡ 10% (Soyacal 20%)	Nutrilipid§ 10% (Nutrilipid 20%)
Concentration (g/dl)	10 (20)	10 (20)	10 (20)	10 (20)	10 (20)
Fat source (g/dl)					
Soybean oil	10 (20)	5 (10)	10 (20)	10 (20)	10 (20)
Safflower oil		5 (10)			
Fatty acid content					
(Percent of total fat)					
Linoleic	50	65.8	54.5	49–60	49–60
Oleic	26	17.7	22.4	21–26	21–26
Palmitic	10	8.8	10.5	9–13	9–13
Stearic	3.5	3.4	4.2	3–5	3–5
Linolenic	9	4.2	8.3	6–9	6–9
Egg phosphatides					
(g/dl)	1.2	1.2	1.2	1.2	1.2
Glycerol (g/dl)	2.25	2.5	2.5	2.21	2.21
Osmolality (mOsm/l)	260	276 (258)	284 (292)	280 (315)	280 (315)
pH	6–8.9	6–9	6–9	6–7.9	6–7.9
Calories (kcal/ml)	1.1 (2.0)	1.1 (2.0)	1.1 (2.0)	1.1 (2.0)	1.1 (2.0)

* Clintec Nutrition Company, Deerfield, IL.
† Abbott Laboratories, North Chicago, IL.
‡ Alpha Therapeutic Corporation, Los Angeles, CA.
§ Kendall-McGaw Laboratories, Santa Ana, CA.

Studies are somewhat conflicting as to whether or not carnitine supplementation facilitates parenteral lipid utilization.[75–78] A nontoxic substance, carnitine is normally synthesized by the liver from methionine and lysine. Pediatric amino acid solutions are lower in methionine than standard solutions. Dose recommendations for oral or intravenous supplementation are generally in the range of 50 to 70 µmol/kg/d (8 to 11 µg/kg/d). Carnitine is not generally available for intravenous or oral use in this country at this time.

An increased risk of kernicterus in infants with elevated serum bilirubin level, altered pulmonary function, and impaired neutrophil function has been reported with intravenous fat doses in excess of 3.6 g/kg/d, or doses given over short infusion times. Intravenous fat may be safely given if the dosage is within the recommended range and if it is given over 24 hours whenever possible. If serum bilirubin levels are greater than 8 to 10 mg/dl (while the serum albumin level is 2.5 to 3 g/dl), lipids should be given only in amounts adequate to prevent essential fatty acid deficiency.[79] If intravenous fat is given in greater amounts or given in bolus doses, the free fatty acid:serum albumin molar ratio should be maintained at less than 6 while bilirubin levels remain elevated.[37] (See Chapter 3 for further discussion on this issue.)

VITAMINS

Recommendations for vitamin administration are given in Table 11-5. These recommendations were established by the Nutrition Advisory Group of the American Medical Association in 1975.[80] They were based on the 1974 Recommended Dietary Allowances (RDAs), which are guidelines for enteral nutrient intake. The vitamin content of Pediatric MVI (Roche Pharmaceuticals) is compared to the current RDAs and Estimated Safe and Adequate Daily Dietary Intake of Selected Vitamins and Minerals for infants and children in Table 11-12.

Subsequent studies have shown the Food and Drug Administration's current dose recommendations to produce serum levels at or above the reference range for α-tocopherol, 25-hydroxycholecalciferol, thiamin, riboflavin, niacin, pyridoxine, folate, pantothenic acid, cyanocobalamin, and biotin.[81–83] There are no reports of toxic vitamin levels using these recommended doses.

Levels of several vitamins may decrease over time in parenteral nutrient admixtures due to light degradation, decomposition in the presence of bisulfite (an antioxidant additive) or varying pH, and adsorbance to plastic or glass. For this reason, it is recommended that multivitamins be added to parenteral nutrient solutions immediately prior to administration and that administration be completed within 24 hours.

Table 11-12 Recommendations for Pediatric Parenteral Daily Vitamin Dosage

	Age (years)	A IU	D IU	E mg	K µg	C mg	B1 mg	B2 mg	B6 mg	B12 µg	Niacin mg	FA µg	PA mg	Biotin µg
Infants	Preterm	1400	400	5	5µg/kg	50	0.6	0.8	0.6	0.4	10	65	2	3
	0.0–0.5	1400	400	3	5	30	0.3	0.4	0.3	0.5	6	30	2	35
	0.5–1.0	2000	400	4	10	35	0.4	0.5	0.6	1.5	8	45	3	50
Children	1–3	2000	400	6	15	40	0.7	0.8	0.9	2.0	9	100	3	65
	4–6	2500	400	7	20	45	0.9	1.1	1.3	2.5	11	200	3–4	85
	7–10	3300	400	7	30	45	1.0	1.2	1.6	3.0	16	300	4–5	120
Pediatric MVI* (One dose)		2300	400	7	200	80	1.2	1.4	1.0	1.0	17	140	5.0	20

Note: FA, folic acid; PA, pantothenic acid.
* Armour Pharmaceutical Company

Source: Data from references 80, 123, and 124.

MINERALS

Magnesium

Magnesium deficiency is identified by evaluation of serum levels. Although rare, magnesium deficiency may be seen in cases of protein-calorie malnutrition, chronic malabsorption, or cystic fibrosis.[84,85] Repletion dose is 0.2 mEq/kg given intramuscularly or intravenously every 6 hours until symptoms subside. Blood pressure should be monitored with intravenous magnesium repletion, as hypotension may occur.[37]

Parenteral doses of 0.5 mEq/kg/d may be needed to allow adequate retention for prematurely born infants, though general dose recommendations for all other infants and children are 0.25 to 1.0 mEq/kg/d of magnesium with a maximum allowable dose of 25 mEq/d.[37,47,72,86] Upper-range doses may be needed during rapid growth phases, diuretic therapy, or chronic malabsorption. Lower range doses may be indicated if renal function is impaired. Magnesium is added to parenteral admixtures as magnesium sulfate (50% $MgSO_4$), which contains 10 mEq of magnesium per milliliter.

Calcium

Calcium deficiency is not usually identified by low serum levels. If calcium intake is insufficient, serum calcium is maintained at the expense of bone stores in most infants and children. Hypocalcemia is most common during the neonatal period, particularly in infants born prematurely due to their relatively low calcium stores and inappropriately low parathyroid hormone levels.[87]

Parenteral calcium doses for prematurely born infants are generally 20 to 40 mg/kg/d (1 to 2 mEq/kg/d), though up to 60 mg/kg/d (3 mEq/kg/d) has been reported in the literature without evidence of hypercalciuria or other complication of calcium metabolism.[86,88,89] Aluminum intake may be excessive at higher calcium intake levels if calcium gluconate is used.[90] Parenteral calcium needs are given in Table 11-5. For the various age groups, though, most published sources empirically recommend 10 to 50 mg/kg/d (0.5 to 2.5 mEq/kg/d) for all ages.[37,42] Calcium should be administered over 24 hours, as parenteral calcium administered chronically as bolus doses over 20 minutes to 1 hour has been associated with hypercalcemia and hypercalciuria.[91,92] Hypercalciuria and nephrolithiasis have been associated with furosemide therapy and inadequate phosphorus intake.[87,93] Older children receiving cyclic parenteral nutrition may have greater urinary losses of calcium.[94]

Calcium gluconate is generally the additive of choice, though recently there has been some concern regarding aluminum contamination.[90] Calcium gluconate contains 1g of calcium gluconate, providing 5 mEq or 100 mg of calcium per 10 ml.

Phosphorus

Phosphorus depletion has been reported in infants and children. It is character-ized by hypercalciuria (at least 4 mg of calcium per kilogram per day), hypophosphatemia (serum levels less than 4 mg/dl), and undetectable levels of urinary phosphorus excretion.[85,95,96] Parenteral repletion may be accomplished by an initial dose of 5 to 9 mg/kg or 0.15 to 0.3 mmol/kg of phosphorus per kilogram, given over 6 hours.

Recommendations for parenteral administration of phosphorus for children are given in Table 11-5. Phosphorus is added to parenteral nutrient solutions as potas-sium or sodium phosphate salts. Potassium phosphate contains 93 mg (3 mmol) of phosphorus and 4.4 mEq of potassium per milliliter. Sodium phosphate contains 93 mg (3 mmol) of phosphorus and 4 mEq of sodium per milliliter.

The greatest difficulty in providing adequate calcium and phosphorus parenter-ally is their relative insolubility in the same admixture, limited further by increas-ing pH and temperature. Alternating calcium and phosphorus administration causes alternating elevations of serum and urinary excretion of calcium and phos-phorus.[97] Solubility studies and guidelines for simultaneous administration of cal-cium and phosphorus have been published for various amino acid products.[98–101]

TRACE MINERALS

Recommendations for daily parenteral doses are given in Table 11-5.[102] Zinc, copper, chromium, manganese, selenium, and iodine are available singly or in combination for use in parenteral nutrition admixtures. Neither clinical nor bio-chemical deficiency of molybdenum or iodine with parenteral nutrition has been reported in the literature, and they are generally not included in parenteral nutri-tion admixtures. Transdermal absorption of iodine from cleansing or disinfecting solutions or ointments may be an adequate source of iodine.[103] Fluorine is not added, as its role in human nutrition is limited primarily to dental health.

Very low birth weight infants and infants and children with protein-calorie mal-nutrition, thermal injury, neoplasms, chronic diarrhea, enterocutaneous fistulas, or bile salt malabsorption are at greatest risk for developing trace element defi-ciency.[102,104,105] Zinc supplementation without copper supplementation may inter-fere with copper metabolism.[106] Infants and children who develop cholestatic liver disease should receive reduced doses of copper or no copper supplementation, as it is excreted primarily through bile, and its accumulation is potentially hepatotoxic.[37,105] Selenium is present as a contaminant in parenteral dextrose solu-tion and may provide up to 0.9 µg/dl. Parenteral selenium toxicity has not been reported.

Iron deficiency is probably the most common trace mineral deficiency. It mani-fests as microcytic hypochromic anemia and is characterized by low serum hemoglobin and ferritin levels, low hematocrit, and low percent transferrin saturation. Infants and children at risk for iron deficiency include those who are prematurely born, chronically ill, protein-calorie malnourished, have significant unreplaced blood loss, or who receive unsupplemented parenteral nutrition for long periods of time. There is some controversy over whether or not iron should be routinely included in parenteral nutrition therapy. Intramuscular injections of iron may not be the best choice in the small prematurely born infant or the protein-calorie malnourished patient due to small muscle mass and increased risk of sarcoma at the site of injection.[107] Anaphylaxis has been reported in some patients with administration of iron dextran.[108] Several authors report that iron may be safely given daily in parenteral nutrition admixtures or in bolus doses given intravenously over 2 to 3 hours weekly or monthly.[107,109,110] Iron is often only given in treatment of iron deficiency anemia. Iron dextran is available as the source of iron for parenteral use. Guidelines for dosage and administration of iron dextran in treatment of iron deficiency are given in the manufacturer's package insert.

PATIENT MONITORING

Many parameters are monitored to evaluate the child's tolerance and response to TPN. A comprehensive monitoring program includes evaluation of anthropometrics (see Table 11-13), physical laboratory measurement of metabolic and electrolyte status (see Table 11-7), and daily physical examination (including intake and output). Baseline laboratory measurements are crucial in order to avoid or identify complications and to measure trends during nutrition therapy. Metabolic complications that can occur during pediatric nutrition support are summarized in Table 11-8. Laboratory monitoring protocols may vary slightly from one setting to another, but once the patient stabilizes on the nutritional regimen, the need and frequency for some tests can be re-evaluated. Careful ordering of blood tests in infants and children must be followed due to their small blood volume.

Table 11-13 Growth Parameters Monitored during Pediatric Parenteral Nutrition

Parameter	Frequency
Weight	Daily
Height	Weekly (infants)
	Monthly (over 1 year of age)
Head circumference	Weekly (infants)
	Monthly (under 2 years of age)
Triceps skinfold, mid-arm circumference, muscle circumference	Monthly (if trained nurse or nutritionist available)

Cost and blood losses are valid concerns. Careful monitoring can avoid potential complications or at least lead to identification and treatment of actual complications, as well as ensure appropriate growth and development.

Examples of bedside monitoring are listed in Table 11-14. In addition to the daily physical examination, other assessments of the child on TPN should focus on changes in mental and behavioral status, edema, and skin turgor.

PSYCHOSOCIAL ISSUES

The ability of a patient to adapt to the lifestyle changes brought on by dependency on some form of nutrition support will depend on the onset of the problem necessitating PN (acute versus chronic condition), the duration and complexity of the hospitalization, and the duration of nutrition support therapy.[111] In the pediatric patient, another variable influencing coping is the child's developmental level and the stability of the family unit. Parents of an infant born with an unexpected congenital anomaly may find this sudden and unanticipated situation overwhelming. For the family faced with a child who requires parenteral nutrition as a result of trauma, the prospect of long-term PN is one of many changes that will forever alter their lifestyle. The adolescent who has suffered from the chronic pain and alteration in bowel function associated with Crohn's disease may find home PN a relief, a return to normalcy, and a way to regain control over his or her life. Keeping the family informed, providing consistent support through a social worker and/or primary nurse, and involving the family and child (as age-appropriate) in the actual care as soon as possible can lessen the feelings of helplessness and empower the child and family to meet some of their own needs. Family involvement is crucial to the success of home PN, and two caregivers should be identified early in the hospitalization.

A multidisciplinary approach to informing, supporting, and teaching the child and family regarding prognosis for recovery and PN technology and skills is

---

Table 11-14 Bedside Monitoring during Pediatric Parenteral Nutrition

Parameter	Initiation of TPN	When Stable on TPN
Blood Dextrostix/Chemstrip	4×/day	Daily
Urine glucose, protein, ketones, specific gravity, and pH	4×/day	3×/day
Vital signs	Hourly × 4, then every 4 hours	3×/day (hourly if unstable)
Intake and output	Hourly	Hourly
Administration system	Hourly	Hourly
Infusion site/dressing	Hourly	Hourly

essential in preparing the child for discharge. The more obvious team members involved in the care of the PN-dependent patient include the nurse, physician, dietitian, and pharmacist. However, a variety of therapists who support the normal development of the child on PN and assist in maintaining the family's integrity are critical to this pediatric population both in and out of the acute care setting.

For the neonate who is limited or unable to take oral feedings, early involvement in occupational and speech therapy as well as physical therapy is helpful in providing oral stimulation, establishing non-nutritive sucking, and providing sensory stimulation. Prolonged, early oral deprivation can lead to increased oral sensitivity and abnormal tongue movements that can adversely influence the development of future speech patterns.[112] Child life specialists can also assist in developing programs to support normal stimulation and infant development patterns. Eating is such a basic, essential function that many parents, particularly the mother, may feel responsible for their infant's problems and may suffer loss of esteem or feelings of inadequacy at being unable to perform the simple care-giving task of feeding. Social workers can work with the other therapists in supporting parent involvement in "feeding" the PN-dependent infant by encouraging holding, cuddling, and the offering of a pacifier during "normal" feeding times. When possible, the infant on TPN should be offered some type of oral feeding, if only in very small amounts. If totally deprived of oral sustenance, the child may react adversely to food when it is finally introduced.

The infant should be supported in normal developmental tasks such as sucking on fingers or toys in order to learn and develop trust in his or her environment. Other types of tactile and visual stimulation can be provided to distract the infant from manipulating or chewing on tubes and equipment. Totally immobilizing the infant with arm boards and arm and leg restraints to protect equipment can adversely affect the developmental process.

Safety and the need to somewhat limit the mobility of the toddler receiving PN are concerns that can be dealt with by the multidisciplinary team. Normal developmental milestones such as walking and toileting need to be supported as much as possible. Creative strategies to allow toddlers some control and independence in their environment can lessen the negative impact of hospitalization on normal development and promote development of autonomy and initiative. Being in as normal and homelike an environment as possible, having clothes, toys, and photographs from home, sibling visits, and a high level of parent involvement can help the young child deal with the fear of painful procedures, the strange hospital environment, separation from loved ones, and feelings that the illness is a punishment for being "bad." Preparation for discharging the toddler patient to the home should focus on developmental as well as technical aspects of care.

The school-age child who is frequently hospitalized and requires PN needs to maintain involvement in school and with friends, to have some conformity in appearance with peers, and to have as much control over himself or herself and his or her surroundings as possible. In-hospital teachers should be a part of this child's multidisciplinary team. The child needs choices when possible, including input into selection of the type and placement of the CVC and assisting with dressing changes if feasible. An established routine that allows the child to "do" for himself or herself is important to avoid feelings of inferiority. Self-care skills should be taught to this age child early on so that the dependent sick role is not fostered. When discharged on home PN, the child should resume as normal a school and play routine as the illness allows.

With adolescents, just as with the school-age child, control and body image and appearance are important. Nighttime cyclical PN; small, portable pumps; and vests holding fluid bags and pumps are all strategies helpful to the adolescent in lessening his or her sense of isolation and "differentness." The loss of health and the loss of control over bodily functions can lead to role alterations and anger or depression and to poor compliance with the therapeutic regimen. Anxiety experienced by the older child who is dependent on home PN can be related to fear of mechanical pump failure or malfunction, tubing kinking, or disconnection and catheter dislodgement. Sleep disturbances can occur due to anxiety as well as to nocturnal infusions and the associated increase in voiding. The adolescent may worry about what friends may think and how they will react to his or her dependence on technology and change in physical appearance. Delayed growth or late sexual maturation related to nutritional deficiencies can further add to the adolescent's stress as he or she tries to master the developmental task of role identification. Financial worries about the costs of PN technology are also a concern to the older child. Again, support of the multidisciplinary team and family is essential to the child's adjustment to long-term PN.

Pediatric Total Parenteral Nutrition in the Home Care Setting

The technology that supported the hospitalized TPN patient soon propelled high-technology parenteral nutrition into the home, only 4 years after Dudrick's 1964 experiments with beagle pups.[113,114] The high-technology home care trend had its beginnings in three areas: financial, technological, and patient choice.[115]

The diagnostic-related grouping (DRG) era of the 1980s accelerated the movement of adult TPN programs from the hospital to the home setting. Also in the 1980s, home care companies (both hospital-based and private agencies) that provided durable medical equipment (DME), pharmaceuticals, and home clinical services became a growing industry and were later characterized by mergers that allowed agencies to survive the fierce competition between home care companies. Although DRGs do not yet apply to the pediatric population, many third-party payers have established prospective payment systems (PPS) that set a predetermined amount of money per patient, require prior authorization for many services, and set restrictions for hospital length of stay. The PPSs provided a financial incentive for hospitals to discharge pediatric patients "quicker and sicker." Currently, Champus (third-party payer for military and their dependents) and Medicaid (which varies from state to state) have PPS plans that affect the pediatric population in both the hospital and home settings.

The second reason for the trend toward technically complex home care is the availability of small but sophisticated home infusion pumps, the variety of vascular access devices, and easily-stored plastic solution containers. The small, programmable pumps provide freedom and mobility, which can allow the child to return to school with pump, bag, and tubing if necessary. These pumps are user-friendly, compact, and lightweight and can be preset to taper the infusion rate at the start and end of infusion therapy. This feature can allow the child an uninterrupted night's sleep, and multirate settings are maintained even when the pump is not in use. A temporary silence feature on the pump alarm and a long-life battery are other desirable features of the new home pumps. All of these technologic advances have greatly contributed to the convenience and safety of pediatric home TPN.

The last factor that has influenced the movement of pediatric TPN from hospital to home is patient choice. It is widely acknowledged that the home environment is much more supportive of the child's optimal growth and development. In spite of all the obstacles and advance preparation necessary for discharge, children and parents prefer the more normal nurturing home environment rather than the not always pleasant, not always safe hospital environment.

In order to safely support the high-tech child in the home, discharge planning and teaching must begin early in hospitalization, sometimes before the child is considered medically stable. Once metabolically and nutritionally stable, the child is quickly moved toward discharge. The child, if old enough, should be included in teaching and preparation as well as at least one other adult caregiver. For the infant or child too young to fully participate in self-care, two adult caregivers should be identified. The family should be offered a choice of home care providers whenever possible in order to become empowered as the "expert" caregiver outside the acute care setting. This empowerment process is especially critical to the family whose child may have a lifelong dependency on TPN.

The home care agency, whether hospital or community based, should provide the quality and variety of pediatric assessment and clinical services required by the child in the hospital. The home care agency should have quality assurance programs that define and update standards of home care as well as evaluate program outcomes. The Joint Commission on Accreditation of Healthcare Organizations has developed home care standards that address all aspects of patient care and focus on the patient's right to informed decision-making related to home care and the need to ensure continuity of care through care coordination.[116]

Most clinical services are administered by a registered nurse in the home, but home-based or center-based pharmaceutical, dietetic, occupational, physical, and speech therapy services may also be needed by the child on home TPN. Although all home therapies and services must be ordered by a physician, the hospital nutrition support nurse or nurse discharge planner can recommend reputable agencies with pediatric services and specialists. Certain specialty organizations such as the Intravenous Nursing Society (INS), the Oncology Nursing Society (ONS), and the American Society for Parenteral and Enteral Nutrition (ASPEN) have developed standards of patient care for pediatric home TPN and intravenous therapy that can be valuable resources to families and providers in vendor selection. The home health TPN team should be skilled in providing PN to the child in order to promptly recognize and manage the therapy responses and adverse reactions unique to the pediatric population. Team members must be knowledgeable in the developmental and financial impact of long-term TPN on the child and family as well as proficient in managing the technology of home TPN.

Financial Concerns

Often, the third-party payer has a preferred provider relationship with a home care vendor that dictates patient choice. The hospital discharge planner and the family must be aware of such relationships. If the preferred provider does not provide pediatric services, a change in provider can sometimes be negotiated with the payer. Also, the patient's policy may not include home care coverage, and the discharge planner may need to document the higher cost of hospital TPN versus home TPN and request an exception to benefits for the child with long-term TPN needs. Medicaid, which is state administered has requirements that vary from state to state, in particular, for home nurse visits, DME, and nutritional solutions for the home TPN patient. Some states have a special waiver that financially assists technology-dependent children who meet designated criteria. All financial avenues must be explored prior to discharge to ensure safe support of the child on home TPN. Some hospitals, home care agencies, and third-party payers have moved to the case management system that allows a case manager, usually a registered nurse, to identify the most cost-effective utilization of the patient's health care resources as he or she moves from one setting to another.

The home TPN nurse should be included early in the discharge planning process by attending patient care conferences, providing family and patient teaching regarding home care, and making home visits prior to the child's discharge. This nurse can assist the child and family in maintaining vascular access, drawing blood for metabolic monitoring, and selecting the most appropriate infusion devices and infusion schedule for the home setting. The home nurse becomes the family's most consistent link in the care coordination that supports the least disruption in their lifestyle and still maintains the child's quality of life.

Even after clearing the hurdle of learning all the complexities of their child's home care, the family still has the ever-present financial concern of paying for prolonged home TPN.[117] Although home TPN is more cost-effective than TPN in the acute care setting, home costs can range from $6000 to $8000 a month. Private insurance may cover only part of the costs, leaving the family responsible for the remainder. If insurance coverage is provided through a parent's employer, frequent absences from work to care for a TPN-dependent child can jeopardize not only the parent's employment but also payment for insurance premiums. As the child becomes older and reaches maturity, the parent's policy will no longer cover him or her, and this inability to obtain insurance coverage for a lifelong TPN-dependent family member is an ongoing concern. As home care continues to expand, cost-containment measures that will likely affect the child on home TPN will continue to include careful review of claims prior to payment authorization, strict eligibility requirements, and setting of cost ceilings on reimbursement rates.[115]

Lack of respite care is another major concern for the family with a child on home TPN. Very few insurance policies address reimbursement for respite care, and nationally there are very few facilities able to provide respite care for technology dependent children. Therefore, most respite care must be provided by private duty nurses at very expensive rates ($20 to $30 per hour). Theoretically, giving the caregiver a periodic break or respite in caring for a technology dependent child could reduce costs to third-party payers in the long run if it would avoid inappropriate hospital readmission due to caregiver exhaustion. However, the area of respite care needs to be more thoroughly researched before insurance companies revise reimbursement policies to support respite care as a necessity rather than a luxury for the home bound TPN-dependent child.

Other areas of concern for the home TPN patient are symptom management, such as the diarrhea that results from short bowel syndrome, and loss of control over one's life. The OLEY Foundation (214 Hun Memorial, Albany, New York 12208) is a national support group established to support both enteral and parenteral nutrition patients through its *Lifeline* newsletter and various regional activities.

REFERENCES

1. Sutphen JL. Nutritional support of the pediatric patient. *Clin Consult Nutr Supp.* 1981;1:1.

2. Filler RM. Parenteral support of the surgically ill child. In: Suskind RM, ed. *Textbook of Pediatric Nutrition.* New York, NY: Raven Press; 1981:341.

3. Rickard KA, Grosfeld JL, Kirksey A, et al. Reversal of protein-energy malnutrition in children during treatment of advanced neoplastic disease. *Ann Surg* 190:771, 1979.

4. Filler RM, Dietz W, Suskind RM, et al. Parenteral feeding in management of children with cancer. *Cancer.* 1979; 43 (suppl):2117, 1979.

5. Copeland EM, MacFadgen BV, Dudrick SJ. Effect of intravenous hyperalimentation on established delayed hypersensitivity in the cancer patient. *Ann Surg.* 1976;184:60.

6. Copeland EM, Daly JM, Ota DM, et al. Nutrition, cancer, and intravenous hyperalimentation. *Cancer.* 1979;43:2108.

7. Perl M. TPN and the anorexia nervosa patient. *Nutr Supp Serv.* 1981;1:13.

8. Pertschuk MJ, Forster J, Buzby G, et al. The treatment of anorexia nervosa with total parenteral nutrition. *Biol Psychiatry.* 1981;16:539.

9. Ziegler M, Jacobowski O, Hoelzer D, et al. Route of pediatric parenteral nutrition: proposed criteria revision. *J Pediatr Surg.* 1980;15:472.

10. Centers for Disease Control. *Methods of Prevention and Control of Nosocomial Infections. Guidelines for the Prevention and Control of Nosocomial Infections.* Atlanta, GA: Center for Disease Control; 1981.

11. Maki DG, Goldman DA, Rhame FS. Infection control in intravenous therapy. *Ann Intern Med.* 1973;79:867.

12. Ryan JA, Abel RM, Abbott WM, et al. Catheter complications in total parenteral nutrition. A prospective study of 200 consecutive patients. *N Engl J Med.* 1974;290:757.

13. Chathas MK. Percutaneous central venous catheters in neonates. *J Obstet Gynecol Neonatal Nurs.* 1986;15:324.

14. Dolcourt JL, Bose CL. Percutaneous insertion of Silastic central venous catheters. *Pediatrics.* 1982;70:484.

15. Goodwin ML. The Seldinger method of PICC insertion. *J Intravenous Nurs.* 1989;12:238.

16. Brown JM. Peripherally inserted central catheters—use in home care. *J Intravenous Nurs.* 1989;12:144.

17. Pemberton LB, Lyman B, Lander V, Covinsky J, et al. Sepsis from triple versus single lumen catheters during total parenteral nutrition in surgical or chronically ill patients. *Arch Surg.* 1986;121:591.

18. Yeung C, May J, Hughes R. Infection rate for single lumen versus triple lumen subclavian catheters. *Inf Control Hosp Epidemiol.* 1988;9:154.

19. Maki DG, Cobb L, Garman JK, Shapiro JM, Ringer M, Helgerson RB. An attachable silver-impregnated cuff for prevention of infection with central venous catheters: a prospective randomized multicenter trial. *Am J Med.* 1988;85:307.

20. Lawson M, Kavanough T, et al. Comparison of transparent dressing to paper tape dressing over central venous catheter sites. NITA 1986;9:40.

21. Waldron T, ed. Wisconsin studies provide clues for preventing bacteria. *Hosp Inf Control.* 1986;13:149.

22. Hughes CB. A totally implantable central venous system for chemotherapy administration. NITA 1985;8:523.

23. Baumgartner TG. Filters and their implication in health care. *Nutr Supp Serv.* 1985;5:7.

24. Holmes CJ, Dundin RB, Ausman RK, et al. Potential hazards associated with microbial contamination of in-line filters during intravenous therapy. *J Clin Microbiol.* 1980;12:725.

25. Turco SJ. Drug adsorption to membrane filters. *Am J Intravenous Ther Clin Nutr.* 1982;9:6.

26. Wagner DR, Carter A, Long JM. Microbial growth in TPN admixtures. *J Parenter Enter Nutr.* 1987;11:145.

27. Gilbert M, Gallagher SC, Eads M, et al. Microbial growth patterns in a total parenteral nutrition formulation containing lipid emulsion. *J Parenter Enter Nutr.* 1986;10:494.

28. Messing B, Beliah M, Girard-Pipau F, et al. Technical hazards of using nutritive mixtures in bags for cyclical intravenous nutrition. *Gut.* 1982;23:297.

29. Freund HR, Rimon B, Muggia-Sellam M, et al. The "all-in-one" system for TPN causes increased rates of catheter blockade. *J Parenter Enter Nutr.* 1986;10:543.

30. Allwood MC. Release of DEHP plasticizer into fat emulsion from IV administration sets. *Pharma J.* 1985;235:600.

31. Maini B, Blackburn GL, Bestrian BR, et al. Cyclic hyperalimentation: an optimal technique for preserving visceral protein. *J Surg Res.* 1976;20:515.

32. Faubion WC, Baker WL, Iott BA, et al. Cyclic TPN for hospitalized pediatric patients. *Nutr Supp Serv.* 1981;1:24.

33. Rao M, Koenig E, Li S, et al. Estimation of insensible water loss in low birth weight infants by direct calorimetric measurement of metabolic heat release. *Pediatr Res.* 1989;25:295A.

34. Aperia A, Broberger O, Elinder G, Herin P, Zetterstrom R. Postnatal development of renal function in pre-term and full-term infants. *Acta Paediatr Scand.* 1981;70:183.

35. Eunice J, Klavdianou M, Vidyasagar D. Electrolyte problems in neonatal surgical patients. *Clin Perinatol.* 1989;16:219.

36. Groh-Wargo S, Ciaccia A, Moore J. Neonatal metabolic acidosis: effect of chloride from normal saline flushes. *J Parenter Enter Nutr.* 1988;12:159.

37. Kerner JA Jr, ed. *Manual of Pediatric Parenteral Nutrition.* New York, NY: John Wiley and Sons; 1983.

38. Kerner JA Jr, Sunshine P. Parenteral alimentation. *Semin Perinatol.* 1979;3:417.

39. Oh W, Karechi H. Phototherapy and insensible water loss in the newborn infant. *Am J Dis Child.* 1972;124:230.

40. Yeh TF, Voora S, Lillien J. Oxygen consumption and insensible water loss in premature infants in single versus double walled incubators. *J Pediatr.* 1980;97:967.

41. Gruskin AB. Fluid therapy in children. *Urol Clin North Am.* 1976;3:277.

42. Stevenson JG. Fluid administration in the association of patent ductus arteriosus complicating respiratory distress syndrome. *J Pediatr.* 1977;90:257.

43. Brown ER, Stark A, Sosenko I, et al. Bronchopulmonary dysplasia: possible relationship to pulmonary edema. *J Pediatr.* 1978;92:982.

44. Goldman HI. Feeding and necrotizing enterocolitis. *Am J Dis Child.* 1980;134:553.

45. Goldberg RN, Chund D, Goldman SL, et al. The association of rapid volume expansion and intraventricular hemorrhage in the preterm infant. *J Pediatr.* 1980;96:1060.

46. Zlotkin SH, Bryan MH, Anderson GH. Intravenous nitrogen and energy intakes required to duplicate in utero nitrogen accretion in prematurely born human infants. *J Pediatr.* 1981;99:115.

47. Khaldi N, Coran AG, Wesley JR. Guidelines for parenteral nutrition in children. *Nutr Supp Serv.* 1984;4:27.

48. Cochran EB, Phelps SJ, Helms RA. Parenteral nutrition in pediatric patients. *Clin Pharm.* 1988;7:351.

49. Sajbel TA, Dutro MP, Radway PR. Use of separate insulin infusions with total parenteral nutrition. *J Parenter Enter Nutr.* 1987;11:97.

50. Groh-Wargo S. Prematurity/low birth weight. In: Lang C, ed. *Nutritional Support in Critical Care.* Gaithersburg, Md: Aspen Publishers; 1987:287–313.

51. Rubecz I, Mestyan J, Varga P, Klujber L. Energy metabolism, substrate utilization, and nitrogen balance in parenterally fed postoperative neonates and infants. *J Pediatr.* 1981;98:42.

52. Duffy B, Gunn T, Collinge J, et al. The effect of varying protein quality and energy intake on the nitrogen metabolism of parenterally fed very low birth weight (<1600 G) infants. *Pediatr Res.* 1981;15:1040.

53. Anderson TL, Muttart CR, Bilber MA, et al. A controlled trial of glucose versus glucose and amino acids in premature infants. *J Pediatr.* 1979;94:947.

54. Zlotkin SH, Stallings VA, Pencharz PB. Total parenteral nutrition in children. *Pediatr Clin North Am.* 1985;32:381.

55. Heird WC. Essentiality of cyst(e)ine for neonates. Clinical and biochemical effects of parenteral cysteine supplementation. In: Kinney JM, Borum PR, eds. *Perspectives in Clinical Nutrition.* Munich, Germany: Urban Schwarzenberg; 1989:275–282.

56. Gaull GE, Sturman JA, Raiha NCR, Sturman JA. Development of mammalian sulfur metabolism. Absence of cystathionase in human fetal tissues. *Pediatr Res.* 1972;6:538.

57. Zlotkin SH, Bryan H, Anderson H. Cysteine supplementation to cysteine-free intravenous feeding regimens in newborn infants. *Am J Clin Nutr.* 1981;34:914.

58. Heird WC, Hay W, Helms RA, Storm MC, Kashyap S, Dell RB. Pediatric parenteral amino acid mixture in low birth weight infants. *Pediatrics.* 1988;81:41.

59. Heird WC, Dell RB, Helms RA, et al. Amino acid mixture designed to maintain normal plasma amino acid patterns in infants and children requiring parenteral nutrition. *Pediatrics.* 1987;80:401.

60. Coran AG, Drongowski RA. Studies on the toxicity and efficacy of new amino acid solution in pediatric parenteral nutrition. *J Parenter Enter Nutr.* 1987;11:368.

61. Helms RA, Christensen ML, Mauer EC, Storm MC. Comparison of a pediatric versus standard amino acid formulation in preterm neonates requiring parenteral nutrition. *J Pediatr.* 1987;110:466.

62. Chessex P, Zebiche H, Pineault M, Lepage D, Dallaire L. Effect of amino acid composition of parenteral solutions on nitrogen retention and metabolic response in very-low-birth weight infants. *J Pediatr.* 1985;106:111.

63. Adamkin DH, McLead R, Marchildon M, et al. Comparison of two neonatal amino acid formulations in preterm infants—multicenter study. *Pediatr Res.* 1989;25:283A.

64. Abitbol CL, Holliday MA. Total parenteral nutrition in anuric children. *Clin Nephrol.* 1976;5:153.

65. Holliday MA, Wassner S, Ramirez J. Intravenous nutrition in uremic children with protein-energy malnutrition. *Am J Clin Nutr.* 1978;31:1854.

66. Motil KJ, Harmon WE, Grupe WE. Complications of essential amino acid hyperalimentation in children with acute renal failure. *J Parenter Enter Nutr.* 1980;4:32.

67. Takala J. Total parenteral nutrition in experimental uremia: studies of acute and chronic renal failure in the growing rat. *J Parenter Enter Nutr.* 1984;8:427.

68. Helms RA, Phelps SJ, Mauer EC, Christensen ML, Storm MC. Parenteral protein use in liver disease. *Pediatr Res.* 1989;25:115A.

69. Maldonato J, Gil A, Faus MJ, Periago JL, Loscertales M, Molina JA. Differences in the serum amino acid pattern of injured and infected children promoted by two parenteral nutrition solutions. *J Parenter Enter Nutr.* 1989;13:41.

70. Holman RT, Johnson SB, Hatch TF. A case of human linolenic acid deficiency involving neurologic abnormalities. *Am J Clin Nutr.* 1982;35:617.

71. American Academy of Pediatrics, Committee on Nutrition. Commentary on parenteral nutrition. *Pediatrics.* 1983;71:547.

72. Levy JS, Winters RW, Heird WC. Total parenteral nutrition in pediatric patients. *Pediatr Rev.* 1980;2:99.

73. American Academy of Pediatrics, Committee on Nutrition. Prudent life-style for children: dietary fat and cholesterol. *Pediatrics.* 1986;78:51.

74. Ohio Neonatal Nutritionists. *Nutritional Care for High Risk Newborns.* Philadelphia, Pa: George F. Stickley; 1985.

75. Helms RA, Mauer EC, Hay WW Jr, et al. Effect of intravenous L-carnitine on growth parameters and fat metabolism during parenteral nutrition in neonates. *J Parenter Enter Nutr.* 1990;14:448.

76. Schmidt-Sommerfeld E, Penn D, Wolf H. Carnitine deficiency in premature infants receiving total parenteral nutrition: effect of L-carnitine supplementation. *J Pediatr.* 1983;102:93.

77. Winter SC, Szabo-Aczel S, Curry CJR, et al. Plasma carnitine deficiency: clinical observations in 51 pediatric patients. *Am J Dis Child.* 1987;141:660.

78. Coran AG, Drongowshi RA, Baker PJ. The metabolic effects of oral L-carnitine administration in infants receiving total parenteral nutrition with fat. *J Pediatr Surg.* 1985;20:758.

79. American Academy of Pediatric Committee on Nutrition. Use of intravenous fat emulsions in pediatric patients. *Pediatrics.* 1981;68:738.

80. American Medical Association, Nutrition Advisory Group. Multivitamin preparations for parenteral use. *J Parenter Enter Nutr.* 1979;3:258.

81. Moore MC, Greene HL, Phillips B, et al. Evaluation of a pediatric multiple vitamin preparation for total parenteral nutrition in infants and children. I. Blood levels of water-soluble vitamins. *Pediatrics.* 1986;77:530.

82. Greene HL, Moore MEC, Phillips B, et al. Evaluation of a pediatric multivitamin preparation for total parenteral nutrition. II. Blood levels of vitamins A, D, and E. *Pediatrics.* 1986;77:539.

83. Marinier E, Gorski AM, DeCourcy GP, et al. Blood levels of water-soluble vitamins in pediatric patients on total parenteral nutrition using a multiple vitamin preparation. *J Parenter Enter Nutr.* 1989;13:176.

84. Committee on Dietary Allowances, Food and Nutrition Board. *Recommended Dietary Allowances.* 10th ed. Washington, DC: National Academy of Sciences; 1989.

85. Green CG, Doershuk CF, Stern RC. Symptomatic hypomagnesemia in cystic fibrosis. *J Pediatr.* 1985;107:425.

86. James BE, Hendry PG, MacMahon RA. Total parenteral nutrition of premature infants. 1. Requirement for macronutrient elements. *Aust Paediatr J.* 1979;15:62.

87. Greer FR, Tsang RC. Calcium and vitamin D metabolism in term and low-birth-weight infants. *Perinatol Neonatol.* 1986;Jan/Feb:14.

88. Koo WWK, Tsang RC, Steichen JJ, et al. Parenteral nutrition for infants: effect of high versus low calcium and phosphorus content. *J Pediatr Gastroenterol Nutr.* 1987;6:96.

89. Ricour C, Millot M, Balsan S. Phosphorus depletion in children on long-term total parenteral nutrition. *Acta Paediatr Scand.* 1975;64:385.

90. Koo WWK, Kaplan LA, Horn J, Tsang RC, Steichen JJ. Aluminum in parenteral nutrition solution—sources and possible alternatives. *J Parenter Enter Nutr.* 1986;10:591.

91. Changaris DG, Purohit DM, Balentine JD, et al. Brain calcification in severely stressed neonates receiving parenteral calcium. *J Pediatr.* 1984;104:941.

92. Goldsmith MA, Bhatia SS, Kanto AP, et al. Gluconate calcium therapy and neonatal hypercalciuria. *Am J Dis Child.* 1981;135:538.

93. Hufnagle KF, Khan SN, Penn D, et al. Renal calcifications: a complication of long-term furosemide therapy in preterm infants. *Pediatrics.* 1982; 70:360.

94. Wood RJ, Bengoa JM, Sitrin MD, Rosenberg IH. Calciuretic effect of cyclic versus continuous total parenteral nutrition. *Am J Clin Nutr.* 1985;41:614.

95. Vileisis RA. Effect of phosphorus intake in total parenteral nutrition infusates in premature neonates. *J Pediatr.* 1987;110:586.

96. Aladjem M, Lotan D, Biochis H, et al. Changes in the electrolyte content of serum and urine during total parenteral nutrition. *J Pediatr.* 1980;97:437.

97. Kimura S, Nose O, Seino Y, et al. Effects of alternate and simultaneous administrations of calcium and phosphorus on calcium metabolism in children receiving total parenteral nutrition. *J Parenter Enter Nutr.* 1986;10:513.

98. Eggert LD, Rusho WJ, MacKay MW, Chan GM. Calcium and phosphorus compatibility in parenteral nutrition solutions for neonates. *Am J Hosp Pharm.* 1982;39:49.

99. Poole RL, Rupp CA, Kerner JA. Calcium and phosphorus in neonatal parenteral nutrition solutions. *J Parenter Enter Nutr.* 1983;7:358.

100. Fitzgerald KA, MacKay MW. Calcium and phosphate solubility in neonatal parenteral nutrient solutions containing Trophamine. *Am J Hosp Pharm.* 1986;43:88.

101. Fitzgerald KA, MacKay MW. Calcium and phosphate solubility in neonatal parenteral nutrient solutions containing Aminosyn PF. *Am J Hosp Pharm.* 1987;44:1396.

102. Shils ME, Burke AW, Greene HL, et al. Guidelines for essential trace element preparations for parenteral use: a statement by an expert panel. *JAMA.* 1979;241:2051.

103. Pyati SP, Ramamurthy RS, Krauss MT, Pildes RS. Absorption of iodine in the neonate following topical use of povidone iodine. *J Pediatr.* 1977;91:825.

104. Shaw JCL. Trace elements in the fetus and young infant II. Copper, manganese, selenium and chromium. *Am J Dis Child.* 1980;134:74.

105. Triplett WC. Clinical aspects of zinc, copper, manganese, chromium and selenium metabolism. *Nutr Int.* 1985;1:60.

106. American Academy of Pediatrics, Committee on Nutrition. Zinc. *Pediatrics.* 1978;62:408.

107. Reed MD, Bertino JS, Halpin TC. Use of intravenous iron dextran injection in children receiving total parenteral nutrition. *Am J Dis Child.* 1981;135:829.

108. Seashore JH. Metabolic complications of parenteral nutrition in infants and children. *Surg Clin North Am.* 1980;60:1239.

109. Wan KK, Tsallas G. Dilute iron dextran formulation for addition to parenteral nutrient solutions. *Am J Hosp Pharm.* 1980;37:206.

110. Halpin T, Reed M, Bertino J. Use of intravenous iron dextran in children receiving TPN for nutritional support of inflammatory bowel disease. *J Parenter Enter Nutr.* 1980;4:600.

111. Bastian C, Driscoll R. Enteral tube feeding at home. In: Rombeau JL, Caldwell MD, eds. *Enteral and Tube Feeding.* Philadelphia, Pa: WB Saunders; 1984:494–512.

112. Illingworth RS, Lister J. The critical or sensitive period, with special reference to certain feeding problems in infants and children. *Pediatrics.* 1964;65:849.

113. Dudrick SJ, Wilmore DW, Vares JM, Rhodes JD. Tissue maintenance synthesis, and growth with parenteral nutrition. *Surgery.* 1986;64:134.

114. Dudrick SJ, Englert DM, MacFadyen BV, et al. A vest for ambulatory patients receiving hyperalimentation. *Surg Gynecol Obstet.* 1974;139:24.

115. Handy CM. Home care of patients with technically complex nursing needs. *Nurs Clin North Am.* 1988;23:315.

116. Griffin RE, Crocker KS, Wilcox GS, et al. Developments in home nutritional support. *Nutr Supp Serv.* 1988;8:19.

117. Heaphey L. Home nutritional support: current consumer concerns. *Nutr Supp Serv.* 1988;8:24.

118. Nelson WE, Behrman RE, Vaughan VC, eds. *Nelson's Textbook of Pediatrics.* 12th ed. Philadelphia, Pa: WB Saunders; 1983:231.

119. Tilden SJ, Watkins S, Tong TK, Jecvanandam M. Measured energy expenditure in pediatric intensive care patients. *Am J Dis Child.* 1989;143:490.

120. Lowery EH. *Growth and Development of Children.* 6th ed. Chicago: Year Book Medical Publishers; 1973.

121. Ryan JA Jr. Complication of total parenteral nutrition. In: Fischer JE, ed. *Total Parenteral Nutrition.* Boston, Mass: Little, Brown & Co; 1976.

122. Wu PYK, Edwards N, Storm M. Plasma amino acid pattern in normal term breast-fed infants. *J Pediatr.* 1986;109:347.

123. Tsang RC. *Vitamin and Mineral Requirements in Preterm Infants.* New York, NY: Marcel Dekker, Inc; 1985:vii.

124. Committee on Dietary Allowances, Food and Nutrition Board. *Recommended Dietary Allowances.* 10th ed. Washington, DC: National Academy of Sciences; 1989.

Chapter 12

Nutrition Support of Inborn Errors of Metabolism

Phyllis B. Acosta

Nutrition support of infants and children with inborn errors of metabolism requires in-depth knowledge of metabolic processes, the science and application of nutrition, growth and development, and food science. When providing nutrition support for patients with inborn errors, the specific nutrient needs of each patient, based on individual genetic and biochemical constitution, *must* be considered. Nutrient requirements established for normal populations[1,2] may not apply to individuals with inborn errors of metabolism.[3,4] Some chemical compounds, normally not considered essential because they can be synthesized de novo, cannot be synthesized in patients with a metabolic defect. Consequently, dependent on the inborn error, the subsequent organ damage that accrues, and the rate of loss of specific chemicals from the body, several compounds may become conditionally essential. Among these are the amino acids arginine,[5] carnitine,[6] cystine,[7] and tyrosine[8] and the "vitamins" coenzyme Q_{10},[9] lipoic acid,[9] and tetrahydrobiopterin.[10] Failure to adapt nutrient intake to the individual needs of each patient can result in mental retardation, metabolic crises, neurologic crises, growth failure, and, with some inborn errors, death.[4] Quality care is best achieved by an experienced team of specialists in a genetic/metabolic center.

This chapter addresses principles and practical considerations in nutrition support of inborn errors of metabolism; nutrition support of selected inborn errors of amino acid, nitrogen, carbohydrate, lipid, and mineral metabolism; selected areas needing further research; and roles and functions of the dietitian in nutrition support of inborn errors of metabolism. For a detailed guide to nutrition support, see *Nutrition Support Protocols*.[11]

PRINCIPLES AND PRACTICAL CONSIDERATIONS IN NUTRITION SUPPORT

Principles of Nutrition Support[3]

A number of approaches to nutrition support of inborn errors of metabolism are discussed here. The appropriate approach is dependent on the biochemistry and pathophysiology of disease expression. Several therapeutic approaches may be used simultaneously:

1. Correcting the primary imbalance in metabolic relationships: This correction involves reduction, through dietary restriction, of accumulated substrate(s) that are toxic. Examples are phenylketonuria, maple syrup urine disease, and galactosemia, where phenylalanine; leucine, isoleucine, and valine; and galactose are limited, respectively.

2. Providing alternate metabolic pathways to decrease accumulated toxic precursors in blocked reaction sequences: For example, innocuous isovalerylglycine is formed from accumulating isovaleric acid if supplemental glycine is provided to drive glycine-N-transacylase. Isovalerylglycine is excreted in the urine.

3. Supplying products of blocked primary pathways: Some examples are arginine in most disorders of the urea cycle,[12] cystine in homocystinuria,[7] tyrosine in PKU,[8] tetrahydrobiopterin in biopterin synthesis defects,[10] and ether lipids in patients with some peroxisomal disorders.[13]

4. Supplementing conditionally essential nutrients: Examples are carnitine, cystine, and tyrosine in secondary liver disease[14] or with excess excretion of carnitine in organic acidemias.[6]

5. Stabilizing altered enzyme proteins: The rate of biologic synthesis and degradation of holoenzymes is dependent on their structural conformation. In some holoenzymes, saturation by coenzyme increases their biologic half-life and, thus, overall enzyme activity at the new equilibrium. This therapeutic mechanism is illustrated in homocystinuria and maple syrup urine disease. Pharmacologic intake of pyridoxine in homocystinuria and of thiamine in maple syrup urine disease increases intracellular pyridoxal phosphate and thiamine pyrophosphate, respectively, and increases the specific activity of cystathionine β-synthase and branched-chain α-ketoacid dehydrogenase complex, respectively.[15,16]

6. Replacing deficient cofactors: Many vitamin-dependent disorders are due to blocks in coenzyme production and are "cured" by pharmacologic intake of a specific vitamin precursor. This mechanism presumably involves overcoming a partially impaired enzyme reaction by mass action. Impaired re-

actions required to produce methylcobalamin and/or adenosylcobalamin result in homocystinuria and/or methylmalonic aciduria. Daily intakes of appropriate forms of milligram quantities of vitamin B_{12} may cure the disease.[17]

7. Inducing enzyme production: If the structural gene or enzyme is intact but suppressor, enhancer, or promoter elements are not functional, abnormal amounts of enzyme may be produced. The structural gene may be "turned on" or "turned off" to enable normal enzymatic production to occur. In the acute porphyria of type I tyrosinemia, excessive Δ-aminolevulinic acid (ALA) production may be reduced by suppressing transcription of the Δ-ALA synthase gene with excess glucose.[18]

8. Supplementing nutrients that are inadequately absorbed or not released from their apoenzyme: Examples are zinc in acrodermatitis enteropathica[19] and biotin in biotinidase deficiency.[20]

Practical Considerations in Nutrition Support

Nutrients

Diet restrictions required to correct imbalances in metabolic relationships usually require the use of chemically defined or elemental medical foods. These chemically defined products are normally supplemented with small amounts of whole natural protein that supply the restricted amino acid(s). Natural foods seldom supply more than 25%[21] and often much less of the protein requirements of patients with disorders of amino acid or nitrogen metabolism. Other nitrogen-free natural foods that provide energy are limited in their range of nutrients. Consequently, care must be taken to provide nutrients often considered to be food contaminants because their essentiality has been demonstrated through long-term use of total parenteral nutrition.[22] Thus in addition to nutrients for which Recommended Dietary Allowances (RDAs)[1] are established, other nutrients must be supplied in adequate amounts. These include the trace minerals chromium, copper, manganese, and molybdenum and the vitamins biotin, pantothenic acid, choline, and inositol. Other possible conditionally essential nutrients for patients with phenylketonuria have been described.[23]

Osmolality

Chemically defined diets consist of small molecules that may provide an osmolality greater than the physiologic tolerance of the patient. Abdominal cramping, diarrhea, distention, nausea, and vomiting have resulted from use of hyperosmolar feeds. Aside from gastrointestinal distress, more serious consequences can occur in infants, such as hypertonic dehydration, hypovolemia, hypernatremia, and death. Osmolalities of selected chemically defined products intended for use in treating inherited diseases of amino acid metabolism have been published.[24] The neonate *should not* be fed an elemental formula that contains greater than 24 kcal/oz or an osmolality greater than 450 mOsm/kg water.[11]

Maillard Reaction

Medical foods for inborn errors of amino acid or nitrogen metabolism are formulated from L-amino acids or hydrolysates and free sugars. The Maillard reaction is a name given to a complex group of chemical reactions in foods in which reacting amino acids, peptides, and protein condense with sugars, forming bonds for which no digestive enzymes are available. The Maillard reaction is accelerated by heat and is characterized in its initial stage by a light brown color, followed by buff yellow and dark brown in the intermediate and final stages. Caramel-like color and roasted aromas develop. Those who prepare medical foods need to be able to recognize the Maillard reaction because it causes loss of some sugars and amino acids. For this reason, medical foods should not be heated beyond 130°F.

Introduction of Natural Foods

Natural foods should be introduced into the diet of the infant at about 4 months of age if the infant shows developmental readiness by a decrease in tongue thrust. Natural foods are important in the diet as sources of unidentified nutrients, to provide fiber, to enhance the child's acceptance of a variety of tastes and textures, and, when solid foods are eaten, to develop jaw muscles important for speech.

Changes in Nutrition Support Prescription

As soon as nutrition support is well established in an infant or child, the prescription should be fine-tuned routinely and frequently. *Small, frequent changes in prescription work better than large, infrequent changes.* Small, frequent changes prevent "bouncing" of plasma amino acids, glucose, organic acids, or ammonia concentrations and allow the intake to grow with the child, thus precluding the child's "growing out of the prescription."[11]

Monitoring

Successful management of inborn errors of metabolism requires frequent monitoring. Frequent monitoring gives the physician and dietitian data that verify the adequacy of the nutrition support prescription. These data are also useful in motivating patient/parent compliance with the prescription. Patients with insulin-dependent diabetes often monitor blood glucose three times daily, so frequent monitoring of plasma amino acids or other indicated parameters should pose no major problem.

Some centers may wish to draw blood when the patient is fasting to monitor plasma amino acids. Prolonged fasting (>8 hours) may cause spurious elevations of plasma amino acids that could lead to unwarranted diet changes,[25] and blood drawn 15 minutes to 1 hour after a meal may also yield spuriously high values.[26]

INBORN ERRORS OF AMINO ACID METABOLISM

The problem of ensuring adequate nutrition for infants and children with inborn errors of metabolism may be decreased by the use of a protocol—a plan for treatment.[11] Each patient requires individualized medical and nutrition care. Information in Appendix 12-A describes various inborn errors, nutrients to modify, vitamin responsiveness, and medical foods available. Data in Appendix 12-B outlines recommended nutrient intakes for *beginning* therapy,[11] while Appendix 12-C provides information on nutrition support during acute illness, medications and nutrient interactions, and nutrition assessment parameters.

When specific amino acids require restriction, total deletion for 1 to 2 days *only* is the best approach to initiating therapy. Longer term deletion or over-restriction may precipitate deficiency of the amino acid(s).[11] The most limiting nutrient determines growth rate, and over-restriction of an amino acid, nitrogen, or energy will result in further intolerance of the toxic nutrient. Results of amino acid and nitrogen deficiencies are described in Table 12-1. Data outside the parentheses in Appendix 12-B describe amounts of amino acids with which to begin nutrition support. Data within the parentheses indicate the possible range of amino acid requirements, depending on the extent of the enzyme deficit. Only frequent monitoring of plasma amino acids, nutrient intake, and growth can verify the adequacy of intake.[11]

Protein requirements of infants and children with inborn errors of amino acid metabolism are normal if liver or renal function is not compromised. However, the form in which the protein is administered must be altered in order to restrict specific amino acids. Consequently, medical foods formulated from L-amino acids, specially treated casein hydrolysate, or soy protein isolate[27,28] must be used with very small amounts of natural protein to provide amino acid and nitrogen requirements.[21] Because utilization of L-amino acid mixes may differ somewhat from use of amino acids derived from whole protein during digestion, recommended protein intakes of infants and children with inborn errors of amino acid metabolism are greater than National Academy of Sciences/National Research Council (NAS/NRC) RDAs.[1]

Energy intakes of infants and children with inborn errors of metabolism must be adequate to support normal rates of growth. Provision of apparently adequate amino acids and nitrogen without sufficient energy will lead to growth failure. Pratt et al.[29]suggested that calorie requirements may be greater than normal when

Table 12-1 Results of Amino Acid and Nitrogen Deficiencies*

Amino Acid	Manifestations of Deficiency
Arginine	Elevated blood ammonia
	Elevated urinary orotic acid
	Generalized skin lesions
	Poor wound healing
	Retarded growth
Carnitine	Fatty myopathy
	Cardiomyopathy
	Depressed liver function
	Neurologic dysfunction
	Defective fatty acid oxidation
	Hypoglycemia
Citrulline	Elevated blood ammonia
Cysteine	Impaired nitrogen balance
	Impaired sulfur balance
	Decreased tissue glutathione
	Hypotaurinemia
Isoleucine	Weight loss or no weight gain
	Redness of buccal mucosa
	Fissures at corners of mouth
	Tremors of extremities
	Decreased plasma cholesterol
	Decreased plasma isoleucine
	Elevations in plasma lysine, phenylalanine, serine, tyrosine, and valine
	Skin desquamation, if prolonged
Leucine	Loss of appetite, apathy, irritability
	Weight loss or poor weight gain
	Decreased plasma leucine
	Increased plasma isoleucine, methionine, serine, threonine, and valine
Lysine	Weight loss or poor weight gain
	Impaired nitrogen balance
Methionine	Decreased plasma methionine
	Increased plasma phenylalanine, proline, serine, threonine, and tyrosine
	Decreased plasma cholesterol
	Poor weight gain
Phenylalanine	Weight loss or poor weight gain
	Impaired nitrogen balance
	Aminoaciduria
	Decreased serum globulins
	Decreased plasma phenylalanine
	Mental retardation
	Anemia

continues

Table 12-1 continued

Amino Acid	Manifestations of Deficiency
Taurine	Impaired visual function
	Impaired biliary secretion
Threonine	Arrested weight gain
	Glossitis and reddening of the buccal mucosa
	Decreased plasma globulin
	Decreased plasma threonine
Tryptophan	Weight loss or no weight gain
	Impaired nitrogen retention
	Decreased plasma cholesterol
Tyrosine	Impaired nitrogen retention
	Catecholamine deficiency
	Thyroxine deficiency
Valine	Poor appetite, drowsiness
	Excess irritability and crying
	Weight loss or decrease in weight gain
	Decreased plasma albumin
Nitrogen	No or decreased weight gain
	Impaired nitrogen retention

*Data from references 5-8, 11, 14, 29, and 95 to 111.

L-amino acids supply the protein equivalent. Maintenance of adequate energy intake is essential for normal growth and development and to prevent catabolism. If NAS/NRC RDAs[1] for energy cannot be achieved through oral feeds, nasogastric, gastrostomy, or parenteral feeds must be employed. Amino acid solutions designed for specific metabolic defects may be obtained from PharmaThera (Memphis, TN) if parenteral alimentation is required.

Major, trace, and ultra-trace mineral and vitamin intakes should meet NAS/NRC RDAs and Safe and Adequate Daily Dietary Intakes[1] for age. If the medical food mixture fails to supply 100% of requirements for the infant and at least 80% of the requirement for children, appropriate supplements should be given.

The Infant Formula Act (IFA)[30] specifies minimum and maximum concentrations of selected nutrients per 100 kcal of infant formula in the form prepared for consumption (Table 12-2). However, IFA does not address amounts of chromium, molybdenum, and selenium that should be present per 100 kcal, and IFA specifications often differ from those of the NAS/NRC RDAs.[1] Consequently, an infant formula may meet IFA requirements but fail to supply some nutrients in amounts specified by NAS/NRC RDAs[1] (Table 12-2). Data in Appendix 12-D describe formulations and major nutrient composition of medical foods for inborn errors of metabolism.

Table 12-2 Comparison of Nutrient Specifications in Infant Formula Act and 1980 Recommended Dietary Allowances

Nutrients	IFA (per 100 kcal)	RDAs (per 100 kcal)
Protein, g	1.8–4.5	1.9
Fat, g	3.3–6.0	NG
Linoleic acid, mg	300	NG
Arginine, mg	NG	NG
Cystine, mg	NG	See (Met + Cys)
Histidine, mg	NG	29
Isoleucine, mg	NG	72
Leucine, mg	NG	117
Lysine, mg	NG	86
Methionine, mg	NG	43 (Met + Cys)
Phenylalanine, mg	NG	123 (Phe + Tyr)
Threonine, mg	NG	59
Tyrosine, mg	NG	See (Phe + Tyr)
Tryptophan, mg	NG	18
Valine, mg	NG	80
Minerals		
Calcium, mg	60	52
Chloride, mg	55–150	40
Chromium, µg	NG	1.45
Copper, µg	60	73
Iodine, µg	5–75	6
Iron, mg	0.15–3.0	1.45
Magnesium, mg	6	7.25
Manganese, µg	5	73
Molybdenum, µg	NG	4.3
Phosphorus, mg	30	34
Potassium, mg	80–200	51
Selenium, µg	NG	1.49
Sodium, mg	20–60	17
Zinc, mg	0.50	0.44
Calcium/phosphorus ratio	1.1–2.0	1.6
Vitamins		
A, IU	250–750	204
D, IU	40–100	58
E, IU	0.7	0.5
K, µg	4	1.7
B_1, µg	40	44
B_2, µg	60	57
B_6, µg	35	44
B_{12}, µg	0.15	0.07
Biotin, µg	1.5	5.1
C, mg	8	5
Choline, mg	7	NG
Folacin, µg	4	4.34
Inositol, mg	4	NG
Niacin, µg	250	861 NE
Pantothenic acid, µg	300	287

Key: Cys, cystine; Met, methionine; NE, niacin equivalents; NG, none given; Tyr, tyrosine.

INBORN ERRORS OF NITROGEN METABOLISM

The urea cycle contributes large amounts of arginine to the body arginine pool. When the urea cycle is nonfunctional, arginine becomes an essential amino acid.[8] Consequently, arginine supplements must be administered in all disorders of the urea cycle except arginase deficiency (Appendixes 12-A and 12-B). In carbamyl phosphate synthetase (CPS) or ornithine transcarbamylase (OTC) deficiency, L-citrulline may be given in place of L-arginine. When administered in adequate amounts, these amino acids also enhance waste nitrogen excretion.[12]

Protein (nitrogen) restriction has been the primary approach to prevention of elevated blood ammonia (Appendixes 12-A and 12-B). Protein quality is determined by its essential amino acid content. Protein synthesis and nitrogen utilization are more efficient when all essential amino acids are present in appropriate amounts. Severe restriction of natural protein leads to inadequate intake of several essential and conditionally essential amino acids. Because of this, medical foods consisting of essential and conditionally essential amino acids have been devised (Appendix 12-D). Carnitine, cystine, taurine, and tyrosine may not be synthesized in adequate amounts when liver parenchymal cells are damaged, as reported with some urea cycle enzyme defects.[31,32] Any medical food used for therapy of urea cycle disorders should contain carnitine, cystine, taurine, and tyrosine. Over-restriction of an essential amino acid and/or nitrogen leads to decreased protein synthesis and/or body protein catabolism and increased blood ammonia.

Bachmann and Colombo[33] reported that elevated blood ammonia enhances brain uptake of tryptophan. The resulting enhanced serotonin synthesis appears to decrease appetite, which can account for inadequate energy intake that results in body protein catabolism.[34] Unless blood ammonia can be maintained in the normal range, tryptophan content of medical foods designed for urea cycle disorders should be on the low side of normal requirements.

Protein quality of medical foods must also be evaluated based on their mineral and vitamin content since natural protein sources (dairy products, meat, fish and other seafood, poultry) normally supply large amounts of minerals and vitamins, and intracellular minerals are important for protein synthesis. Medical foods devised for patients with urea cycle disorders must supply all minerals and vitamins not contributed by the small quantities of breads/cereals, fruits, fats, and vegetables the patient may ingest. UCD1/2 contains no added chromium, magnesium, or selenium. UCD2 is low in all added minerals and vitamins[35] (Appendix 12-D). Amin-Aid has no minerals or vitamins added and has a high calorie to protein ratio (123:1) that is not appropriate for infants or children, who require a calorie:protein ratio of 60:1 to 40:1, respectively.

Because protein intake is severely restricted, energy (kilocalorie) intake should be increased to prevent use of muscle protein for energy purposes and thus prevent catabolism of body protein (Appendix 12-B). Energy is the first requirement of the body and inadequate energy intake for protein synthesis and other needs will lead to elevated blood ammonia.[12]

Waste nitrogen excretion is enhanced through treatment with sodium benzoate and/or sodium phenylacetate.[36] Sodium benzoate is conjugated with glycine primarily in hepatic and renal cell mitochondria to form hippurate, which is cleared by the kidney.[37] Sodium phenylacetate conjugates with glutamine in kidney and liver cells to form phenylacetylglutamine, which is excreted by the kidney.[37,38] Phenylacetic acid conjugates with taurine in the kidney.[39]

Concerns with the Use of Sodium Benzoate and/or Sodium Phenylacetate

Chronic exposure of mammalian cortical neuronal cultures with 0.6 mmol phenylacetate has a detrimental effect on their growth and function. Detrimental effects may be mediated by deficiencies of pantothenate, niacin, folate, and vitamin B_{12}, which are all required for conjugation reactions by cytochrome P-450 systems.[40]

The synthesis of hippurate from benzoate and glycine requires adenosine triphosphate (ATP) and coenzyme A (CoA).[41] If glycine is inadequate, benzoyl CoA will accumulate and can impair hepatic gluconeogenesis and lipogenesis,[42] possibly due to CoA sequestration. An oral dose of 4 g sodium benzoate given to healthy adults depleted the metabolic pool of glycine, as indicated by an increased urinary excretion of pyroglutamic acid (5-oxoproline).[43] Inadequate available glycine for heme and glutathione synthesis could have serious pathologic effects. Cyr et al.[44] found that benzoyl CoA accumulated in isolated hepatocytes when incubated with benzoate. Synthesis of urea and orotate were depressed in this system. The authors suggested that benzoate potentiates ammonia toxicity by blocking the urea cycle through sequestration of CoA. Batshaw et al.[45] and Hayman and coworkers[34] reported that sodium benzoate increased tryptophan uptake by the brain and increased serotonin flux. The suggestion was made that clinical symptoms of sodium benzoate intoxication are related to this alteration in serotonin metabolism.

Glycine is readily made from serine. Tetrahydrofolate (FH_4) is required for this reaction to occur. Glycine can also be synthesized from glutamate. Pyridoxal phosphate (PLP) and an aldolase are required for this set of reactions. Because of the several coenzymes required to maintain serine (nicotinamide-adenine dinucleotide [NAD], PLP) and glycine (FH_4, PLP) pools and the use of CoA in synthesis of hippurate, folate, pantothenate, pyridoxine, and niacin should be administered at three to five times their RDAs for age when sodium benzoate is given therapeutically.

INBORN ERRORS OF CARBOHYDRATE METABOLISM

Galactosemias and Hereditary Fructose Intolerance

Deletion of galactose in most forms of galactosemia and fructose in hereditary fructose intolerance must be accompanied by adequate intakes of protein, energy, minerals, and vitamins (Appendixes 12-A and 12-B). Both galactose and fructose bind with phosphate in patients with galactosemia and hereditary fructose intolerance.[46–49] This intracellular sequestering of phosphorus in combination with excess urinary phosphate loss (Fanconi syndrome) suggests the need for increased phosphorus intake. If the patient with galactose-1-phosphate uridyl transferase or aldolase B deficiency has any residual enzyme activity, pharmacologic doses of folic acid may extend the enzymes' half-life[50] and provide for better outcomes.

Therapy of galactosemia due to galactose-1-phosphate uridyl transferase deficiency, while lifesaving, has resulted in less than optimum outcomes.[51] Poor outcomes may be the result of small but significant intakes of naturally occurring galactose in fruits, vegetables, grains, and other foods[52–63] and/or from ongoing deficiencies of riboflavin,[64] phosphorus,[65] and inositol.[66]

Infant formulas made from soy protein isolate, without added lactose, contain significantly less galactose[67] than formulas made from hydrolyzed casein.[67] One such formula (RCF) may be used long-term after Isomil or ProSobee is discontinued as a source of protein, minerals, and vitamins. Deletion of milk, milk products, products containing milk, and organ meats; careful label reading for the presence of lactose, casein, or whey; and examination of all drug ingredients should be practiced before suggesting the use of any food or drug.

Glycogen Storage Diseases

Outcomes of patients with glycogen storage disease have been significantly improved by two recent therapeutic approaches.[68,69] These are continuous nasogastric feeding and administration of raw cornstarch (Appendix 12-A).[68–73] Both therapeutic modalities aim at maintaining normal blood glucose at all times.[72–76] High-protein diets[77–79] and L-alanine supplements[80] have been found beneficial in muscle phosphorylase deficiency (Appendix 12-B).

INBORN ERRORS OF LIPOPROTEIN METABOLISM

Abetalipoproteinemia, hypobetalipoproteinemia, lecithin:cholesterol acyl tranferase (LCAT) deficiency, and type I hyperlipoproteinemia all require stringent restriction of triglycerides with long-chain fatty acids.[81–84] In all four disorders care must be taken to provide adequate linoleic and α-linolenic acids to prevent deficiency (Appendix 12-B). Medium-chain triglycerides (MCT) may be used as a calorie source. In the abeta- and hypobetalipoproteinemias, all the fat-soluble vitamins require supplementation.[81–83] In particular, pharmacologic doses of vitamin E are necessary to prevent myopathy and neurologic degeneration[83] in abetalipoproteinemia.

Restriction of total fat, cholesterol, and saturated fat[85, 86] is used to treat types IIa, IIb, and III hyperlipoproteinemia. Natural fiber in the form of whole grains, legumes, fruits, and vegetables should be increased in the diets of children with types IIb and III hyperlipoproteinemias. Mono- and disaccharides are restricted in the diets of patients with type IIb and type III hyperlipoproteinemias.[87] When cholestyramine or colestipol is used, total dietary fat, fat-soluble vitamins, vitamin B₁₂, and iron may all need to be increased in the diet.[40] Great care must be taken to ensure an adequate diet since growth failure and nutritional dwarfing may otherwise result.[88]

INBORN ERRORS OF MINERAL METABOLISM

Acrodermatitis enteropathica, characterized by mental depression, circumoral and acral dermatitis, alopecia, diarrhea, failure to thrive, and death, is a rare inher-

---

Table 12-3 Research Approaches Related to Nutrition Therapy of Inborn Errors of Metabolism

1. Investigations of how vitamins may affect active cofactor concentrations and activate specific deficient enzymes.
2. Studies of the pathogenesis of the clinical manifestations of inborn errors, designed to develop rationale for better diet therapy.
3. Longitudinal studies of the adequacy of nutrition therapies in maintaining normal growth and development while maximizing therapeutic response.
4. Studies of the development of secondary nutrient deficiencies in patients on therapeutic diets, due to interference with the availability of other nutrients, such as trace elements.
5. Investigation of possible injurious effects of specific components of therapeutic diets.
6. Attempts to improve nutrition therapies of inborn errors to eliminate metabolic problems not completely controlled, such as hyperlipidemia and hyperuricemia in glycogen storage disease or carnitine wasting in renal Fanconi syndrome or the organic acidemias.
7. Development of methods for improving the palatability or acceptability of nutrition therapies, such as by the substitution of specific amino acid-deficient peptides for amino acid mixtures.
8. Development of animal models for the study of nutrition therapies of inborn errors, either by a search for heterozygotes or through the use of recombinant DNA methods.
9. Investigations of how vitamins may affect active cofactor concentrations and activate specific deficient enzymes.
10. Studies of the pathogenesis of the clinical manifestations of inborn errors, designed to develop rationale for better diet therapy.

Source: Data from reference 92.

ited disorder affecting zinc absorption.[19] Large supplements of zinc given two to three times daily cure all the symptoms of this disorder (Appendix 12-B).

Wilson's disease is a rare disorder that results in accumulation of copper in the brain, liver, and kidneys, resulting in neurologic deterioration and liver and renal failure.[89] Therapy includes restriction of foods high in copper and the use of D-penicillamine (Appendix 12-C). Zinc and pyridoxine supplements should be administered when D-penicillamine is used.[90,91]

Table 12-4 Roles and Functions of the Dietitian in Nutrition Support of Inborn Errors of Metabolism

During Screening

1. Evaluate nutrient intake of subjects who have a positive screen.

During Acute Care and/or the Diagnostic Work-Up

1. Evaluate nutrient intake during the diagnostic work-up.
2. Recommend nutrition support during medical management of the critically ill infant or child.
3. Coordinate implementation of the nutrition support plan with the hospital dietitian.
4. Educate physicians and nurses concerning the need for the patient to meticulously adhere to the nutrition support plan.
5. Educate parents/caretakers about the disorder and the initial nutrition support plan.

During Long-Term Follow-Up

1. Manage case.
2. Educate parents/caretakers about symptoms of impending acute illness and priority actions to take.
3. Corroborate teaching by physician, nurse and counselor about the mode of inheritance, likelihood of recurrence with another pregnancy, expectations for child, carrier status of normal children.
4. Educate parents/caretakers and patient about goals of nutrition support.
5. Educate parents/caretakers and patient about nutrition support: how and where to obtain medical food, medical food preparation, menu planning, meal preparation, record keeping, anticipatory guidance concerning growth and developmental feeding behaviors.
6. Evaluate nutrition status and feeding abilities of the patient on a continuing basis.
7. Develop the prescription for nutrition support and make changes in the nutrition support prescription as indicated.
8. Implement the nutrition support plan.
9. Maintain clinical summary sheets and growth charts.
10. Present patient nutrition data at team conferences.
11. Maintain up-to-date files on formulation and nutrient composition of foods.
12. Develop and standardize special recipes.
13. Develop education materials for parents, patients, and professionals.
14. Coordinate care with public health nutritionist and/or home health care agency.
15. Conduct ongoing clinical research.

AREAS NEEDING FURTHER RESEARCH

Recently the National Institutes of Health recognized the need for research on nutrition therapy of inborn errors of metabolism by issuing a request for applications (RFA).[92] The goals listed in the RFA were (1) to improve the effectiveness of currently utilized nutrition therapies of inborn errors by making them safer, more palatable, and less likely to lead to secondary deleterious consequences and, (2) to develop new rational diet therapies based on knowledge of pathogenesis. Research approaches outlined in Table 12-3 were identified for support, and investigations utilizing these approaches were encouraged. Other approaches for meeting the goals of the RFA were not excluded.

FUNCTIONS OF THE DIETITIAN IN NUTRITION SUPPORT OF INBORN ERRORS OF METABOLISM

The roles of the dietitian in nutrition support of inborn errors of metabolism are outlined in Table 12-4. The dietitian, because of her or his central role in therapy, is often the case manager,[93] coordinating clinic care and acting as liaison with the public health nutritionist[94] and/or home health agency. The crucial role of the dietitian in long-term management of the patient with an inborn error of metabolism mandates excellent interpersonal skills as well as a knowledge base far in excess of entry level requirements. Without this knowledge and the capability to transmit this knowledge to patients, parents, and professionals, outcomes may be poor, or death may occur.

REFERENCES

1. Committee on Dietary Allowances, Food and Nutrition Board. *Recommended Dietary Allowances.* 10th rev. ed. Washington, DC: National Academy of Sciences; 1989.
2. FAO/WHO/UNU Expert Consultation. *Energy and Protein Requirements.* Geneva: World Health Organization; 1985.
3. Elsas LJ, Acosta PB. Nutrition support of inherited metabolic diseases. In: Shils ME, Young VR, eds. *Modern Nutrition in Health and Disease.* 7th ed. Philadelphia, Pa: Lea & Febiger; 1988:1337–1379.
4. Martin SB, Acosta PB. Nutrition support of phenylketonuria and maple syrup urine disease. *Top Clin Nutr.* 1987;2:9–24.
5. Goldblum OM, Brusilow SW, Maldonado YA, Farmer ER. Neonatal citrullinemia associated with cutaneous manifestations and arginine deficiency. *J Am Acad Dermatol.* 1986;14:321–326.
6. Borum PR, Bennett SG. Carnitine as an essential nutrient. *J Am Col Nutr.* 1986;5:177–182.
7. Sansaricq C, Garg S, Norton PM, Phansalkar SV, Snyderman SE. Cystine deficiency during dietotherapy of homocystinemia. *Acta Paediatr Scand.* 1975;64:215–218.
8. Laidlaw SA, Kopple JD. Newer concepts of the indispensable amino acids. *Am J Clin Nutr.* 1987;46:593–605.

9. Przyrembel H. Therapy of mitochondrial disorders. *J Inherited Metab Dis.* 1987;10:129–146.

10. Blau N. Inborn errors of pterin metabolism. *Ann Rev Nutr.* 1988;8:185–209.

11. Acosta PB. *Nutrition Support Protocols.* Columbus, Ohio: Ross Laboratories; 1989.

12. Batshaw ML, Monahan PS. Treatment of urea cycle disorders. In: Tada K, Colombo JP, Desnick RJ, eds. *Recent Advances in Inborn Errors of Metabolism.* New York, NY: Karger; 1987:242–250.

13. Holmes RD, Wilson GN, Hajra A. Oral ether lipid therapy in patients with peroxisomal disorders. *J Inherited Metab Dis.* 1987;10(suppl 2):239–241.

14. Rudman DA, Feller A. Evidence for deficiencies of conditionally essential nutrients during total parenteral nutrition. *J Am Col Nutr.* 1986;5:101–106.

15. Elsas LJ, Danner D, Lubitz D, Fernhoff P, Dembure P. Metabolic consequences of inherited defects in branched chain α-ketoacid dehydrogenase: mechanism of thiamine action. In: Walser M, Williamson JR, eds. *Metabolism and Clinical Implications of Branched Chain Amino and Ketoacids.* New York, NY: Elsevier/North Holland; 1981:369–382.

16. Barber GW, Spaeth GL. Pyridoxine therapy in homocystinuria. *Lancet.* 1967;1:337–340.

17.
   Rosenberg LE, Fenton WA. Disorders of propionate and methylmalonate metabolism. In: Scriver CR, Beaudet AL, Sly WS, Valle D, eds. *The Metabolic Basis of Inherited Disease.* 6th ed. New York, NY: McGraw-Hill Information Services; 1989:821-844.

18. Bonkowsky HL, Magnussen CR, Collins AR, Donerty JM, Ress RA, Tschudy DP. Comparative effects of glycerol and dextrose on porphyrin precursor excretion in acute intermittent porphyria. *Metabolism.* 1976;25:405–414.

19. Aggett PJ. Acrodermatitis enteropathica. *J Inherited Metab Dis.* 1983;6(suppl 1):39–43.

20. Wolf B, Heard GS. Disorders of biotin metabolism. In: Scriver CR, Beaudet AL, Sly WS, Valle D, eds. *The Metabolic Basis of Inherited Disease.* 6th ed. New York, NY: McGraw-Hill Information Services Co; 1989:2083–2103.

21. Stepnick-Gropper S, Acosta PB, Clarke-Sheehan N, Wenz E, Cheng M, Koch R. Trace element status of children with PKU and normal children. *J Am Diet Assoc.* 1988;88:459–465.

22. Chipponi JX, Bleier JC, Santi MT, Rudman D. Deficiencies of essential and conditionally essential nutrients. *Am J Clin Nutr.* 1982;35:1112–1116.

23. Acosta PB, Stepnick-Gropper S. Problems related to diet management of maternal phenylketonuria. *J Inherited Metab Dis.* 1986;9(suppl 2):183–201.

24. Martin SB, Acosta PB. Osmolalities of selected enteral products and carbohydrate modules used to treat inherited metabolic disorders. *J Am Diet Assoc.* 1987;87:48–52.

25. Guttler F, Olesen ES, Wamberg E. Diurnal variations of serum phenylalanine in phenylketonuric children on low phenylalanine diet. *Am J Clin Nutr.* 1969; 22:1568–1570.

26. Stepnick-Gropper S, Acosta PB. The effect of simultaneous ingestion of L-amino acids and whole protein on plasma amino acid concentrations and urea nitrogen concentrations in humans. *JPEN.* 1991;5:48–53.

27. Sarett HP, Knauff KH. Development of special formulas for the dietary management of inborn errors of metabolism. In: Wapnir RA, ed. *Congenital Metabolic Diseases.* New York, NY: Marcel Dekker; 1985:169–185.

28. Acosta PB. Construction of an amino acid-restricted diet. In: Kelley VC, ed. *Practice of Pediatrics.* Philadelphia, PA: Harper & Row; 1983.

29. Pratt EL, Snyderman SE, Cheung MW, Norton P, Holt LE: The threonine requirement of the normal infant. *J Nutr.* 1955;56: 231–251.

30. Young FE, Heckler MM. Nutrient requirements for infant formulas. *Fed Reg.* 1985;50:45106–45108.

31. LaBrecque DR, Latham PS, Riely, Hsia YE, Klatskin G. Heritable urea cycle enzyme deficiency-liver disease in 16 patients. *J Pediatr.* 1979;94:580–587.

32. Zimmerman A, Baumgartner R. Severe liver fibrosis in argininosuccinic aciduria. *Arch Pathol Lab Med.* 1986;110:136–140.

33. Bachmann C, Colombo JP. Increased tryptophan uptake into the brain in hyperammonemia. *Life Sci.* 1983;33:2417–2424.

34. Hayman SL, Porter CA, Page TJ, Iwata BA, Kissel R, Batshaw ML. Behavior management of feeding disturbances in urea cycle and organic acid disorders. *J Pediatr.* 1987;111:558–562.

35. Mead Johnson Nutritionals. *Dietary Management of Metabolic Disorders.* Evansville, Ind: Mead Johnson Nutritionals; 1989.

36. Brusilow SW, Tinker J, Batshaw ML. Amino acid acylation: a mechanism of nitrogen excretion in inborn errors of urea synthesis. *Science.* 1980;207:659–661.

37. Moldave K, Meister A. Synthesis of phenylacetylglutamine by human tissue. *J Biol Chem.* 1957;229:463–476.

38. Ambrose AM, Power FW, Sherwin CP. Further studies on the detoxication of phenylacetic acid. *J Biol Chem.* 1933;101:669–675.

39. James MO, Smith RL, Williams RT, Reidenberg M. The conjugation of phenylacetic acid in man, subhuman primates and some non-primate species. *Proc R Soc Lond.* 1972;182:25–35.

40. Zeman FJ. Drugs and nutritional care. In: *Clinical Nutrition and Dietetics.* Lexington, Mass: DC Heath & Co; 1983:49–75.

41. Gatley SJ, Sherratt HSA. The synthesis of hippurate from benzoate and glycine by rat liver mitochondria. *Biochem J.* 1977;166:39–47.

42. McCune SA, Durant PJ, Flanders LE, Harris RA. Inhibition of hepatic gluconeogenesis and lipogenesis by benzoic acid, p-tert.-butylbenzoic acid and a structurally related hypolipidemic agent SC-33459. *Arch Biochem Biophys.* 1982;214:124–133.

43. Jackson AA, Badaloo AV, Forrester T, et al. Urinary excretion of 5-oxo-proline (pyroglutamic aciduria) as an index of glycine insufficiency in normal man. *Br J Nutr.* 1987;58:207–214.

44. Cyr DM, Maswoswe SM, Trembloy GC. Inhibition of the urea cycle and *de novo* pyrimidine biosynthesis by sodium benzoate. *J Inherited Metab Dis.* 1987;10(suppl 2):308–310.

45. Batshaw ML, Hyman SL, Coyle JT, Bachmann C. Effect of sodium benzoate (SB) on brain serotonin (5-HT) metabolism in experimental hyperammonemia (HA). *Pediatr Res.* 1986;20:326A.

46. Komrower GM. Galactosaemia—thirty years on. The experience of a generation. *J Inherited Metab Dis.* 1982;5(Suppl 2):96–104.

47. Sardharwalla IB, Wraith JE. Galactosemia. *Nutr Health.* 1987;5:175–188.

48. Odievre M, Gentil C, Gautier M, Alagille D. Hereditary fructose intolerance in childhood. *Am J Dis Child.* 1978;132:605–608.

49. Kogut MD, Roe TF, Ng W, Donnell GN. Fructose-induced hyperuricemia: observations in normal children and in patients with hereditary fructose intolerance and galactosemia. *Pediatr Res.* 1975;9:774–778.

50. Rosensweig NS, Herman RH, Stifel FB, Herman YF. Regulation of human jejunal glycolytic enzymes by oral folic acid. *J Clin Invest.* 1969;48:2038–2042.

51. Waggoner DD, Buist NRM, Donnell GN. Long-term prognosis in galactosaemia; Results of a survey of 350 cases. *J Inherited Metabolic Disease.* 1990;13:802–818.

52. Ash ASF, Reynolds TM. Water-soluble constituents of fruit. III. An examination of the sugars and polyols of apricots, peaches, pears, and apples by paper chromatography. *Aust J Chem.* 1955;8:276–279.

53. Cerbulis J. Sugars in Caracas cacao beans. *Arch Biochem Biophys.* 1954;49:442–450.

54. Fry SC. Phenolic components of the primary cell wall. Feruloylated disaccharides of D-galactose and L-arabinose from spinach polysaccharide. *Biochem J.* 1982;203:493–504.

55. Grierson D, Tucker GA, Robertson NG. The molecular biology of ripening. In: Friend J, Rhodes MJC, eds. *Recent Advances in the Biochemistry of Fruits and Vegetables.* New York, NY: Academic Press; 1981:149–160.

56. John MA, Dey PM. Postharvest changes in fruit cell wall. *Adv Food Res.* 1986;30:139–193.

57. Owens HS, Stark JB, Goodban AE, Walker HG. Application of compositional knowledge to beet sugar technology. *J Agric Food Chem.* 1955;3:350–353.

58. Panoyotatos N, Villemez CL. The formation of a β-[1 - 4]-D-galactan chain catalyzed by a *Phaseolus aureus* enzyme. *Biochem J.* 1973;133:263–271.

59. Pressey R. β-galactosidases in ripening tomatoes. *Plant Physiol.* 1983;71:132–135.

60. Schwarz V, Simpson NIM. Galactose content of foods for galactosaemic infants. *Lancet.* 1962;2:611–612.

61. Shallenberger RS, Moyer JC. Relation between changes in glucose, fructose, galactose, sucrose and stachyose and the formation of starch in peas. *J Agric Food Chem.* 1961;9:137–140.

62. Wood PJ, Siddiqui IR. Isolation and structural studies of a water-soluble galactan from potato (solanum tuberosum) tubers. *Carbohydr Res.* 1972;22:212–220.

63. Yokotsuka T. Soy sauce biochemistry. *Adv Food Res.* 1986;30:196–329.

64. Prchal JT, Conrad ME, Skalka HW. Association of presenile cataracts with heterozygosity for galactosaemic states and with riboflavin deficiency. *Lancet.* 1978;1:12–13.

65. Pennington JS, Prankerd TAJ. Studies of erythrocyte phosphate ester metabolism in galactosemia. *Clin Sci.* 1958;17:385–391.

66. Wells WW, McIntyre JP, Schlichter DJ, Wacholtz MC, Spieker SE. Studies on myo-inositol metabolism in galactosemia. *Ann NY Acad Sci.* 1969;165:599–608.

67. Mead Johnson Nutritionals. *Galactosemia in Infancy.* Evansville, Ind: Mead Johnson and Co; 1976:1–15.

68. Greene HL, Slonim AE, Burr IM, Moran JR. Type I glycogen storage disease: five years of management with nocturnal intragastric feeding. *J Pediatr.* 1980;96:590–595.

69. Ullrich K, Schmidt H, van Teeffelen-Heithoff A. Glycogen storage disease type I and III and pyruvate carboxylase deficiency: results of long-term treatment with uncooked cornstarch. *Acta Pediatr Scand.* 1988;77:531–536.

70. Greene HL, Ghishan FK, Brown B, McClenathan DT, Freese D. Hypoglycemia in type IV glycogenosis: hepatic improvement in two patients with nutritional management. *J Pediatr.* 1988;112:55–58.

71. Borowitz SM, Greene HL. Cornstarch therapy in a patient with type III glycogen storage disease. *J Pediatr Gastroenterol Nutr.* 1987;6:631–634.

72. Chen YT, Cornblath M, Sidbury JB. Cornstarch therapy in type I glycogen-storage disease. *N Engl J Med.* 1984;310:171–175.

73. Chen YT, Leinhas J, Coleman RA. Prolongation of normoglycemia in patients with type I glycogen storage disease. *J Pediatr.* 1987;111: 567–570.

74. Fernandes J, Leonard JV, Moses SW, et al. Glycogen storage disease: recommendation for treatment. *Eur J Pediatr.* 1988;147:226–228.

75. Schwenk WF, Haymond MW. Optimal rate of enteral glucose administration in children with glycogen storage disease type I. *N Engl J Med.* 1986;314:682–685.

76. Williams JC. Nutritional goals in glycogen storage disease. *N Engl J Med.* 1986;314:709–710.

77. Slonim AE, Coleman RA, Moses WS. Myopathy and growth failure in debrancher enzyme deficiency: improvement with high-protein nocturnal enteral therapy. *J Pediatr.* 1984;105:906–911.

78. Slonim AE, Coleman RA, Moses S, Bashan N, Shipp E, Mushlin P. Amino acid disturbances in type III glycogenosis: differences from type I glycogenosis. *Metabolism.* 1983;32:70–74.

79. Slonim AE, Goans PJ. Myopathy in McArdle's syndrome. Improvement with a high protein diet. *New Engl J Med.* 1985;312:355–359.

80. Slonim AE, Schiff MJ. Alanine is an effective fuel in McArdle's disease. *Clin Res.* 1989;37:461A.

81. Assmann G, Schmitz G, Brewer HB. Familial high density lipoprotein deficiency. In: Scriver CR, Beaudet AL, Sly CS, Valle D, eds. *The Metabolic Basis of Inherited Disease.* 6th ed. New York, NY: McGraw-Hill Information Services Co; 1989:1267–1282.

82. Brunzell JD. Familial lipoprotein lipase deficiency and other causes of the chylomicronemia syndrome. In: Scriver CR, Beaudet AL, Sly CS, Valle D, eds. *The Metabolic Basis of Inherited Disease.* 6th ed. New York, NY: McGraw-Hill Information Services Co; 1989:1165–1180.

83. Kane JP, Havel RJ. Disorders of the biogenesis and secretion of lipoproteins containing the β-lipoproteins. In: Scriver CR, Beaudet AL, Sly CS, Valle D, eds. *The Metabolic Basis of Inherited Disease.* 6th ed. New York, NY: McGraw-Hill Information Services Co; 1989:1139–1164.

84. Norum KR, Gjone E, Glomset JA. Familial lecithin: cholesterol acyltransferase deficiency, including fish eye disease. In: Scriver CR, Beaudet AL, Sly CS, Valle D, eds. *The Metabolic Basis of Inherited Disease.* 6th ed. New York, NY: McGraw-Hill Information Services Co; 1989:1181–1194.

85. Goldstein JL, Brown MS: Familial hypercholesterolemia. In: Scriver CR, Beaudet AL, Sly CS, Valle D, eds. *The Metabolic Basis of Inherited Disease.* 6th ed. New York, NY: McGraw-Hill Information Services Co; 1989:1215–1250.

86. Mahley RW, Rall SC. Type III hyperlipoproteinemia. In: Scriver CR, Beaudet AL, Sly CS, Valle D, eds. *The Metabolic Basis of Inherited Disease.* 6th ed. New York, NY: McGraw-Hill Information Services Co; 1989:1195–1213.

87. Schaefer EJ, Levy RI. Pathogenesis and management of lipoprotein disorders. *New Engl J Med.* 1985;312:1300–1310.

88. Lifshitz F, Moses N. Growth failure a complication of dietary treatment of hypercholesterolemia. *Am J Dis Child.* 1989;143:537–542.

89. Danks D. Disorders of copper transport. In: Scriver CR, Beaudet AL, Sly CS, Valle D, eds. *The Metabolic Basis of Inherited Disease.* 6th ed. New York, NY: McGraw-Hill Information Services Co; 1989:1411–1431.

90. Walshe JM. Hudson memorial lecture: Wilson's disease: genetics and biochemistry—their relevance to therapy. *J Inherited Metab Dis.* 1983;6(suppl 1):51–58.

91. *Physicians' Desk Reference.* Des Moines, Iowa: Edward R. Barnhart; 1989:1299.

92. Levin EY, de la Cruz F. Nutritional therapy of inborn errors of metabolism RFA: 89-HD/DK-01. Bethesda, Md: National Institute of Child Health and Human Development; 1988.

93. Belsten LM, Rarback S, Wellman NS. The metabolic nutritionist as a team member and case manager. *Top Clin Nutr.* 1987;2:76–81.

94. Stephens-Hitchcock E, Walker EJ. The public health approach to the treatment and follow-up of children with metabolic disorders. *Top Clin Nutr.* 1987;2:82–86.

95. Snyderman SE, Boyer A, Phansalkar SV, Holt LE. Essential amino acid requirements of infants: tryptophan. *Am J Dis Child.* 1961;102:163–167.

96. Snyderman SE, Norton PM, Fowler DI, Holt LE. The essential amino acid requirements of infants: lysine. *AMA J Dis Child.* 1959;97:175–185.

97. Barbul A. Arginine: biochemistry, physiology and therapeutic implications. *J Parenter Enter Nutr.* 1986;10:227–238.

98. Milner JA. Metabolic aberrations associated with arginine deficiency. *J Nutr.* 1985;115:516–523.

99. Visek WJ. Arginine needs, physiological state and usual diets. A reevaluation. *J Nutr.* 1986;116:36–46.

100. Visek WJ, Shoemaker JD. Orotic acid, arginine, and hepatotoxicity. *J Am Col Nutr.* 1986; 5:153–166.

101. Zieve L. Conditional deficiencies of ornithine or arginine. *J Am Col Nutr.* 1986;5:167–176.

102. Gilbert EF. Carnitine deficiency. *Pathology.* 1985;17:161–169.

103. Rebouche CJ, Paulson DJ. Carnitine metabolism and function in humans. *Annu Rev Nutr.* 1986;6:41–66.

104. Snyderman SE, Roitman E, Boyer A, Norton PM, Holt LE. The essential amino acid requirements of infants. IX. Isoleucine. *Am J Clin Nutr.* 1964;15:313–321.

105. Snyderman SE, Roitman E, Boyer A, Holt LE. The essential amino acid requirements of infants: leucine. *Am J Dis Child.* 1961;102:157–162.

106. Snyderman SE, Boyer A, Norton PM, Roitman E, Holt LE. The essential amino acid requirements of infants. X. Methionine. *Am J Clin Nutr.* 1964;15:322–330.

107. Snyderman SE, Pratt EL, Cheung MW, et al. The phenylalanine requirement of the normal infant. *J Nutr.* 1955;56:253–263.

108. Ament ME, Geggel HS, Heckenlively JR, Martin DA, Kopple J. Taurine supplementation in infants receiving long-term total parenteral nutrition. *J Am Col Nutr.* 1986;5:127–135.

109. Sturman JA, Wen GY, Wisniewski HM, Neuringer MD. Retinal degeneration in primates raised on a synthetic human infant formula. *Int J Dev Neurosci.* 1984;2:121–129.

110. Snyderman SE, Holt LE, Smellie F, Boyer A, Westall RG. The essential amino acid requirements of infants: valine. *Am J Dis Child.* 1959;97:186–191.

111. Snyderman SE, Holt LE, Dancis J, Roitman E, Boyer A, Balis ME. "Unessential" nitrogen: a limiting factor for human growth. *J Nutr.* 1962;78:57–72.

112. Scriver CR, Kaufman S, Woo SLC. The hyperphenylalaninemias. In: Scriver CR, Beaudet AL, Sly WS, Valle D, eds. *The Metabolic Basis of Inherited Disease.* 6th ed. New York, NY: McGraw-Hill Information Services Co; 1989:495–546.

113. Acosta PB. The contribution of therapy of inherited amino acid disorders to knowledge of amino acid requirements. In: Wapnir RA, ed. *Congenital Metabolic Diseases.* New York, NY: Marcel Dekker; 1985:115–135.

114. Goldsmith LA, Laberge C. Tyrosinemia and related disorders. In: Scriver CR, Beaudet AL, Sly WS, Valle D, eds. *The Metabolic Basis of Inherited Disease.* 6th ed. New York, NY: McGraw-Hill Information Services Co; 1989:547–562.

115. Danner D, Elsas LJ. Disorders of branched chain amino acid and ketoacid metabolism. In: Scriver CR, Beaudet AL, Sly WS, Valle D, eds. *The Metabolic Basis of Inherited Disease.* 6th ed. New York, NY: McGraw-Hill Information Services Co; 1989:671–692.

116. Sweetman L. Branched chain organic acidurias. In: Scriver CR, Beaudet AL, Sly WS, Valle D, eds. *The Metabolic Basis of Inherited Disease.* 6th ed. New York, NY: McGraw-Hill Information Services Co; 1989:791–819.

117. de Sousa C, Chalmers RA, Stacey TE, Tracey BM, Weaver CM, Bradley D. The response to L-carnitine and glycine therapy in isovaleric acidaemia. *Eur J Pediatr.* 1986;144:451–456.

118. Naglak M, Salvo R, Madsen K, Dembure P, Elsas L. The treatment of isovaleric acidemia with glycine supplement. *Pediatr Res.* 1988;24:9–13.

119. Mudd SH, Levy HL, Skovby F. Disorders of transsulfuration. In: Scriver CR, Beaudet AL, Sly WS, Valle D, eds. *The Metabolic Basis of Inherited Disease.* 6th ed. New York, NY: McGraw-Hill Information Services Co; 1989:693–734.

120. Carey MC, Fennelly JJ, FitzGerald O. Homocystinuria II. Subnormal serum folate levels, increased folate clearance and effects of folic acid therapy. *Am J Med.* 1968;45:26–31.

121. Schaumburg H, Kaplan J, Windebank A, Vick N, Rasmus S, Pleasure D, Brown MJ. Sensory neuropathy from pyridoxine abuse. A new megavitamin syndrome. *N Engl J Med.* 1983;309:445–448.

122. Goodman SI, Frerman FE. Organic acidemias due to defects in lysine oxidation: 2-ketoadipic acidemia and glutaric acidemia. In: Scriver CR, Beaudet AL, Sly WS, Valle D, eds. *The Metabolic Basis of Inherited Disease.* 6th ed. New York, NY: McGraw-Hill Information Services Co; 1989:845–853.

123. Warman ML, Levy HL, Perry TL. Clinical and biochemical studies in three sibs with glutaric aciduria type I: response to dietary therapy. *Am J Hum Genet.* 1988;43:A17.

124. Seccombe DW, James L, Booth F. L-carnitine treatment in glutaric aciduria type I. *Neurology.* 1986;36:264–267.

125. Lipkin PH, Roe CR, Goodman SI, Batshaw ML. A case of glutaric acidemia type I. Effect of riboflavin and carnitine. *J Pediatr.* 1988;112:62–65.

126. Travis S, Mathias MM, Dupont J. Effect of biotin deficiency on the catabolism of linoleate in the rat. *J Nutr.* 1972;102:767–772.

127. Roe CR, Hoppel CL, Stacey TE, Chalmers RA, Tracey BM, Millington DS. Metabolic response to carnitine in methylmalonic acidura. *Arch Dis Child.* 1983;58:916–920.

128. Wolf B. Reassessment of biotin-responsiveness in "unresponsive" propionyl CoA carboxylase deficiency. *J Pediatr.* 1980;97:964–967.

129. Brusilow SW, Horwich AL. Urea cycle enzymes. In: Scriver CR, Beaudet AL, Sly WS, Valle D, eds. *The Metabolic Basis of Inherited Disease.* 6th ed. New York, NY: McGraw-Hill Information Services Co; 1989:629–663.

130. Ohtani Y, Ohyanagi K, Yamamoto Y, Matsuda I. Secondary carnitine deficiency in hyperammonemic attacks of ornithine transcarbamylase deficiency. *J Pediatr.* 1988;112:409–414.

131. Segal S. Disorders of galactose metabolism. In: Scriver CR, Beaudet AL, Sly WS, Valle D, eds. *The Metabolic Basis of Inherited Disease.* 6th ed. New York, NY: McGraw-Hill Information Services Co; 1989:453–480.

132. Garibaldi LR, Canini S, Superti-Furga A, et al. Galactosemia caused by generalized uridine diphosphate galactose-4-epimerase deficiency. *J Pediatr.* 1983;103:927–930.

133. Sardharwalla IB, Wraith JE, Bridge C, Fowler B, Roberts SA. A patient with severe type of epimerase deficiency galactosaemia. *J Inherited Metab Dis.* 1988;11(suppl 2):249–251.

134. Hers H-G, Van Hoof F, deBarsy T. Glycogen storage diseases. In: Scriver CR, Beaudet AL, Sly WS, Valle D, eds. *The Metabolic Basis of Inherited Disease.* 6th ed. New York, NY: McGraw-Hill Information Services Co; 1989:425–452.

135. Gitzelmann R, Steinmann B, van den Berghe G. Disorders of fructose metabolism. In: Scriver CR, Beaudet AL, Sly WS, Valle D, eds. *The Metabolic Basis of Inherited Disease.* 6th ed. New York, NY: McGraw-Hill Information Services Co; 1989:399–424.

136. Mock DM, Perman JA, Thaler MM, Morris RC. Chronic fructose intoxication after infancy in children with hereditary fructose intolerance. *N Engl J Med.* 1983;309:764–770.

137. Pineda O, Torun B, Viteri FE, Arroyave G. Protein quality in relation to estimates of essential amino acid requirements. In: Bodwell CE, Adkins JS, Hopkins DT, eds. *Protein Quality in Humans: Assessment and In Vitro Estimation.* Westport, Conn: Avi Publication Co; 1981:29–42.

138. Torun B, Pineda O, Viteri FE, Arroyave G. Use of amino acid composition data to predict nutritive value for children with specific reference to new estimates of their essential amino acid requirements. In: Bodwell CE, Adkins JS, Hopkins DT, eds. *Protein Quality in Humans: Assessment and In Vitro Estimation.* Westport, Conn: Avi Publication Co; 1981:374–389.

139. Bower BD, Smallpiece V. Lactose-free diet in galactosaemia. *Lancet.* 1955;2:873.

140. Bell L, Sherwood WG, Chir B. Current practices and improved recommendations for treating hereditary fructose intolerance. *J Am Diet Assoc.* 1987;87:721–728.

141. American Academy of Pediatrics, Committee on Nutrition. Commentary on breastfeeding and infant formulas, including standards for formulas. *Pediatrics.* 1976;57:278–285.

142. Holman RT, Johnson SB, Hatch TF. A case of human linolenic acid deficiency involving neurological abnormalities. *Am J Clin Nutr.* 1982;35:617–623.

143. Pellock JM. Efficacy and adverse effects of antiepileptic drugs. *Pediatr Clin North Am.* 1989;36:435–448.

144. Millington DS, Roe CR, Maltby DA, Inoue I. Endogenous catabolism is the major source of toxic metabolites in isovaleric acidemia. *J Pediatr.* 1987;110:56–60.

145. Petrowski S, Nyhan WL, Reznik V, et al. Pharmacologic amino acid acylation in the acute hyperammonemia of propionic acidemia. *J Neurogenet.* 1987;4:87–96.

146. Bachmann C. Treatment of congenital hyperammonemias. *Enzyme.* 1984;32:56–64.

147. Ross Laboratories. *Ross Laboratories Product Handbook.* Columbus, Ohio: Ross Laboratories; 1988.

148. Mead Johnson Nutritionals. *Dietary Management of Metabolic Disorders.* Evansville, Ind: Bristol-Myers Co; 1989.

Appendix 12-A

Nutrition Support of Inborn Errors of Metabolism

Inborn Errors of Amino Acid Metabolism

Aromatic Amino Acids

Inborn Error and Defect	Nutrient(s) to Modify	Vitamin-Responsive	Medical Foods Available
Phenylketonuria and hyperphenylalaninemia (phenylalanine hydroxylase)[112]	Restrict PHE, increase TYR (see Appendix 12-B).[113] See Chapters 4 and 5 for other nutrient needs.	No	Analog XP; Lofenalac; Maxamaid XP; Maxamum XP; Phenyl-Free; PKU 1, 2, 3
Hyperphenylalaninemia (dihydropteridine reductase; GTP cyclohydrolase I; pyruvoyltetrahydrobiopterin synthase)[10,112]	Same as for phenylketonuria[113]	Yes. Tetra-hydrobiopterin 2 mg/kg/d[10]	Same as for phenylketonuria
Tyrosinemia type I (fumarylacetoacetate hydrolase)[114]	Restrict PHE and TYR; restrict MET if plasma MET level is above normal. Provide greater than normal energy intake (see Appendix 12-B). See Chapters 4 and 5 for other nutrient needs.	No	Analog XPHEN, TYR, MET; Maxamaid XPHEN, TYR
Tyrosinemia type II (tyrosine aminotransferase)[114]	Restrict PHE and TYR (see Appendix 12-B).[11,114] See Chapters 4 and 5 for other nutrient needs.	No	Analog XPHEN, TYR; Low PHE/TYR Diet Powder; Maxamaid XPHEN, TYR; TYR 1, 2

Key: ALA, alanine; BCAAs, branched-chain amino acids; CYS, cystine; EAAs, essential amino acids (includes conditionally essential cystine and tyrosine); GLY, glycine; GTP, guanosine triphosphate; ILE, isoleucine; IM, intramuscular; LEU, leucine; LYS, lysine; MCT, medium-chain triglycerides; MET, methionine; MSUD, maple syrup urine disease; PHE, phenylalanine; PUFAs, polyunsaturated fatty acids; THR, threonine; TRP, tryptophan; TYR, tyrosine; VAL, valine.

Inborn Error and Defect	Nutrient(s) to Modify	Vitamin-Responsive	Medical Foods Available
Branched-Chain Amino Acids			
Maple syrup urine disease (branched-chain ketoacid dehydrogenase complex)[115]	Restrict ILE, LEU, VAL (see Appendix 12-B).[3,11,113] Maintain protein and energy intakes at or above NAS/NRC RDAs for age. See Chapters 4 and 5 for other nutrient needs.	Yes. Thiamine-responsive if any residual enzyme activity.[15] Response to thiamine inadequate to alleviate need for restriction of BCAAs.[115] 300 mg oral thiamine/day.[115]	Analog MSUD; Maxamaid MSUD; Maxamum MSUD; MSUD Diet Powder; MSUD 1,2
Isovaleric acidemia (isovaleryl-CoA dehydrogenase)[116], β-methylcrotonyl-glycinuria (3-methylcrotonyl CoA carboxylase)[116]	Restrict LEU[3]; supplement with L-carnitine and GLY[117,118] (see Appendix 12-B). Maintain protein and energy intakes at or above NAS/NRC RDAs for age. See Chapters 4 and 5 for other nutrient needs.	No	Analog XLEU; Maxamaid XLEU
Sulfur Amino Acids			
Homocystinuria, pyridoxine-nonresponsive (cystathionine-β-synthase)[119]	Restrict MET[3,11]; increase CYS[7]; supplement folate (see Appendix 12-B).[120] Maintain protein and energy intakes at or above NAS/NRC RDAs for age. See Chapters 4 and 5 for other nutrient needs.	No	Analog XMET; Hom 1, 2; Low Methionine Diet Powder, Maxamaid XMET; Maxamum XMET

Homocystinuria, pyridoxine-responsive (cystathionine-β-synthase)[16,119]	See Chapters 4 and 5 for nutrient needs.	Yes. 25 to 1000 mg of ORAL pyridoxine daily. Use smallest amount that results in biochemical normalcy as excess causes peripheral neuropathy.[121]	None indicated

Other Inborn Errors of Amino Acid Metabolism

Glutaric aciduria type I (glutaryl-CoA dehydrogenase)[122]; ketoadipic aciduria (2-keto-adipic acid dehydrogenase)[122]	Restrict LYS and TRP[123]; supplement L-carnitine[124] (see Appendix 12-B). Maintain protein and energy intakes at or above NAS/NRC RDAs for age. See Chapters 4 and 5 for other nutrient needs.	Yes. Some patients have a partial response to *oral* riboflavin, 100–300 mg daily.[125]	Analog XLYS, TRY; Maxamaid XLYS, TRY; Maxamum XLYS, TRY
Methylmalonic acidemia (methylmalonyl-CoA mutase⁰ or ⁻)[17]	Restrict ILE, MET, THR, VAL,[11] long-chain unsaturated fatty acids[126]; supplement L-carnitine[127] (see Appendix 12-B). Provide greater than normal energy intake. See Chapters 4 and 5 for other nutrient needs.	No	Analog XMET, THRE, VAL, ISOLEU; Maxamaid XMET, THRE, VAL, ISOLEU; Maxamum XMET, THRE, VAL, ISOLEU; OS 1, 2
Methylmalonic acidemia (cobalamin reductase, adenosyltransferase)[17]	Minimum restriction of ILE, MET, THR, VAL; supplement L-carnitine (see Appendix 12-B). See Chapters 4 and 5 for other nutrient needs.	Yes. 1–2 mg adenosylcobalamin daily.[17]	None indicated

Inborn Error and Defect	Nutrient(s) to Modify	Vitamin-Responsive	Medical Foods Available
Propionic acidemia[17] (propionyl-CoA carboxylase)	Restrict ILE, MET, THR, VAL,[11] long-chain unsaturated fatty acids[126]; provide greater than normal energy intake; supplement L-carnitine[127] (see Appendix 12-B). See Chapters 4 and 5 for other nutrient needs.	Questionable. Some clinicians supplement with 5–10 mg oral D-biotin daily.[128]	Analog XMET, THRE, VAL, ISOLEU; Maxamaid XMET, THRE, VAL, ISOLEU; Maxamum XMET, THRE, VAL, ISOLEU; OS 1, 2

Inborn Errors of Nitrogen Metabolism

Inborn Error and Defect	Nutrient(s) to Modify	Vitamin-Responsive	Medical Foods Available
Carbamylphosphate synthetase deficiency; ornithine transcarbamylase deficiency[129]	Restrict protein[12]; supplement with EAAs,[12] L-carnitine,[135] L-citrulline[12]; provide greater than normal energy intake (see Appendix 12-B). See Chapters 4 and 5 for other nutrient needs.	No	Amin-Aid, UCD1, 2; Protein-Free Diet Powder
Citrullinemia (argininosuccinate synthetase)[129]; argininosuccinic aciduria (argininosuccinate lyase)[129]	Restrict protein[12]; supplement with EAAs,[12] L-arginine,[12] L-carnitine[135]; provide greater than normal energy intake (see Appendix 12-B). See Chapters 4 and 5 for other nutrient needs.	No	Amin-Aid; UCD1, 2; Protein-Free Diet Powder
Argininemia (arginase)[129]	Restrict protein[12]; supplement with EAAs,[12] L-carnitine[130]; provide greater than normal energy intake (see Appendix 12-B). See Chapters 4 and 5 for other nutrient needs.	No	Amin-Aid; UCD1, 2; Protein-Free Diet Powder

Inborn Errors of Carbohydrate Metabolism
Galactosemias

Inborn Error and Defect	Nutrient(s) to Modify	Vitamin-Responsive	Medical Foods Available
Epimerase deficiency[131]	Delete galactose. Add specific known amount of galactose[132,133] (see Appendix 12-B). Maintain normal energy and	No	Isomil, ProSobee for infants; RCF for children

Disorder	Treatment		Products
(continued)	protein intakes for age. See Chapters 4 and 5 for other nutrient needs.		
Galactokinase deficiency[131]	Delete galactose.[131] Maintain normal energy and protein intakes for age. See Chapters 4 and 5 for other nutrient needs.	No	Isomil, ProSobee for infants; RCF for children
Galactose-1-phosphate uridyl transferase deficiency[131]	Delete galactose.[131] Maintain normal energy and protein intakes for age. See Chapters 4 and 5 for other nutrient needs.	No	Isomil, ProSobee for infants; RCF for children

Glycogen Storage Diseases

Disorder	Treatment		Products
Type Ia (glucose-6-phosphatase), type Ib (defective glucose-6-phosphate transport)[134]	Modify type of carbohydrate[71–73] and frequency of feeds[68] (see Appendix 12-B). Maintain normal energy and protein intakes for age. Avoid lactose, fructose, and sucrose.[134] See Chapters 4 and 5 for other nutrient needs.	No	ProViMin, RCF for infants and children
Type III (amylo-1, 6-glucosidase)[134]	Provide high protein[77]; supplement with L-ALA[78]; modify type of carbohydrate[69,71] and frequency of feeds[77] (see Appendix 12-B). Avoid lactose, fructose, and sucrose.[134] Provide normal energy intake for age. See Chapters 4 and 5 for other nutrient needs.	No	ProViMin, RCF for infants and children
Type IV (α-1, 4-glucan: α-1, 4-glucan 6-glucosyltransferase)[134]	Provide high protein unless cirrhosis present; modify type of carbohydrate and frequency of feeds[70] (see Appendix 12-B). Provide normal energy intake for age. See Chapters 4 and 5 for other nutrient needs.	No	ProViMin; RCF

Inborn Error and Defect	Nutrient(s) to Modify	Vitamin-Responsive	Medical Foods Available
Type V (muscle phosphory-lase)[134]	Provide high protein[79]; supplement L-ALA[80] (see Appendix 12-B). Provide normal energy intake for age. See Chapters 4 and 5 for other nutrient needs.	No	Mono- and Disaccharide-Free Diet Powder; ProViMin; RCF
Hereditary Fructose Intolerance			
Hereditary fructose intoler-ance (aldolase B)[135]	Restrict fructose[136]; restrict protein if liver damage[48] (see Appendix 12-B). Maintain energy intake at NAS/NRC RDA for age. See Chapters 4 and 5 for other nutrient needs.	No	Enfamil; Similac for infants; ProViMin, RCF, or whole cow's milk for children
Inborn Errors of Lipoprotein Metabolism			
Abetalipoproteinemia and hypobetalipoproteinemia (absence and decrease in apoB)[83]	Restrict triglycerides with long-chain fatty acids; supplement with vitamins A, D, E, K[83,87] (see Appendix 12-B). See Chapters 4 and 5 for other nutrient needs. Maintain protein and energy intakes at NAS/NRC RDAs for age.	No	ProViMin, MCT
Lecithin: cholesterol acyltransferase deficiency (LCAT)[84]	Restrict fat[84,87] (see Appendix 12-B). See Chapters 4 and 5 for other nutrient needs. Maintain protein and energy intakes at NAS/NRC RDAs for age.	No	ProViMin, MCT
Hyperlipoproteinemias			
Type I (extrahepatic lipopro-tein lipase; apo CII absent or decreased)[82]	Restrict triglycerides with long-chain fatty acids[81,87] (see Appendix 12-B). See Chapters 4 and 5 for other nutrient	No	ProViMin, MCT

Type IIa (LDL receptors absent or defective)[85]	needs. Maintain protein and energy intakes at NAS/NRC RDAs for age. Restrict cholesterol, saturated fat; increase PUFAs[85,87,88] (see Appendix 12-B). See Chapters 4 and 5 for other nutrient needs. Maintain protein and energy intakes at NAS/NRC RDAs for age.	No	Enfamil, Similac for infants; ProViMin, RCF for children
Type IIb[85]	Restrict cholesterol, saturated fat, mono- and disaccharides, alcohol. Increase fiber and PUFAs[85,87,88] (see Appendix 12-B). See Chapters 4 and 5 for other nutrient needs. Maintain normal protein and energy intakes.	No	Mono- and Disaccharide-Free Diet Powder, ProViMin, RCF
Type III (hepatic lipoprotein lipase; homozygous for abnormal apo E2; remnant receptor defect)[86]	Restrict cholesterol, saturated fat, mono- and disaccharides, alcohol. Increase PUFAs and fiber. Restrict energy if patient is overweight.[86,87] Maintain normal protein intake (see Appendix 12-B). See Chapters 4 and 5 for other nutrient needs.	No	Enfamil, Similac for infants; ProViMin, RCF for children

Inborn Errors of Mineral Metabolism

Acrodermatitis enteropathica (defect in intestinal zinc absorption)[19]	Give zinc supplements[19] (see Appendix 12-B). See Chapters 4 and 5 for other nutrient needs. Maintain normal protein and energy intakes.	No	None indicated
Wilson's disease: hepatolenticular degeneration (excessive accumulation of copper)[89,90]	Restrict dietary copper (see Appendix 12-B). See Chapters 4 and 5 for other nutrient needs. Maintain normal protein and energy intakes.	No	None indicated

Appendix 12-B

Recommended Nutrient Intakes (with Ranges) for Beginning Therapy

Age (years)

Nutrients to Modify	0.0 < 0.5	0.5 < 1.0	1 < 4	4 < 7	7 < 11	11 < 19
Inborn Errors of Amino Acid Metabolism						
Aromatic Amino Acids						
Phenylketonuria and hyperphenylalaninemia[3,4,11,113]						
PHE, mg	55 (70–20)/kg	30 (50–15)/kg	325 (200–450)/day	425 (225–625)/day	450 (250–650)/day	500 (300–750)/day
TYR, mg	195 (210–180)/kg	185 (200–170)/kg	2800 (1400–4200)/day	3150 (1750–4550)/day	3500 (2100–4900)/day	3850 (2100–5600)/day
Protein, g	3.0–2.5/kg	2.5–2.25/kg	25/day	30/day	35/day	50–65/day
Energy, kcal	120/kg	110/kg	900–1800/day	1300–2300/day	1650–3300/day	1500–3300/day
Tyrosinemia type I[3,11]						
PHE, mg	75 (95–45)/kg	55 (75–30)/kg	600 (500–700)/day	650 (550–750)/day	700 (600–800)/day	800 (700–900)/day
TYR, mg	75 (95–45)/kg	55 (75–30)/kg	400 (300–500)/day	450 (350–550)/day	500 (400–600)/day	550 (450–650)/day
MET, mg	40 (50–20)/kg	30 (40–20)/kg	300 (200–400)/day	350 (250–450)/day	400 (300–500)/day	400 (300–500)/day
Protein,† g	3.0–2.5/kg	2.5–2.25/kg	25/day	30/day	35/day	50–65/day
Carbohydrate			60%–80% of calories			
Energy, kcal			110%–120% of NAS/NRC RDA for age			
Branched-Chain Amino Acids						
Tyrosinemia type II[3,11]						
PHE, mg	100 (125–65)/kg	80 (105–45)/kg	450 (400–500)/day	500 (450–550)/day	550 (500–600)/day	600 (550–700)/day
TYR, mg	75 (100–40)/kg	55 (80–20)/kg	400 (350–450)/day	450 (400–500)/day	500 (450–550)/day	550 (400–550)/day
Protein, g	3.0–2.5/kg	2.5–2.25/kg	25/day	30/day	35/day	50–65/day
Energy, kcal	120/kg	110/kg	900–1800/day	1300–2300/day	1650–3300/day	1500–3300/day
Maple syrup urine disease[3,4,11,113]						
ILE, mg	60 (90–30)/kg	50 (70–30)/kg	50 (70–20)/kg	25 (30–20)/kg	25 (30–20)/kg	25 (30–10)/kg
LEU, mg	80 (100–40)/kg	80 (75–40)/kg	55 (70–40)/kg	50 (65–35)/kg	45 (60–30)/kg	40 (50–15)/kg
VAL, mg	70 (95–40)/kg	55 (80–30)/kg	58 (85–30)/kg	40 (60–30)/kg	28 (30–25)/kg	22 (30–15)/kg
Protein, g	3.0–2.5/kg	2.5–2.25/kg	25/day	30/day	35/day	50–65/day
Energy, kcal			100%–105% of NAS/NRC RDA for age			

Key: ARG, arginine; CIT, citrulline; CYS, cystine; GLY, glycine; ILE, isoleucine; LYS, lysine; MET, methionine; MUFA, monounsaturated fatty acid; PHE, phenylalanine; PUFA, polyunsaturated fatty acid; THR, threonine; TRP, tryptophan; TYR, tyrosine; VAL, valine.

Nutrients to Modify	Age (years)					
	0.0 < 0.5	0.5 < 1.0	1 < 4	4 < 7	7 < 11	11 < 19
INBORN ERRORS OF AMINO ACID METABOLISM						
Isovaleric acidemia and beta-methylcrotonylglycinuria[3,113,117,118]						
LEU, mg	95 (110–65)/kg	75 (90–50)/kg	975 (800–1150)/day	1275 (1050–1500)/day	1445 (1190–1700)/day	1955 (1610–2300)/day
L-Carnitine, mg	300–100/kg	300–100/kg	300–100/kg	300–100/kg	300–100/kg	300–100/kg
GLY, mg	125 (150–100)/kg	125 (150–100)/kg	125 (150–100)/kg	125 (150–100)/kg	125 (150–100)/kg	125 (150–100)/kg
Protein, g	3.0–2.5/kg	2.5–2.25/kg	25/day	30/day	35/day	50–65/day
Energy, kcal	------- 100%–105% of NAS/NRC RDA for age -------					
Sulfur Amino Acids						
Homocystinuria, cystathionine-β-synthase deficiency (pyridoxine-nonresponsive)[3,7,11,113,120]						
MET, mg	35 (50–20)/kg	28 (40–15)/kg	20 (30–10)/kg	15 (20–10)/kg	15 (20–10)/kg	15 (20–10)/kg
CYS, mg	300–250/kg	250–200/kg	150 (200–100)/kg	150 (200–100)/kg	150 (200–100)/kg	75 (150–25)/kg
Folate, mg	------- 0.5–1.0/day -------			1–3/day		
Protein, g	3.0–2.5/kg	2.5–2.25/kg	25/day	30/day	35/day	50–65/day
Energy, kcal	120/kg	115/kg	900–1800/day	1300–2300/day	1650–3300/day	1500–3300/day
Other Amino Acids						
Glutaric aciduria type I and ketoadipic aciduria[95,96,113,124,125,137,138]						
LYS, mg	85 (100–70)/kg	65 (90–40)/kg	55 (80–30)/kg	50 (75–25)/kg	45 (65–25)/kg	40 (60–20)/kg
TRP, mg	25 (40–10)/kg	15 (30–10)/kg	12 (16–8)/kg	12 (16–8)/kg	8 (10–5)/kg	6 (8–4)/kg
L-carnitine, mg	125–115/kg	125–115/kg	125–115/kg	125–115/kg	125–115/kg	125–115/kg
Riboflavin, mg	------- 300–100/day, administer orally -------					
Protein, g	3.0–2.5/kg	2.5–2.25/kg	25/day	30/day	35/day	50–65/day
Energy, kcal	120/kg	115/kg	900–1800/day	1300–2300/day	1650–3300/day	1500–3300/day
Propionic acidemia and methylmalonic acidemia[17,126-128]						
ILE, mg	95 (120–60)/kg	70 (90–40)/kg	610 (485–735)/day	795 (630–960)/day	900 (715–1090)/day	1215 (965–1470)/day
MET, mg	35 (50–15)/kg	25 (40–10)/kg	330 (275–390)/day	435 (360–510)/day	495 (410–580)/day	665 (550–780)/day
THR, mg	90 (135–50)/kg	55 (75–20)/kg	505 (415–600)/day	660 (540–780)/day	745 (610–885)/day	1010 (830–1195)/day
VAL, mg	85 (105–60)/kg	55 (75–30)/kg	690 (550–830)/day	900 (720–1080)/day	1020 (815–1225)/day	1380 (1105–1655)/day
D-Biotin, mg	------- 5–10/day for propionic acidemia					
Adenosylcobalamin, mg	------- 1–2 daily for cobalamin-responsive methylmalonic acidemia					
L-carnitine, mg	300–100/kg	300–100/kg	300–100/kg	300–100/kg	300–100/kg	300–100/kg
Protein,[†] g	3.0–2.5/kg	2.5–2.25/kg	25/day	30/day	35/day	50–65/day

Energy, kcal — 100%–105% of NAS/NRC RDA for age

Inborn Errors of Nitrogen Metabolism

Citrullinemia; argininosuccinic aciduria[5,12,129,130]

ARG, mg	700–350/kg	500–250/kg	500–250/kg	400–200/kg
Protein,‡ g	1.6–1.25/kg	1.0–0.86/kg	0.82–0.79/kg	0.79–0.61/kg
L-Carnitine, mg	100–50/kg	100–50/kg	100–50/kg	100–50/kg
Energy, kcal	100%–105% of NAS/NRC RDA for age			

Carbamylphosphate synthetase deficiency; ornithine transcarbamylase deficiency[5,12,129,130]

CIT, mg	700–350/kg	500–250/kg	500–250/kg	400–200/kg
Protein,‡ g	1.6–1.25/kg	1.0–0.86/kg	0.86–0.82/kg	0.79–0.61/kg
L-Carnitine	100–50/kg	100–50/kg	100–50/kg	100–50/kg
Energy, kcal	100%–105% of NAS/NRC RDA for age			

Argininemia[5,12,129,130]

Protein,‡ g	1.6–1.25/kg	1.25–1.0/kg	0.86–0.82/kg	0.79–0.61/kg
L-Carnitine, mg	100–50/kg	100–50/kg	100–50/kg	100–50/kg
Energy, kcal	100%–105% of NAS/NRC RDA for age			

Inborn Errors of Carbohydrate Metabolism

Galactosemias

Epimerase deficiency[132,133]

Galactose, mg	1000–1500/day	500–1000/day			
Protein, g	2.2/kg	2.0/kg	30/day	23/day	34/day	45–65/day
Energy, kcal	120/kg	115/kg	1300–2300/day	900–1800/day	1650–3300/day	1500–3300/day

Galactokinase deficiency[139]

Galactose, mg	<50/day	<100/day	<100/day	<100/day	
Protein, g	2.2/kg	2.0/kg	30/day	23/day	34/day	45–65/day
Energy, kcal	120/kg	115/kg	1300–2300/day	900–1800/day	1650–3300/day	1500–3300/day

Galactose-1-phosphate uridyl transferase deficiency[139]

Galactose, mg	<50/day	<100/day	<100/day		
Protein, g	2.2/kg	2.0/kg	30/day	23/day	34/day	45–65/day
Energy, kcal	120/kg	115/kg	1300–2300/day	900–1800/day	1650–3300/day	1500–3300/day

Nutrients to Modify	Age (years)					
	0.0 < 0.5	0.5 < 1.0	1 < 4	4 < 7	7 < 11	11 < 19

Glycogen Storage Diseases

Glucose-6-phosphatase deficiency (von Gierke's disease, type Ia); type Ib[68,72–75]

Carbohydrate 60%–70% of calories. Provide at least 50% of carbohydrate as uncooked cornstarch every 4 hours during the day and via continuous tube feeding at night. During the first 3 months of life feed every 2 hours and use Polycose instead of uncooked cornstarch; gradually change to raw cornstarch over 3 months.

Nutrient	0.0 < 0.5	0.5 < 1.0	1 < 4	4 < 7	7 < 11	11 < 19
Protein,† g	2.2/kg	2.0/kg	23/day	30/day	34/day	45–65/day
Energy, kcal	120/kg	115/kg	900–1800/day	1300–2300/day	1650–3300/day	1500–3300/day

Amylo-1,6-glucosidase deficiency (Cori's disease, type III)[71,78]

Nutrient	0.0 < 0.5	0.5 < 1.0	1 < 4	4 < 7	7 < 11	11 < 19
Protein, g	4.4/kg	4.0/kg	4.0/kg	3.5/kg	3.0/kg	2.5/kg
L-Alanine, mg	500–400/kg	400–300/kg	300–200/kg	200–100/kg	200–100/kg	200–100/kg

Carbohydrate 40%–50% of calories. Provide about one half as uncooked cornstarch every 6 hours throughout day and night. During the first 3 months of life feed every 2 hours and use Polycose instead of cornstarch; over 3 months gradually change to raw cornstarch.

Nutrient	0.0 < 0.5	0.5 < 1.0	1 < 4	4 < 7	7 < 11	11 < 19
Energy, kcal	120/kg	110/kg	900–1800/day	1300–2300/day	1650–3300/day	1500–3300/day

Alpha-1, 4-glucan:alpha–1, 4-glucan 6-glucosyltransferase deficiency (Andersen's disease, type IV)[70,77]

Nutrient	0.0 < 0.5	0.5 < 1.0	1 < 4	4 < 7	7 < 11	11 < 19
Protein, g	High protein as for type III unless cirrhosis present					
Carbohydrate	Uncooked cornstarch every 4–5 hours to maintain normoglycemia. See under type III					
Energy, kcal	120/kg	110/kg	900–1800/day	1300–2300/day	1650–3300/day	1500–3300/day

Muscle phosphorylase deficiency (McArdle's disease, type V)[79,80]

Nutrient	0.0 < 0.5	0.5 < 1.0	1 < 4	4 < 7	7 < 11	11 < 19
Protein, g	High protein as for type III					
L-Alanine, mg	Same as for type III					
Energy, kcal	120/kg	110/kg	900–1800/day	1300–2300/day	1650–3300/day	1500–3300/day

Hereditary Fructose Intolerance[136,140]

Nutrient	0.0 < 0.5	0.5 < 1.0	1 < 4	4 < 7	7 < 11	11 < 19
Fructose, mg	<10/kg	<10/kg	<10/kg	<20/kg	<30/kg	<40/kg
Protein	Restriction only with liver damage					
Energy, kcal	120/kg	110/kg	900–1800/day	1300–2300/day	1650–3300/day	1500–3300/day

Inborn Errors of Lipid Metabolism

Abetalipoproteinemia and hypobetalipoproteinemia[83,141,142]

Long-chain triglycerides with linoleic and α-linolenic acids	>3%<5% of calories					
Vitamin A	1000–2000/day					5000–10,000/day
E, mg	Use water-miscible form to supplement					
K	Supplement with water-miscible form if bruising, bleeding, or hypoprothrombinemia present					
Protein, g	2.2/kg	2.0/kg	23/day	30/day	35/day	44–56/day
Energy, kcal	120/kg	115/kg	900–1800/day	1300–2300/day	1650–3300/day	1500–3300/day

LCAT deficiency[84,141,142]

Long-chain triglycerides	>3%<5% of calories					
Linoleic acid	3% of calories					
α-linolenic acid	1% of calories					
Protein, g	2.2/kg	2.0/kg	23/day	30/day	35/day	44–56/day
Energy, kcal	120/kg	115/kg	900–1800/day	1300–2300/day	1650–3300/day	1500–3300/day

Hyperlipoproteinemias

Type I[82,87,141,142]

Long-chain triglycerides	<15% of calories					
Linoleic acid	3% of calories					
α-linolenic acid	1% of calories					
Protein, g	2.2/kg	2.0/kg	23/day	30/day	35/day	44–56/day
Energy, kcal	120/kg	115/kg	900–1800/day	1300–2300/day	1650–3300/day	1500–3300/day

Type IIa[85,87,88]

Total fat	<30% of calories					
Cholesterol, mg	<100/1000 kcal. Never >300/day					
Saturated fat	<10% of calories					
PUFAs	<15% of calories					
MUFAs	<10% of calories					
Protein, g	2.2/kg	2.0/kg	23/day	30/day	35/day	44–56/day
Energy, kcal	120/kg	115/kg	900–1800/day	1300–2300/day	1650–3300/day	1500–3300/day

Type IIb[85,87,89]

Cholesterol, mg	<100/1000 kcal. Never >300/day
Total fat	<30% of calories
Saturated fat	<10% of calories
PUFAs	15% of calories

Nutrients to Modify	Age (years)					
	0.0 < 0.5	0.5 < 1.0	1 < 4	4 < 7	7 < 11	11 < 19
MUFAs	<10% of calories					
Fiber	Increase					
Mono- and disaccharides	Restrict					
Protein, g	2.2/kg	2.0/kg	23/day	30/day	35/day	44–56/day
Energy, kcal	120/kg	115/kg	900–1800/day	1300–2300/day	1650–3300/day	1500–3300/day
Type III[86–89]						
Cholesterol, mg	<100/1000 kcal. Never >300/day					
Saturated fat	<10% of calories					
PUFAs	15% of calories					
Fiber	Increase					

Inborn Errors of Mineral Metabolism

	Age (years)					
Acrodermatitis enteropathica[19]	35–100 mg elemental zinc daily; give in two or three doses					
Protein, g	2.2/kg	2.0/kg	23/day	30/day	35/day	44–56/day
Energy, kcal	120/kg	115/kg	900–1800/day	1300–2300/day	1650–3300/day	1500–3300/day
Wilson's disease[89–91]						
Copper, mg	0.3/day	0.4/day	0.5/day	0.8/day	1.0/day	1.0/day
Zinc, mg	20/day	20/day	20/day	30/day	30/day	30/day
Protein, g	2.2/kg	2.0/kg	23/day	30/day	35/day	44–56/day
Energy, kcal	120/kg	115/kg	900–1800/day	1300–2300/day	1650–3300/day	1500–3300/day
Pyridoxine, mg			25/day			

* ARG, arginine; CIT, citrulline; CYS, cystine; GLY, glycine; ILE, isoleucine; LCAT, lecithin: cholesterol acyl transferase; LEU, leucine; LYS, lysine; MET, methionine; MUFA, monounsaturated fatty acid; PHE, phenylalanine; PUFA, polyunsaturated fatty acid; THR, threonine; TRP, tryptophan; TYR, tyrosine; VAL, valine.

† Protein may need to be decreased by 5–10% if liver damage with hyperammonemia is present.

‡ Total protein intake may be somewhat greater with the use of Ucephan®.

Appendix 12-C

Nutrition Support during Acute Illness; Medications and Nutrient Interactions and Nutrition Assessment Parameters

Inborn Errors of Amino Acid Metabolism
Aromatic Amino Acids

Inborn Error and Defect	Nutrition Support during Acute Illness	Medications and Nutrient Interaction	Nutrition Assessment Parameters
Phenylketonuria and hyperphenylalaninemia (phenylalanine hydroxylase)	Delete dietary PHE 1–2 days ONLY. For infant offer Pedialyte to maintain electrolyte balance if needed. Give fruit juices and sugar-sweetened, caffeine-free soft drinks with added Polycose or Moducal if tolerated to maintain energy intake at 100% RDA for age. If necessary give IV glucose, lipid and L-amino acids free of PHE to maintain anabolism. Return to oral medical food and complete diet as rapidly as tolerated.[11]	No medication required with early and continuing meticulous therapy throughout life	Plasma PHE and TYR; dietary intake of PHE, TYR, protein, energy, minerals, vitamins.[11] See Chapter 2 for other routine assessment parameters and standards.
Hyperphenylalaninemia (dihydropteridine reductase; GTP cyclohydrolase I; pyruvoyltetrahydro-biopterin synthase)	Same as above	L-DOPA, 5-hydroxy-tryptophan, carbidopa[10]	Plasma PHE and TYR; dietary intake of PHE, TYR, protein, energy, minerals, vitamins. See Chapter 2 for other routine assessment parameters and standards.
Tyrosinemia type I (fumarylacetoacetate hydrolase)	Delete dietary PHE, TYR, MET, 1–2 days *only*. For infant offer Pedialyte to maintain electrolyte balance if needed. Give fruit juices and sugar-sweetened, caffeine-free soft drinks with added Polycose or Moducal if tolerated to maintain energy intake at 120%–130% RDA for age.		Plasma PHE, TYR, MET; plasma bicarbonate, phosphate, potassium, plasma alkaline phosphatase, electrolytes; liver enzymes; urinary succinylacetone; dietary intake of PHE, TYR, MET, protein, energy, minerals, vitamins. Liver imaging studies.[3,11] See Chapter 2 for other

Disorder	Nutrition intervention	Drug-nutrient interaction	Assessment/Monitoring
	If necessary, give IV glucose, lipid, and L-amino acids free of PHE, TYR and MET to maintain anabolism. Return to oral medical food and complete diet as rapidly as tolerated.[3,11]		routine assessment parameters and standards.
Tyrosinemia type II (tyrosine amino transferase)	Delete PHE and TYR 1–2 days *only*. For infant offer Pedialyte to maintain electrolyte balance if needed. Give fruit juices and sugar-sweetened, caffeine-free soft drinks with added Polycose or Moducal if tolerated to maintain energy intake at 100% RDA for age. If necessary give IV glucose, lipid, and L-amino acids free of PHE and TYR to maintain anabolism. Return to oral medical food and complete diet as rapidly as tolerated.		Plasma PHE and TYR; urinary N-acetyl-tyrosine, p-tyramine, p-hydroxyphenylorganic acids; dietary intake of PHE, TYR, protein, energy, minerals, vitamins. See Chapter 2 for other routine assessment parameters and standards.

Branched-Chain Amino Acids

Disorder	Nutrition intervention	Drug-nutrient interaction	Assessment/Monitoring
Maple syrup urine disease (branched-chain ketoacid dehydrogenase complex)	Delete dietary BCAAs 1–2 days *only*. For infant offer Pedialyte to maintain electrolyte balance if needed. Give fruit juices and sugar-sweetened, caffeine-free soft drinks with added Polycose or Moducal if tolerated to maintain energy intake at 100%–120% of RDA for age. If necessary, give IV glucose, lipid and L-amino acids free of BCAA's. Return to oral medical food and complete diet as rapidly as tolerated.[3,11]	Anticonvulsants if seizures occur. Phenobarbital and phenytoin lead to accelerated metabolism of vitamin D and vitamin D deficiency that responds to 1,25-dihydroxy-vitamin D.[143]	Plasma BCAAs, ALA, ALLO; urine ketoacids of BCAAs. Bone radiographs of lumbar vertebrae, cation/anion gap; dietary intake of BCAAs, protein, energy, minerals, vitamins.[11] See Chapter 2 for other routine assessment parameters and standards.

Inborn Error and Defect	Nutrition Support during Acute Illness	Medications and Nutrient Interaction	Nutrition Assessment Parameters
Isovaleric acidemia (isovaleryl-CoA dehydrogenase); beta-methylcrotonylglycinuria (3-methylcrotonyl CoA carboxylase)	Delete dietary LEU 1–2 days *only*. Increase GLY and L-carnitine. For infant offer Pedialyte to maintain electrolyte balance if needed. Give fruit juices and sugar-sweetened, caffeine-free soft drinks with added Polycose or Moducal if tolerated to maintain energy intake at 105%–110% of RDA for age. If necessary, give IV glucose, lipid, and L-amino acids free of LEU. Return to oral medical food and complete diet as rapidly as tolerated.[144]	Benzoates, salicylates are *contraindicated*.[101]	Plasma BCAAs, L-carnitine, GLY; isovalerylglycine; CBC/differential. Bone radiographs of lumbar vertebrae. Urinary isovaleryl-glycine, beta-hydroxyisovaleric acid, cation/anion gap. Dietary intake of BCAAs, protein, energy, minerals, vitamins. See Chapter 2 for other routine assessment parameters and standards.

Sulfur Amino Acids

Inborn Error and Defect	Nutrition Support during Acute Illness	Medications and Nutrient Interaction	Nutrition Assessment Parameters
Homocystinuria, pyridoxine-nonresponsive (cystathionine-beta-synthase)	Delete dietary MET 1–2 days *only*. For infant offer Pedialyte to maintain electrolyte balance if needed. Give fruit juices and sugar-sweetened, caffeine-free soft drinks with added Polycose or Moducal if tolerated to maintain energy intake at 100% RDA for age. If necessary, give IV glucose, lipid, and L-amino acids free of MET. Return to oral medical food and complete diet as rapidly as tolerated.[11]	Anticonvulsants if seizures occur. Phenytoin and phenobarbital accelerate metabolism of vitamin D and cause vitamin D deficiency that responds to 1,25-dihydroxy-vitamin D.[143]	Plasma MET, CYS, HOMOCYS; erythrocyte folate; bone radiographs of lumbar vertebrae; dietary intake of MET, CYS, protein, energy, minerals, vitamins.[11] See Chapter 2 for other routine assessment parameters and standards.

Other Inborn Errors of Amino Acid Metabolism

Glutaric aciduria type I (glutaryl-CoA dehydrogenase); ketoadipic aciduria (2-ketoadipic acid dehydrogenase)	Delete LYS and TRP 1–2 days *only*. For infant offer Pedialyte to maintain electrolyte balance if needed. Increase L-carnitine. Maintain energy intake at 100% of RDA for age. Give fruit juices and sugar-sweetened, caffeine-free soft drinks with added Polycose or Moducal if tolerated. If necessary give IV glucose, lipid, and L-amino acids free of LYS and TRP to maintain anabolism. Return to medical food and complete diet as rapidly as tolerated.	Baclofen-Geneva Generics, Inc.[122] Valproic acid depresses appetite and causes an increase in plasma glycine.[143]	Plasma LYS, TRP; L-carnitine; urinary glutaric acid; dietary intake of LYS, TRP, protein energy, minerals, vitamins. See Chapter 2 for other routine assessment parameters and standards.
Propionic acidemia (propionyl-CoA carboxylase), methylmalonic acidemia (methylmalonyl CoA mutase⁰ or⁻)	Delete ILE, MET, THR, VAL, 1–2 days *only*. Increase L-carnitine. For infant offer Pedialyte to maintain electrolyte balance if needed. Give sugar-sweetened, caffeine-free soft drinks with added Polycose or Moducal if tolerated to maintain energy intake at 105% of RDA for age. If necessary, give IV glucose, lipid, and L-amino acids free of ILE, MET, THR, and VAL to maintain anabolism. Return to oral medical food and complete diet as rapidly as tolerated.[11]	Phenylacetate during acute illness if accompanied by elevated blood ammonia[145]; supplement folate, pantothenate, pyridoxine, and vitamin B$_{12}$ at three to five times RDA for age when phenylacetate used.	Plasma ILE, MET, THR, VAL, GLY, L-carnitine (free and ester); blood ammonia, cation/anion gap; urinary metabolites of propionate or methylmalonate, CBC/differential; plasma prealbumin or RBP; bone radiographs; dietary intake of ILE, MET, THR, VAL, protein, minerals, vitamins.[11] See Chapter 2 for other routine assessment parameters and standards.

Inborn Errors of Nitrogen Metabolism

Urea cycle disorders	Blood NH$_3$ > 200 µmol/L. Delete protein 1–2 days *only*. Increase L-ARG or L-CIT if not arginase deficient. Give fruit	UCEPHAN: Folate, niacin, pantothenate, pyridoxine,	Plasma amino acids, blood ammonia; plasma prealbumin or RBP; plasma triglycerides; urinary pyroglutamic

Inborn Error and Defect	Nutrition Support during Acute Illness	Medications and Nutrient Interaction	Nutrition Assessment Parameters
	juices and caffeine-free soft drinks with added Polycose or Moducal if tolerated to maintain energy intake at 105%–115% of RDA for age. If necessary, give IV L-ARG or L-CIT, glucose, and lipid to maintain caloric intake.[146] Return to oral medical food and complete diet as rapidly as tolerated.	vitamin B$_{12}$ (administer at three to five times RDA for age). Anticonvulsants for seizures. Phenobarbital and phenytoin lead to accelerated metabolism of vitamin D and vitamin D deficiency that responds to 1,25-dihydroxyvitamin D.[143]	acid,[43] 3-methyl-histidine[46]; dietary intake of protein, energy, minerals, vitamins. See Chapter 2 for other routine assessment parameters and standards.

Inborn Errors of Carbohydrate Metabolism
Galactosemias

Inborn Error and Defect	Nutrition Support during Acute Illness	Medications and Nutrient Interaction	Nutrition Assessment Parameters
Epimerase deficiency	Same as for normal infant. Avoid drugs containing galactose or lactose.		Erythrocyte galactose-1 phosphate and UDP-galactose[131-133]; dietary intake of galactose, protein, energy, minerals, vitamins. See Chapter 2 for other routine assessment parameters and standards.
Galactokinase deficiency	Same as for normal infant. Avoid drugs containing galactose or lactose.		Urinary galactose; routine eye examinations for cataracts.[131] See Chapter 2 for other routine assessment parameters and standards.
Galactose-1-phosphate	Same as for normal infant. Avoid drugs containing galactose or lactose.		Erythrocyte galactose-1-phosphate; routine eye examinations for

		cataracts; liver enzymes[131]; dietary intake of galactose, protein, energy, minerals, vitamins. See Chapter 2 for other routine assessment parameters and standards.

Glycogen Storage Diseases

Type Ia, III, IV	Give oral carbohydrate and/or IV glucose to maintain normoglycemia.	Blood glucose; liver enzymes; dietary intake of carbohydrate,[74,75] protein, energy, minerals, vitamins. See Chapter 2 for other routine assessment parameters and standards.

Inborn Errors of Lipoprotein Metabolism

Abetalipoproteinemia and hypobeta-lipoproteinemia	Same as normal individual except restrict fat.	Plasma concentrations of retinol; RBP; tocopherol; 1,25-dihydroxycholecalciferol; clotting time[83]; dietary intake of energy, protein, linoleic and linolenic acids, total fat, minerals, vitamins.[88] See Chapter 2 for other assessment parameters and standards.
Lecithin:cholesterol acyl transferase	Same as normal individual except restrict fat.	Plasma lipoproteins; plasma albumin[84]; dietary intake of energy, protein, linoleic and linolenic acids, total fat, minerals, vitamins.[88]

Hyperlipoproteinemias

Type I	Same as normal individual except restrict fat.	Plasma chylomicrons (triglycerides)[82]; dietary intake of energy, protein, linoleic and linolenic acids, total fat, minerals, vitamins.[84]

Inborn Error and Defect	Nutrition Support during Acute Illness	Medications and Nutrient Interaction	Nutrition Assessment Parameters
Type IIa, IIb	Same as normal individual except restrict cholesterol, saturated fat; increase PUFAs.	Cholestyramine, colestipol, lovastatin. Cholestyramine and colestipol cause fecal loss of fat, fat-soluble vitamins, folate, vitamin B₁₂, and iron.[40,87]	Plasma LDL cholesterol; plasma ferritin, erythrocyte B₁₂ and folate, plasma RBP; dietary intake of energy, protein, total fat, PUFAs, MUFAs, fiber, mono- and disaccharides, minerals, vitamins.[40,85,88] See Chapter 2 for other routine assessment parameters and standards.
Type III	Same as for normal individual except restrict cholesterol, saturated fat; increase PUFAs.	Nicotinic acid, clofibrate, gemfibrozil, mevinolin[87]	Plasma LDL, VLDL, and cholesterol; blood glucose, uric acid; dietary intake of energy, protein, total fat, saturated fat, PUFAs, mono- and disaccharides, fiber, minerals, vitamins.[86,88] See Chapter 2 for other routine assessment parameters and standards.
Inborn Errors of Mineral Metabolism			
Acrodermatitis enteropathica	Same as for normal individual.		Plasma neutrophil, or urinary zinc[19]; dietary intake of energy, protein, minerals, vitamins. See Chapter 2 for other routine assessment parameters and standards.

| Wilson's disease | Dependent on etiology of acute illness. | D-penicillamine binds other divalent minerals such as zinc and causes excess excretion.[89] D-penicillamine increases the pyridoxine requirement to 25 mg/d.[90,91] | Plasma copper, ferritin, prealbumin.[89,90] Dietary intake of energy, protein, copper, zinc, other minerals and vitamins. See Chapter 2 for other routine assessment parameters and standards. |

Note: ARG, arginine; BCAA, branched-chain amino acid; CBC, complete blood count; CIT, citrulline; CYS, cystine; GLY, glycine; GTP, guanosine triphosphate; HOMOCYS, homocystine; ILE, isoleucine; LCAT, lecithin:cholesterol acyl transferase; IV, intravenous; LEU, leucine; LDL, low-density lipoprotein; LYS, lysine; MET, methionine; MUFA, monounsaturated fatty acid; PHE, phenylalanine; PUFA, polyunsaturated fatty acid; RBP, retinol-binding protein; THR, threonine; TRP, tryptophan; TYR, tyrosine; UDP, uridine diphosphate; VAL, valine; VLDL, very low density lipoprotein.

Appendix 12-D

Formulation and Nutrient Composition of Medical Foods

Inborn Errors of Amino Acid Metabolism
Aromatic Amino Acids

Product	Modified Nutrient(s) (mg/100 g)	Protein Equiv, g Source (per 100 g)	Fat, g Source (per 100 g)	Carbohydrate, g Source (per 100 g)	Energy kcal (per 100 g)	Minerals Not Added	Vitamins Not Added
Phenylketonuria and Hyperphenylalaninemia							
Analog XP§	PHE—0; TYR—1370; TRP—300; added L-carnitine, taurine	13.0 L-amino acids	20.9 Peanut oil, refined lard, coconut oil	59.0 Corn syrup solids	475	None	None
Lofenalac‖	PHE—80; TYR—800; TRP—195; added L-carnitine, taurine	15.1 Enzymically hydrolyzed casein, L-amino acids	18.0 Corn oil	60.0 Corn syrup solids, modified tapioca starch	460	Chromium Molybdenum Selenium	None
Maxamaid XP§	PHE—0; TYR—2650; TRP—570	25 L-amino acids	< 1.0 None added	62 Sucrose, hydrolyzed corn starch	350	Chromium Selenium	K
Maxamum XP§	PHE—0; TYR—4030; TRP—890; added L-carnitine, taurine	39 L-amino acids	< 1.0 None added	45 Sucrose, hydrolyzed corn starch	340	None	None
Phenyl-Free‖	PHE—0; TYR—940; TRP—280	20 L-amino acids	6.8 Corn & coconut oils solids, modified tapioca starch	66 Sucrose, corn syrup	410	Chromium, Inadequate selenium	None
PKU 1‖	PHE—0; TYR—3400; TRP—1000	50 L-amino acids	0 None added	19 Sucrose	280	Chromium Selenium	None
PKU 2‖	PHE—0; TYR—4500; TRP—1400	67 L-amino acids	0 None added	7 Sucrose	300	Chromium Selenium	None
PKU 3‖	PHE—0; TYR—6000; TRP—1400	68 L-amino acids	0 None added	3 Sucrose	290	Chromium Selenium	None
Tyrosinemia I							
Analog XPHEN, TYR, MET§	PHE—0; TYR—0 MET—0; added L-carnitine, taurine	13 L-amino acids	20.9 Peanut oil, refined lard, coconut oil	59.0 Corn syrup solids	475	None	None

Product	Modified Nutrient(s) (mg/100 g)	Protein Equiv, g Source (per 100 g)	Fat, g Source (per 100 g)	Carbohydrate, g Source (per 100 g)	Energy kcal (per 100 g)	Minerals Not Added	Vitamins Not Added
Maxamaid XPHEN, TYR§	PHE—0 TYR—0	25 L-amino acids	<1.0 None added	62 Sucrose, hydrolyzed corn starch	350	Chromium Selenium	K
Tyrosinemia Type II Analog XPHEN, TYR§	PHE—0; TYR—0; added L-carnitine, taurine	13.0 L-amino acids	20.9 Peanut oil, refined lard, coconut oil	59.0 Corn syrup solids	475	None	None
Low PHE/TYR Diet Powder‖	PHE—75; TYR < 38	15 Enzymatically hydrolyzed casein, L-amino acids	18 Corn oil	60 Corn syrup solids, modified tapioca starch	460	Chromium, Molybdenum, Selenium	None
Maxamaid XPHEN, TYR§	See under Tyrosinemia Type 1						
TYR 1‖	PHE—0; TYR—0	47 L-amino acids	0 None added	21 Sucrose	270	Chromium Selenium	None
TYR 2‖	PHE—0; TYR—0	63 L-amino acids	0 None added	12 Sucrose	300	Chromium Selenium	None
Branched-Chain Amino Acids							
Maple Syrup Urine Disease Analog MSUD§	ILE—0; LEU—0; VAL—0; added L-carnitine, taurine	13.0 L-amino acids	20.9 Peanut oil, refined lard, coconut oil	59.0 Corn syrup solids	475	None	None
Maxamaid MSUD§	ILE—0; LEU—0; VAL—0	25 L-amino acids	< 1.0 None added	62 Sucrose, hydrolyzed corn starch	350	Chromium Selenium	K
Maxamum MSUD§	ILE—0; LEU—0; VAL—0; added L-carnitine, taurine	39 L-amino acids	< 1.0 None added	45 Sucrose, hydrolyzed corn starch	340	None	None
MSUD Diet Powder‖	ILE—0; LEU—0; VAL—0; added L-carnitine, taurine	9.9 L-amino acids	20 Corn oil	63 Corn syrup solids, modified tapioca starch	470	Chromium Molybdenum Selenium	None
MSUD 1‖	ILE—0; LEU—0; VAL—0	49 L-amino acids	0 None added	29 Sucrose	280	Chromium Selenium	None
MSUD 2‖	ILE—0; LEU—0; VAL—0	54 L-amino acids	0 None added	22 Sucrose	310	Chromium Selenium	None

Isovaleric Acidemia and Beta-Methylcrotonylglycinuria

Product	Modifications	Protein	Fat	CHO		Minerals	
Analog XLEU§	LEU—0; added L-carnitine, taurine	13.0 L-amino acids	20.9 Peanut oil, refined lard, coconut oil	59.0 Corn syrup solids	475	None	None
Maxamaid XLEU§	LEU—0	25 L-amino acids	<1.0 None added	62 Sucrose, hydrolyzed corn starch	350	Chromium Selenium	K

Sulfur Amino Acids

Homocystinuria Pyridoxine-Nonresponsive

Product	Modifications	Protein	Fat	CHO		Minerals	
Analog XMET§	MET—0; CYS—390; added L-carnitine, taurine	13.0 L-amino acids	20.9 Peanut oil, refined lard, coconut oil	59.0 Corn syrup solids	475	None	None
HOM 1‖	MET—0; CYS—2500	52 L-amino acids	0 None added	18 Sucrose	280	Chromium Selenium	None
HOM 2‖	MET—0; CYS—3400	69 L-amino acids	0 None added	5 Sucrose	300	Chromium Selenium	None
Low Methionine Diet Powder‖	MET—155; CYS 140; added L-carnitine, taurine	15.5 Soy protein isolate, L-amino acids	28 Coconut & corn oils	51 Corn syrup solids	520	Chromium Molybdenum Selenium	None
Maxamaid XMET§	MET—0; CYS—750	25 L-amino acids	<1.0 None added	62 Sucrose, hydrolyzed corn starch	350	Chromium Selenium	K
Maxamum XMET§	MET—0; CYS—1180; added L-carnitine, taurine	39 L-amino acids	<1.0 None added	45 Sucrose, hydrolyzed corn starch	340	None	None

Other Inborn Errors of Amino Acid Metabolism

Glutaric Aciduria Type I and Ketoadipic Aciduria

Product	Modifications	Protein	Fat	CHO		Minerals	
Analog XLYS, TRY§	LYS—0; TRP—0; added L-carnitine, taurine	13.0 L-amino acids	20.9 Peanut oil, refined lard, coconut oil	59.0 Corn syrup solids	475	None	None

Product	Modified Nutrient(s) (mg/100 g)	Protein Equiv, g Source (per 100 g)	Fat, g Source (per 100 g)	Carbohydrate, g Source (per 100 g)	Energy kcal (per 100 g)	Minerals Not Added	Vitamins Not Added
Maxamaid XLYS, TRY§	LYS—0; TRP—0	25 L-amino acids	<1.0 None added	62 Sucrose, hydrolyzed corn starch	350	Chromium Selenium	K
Maxamum XLYS, TRY§	LYS—0; TRP—0; added L-carnitine, taurine	39 L-amino acids	<1.0 None added	45 Sucrose, hydrolyzed corn starch	340	None	None
Methylmalonic Acidemia and Propionic Acidemia							
Analog XMET THRE, VAL, ISOLEU§	ILE—<35; MET—0; THR—0; VAL—0; added L-carnitine, taurine	13.0 L-amino acids	20.9 Peanut oil, refined lard, coconut oil	59.0 Corn syrup solids	475	None	None
Maxamaid XMET, THRE, VAL, ISOLEU§	ILE—<70; MET—0; THR—0; VAL—0	25 L-amino acids	<1.0 None added	62 Sucrose, hydrolyzed corn starch	350	Chromium Selenium	K
Maxamum XMET, THRE, VAL, ISOLEU§	ILE—<110; MET—0; THR—0; VAL—0; added L-carnitine, taurine	39 L-amino acids	<1.0 None added	45 Sucrose, hydrolyzed corn starch	340	None	None
OS1‖	ILE—<100; MET—0; THR—0; VAL—0	42 L-amino acids	0 None added	29 Sucrose	280	Chromium Selenium	None
OS2‖	ILE—<150; MET—0; THR—0; VAL—0	56 L-amino acids	0 None added	20 Sucrose	300	Chromium Selenium	None
Inborn Errors of Nitrogen Metabolism							
Amin-Aid¶	Essential amino acids	3.7 L-amino acids	10.7	85	454	All	All
Protein-Free Diet Powder‖	Added L-carnitine, taurine	0 None added	22 Corn oil	72 Corn syrup solids, modified tapioca starch	490	Chromium Molybdenum Selenium	None
UCD 1‖	Essential amino acids + CYS, TYR	56 L-amino acids	0 None added	8 Sucrose	260	Chromium Magnesium Selenium	None
UCD 2‖	Essential amino acids	67 L-amino acids	0 None added	6 Sucrose	290	Chromium Magnesium Selenium	None

Inborn Errors of Carbohydrate Metabolism

Galactosemias

Product	Nutrient	Protein	Fat	Carbohydrate	Energy	Minerals	Vitamins
RCF§	Carbohydrate	4.0/100 ml concentrate; soy protein isolate, L-amino acids	7.2/100 ml concentrate, soy and coconut oils	0.008/100 ml concentrate. None added	81/100 ml concentrate	Chromium Molybdenum	None

Glycogen Storage Diseases

Product	Nutrient	Protein	Fat	Carbohydrate	Energy	Minerals	Vitamins
Type Ia, Ib, III, IV, V ProViMin§	Carbohydrate, fat	73.0 Casein, L-amino acids	1.4 Coconut oil	2.0 None added	313	Chromium Molybdenum	None
RCF§	See under Galactosemias						
Type V Mono- and Disaccharide-Free Diet Powder‖	Carbohydrate	22.0 Enzymically hydrolyzed casein, L-amino acids	33.0 Fractionated coconut oil, corn oil	33.0 Modified tapioca starch	490	Chromium Molybdenum Selenium	None

Inborn Errors of Lipoprotein Metabolism

Product	Nutrient	Protein	Fat	Carbohydrate	Energy	Minerals	Vitamins
MCT Oil‖	Fatty acids	None	99 Triglycerides of medium chain fatty acids	None	767/ 100 ml	All	All
ProViMin§	See under Glycogen storage disease						
RCF§	See under Galactosemias						

Key: CYS, cystine; ILE, isoleucine; LEU, leucine; LYS, lysine; MET, methionine; PHE, phenylalanine; TRP, tryptophan; TYR, tyrosine; VAL, valine.
Note: For most recent formulation and nutrient composition, review label.
§ Ross Laboratories, 625 Cleveland Avenue, Columbus, OH 43216.
‖ Mead Johnson Nutritionals, 2400 W. Lloyd Expressway, Evansville, IN 47721.
¶ Kendall McGaw Laboratories, Inc. 2525 McGaw Avenue, Irvine, Ca 92714.

Source: Data from references 11, 147, and 148.

Chapter 13

Failure To Thrive

Karen E. Peterson

Failure to thrive (FTT) is a serious condition affecting the growth and nutritional status of infants and young children. FTT is characterized by growth delay and is often accompanied by illness, decreased activity, cognitive delay, poor school performance, and behavioral and social problems.[1-3] FTT is reported in 1% to 5% of children admitted to pediatric teaching hospitals[4,5] and in 7% to 10% of low-income preschool children seen in community-based settings in the United States.[6-9]

DEFINITION

FTT, a term used in industrialized countries, is not distinct from protein-energy malnutrition (PEM) described in children in developing countries. Although FTT and PEM have been described in separate literatures, they clearly constitute the single syndrome of childhood undernutrition. The severity and relative importance of risk factors associated with undernutrition may vary in each setting, but patterns of growth delay and broad categories of risk appear to be similar for FTT and PEM.

FTT is defined both by anthropometry and by diagnostic categories related to the etiology of undernutrition. No consensus exists on anthropometric indicators of FTT.[10,11] Deficits in attained size and in growth velocity, relative to healthy reference children, are used to define FTT. The anthropometric indicators and cutoff values vary across texts and studies[10] and with the clinical or public health purpose.[11,12] In general, however, children considered at risk for FTT are those whose measures fall at the bottom of the growth chart.

Percentile Definitions

Growth criteria for selection of FTT samples in hospital or clinic case series and case control studies have included admission weight less than the 3rd or 5th percentile on reference growth charts or less than 80% to 85% of the 50th percentile weight-for-age. The prevalence of undernutrition in the national Pediatric Nutrition Surveillance System is defined as weight-for-age, height-for-age, and weight-for-height below the 5th percentile on National Center for Health Statistics (NCHS) growth charts (see Table 13-1).[13] Low weight-for-age may reflect short stature due to chronic undernutrition and/or low weight-for-height due to acute undernutrition that precedes or is superimposed on chronic undernutrition. All three indicators are appropriate to estimate the prevalence of undernutrition in groups of children.[11] By definition, 5% of children in the reference population have growth measures below the 5th percentile and are growing normally. In nutrition surveys and surveillance, the proportion of children with anthropometric measures below the 5th percentile in excess of the 5% expected reflects undernutrition in the group.

Standard Deviation Score Definitions

The standard deviation (SD) score, also called the Z score, corresponds to percentile on reference growth charts but expresses an individual's weight and height measurements in SD units. SD scores show how far an observation is from the median, or 50th percentile, of reference growth charts, for children of the same age and sex.[14]

$$Z = \frac{\text{measurement value} - \text{median for age value of reference population}}{\text{standard deviation for age of reference population}}$$

Percentiles and equivalent SD scores for weight-for-age, height-for-age, and weight-for-height can be easily calculated using low-cost computer software developed by the Centers for Disease Control (CDC) and the World Health Organization (WHO).[15]

Table 13-1 Indicators of Undernutrition Used in National Pediatric Nutrition Surveillance System

Indicator	Cut-Off Value on NCHS Growth Charts	Interpretation
Low weight-for-age	< 5th percentile	Underweight
Low weight-for-height	< 5th percentile	Underweight (wasting, acute undernutrition)
Low height-for-age	< 5th percentile	Short stature (stunting, chronic undernutrition)

Source: US DHHS, PHS, Centers for Disease Control, Center for Health Promotion and Education, Division of Nutrition, *Pediatric Nutrition Surveillance Manual*, 1985.

Both percentiles and SD scores express the distribution of reference growth data around the 50th percentile. An SD score of 0.00 is equivalent to the 50th percentile; −1.65 SD corresponds to the 5th percentile cut-off used in the national Pediatric Nutrition Surveillance System.[13] A cut-off of −2.0 SD below the NCHS reference median weight-for-age, height-for-age, and weight-for-height is currently recommended by WHO[16,17] to discriminate between well and poorly nourished children. This cut-off corresponds to a percentile of 2.3 on reference growth charts. This cut-off can be used to compare domestic and international nutrition data, and it may be useful in assessing the nutritional status of immigrant and refugee groups in the United States.[11]

SEVERITY OF UNDERNUTRITION

The severity of undernutrition is commonly classified with percent of median indicators.[18,19] The Gomez[18] criteria express weights of individual children as a percentage of the 50th percentile weight-for-age of reference growth standards (see Table 13-2); the degree of underweight is categorized as mild, moderate, or severe (grades I, II, or III undernutrition). The Waterlow[19] criteria examine the relationship of weight to height or length to ascertain the degree of wasting, or acute undernutrition (see Table 13-3). Height or length-for-age is compared with reference standards to determine the severity of stunting, or chronic undernutrition.

The Gomez and Waterlow criteria can be used to categorize the severity of undernutrition if no computer software is available in the clinical setting. However, these criteria are age-biased and underestimate the prevalence and severity of undernutrition with increasing age.[20] SD scores for anthropometric measures are adjusted for age, and progressive decrements in SD score (−2.0, −3.0, −4.0) calculated from CDC/WHO computer software[15] should be used to describe the relative severity of undernutrition if possible.[14]

Table 13-2 Classification of Severity of Underweight

Grade of Malnutrition	Percent of Median Weight-for-Age
Normal	90–110
I. Mild	75–89
II. Moderate	60–74
III. Severe	<60

Source: Data from reference 18.

Table 13-3 Classification of Severity of Wasting and Stunting

Grade of Malnutrition	Percent of Median Weight-for-Height (Wasting)	Percent of Median Height-for-Age (Stunting)
Normal	90–110	95
I. Mild	80–89	90–94
II. Moderate	70–79	85–89
III. Severe	<70	<85

Source: Data from reference 19.

GROWTH FALTERING

Growth faltering may also be considered evidence of FTT. Faltering is defined in clinical practice as a decrease in weight-for-age of approximately two major centiles, or 2 SD, over a period of 3 months in infants and a 6-month period in preschool children aged 12 or more months.[20–22] SD scores are also used to measure the change in growth rate. When SD scores for an individual's measures are compared over time, a negative change in SD score indicates a slowing of growth rate. A positive difference in SD score indicates catch-up growth, compared to healthy children of the same age and sex. In the example in Table 13-4, the weight-for-age percentile of the child improved with nutritional rehabilitation, indicated by a positive change in SD score. At presentation the child was moderately to severely malnourished (SD = −3.3) but had reached the normal range at follow-up.

DIAGNOSTIC CATEGORIES OF UNDERNUTRITION

Diagnostic categories of undernutrition based on clinical assessment focus on the symptoms and etiology of undernutrition. The clinical manifestations of PEM

Table 13-4 SD Scores as Measures of Size and Catch-Up Growth

	Presentation	9 Months
Age in months	7.3	17.1
Weight in Kg	4.8	10.0
Percentile	0.05	28.5
SD score	−3.3	−0.6
SD difference		+2.7

Source: Adapted from Peterson KE, Rathbun JM, Herrera MG, Growth data analysis in FTT treatment and research, in *New Directions in Failure-to-Thrive: Implications for Research and Practice* (pp 157–178) by D Drotar (ed) with permission of Plenum Press, © 1985.

have been classified into two types,[19] marasmus and kwashiorkor. Marasmus results when energy alone is deficient. The dietary antecedents of kwashiorkor are not well understood, but a low ratio of protein intake relative to energy intake appears to contribute to cases reported in North America.[23] In a case series of 16 children admitted to an urban United States hospital for severe primary protein-calorie malnutrition, 15 children had marasmus and 1 child had marasmic kwashiorkor.[24]

Diagnostic categories of FTT are not related to the underlying energy or protein deficit but refer instead to the complex array of biologic and social factors associated with undernutrition in the United States. Thus FTT is not a syndrome distinct from "primary undernutrition," resulting from inadequate food intake. Growth delay is ultimately the result of inadequate nutrient availability relative to requirements, and diagnostic categories of FTT describe the etiologic factors that promote this imbalance. FTT is categorized as organic, nonorganic, or of mixed etiology.[2,25] Organic causes of FTT can be traced to prenatal influences (minor congenital anomalies, in utero toxin exposure, prematurity, intrauterine growth retardation) or to ongoing or recurring illness after the neonatal period.[2] Gastrointestinal or central nervous system disturbances comprise 80% of cases of organic origin.[4] In nonorganic FTT, inadequate nutrient intake or retention appears to be the outcome of individual temperament, difficult or impoverished feeding and nonfeeding interactions between the child and caregiver, and family poverty, stress, or loss.[2] Both organic and nonorganic factors contribute to FTT of mixed etiology,[25] and the organic disturbance itself may constitute a stress for the family.

The majority of FTT cases referred to tertiary care centers in the United States appear to be psychosocial in origin or due to mixed etiology.[2,25] Of 82 children hospitalized in a tertiary care facility for FTT, 28% were classified as exhibiting growth delay attributable to organic causes, 46% were classified as nonorganic FTT, and 26% were classified as mixed etiology FTT.[25] Among children referred to a network of outpatient growth and nutrition clinics, psychosocial or a mixed etiology was reported in over 93% of the children diagnosed with FTT.[26]

NUTRITIONAL MANAGEMENT OF FAILURE TO THRIVE

Nutrition services provided to children with FTT take place in the context of multidisciplinary, family-focused care that addresses the biologic and social risk factors and consequences of undernutrition.[2,26,27] The treatment team includes, in addition to the dietitian or trained nutritionist, a physician and/or a nurse practitioner, a social worker and/or a psychologist, specialty consultants, and practitioners in community agencies. Family members are key participants in the assessment of growth delay and in the design and implementation of treatment strategies. Within this multidisciplinary context, nutritional management of FTT includes three components:

1. anthropometric and dietary assessment
2. provision of energy and protein to meet catch-up growth requirements
3. concrete, individualized nutritional instruction

ASSESSMENT

Anthropometry

The NCHS growth charts[28] are the appropriate ones to use in the screening and diagnosis of children in the United States who are failing to thrive. The NCHS charts are also appropriate to assess the growth of children who are refugees or immigrants to the United States. Based on a review of 55 reference growth charts, the WHO Consultation on Growth Charts has recommended the use of the NCHS charts for assessment of child growth in both industrialized and developing countries.[29] The alternative use of reference growth data from developing countries may not yield an accurate assessment. For instance, their use to assess growth of refugee children is inappropriate, because these data may include measures of acutely or chronically malnourished children, or children who show evidence of intergenerational stunting.

Techniques for obtaining anthropometric measurements are described in Chapters 1 and 2. Anthropometric data should be collected regularly according to a protocol that is simultaneously appropriate for clinical and research purposes. Growth in the child with FTT is the final outcome measure for all treatments, so consistent and accurate technique is imperative. Personnel obtaining measures should be clearly designated and well trained. Anthropometric measures are obtained at presentation to the clinic or hospital, and thereafter according to the schedule in Table 13-5. Routine use of upper arm measurements may not be indicated unless mandated by specific clinical or research protocols. In malnourished children with edema, triceps skinfold and mid-arm muscle circumference provide a better index of nutritional status than weight-for-height, because the arm is relatively free of edema.[30]

Table 13-5 Anthropometric Assessment Guidelines

	Initial Visit	Hospitalization		Outpatient Visit
		Daily	Weekly	
Weight-for-age	X	X		X
Height-for-age	X		X	X
Weight-for-height	X		X	X
Head circumference	X		X	X

In the evaluation of FTT, the child's growth record over time must be examined. A single weight less than the 5th percentile is less informative than a deviation from a previously established growth channel. Some normal shifting of percentiles may occur, especially during the first 2 years of life.[31] In healthy reference children, a shift toward the 50th percentile is more likely than a shift away from the 50th percentile.[32] A weight decrement of more than two major centiles from a previously established growth channel over a period of 3 to 6 months should be considered evidence of growth failure.[33,34] In addition, the relationship of weight to height must be evaluated. A child with a weight:height ratio less than the 5th percentile may be wasted, or acutely malnourished. A drop in weight followed by a decrease in height percentiles indicates the child is passing from a state of acute to chronic malnutrition. Stunting is an adaptive physiologic phenomenon that preserves an adequate weight:height ratio at the expense of linear growth. Stunted growth may reflect micronutrient deficiencies, including zinc.[35] Short stature has also been reported in association with elevated lead levels.[36,37]

Some children are both underweight and short relative to reference standards (weight and height less than the 5th percentile) but have weight:height ratios within the normal range. These children may be genetically small, may have suffered a nutritional insult earlier in life that impaired potential for full catch-up growth, or may be proportionally stunted in the face of persistent undernutrition. In children consuming adequate diets and without a history of growth delay, constitutional growth deficit can be excluded by assessing midparental height (average height of both parents at any time between 25 and 45 years of age) using the Tanner-Whitehouse charts.[38] From ages 2 to 9, the child's height correlates well with the mean of parents' heights (average correlation coefficients are 0.53 for boys and 0.49 for girls).[38] Any child whose height falls more than 2.5 SD below that expected using the Tanner standards should be evaluated for FTT.[1]

Among certain groups in industrialized countries, use of midparental height to assess constitutional growth deficit may be inappropriate. The correlation of child and parental heights is based on the assumption that parents grew normally and realized their genetic potential.[39] Children of parents who suffered FTT as children, immigrants from less developed countries, and families who have been chronically impoverished may show evidence of intergenerational stunting. The secular trend in height among immigrants to industrialized countries and studies of children in developing countries suggests that differences in growth among well-nourished children of different ethnic groups are smaller than disparities noted between children of differing social classes.[40,41] With adequate nutrition and improvement of poor socioeconomic circumstances, children of families showing intergenerational growth deficits may exceed growth predicted by assessment of midparental height alone.

Premature and small-for-gestational-age (SGA) infants comprise a heterogeneous group of children who are small relative to reference standards at birth but who exhibit different patterns of growth in infancy and early childhood. Potential for catch-up growth in high-risk infants varies with birthweight,[42,43] degree of prematurity, severity of perinatal medical illness, and ponderal index classification, which reflects timing and duration of intrauterine growth retardation, as described in Chapter 3. Premature infants without serious medical problems and asymmetric SGA babies may show rapid catch-up growth in the first 6 to 9 months of life.[43–45] Nutritional rehabilitation should be targeted to support maximal growth rates during this period.[46] Symmetric SGA infants and more severely affected premature infants may not show catch-up growth but should be nutritionally supported so that their growth rates parallel reference curves.[46] (Guidelines for nutritional management of premature and SGA infants appear in Chapter 3.) After 24 months, catch-up growth in United States' children with low birth weights appears limited, and these children are likely to remain shorter and lighter throughout childhood.[42] A recent report of a multicenter longitudinal study of low-birth-weight infants suggests postnatal catch-up growth in the first year of life may be influenced by race/ethnicity and/or socioeconomic status. In a diverse sociodemographic cohort of 608 infants, growth curves paralleled those of term infants, but no catch-up growth was noted in the first 12 months,[47] in contrast with earlier reports of catch-up growth in white middle- and upper-class European infants.[48]

In growth monitoring of the premature infant during infancy and early childhood, the age at measurement should be corrected for the number of weeks the child was premature. Corrected age is postnatal age less the number of weeks the child was premature (the difference between 40 weeks and gestational age). The difference between growth percentiles for corrected and uncorrected postnatal age is statistically significant from 18 months to 3 years, depending on the growth parameter.[45] Severity of growth deficit in premature infants will be overestimated if uncorrected ages are used to analyze anthropometric data. Age at measurement should be corrected for prematurity to 18 months for head circumference, 24 months for weight, and 3.5 years for height.[45]

Dietary Assessment

A complete diet history is obtained on all children who meet anthropometric criteria for risk of FTT. The diet history follows general nutrition assessment guidelines described in Chapter 2, Exhibit 2-2. Careful attention should be paid to the child's feeding history, including breastfeeding and/or method of formula preparation, volume of formula/breast milk consumed, age at introduction and acceptance of solid foods, ability to feed independently (use of cup, fingers, cutlery), and identification of the primary caregiver in the feeding settings (parent, sibling, day care provider).[49] A 3- to 7-day dietary record may provide additional information about exact amounts and types of foods eaten, and variations in total intake of the child from day to day.

Observation of the family mealtime or feeding situation can identify behavior problems in the child and caregiver that may contribute to inadequate caloric intake. Assessment of the feeding capacities of the child includes noting the duration and pace of feeding preferred, ability to remain focused on feeding, and readiness for self-feeding. In the caregiver, observe the technical ability and ease in feeding and the flexibility of response to the child's needs. Areas of concern include the location of feedings; mealtime atmosphere (tension level, noise level); size and preparation of meal; positioning of breast or bottle; technical difficulties with sucking, swallowing, and burping; and control issues between child and caregiver.

After determining the caloric content of the diet, assess whether the intake of the child is adequate for growth. Recommended dietary allowances for energy and protein for healthy infants and children are detailed in Chapter 2. Requirements will vary somewhat for active, irritable, or infected infants as well as for infants with ongoing losses like vomiting and diarrhea. Children with organic or mixed etiology FTT associated with chronic diseases including cardiac impairment, cystic fibrosis, and malabsorption syndromes often have elevated caloric requirements. Adequacy of other nutrients, such as protein, calcium, iron, and zinc, should be evaluated. If the history reveals inadequate caloric intake and no history of vomiting, bulky stools, or increased metabolic rate, the assessment should pursue the cause of inadequate caloric intake. The dietary history may highlight feeding interactions and nutritional misperceptions that contribute to inadequate intake. However, if a careful nutritional history and feeding observations show adequate caloric intake, organic causes should be sought.

Assessment of Associated Risk Factors

The dietitian or trained nutritionist should review other team members' assessments of social and medical factors[2,27] in order to integrate this information into a nutrition treatment plan. Key characteristics documented in the medical record are listed in Table 13-6.

NUTRITIONAL REHABILITATION

Children with FTT who are severely malnourished may require management of dehydration with parenteral alimentation. However, most children can be fed orally, and gastrointestinal mucosal structure and function will improve more rapidly in children who are fed.[50]

Initial energy intakes in malnourished children should be low: 25 kcal/kg in infants and 50 kcal/kg in children.[50] Energy intake is advanced daily in 20 to 25 kcal/kg increments, as long as stool consistency is improving and wet stool weights are less than 150 g/d in younger infants and 200 g/d in older infants.[50] If

Table 13-6 Assessment of FTT: Review of Health and Social Factors Documented in Medical Record

Health History	Social History	Biochemical Data	Clinical Exam	Caregiver–Child Interaction
Individual: Gestational age Birth weight Illness Hospitalizations Medications *Family:* Mental illness Alcohol/drug abuse Genetic disorder Malabsorption or maldigestion Chronic or metabolic disorder Eating disorder	Multiple caregivers Support systems available to caregiver Maturity of caregiver Social environment (marital dissatisfaction, financial stress, disorganized lifestyle) History of abuse or neglect of child, sibling, or caregivers	Hematocrit (hct), hemoglobin (hb) Albumin/transferrin BUN or creatinine Lead (Pb), free erythrocyte protoporphyrin (FEP) Tuberculin test Alkaline phosphatase Stool for pH, reducing substances, ova and parasites	Nausea, vomiting, and/or chalasia Diarrhea, steatorrhea, or constipation Stool size, frequency, consistency, color, odor Acute or recurring illness or infections Clinical manifestations of malnutrition Rumination Signs of abuse or neglect	Evidence of bonding (richness of interaction, eye and physical contact, sense of mutual pleasure, warmth and affection, consistency of response) Caregiver's attentiveness to child's cues Appropriateness of caregiver's expectations Clarity of child's cues to caregiver

Note: BUN, blood urea nitrogen.
Source: Data from references 2 and 49.

stool output is excessive, energy intake should be reduced to the previous level for 1 to 2 days, then advanced slowly. Commercial formulas are recommended for initial therapy because nutrients are balanced and intake can be monitored.[50] Additional potassium up to 5 mEq/kg/d may be required for the first week of nutritional rehabilitation of kwashiorkor.[51] Zinc supplementation in the range of 1.6 to 9.8 mg/kg/d may improve weight gain without increasing energy intake.[52]

Once the child is stabilized, long-term catch-up growth in FTT depends on the provision of calories and protein in excess of normal requirements. Total energy needs may be 50% greater than normal.[53] Murray and Glassman note that many children with FTT will not gain weight unless intakes are in excess of 150 kcal/kg; they suggest that realimentation begin at that level and be adjusted upward to achieve a weight gain of 30 g/d in the infant and 60 to 90 g/d in the young child.[54] In developing countries malnourished children demonstrate catch-up growth on intakes ranging from 3.1 to 4.4 g/kg of protein and 150 to 240 kcal/kg.[53,55,56] Guidelines for estimating individual catch-up growth requirements are detailed in Table 13-7.

Table 13-7 Estimating Catch-Up Growth Requirements*

$$\text{Catch-up Growth Requirement (kcal/kg/day)} = \frac{\text{Calories Required for Weight Age (kcal/kg/day)} \times \text{Ideal Weight for Age (kg)}}{\text{Actual Weight (kg)}}$$

1. Plot the child's height and weight on the NCHS growth charts.
2. Determine at what age the present weight would be at the fiftieth percentile (weight age).
3. Determine recommended calories for weight age (see Chapter 2).
4. Determine the ideal weight (fiftieth percentile) for the child's present age.
5. Multiply the value obtained in (3) by the value obtained in (4).
6. Divide the value obtained in (5) by actual weight.

Estimated protein requirements during catch-up growth can be similarly calculated:

$$\text{Protein Requirement (g/kg/day)} = \frac{\text{Protein Required for Weight Age (g/kg/day)} \times \text{Ideal Weight for Age (kg)}}{\text{Actual weight (kg)}}$$

* Guidelines are used to estimate catch-up growth requirements; precise individual needs will vary and be mediated by medical status and diagnosis.
Source: Adapted with permission from Peterson K, Washington JS, and Rathbun J, Team management of failure-to-thrive, in *Journal of the American Dietetic Association* (1984;84:810–815), copyright © 1984, American Dietetic Association.

Table 13-8 Caloric Supplementation

Infants

Formula: Increase caloric density in 2 kcal/oz increments

20 kcal/oz	Normal dilution
24 kcal/oz	Increased concentration (13:8)
28–30 kcal/oz	Carbohydrate additive, vegetable oil, medium chain triglycerides

High calorie strained baby foods: Read labels to determine caloric content.
Plain meats, high meat dinners, sweet potatoes, peas, mixed vegetables, peaches, bananas, pudding are higher than other choices
Strained foods may be fortified with infant cereal, dry milk powder, carbohydrate additives, vegetable oil

Toddlers

Beverages: 25–30 kcal/oz: Increase in 5 kcal/oz steps.

Milk drinks	Dry milk or instant breakfast powder
Juices	Carbohydrate additives

Solid foods: Increase caloric density of foods preferred by the child.

Semisolids	Carbohydrate additives, vegetable oil
Entrees	Gravies, sauces, grated cheese, margarine
Snacks (crackers, bread)	Cream cheese, peanut butter

Source: Adapted from Rathbun JM and Peterson KE, Nutrition in failure-to-thrive, in *Pediatric Nutrition: Theory and Practice* (pp 627–643) by RJ Grand, JL Sutphen, and WH Dietz (eds), with permission of Butterworth Publishers, © 1987.

Increases in caloric density of the diet (Table 13-8) are often necessary to ensure adequate caloric intake without increases in volume; these should proceed gradually. For infants who are formula fed, the caloric density of formula can be increased slowly, in 2-kcal steps from 20 kcal/oz of standard formula up to 28 to 30 kcal/oz. Caloric density may be increased up to 24 kcal/oz by concentrating formula using the dilution of one 13-oz can of concentrate and 8 oz of water. This concentration is well tolerated and often sufficient to promote the required catch-up growth. The caloric density should not be increased by concentration over 24 kcal/oz because high osmolality and renal solute load can lead to dehydration, diarrhea, and loss of nutrients in young infants. Other additives can be used to increase caloric density over 24 kcal/oz, in 2-kcal steps, to a maximum of 28 to 30 kcal/oz. These include rice cereal, vegetable oil, and a carbohydrate additive. The proportion of calories from carbohydrate, protein, and fat should remain within recommended guidelines. Each change to increase the caloric density should be monitored over a 2- to 3-day period for weight gain, as well as signs of intolerance such as vomiting or diarrhea. If the increase is not tolerated, go back to the previous step for 2 to 3 more days.

The caloric density of baby foods can be enhanced by choosing foods high in calories and by judicious but regular addition of infant cereal, vegetable oil, or a carbohydrate additive to baby foods.

For the toddler, the caloric density of milk can be increased by concentration, provided the child's current intake does not exceed the recommended number of portions for age. By adding 2 T nonfat dry milk to 8 oz whole milk, the caloric density can be increased to 24 kcal/oz, but not beyond that point. A carbohydrate additive can also be combined with juices in a stepwise fashion to increase calories to 28 to 30 kcal/oz. Frappes may be prepared for older children with whole milk combined with powdered milk and flavoring or instant breakfast. An excessive intake of juices or other liquids should be avoided as this may compromise solid food intake.

To increase the caloric density of solids fed to toddlers, offer small frequent feeding of foods preferred by the child. Add something extra—cheese, peanut butter, or other ingredients including cereal, vegetable oil, or carbohydrate additives. One to 2 weeks of refeeding may be required to demonstrate initial weight gain. Efforts to promote catch-up growth should be sustained until the child regains previous growth percentiles. Parents must be educated regarding the catch-up growth process and long-term growth goals. The baseline appearance of a cachectic child may bias the family's perception of recovery. The misperception that the recovering child is too plump may result in an abrupt diet change and abandonment of high-calorie feedings. Once the child has attained an appropriate weight:height ratio, growth velocity will decelerate to normal rates for age and intake will usually decrease voluntarily to recommended energy intakes for age.[49]

Maladaptive feeding practices are often observed in children with FTT. Improper preparation of formula may decrease total caloric intake. Excessive intake of juices and soft drinks can dampen appetite and promote overall deficits in calories, protein, and calcium. In some instances, sweets have been offered in excessive amounts in hopes of providing the child with "fattening" foods. Families whose child has FTT benefit from concrete feeding guidelines that describe how to prepare foods and offer them to the child. The child who constantly drinks or eats between meals may be able to increase overall energy intake by taking only three to four regular, nutritious snacks of high-calorie, high-protein foods each day. Explicit limits may allow the process of interminable feeding in some of these families to stop, making way for play and enjoyment for parents and child in the nonfeeding situation. In this effort, however, clinical emphasis must always be on appropriate provision of nutrients, as well as on limit setting. Long-term nutritional follow-up is imperative to provide the opportunity to reinforce nutritional instructions and to reassess and adapt meal plans to meet the growing child's changing nutritional needs.

Concrete nutritional instructions may be more effective when accompanied by techniques for behavior change. Concrete interventions may include decreasing distractions in the feeding environment of a hypersensitive infant, introducing finger foods to the toddler in control struggles over "being fed," using a behavior modification program to decrease rumination, or encouraging positive feeding behaviors through use of rewards (e.g., hugs, congratulations). In the older child who refuses food, a prescription for specific times and durations of meals and snacks may be indicated. These children often need to learn the importance of eating when they are hungry and stopping when they are full.[57] Such behavior guidelines also alter the interaction of the child and caregiver during feeding. Feeding is the historic battleground in the home with FTT. To the extent that this can be converted to a place of business, that of eating, the family may experience relief.

Community-based management of growth delay must be coordinated, interdisciplinary, and family focused. Nutrition assessment and treatment plans should be reviewed with the primary physician and integrated with treatment plans of other team members. Written permission for concentration and use of special additives in infant formula should be obtained from the child's primary physician. Community-based referrals mirror the multidisciplinary case management of growth delay and include the Special Supplemental Food Program for Women, Infants, and Children (WIC) and food assistance programs, liaisons with public health nurses who can reinforce nutrition care plans in the home, and appropriate referrals to address psychosocial and developmental risk factors associated with growth delay in early childhood.

PROGNOSIS

Studies of sequelae of early FTT highlight significant long-term physical, cognitive, and behavioral morbidity in the absence of treatment. In uncontrolled studies, one fifth to one third of children hospitalized for FTT had weights less than the 3rd to 10th percentile. In Elmer's investigation, which controlled the analysis for midparental height, 60% of children were at less than the 3rd percentile for both height and weight on follow-up.[58] Only 5 of 15 children were within 1 cm of height predicted by midparental height. In Chase and Martin's controlled study, 68% of heights, 53% of weights, and 37% of head circumferences fell below the third percentile in cases studied $3^1/_2$ years after hospitalization for FTT.[59] In the rural outpatient setting, weights and head circumferences but not heights of female subjects described by Mitchell were significantly lower at follow-up compared with female controls.[6] Mean measures of boys did not differ significantly from controls at follow-up.

However, children who received intensive treatment for FTT of varying etiologies have demonstrated catch-up growth during the treatment. Rapid catch-up growth was documented for 55 of 57 children hospitalized with caloric-deprivation FTT,[24,60] suggesting that the effectiveness of treatment during hospitalization was related to nutritional rehabilitation. Catch-up growth also may depend on the severity of undernutrition and on the number and severity of documented medical and social factors and how effectively they can be treated. Normalization of growth has been reported in cases of organic FTT if diseases were amenable to treatment.[61] Catch-up growth in nonorganic FTT appears to be greatest among children who receive intensive psychologic and/or social intervention.[61,62] Among 1,286 children diagnosed with FTT followed in specialty outpatient clinics, catch-up growth was not differentially associated with diagnostic categories or with individual social risk factors.[26] However, the multidisciplinary treatment provided in these clinics addressed both medical and social factors, so that catch-up growth may have been demonstrated regardless of diagnosis. Catch-up growth at 4 and 12 months of treatment was associated with age, gestational age, and initial nutritional status.[26]

RESEARCH PRIORITIES

Research priorities in FTT include documentation of nutrient intake, feeding history, and behaviors of children with FTT, compared with healthy controls, since the few studies[63] that document these factors are small cross-sectional or case series studies.

The epidemiology of FTT in the United States requires investigation in case control or longitudinal multivariate studies that measure the relative contribution and interaction of biologic and social factors to growth delay.[11] Similarly, the functional consequences of undernutrition in the United States should be documented and related to appropriate nutritional indicators and cut-offs.[11]

Patterns of catch-up growth during nutritional rehabilitation require more research, including the role of risk factors as well as effectiveness of different clinic and community-based interventions. Operational research is also needed on multidisciplinary models to treat children with FTT within the context of community-based, family-centered care provided under Public Law 99-457 to children with special health care needs.

REFERENCES

1. Bithoney W, Rathbun J. Failure to thrive. In: Levine MD, Carey WB, Crocker AC, Rathbun J, eds. *Developmental Behavioral Pediatrics*. Philadelphia, Pa: WB Saunders Co; 1983.

2. Rathbun JM, Peterson KE. Nutrition in failure-to-thrive. In: Grand RJ, Sutphen JL, Dietz WH, eds. *Pediatric Nutrition: Theory and Practice*. Boston, Mass: Butterworth Publishers; 1987:627–643.

3. Frank DA, Ziesel SH. Failure-to-thrive. *Pediatr Clin North Am*. 1988;35:1187–1206.

4. Berwick D. Nonorganic failure to thrive. *Pediatr Rev.* 1980;1:265.

5. English P. Failure to thrive without organic reason. *Pediatr Ann.* 1978;7:774.

6. Mitchell WG, Gorrell RW, Greenberg RA. Failure-to-thrive: a study in a primary care setting: epidemiology and follow-up. *Pediatrics.* 1980;65:971–976.

7. Massachusetts Department of Public Health Office of Nutrition. *Nutrition Counts.* Boston, Mass: Massachusetts Department of Public Health; 1990.

8. Dietz WH. Undernutrition of children in Massachusetts. *J Nutr.* 1990;120:948–954.

9. Guyer B, Wehler CA, Anderka MT, et al. Anthropometric evidence of malnutrition among low-income children in Massachusetts in 1983. *Mass J Commun Health.* 1986;2(2):3-9.

10. Wilcox WD, Nieburg P, Miller DS. Failure to thrive: a continuing problem of definition. *Clin Pediatr.* 1989;28:391–394.

11. Peterson KE, Chen LC. Defining undernutrition for public health purposes in the United States. *J Nutr.* 1990;120:933–942.

12. Habicht JP, Pelletier DL. The importance of context in choosing nutritional indicators. *J Nutr.* 1990;120:1519–1524.

13. Center for Health Promotion and Education, Division of Nutrition. *Pediatric Nutrition Surveillance Manual.* Atlanta; Ga: Centers for Disease Control, 1985:42.

14. Waterlow JC, Buzina R, Keller W, Lane JM, Nichaman MZ, Tanner JM. The presentation and use of height and weight data for comparing the nutritional status of groups of children under the age of ten years. *Bull WHO.* 1977;55:486–498.

15. Dean AG, Dean JA, Burton AH, Dicker RC. Epi Info, V.5: a word processing, database, and statistics program for epidemiology on microcomputers. Stone Mountain, Ga: USD, Inc;1990.

16. Gueri M, Gurney JM, Jutsum P. The Gomex classification, time for a change? *Bull WHO.* 1980;58:773–777.

17. WHO Working Group. Use and interpretation of anthropometric indicators of nutritional status. *Bull WHO.* 1986;64:929–941.

18. Gomez F, Galvan R, Frenk S, Munoz JC, Chavez R, Vasquez J. Mortality in second and third degree malnutrition. *J Trop Pediatr.* 1956;2:77.

19. Waterlow J. Classification and definition of protein calorie malnutrition. In: Beaton G, Bengoa, eds. *Nutrition in Preventative Medicine.* Geneva: World Health Organization; 1976. WHO Monograph Series No. 62.

20. Peterson KE, Rathbun JM, Herrera MG. Growth data analysis in FTT treatment and research. In: Drotar D, ed. *New Directions in Failure-to-Thrive: Implications for Research and Practice.* New York: Plenum Press; 1985:157–178.

21. Kristiansson B, Karlberg J, Fallstrom SP. Infants with low rate of weight gain. I. A study of organic factors and growth patterns. *Acta Paediatr Scand.* 1981;70:655–662.

22. Massachusetts Department of Public Health, Massachusetts Application, PL 99-457, Part H, Early Intervention, U.S. Department of Education; Boston, Mass: Massachusetts Department of Public Health; 1991.

23. Roussouw JE. Kwashiorkor in North America. *Am J Clin Nutr.* 1989;49:588–592.

24. Listernick R, Cristoffel K, Pace J, Chiaramonte J. Severe primary malnutrition in U.S. children. *Am J Dis Child.* 1985;138:1157–1160.

25. Homer C, Ludwig S. Categorization of etiology of failure to thrive. *Am J Dis Child.* 1981;135:848–851.

26. Massachusetts Department of Public Health. *Catching Up: Report of the Massachusetts Growth and Nutrition Clinics, FY 1985-1989.* Boston, Mass: Massachusetts Department of Public Health; 1991.

27. Peterson KE, Washington JS, Rathbun JM. Team management of failure to thrive. *J Am Diet Assoc.* 1984;84:810.

28. Hamill PVV, Drizd TA, Johnson CL, Reed RB, Roche AF. 1976 NCHS growth charts. Monthly vital statistics report 25, no. 3 (suppl) DHEW publication no. (HRA) 76; Washington, DC: U.S. Department of Health and Human Services; 1976.

29. World Health Organization. A growth chart for use in maternal and child health care. Geneva: World Health Organization; 1978.

30. Blackburn GL, Thornton PA. Nutritional assessment of the hospitalized patient. *Med Clin North Am.* 1979;63:1103–1115.

31. Smith DW, Truog W, Rogers JE, Greitzer LF, McCann JJ, Harvey MAS. Shifting linear growth during infancy: illustrations of genetic factors in growth from fetal life through infancy. *J Pediatr.* 1976;89:225–230.

32. Berkey CS, Reed RB, Valadian I. Longitudinal growth standards for preschool children. *Ann Hum Biol.* 1983;10:57–67.

33. Fomon SJ. Normal growth, failure to thrive and obesity. In: *Infant Nutrition.* Philadelphia, Pa: WB Saunders; 1974.

34. Karlberg P, Engstrom I, Karlberg J, Kristiansson B. Evaluation of growth during the first two years of life. In: Kristiansson B, ed. *Low Rate of Weight Gain in Infancy and Early Childhood.* Goteborg, Sweden: Department of Paediatrics, University of Goteborg; 1980.

35. Walravens PA, Krebs NF, Hambidge KM. Linear growth of low income preschool children receiving a zinc supplement. *Am J Clin Nutr.* 1983;38:195–201.

36. Bithoney WG. Elevated lead levels in children with nonorganic failure to thrive. *Pediatrics.* 1986;78:5.

37. Schwartz J, Angle C, Pitcher H. Relationship between childhood blood lead levels and stature. *Pediatrics.* 1986;77:281–288.

38. Tanner JM, Goldstein H, Whitehouse RH. Standards for children's height at ages 2–9 years allowing for height of parents. *Arch Dis Child.* 1970;45:755–762.

39. Tanner JM. Catchup growth in man. *Br Med Bull.* 1981;37:233–238.

40. Habicht JF, Martorell R, Yarbrough C, Malina RM, Klein RE. Height and weight standards for preschool children: are there really ethnic differences in growth potential? *Lancet.* 1974;1:611–614.

41. Martorell R. Child growth retardation: a discussion of its causes and its relationship to health. In: Blaxter K, Waterlow JC, eds. London: John Libbey; 1985.

42. Binkin NJ, Yip R, Fleshood L, Trowbridge FL. Birth weight and childhood growth. *Pediatrics.* 1988;82:828–834.

43. Fitzhardinge PM, Inwood S. Long-term growth in small-for-date children. *Acta Paediatr Scand* 1989 *[suppl].*;349:27–33.

44. Villar J, Smeriglio V, Martorell R, et al. Heterogenous growth and mental development of intrauterine growth-retarded infants during the first 3 years of life. *Pediatrics.* 1984;74:783–791.

45. Altigani M, Murphy JF, Newcombe RG, Gray OP. Catchup growth in preterm infants. *Acta Paediatr Scand.* 1989 (suppl); 357:3–19.

46. Peterson KE, Frank DA. Feeding and growth of premature and small-for-gestational-age infants. In: Taeusch HW, Yogman MW, eds. *Follow-Up Management of the High-Risk Infant.* Boston, MA: Little, Brown & Co; 1987.

47. Casey PH, Kraemer HC, Bernbaum J, et al. Growth patterns of low birth weight preterm infants: a longitudinal analysis of a large, varied sample. *J Pediatr.* 1990;117:298–307.

48. Brandt I. Growth dynamics of low-birth-weight infants with emphasis on the perinatal period. In: Falkner F, Tanner JM, eds. *Human Growth.* 2nd ed. Vol 1. *A Comprehensive Treatise.* New York, NY: Plenum Press; 1986:415–475.

49. The Quality Assurance Committee, Dietitians in Pediatric Practice and Woolridge NH, ed. *Quality Assurance Criteria for Pediatric Nutrition Conditions: A Model.* Chicago, IL: The American Dietetic Association; 1988.

50. McLean WC. Protein-energy malnutrition. In: Grand RJ, Sutphen JL, Dietz WH, eds. *Pediatric Nutrition: Theory and Practice.* Boston, MA: Butterworth Publishers; 1987:421–431.

51. MacLean WC, Lopez de Romano G, Massa E, et al. Nutritional management of chronic diarrhea and malnutrition: primary reliance on oral feeding. *J Pediatr.* 1980;97:316–323.

52. Golden MHN, Golden BE. Effects of zinc supplementation on the dietary intake, rate of weight gain, and energy cost of tissue deposition in children recovering from severe malnutrition. *Am J Clin Nutr.* 1981;34:900–908.

53. Whitehead RG. Protein and energy requirements of young children living in developing countries to allow catchup growth after infections. *Am J Clin Nutr.* 1977;30:1545.

54. Murray C, Glassman M. Nutrient requirements during growth and recovery from failure to thrive. In: Accardo PJ, ed. *Failure to Thrive in Infancy and Early Childhood.* Baltimore, Md: University Park Press; 1981.

55. Ashworth A, Feacham RG. Interventions for the control of diarrheal disease among young children: prevention of low birth weight. *Bull WHO.* 1985;63:165–184.

56. Kerr D, Ashworth A, Picou D, et al. Accelerated recovery from infant malnutrition with high calorie feeding. In: Gardner LI, Amacher P, eds. *Endocrine Aspects of Malnutrition.* Santa Ynez, Calif: The Kroc Foundation; 1973.

57. Chatoor I, Egan J. Nonorganic failure to thrive and dwarfism due to food refusal: a separation disorder. *J Am Acad Child Psychiatry.* 1983;22:294.

58. Elmer E, Gregg GS, Ellison P. Late results of failure to thrive. *Clin Pediatrics.* 1968;8(10):584–588.

59. Chase HP, Martin HP. Undernutrition and child development. *N Engl J Med.* 1970;282:933.

60. Ellerstein NS, Ostrov BE. Growth patterns in children hospitalized because of caloric-deprivation failure to thrive. *Am J Dis Child.* 1985;139:164–166.

61. Kristiansson B, Fallstrom SP. Growth at the age of 4 years subsequent to early failure to thrive. *Child Abuse Neglect.* 1987;11:35–40.

62. Bithoney WG, McJunkin J, Michalek J, Egan H, Snyder J, Munier A. Prospective evaluation of weight gain in both nonorganic and organic failure-to-thrive children: an outpatient trial of a multidisciplinary team intervention strategy. *Dev Behav Pediatr.* 1989;10:27–31.

63. Pollitt E. Failure to thrive: socioeconomic, dietary intake and mother–child interaction data. *Fed Proc.* 1975;34:1593–1597.

Chapter 14

Pediatric Acquired Immunodeficiency Syndrome

Linda M. Gallagher, Sylvia Evans, and Mary E. Smaha

The first cases of pediatric acquired immunodeficiency syndrome (AIDS) were reported in 1982, and since that time over 3471 cases in children under the age of 13 years have been reported to the Centers for Disease Control (CDC).[1]

Although pediatric cases account for only 1.7% of total reported cases of AIDS, 782 new pediatric diagnoses of AIDS were reported to the CDC in 1990, and 342 new cases were diagnosed in 1991.[1] The prognosis for symptomatic children with AIDS is poor, with a median life expectancy of only 2 years after diagnosis.[2,3] As of December 1991, 1850 children or 53% of those reported to the CDC had died.[1]

The medical, nutritional, and social implications of AIDS are numerous, and management requires an approach that is both coordinated and comprehensive. This chapter will provide a brief overview of pediatric AIDS and discuss the goals and strategies of its nutritional management.

AIDS is caused by the human immunodeficiency virus-1 (HIV-1), a type of retrovirus. The HIV enters the cell and after replication induces cell dysfunction or death. Cells of the immune system are the most commonly affected.

The immune system is comprised of lymphocytes and other white blood cells. Lymphocytes can be divided into the B cells, which are responsible for humoral immunity (via immunoglobulin production), and the T cells, which are necessary for cell-mediated immunity. The T cells can be further classified as either helper (CD4) or suppressor T cells (CD8). The helper T cell enhances the operation of the entire immune system, whereas the suppressor T cell shuts down the immune response after the foreign antigens have been destroyed. In healthy individuals there are twice as many helper T cells as suppressor T cells. AIDS patients commonly have a significant reversal of the helper:suppressor ratio.[4]

HIV preferentially infects the helper T cells. When stimulated by a foreign antigen, the infected lymphocyte will reproduce the virus instead of itself, and this new virus subsequently infects other helper T cells, essentially becoming a part of every cell it infects.

DEFINITIONS FOR AIDS SURVEILLANCE OF CHILDREN

The term "AIDS" is employed by the CDC to refer to those individuals who typically display specific "indicator" diseases as a result of HIV infection.[5] AIDS-related complex (ARC) has often been used to refer to symptomatic children whose manifestations do not meet the CDC definition for AIDS. However, because confusion can easily occur as to whether a child has AIDS or ARC, the more appropriate term, HIV infection, should be used to cover the entire spectrum from healthy to very ill child.[5]

As indicated by Table 14-1, the current CDC definition is a complex one, with criteria dependent on the results of the laboratory tests and medical findings.[6] Because maternal antibody is easily transmitted across the placenta, children less than 15 months of age must have additional clinical evidence in order to be considered truly infected. Only those patients who meet the strict diagnostic criteria are classified as having AIDS. The number of children with seropositive HIV infection who are at a high risk of developing AIDS is probably two to three times the number of AIDS cases actually reported to the CDC.[7]

DIAGNOSIS

Identifying HIV infection in children can be difficult since there is a lack of widely available specific diagnostic methods for this age group. In infants and young children a positive antibody titer may be a nonconclusive diagnostic tool since an infected mother almost always passes HIV antibody to her infant and it can take as long as 15 months for a noninfected child to actually become seronegative.[5]

Several assays have been developed to detect a viral structural protein of the HIV. The enzyme-linked immunosorbent assay (ELISA) is a test particularly useful in the screening of blood products. Although highly sensitive, positive results should be further evaluated, typically by repeating the ELISA and then performing a more specific test such as the Western blot. In the Western blot, serum reacts with the viral antigens, allowing evaluation of the banding pattern of antibody to specific viral proteins.[5]

The HIV culture method is useful only in those children who display detectable antigen in their serum.[5] This assay is becoming a readily available method for early diagnosis. Other available methods for detecting antibody are through immunofluorescence assay and radioimmunoassay. These IgG-specific assays detect antibodies to the major viral envelope proteins (gp160, gp120, gp41), core proteins (p24, p17), or reverse transcriptase (gp51).[8]

The polymerase chain reaction (PCR), a gene amplification technique, is another HIV diagnostic tool for documenting HIV infection. Relatively small amounts of nonreplicating virus can be detected with PCR.[8] This method provides

Table 14-1 Surveillance Case Definition in AIDS

I. Without laboratory evidence of HIV infection (tests not done or inconclusive), a patient with AIDS:

   A. *Does not have another cause of immunodeficiency*

and

   B. *Has had one of the following AIDS indicator diseases definitively diagnosed:*
      1. Candidiasis of the esophagus, trachea, bronchi, or lungs
      2. Extrapulmonary cryptococcosis
      3. Cryptosporidiosis with diarrhea >1 month
      4. Cytomegalovirus disease of an organ other than liver, spleen, lymph nodes in patient >1 month of age
      5. Herpes Simplex Virus infection causing a mucocutaneous ulcer persisting >1 month or bronchitis, pneumonitis, or esophagitis in a patient >1 month of age
      6. Primary lymphoma of the brain in a patient <60 years of age
      7. Kaposi sarcoma in a patient <60 years of age
      8. Lymphoid interstitial pneumonia and/or pulmonary lymphoid hyperplasia in a child <13 years of age
      9. *Mycobacterium avium* complex or *M. kansasii* disease disseminated to site other than lungs, skin, or cervical or hilar lymph nodes
     10. *Pneumocystis carinii* pneumonia
     11. Progressive multifocal leukoencephalopathy
     12. Toxoplasmosis of the brain in a patient >1 month of age

II. With laboratory evidence of HIV infection, a patient with AIDS:

   A. *Has had one of the already-listed AIDS indicator diseases definitively diagnosed or one of the following AIDS indicator diseases definitively diagnosed:*
      1. Multiple or recurrent bacterial infections (at least two within 2 years) in a child <13 years of age
      2. Coccidioidomycosis disseminated to a site other than lungs or cervical or hilar lymph nodes
      3. HIV encephalopathy
      4. Histoplasmosis disseminated to a site other than lung or cervical or hilar lymph nodes
      5. Isosporiasis with diarrhea >1 month duration
      6. Kaposi sarcoma
      7. Primary lymphoma of brain
      8. Other non-Hodgkin lymphoma of B-cell or unknown immunologic phenotype
      9. Disseminated nontubercular mycobacterial disease involving a site other than lungs, skin, or cervical or hilar lymph nodes
     10. Tuberculosis involving at least one site other than lungs
     11. Recurrent nontyphoid *Salmonella* bacteremia
     12. HIV wasting syndrome

or

   B. *One of the following AIDs indicator diseases diagnosed presumptively:*
      1. Esophageal candidiasis
      2. Cytomegalovirus retinitis with loss of vision
      3. Kaposi sarcoma
      4. Lymphoid interstitial pneumonia or pulmonary hyperplasia in a child <13 years of age

    5. Acid-fast infection disseminated to a site other than lungs, skin, or cervical or hilar
       lymph nodes
    6. *Pneumocystis carinii* pneumonia
    7. Toxoplasmosis of the brain in a patient >1 month of age

III. With laboratory evidence against HIV infection (negative test results), a patient with AIDS:

    A. *Does not have another cause of underlying immunodeficiency (listed in section I, above)*

and

    B. *Has had Pneumocystis carinii pneumonia definitively diagnosed*

or

    Has had definitive diagnosis of one of the AIDS indicator diseases listed in section I, above, *plus* a T-helper lymphocyte count <400/mm

Source: Centers for Disease Control, *MMWR* (1987;36:1S–15S).

---

direct evidence of HIV infection as opposed to serologic testing, which is dependent on the response by the host to the virus. The PCR is a promising new method but is not yet widely available.

EPIDEMIOLOGY

The racial distribution of pediatric AIDS in the United States is 52% black, 26% Hispanic, and 22% white.[1] Approximately 80% of all cases are acquired perinatally.[9] The exact mechanism for perinatal transfer is unclear, but it appears that the virus can be acquired in utero from maternal blood during delivery, and from breast milk.[4,9–11] The majority of all HIV-infected mothers are themselves asymptomatic at the time of delivery.[12] Approximately one third of women with HIV infection will give birth to offspring who will become AIDS victims.[13]

Blood transfusions represent 9% of childhood-acquired AIDS.[1] Five percent of pediatric AIDS cases can be linked to blood products received as treatment for coagulation disorders.[1] Approximately 40% to 80% of hemophiliacs who received clotting factor prior to 1985 are positive for HIV.[14–16]

Table 14-2 compares the risk factors for AIDS. Fifty percent of pediatric AIDS cases are diagnosed during the first year of life, and 82% by age 3.[17] Symptoms typically present between the ages of 4 and 6 months in those children diagnosed by age 1.[5] The incubation period of HIV infection is shorter in children than in adults, and the laboratory manifestations and spectrum of illness are also different. For all individuals infected with HIV, however, the disease course is ultimately plagued by progressive immunologic dysfunction and clinical deterioration.

Table 14-2 Risk Factors in Pediatric AIDS

	Infants and Children Less than 13 Years (%)
Parent with AIDS; mother in high-risk group	85
Blood product recipient (1979–1985)	8
Hemophiliac/coagulation disorder	5
Undetermined risk factor	2

Source: Adapted from US DHHS, Centers for Disease Control, Division of HIV/AIDS, HIV/AIDS Surveillance, 1992.

CLINICAL MANIFESTATIONS

There is a wide array of clinical features (Table 14-3) in the HIV-infected child, ranging from those with no symptoms to those with severe illness. At least half of children with documented AIDS present with a combination of symptoms that include lymphadenopathy, hepatosplenomegaly, failure to thrive, and bacterial infections.[5] Serious bacterial infections such as sepsis, pneumonia, meningitis, and cellulitis are a recurrent problem in the HIV-infected child.

Opportunistic infections are diseases that only occur when the immune system is compromised or destroyed, at which time such pathogens have the opportunity to cause disease.[3] The most common opportunistic infection associated with pediatric AIDS, *Pneumocystis* pneumonia, has occurred in 52% of pediatric cases reported to the CDC.[5] Children who develop *Pneumocystis carinii* infection generally display AIDS symptomatology at an earlier age and have a shorter median life

Table 14-3 Common Clinical Symptoms in Pediatric AIDS

Infections
  Opportunistic
  Bacterial
  Viral
Failure to thrive
Diarrhea
Hepatosplenomegaly
Lymphadenopathy
Chronic interstitial pneumonitis
Central nervous system abnormalities (e.g., HIV encephalopathy)
Oral esophageal ulcers
Laboratory abnormalities: hypergammaglobulinemia, abnormal T cell function

expectancy than children with other types of opportunistic infections such as *Candida* esophagitis, cytomegalovirus, and cryptosporidiosis.[5]

Lymphocytic interstitial pneumonitis (LIP) is commonly associated with pediatric AIDS, infecting approximately one half of all such patients. This disease induces inflammatory changes in lung tissue and leads to restrictive airway disease with resultant hypoxemia and low carbon dioxide diffusion. The prognosis for children with LIP is generally better than that of children with opportunistic infections (median survival of 91 months in LIP versus 14 months in *Pneumocystis carinii* infection).[5]

Blood abnormalities are common in children infected by HIV. Thrombocytopenia, anemia, immune leukopenia, and neutropenia have been reported.[5] Neurologic dysfunction may also occur in infected children. It may present as a progressive encephalopathy characterized by cognitive or motor regression or ataxia, weakness, or impaired brain growth. A direct invasion of the brain by the HIV is postulated since the HIV antigen has been isolated from cerebrospinal fluid.[5]

CONTROL OF INFECTIONS

Infants and children infected with HIV infection are hospitalized an average of two to three times per year at an annual cost per child of $50,000.[2]

Aggressive management of recurrent infections is important in order to deter severe illness. Some centers use prophylactic antibiotics to ward off potential infections, but this carries a risk of side effects and the emergence of resistant bacterial strains.

Because of a poorly functioning immune system with an inability to produce effective antibodies, the HIV-infected child is sensitive to many life-threatening infections. Children with significant defects in B cell function may benefit from intravenous immunoglobulin (IVIG) therapy in an attempt to decrease the incidence of bacterial infections. Such infusions, generally given in 2- to 4-week intervals, will not reverse the humoral immunity defect but will provide a supply of functioning antibody. The yearly cost of IVIG is approximately $30,000 per child, and clinical trials are in progress to assess the effect of such antibody infusions.[17]

The ideal goal in treating the HIV-infected child is to inhibit retrovirus replication and prevent immune system dysfunction. Zidovudine (formerly known as azidothymidine [AZT]) is the most common antiviral agent currently in use in AIDS management. It is thought to inhibit reverse transcriptase and/or terminate the chain after incorporation into the viral DNA.[5] Although shown effective, it can be quite toxic, inducing such symptoms as severe anemia, central nervous system disturbance, macrocytosis, and nausea.[18] The HIV antigen has been shown to decrease during AZT therapy, but it returns after treatment is stopped. It is currently considered a lifelong treatment. Studies thus far indicate that AZT-treated patients have a 6% mortality rate after 36 weeks of therapy and a 10% rate after 1 year.[5]

Another antiretroviral agent, dideoxycytidine (ddC), is undergoing trials as a single agent and in combination with AZT. The hope is that a regimen that reduces the myelosuppression associated with AZT while maximizing antiretroviral treatment can be produced.[5] Other promising therapeutic agents include dideoxyinosine (ddI) and soluble CD4 antigen, both of which are under investigation.

Efforts to develop a vaccine against HIV are complicated by the numerous subtypes of the virus and the uncertain role that antibodies and cell-mediated immunity play in the defense against HIV.

NUTRITIONAL IMPLICATIONS

The provision of adequate nutrition is an extremely important aspect in the care of the child who is HIV positive or has AIDS. Although there is little research published on the role of nutrition in improving patients' prognosis, it can be inferred that suboptimal nutrition in already immunosuppressed children will only further decrease their resistance to infections. It is well known that severe malnutrition has a deleterious effect on immune function. Impaired cellular immunity can be expected in the face of protein-calorie malnutrition.[19] Also, deficiencies of vitamins (e.g., pyridoxine, folate, and vitamins A, C, and E) or minerals (e.g., zinc, iron, copper, selenium) can result in specific abnormalities in immune function.[20] As is frequently observed in other chronic disease states, the cachexia associated with AIDS is often severe and debilitating. Significant failure to thrive is a very common clinical manifestation, and its impact in the clinical progression of AIDS is not well defined.

The nutritional status of children with AIDS is challenged throughout the disease course by a myriad of unanticipated developments, such as neurologic deterioration, malabsorption, and systemic infection. It appears that HIV infection does not affect birth weight,[13,21] but events after birth result in poor growth in symptomatic HIV-infected children.[21] Wasting may occur at any time during the course of the disease, and many factors have been implicated in the pathogenesis of weight loss and body composition changes associated with AIDS. Anorexia has been observed in the context of systemic infection, anxiety, depression, or secondary to drug therapy. Impaired food intake has occurred in patients with severe oral candidiasis (the most common fungal infection in children), dysphagia, odynophagia (fear of pain), or diarrhea and viral esophagitis from disseminated cytomegalovirus (CMV) or herpes simplex virus (HSV). Both adults and children have demonstrated intestinal dysfunction. Carbohydrate and fat malabsorption and increased bile salt deconjugation, which may contribute to malabsorption of long-chain fatty acids secondary to bile salt depletion, have been documented.[22–25]

A hypermetabolic resting energy expenditure (REE) >110% of estimated basal energy expenditure (EBEE) has been noted in stable, malnourished HIV-infected adults with a previous history of wasting and with infections such as *Mycobacterium avium-intracellulare* (MAI) and/or *Pneumocystis carinii* pneumonia (PCP).[26] Yet a compensatory hypometabolism—i.e., starvation-type response—has been noted in clinically stable AIDS patients in the absence of severe wasting, presumably representing a normal metabolic response to a relative energy deficit with clinical or subclinical malabsorption.[27,28] Finally, body composition studies in adult malnourished AIDS patients have demonstrated a relative increase in protein catabolism over fat catabolism, consistent with metabolic changes due to stress (sepsis, surgery, trauma). Kotler et al. have noted a clinical picture including progressive depletion in body potassium and body cell mass, increased extracellular water, and wide ranges in body fat content, a response that mimics that seen in other chronic debilitating illnesses.[29] Clearly, malnutrition in adults and children with AIDS is common and multifactorial; understanding the "wasting syndrome" in AIDS is important in designing effective nutrition support for patients affected with this disease.

Protein-calorie malnutrition from AIDS is a major contributor to increased morbidity in AIDS patients;[30] however, there have been few published studies of nutritional support in adult or pediatric AIDS patients.[21,27,31–33] A few studies have indicated that effective nutritional management of AIDS patients is possible. Preliminary results using megestrol acetate, a synthetic orally active progesterone, in symptomatic HIV-infected patients with a history of weight loss but no significant gastrointestinal involvement have demonstrated potential benefit in terms of appetite stimulation and weight gain.[33] Further, short-term energy balance and repletion of body-cell-mass have been achieved with enteral or parenteral nutritional support in some adults and children successfully treated for complications of AIDS.[21,31,32] In our institution, accelerated growth has been possible in some HIV-infected children receiving nutritional support in the absence of serious complications of AIDS.[21] The similarities between death from wasting in AIDS and historical accounts of death from starvation suggest that successful attempts to maintain body cell mass could prolong survival of patients with AIDS.[34] Although further research is necessary to design strategies for the successful management of wasting in AIDS, it is clear that early nutritional assessment and intervention may aid in optimizing nutritional status and enhancing quality of life in a disease characterized by nutritional complications.

A thorough nutritional assessment and care plan should be completed on all HIV-infected children, symptomatic and asymptomatic. An initial nutritional assessment for the asymptomatic child provides the dietitian with valuable baseline information and allows for prophylactic measures to be taken before nutritional deterioration begins. Further, ongoing monitoring of immunologic, anthropometric, gastrointestinal, medicinal, laboratory, and nutritional information is important to detect changes in the patient's medical and nutritional status as the disease progresses. An understanding of how the clinical manifestations (Table 14-3) of AIDS can affect a child's nutritional requirements helps the nutritionist estimate individual energy and nutrient needs and translate them into an acceptable nutrition care plan.

ENERGY REQUIREMENTS

In many instances energy requirements will exceed the Recommended Dietary Allowance (RDA) for age due to the increased metabolic needs that accompany various infections. It is important to provide for additional energy requirements due to stress, fever, and/or increased respiratory rates, as well as provide sufficient calories for growth.

Calculations that may be used to determine energy requirements include the Peterson/Washington formula (see Chapter 13, Table 13-7) for infants and young children. For an older child or adolescent, adjustment of basal energy needs may be used to calculate energy requirements. Based on clinical experience, it appears that providing approximately one and a half times the RDA for energy can promote weight gain if malabsorption and diarrhea are not debilitating. It is important, however, not to assume that each patient's energy requirements will be met by implementing a calculation of energy needs. Observing individual weight gain and growth will reveal if these estimations are adequate. In some patients, despite seemingly adequate intake, all growth (including brain growth) stops or slows dramatically. The reason for this growth failure is not clearly understood at this point in time.

CLINICAL MANIFESTATIONS AND FORMULA AND MEAL SELECTIONS

When suggesting a formula or specific meal plan for a child who has AIDS, it is important to evaluate his or her clinical manifestations. There is no one formula or special diet that is universally appropriate for HIV-infected children.

Children who are experiencing diarrhea and malabsorption may need to eliminate certain foods or ingredients from their diets. Although the nature and etiology of carbohydrate malabsorption in HIV-infected children are not well defined, gastrointestinal dysfunction and disaccharide intolerances, especially to lactose, are common in these children.[35,36] In the presence of lactose intolerance a lactose-restricted diet (lactose-free or lactose-reduced, depending upon degree of tolerance) is necessary to alleviate symptoms of diarrhea, abdominal pain or distention, or poor weight gain. Unfortunately, a lactose-restricted diet limits nutrient-dense dairy products. Lactose-free formulas and supplements (Table 14-4) and commercially prepared lactose-reduced dairy products and enzyme substitutes may aid in maximizing the nutritional quality of the diet. However, for the older child on table foods, use of a strict diet is generally counterproductive due to restricted food choices and subsequent poor intake. Fortunately, many children with lactose malabsorption are asymptomatic and the lactose-free diet may not be necessary.

In the presence of enteropathy, fat and/or protein malabsorption may also be a problem. Formulas or enteral products (Table 14-4) made with hydrolyzed protein and/or an altered fat such as medium-chain triglyceride (MCT) oil may be warranted. The disadvantage of these products is their lack of palatability. Their medicinal or metallic taste may be poorly accepted by the child who has previously been receiving a sweeter-tasting formula. The addition of flavor packets may improve acceptance by some patients.

In order to meet the increased energy and protein needs of these children, calorically dense and high-quality-protein foods should be offered. This is especially important since the amount of food consumed is often suboptimal in children with oroesophageal ulcers, soreness, and inflammation. This is particularly evident in infants and young children who have not yet experienced eating as a pleasurable activity. The pain associated with eating can lead to an intense fear of food and delays in the introduction of age-appropriate foods. Offering soft foods such as milkshakes, puddings, cream soups, and casseroles may cause less pain and anxiety. Highly spiced or acidic foods should be avoided, and a lukewarm temperature may be tolerated better than very cold or hot items.

Altered taste may also contribute to a reduction in a child's intake. Certain medications, such as pentamidine used to treat *Pneumocystis carinii*, may cause patients to experience a bitter or metallic taste in their mouths. The side effects of anorexia, nausea/vomiting, epigastric distress, diarrhea, and/or glossitis associated with some drugs may also lead to a refusal to eat.

Dysphagia, developmental delay, and poor gross motor control secondary to neurologic complications associated with the AIDS virus may be other contributors to poor intake. Close attention should be paid to these patients not only to ensure adequate intake but also to prevent any problems with aspiration or self-inflicted burns due to spillage.

High-calorie and high-protein food ideas may be found in Exhibit 14-1. Offering six small meals throughout the day may promote adequate intake; however, it is important to remember that each child's meal plan should be individualized to meet his or her specific needs, preferences, and tolerance to certain food items.

If a child's intake by mouth is inadequate, it may be necessary to pass a nasogastric tube or place a gastrostomy tube and provide supplemental tube feedings to prevent further weight loss or dehydration. There are preliminary re-

Table 14-4 Lactose-Free Supplements

Calories Kcal/cc	Supplement	Company	Flavors
1.00	Pediasure+@	Ross	vanilla
1.00	Sustacal@	Mead Johnson	chocolate, strawberry, vanilla, egg nog
1.0	Peptamen	Clintec Nutrition	strawberry, orange, vanilla
1.0	Tolerex	Sandoz	unflavored
1.06	Ensure@	Ross	chocolate, strawberry, vanilla, egg nog, coffee, black walnut
1.0	Entrition*@	Clintec Nutrition	unflavored
1.06	Isocal*@	Mead Johnson	unflavored
1.06	Osmolite*@	Ross	unflavored
1.06	Resource@	Sandoz	chocolate, vanilla, strawberry
1.2	Isosource@	Sandoz	vanilla
1.0	Nutren 1.0@	Clintec Nutrition	unflavored, chocolate, strawberry, vanilla
1.5	Complete Regular*	Sandoz	natural food
1.5	Ensure Plus@	Ross	chocolate, strawberry, vanilla
1.5	Nutren 1.5@	Clintec Nutrition	unflavored, vanilla, chocolate, strawberry
1.5	Resource Plus@	Sandoz	varied
2.0	Nutren 2.0@	Clinitec Nutrition	unflavored, vanilla, chocolate, strawberry
2.0	Magnacal@	Sherwood Medical	vanilla

Note:
+Virtually lactose free
@Contains casein and should be avoided if sensitive to milk protein
*These products are usually not preferred for oral use because they are unflavored
*Milk Substitutes:***
  Edensoy
  Vitasoy
  RiceDream
  Almond Amasake
  "nut" milk
  West Soy milk
Infant soy formulas:
  Isomil
  Prosobee
  Nursoy
Non-Dairy Cream:
  Coffee Rich
  Coffee Mate@
  Creamora@

** Soy milks are found most easily in large supermarkets or Health Food Stores. To be nutritionally similar to milk, soy milk must be fortified with calcium. Compare the labels of products to select a soy milk that resembles milk as some soy drinks are not nutritionally equivalent to milk. Soy milk may be slightly "beany in flavor."

Editors' Note: Milk substitutes such as soy beverages, soy milks, nut milks, and nondairy creamers should *not* be used as a substitute for human breast milk or infant formulas.

Source: Department of Nutrition and Food Service, Children's Hospital, Boston, MA, May 1992.

Exhibit 14-1 Hints for Adding Calories to the Diet

- Add cooked and diced meat, shrimp, tuna, or crabmeat to soups, casseroles and baked potatoes or add to lactose-free sauces and serve over rice, cooked noodles, toast or hot biscuits.
- Add chopped, hardcooked eggs to salads and casseroles. Add an extra egg to lactose-free French toast and pancake batter.
- Cooked dried peas and beans and bean curd (tofu) can be added to soups, pastas, casseroles, and grain dishes.
- Choose dessert recipes that contain eggs such as sponge cake, bread pudding or pudding made with milk substitute.
- Add peanut butter and margarine to bread, crackers, celery sticks, or lactose-free pancakes and waffles.
- Add lactose-free margarine or corn oil to hot foods such as soups, vegetables, mashed potatoes, cooked cereal, rice, or pasta. Put margarine on pasta before topping with spaghetti sauce. Spread margarine on bread while it is hot so the fat will melt into the crevices (and more margarine will be used!).
- Meat, poultry, and fish that are breaded and fried are higher in calories than when baked or broiled (some breadings contain lactose, read label carefully).
- Mayonnaise has 100 calories per tablespoon . . . almost twice as much as salad dressing. Use it in salads and on sandwiches.
- Top lactose-free puddings, pies, hot chocolate, fruit, and jello with a non-dairy whipped topping (eg, Cool Whip).
- Add raisins, dates, chopped nuts and brown sugar or maple syrup to hot or cold cereals.
- Add lactose-free granola to cookie, muffin, or bread batters and sprinkle on pudding and lactose-free ice cream.
- Instead of drinking water, select beverages that contain calories such as juice or frappes made with a milk substitute.
- Eat small frequently scheduled meals throughout the day. Six feedings a day may help to meet caloric requirements without too much effort.
- Notice the time of day when appetite is best and plan for higher calorie foods then. Eat a good snack before bedtime.

Lactose-Free, High Protein Foods

Meat, fish, poultry	Peanut butter
Eggs	Tofu
	Soy infant formula, soy milk

Lactose-Free, High Calorie Foods

Fats—Kosher margarine, oils, mayonnaise, bacon	Desserts—Tofutti, fruit pie, milk-free pudding, Angel cake, milk-free cookies
Fried Foods (check breading ingredients)	Fruits—dried or canned in heavy syrup
	Sweets—jam, jelly, syrup, milk-free candies

continues

Exhibit 14-1 continued

Lactose-Free Snack Ideas

Peanut butter/crackers	Nuts and seeds
Cereal/milk substitute	Fruited jello/cool whip
Plain potato chips	Tofutti ice cream
Lactose-free pudding	Sugar wafers
Popcorn/milk-free margarine topping	Popsicles
Angel cake/milk-free glaze	Ritz crackers
Bananas	Plain corn chips
Peanut butter/celery sticks	Gorp**
Marshmallows	Granola bar (if lactose free)

Lactose-free cookies, cake, muffins, donuts, sweet rolls, puddings and sandwiches filled with meat or peanut butter

Lactose-Free, High Calorie Recipes

SUPER PUDDING

1 cup Coffee Rich
1 cup Soy milk
1 package lactose-free instant pudding
Mix together in a blender.

FRUIT FREEZE

1 1/2 cups fruit sorbet
1/2 cup Coffee Rich/milk substitute
1 tablespoon corn syrup (eg, Karo)
2–3 ice cubes
Mix together in blender. For variation, add banana, pineapple, or any desired fruit. Freeze in ice cube trays or acceptable container.

GORP SNACK MIX**

Choose any of the following ingredients and mix together in any desired amounts: peanuts, raisins, banana chips, cheerios, dried fruit (dates, figs, apricots, pineapple), shredded coconut, granola (check label for lactose), almonds, cashews, sunflower seeds, semi sweet chocolate chips (check label for lactose, whey or milk fat)

**Note: This recipe may not be appropriate for young children who could choke on the small pieces.

Source: Department of Nutrition and Food Service, Children's Hospital, Boston, MA, May 1992.

ports that gastrostomy tube feedings may significantly improve growth when dietary interventions are successful.[21] In addition, a multivitamin and mineral preparation should also be given if intake is suboptimal. Therapeutic doses of specific vitamins or minerals should only be given if there is medical evidence that they are necessary. Total parenteral nutrition, despite its associated risks, may need to be initiated if hydration, electrolyte balance, and weight gain cannot be achieved enterally due to excessive diarrhea or other medical complications (see Chapters 10 and 11 for further information on tube feedings and parenteral nutrition, respectively).

In conclusion, nutritional intervention for both asymptomatic and symptomatic HIV-infected children is an important component of medical care. No one diet or all-encompassing formula can be recommended for these children. Each patient's nutritional care plan should be based on individual clinical manifestations, diet history, personality, and social situation. Further, research is needed to clarify the nutritional requirements of these children, as well as the effect of infection with the AIDS virus on growth potential. The provision of high-quality formulas, foods, and supplements, along with consistent nutritional care, may contribute to such important outcomes as improvement in quality of life, improved growth, and greater resistance to infections. Further clinical research will likely define the nutritional requirements and growth patterns of these children. This additional information will allow for the formulation of more specific nutritional guidelines. The positive outcomes associated with the provision of adequate nutrition are well worth striving for when caring for the child who is HIV positive.

REFERENCES

1. Centers for Disease Control, Division of HIV/AIDS. *HIV/AIDS Surveillance*. Atlanta, Ga: Centers for Disease Control; January 1992:1–22.

2. Oleske J, Connor E, Boland M. A perspective on pediatric AIDS. *Pediatr Ann*. 1988;17:319–321.

3. Abrams D. Clinical experiences with AIDS in San Francisco. *Contemp Dial Neph*. 1985;6:28–34.

4. Rogers MF. AIDS in children: a review of the clinical, epidemiological, and public health aspects. *J Pediatr Infect Dis*. 1985;4:230–236.

5. Falloon J, Eddy J, Pizzo P. Human immunodeficiency virus infection in children. *J Pediatr*. 1989;114:1–30.

6. Centers for Disease Control: Revision of the CDC surveillance case definition for acquired immunodeficiency syndrome. *MMWR*. 1987;36:(suppl):3S–15S.

7. Barrett DJ. The clinician's guide to pediatric AIDS. *Contemp Pediatr*. 1988;5:24.

8. Nicholas SW, Sondheimer DL, Willoughby AD, et al. Human immunodeficiency virus infection in childhood, adolescence, and pregnancy: a status report and national research agenda. *Pediatrics*. 1989;83:293–308.

9. Rogers MF. Pediatric HIV infection: epidemiology, etiopathogenesis and transmission. *Pediatr Ann*. 1988;17:324–331.

10. Ziegler JB, Cooper DA, Johnson RO, et al. Postnatal transmission of AIDS-associated retrovirus from mother to infant. *Lancet.* 1985;1:896–898.

11. Rubinstein A, Bernstein L. The epidemiology of pediatric acquired immunodeficiency syndrome. *Clin Immunol Immunopathol.* 1985;40:115–121.

12. Scott GB, Fischl MA, Slimas N, et al. Mothers of infants with acquired immunodeficiency syndrome: evidence for both symptomatic and asymptomatic carriers. *JAMA.* 1985;253:363–366.

13. Hutto C, Parks WP, Lai S, et al. A hospital-based prospective study of perinatal infection with human immunodeficiency virus type 1. *J Pediatr.* 1991;118:347–353.

14. Hilgartner MW. HIV transmitted by blood products. In: *Report of the Surgeon General's Workshop on Children with HIV Infection and Their Families.* Rockville, Md: DHHS publication no. (HRS-D-MC 87-1) 26, 1987.

15. Lange JMA, Van den Berg H, Dooren LJ, et al. HTLV-III/LAV infection in 9 children infected by a single plasma donor: clinical outcome and recognition patterns of viral proteins. *J Infect Dis.* 1986;154:171–174.

16. Feorino PM, Jaffe HW, Palmer E, et al. Transfusion-associated acquired immunodeficiency syndrome. *N Engl J Med.* 1985;312:1293–1296.

17. Cooper ER. AIDS in children: an overview of the medical, epidemiological, and public health problems. *New Engl J Public Policy.* 1988;4:121–132.

18. Richman DD, Fischl MA, Grieco MH, et al. The toxicity of azidothymidine (AZT) in the treatment of patients with AIDS and AIDS-related complex: a double-blind, placebo-controlled trial. *N Engl J Med.* 1987;317:192–197.

19. Chandra RK. Mucosal immune responses in malnutrition. *Ann NY Acad Sci.* 1983;409:345–352.

20. Cunningham-Rundles S. Effects of nutritional status on immunological function. *Am J Clin Nutr.* 1982;35:1202–1210.

21. Miller TL, Evans S, Morris V, Cooper E, McIntosh K, Winter H. Improvement in nutritional status of HIV-infected children by gastrostomy tube feedings. *Gastroenterology.* 1992;102:A666.

22. Kotler DP, Gaetz HP, Lange M. Klein EB, Holt P. Enteropathy associated with the acquired immunodeficiency syndrome. *Ann Intern Med.* 1984;101:421–428.

23. Gillin JS, et al. Malabsorption and mucosal abnormalities of the small intestine in the acquired immunodeficiency syndrome. *Ann Intern Med.* 1985;102:619–622.

24. Martin SR, Nurko S, Chanock SJ, McIntosk K, Winter H. Gastrointestinal manifestations of congenital acquired immunodeficiency syndrome in children. *Pediatr Res.* 1987;21:272A. Abstract.

25. Kotler DP, Haroutiounian G, Greenburg R, Setchell K, Balistier WF. Increased bile salt deconjugation in AIDS. *Gastroenterology.* 1985;88:1455A. Abstract.

26. Melchior JC, Salmon D, Rigaud D, et al. REE is increased in stable, malnourished HIV-infected patients. *Am J Clin Nutr.* 1991;53:437–441.

27. Kotler DP, Tierney A, Brenner S, Couture S, Wang J, Pierson R. Preservation of short-term energy balance in clinically stable patients with AIDS. *Am J Clin Nutr.* 1990;51:7–13.

28. Stein TP, Nutinsky C, Condoluci D, Schluter MD, Leskiw MJ. Protein and energy substrate metabolism in AIDS patients. *Metabolism.* 1990;39:876–881.

29. Kotler DP, Wang J, Pierson RN. Body composition studies in patients with the acquired immunodeficiency syndrome. *Am J Clin Nutr.* 1985;42:1255–1265.

30. Chlebowski RT. Significance of the altered nutritional status in acquired immune deficiency syndrome (AIDS). *Nutr Cancer.* 1985;7:85–91.

31. Kotler DP, Tierney AR, Culpepper-Morgan JA, Wang J, Pierson RN. Effect of home total parenteral nutrition upon body composition in AIDS. *Clin Res.* 1989;37:331A. Abstract.

32. Kotler DP, Tierney AR, Ferraro R, et al. Enteral alimentation and repletion of body cell mass in malnourished patients with acquired immunodeficiency syndrome. *Am J Clin Nutr.* 1991;53:149–154.

33. Von Roenn JH, Murphy RL, Weber KM, Williams L, Weitzman S. Megestrol acetate for treatment of cachexia associated with human immunodeficiency virus (HIV) infection. *Ann Intern Med.* 1988;109:840–841.

34. Kotler DP, Tierney AR, Wang J, Pierson R. Magnitude of body-cell-mass depletion and the timing of death from wasting in AIDS. *Am J Clin Nutr.* 1989;50:444–447.

35. Yolken RH, Hart W, Oung I, et al. Gastrointestinal dysfunction and disaccharide intolerance in children infected with the human immunodeficiency virus. *J Pediatr.* 1991;118:359–363.

36. Miller TL, Orav EJ, Martin SR, Cooper ER, McIntosh K, Winter HS. Malnutrition and carbohydrate malabsorption in human immunodeficiency virus-1 infected children. *Gastroenterology.* 1991;100:1296–1302.

Chapter 15

Developmental Disabilities

Harriet H. Cloud

The nutritional needs of the child with developmental disabilities are as variable as they are for the child who is normal. They primarily involve energy, growth, regulation of the biochemical processes, and repair of cells and body tissue.

DEFINITION OF DEVELOPMENTAL DISABILITIES

A developmental disability was defined in Public Law 95-602, the Developmental Disabilities Assistance and Bill of Rights Act,[1] as a severe chronic disability of a person that

- is attributable to a mental or physical impairment or combination of mental and physical impairments
- is manifested before the person attains age 22
- is likely to continue indefinitely
- results in substantial functional limitations in three or more areas of major life activity (self-care, receptive and expressive language, learning, mobility, capacity for independent living, and economic self-sufficiency)
- reflects the person's need for a combination of special interdisciplinary, or generic care, treatments, or other services that are lifelong or of extended duration and are individually planned and coordinated

The etiology of developmental disabilities has been traced to chromosomal aberrations such as Down syndrome (trisomy 21) and Prader-Willi syndrome, neurologic insults in the prenatal period, infectious diseases, trauma, congenital defects such as cleft lip and palate, neural tube defects such as spina bifida, inborn errors of metabolism, and other syndromes of lesser incidence.[2]

Nutrition considerations that involve the child with developmental disabilities include assessment of growth and the problems surrounding energy balance. This can lead to either failure to thrive, obesity, or slow growth rate in height. The second major consideration includes feeding from the standpoint of oral motor problems, developmental delays of feeding skills, inability to self-feed, behavioral problems, and tube feedings. Other areas for nutritional consideration include drug-nutrient interaction, constipation, dental caries, urinary tract infections, and food or nutrition misinformation the parent has related to hyperactivity and attention deficit disorders. Table 15-1 includes a list of developmental disorders and their nutrition considerations.

Table 15-1 Developmental Disabilities or Conditions Predisposing to Them and Their Nutritional Considerations

Condition	Nutrition Problems	Treatment Goal
Down syndrome	Poor suck in infancy Constipation Failure to thrive Marked weight gain	Ability to suck vigorously Increased fiber and fluids Increased calories or decreased calories Increased activity
Prader-Willi syndrome	Failure to thrive in infancy Weak suck Obesity Hyperglycemia	Early identification Weight maintained for height Decreased calories Environmental control
Cornelia De Lange syndrome	Failure to thrive Feeding problems	Increased calories Early assessment and intervention
Cerebral palsy	Oral motor feeding problems	Assessment of problem Oral motor facilitation Texture progression Calorie progression
Spina bifida	Obesity Constipation Urinary tract infection Feeding problems	Weight loss or maintenance Kilocalories per centimeter of height Adequate fluid intake
Seizure disorders	Feeding problems Weight loss Drug–nutrient interaction Dental problems	Increased calories Vitamin D supplementation if Dilantin is given

NUTRITIONAL NEEDS OF THE CHILD WITH DEVELOPMENTAL DISABILITIES

Energy needs for the child with developmental disabilities vary as they do for normal children; very little specific information is available for either. A decreased energy need is most apparent in chromosomal aberrations such as Down syndrome, conditions accompanied by limited gross motor activity such as in spina bifida, and syndromes characterized by low muscle tone such as is found in Prader-Willi syndrome.

Energy needs of infants and children with developmental disabilities are highly individualized and vary widely. For the child with Down syndrome, Prader-Willi syndrome, or spina bifida, the growth rate has been found to be slower, basal energy needs lower, and motor activity diminished when compared to the child who is not developmentally disabled. As a result these children tend to become overweight and obese when fed according to normal standards. Determination of energy needs for children with these developmental disabilities, who tend to be short, led to the recommendation that energy needs be calculated per centimeter of height (see Table 15-2).[3]

Children with cerebral palsy often tend to be seriously underweight for height. Few studies have been conducted to estimate the energy needs of the child with cerebral palsy, and those have estimated energy needs utilizing indirect calorimetry. Two other methods for determining energy needs of this population include using a nomogram for calculating body surface area and standards based on cal/m^2/h.[4] This method can be used for males and females 6 years of age and above. Table 15-3 includes basal metabolic rates for infants and children from 1 week of age to 16 years and is based on weight.[4]

Table 15-2 Energy Needs of Selected Populations of Children with Developmental Disabilities

Down syndrome	16.1 kcal/cm: male 1–3 years
	14.3 kcal/cm: female 1–3 years
Prader-Willi syndrome	10–11 kcal/cm: maintenance
	8–9 kcal/cm: weight loss
Spina bifida	7 kcal/cm: weight loss
	Maintenance: 50% of the kilocalorie level of normal children after 8 years of age
Cerebral palsy	13.9 kcal/cm: 5–11 years, mild to moderate activity
	11.1 kcal/cm: 5–11 years, several restrictions on activity

Source: Reprinted from *Nutrition and Feeding for the Developmentally Disabled* by C Rokusek and E Heindicles with permission of the South Dakota University Affiliated Program, Interdisciplinary Center for Disabilities, © 1985.

Table 15-3 Basal Metabolic Rates: Infants and Children

| Age 1 Week to 10 Months | | Age 11 to 36 Months | | | Age 3 to 16 Years | | |
| Metabolic Rate | | Metabolic Rate | | | Metabolic Rate | | |
Weight (kg)	(kcal/h) M/F	Weight (kg)	(kcal/h) M	F	Weight (kg)	(kcal/h) M	F
3.5	8.4	9.0	22.0	21.2	15	35.8	33.3
4.0	9.5	9.5	22.8	22.0	20	39.7	37.4
4.5	10.5	10.0	23.6	22.8	25	43.6	41.5
5.0	11.6	10.5	24.4	23.6	30	47.5	45.5
5.5	12.7	11.0	25.2	24.4	35	51.3	49.6
6.0	13.8	11.5	26.0	25.2	40	55.2	53.7
6.5	14.9	12.0	26.8	26.0	45	59.1	57.8
7.0	16.0	12.5	27.6	26.9	50	63.0	61.9
7.5	17.1	13.0	28.4	27.7	55	66.9	66.0
8.0	18.2	13.5	29.2	28.5	60	70.8	70.0
8.5	19.3	14.0	30.0	29.3	65	74.7	74.0
9.0	20.4	14.5	30.8	30.1	70	78.6	78.1
9.5	21.4	15.0	31.6	30.9	75	82.5	82.2
10.0	22.5	15.5	32.4	31.7			
10.5	23.6	16.0	33.3	32.6			
11.0	24.7	16.5	34.0	33.4			

Source: Reprinted from *Metabolism* by PL Altman and DS Dittmer (eds) with permission of the Federation of American Societies for Experimental Biology, © 1968.

The information in determining the basal energy need must be modified for growth and activity level. The Recommended Dietary Allowances (RDAs) are generally not appropriate to use in determining the energy levels of children with developmental disabilities. A more appropriate strategy would be to utilize basal energy needs with an individualized percentage added for growth rates and energy levels which encompasses slower growth rates and lowered motor activity. The dearth of research in this area makes it difficult to develop standards and requires that the dietitian and physician evaluate the child's nutritional needs carefully.

Protein, Carbohydrates, and Fats

Careful monitoring of protein intake is essential in the child with developmental disabilities. It is generally recommended that 15% to 20% of the total calories come from protein, which may be difficult for the child with an oral motor feeding problem such as a child with cerebral palsy. These children often suffer from serious malnutrition manifested by little or no weight gain and limited growth in height. One recent study of an aggressive tube-feeding approach in 10 seriously malnourished cerebral palsy children (ages 2 to 15 years) resulted in weight gain.[5] The tube-feeding formula provided one kilocalorie per milliliter, with 16% of calories from protein.

Carbohydrates are the primary source of energy for all individuals. According to the usual pediatric dietary recommendations, at least 50% of calories should come from carbohydrates, with no more than 10% coming from sucrose.

Children with developmental disabilities often have a high percentage of their carbohydrate calories coming from foods highly concentrated in sucrose, such as candy, carbonated beverages, cookies, etc. Dietary counseling related to better food choices of carbohydrate is frequently required, just as it is for normal children.

Fats should provide 30% to 35% of the total caloric intake, increasing palatability and satiety as well as providing a supply of the essential fatty acids. For the child who tends to be overweight and obese, fat intake should be carefully evaluated and controlled. For the underweight child, fat can provide an important source of supplemental calories.

Vitamins and Minerals

Research findings do not indicate that vitamin and mineral needs for the child with developmental disabilities are higher than normal. Studies have been completed for the vitamin needs of the child with Down syndrome, spina bifida, fragile X syndrome, and autism.[6–10]

The child with Down syndrome was the subject of research related to the effect of "megavitamin" supplementation, leading to an apparent increase in intelligence quotient scores. The parents of the child with Down syndrome, like those of children with other developmental disabilities, are vulnerable to this sort of nutrition fallacy. Subsequent studies[11] have not found that megavitamin therapy improves intelligence, physical appearance, or growth. Other studies have measured vitamin A, retinol-binding protein, and vitamin B_6 in children with Down syndrome. Most research studies have been limited in size.

Studies involving children with spina bifida have involved ascorbic acid saturation and the impact of supplementation of ascorbic acid for producing an acidic urinary ph. Concern was shown in recent studies related to the effect of supplemental ascorbic acid on serum vitamin B_{12} levels. No evident B_{12} deficiency developed in one study of 40 children[12] receiving long-term vitamin C supplementation.

Recently the literature has reflected a growing interest in vitamin supplementation in the prevention of spina bifida.[13] Nutritional deficiencies identified as possible etiologic factors include folic acid, multivitamins, and zinc.[14] A British study[15] supplemented 234 mothers with a multivitamin/iron preparation 1 month prior to conception. Vitamins included were A, D, thiamine, riboflavin, pyridoxine, niacin, ascorbic acid, and folic acid. Supplemented mothers had a recurrence rate of 0.9% compared to 5.1% of the 219 mothers without supplementation. Numerous variables were present in the study. Causal relationships for the reduced rates of recurrence remain unclear and this issue presently continues to be controversial.

A special concern regarding adequacy of vitamin and mineral intake is the effect of certain medications commonly prescribed to developmentally disabled children on utilization of certain vitamins and minerals. Among these medications are antibiotics, anticonvulsants, antihypertensives, cathartics, corticosteroids, stimulants, sulfonamides, and tranquilizers (see Table 15-4). Their nutritional effect can include nausea and vomiting, gastric distress, constipation, and interference with the absorption of vitamins and minerals. In some cases, vitamin and mineral supplements are recommended.

NUTRITION ASSESSMENT

Assessment of the child with developmental disabilities includes all components of nutrition assessment for normal children (as addressed in Chapter 2) plus the inclusion of an evaluation of feeding skills and development. Guidelines for nutrition assessment of the child with developmental disabilities were developed by nutritionists from University Affiliated Programs throughout the United States for persons with developmental disabilities. A copy of these guidelines is included in Table 15-5.

Taking anthropometric measurements of children who are unable to stand and who have gross motor handicaps will require some ingenuity. Weights may be difficult to obtain on standing calibrated balance beam scales for the child with spina bifida or cerebral palsy. Chair scales are available for use in both clinics and schools, and bed scales are indicated for the severely affected. Recumbent boards can be constructed or commercially obtained. Alternate measures for height measurements include arm span, knee-to-ankle height, or sitting height.[16,17]

Standards for comparison of weight, height, and head circumference are found on the 1979 National Center for Health Studies (NCHS) growth charts.[18] Since these standards were developed on a normal population, the child with developmental disabilities may plot as short, especially when length or height for age is considered. This is particularly true for children with chromosomal aberrations such as Down syndrome or those with a neural tube defect such as spina bifida. Growth curves have been developed for children with Down syndrome,[19] Prader-Willi syndrome,[20] and Turner syndrome;[21] however, for the most part the NCHS charts are used. Proper interpretation is needed.

Table 15-4 Drug-Nutrient Interactions of Medications Frequently Used for Children with Developmental Disabilities

Drug	Indications for Use	Drug–Nutrient Interactions	Prevention of Nutritional Effect
Anticonvulsants			
Diphenylhydantoin (Dilantin) Phenolbarbitol	Treatment of seizures	Altered metabolism and absorption of Vitamins D, K, folate, B_{12}, B_6, calcium. May produce gastrointestinal side effects such as nausea, vomiting, diarrhea, and lethargy.	Vitamin D supplement recommended. Emphasize high-folate food sources. Folic acid supplement indicated only when drug levels and seizure frequency closely monitored.
Carbamazepine (Tegretol) Valproic acid (Depakane)			
Antibiotics			
Chloramphenicol Tetracycline	Treatment of infections	Both may alter intestinal function by decreasing flora and causing irritations. Other side effects include nausea, vomiting.	Decrease milk intake. Provide a multivitamin supplement. *Do not give* with iron supplement within 2 hours. Encourage increased fluids.
Laxatives			
Mineral oil	Constipation	Decreased absorption of fat-soluble vitamins. Indigestion, flatulence, weight loss, anorexia.	Vitamin supplementation and taking 2 hours away from food. Utilization of a high-fiber liquid beverage is an acceptable strategy.
Stimulants			
Dexedrine Methylphenidate (Ritalin)	Attention deficit disorders, hyperactivity	Decreased appetite. Decreased intake. Poor growth.	Take 1/2 hour before meals.

Source: Data from reference 32.

Weight for age, interpreted for the developmentally disabled, is also an important indicator of nutritional status and requires comparison with height for age. Again, it is the child with Down syndrome, spina bifida, cerebral palsy, Cornelia De Lange syndrome, and chromosomal aberrations in general whose height/weight relationship should be carefully monitored. Early identification of inappro-

Table 15-5 Guides for Nutritional Assessment of the Mentally Retarded and Developmentally Disabled

I. Anthropometric
   A. Purpose. To collect data related to growth and body composition
   B. Levels of assessment
      1. Minimal
         a. Weight*
            (1) Conditions: no shoes, light clothing
            (2) Suggested standard: reference data assembled by National Center for Health Statistics
         b. Height*
            (1) Conditions: recumbent length†
            (2) Suggested standard: reference data assembled by National Center for Health Statistics
         c. Head circumference*
            (1) Conditions: up to age 6 years
            (2) Suggested standard: reference data assembled by National Center for Health Statistics
      2. In-depth
         a. Skinfold triceps and subscapular desirable*
            (1) Conditions: obtain duplicate readings
            (2) Suggested standard: reference data assembled by Fomon and National Center for Health Statistics
         b. Arm circumference*
            (1) Conditions: desirable, if possible
            (2) Suggested standard: Gurney and Jelliffe nomogram
   C. Equipment specification and maintenance
      1. Calibrated weight scale (balance-type)
      2. Measuring board (stadiometer) for measuring recumbent length or vertical surface with leveler for measuring standing height
      3. Narrow flexible steel or plastic coated tape measure for measuring circumference of head and arm
      4. Calibrated calipers
II. Clinical
   A. Purpose: To observe clinical signs of chronic or subacute disease
   B. Levels of assessment
      1. Minimal: review of past and present records of medical and dental examinations for signs suggestive of poor nutritional status
      2. In-depth
         a. Collection of health history with special attention to areas of nutritional risk, e.g.,
            (1) Prenatal; pattern and total amount of maternal weight gain, complications of pregnancy, etc.
            (2) Postnatal; client or family history of diabetes, coronary heart disease, infections, anemia, constipation, diarrhea, hyperactivity, food intolerances, pica, inborn errors of metabolism, malabsorption syndromes, etc.
         b. Observation
            (1) General appearance
            (2) Speech
            (3) Oral hygiene

continues

Table 15-5 continued

    C. Suggested standards
       1. Fomon
       2. Christakis
       3. Goldsmith
  III. Biochemical
    A. Purpose: To obtain objective data related to present nutrition status or recent dietary intake
    B. Levels of assessment
       1. Minimal
         a. Complete blood count
         b. Routine urinalysis including microscopic
         c. Semi-quantitative amino acid screening[‡]
       2. In-depth
         a. Serum total protein and albumin
         b. Fasting blood glucose
         c. Serum urea nitrogen
         d. Transferrin saturation
         e. Organic acids as primary screening for metabolic disorders
         f. Quantitative urinary and plasma amino acid screening
       3. Other tests to respond to special conditions or problems (examples only)

Condition/problem	Tests[§]
a. Anticonvulsants	Folic acid, ascorbic acid, calcium, vitamin D, alkaline phosphatase, phosphorus, vitamin B_6
b. Prader-Willi Syndrome	Glucose tolerance test
c. Pica	Lead, hemoglobin

    C. Suggested standards
       1. Fomon
       2. Christakis
  IV. Dietary
    A. Purpose: To determine a usual dietary pattern and/or nutrient intake
    B. Criteria for dietary assessment
       1. Family income
       2. Mechanical feeding problems
       3. Growth deviations
       4. Age
       5. Specific nutritional disorders or inborn errors of metabolism
       6. Feeding behavior problems
       7. Response to parents' or other professionals' concerns
    C. Levels of assessment
       1. Minimal
         a. Twenty-four hour recall using food models and/or measures and food frequency with verbal questioning
         b. Feeding history questionnaire to include parents' concerns regarding nutrition status
       2. In-depth
         a. Three-day dietary intake kept by parent
          (1) Verbal instruction in dietary record keeping
          (2) Kept during two week days and week-end day
          (3) Dietary supplements and/or medications included

(4) Occurrences affecting validity recorded, i.e., illness or holidays
(5) Quantity, preparation and brand names of food included
(6) Where, when and with whom client eats included
   b. Activity record (as needed)
   c. Pertinent historical information related to feeding
   d. Present influences on dietary intake
3. Other
   Certain conditions (i.e., inborn errors of metabolism or syndromes) may require further dietary investigation necessitating more detailed data collection
   D. Suggested standards
      1. Recommended Dietary Allowances
      2. Fomon
      3. FAO
V. Behavioral and Feeding Skill Development
   A. Purpose: To determine the influence of level of feeding development and behavior on nutritional status
   B. Levels of assessment
      1. Minimal
         a. Parental perception of feeding skills and behavior
         b. Professional perception of feeding skills and behavior
      2. In depth
         a. Review of past history and interview to determine feeding skill development and present level of functioning
         b. Observations‖
            (1) Physical
               (a) Oral structure and function including primitive reflexes, sucking, swallowing, biting, chewing, occlusion and caries
               (b) Neuromuscular development including gross and fine motor skills, head and trunk control, eye-hand coordination and position for feeding
            (2) Behavioral
               (a) Parent (caregiver)-child interaction
               (b) Reinforcement patterns (positive and negative)
               (c) Environmental influences
   C. Suggested standards
      1. Gesell and Amatruda
      2. Vineland Social Maturity Scale

* Measurement to be made by well-trained, motivated personnel.

† Standards for recumbent length for normal children are available only up to 2 years of age; however, this method yields more accurate measurement of physically handicapped children over 2 years, especially when they are unable to stand without support.

‡ Screening with multiple Guthrie tests and/or thin layer chromatography or chomatography alone.

§ Professional judgment is warranted and a current search of literature should be done to determine appropriateness of tests before they are used.

‖ Observations both at home and outside home with and without primary care-giver and/or conjoint professional assessments are valuable.

Source: Reprinted from Smith MAH. Nutritional assessment of the mentally retarded and developmentally disabled. In: *Proceedings of the Third National Workshop for Nutritionists from the University Affiliated Facilities* (p 129) with permission of The Boling Child Center for Developmental Disabilities, University of Tennessee Center for Health Sciences, © 1976.

priate relationships is critical so that early nutrition counseling related to energy balance can be given.

Growth velocity is an important anthropometric assessment parameter (see also Chapter 1 and 2). Growth velocity information assists the dietitian in evaluating changes in rate of growth over a specified period of time. Incremental growth curves are available for plotting growth velocity.[22] Skinfold thickness is a useful measurement for estimating body fat and is recommended along with arm circumference in the nutrition assessment guidelines previously cited.

Biochemical measures for the child with developmental disabilities should include at a minimum hemoglobin and hematocrit levels, complete blood count, urinalysis, and semiquantitative amino acid screening. The occurrence of this in an assessment would depend upon biochemical testing the child has received in the primary health care facility. Other tests may be indicated for children on an anticonvulsant medication, who may have low serum levels of folic acid, ascorbic acid, calcium, vitamin D, alkaline phosphatase, phosphorus, and pyridoxine. A glucose tolerance test is recommended for the individual with Prader-Willi syndrome.[23]

The methods used to obtain dietary information about the child with developmental disabilities are identical to those used with the normal child; remember that the parent must be interviewed for the infant and young child, and often for the older child who has a degree of mental retardation, making it difficult to obtain the food intake. It is highly recommended that written dietary records be analyzed with computer software.

In addition to dietary information, an assessment of feeding skills and identification of feeding problems that influence the child's food intake is indicated. This part of the evaluation may include such members of the health care team as the physical therapist, occupational therapist, dentist, and the psychologist. Observation of an actual feeding session is critical and may utilize an evaluation tool such as the Developmental Feeding Tool from the Boling Center for Developmental Disabilities, University of Tennessee in Exhibit 15-1.[24]

The feeding evaluation should include assessment of the oral mechanism, neuromuscular development, head and trunk control, eye-hand coordination, position for feeding, and social-behavioral components, which include the interaction between child and caregiver. Children with developmental disabilities frequently have oral motor feeding problems and positioning problems and tend to be very easily distracted.

MANAGEMENT OF NUTRITION CONCERNS

Once the nutritional problems have been identified for the child with developmental disabilities, various types of intervention programs may be implemented.

Exhibit 15-1 Developmental Feeding Tool (DFT)

Date _____

Staff member _____

Child's name _____

Birth date _____ Age _____ Sex _____ Race _____

Head circumference (cm) _____ (%ile NCHS) _____ Hand dominance _____

Height (cm) _____ (%ile NCHS) _____ Weight (kg) _____ (%ile NCHS) _____

Weight for height (%ile NCHS) _____ Hematocrit _____ Urine screen _____

Parent/Guardian _____

Address _____

City _____ State _____ Zip _____

County_____ Telephone _____

Referrer _____

Yes	No		Yes	No	
		PHYSICAL	___	___	24. Head (Normal)*
		Size	___	___	25. Eyes (Normal)*
___	___	1. Weight (Avg. %ile NCHS)	___	___	26. Ears (Normal)*
___	___	2. Underweight	___	___	27. Nose (Normal)*
___	___	3. Overweight	___	___	28. Teeth/gums (Normal)*
___	___	4. Stature (Avg. %ile NCHS)	___	___	29. Palate (Normal)*
___	___	5. Short (below 5th %ile for	___	___	30. Skin (Normal)*
		ht. NCHS)	___	___	31. Muscles (Normal)*
___	___	6. Tall (above 95th %ile for	___	___	32. Arms/hands (Normal)*
		ht. NCHS)	___	___	33. Legs/feet (Normal)*
___	___	7. Abnormal body propor-			**NEUROMOTOR/**
		tions*			**MUSCULAR**
___	___	8. Head circumference (Avg.			**Tonicity**
		%ile NCHS)	___	___	34. Body tone (Normal)*
___	___	9. Microcephalic			**Head and Trunk Control**
___	___	10. Macrocephalic	___	___	35. Head control (Normal)*
		Laboratory	___	___	36. Lifts head in prone
___	___	11. Hematocrit (Normal)	___	___	37. Head lags when pulled to
___	___	12. Urine screen (Normal)*			sitting
		Health Status	___	___	38. Head drops forward
___	___	13. Bowel problems*	___	___	39. Head drops backward
___	___	14. Diabetes	___	___	40. Trunk control (Normal)*
___	___	15. Vomiting			**Upper Extremity Control**
___	___	16. Dental caries	___	___	41. Range of motion (Normal)*
___	___	17. Anemia	___	___	42. Approach to object
___	___	18. Food allergies/intolerance*			(Normal)*
___	___	19. Medications*	___	___	43. Grasp of object (Normal)*
___	___	20. Vitamin/mineral supple-	___	___	44. Release of object
		ments*			(Normal)*
___	___	21. Ingests non-food items	___	___	45. Brings hand to mouth
___	___	22. Therapeutic diet*	___	___	46. Dominance established
___	___	23. General appearance			
		(Normal)*			

continues

Exhibit 15-1 continued

Yes No

Reflexes

___ ___ 47. Grossly normal

___ ___ 48. Asymmetrical tonic neck reflex*

___ ___ 49. Symmetrical tonic neck reflex*

___ ___ 50. Moro reflex*

___ ___ 51. Grasp reflex*

Body Alignment

___ ___ 52. Scoliosis

___ ___ 53. Kyphosis

___ ___ 54. Lordosis

___ ___ 55. Hip subluxation or dislocation suspected

Position in Feeding

___ ___ 56. Mother's lap

___ ___ 57. Infant seat

___ ___ 58. High chair

___ ___ 59. Table and chair

___ ___ 60. Wheelchair

___ ___ 61. Other adaptive chair*

ORAL/MOTOR

Facial Expression

___ ___ 62. Symmetrical structure/function*

___ ___ 63. Muscle tone lips/cheeks (Normal)

___ ___ 64. Hypertonic muscle tone of lips

___ ___ 65. Hypotonic muscle tone of lips

Oral Reflexes

___ ___ 66. Gag (Normal)*

___ ___ 67. Bite (Normal)*

___ ___ 68. Rooting (Normal)*

___ ___ 69. Suck/swallow (Normal)*

Respiration

___ ___ 70. Mouth

___ ___ 71. Nose

___ ___ 72. Thoracic

___ ___ 73. Abdominal

___ ___ 74. Regular rhythm*

Oral Sensitivity

___ ___ 75. Inside mouth (Normal)*

___ ___ 76. Outside mouth (Normal)*

___ ___ 77. Hypersensitivity*

Yes No

___ ___ 78. Hyposensitivity*

___ ___ 79. Intolerance to brushing teeth

FEEDING PATTERNS

Bottle-feeding

___ ___ 80. Suckling tongue movements

___ ___ 81. Sucking tongue movements

___ ___ 82. Firm lip seal*

___ ___ 83. Coordinated suck-swallow-breathing

___ ___ 84. Difficulty swallowing*

Cup-drinking

___ ___ 85. Adequate lip closure*

___ ___ 86. Loses less than $1/2$ total amount*

___ ___ 87. Wide up-and-down jaw movements

___ ___ 88. Stabilizes jaw by biting edge of cup

___ ___ 89. Stabilizes jaw through muscle control

___ ___ 90. Drinks through a straw

Feeding patterns—Spoon feeding

___ ___ 91. Suckles as food approaches

___ ___ 92. Cleans food off lower lip

___ ___ 93. Cleans food off spoon with upper lip

Feeding Patterns—Chewing

___ ___ 94. Munching pattern

Lateralizes tongue:

___ ___ 95. When food placed between molars

___ ___ 96. When food placed center of tongue

___ ___ 97. To move food from side to side

___ ___ 98. Vertical jaw movements

___ ___ 99. Rotary jaw movements

___ ___ 100. Lip closure during chewing*

Isolated, Voluntary Tongue Movements

___ ___ 101. Protrudes/retracts tongue

Yes	No		
___	___	102.	Elevates tongue outside mouth
___	___	103.	Elevates tongue inside mouth
___	___	104.	Depresses tongue outside mouth
___	___	105.	Depresses tongue inside mouth
___	___	106.	Lateralizes tongue outside mouth
___	___	107.	Lateralizes tongue inside mouth

Special Oral Problems

Yes	No		
___	___	108.	Drools*
___	___	109.	Thrusts tongue when utensil placed in mouth*
___	___	110.	Thrusts tongue during chewing/swallowing*
___	___	111.	Other oral-motor problem*

NUTRITION HISTORY

Past Status

Yes	No		
___	___	112.	Feeding problems birth–1 year*
___	___	113.	Breast fed
___	___	114.	Bottle fed
___	___	115.	Weaned

Current Status

Yes	No		
___	___	116.	Eats blended food
___	___	117.	Eats limited texture
___	___	118.	Eats chopped table foods
___	___	119.	Eats table foods
___	___	120.	Feeds unassisted
___	___	121.	Feeds with partial guidance
___	___	122.	Feeds with complete guidance
___	___	123.	Drinks from a cup unassisted
___	___	124.	Drinks from a cup assisted
___	___	125.	Finger-feeds
___	___	126.	Uses a spoon
___	___	127.	Uses a fork

Yes	No		
___	___	128.	Uses a knife
___	___	129.	Average rate of eating
___	___	130.	Fast rate of eating
___	___	131.	Slow rate of eating

Diet Review

Yes	No		
___	___	132.	Appetite normal
___	___	133.	Eats 3 meals/day
___	___	134.	Snacks daily

Dietary Intake, Current

Yes	No		
___	___	135.	Milk/dairy products, 3–4/day
___	___	136.	Vegetables, 2–3/day
___	___	137.	Fruit, 2–3/day
___	___	138.	Meat/meat substitute, 2–3/day
___	___	139.	Bread/cereal, 3–4/day
___	___	140.	Sweets/snacks, 1–2/day
___	___	141.	Liquids, 2 cups/day

SOCIAL/BEHAVIORAL

Child-Caregiver Relationship

Yes	No		
___	___	142.	Child responds to caregiver
___	___	143.	Caregiver affectionate to child

Social Skills

Yes	No		
___	___	144.	Eye contact
___	___	145.	Smiles
___	___	146.	Gestures, i.e., waves byebye
___	___	147.	Clings to caregiver
___	___	148.	Interacts with examiner
___	___	149.	Responds to simple directions
___	___	150.	Seeks approval
___	___	151.	Toilet trained
___	___	152.	Knows own sex

Behavior Problems

Yes	No		
___	___	153.	Self abusive
___	___	154.	Hyperactive
___	___	155.	Aggressive

COMMENTS _____

_____
_____

* List or specify on Comments section.

Source: Smith MAH, Connolly B, McFadden S, et al. Developmental feeding tool. In: Smith MAH (ed). *Feeding Management for a Child with a Handicap.* Memphis, TN: Child Development Center, University of Tennessee Center for Health Sciences: 69–70.

First, though, the motivation level and degree of understanding of the parents and the family must be taken into consideration. Indeed, the new guidelines for intervention of the Surgeon General's report[25] on case management for children with developmental disabilities specify that all approaches should be family based. They should also be community centered and comprehensive in scope. The point is to take into account all aspects of a child's treatment program, to avoid issuing an isolated set of instructions relevant only to the treatment goals of one discipline among the many involved in a child's care. This is an important philosophical consideration for the dietitian who would be working with this particular population. The parent or another designated family member may be an individual's case manager, or another health care professional may be the case manager. Nutrition intervention would then become a part of the total intervention package rather than something standing alone, and indeed, it will work better if it is a part of that package.

Another important consideration is whether or not the family gives a high priority to a particular intervention procedure; this applies, again, to any discipline, but in this case particularly to nutrition. For example, consider an obese spina bifida child who has frequent urinary tract infections and a major problem with constipation. The family of this child may give a lower priority to weight management until the other problems have been taken care of. If that is the case, then suggestions should be withheld. When it is determined that suggestions should be given to the family related to any kind of nutritional problem, the coping and educational level of the family should be considered. Often parents of the developmentally disabled child have difficulty coping with the fact that they have a developmentally disabled child and may not be able to deal with too many suggestions at once.

It has been the author's experience that it is better to give one or two specific nutrition activities for a parent to work on at first; then set up frequent follow-up visits for evaluation and providing more suggestions. Also, be available to the parent by telephone for reinterpretation of what it was you might have said during the visit. This is particularly true when parents are distraught. Such parents may find it difficult to follow through on several suggestions given at one time, and as a result they may not attempt anything.

An important consideration for working on nutrition problems with this particular population is the cost of some of the intervention suggestions. The nutritionist should determine if there is a community resource or insurance that can pay for the nutrition suggestions made.

The general principle in the management of nutritional concerns is the importance of the interdisciplinary approach. Again, it has been the author's experience that most children with developmental disabilities have problems requiring input from the physician, physical therapist, occupational therapist, social worker, psychologist, and nurse, in addition to the nutritionist. Pulling that team together in addressing these problems is important in order to have successful nutrition intervention. Some examples of the interdisciplinary approach include working with the occupational therapist in control of oral motor problems for the child with a feeding problem, with the physical therapist or occupational therapist on positioning, and with the psychologist on behavioral problems. All of these problems influence how the nutrition problem is addressed. Communication is a key element in the success of the interdisciplinary approach, which mandates group discussions, correspondence between groups, and good documentation. If one is fortunate, all the disciplines may be in the same facility. The success of an interdisciplinary effort can be phenomenal and can bring about very positive changes in the nutritional problems, so it is worth the effort to ensure lines of communication are maintained.

MANAGEMENT OF NUTRITIONAL PROBLEMS

Obesity

Weight management of the child with developmental disabilities is indicated in any child who tends to plot in the > 75th percentile for weight/height relationship. Conditions that predispose to obesity are low muscle tone, limited physical activity, isolation, and slow growth in height, all of which are found in children with Down syndrome, Prader-Willi syndrome, spina bifida, Turner syndrome, Klinefelter syndrome, and mental retardation. The energy needs of such children are outlined in Table 15-2.

Prevention is the best nutrition intervention to avoid obesity. Counseling in appropriate feeding practices and frequent monitoring of height and weight are essential in a prevention program. Important topics to cover in counseling the parent for preventive weight management include

- growth curves and growth rates
- learning to identify true hunger cues
- increasing activity
- selecting nutritious "lowered" calorie foods
- food preparation practices
- the place of or emphasis on food in the family
- serving sizes

Successful programs for the obese individual should be individually planned and include a written diet. For the school-age child successful management will require contact with the child's school to determine food available through the school food service. Often the family is unaware that school lunch programs may provide low-fat milk, select menus, and salad bars as well as the traditional school lunch.

Childhood weight management must be carefully planned in order to avoid poor growth or nutritional deficiencies. Dietary records maintained by the parent and others caring for the child such as teachers, day care workers, family, and friends are useful for monitoring intake. The diet plan for the older developmentally disabled child who is also mentally retarded must be presented in a way the child can understand. The interdisciplinary approach of working with a special education teacher to present written or pictorial information in an understandable format is necessary for success in this area.

Lack of exercise is often common in the child or adolescent with developmental disabilities. The availability of exercise programs for such children varies from school system to school system, as does the availability of general community-based programs of exercise. Exploring and coordinating community exercise resources is an important part of the dietitian's role in providing good nutritional care.[26]

Behavioral considerations are also an important consideration of weight management programs for the child with developmental disabilities. Important behavioral assessments to make include speed of eating, meal frequency, length of time spent eating, and where meals are taken. Three important behavior modifications to emphasize in the weight management plan include establishing a reward system for compliance with diet, increasing exercise, and targeting eating behaviors to change.

Intervention for obesity for the child with Prader-Willi syndrome requires special involvement of both the family and health care providers.[27] Total environmental control of food access plus a low-calorie diet combined with consistent behavior management techniques and physical exercise are necessary. Environmental control may include locking the refrigerator, cupboards, and the kitchen. Individuals with Prader-Willi syndrome often hide and hoard food and exhibit emotional outbursts when food is withheld.

It has been estimated that the caloric needs of the child with Prader-Willi syndrome are 37% to 77% of normal for weight maintenance, that weight loss occurs at 8 to 9 calories per centimeter of height, and that maintenance of appropriate weight can be accomplished at 10 to 11 calories per centimeter of height.[27]

Several hypocaloric regimens have been used in various centers with variable success. The use of a modified diabetic exchange list has been successful along with a balanced low-calorie diet, a ketogenic diet, and a protein-sparing modified fast.[27]

Increasing physical activity and exercise is an important strategy, and daily exercise routines should be begun early to prevent problems secondary to hypotonia. Adaptive physical education programs in the school should be used with the school-age child.

Failure To Thrive

Failure to thrive, which is defined as inadequate weight gain for height, is frequently found in the child with developmental disabilities. It may result from (1) impaired oral motor function and resultant feeding problems; (2) excessive energy needs, such as occur in cerebral palsy and heart disease and with gastrointestinal problems; (3) infections and frequent illnesses; (4) medications that may affect appetite; and (5) parental inadequacy related to feeding.

Nutrition intervention must begin with a careful assessment, including a feeding evaluation with the opportunity for observation of parent/caregiver–child interaction. Management strategies will be individualized but will generally require increasing calories through either increasing formula concentration for the infant, use of supplemental formulas, or providing energy-dense foods through carbohydrate or fat supplements (see Table 15-6).

Some children with developmental disabilities with failure to thrive require medical evaluation to determine the need for tube feeding or total parenteral nutrition on a temporary basis following a surgical procedure for a gastrointestinal disorder. Usually this will be followed with a return to oral feeding.

Constipation

Constipation, defined as infrequent bowel movements of hard stools, often afflicts children with developmental disabilities, for various reasons, among them lack of activity, generalized hypotonia, and limited bowel muscle function. It can also result from insufficient fluid intake, lack of fiber in the diet, frequent vomiting, and medications. Parents frequently report using laxatives, mineral oil, and

---

Table 15-6 Food That Can Be Added to Pureed Foods to Increase Calories

Food	Calories
Infant cereal	9/T
Nonfat dry milk	25/T
Cheese	120/oz
Margarine	101/T
Evaporated milk	40/oz
Vegetable oils	110/T
Strained infant meats	100–150/jar
Glucose polymers, powdered or liquid	30/T

enemas on a regular basis to correct the problem. As a rule, laxatives and enemas are not recommended since they can lead to dependency, and mineral oil decreases the absorption of the fat-soluble vitamins A, D, E, and K.[3]

Treatment includes adjusting the diet to increase fiber and fluid content. Usual recommendations are as follows:

- Maintain adequate fluid intake, exceeding the daily requirement for age and including water and diluted fruit juice.

- Increase fiber content of the diet by replacing white bread and canned fruits with whole-grain breads and cereals, raw vegetables, fresh fruits, dried fruits, commercial fiber-rich beverages, and cereals fortified with 1 to 2 T unprocessed bran.

- Increase daily exercise.

Feeding Problems

Most feeding problems are the result of oral motor difficulties (see Table 15-7) caused by neuromotor dysfunction, developmental delays, positioning problems, a poor mother-child relationship, and sensory defensiveness.[28] All of these problems may contribute to such behavioral problems as refusal to eat, mealtime tantrums, resistance to texture changes, etc.

Intervention for feeding problems lends itself best to the team approach, utilizing occupational therapy, physical therapy, speech, nursing, psychology, nutrition, and social work.[28] A single written care plan developed by the team, prioritized with the parent's assistance according to the child's needs, should be

---

Table 15-7 Feeding Problems Commonly Encountered

Problem	Description
Tonic bite reflex	Strong jaw closure when teeth and gums are stimulated
Tongue thrust	Forceful and often repetitive protrusion of an often bunched or thick tongue, in response to oral stimulation
Jaw thrust	Forceful opening of the jaw to its maximal extent during eating, drinking, attempts to speak, or general excitement
Tongue retraction	Pulling back the tongue within the oral cavity at presentation of food, spoon, or cup
Lip retraction	Pulling back the lips in a very tight smile-like pattern at the approach of the spoon or cup toward the face
Sensory defensiveness	A strong adverse reaction to sensory input (touch, sound, light)

Source: Reprinted from Lane SJ, Cloud HH, Feeding problems and intervention: An interdisciplinary approach, in *Topics in Clinical Nutrition* (1988;3[3]:26), copyright © 1988, Aspen Publishers, Inc.

provided.[29] Nutritional intervention may involve increasing calories, altering the texture of foods offered, and determining tube-feeding formulas. Additional nutrition education and counseling, oral motor therapy, and behavior management counseling are part of the feeding plan.

Dental Disease

Dental health care contributes to overall improved nutritional status but is often an unmet need in children and adolescents who are developmentally disabled. Dental caries and gum disease are prevalent in this population and are caused by plaque formation, tooth susceptibility, sugar consumption, and medication. Prevention and intervention include home care, professional treatment, and nutritional intervention.

Nutritional intervention involves decreasing the sucrose intake of the diet by eliminating candy, sugar-containing gum, sugar-containing carbonated beverages, cookies, cakes, and highly sweetened foods. Supplying adequate fluoride in the drinking water is helpful in the prevention of caries. In communities where the water supply is not fluoridated, toothpaste and topical application of fluoride can be used.

Gingival disease is often found where dental hygiene is poor. Children taking Dilantin for seizures may suffer gingival hyperplasia, a side effect of the drug. Nutrition counseling to decrease sucrose intake, increase intake of raw fruits and vegetables, and improved snacking practices, coupled with good dental hygiene instruction from the dentist and regular dental care, are important components of dental intervention problems.

OTHER NUTRITIONAL CONSIDERATIONS

A ketogenic diet has been developed for children with intractable epileptic seizures nonresponsive to anticonvulsants.[30,31] Generally this is recommended for children under age 10. This diet is high in fat and very low in protein and carbohydrates. It is thought that the ketosis produced by the low carbohydrate content decreases the number and severity of the seizures. Generally a 4:1 ratio of fat to carbohydrate is required. Fluids are limited and protein kept low. Historically the diet was high in saturated fat content; however, in recent years corn oil and MCT oil has been used.[30,31] One study of 50 children[31] showed excellent results in seizure control utilizing an emulsion of MCT oil to which a variety of flavorings were added. Daily vitamin and mineral supplements are required since the diet is low in calcium, iron, vitamin C, and other vitamins and minerals. The expense of the diet, compliance problems, and lack of palatability have made its use controversial.

CONCLUSION

The nutritional needs of the child with developmental disabilities are important considerations in their treatment and program planning. The goal is to ensure a nutritional intake adequate for growth and provide enough energy for participation in therapy. Research is needed to better define the nutritional requirements of this population. The RDAs for normal children are often inappropriate for this population.

Dietitians in programs serving this population are challenged to defend the cost-effectiveness of nutritional care and to develop nutrition education materials and programs specifically adapted for these children and adolescents, in collaboration with special education professionals.

REFERENCES

1. Developmental Disabilities Assistance and Bill of Rights Act, Public Law 95-602, 1978, no. 503, no. 102.
2. Cloud H. Nutrition assessment of the individual with developmental disabilities. *Top Clin Nutr.* 1987;2:4.
3. Rokursek C, Heindicles E. *Nutrition and Feeding for the Developmentally Disabled.* Vermillion, SD: South Dakota Department of Education and Cultural Affairs; 1985.
4. Walker WA, Hendricks KM. Estimation of energy needs. In: *Manual of Pediatric Nutrition.* Philadelphia, Pa: WB Saunders, 1985.
5. Patrick J, Boland M, Staski D, Murray G. Rapid correction of wasting in children with cerebral palsy. *Dev Med Child Nutr.* 1986;28:734–739.
6. Bennett FC, McClelland S, Kriegsmann E, Andrus L, Sells C. Vitamin and mineral supplementation in Down's Syndrome. *Pediatrics.* 1983;72:707–713.
7. Bidder RT, Gray P, Newcombe RG, Evans BK, Hughes M. The effects of multivitamins and minerals on children with Down syndrome. *Dev Med Child Neurol.* 1989;31:532–537.
8. Ekvall SM. Myelomeningocele: nutrition implications. *Top Clin Nutr.* 1988;3:41–54.
9. Esterman P, Gerber E, Ekvall S. Infantile autism. In: Palmer S, Ekvall S, eds. *Pediatric Nutrition.* Springfield, Ill: Charles C Thomas; 1978:90–94.
10. Chundley AE, Hagerman RJ. Fragile X Syndrome. *J Pediatr.* 1987;110:821–831.
11. Van Dyke DD. Medical problems in infants and young children with Down syndrome: implications for early services. In: Blackman J, ed. *Infants and Young Children with Down Syndrome.* Gaithersburg, Md: Aspen Publishers; 1989:39–50.
12. Ekvall S, Chen IW, Brzian R. The effect of supplemental ascorbic acid on serum vitamin B_{12} levels in myelomeningocele patients. *Am J Clin Nutr.* 1981;34:1356–1361.
13. Lawrence KM, James N, Campbell H. Blood folate levels and quality of the maternal diet. *Br Med J.* 1980;285:216.
14. Bergman KE, Makoseh J, Tews KH. Abnormalities of hair zinc concentrations in mothers of newborn infants with spina bifida. *Am J Clin Nutr.* 1980;33:2145–2150.

15. Smithells RN, Nevin NC, Seller MJ, et al. Further experience of vitamin supplementation for prevention of neural tube defect recurrences. *Lancet.* 1983;1:1027.

16. Roche AF. Growth assessment of handicapped children. *Diet Curr.* 1979;6:25–30.

17. Cloud HH. Nutrition assessment of the individual with developmental disabilities. *Top Clin Nutr.* 1987;2:53–62.

18. Hamill P, Drizd, TA, Johnson CL, et al. Physical growth: National Center for Health Statistics percentiles. *Am J Clin Nutr.* 1979;32:607–629.

19. Cronk C, et al. Growth charts for children with Down syndrome: 1 month to 18 years of age. *Pediatrics.* 1988;81:102.

20. Grunsway LR, Alexander RC, eds. Management of Prader-Willi syndrome. New York, NY: Springer-Verlag; 1988.

21. Lyon AJ, Preese MA. Growth curve for girls with Turner syndrome. *Arch Dis Child.* 1985; 60:932–935.

22. Roche AF, Hines JH. Incremental growth charts. *Am J Clin Nutr.* 1980; 33:2041–2052.

23. Smith MAH. Nutritional assessment of the Mentally Retarded and Developmentally Disabled. Proceedings of the Third National Workshop for Nutritionists from the Univ. Affiliated Facilities. Memphis, Tenn: The Boling Child Development Center, University of Tennessee Center for Health Sciences; 1976.

24. Smith MAH, Connolly B, McFadden S, et al. Developmental feeding tool. In: *Feeding Management for a Child with a Handicap.* Memphis, Tenn: The Boling Child Development Center, University of Tennessee Center for Health Sciences; 1982:69.

25. U.S. Department of Health and Human Services, Public Health Service. *Surgeon General's Report: Children with Special Health Care Needs, Campaign '87. Committment to Family-Centered, Community-Based, Coordinated Care.* DHHS publication no. (HRS) D/MC, 87-2.

26. American Dietetic Association. Nutrition services for children with special health care needs. *J Am Diet Assoc.* 1989;89:1133–1137.

27. McCammon S, Rues J, Cannon S. Prader-Willi syndrome: intervention approaches based on differential phase characteristic. *Top Clin Nutr.* 1988;3:1–8.

28. Lane SJ, Cloud HH. Feeding problems and intervention: an interdisciplinary approach. *Top Clin Nutr.* 1988;3:23–32.

29. Lucas B. Children with developmental disorders: nutrition issues. *Newsletter of The Dietetic in Developmental & Psychiatric Disorder Practice Group of The American Dietetic Association.* 1989; winter.

30. Woody RC. Corn oil ketogenic diet for children with intractable seizures. *J Child Neurol.* 1988;3:21.

31. Sills MA, Forsythe WI, Hoidukewych D, MacDonald A, Robinson M. The medium chain triglyceride diet and intractable epilepsy. *Arch Dis Child.* 1986;61:1168–1172.

32. Roe A. *Handbook: Interactions of Selected Drugs and Nutrients in Patients.* 3rd ed. Chicago, Ill. American Dietetic Assocation; 1982.

Chapter 16

Pulmonary Diseases

Nancy H. Wooldridge

CYSTIC FIBROSIS

Cystic fibrosis (CF), a genetic disorder of children, adolescents, and young adults characterized by widespread dysfunction of the exocrine glands, is the most common lethal hereditary disease of the Caucasian race.[1] Characteristic of the disease is the production of abnormally thick and viscous mucus, which affects various organs of the body. In the lungs, the thick mucus clogs the airways, causing obstruction and subsequent bacterial infections. The thick mucus prevents the release of pancreatic enzymes into the small intestine for the digestion of foods. Blockage of ducts eventually causes pancreatic fibrosis and cyst formation. About 85% of CF patients have pancreatic involvement exhibited by such gastrointestinal symptoms as frequent, foul-smelling stools, increased flatus, and abdominal cramping. In a small percentage of patients, the ducts and tubules of the liver are obstructed by mucus, resulting in liver disease similar to cirrhosis. Another complication of CF is diabetes, particularly seen in the adolescent and young adult population. A unique characteristic of the disease is an increased loss of sodium and chloride in the sweat. Sterility in males and decreased fertility in females is also seen.

The life expectancy of CF patients has greatly improved since the disease was first described as a distinct clinical entity by Andersen in 1938.[2] During the 1930s to 1950s, CF patients usually died at an early age of malabsorption and malnutrition. With pancreatic enzyme therapy, antibiotic therapy, and earlier diagnosis, the prognosis of CF patients has greatly improved over the years. The Cystic Fibrosis Foundation currently reports the median age of survival to be 28 years.[3]

Genetics

CF is transmitted as an autosomal recessive trait. Both parents are carriers of the defective gene but exhibit no symptoms of the disease themselves. Each offspring of two carriers of the defective gene has a 25% chance of having the disease.

The defective gene in CF has recently been discovered on chromosome 7.[4] It is hoped that this new discovery will lead to improved treatment of CF patients and ultimately to a cure for the disease.

Incidence

The incidence of CF in whites is 1 in 2000 live births, with a carrier rate of 1 in 20. The incidence is 1 in 17,000 births among blacks. The disease is rarely seen in Orientals and American Indians.[5]

Manifestations

Manifestations of the disease are numerous and are quite variable from patient to patient. A summary of common manifestations of CF is depicted in Table 16-1. Any child who repeatedly exhibits any of these symptoms should be tested for CF. In addition, CF should be ruled out when a child tastes salty when kissed or experiences heat prostration.

Diagnosis

The definitive diagnosis of CF is made when elevated levels of chloride and sodium are found in the patient's sweat, as measured by a quantitative pilocarpine iontophoresis sweat test, and at least one of the following:

1. evidence of pulmonary involvement
2. evidence of pancreatic insufficiency
3. a positive family history

Table 16-1 Manifestations of Cystic Fibrosis

Pulmonary	*Gastrointestinal*
Chronic cough	Failure to thrive
Repeated bronchial infections	Steatorrhea
Increased work of breathing	Hypoalbuminemia
Digital clubbing	Rectal prolapse
Bronchospasm	Frequent, foul-smelling stools
Cyanosis	Abdominal cramping
Chronic pneumonia	Voracious appetite
Nasal polyps	Anemia
	Vitamin deficiency

Practitioners in the community have become more familiar with CF and with the many ways the disease may manifest itself. Therefore, patients are usually diagnosed during infancy and early childhood. However, because of the variability of the disease, the diagnosis may not be recognized in some patients until adolescence or young adulthood.

Management

Rigorous daily management is required to control the symptoms of the disease. The pulmonary symptoms are controlled by daily chest percussion and vibration treatments and by the timely use of oral and intravenous antibiotics.

Pancreatic enzyme replacement therapy is a crucial part of the management of the gastrointestinal symptoms. Enzymes are often required with each meal and snack. Dosage is very individualized, depending on factors such as the extent of pancreatic involvement, the patient's dietary intake, and the patient's age. Vitamin and mineral supplementation is also recommended. Providing adequate nutrition for normal growth and development is one of the primary goals of disease management in CF.

Effects on Nutritional Status

Chronic Energy Deficit

Many aspects of the disease of CF stress the nutritional status of the patient directly or indirectly by affecting the patient's appetite and subsequent intake. Aspects of pulmonary and gastrointestinal involvement affecting nutritional status are summarized in Table 16-2. Gastrointestinal losses occur in spite of pancreatic enzyme replacement therapy. Also, catch-up growth requires additional calories. All of these factors contribute to a chronic energy deficit, which can lead to a marasmic type of malnutrition. The primary goal of nutritional therapy is to overcome this energy deficit.

Table 16-2 Aspects of Cystic Fibrosis Which Affect Nutritional Status

Pulmonary	Gastrointestinal
Increased work of breathing	Malabsorption of fat
Chronic cough	Loss of fat-soluble vitamins
Cough-emesis cycle	Loss of essential fatty acids
Chronic antibiotic therapy	Malabsorption of protein
Fatigue, anxiety	Loss of nitrogen
Decreased tolerance for exercise	
Repeated pulmonary infections	

Appetite

Many references have been made to the voracious appetites of CF patients. This may be true of undiagnosed and untreated patients, particularly infants. In practice, however, dietetic professionals are usually dealing with patients who have very poor appetites. Studies have shown variable intakes in the CF population, but the intakes are usually less than adequate and are associated with a less than normal growth pattern.[6-11] Table 16-2 delineates some aspects of CF that contribute to this poor appetite and failure to thrive.

Nutritional Screening and Assessment

Since nutrition plays such an important role in the treatment of CF, routine nutritional screening and thorough assessments are very important. In this section, anthropometric, dietary, biochemical, and clinical evaluations will be discussed. Examples of a nutrition assessment form and a CF nutrition flow sheet, developed by a group of CF nutritionists, appear in Exhibits 16-1 and 16-2.

Anthropometric

Monitoring growth parameters is an important component of the screening, assessment, and follow-up of CF patients. As with any child, CF patients should be weighed and measured routinely using appropriate techniques and equipment, such as those described by Fomon.[12] Weight-for-age, recumbent length or height-for-age, weight-for-height, and head circumference should be accurately measured and plotted on the National Center for Health Statistics (NCHS) growth curves at each clinic visit or hospitalization.[13] The detailed NCHS weight/height tables should be employed in determining weight/height percentiles for the preadolescent and adolescent patient.[14] (See Chapter 2, Nutrition Assessment, for additional information.)

Growth charts are wonderfully simple and readily accessible screening and assessment tools. Although they are intended for use with a healthy population of children, NCHS growth charts provide a way to monitor the growth of CF patients. General recommendations of cases needing further attention include the following:

1. weight-for-age less than the 5th percentile and greater than the 95th percentile
2. length- or height-for-age less than the 5th percentile and greater than the 95th percentile
3. weight-for-height less than the 5th percentile or greater than the 95th percentile
4. a crossing of percentile levels in either an upward or downward direction

Exhibit 16-1 Nutrition Assessment, Cystic Fibrosis

Date of assessment: _____

Name: _____   C.F. Center: _____

Date of Birth: _____   Physician: _____

Admitting Dx (other than CF) _____   Age of dx: _____

I. DIET HISTORY

Pancreatic enzymes—type:_____ Number with meals: ____ Number with snacks: ___

How are enzymes taken? _____

Use or avoidance of enzymes in school or other settings: _____

Vitamins—type and dosage: _____ NaCl tablets:_____

Nutrition supplements—type and amount: _____ Oral, tube, or IV: _____

Food allergies/intolerances: _____ Type of tube feeding:_____

Special diet: _____Frequency of tube feeding:_____

Food assistance (WIC, Food Stamps, etc.): _____

Milk/formula—type: _____ amount: _____ preparation:_____

Problems with vomiting or reflux:_____

Any behavioral problems related to meals and eating: _____

_____

Appetite: Excellent _____ Good _____ Fair_____ Poor _____

Parental/guardian concerns:_____

_____

Status of diet education: _____

_____

II. PHYSICAL ASSESSMENT/ANTHROPOMETRICS:

	Date	Value	Percentile
height or length:			
weight:			
weight for length:			
height age (if less than 5 months old):			
head circumference:			
triceps skinfold:			
mid-arm circumference:			
mid-arm muscle area:			
mid-arm fat area:			
subscapular or calf:			

Weight Changes: +/– _____ kg.   in _____ months

III. PHYSICAL ACTIVITY

Type: _____

PT Frequency: _____

Duration: _____

When (i.e., before or after meals, . . .) _____

_____

Use of O_2: _____

Sleep problems:_____

Hemoptysis: _____

Exhibit 16-1 continued

IV. STOOL PATTERN

Number of stools: _____

Consistency: _____

Change in bowel status: _____

Problems with rectal prolapse, constipation, sticky bowel, GI distress, bloating, etc.:___

_____

_____

V. LABORATORY STUDIES

	Lab Normals	Date	Value
Total Protein			
Albumin			
Prealbumin			
Hematocrit			
Hemoglobin			
Transferrin			
72 hour fecal fat			
Bentiromide test (PABA)			
Sodium			
Potassium			
Chloride			
Glucose			
hgb A_1C			
BUN			
Creatinine			
Prothrombin time			
Vitamin A			
Vitamin E			
Zinc			
Magnesium			
Cholesterol			
Triglycerides			
CO_2			
Others			

VI. ASSESSMENT OF NUTRITIONAL STATUS

	Calories	Protein	Fat	Carbohydrates
Estimated Daily Requirement*:				
Estimated Daily Intake:				
Intake as Percent of Requirement:				

Calorie Intake Goal (cal/day): _____

Estimated Fluid Requirement: _____

IBW or Desirable Weight: _____

Actual Weight as Percent of Desirable: _____

Drug–Nutrient Interactions: _____

continues

Exhibit 16-1 continued

Assessment of Nutritional Status: _____
_____
_____
_____
_____
_____

Recommendations/Instructions: _____
_____
_____
_____
_____
_____
_____

Dietitian: _____
_____

Notes:

1. Caloric requirement was determined using (Check one)
   _____ 150 calories/kg actual weight for infant
   _____ Resting Energy Expenditure (REE) × 1.5 (no acute illness, mild CF)
   _____ REE × 1.75 (infection, recent weight loss, moderate CF)
   _____ REE × 2.0 (acute illness, severe wasting, significant malabsorption)
   _____ RDA for age × 1.3 (moderate disease)
   _____ RDA for age × 1.5 (severe disease)
   _____ WHO BMR Equation
   _____ Other:_____

2. _____ Protein requirement was determined using (Check one)
   _____ 2.2 gm protein/kg infant (2 × RDA)
   _____ 1.2 gm protein/kg child (2 × RDA)
   _____ 1.0 gm protein/kg teenager, adult (2 × RDA)
   _____ Calories/150 × 6.25
   _____ Other:_____

3. Desirable weight was determined using (Check one)
   _____ 50th Percentile Weight for Height on NCHS Growth Chart
   _____ Metropolitan Life Insurance Table for Small Frame
   _____ Metropolitan Life Insurance Table for Medium Frame
   _____ Male 106 lbs first 5 feet + 6 lbs per inch
   _____ Female 100 lbs first 5 feet + 5 lbs per inch
   _____ Other: _____

Source: Courtesy of Patricia Murray, RD, MEd, Londonderry, NH.

Other anthropometric measurements, such as triceps skinfold, mid-arm circumference, and mid-arm muscle circumference, can be monitored. These measurements are particularly beneficial when monitoring the effects of nutrition intervention over long periods of time.

Most growth studies have found CF patients to be smaller and lighter than their age- and sex-matched peers.[11,15–18] For example, Sproul and Huang found the 50th percentile for CF patients from infancy to adolescence for height and weight to be between the 3rd and 10th percentiles on the growth charts for healthy children.[15] These same investigators noted an absence of the adolescent growth spurt in the CF population. Growth deficiencies significantly correlated with the severity of respiratory disease but did not correlate with pancreatic insufficiency.

Wooldridge et al. found poor growth in a total population of treated CF patients less than 3 years of age in the absence of pulmonary disease, as indicated by good Shwachman and Brasfield (X-ray) scores.[19–21] Ressler et al. recently studied this same population of CF children, now aged 8–11 years, and found that their heights and weights continued to be significantly smaller than those of their age- and sex-matched unaffected peers. The decrease in growth did not correlate with pulmonary status.[22]

In contrast, the Toronto CF clinic reports that its patients conform to the normal distribution for height in both males and females and for weight in males.[23,24] This clinic has advocated a high-calorie diet with 40% of total calories as fat, coupled with high doses of pancreatic enzymes, as part of its routine medical care since the early 1970s.[25]

Adequate diet and pancreatic enzyme supplementation play a significant role in the proper nutrition of these patients. However, it seems that in spite of treatment, growth may be a problem for CF children from an early age in spite of good pulmonary function. And as the pulmonary disease progresses, the magnitude of the growth problem increases.

Dietary

As part of the nutritional assessment, dietary analysis provides important information about what and how much the CF patient is eating. Several methods of gathering the data can be utilized, including a 24-hour dietary recall, a 3- to 7-day food record, and a food frequency form. The health professional should analyze the diet's adequacy in terms of calories, protein, and other nutrients by looking for a variety of foods in adequate amounts. As shown in Table 16-3, the Cystic Fibrosis Foundation recommends a 50% to 100% increase in calories above what is normally recommended for a healthy child. The recommendation for protein is 2 to 2$^1/_2$ times the Recommended Dietary Allowance (RDA).[1,26]

Exhibit 16-2 Cystic Fibrosis Nutrition Flow Sheet

Patient Name: _____						
Date of Birth: _____						
Diagnosis (other than CF): _____						
Date:						
Height						
Weight						
Height %						
Weight %						
Height/Weight %						
IBW						
Oral Intake						
Caloric Needs						
% of Needs						
Protein Intake						
Protein Needs						
% of Needs						
Supplements/Tube feeding						
Skinfold measurement						
Skinfold measurement %						
Other:						
Plan or Comments:						

Source: Courtesy of Patricia Murray, RD, MEd, Londonderry, NH.

Biochemical

Undiagnosed infants, particularly those who are breastfed or who are on soy formula, often present with hypoalbuminemia and subsequent edema. The malabsorption of undiagnosed CF causes the inadequate absorption of protein. The low protein content of breast milk as compared to modified cow milk formulas further compromises the infant's protein status. For reasons as yet unclear, the CF infant

Table 16-3 Recommended Caloric Intake, Protein Intake, and Vitamin and Mineral Supplementation in CF

Nutrient	Recommended Amount
Calories	150%–200% of the RDA[1,26]
Protein	200%–250% of the RDA[1,26]
Vitamin A*	5000–10,000 IU/d[40,41]
Vitamin D†	400–800 IU/d[40,41]
Vitamin E	1 IU/kg of body weight,[40,41] in water-miscible form
Vitamin K	5.0 mg every third day[40] or 2.5–5.0 mg weekly[41] or 5.0 mg twice a week[1]
Water-soluble vitamins	Give RDA, twice the RDA[1], or multivitamin plus normal diet[41]
Sodium and chloride, at times of increased sweating	2–4 g sodium chloride

* Can be provided by 1–2 multivitamins per day; however, Chase states emulsified alcohol is better absorbed.
† Can be provided by 1–2 multivitamins per day.

Source: Data from references 1, 26, 40, and 41.

does not utilize soy protein effectively. Upon diagnosis and the initiation of pancreatic enzyme therapy, the hypoalbuminemia is usually corrected because the patient is no longer malabsorbing protein. It is wise to check an albumin level in newly diagnosed infants.

Any time an inadequate protein intake is suspected, it may be beneficial to assess the albumin level. However, it is important to remember that besides malnutrition, other causes of an abnormal albumin value include infection and other physiologic stress, fluid overload, congestive heart failure, and severe hepatic insufficiency.[27] CF patients, who chronically have inadequate calorie intakes, usually have a marasmic type of malnutrition. Their visceral protein levels are usually in the normal range, while somatic protein stores are low.[27]

The long-term antibiotic therapy that is so common in the treatment of CF alters the gut flora. Since an important source of vitamin K is microbiologic synthesis in the gut, vitamin K status is affected. For this reason it is important to routinely monitor prothrombin times.

Other biomedical indexes that may need to be monitored include measures of iron status, such as ferritin, serum iron, total iron-binding capacity, and vitamin levels, particularly of the fat-soluble vitamins. Many CF centers also use various diagnostic tests to assess exocrine pancreatic function, including duodenal aspirations, fecal fat studies, and stool trypsin studies.

Clinical

Stool Pattern. The patient's stool pattern should be monitored carefully at each clinic visit, because this is a good indication of the adequacy of the enzyme therapy. Questions to be asked during a nutrition screening and assessment should include the following:

1. number of stools per day
2. consistency of stools
3. presence of oily discharge
4. rectal prolapse
5. foul-smelling, floating stools and/or flatus
6. abdominal cramping

Enzyme Therapy. Important aspects of enzyme replacement therapy that need to be checked every clinic visit and hospitalization are

1. type
2. brand
3. amount taken
4. when taken
5. method of administration
6. timing with meals

Other Medications. It is important to note other medications the patient may be taking at each clinic visit, including antibiotics, diuretics, cardiac medications, vitamins, and minerals.

Pulmonary Status. The pulmonary status of the patient will directly influence the patient's nutritional status. The nutritional professional needs to note the presence of an acute pulmonary exacerbation and chronic disease. Older CF patients will be able to have pulmonary function tests to assess the extent of their pulmonary involvement. The Brasfield or X-ray score is also a quantitative measure of pulmonary status, designed as a simple, reproducible tool for scoring chest roentgenograms. The perfect X-ray score is 25.[21]

Other Medical Complications. Evidence of other medical problems should be noted, including diabetes mellitus, liver disease, and lactose intolerance. These conditions will also have a direct impact on the patient's nutritional status.

Nutritional Management

Adequate Diet for Normal Growth and Development

In the past, the gastrointestinal symptoms of the disease, such as increased number of bulky, foul-smelling stools, increased flatus, and abdominal cramping, were treated with a low-fat diet. Today, with the advent of better enzyme replacement therapy, fat restriction is no longer routinely imposed on all patients. Health professionals now appreciate the tremendous energy demands of the disease, although the specific energy, protein, and nutrient requirements of CF patients have not been determined quantitatively. It is difficult to meet the high-energy needs within the confines of a fat restriction.

The present recommendation is to allow as much fat in the diet as the individual patient can tolerate. Individuals may identify particular food items that cause them an increase in gastrointestinal symptoms, such as flatus or abdominal cramping. The patient can either avoid these food items or try taking additional enzymes with these particular foods.

Age-specific considerations in the nutritional management of CF are summarized in Table 16-4. In practice, it is easy for a CF patient to achieve the recommended protein intake because the average American diet is so high in protein. It is much more difficult to achieve the calorie intake that is recommended.

To close the gap between caloric needs and the amount of calories the patient is able to consume, calorically dense foods can be added to the patient's diet. Margarine, cheese, sour cream, and cream cheese can easily be added to the patient's favorite foods, if the patient can tolerate the added fat. Exhibit 16-3 depicts one approach to increasing calories and protein.

Supplements. Milkshakes and other high-calorie drinks can be used as supplemental feedings. Commercial oral feedings can also be used to boost calories but add additional expense and in some instances are difficult for the family to obtain.

Tube Feedings. Oftentimes, in spite of vigorous efforts by the patient, the patient's family, and dietetic professionals, it is very difficult to meet the patient's caloric needs by the oral route alone. At these times, alternate routes of supplemental feedings need to be considered.

CF centers have reported using various forms of tube feedings, including nasogastric, gastrostomy, and jejunostomy feedings. Tube feedings are sometimes administered on a continuous basis while the patient is asleep. Some centers use a partially predigested formula with or without enzymes; others use an isotonic formula with enzymes. Enzyme administration poses a problem with nocturnal tube feedings. Mixing enzymes directly into the feeding causes the product to begin to break down and may clog the feeding tube. Many centers instruct patients to take pancreatic enzymes prior to the initiation of the feeding and if/when they wake up during the night.

Table 16-4 Nutritional Management of CF Patients

1. Infants
   • Breast milk, standard iron-fortified infant formula, or special formulas such as Alimentum* and Pregestimil† (protein hydrolysate formulas with medium-chain triglycerides) or Portagen† (intact protein formula with 85% of fat from medium-chain triglycerides) can be recommended.
   • Pancreatic enzymes should be given prior to feedings with any of the milks or formulas listed above.
   • Vitamin supplements and a source of fluoride should be given.
   • Introduction of solid foods should proceed as with a healthy infant. Some of the high-calorie, starchy vegetables and dessert baby foods can also be added to the diet to increase calorie intake. Salt supplementation may be needed.
2. Toddlers
   • Toddlers' diets should be based on a normal diet with a variety of foods.
   • Parents should be forewarned of the normal decrease in growth and appetite during this age.
   • Regular meal times and snack times should be encouraged.
   • Excessive snacking and drinking between meals should be discouraged.
   • Pancreatic enzymes and vitamins are continued.
3. Preschool and school age
   • A normal healthy diet with a variety of foods again should form the basis of the diet.
   • Parents lose control of what child eats away from home at preschool and school.
   • Arrangements need to be made for child to take enzymes during the school day.
   • Vitamins are continued.
4. Adolescents
   • Patients begin exercising more independence in food choices.
   • Parents can provide appropriate food environment at home.
   • Patients can be taught to include quick-to-prepare high-calorie foods in daily diet.
   • Snack and fast foods can add a significant amount of calories to the diet and should not be discouraged.
   • Importance of high-calorie intake and enzyme and vitamin therapy should be emphasized by health professionals directly to patient and not via the parents.

* Ross Laboratories, Columbus, Ohio.
† Mead Johnson Nutritionals, Bristol-Myers Institutional Products, Evansville, Indiana.

Numerous studies have been conducted on the effectiveness of these various types of feedings, with varying results.[28–33] Patients do gain weight on these types of feedings; however, the weight is lost when the feedings are discontinued. The studies' results emphasize the need to begin these types of therapies early in the course of malnutrition. Levy et al. have developed a prognostic equation that can help to determine which malnourished CF patients are likely to benefit from intensive nutritional support.[34] Most of the studies reported in the literature have been unable to discern the long-term effect of improved nutritional status on the progression of the pulmonary disease. Shepherd et al. in a study of 10 undernourished

Exhibit 16-3 Instructional Handout on Increasing Calories

Calorie-Protein
BOOSTERS

—Some ways to hide extra calories and protein—

Powdered Milk (33 cal/tbsp, 3 gm pro/tbsp)
Add 2-4 tbsp to 1 cup milk. Mix into puddings, potatoes, soups, ground meats, vegetables, cooked cereal.

Eggs (80 cal/egg, 7 gm pro/tbsp)
Add to casseroles, meat loaf, mashed potato, cooked cereal, macaroni & cheese. Add extra to pancake batter and french toast. (Do not use raw eggs in uncooked items.)

Butter or margarine (45 cal/tsp)
Add to puddings, casseroles, sandwiches, vegetables, cooked cereal.

Cheeses (100 cal/oz, 7 gm pro/oz)
Give as snacks, or in sandwiches. Add melted to casseroles, potatoes, vegetables, soup.

Wheat germ (25 cal/tbsp)
Add a tablespoon or two to cereal. Mix into meat dishes, cookie batter, casseroles, etc.

Mayonnaise or Salad Dressings (45 cal/tsp)
Use liberally on sandwiches, on salads, as a dip for raw vegetables or sauce on cooked vegetables.

Evaporated milk (25 cal/tbsp, 1 gm pro/tbsp)
Use in place of whole milk, in desserts, baked goods, meat dishes and cooked cereals.

Sour Cream (26 cal/tbsp)
Add to potatoes, casseroles, dips; use in sauces, baked goods, etc.

Sweetened condensed milk (60 cal/tbsp, 1 gm pro/tbsp)
Add to pies, puddings, milkshakes. Mix 1-2 tbsp with peanut butter and spread on toast.

Peanut butter (95 cal/tbsp, 4 gm pro/tbsp)
Serve on toast, crackers, bananas, apples, celery.

Carnation Instant Breakfast (130 cal/pckt, 7 gm pro/pckt)
Add to milk, milkshakes.

Gravies (40 cal/tbsp)
Use liberally on mashed potatoes, meats.

High Protein Foods	★ MEATS—Beef, Chicken, Fish, Turkey, Lamb ★ MILK & CHEESE—Yogurt, Cottage Cheese, Cream Cheese ★ EGGS ★ PEANUT BUTTER (with Bread or Crackers) ★ DRIED BEANS & PEAS (with Bread, Cornbread, Rice)

Source: Courtesy of Kathy Barnhill Moates, Director of Nutrition, Pediatric Pulmonary Center, University of Alabama, Birmingham, AL.

CF patients showed fewer pulmonary infections per year and a significant reversal of the trend for deteriorating lung function with nutrition support.[35] As previously mentioned, the Toronto Clinic places a heavy emphasis on nutritional guidance and intervention in CF. The median age of survival in Toronto is 30 years, as compared to 21 years in the Boston Clinic, although these two groups of patients have very similar age-specific pulmonary function.[21] In order to establish the effects of nutrition intervention on pulmonary function, multicenter studies that control for the many variables involved are needed. If no long-term effect on pulmonary function or survival is demonstrated, the validity of more invasive nutrition interventions may be questioned.[12]

Parenteral Nutrition. The use of parenteral nutrition in the treatment of CF has also been studied. Conflicting results of its effectiveness have been reported.[36–38] Parenteral nutrition is more expensive than enteral feedings and does carry its own risks. One such risk is the increased rate of carbon dioxide production with high-carbohydrate infusions, which significantly raises the respiratory quotient.[39]

Adequate Vitamin and Mineral Status

Vitamins. Much of the focus on nutritional research in CF has been on fat-soluble vitamin status because of the well-documented fat malabsorption in CF.[40] Water-soluble vitamins have received less attention in clinical research in CF. Various researchers' recommendations for vitamin supplementation are shown in Table 16-3. Recommendations vary because specific nutrient requirements have not been established for CF patients. Quantification of vitamin stores is difficult to ascertain in CF patients. Values are altered by antibiotics and vitamin therapy.

In practice, most centers advise patients to take a multivitamin supplement that supplies twice the vitamin RDAs and extra vitamin E and vitamin K in water-miscible forms. Extra vitamin K supplements are particularly recommended for infants, whose gut flora may not yet be mature, and for older patients in the following situations: (1) after a bleeding episode, (2) with long-term (over 1 month) antibiotic therapy, and (3) prior to surgery. When prothrombin times are abnormal, intramuscular vitamin K may be recommended.

Minerals. Minerals such as zinc, iron, and selenium have been studied in the CF population.[41] Much more study is needed before specific supplementation recommendations can be made. These minerals as well as other macro- and micronutrients are important in the overall nutriture of the CF patient, and therefore eating a variety of foods should be encouraged.

Additional salt should be added to the diet during times of increased sweating, such as

1. during hot weather
2. with fevers

3. with profuse diarrhea

4. during strenuous physical activity

The additional salt compensates for the increased loss of sodium and chloride through the sweat. In most instances, liberal use of the salt shaker and the inclusion of highly salty foods in the diet will supply the needed sodium and chloride. Salt supplements may be used in instances of very heavy sweating.

Adequate Pancreatic Enzyme Replacement Therapy

Types of Available Enzymes. There are many different brands and types of pancreatic enzymes available (Table 16-5). They contain varying amounts of lipase, which breaks down fat; protease, which breaks down protein; and amylase, which breaks down carbohydrate.

The nonproprietary name of these products is pancrelipase. Most of the products feature an enteric coating, which protects the enzymes from inactivation in the acid environment of the stomach. The enzymes become activated in the alkaline pH of the duodenum. Pancreatic enzymes are also available in powder and capsule forms.

Dosage. The proper dosage of pancreatic enzymes for an individual patient is derived by a trial-and-error process, which begins by choosing an enzyme and a beginning dose, based on the physician's and/or dietitian's recommendations. Dosage at snack time depends on the size and type of snack. Careful monitoring of the patient's growth, stool pattern, and the absence or presence of gastrointestinal symptoms is necessary to determine the adequacy of therapy. This monitoring and making necessary adjustments in the dosage needs to be continued throughout the patient's treatment.

Administration. Enzymes should be taken within an hour *prior* to meals and snacks, to be most effective. The enterically coated enzymes should not be chewed or crushed. Some patients may require additional enzymes with some higher-fat foods such as pizza.

Most of the enzymes are available in capsule form. For infants and small children who are unable to swallow a capsule, the capsule can be broken open and the contents mixed with a soft food such as applesauce. When the enterically coated enzymes are mixed with a higher-pH food such as pudding or milk, the enzymes will become activated and begin breaking down the food. Powdered enzymes are already in an activated form. Mixing enzymes directly into a tube feeding or infant formula causes the feeding to begin enzymatic digestion. This may cause the feeding to take on an unpleasant color, taste, or odor.

Patient Compliance. Administering enzymes to a very young infant can be a frustrating endeavor for the parent and/or caretaker, primarily because of the infant's natural extrusion reflex. After a few months of age, taking enzymes becomes part of a CF patient's daily routine. In the preadolescent and adolescent age

Table 16-5 Pancreatic Enzymes

Product (Manufacturer)	Form	Lipase USP Units	Protease USP Units	Amylase USP Units
Cotazym (Organon, Inc.)	Powder in a capsule	8000	30,000	30,000
Cotazym-S (Organon, Inc.)	Enteric-coated spheres	5000	20,000	20,000
Creon (Reid-Rowell)	Enteric-coated microspheres in capsules	8000	13,000	30,000
Entolase (AH Robins)	Enteric-coated microbeads in hard gelatin capsules	4000	25,000	20,000
Entolase-HP (AH Robins)	Enteric-coated microbeads in hard gelatin capsules	8000	50,000	40,000
Ku-Zyme HP (Schwarz)	Capsules	8000	30,000	30,000
Pancrease (McNeil)	Enteric-coated microspheres	4000	25,000	20,000
Pancrease MT4 (McNeil)	Enteric-coated microtablets capsules	4000	12,000	12,000
Pancrease MT10 (McNeil)	Enteric-coated microtablets capsules	10,000	30,000	30,000
Pancrease MT16 (McNeil)	Enteric-coated microtablets capsules	16,000	48,000	48,000
Ultrase MT12 (Scandipharm, Inc.)	Enteric-coated minitablets	12,000	39,000	39,000
Ultrase MT20 (Scandipharm, Inc.)	Enteric-coated minitablets	20,000	65,000	65,000
Ultrase MT24 (Scandipharm, Inc.)	Enteric-coated minitablets	24,000	78,000	78,000
Viokase Powder (AH Robins)	Powder (1/4 tsp)	16,800	70,000	7,000
Viokase Tablet (AH Robins)	Tablet	8000	30,000	30,000
Zymase (Organon, Inc.)	Enteric-coated spheres	12,000	24,000	24,000

groups, patient compliance with enzyme administration can become a big issue. Sometimes schools require the patient to come to the school office for medications, and this may be a source of embarrassment and alienation for the patient. The lack of compliance needs to be discussed with the patient, and a solution must be found that is agreeable to the patient, parents, and school authorities.

Pancreatic enzyme therapy is very expensive and contributes significantly to the overall cost of this disease. Enzymes are often covered by third-party payers and programs such as State Children's Rehabilitation Services.

Referral to Food/Nutrition and Other Resources

Referral to food and nutrition resources such as the Women, Infants, and Children (WIC) program and the Food Stamp Program should be made based on the individual patient's needs. In some states, referrals can be made to the State Children's Rehabilitation Services for aid in obtaining supplemental feedings.

CF has a tremendous impact on patients and their families emotionally, physically, and financially. Most CF centers provide an interdisciplinary team approach to the care of these patients and their families in order to better help them meet their many needs.

Drug–Nutrient Interactions

Prolonged antibiotic therapy can alter the gut flora and subsequently influence vitamin K status. Bronchodilators containing theophylline are often prescribed for CF patients. Theophylline levels must be monitored carefully to determine proper dosage, because toxic levels of theophylline can cause nausea and vomiting and consequently interfere with intake.

As the CF patient's pulmonary disease progresses, cor pulmonale, or right-sided heart failure, develops. Diuretics are often prescribed at this point. Electrolyte and fluid status need to be carefully monitored.

Identification of Areas Needing Further Research

There are many unanswered questions about CF in general and more specifically in regard to nutrition. Much more research is needed to determine specific nutrient requirements of CF patients in regard to energy, protein, vitamins, and minerals. The most appropriate method for delivering these nutrients must be determined. Can it be done by oral means alone, or should more invasive nutrition therapy such as gastrostomy feedings, jejunostomy feedings, or parenteral nutrition become a part of routine nutritional care? The most appropriate time for nutrition intervention in the course of the disease must be determined. What are the psychosocial and emotional benefits and drawbacks with more invasive nutritional therapy? What effect does improved nutritional status have on the progression of the pulmonary disease, the ultimate killer of the vast majority of CF patients? What constitutes normal growth for a CF patient?

CF is a complicated disease affecting many organs of the body. Proper nutritional care is an integral part of its therapy. The disease process is highly variable, and thus every patient and family deserves individualized treatment and support from an interdisciplinary team of health professionals.

BRONCHOPULMONARY DYSPLASIA

Bronchopulmonary dysplasia (BPD) was first described by Northway in 1967 as a form of chronic lung disease seen in infants with severe hyaline membrane disease who required mechanical ventilation and high concentrations of oxygen for prolonged periods of time.[42] Northway's definition included four stages of the disease based on radiographic findings, with stage IV being defined as the period of chronic lung disease, characterized by severe functional and morphologic lung damage.[42]

Today's definition of BPD usually includes infants who have had an acute lung injury with minimal clinical and radiographic findings as well as those with major radiographic abnormalities. There is no standard nomenclature used in defining BPD. This chronic disease is seen in young infants, the vast majority being premature infants who require respiratory support during the first 2 weeks of life or longer. The use of intermittent positive pressure ventilation (IPPV) and high concentrations of oxygen is associated with the occurrence of BPD.

More and more preterm infants are surviving with the aid of mechanical ventilation today. Consequently, BPD has become one of the most common sequelae of newborn intensive care unit stays.

The disease is characterized by signs of respiratory distress such as chest retractions, tachypnea, crackles, and wheezing. Supplemental oxygen therapy may be required, and there will be changes on the patient's chest radiograph. Pulmonary complications of BPD may include recurrent atelectasis, pulmonary infections, and respiratory failure requiring mechanical ventilation. Other complications of BPD include cor pulmonale, poor growth, and developmental delays including delayed feeding skills.

The primary goal of BPD management is to provide the patient with the necessary pulmonary support during the acute and chronic phases of the disease to minimize lung damage and to maintain optimal oxygen saturation. This may include mechanical ventilation, supplemental oxygen, and diuretic therapy. Of almost equal importance is the provision of adequate nutrition not only for growth and development but also to compensate for the demands of the disease. Growth of new lung tissue can occur in humans until about 8 years of age. Theoretically, a BPD patient can "outgrow" the disease if proper pulmonary and nutritional support can be provided.

Effects on Nutritional Status

Increased Nutrient Requirements

Effects of Prematurity. In light of the fact that most babies who develop BPD are premature infants, it is easy to see that these infants have little fat, glycogen, or other nutrients in reserve. Faced with the demands of prematurity and the stress of BPD, the infant can quickly develop a state of negative nutrient balance.

Effects of Bronchopulmonary Dysplasia. Four factors increase the caloric requirements of BPD patients:

1. increased basal metabolic rate
2. increased work of breathing
3. chronic illness/infections
4. respiratory distress/metabolic complications

Weinstein and Oh reported that resting oxygen consumption was approximately 25% higher in eight infants with BPD when compared to controls.[43]

Infants with BPD are very fluid sensitive because of the acute lung disease and cor pulmonale. Fluid restrictions are imposed, which places a limitation on the provision of calories.

These infants must be adequately oxygenated in order for growth and tissue repair to occur. Frequent intubations and mechanical ventilation interfere with the normal feeding sequence and feeding skill development. This may cause severe problems with oral intake later.

Treatment of the BPD patient usually includes a wide array of medications, including diuretics, bronchodilators, cardiac medications, and steroids. The impact of these drugs on the patient's nutritional status is further discussed in the "Drug-Nutrient Interaction" section.

Nutrition Assessment

Anthropometric

Obtaining daily weights in a BPD patient is essential during the early hospitalization(s) and critical stages of the disease. Weight data help to identify fluid overload in a patient as well as growth.

Monitoring weight, length, and head circumference on a regular basis during the follow-up period will provide the necessary data to assess whether the patient is achieving growth. Measurements should be made using appropriate techniques and equipment and be plotted on appropriate growth charts, using either the NCHS growth charts and correcting for gestational age or the Babson growth charts that allow assessment of infants of varying gestational age.[13,44] Other easily obtained and useful measurements are the mid-arm circumference and triceps skinfold.

It is unrealistic to expect true growth to occur when life-threatening events such as respiratory failure, necrotizing enterocolitis, or other serious problems of prematurity are taking place. The patient must be fairly stable for growth to occur. This is supported by a study by Shankaran et al., who found a poor pattern of growth in BPD patients to be related to the severity of pulmonary disease.[45] Similarly, Kurzner et al. found resting metabolic rate to be inversely correlated with body weight in infants with BPD.[46]

Dietary

The BPD patient's dietary intake needs to be evaluated for calories, protein, fluid, and caloric distribution of fat, protein, and carbohydrate. The type of feeding—enteral versus parenteral—should be noted, as well as vitamin and mineral supplementation. This can then be compared to the patient's estimated nutrient and fluid requirements. Exhibit 16-4 contains an example of a neonatal intensive care unit (NICU) data collection form.

Of particular importance in the nutrition assessment of BPD patients is careful monitoring of the patient's ability to suck and swallow and feeding skill development. The sucking reflex does not develop until about 34 weeks of gestation. Alternate methods of feeding will need to be utilized until this reflex develops. Neurologic impairment may prevent the patient from being able to swallow. Noxious stimuli to the patient's mouth, such as frequent intubations and suctioning, may seriously affect normal feeding skill development. Maintaining adequate oxygenation during feedings is essential. It is important to note whether the patient tires during feedings and whether he or she turns blue around the mouth or fingertips, indicating a drop in oxygen saturation. It is imperative that these problems be identified early and appropriate intervention instituted.

Biochemical

Biochemical monitoring of the BPD patient is summarized in Exhibit 16-5. Frequencies of measurement depend on the patient's clinical status, the type and amount of diuretic therapy, and the protocol of the individual institution.

Exhibit 16-4 NICU Data Collection Form

Hx: GA _____ Multi Ges _____ Apgars _____
BWt _____ BL _____ BHC _____
Maternal Hx _____

Initial Dx _____

ID Stamp
Admit Date: _____
Address:_____
Phone: _____
Parents: _____
Insurance: _____

Current Problems _____
_____
_____
_____
_____

DATE:							
ANTHROPOMETRICS							
Weight, kg							
Length, cm							
HC, cm							
F/N							
Goals							
Kcal/kg/d							
Pro/kg/d							
cc/kg/d							
Present Intake							
cc/kg/d							
Kcal/kg/d							
Pro/kg/d							
Fat/kg/d							
%kcal enteral							
Kcal distrib							
Enteral							
Formula							
Additives							
Kcal/cc							
Route							
Rate							
IN (Total Intake)cc							
Parenteral							
Days on TPN							
Route							
Rate							
Glucose conc							
Fat conc							
Pro source							
g lipid/kg/hr							
mg glucose/kg/hr							
NPC:N							
Ca:PO4							
IN Parenteral							
Intralipid							
IV Fluids							
_____TPN Audit							_____ F/U day

continues

Exhibit 16-4 continued

DATE							
BIOCHEMICAL							
FBP							
Glucose							
Ca/PO4							
Mg							
Alk Phos							
GGT/SGOT							
Bili T/D							
TG/Chol							
Hct/Hgb							
T Pro/Alb							
Prealb							
TOLERANCE:							
Stools							
pH/Red sub							
Urine cc							
Emesis							
Residuals							
Dstix							
Abd girth							

MEDICATIONS: _____

COMMENTS/PLANS: _____

Source: Courtesy of Florence Atwood, MS, RD, Clinical Nutrition Specialist, The Children's Hospital, Birmingham, AL.

Exhibit 16-5 Biochemical Monitoring of the BPD Patient

Electrolytes: 1. Chloride								
2. Potassium								
3. Sodium								
Minerals: 1. Calcium								
2. Phosphorus								
3. Magnesium								
Other: 1. Albumin								
2. Alkaline phosphatase								
3. Hematocrit								
4. Hemoglobin								
5. $PaCO_2$								
6. pH								
Medications: Theophylline								

Clinical

The patient's pulmonary status will have a great impact on the patient's nutritional needs. Noting the patient's pulmonary status is an important component of the nutrition assessment. The following information should be noted:

1. ventilator dependency
2. use of supplemental oxygen
3. partial pressure of oxygen, arterial
4. presence of tachypnea, rales, rhonchi
5. presence of bronchiolitis/pneumonia

Other medical conditions, such as cor pulmonale and the patient's medication regimen, should also be noted. The NICU data collection form found in Exhibit 16-4 lists the type of data needed to determine the patient's tolerance of the feedings, and Table 16-6 lists drug-nutrient interactions of medications commonly prescribed for BPD patients.

Table 16-6 BPD-Drug-Nutrient Interactions

Medication	Nutrients Affected	Other Effects
Diuretics (e.g., furosemide)	↓ Na, ↓ K, ↓ Cl ↓ Mg, ↓ Ca ↓ Zn	Volume depletion Metabolic alkalosis Anorexia Diarrhea Hyperuricemia Gastrointestinal irritant
Bronchodilators (e.g., theophylline)		Gastrointestinal distress Nausea Vomiting Diarrhea
Steroids (e.g., prednisone)	↓ Ca, ↓ P	Growth suppression
Digitalis, cardiac glycosides (e.g., digoxin)	↓ K, ↓ Mg ↓ Ca, ↓ Zn	Glucose malabsorption Anorexia Nausea Vomiting Diarrhea

Nutrition Management

Determination of Caloric Requirements

As has already been discussed, the patient with BPD has high energy and nutrient needs. At the same time, numerous constraints are placed on the delivery of the calories and nutrients, such as fluid restrictions, sodium restrictions, gastrointestinal immaturity, and renal immaturity.

Oh describes three phases of nutritional management of infants with BPD, which are summarized below.[47] The estimated caloric requirements of each phase and the components of the energy expenditure are depicted in Table 16-7.

Acute Phase. The BPD patient during this phase is critically ill and at risk for clinical morbidities such as patent ductus arteriosus and necrotizing enterocolitis. No calories are needed for specific dynamic action or for growth. Efforts should be made to keep thermal losses to a minimum. Possible feeding complications during this phase include fluid overload and hyperglycemia. Caloric provision is often relegated to secondary importance behind these two problems and electrolyte imbalance.

Table 16-7 Calorie Requirements (kcal/kg/d) of Infants with Bronchopulmonary Dysplasia at Various Periods* of Nutritional Management

Component	Acute	Intermediate	Convalescent
Basal metabolic rate	45	60	60
Stool losses	0–10	10	10
Thermal stress	0–10	0–10	10
Activity	5	5	10
Specific dynamic action	0	0–5	10
Growth allowance	0	20–30	20–30
Total	50–70	95–120	120–130

*Acute = clinical illness, oral feeding difficult; intermediate = clinical improvement, gradual introduction of oral feeding; convalescent = recovery, oral feeding exclusively

Source: Reprinted with permission of Ross Laboratories, Columbus, OH 43216, from *Bronchopulmonary Dysplasia and Related Chronic Respiratory Disorders* by PM Farrell and LM Taussig, © 1986 Ross Laboratories.

Intermediate Phase. This phase is characterized by a period of clinical improvements and a gradual introduction of oral feeding. Again, thermal losses should be kept to a minimum. Fluid overload continues to be a possible complication.

Convalescent Phase. This is a period of recovery. Usually, but not always, the patient is exclusively feeding orally. Minimizing thermal losses continues to be important, as well as monitoring activity, growth, and adequate oxygenation of tissues.

Continued monitoring of intake, growth, and development is important. Nutritional recommendations must be individualized according to each patient's needs.

Determination of Protein Requirements

Adequate protein is necessary to achieve growth, but the immature kidney cannot handle high-protein loads. Protein should constitute about 8% to 12% of the total calories, with the remainder of the calories evenly divided between carbohydrate and fat.

Provision of Adequate Calories and Protein

Translating these calorie and protein requirements into a feeding order can be very difficult in light of the restrictions previously described. This discussion will be divided into parenteral and enteral routes of feeding.

Parenteral Nutrition. During the acute phase of BPD, parenteral nutrition is often employed. Niermeyer states that a solution of 1% to 1.5% of amino acids and 10% dextrose solution in water (D10W) to 12.5% dextrose solution in water (D12.5W) administered at a rate of about 120 ml/kg/d via a peripheral vein will usually meet protein and energy demands.[48] Lipids may be given to provide a concentrated source of noncarbohydrate calories with negligible osmotic effects. Fatty acid deficiency can be avoided by providing 2% to 4% of the nonprotein calories as linoleic acid (0.5 to 1.0 g/kg/d of available emulsions).[49] If feeding intolerance is prolonged, central venous access may be necessary to deliver more concentrated glucose and protein solutions (15% dextrose solution in water [D15W] to 20% dextrose solution in water [D20W] and 1.5% to 2.5% amino acids). Lipids should constitute 20% to 50% of total calories.[48]

Studies have raised concern about the effect of intravenous fat in pulmonary-compromised patients.[50,51] Other studies have shown that the possible adverse effect of lipid infusion is related to the maturity of the infant and the rate of the infusion.[52,53] The use of parenteral fat emulsions should be carefully monitored in patients with underlying infection, pulmonary disease, and/or hyperbilirubinemia.[49] The American Academy of Pediatrics recommends starting lipids in the low-birth-weight infant at 0.5 to 1.0 g/kg/d and increasing by 0.5 g/kg/d to a maximum of 2.0 to 3.0 g/kg/d and not exceeding an infusion rate of 0.25 g/kg/h around the clock.[54] Serum triglyceride levels should be kept below 150 mg/dl.[54] Wells et al. accepted the following laboratory parameters as indicating tolerance of a 20% soybean/safflower-based lipid by very low birth weight infants in their study: triglyceride level 200 mg/dl, free fatty acids level 1 mEq/L, and serum cholesterol level 150 mEq/dl. [55] These authors also found that lipids could be infused over a 20-hour period at rates of 0.15 g/kg/h or less.[55]

High-glucose loads result in an increase in the respiratory quotient and a consequent increase in carbon dioxide production. Infants with borderline respiratory function may not be able to excrete this additional carbon dioxide, and respiratory acidosis could result.

Enteral Nutrition. Enteral feedings must be begun at a slow rate and may initially be diluted to allow the immature intestine of the premature infant to adapt to the feedings. During this transitional phase, parenteral nutrition is often continued in order to meet the increased caloric needs of the patient. It is very important to maintain the delivery of adequate calories while tolerance to enteral feedings is being established.

This transitional phase can become very tricky. An infant must be hungry before an oral feeding will be readily accepted. Continuous infusions of nutritional solutions may suppress natural hunger sensations. Hunger is particularly important when feeding skills are being developed. An appropriate schedule of parenteral feedings, enteral tube feedings, and oral feedings must be determined by members of the interdisciplinary health care team to best suit the individual patient's needs.

Intestinal adaptation usually results in tolerance of an infant formula concentrated to 24 cal/oz (0.8 cal/mL). In order to meet some infants' very high energy needs, it may become necessary to further concentrate the formula to 26 to 30 cal/oz by adding carbohydrate in the form of glucose polymers or rice cereal and/or lipids. When modulating formulas in this manner, it is important to maintain a proper balance of nutrients. Caloric distribution should continue to be approximately 8% to 12% protein, 40% to 50% carbohydrate, and 40% to 50% fat. Excessive osmolality and renal solute load should be avoided. An example of a modulated formula is given in Table 16-8.

When infants are receiving high-calorie formulas, careful monitoring is warranted. Increasing the caloric density may increase the potential renal solute load while fluid intake is limited. When the infant is growing and nitrogen is being utilized to form new tissue, the infant usually handles the solute load. However, if growth ceases or if there is increased fluid loss, such as with a febrile illness, renal solute load may become a problem for these infants, and azotemia may result.

The infant may be unable to consume an adequate amount of formula by mouth. It may be necessary to deliver the balance of the formula via a tube feeding to achieve adequate intake.

Maintenance of Adequate Vitamin and Mineral Status

Calcium and Phosphorus. As previously stated, infants born prematurely are born without the benefit of the calcium and phosphorus accretion of the third trimester of gestation. In addition, the calcium and phosphorus status of premature

Table 16-8 Example of a Modulated Formula

	Carbohydrate (g)	Protein (g)	Fat (g)
30 ml Similac 24*	2.55	0.66	1.29
1 g Sumacal, powder†	0.96	—	—
1 ml Microlipid†	—	—	0.50
Total	3.51	0.66	1.79
Calories/g	× 4	× 4	× 9
	14.04	2.64	16.11
% Total calories	43	8	49

Total calories = 32.79/31 ml
              1.05 cal/ml

* Ross Laboratories, Columbus, Ohio.
† Sherwood Medical, St. Louis, Missouri.

infants with BPD is further compromised by diuretic and steroid therapy and feeding delays. The adequacy of calcium and phosphorus intake should be assessed. Adequate amounts can generally be administered in parenteral solutions. Preterm human milk can be fortified with a commercial human milk fortifier.

Trace Minerals. Particular attention should be given to the following trace minerals, which are components of an antioxidant enzyme system: copper, zinc, selenium, and manganese.

Vitamins A and E. Many studies have examined the role of vitamin A (retinol) in animals and premature infants who develop chronic lung disease. Vitamin A is essential in the respiratory tract for maintenance of the integrity and differentiation of epithelial cells. Deficiency of vitamin A results in loss of cilia and other changes in the airways, which resemble the changes seen in BPD.

Adequate vitamin E status is particularly important in premature infants with BPD since vitamin E is a major antioxidant, protecting lipid-containing cell membranes from oxidation. Infants will most likely receive adequate vitamin E when fed human milk or commercial formulas. Large doses of vitamin E appear to offer no additional protection against BPD. If for medical reasons the infant is not fed parenterally or enterally, the premature infant with BPD is at increased risk for developing vitamin E deficiency. Also at risk for vitamin E deficiency is the infant maintained by parenteral nutrition that includes large amounts of polyunsaturated fatty acids but little vitamin E.

Addressing Feeding Difficulties

The patient's ability to suck and swallow needs to be assessed. Feeding behavior should be assessed for age appropriateness based on corrected age.

BPD patients are susceptible to developing feeding difficulties because of their usual prematurity and also because of the nature of the life-sustaining respiratory therapy they receive. Intubations and suctioning are noxious stimuli to the oral area and can interfere with normal feeding development. Supplemental oxygen is usually delivered by nasal cannula and does not interfere with oral feedings.

Occupational therapists have a tremendous role to play in identifying feeding problems and designing treatment plans. Non-nutritive sucking can be instituted during a tube feeding so that the infant can begin to associate feelings of satiety with sucking. In some instances, feedings thickened with rice cereal may be easier for infants to handle. Overlooking problems in the development of feeding skills can result in serious aversions to eating or decreased and inadequate intake.

When critical steps in feeding skill development have been missed, it may be necessary to design a program that breaks eating down into small steps and orienting the child to each step. Instead of feeding according to chronologic age, it is more important to feed the child according to his or her stage of feeding development. A behavioral program may be necessary to help the patient overcome fears related to eating or when food refusal is used manipulatively.

Referral to Food/Nutrition Resources

Caring for a BPD patient can be very draining for the patient's family from an emotional, physical, and financial standpoint. It is important to assess the patient's and family's needs in regard to food/nutrition resources. Appropriate referrals must be made. Often this can be done in cooperation with the nurse and/or social worker (see also Chapter 8, Community Nutrition).

Identification of Areas Needing Further Research

Effects of early onset of respiratory failure and vigorous ventilator support on nutrient/energy requirements for BPD patients need to be assessed at various stages of the disease, particularly regarding energy, protein, vitamins A and E, and minerals such as calcium and phosphorus. Assimilation and absorption of nutrients in BPD patients and whether or not a deficiency of one of these nutrients plays a role in the etiology of the disease also need to be determined. Suggestions for further research are as follows:

- general growth studies of BPD patients
- establishing appropriate growth for BPD patients at various stages of the disease
- determining appropriate methods and timing of nutrition intervention in BPD treatment
- establishing nutritional requirements of BPD patients at various stages of the disease
- establishing treatment that will ensure appropriate development of feeding skills

---

REFERENCES

1. Doershuk CF, Dooley RR, Hilman BC, et al. *Guide to Diagnosis and Management of Cystic Fibrosis*. Indianapolis, Ind: Cystic Fibrosis Foundation; 1981.

2. Andersen DH. Cystic fibrosis of the pancreas and its relation to celiac disease: a clinical and pathologic study. *Am J Dis Child*. 1938;56:344.

3. *Patient Registry 1990 Annual Data Report*. Bethesda, Md: Cystic Fibrosis Foundation, January 1992.

4. Riordan JR, Rommens JM, Kerem B, et al. Identification of the cystic fibrosis gene: cloning and characterization of complementary DNA. *Science*. 1989;245:1066.

5. Taussig LM, ed. *Cystic Fibrosis*. New York, NY: Thieme-Statton; 1984.

6. Dodge JA. Nutritional requirements in cystic fibrosis: a review. *J Pediatr Gastroenterol Nutr*. 1988;7(suppl 1):S8.

7. Parsons HG, Beaudry P, Dumas A, Pencharz PB. Energy needs and growth in children with cystic fibrosis. *J Pediatr Gastroenterol Nutr*. 1983;2:44.

8. Luder EL, Gilbride JA. Teaching self-management skills to cystic fibrosis patients and its effect on their caloric intake. *J Am Diet Assoc.* 1989;89:359.

9. Hodges P, Sauriol D, Man SFP, et al. Nutrient intake of patients with cystic fibrosis. *J Am Diet Assoc.* 1984;84:644.

10. Hubbard VS, Mangrum PJ. Energy intake and nutrition counseling in cystic fibrosis. *J Am Diet Assoc.* 1982;80:127.

11. Soutter VL, Kristidis P, Griuca MA, Gaskin KJ. Chronic undernutrition/growth retardation in cystic fibrosis. *Clin Gastroenterol.* 1986;151:137.

12. Fomon SJ. *Infant Nutrition.* Philadelphia, Pa: WB Saunders; 1974.

13. National Center for Health Statistics. *NCHS Growth Curves for Children 0-18 Years.* Washington, DC: Health Resources Administration; 1977. US Vital and Health Statistics, series 11, no. 165.

14. National Center for Health Statistics. *Height and Weight of Youths 12-17 Years.* Washington, DC: Health Services and Mental Health Administration; 1973. US Vital and Health Statistics, series 11, no. 124.

15. Sproul A, Huang N. Growth patterns in children with cystic fibrosis. *J Pediatr.* 1964;65:664.

16. Berry HK, Kellogg FW, Hunt MM, et al. Dietary supplement and nutrition in children with cystic fibrosis. *Am J Dis Child.* 1975;129:165.

17. Yassa JG, Prosser R, Dodge JA. Effects of an artificial diet on growth of patients with cystic fibrosis. *Arch Dis Child.* 1978;53:783.

18. Dodge JA, Yassa JG. Food intake and supplementary feeding programmes. In: Sturgess JM, ed. *Perspectives in Cystic Fibrosis.* Toronto: Canadian Cystic Fibrosis Foundation; 1980.

19. Wooldridge NH, Bonner JL, Brasfield D, Tiller RE. Evaluation of growth in young children with cystic fibrosis. *CF Club Abstr.* 1982;23:146.

20. Shwachman H, Kulczycki LL. Long-term study of one hundred and five patients with cystic fibrosis. *Am J Dis Child.* 1958;96:6.

21. Brasfield D, Hicks G, Soong S, Tiller RE. The chest roentgenogram in cystic fibrosis: a new scoring system. *Pediatrics.* 1979;63:24.

22. Ressler MQ, Wooldridge NH, Moates KB, Craig CB, Lyrene RK. Evaluation of growth in children with cystic fibrosis from birth through pre-adolescence. *J Amer Diet Assoc.* 1991;91:A-125.

23. Gurwitz D, Corey M, Francis PWI, et al. Perspectives in cystic fibrosis. *Pediatr Clin North Am.* 1979;26:603.

24. Corey M, McLaughlin FJ, Williams M, Levison H. A comparison of survival, growth, and pulmonary function in patients with cystic fibrosis in Boston and Toronto. *J Clin Epidemiol.* 1988;41:583.

25. Crozier DN. Cystic fibrosis—a not so fatal disease. *Pediatr Clin North Am.* 1974;21:935.

26. National Research Council. *Recommended Dietary Allowances.* Washington, DC: National Academy Press, 1989.

27. Weinsier RL, Heimburger DC, Butterworth CE. *Handbook of Clinical Nutrition.* St Louis, Mo: CV Mosby; 1989.

28. Shepherd RW, Thomas BJ, Bennett D, et al. Changes in body composition and muscle protein degradation during nutritional supplementation in nutritionally growth-retarded children with cystic fibrosis. *J Pediatr Gastroenterol Nutr.* 1983;2:439.

29. Bertrand JM, Morin CL, Lasalle R, et al. Short-term clinical, nutritional and functional effects of continuous elemental enteral alimentation in children with cystic fibrosis. *J Pediatr.* 1984;104:41.

30. O'Loughlin E, Forbes D, Parsons H, et al. Nutritional rehabilitation of malnourished patients with cystic fibrosis. *Am J Clin Nutr*. 1986;43:732.

31. Moore MC, Greene HL, Donald WD, Dunn GD. Enteral tube feeding as adjunct therapy in malnourished patients with cystic fibrosis: a clinical study and literature review. *Am J Clin Nutr*. 1986;44:33.

32. Boland MP, Stoski DS, MacDonald NE, et al. Chronic jejunostomy feeding with a non-elemental formula in undernourished patients with cystic fibrosis. *Lancet*. 1986; 1(8475):232–234.

33. Levy LD, Durie PR, Corey ML. Effects of long-term nutritional rehabilitation on body composition and clinical status in malnourished children and adolescents with cystic fibrosis. *J Pediatr*. 1985;107:225.

34. Levy L, Durie P, Pencharz P, Corey M. Prognostic factors associated with patient survival during nutritional rehabilitation in malnourished children and adolescents with cystic fibrosis. *J Pediatr Gastroenterol Nutr*. 1986;5:97.

35. Shepherd RW, Holt TL, Thomas BJ, et al. Nutritional rehabilitation in cystic fibrosis: controlled studies of effects on nutritional growth retardation, body protein turnover, and course of pulmonary disease. *J Pediatr*. 1986;109:788.

36. Shepherd R, Cooksley WGE, Cooke WDD. Improved growth and clinical, nutritional and respiratory changes in response to nutritional therapy in cystic fibrosis. *J Pediatr*. 1980;97:351.

37. Mansell AL, Cuttart CR, Loeff DE, Heird WC. Short-term pulmonary effects of total parenteral nutrition in children with cystic fibrosis. *J Pediatr*. 1984;104:700.

38. Lester LA, Rothberg RM, Dawson G, et al. Supplemental parenteral nutrition in cystic fibrosis. *J Parenter Enter Nutr*. 1986;10:289.

39. Askanasi J, Rosenbaum SH, Hyman AI, et al. Respiratory changes induced by the large glucose loads of total parenteral nutrition. *JAMA*. 1980;243:1444.

40. Chase HP, Long MA, Lavin MH. Cystic fibrosis and malnutrition. *J Pediatr*. 1979;95:337.

41. Farrell PM, Hubbard VS. Nutrition in cystic fibrosis: vitamins, fatty acids and minerals. In: Lloyd-Still JD, ed. *Textbook of Cystic Fibrosis*. Littleton, Mass: John Wright, 1983.

42. Northway WH, Rosan RCC, Porter DY. Pulmonary disease following respiratory therapy of hyaline membrane disease. *N Engl J Med*. 1967;276:357.

43. Weinstein MR, Oh W. Oxygen consumption in infants with bronchopulmonary dysplasia. *J Pediatr*. 1981;99:958.

44. Babson SG, Brenda GI. Growth graphs for the clinical assessment of infants of varying gestational age. *J Pediatr*. 1976;89:814.

45. Shankaran S, Szego E, Eizert D, Siegel P. Severe bronchopulmonary dysplasia—predictors of survival and outcome. *Chest*. 1984;86:607.

46. Kurzner WI, Garg M, Bautista DB, et al. Growth failure in infants with bronchopulmonary dysplasia: nutrition and elevated resting metabolic expenditure. *Pediatrics*. 1988;81:379.

47. Oh W. Nutritional management of infants with bronchopulmonary dysplasia. In: Farrell PM, Taussig LM, eds. *Bronchopulmonary Dysplasia and Related Chronic Respiratory Disorders*. Columbus, Ohio: Ross Laboratories; 1986:96–105.

48. Niermeyer S. Nutritional and metabolic problems in infants with bronchopulmonary dysplasia. In: Bancalari E, Stocker JT, eds. *Bronchopulmonary Dysplasia*. Washington, DC: Hemisphere Publishing Corp; 1988:313–336.

49. American Academy of Pediatrics, Committee on Nutrition. Use of intravenous fat emulsions in pediatric patients. *Pediatrics*. 1981;68:738.

50. Green HL, Hazlett D, Demarec R. Relationship between intralipid-induced hyperlipemia and pulmonary function. *Am J Clin Nutr.* 1976;29:127.

51. Friedman Z, Marks KH, Maisels J, et al. Effect of parenteral fat emulsion on the pulmonary and reticuloendothelial systems in the newborn infant. *Pediatrics.* 1978;61:694.

52. Perira GR, Foxx WW, Stanely CA, et al. Decreased oxygenation and hyperlipemia during intravenous fat infusions in premature infants. *Pediatrics.* 1980;66:26.

53. Stahl GE, Spear MC, Egler JM, et al. The effect of lipid infusion rate on oxygenation in premature infants. *Pediatr Res.* 1984;18:406A.

54. American Academy of Pediatrics, Committee on Nutrition. Nutritional needs of low-birth-weight infants. *Pediatrics.* 1985;75:976.

55. Wells DH, Ferlauto JJ, Forbes DJ. Lipid tolerance in the very-low-birth-weight infant on intravenous and enteral feedings. *J Parenter Enter Nutr.* 1989;13:623.

SUGGESTED READING

Adams E. Nutrition care in cystic fibrosis. *Nutrition News.* 1988;3.

Allen AM, Moore AO. *Food Medication Interactions.* Tempe, Ariz: Ann Moore Allen.

Bancalari E, Gerhardt T. Bronchopulmonary dysplasia. *Pediatr Clin North Am.* 1986;33:1.

Bureau of Maternal and Child Health Resources Development. Guidelines for the care of children with chronic lung disease (bronchopulmonary dysplasia). In: Polgar G, ed. *Pediatric Pulmonology.* New York, NY: Alan R Liss; 1989:3–13.

Doershuk CF, Boat TF. Cystic fibrosis. In: Behrman RE, Vaughan VC, Nelson WE, eds. *Nelson Textbook of Pediatrics.* Philadelphia, Pa: WB Saunders; 1983:1006–1099.

Durie PR, Couper R. Pancreatic function testing and assessment. In: *Pediatric Pulmonology.* New York, NY: Alan R Liss; 1988:75–77.

Frank L. Nutrition: influence on lung growth, injury and repair, and development of bronchopulmonary dysplasia. In: Bancalari E, Stocker FT, eds. *Bronchopulmonary Dysplasia.* New York, NY: Hemisphere Publishing Corp; 1988:78–109.

Handen BL, Mandell F, Russo DCC. Feeding induction in children who refuse to eat. *Am J Dis Children.* 1986;140:52.

Lyrene RK, Guthrie RD, Hodson WA. Chronic lung disease in infancy. In: Kelly VC, ed. *Practice of Pediatrics.* Philadelphia, Pa: Harper & Row; 1981:1–11.

Wooldridge NH, Moyer-Mileur L. Pulmonary disease. In: Wooldridge NH, Spinozzi N, eds. *Quality Assurance Criteria for Pediatric Nutrition Conditions: A Model.* Chicago: The American Dietetic Association; 1988, 1990:119–128, XIIS-1–XIIS-14.

RESOURCES

Pamphlets

Luder E. *Living with Cystic Fibrosis: Family Guide to Nutrition.* Springhouse, Pa: McNeil Pharmaceutical, 1987.

Nutritional Guidelines for Adults with Cystic Fibrosis. Booklet available from Cystic Fibrosis Program, the Childrens Hospital, 300 Longwood Avenue, Boston, MA 02146.

Power Pack Packet: Rocket Fueled Ideas for Your High Calorie High Protein Diet. Available from Pediatric Pulmonary Center, 1600 7th Avenue South, Suite 656, Birmingham, AL 35233.

Cookbooks

A Way of Life: Cystic Fibrosis Nutrition Handbook and Cookbook. Available from Pediatric Pulmonary Center, S4/120, Food and Nutrition Services, University of Wisconsin Hospital and Clinics, 600 Highland Avenue, Madison, WI 53792. (Cost: $5)

Fat and Loving It—A Cookbook for Cystic Fibrosis. Available from Gail Farmer, P.O. Box 5127, Belmont, CA 94002. (Cost: $10)

Videotapes

Barnhill K. *The Food Diet: A Way of Living* [Videotape]. Birmingham, Ala: Board of Trustees, University of Alabama; 1988.

Nutritionist's Experience at CF Camp [videotape]. Santa Clara, Calif: Kaiser-Permanente Medical Program.

The Adventure of Mr. Enzyme [videotape]. Springhouse, Pa: McNeil Pharmaceutical; 1990.

Computer Program

Interactive Apple Computer Program for CF Patients. Pittsburgh, Pa: University of Pittsburgh School of Medicine.

Other

Cystic Fibrosis Foundation, 6931 Arlington Road, Bethesda, MD 20814, 1-800-FIGHT CF.

Chapter 17

Gastrointestinal Disorders

Linda J. Boyne and Leo A. Heitlinger

The gastrointestinal tract is the site of the assimilation of macro- and micronutrients, vitamins, and minerals. The function of the gastrointestinal tract may be disrupted by disease and result in alterations in nutritional requirements. The intent of this chapter is to provide ready information to the reader on the evaluation of gastrointestinal symptoms in the pediatric population, ages birth to 18 years. The tests commonly used to evaluate gastrointestinal symptoms are presented. Most of the information is provided in easy-to-read tabular form.

Guidelines for therapeutic diets for acute diarrhea, celiac disease, and constipation are presented. Since pancreatic insufficiency and cholestatic liver disease are associated with malabsorption of fat-soluble vitamins, recommended doses for supplementation in these conditions are addressed. Finally, the special nutritional needs of the liver transplant recipient are discussed.

SITES OF NUTRIENT ABSORPTION

The gastrointestinal tract may be thought of as a tube that processes and absorbs nutrients. Many nutrients are absorbed throughout the intestinal tract, while others are absorbed only from specific sites. Absorption of the latter class of nutrients is particularly vulnerable to disease or surgical resection. In Figure 17-1 the principal sites of absorption of macro- and micronutrients, vitamins, and minerals are presented.

COMMON SYMPTOMS OF GASTROINTESTINAL DISEASE

Most symptoms of gastrointestinal disease can arise from disorders located in a specific region of the bowel, the entire bowel, or distant sites; e.g., vomiting can occur due to pyloric stenosis, gastroenteritis, or brain tumor. In Figure 17-2, con-

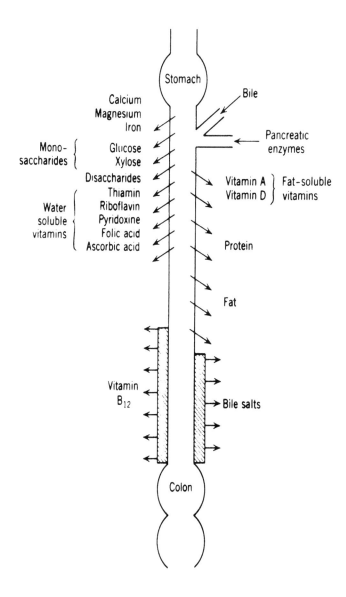

Figure 17-1 Principal sites of absorption of nutrients. *Source:* Reprinted from *Handbook of Physiology*, Vol 3, ed 6 by CC Booth with permission of the American Physiological Society, © 1968.

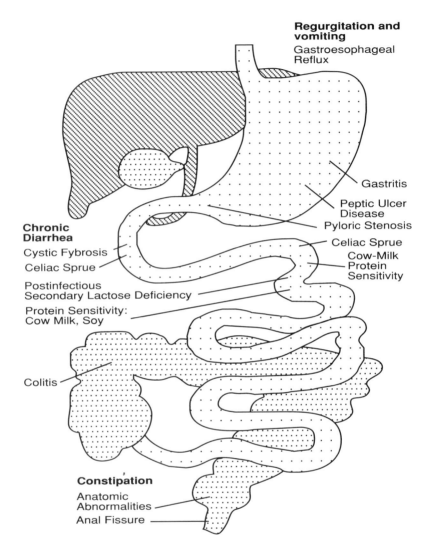

Regurgitation and vomiting
Gastroesophageal Reflux

Gastritis

Peptic Ulcer Disease
Pyloric Stenosis
Celiac Sprue
Cow-Milk Protein Sensitivity

Chronic Diarrhea
Cystic Fybrosis
Celiac Sprue

Postinfectious Secondary Lactose Deficiency

Protein Sensitivity: Cow Milk, Soy

Colitis

Constipation
Anatomic Abnormalities
Anal Fissure

Figure 17-2 The site of pathology within the gastrointestinal tract varies with the disease process. *Source:* Reprinted with permission of Ross Laboratories, Columbus, OH 43216 from *Problems Relating to Feedings in First Two Years,* p. 11, © 1977 Ross Laboratories.

ditions that involve portions of the gastrointestinal tract rather than the entire tract are presented. In the accompanying table (Table 17-1) common symptoms are grouped according to their most common location of origin. The differential diagnosis of these symptoms and treatment of the etiology of symptoms are presented.

Table 17-1 Common Pediatric Gastrointestinal Disorders

Presenting Symptom	Differential Diagnosis	Treatment
Stomach and Esophagus Vomiting/regurgitation	*Structural:* Congenital anomaly of the gastrointestinal tract	Surgery
	Inflammatory: Peptic disease	Medications, e.g., antacids; avoid caffeine-containing foods, alcohol, smoking
	Functional: Gastroesophageal reflux	Infants: positioning, thickened feeds, prokinetics. Surgical treatment if above fails, e.g., fundoplication. Medications, e.g., antacids; avoid caffeine-containing foods, alcohol, smoking
Dysphagia (choking after eating), odynophagia (pain with swallowing)	*Structural:* Congenital anomalies	Surgery
	Inflammatory: Peptic strictures	Medications, e.g., antacids; dilatation, fundoplication
	Functional: Esophageal spasms	Calcium channel blockers and nitrates; avoid extreme temperatures in foods
Pancreas and liver Jaundice	*Structural:* Extrahepatic biliary tract obstruction, e.g., biliary atresia	Surgical correction; fat soluble vitamin supplementation (fat source: MCT); choleretic agents, e.g., phenobarbital, cholestyramine, ursodeoxycholate
Failure to tolerate feeds, persistent bilious vomiting, and distended upper abdomen	Annular pancreas	Surgery
Recurrent abdominal pain, jaundice	Gallstones	Surgery, lithotripsy, dissolution therapy
	Choledochal cyst	Surgery

continues

Table 17-1 continued

Presenting Symptom	Differential Diagnosis	Treatment
	Inflammatory:	
Anorexia, nausea, vomiting, jaundice	Hepatitis	Diet as tolerated; steroids for autoimmune hepatitis
Abdominal pain	Pancreatitis	NPO; nasogastric suctioning; TPN if prolonged course. Medications: pain control (e.g., meperidine), H_2 antagonists (i.e., cimetadine), pancreatic enzyme replacement. When improved, high CHO, low-fat diet. Elemental diet may be beneficial.
	Functional:	
	Hereditary metabolic disorders	See Chapter 12
Meconium ileus, failure to thrive, chronic diarrhea	Pancreatic insufficiency, e.g., cystic fibrosis, Shwachman/Diamond syndrome	Enzyme replacement therapy; fat soluble vitamin supplementation; high-calorie, high-fat diet
Small bowel and colon		
	Structural:	
Failure to thrive, diarrhea	Short bowel syndrome	TPN progressing to MCT-predominate hydrolysate formula; vitamin and mineral supplements
Abdominal distention, steatorrhea	Lymphangiectasia, protein-losing enteropathy	Surgical excision, if possible. Fat soluble vitamin supplementation. High-calorie, high-protein, low-LCT diet; high-MCT diet or TPN may be necessary.
Anemia, gastrointestinal bleeding	Congenital malformations, e.g., Meckel's diverticulum, duplication cysts	Surgery
	Inflammatory:	
Diarrhea, vomiting	Infectious enteropathies	Oral rehydration solutions, followed by lactose and/or sucrose restrictions†
Failure to thrive, abdominal distention, steatorrhea	Gluten-sensitive enteropathy (celiac disease)	Gluten-free diet
Failure to thrive, vomiting, diarrhea	Dietary protein intolerance	Hydrolysate formula, elimination diet
Postprandial abdominal pain	Inflammatory bowel disease, small bowel (Crohn's) disease	High-calorie diet; B_{12} supplementation if ileum affected

Presenting Symptom	Differential Diagnosis	Treatment
Rectal bleeding, diarrhea, tenesmus	Ulcerative colitis or Crohn's disease of the colon	High-calorie diet; folate supplementation; low-residue diet,‡ if strictures or active colitis; other foods as tolerated
	Functional:	
Fermentive diarrhea after introduction of sucrose-containing foods	Congenital enzyme deficiency, e.g., sucrase/isomaltase deficiency	Dietary restrictions of sucrose-containing foods
Severe, watery diarrhea from first day of life	Lactase deficiency	Dietary restrictions with calcium supplement or enzyme replacement, i.e., Lactaid, Lactrase
Chronic diarrhea, normal growth pattern	Irritable bowel syndrome (chronic nonspecific diarrhea, toddler's diarrhea, or spastic colon)§	Normal diet for age, increased fiber intake, decreased intake of sorbitol-containing beverages (apple and pear juice)
	Structural:	
Constipation	Hirschsprung's disease; post NEC strictures	Surgery
	Functional:	
	Constipation	Complete bowel clean out using saltwater enemas, mineral oil; high-fiber diet, bowel habit training. In infants, increase CHO content of diet using sucrose, dextrimaltose

Key: LCT, long-chain triglycerides; MCT, medium-chain triglycerides; NEC, necrotizing enterocolitis; TPN, total parenteral nutrition.

† The use of oral rehydration solutions should be closely monitored. Oral rehydration solutions should be used for 6–8 hours, then infant refeeding should begin to prevent further weight loss. To refeed, oral rehydration solutions may be alternated with a full-strength lactose-free formula for the first few feedings, or a concentrated formula may be reconstituted with the rehydration solution. Studies have shown that early refeeding does not exacerbate the diarrhea and the child recovers more quickly. Frequently the cow milk–based formula the child may have been consuming prior to the enteropathy may be used instead of a lactose-free formula. If a lactose-free formula is preferred, the previous formula may be reintroduced after a period of one or more weeks.

‡ The use of milk or a low-residue diet should be dictated by the individual tolerance of the patient.

§ This disorder often follows a bout of infectious enteropathy or antibiotic therapy and is exacerbated by increased fluid intake or strict elimination diets. A good rule of thumb is "to feed the child, not the diarrhea."

DIAGNOSTIC TESTS

A myriad of tests are available to evaluate gastrointestinal function. The tests most commonly performed are presented in Table 17-2. For each test the procedure and potential diagnoses are listed.

Table 17-2 Common Diagnostic Tests for Pediatric Gastrointestinal Disorders

Test	Procedure	Diagnosis
Barium swallow	Swallow barium sulfate; upper gastrointestinal tract and small bowel visualized by fluoroscopy. NPO 4 hours.	Hiatal hernia, stricture, dysmotility disorders, varices
Esophageal pH monitoring	8 French tube with pH sensor on end, inserted for 24 hours. Infants fed 1/2 formula, 1/2 apple juice every 4 hours. Older child fed applesauce, and apple juice added to diet.	Gastroesophageal reflux
Esophago-gastro-duodenoscopy (EGD)	Fiberoptic tube into upper gastrointestinal tract; lining visualized and biopsies taken. NPO.	Esophagitis, gastritis, duodenitis, peptic ulcer disease, caustic substance ingestions
Upper GI with small bowel follow-through	Swallow barium sulfate; look for strictures and mucosal lesions by fluoroscopy. NPO.	Inflammatory and structural lesions
Breath hydrogen	Oral sugar load of 1 g/kg to a maximum of 25 g. End expiratory breath collection. NPO.	Lactose or other sugar intolerance. Peak after 90 minutes, rise of >20 ppm is positive.
D-xylose	D-xylose administered in AM after fast after midnight. Dose: 0.35 g/kg. Blood drawn 1 hour after administration.	Malabsorption syndrome. Normal if > 20 mg/dL.
Quantitative fecal fat	Diet with > 30% total calories as fat for 2 days prior to stool collection. Three-day stool collection after charcoal marker noted in stool. (Do not use diaper creams, e.g., A&D ointment. Reverse disposable diaper for easier collection.)	Pancreatic insufficiency, e.g., cystic fibrosis; mucosal atrophy, e.g., celiac disease
Barium enema	Barium sulfate by enema. Lumen and mucosa of colon visualized by fluoroscopy.	Colitis, polyps, Hirschsprung's disease
Colonoscopy	Insertion of flexible fiberoptic tube via anus into large bowel. Visual examination of colonic lining, biopsies obtained (is alternative to barium enema). NPO.	Colitis, polyps
Liver and pancreas tests		
Bilirubin	Blood (serum) test to determine *excretory* function of liver	Hepatitis, biliary tract disease

Test	Procedure	Diagnosis
Biliary tract nuclear scan	Intravenous injection of a bile salt analogue; images obtained over liver and bowel for 24 hours	Obstructive lesions of biliary tree (e.g., impacted gall stones, biliary atresia); poor uptake is indicative of hepatitis
Plasma ammonia level	Blood (plasma) test to determine *detoxification* capabilities of liver	Hepatic encephalopathy, hepatic failure, Reye's syndrome
Prothrombin time	Blood (whole blood) test to determine *synthetic* function of liver; vitamin K dependent, clotting factors	If prothrombin time is prolonged and patient is not on antibiotics, hepatic protein synthesis diminishes.
Ultrasonography	Study to determine gross structure of liver, evaluate liver and biliary systems	Gallstones, pancreatic pseudocysts, biliary tract anomalies, biliary tract obstructions, hepatic tumors
Aminotransferase levels	Blood (serum) test to determine inflammation of liver due to virus, toxin	Infectious, toxic, or autoimmune hepatitis
Serum amylase and lipase levels	Blood (serum) test to determine pancreatic inflammation or obstruction	Acute or chronic pancreatitis. Amylase is elevated in mumps, pregnancy and lactation, pelvic inflammatory disease, and small bowel disease.
Liver-spleen nuclear scan	Intravenous injection of a marker of blood flow. Poor uptake by liver and uptake by spleen, lung, and bone marrow indicative of portal hypertension	Obstruction of extrahepatic blood vessels (e.g., portal vein thrombosis), cirrhosis, hepatic failure
Computed tomography scan of abdomen	Multiple radiographs of abdomen with or without intraluminal and/or intravenous contrast. Computer reconstructs multiple images to generate "slices" through the abdomen. NPO.	Demonstration of organ size, consistency, blood flow, and function (kidney); identification of tumors and areas of inflammation (e.g., abscess)

THERAPEUTIC DIETS

Acute Diarrhea

Acute diarrhea, namely, diarrhea of less than 7 days duration, is among the most common reasons for seeking the assistance of a pediatrician. Under most circumstances a normal diet should be continued throughout the illness. When dehydration is imminent, the use of maintenance glucose-electrolyte solutions may prevent progression of the illness. When patients become dehydrated, oral rehydration solutions or intravenous fluids may be required. The composition of commonly used oral maintenance and rehydration solutions is presented in Table 17-3.

Celiac Disease

Celiac disease is uncommon in the United States. The principal therapy is the removal of gluten-containing foods from the diet. The infant foods to use and avoid are presented in Table 17-4.

Table 17-3 Composition of Oral Electrolyte-Glucose Solutions (Concentration When Reconstituted)

Solution	Na^+ (mEq/l)	K^+ (mEq/l)	Cl^- (mEq/l)	Carbohydrate (g/l)	Osmolality (mOsM/l)
Rehydration					
WHO-ORS*	90	20	80	20[1]	310
Rehydralyte[†]	75	20	65	25[1]	310
Maintenance					
Infalyte[‡]	50	25	45	0[1]	200
Ricelyte[§]	50	25	45	20[2]	290
Pedialyte[†]	45	20	35	25[1]	270
Resol[ǁ]	50	20	50	20[1]	269
Other clear liquids					
Cola[¶]	2	0.1		50–150[3]	550
Gingerale[¶]	3	1		50–150[3]	540
Apple juice[¶]	3	28		100–150[4]	700
Chicken broth	250	8		0	450
Tea	0	0		0	5

* Continued use of this product without the addition of free water could lead to hypernatremia.
[†] Ross Laboratories, Columbus, OH.
[‡] Pennwalt, Rochester, NY.
[§] Mead Johnson, Evansville, IN.
[ǁ] Wyeth-Ayerst Laboratories, Philadelphia, PA.
[¶] These products also contain fructose.
[1] Containing glucose
[2] Containing rice-syrup-solids
[3] High fructose syrup
[4] Sucrose

Source: Adapted with permission from *AAP News* (1989; 5[9]:5), Copyright © 1989, American Academy of Pediatrics.

Table 17-4 Gluten-Free Diet for Infants with Celiac Disease

	Use	*Avoid*
Formula	Breast milk or iron-fortified infant formula	None
Dry cereal	Beech-Nut, Mead Johnson: Rice Cereal; Gerber: Rice Cereal with Bananas; Heinz: Instant Rice Cereal	All others
Jarred cereal	Beech-Nut, Gerber: Strained Rice with Applesauce and Bananas; Gerber: Junior Rice with Mixed Fruit; Heinz: Instant Rice Cereal with Bananas and Apple Juice, Rice Cereal with Pears and Apple Juice; Mead Johnson: Bananas 'n Rice	All others
Fruits, juices	All plain	None
Vegetables	All except those to avoid, plus Mead Johnson: Peas 'n Rice, Carrots 'n Rice	Gerber: Mixed Vegetables, Strained Creamed Spinach, Junior Creamed Green Beans
Meats	All plain meats, egg yolks Beech-Nut: Chicken Rice Dinner, Turkey Rice Dinner, Vegetable Chicken Dinner, Cottage Cheese with Pineapple	None All other dinners and high meat dinners
Teething, finger foods	Gluten-free rice wafers, rice cakes; Gerber: Turkey, Chicken, or Meat Sticks	

Note: Gluten or possible gluten-containing foods are those that have the following ingredients listed on a food label: wheat, rye, oats, barley; flour or cereal products; malt, malt flavor; hydrolyzed vegetable or plant protein; modified food starch; or gluten-containing flavorings, vegetable gums, emulsifiers, or stabilizers. Gluten may be present in foods either as a basic ingredient or added during preparation/processing by the manufacturer. Reading food labels is very important in *strict* adherence to a gluten-free diet.

Source: Reprinted with permission from Merritt RJ and Hack S, Infant feeding and enteral nutrition, in *Nutrition in Clinical Practice* (1988;3:47–64), Copyright © 1988, American Society for Parenteral and Enteral Nutrition.

Constipation

Constipation is common in childhood. High-fiber diets are recommended as the first line of therapy. When fiber alone fails, lubricants and laxatives may be required. The fiber content of common foods is presented in Table 17-5.

Table 17-5 Good Sources of Dietary Fiber

Food	Grams of Fiber
Apple, 1 med. w/ skin	2.2
Apple, 1 med. w/o skin	2.0
Apricot, dried, 3 oz	7.8
Blueberries, 1 cup raw	4.4
Dates, dried, 10	4.2
Kiwi, 3 oz	3.4
Pear, 1 med. raw	4.1
Prunes, dried, 3 oz	7.2
Prunes, stewed, 3 oz	6.6
Raisins, 3 oz	5.3
Raspberries, 1 cup	5.8
Strawberries, raw, 1 cup	2.8
Avocado, California, raw, 1 med.	3.0
Beans, black, boiled, 1 cup	7.2
Beans, greater northern, boiled, 1 cup	6.0
Beans, kidney, boiled, 1 cup	6.4
Beans, lima, boiled, 1 cup	6.2
Beans, baby lima, boiled, 1 cup	7.8
Beans, navy, boiled 1 cup	6.6
Beans, green, canned 1/2 cup	6.8
Broccoli, boiled, 1/2 cup	2.2
Chickpeas (garbanzo beans), 1 cup	5.7
Cowpeas (blackeye peas), 1 cup	4.4
Lentils, boiled, 1 cup	7.9

Cereals, ready to eat:	Grams/Ounce
Fiber One	10
All Bran	10
100% Bran with Oat Bran	8
100% Bran with Wheat Bran	8
Nutrific Oatmeal Flakes	6
Natural Raisin Bran	6
40% Bran	6
Benefit	5
Raisin Bran	5
Fruitful Bran	5
Oatmeal Raisin Crisp	4
Meuslix	4
Cracklin' Oat Bran (high in fat)	4

Note: Data for sections on fruits and vegetables from references 2 and 3; data for section on ready-to-eat cereals from manufacturers' labels as of August 1989. Section of Gastroenterology, Columbus Children's Hospital, Columbus OH 43205.

Pancreatic Insufficiency and Cholestatic Liver Disease

Fat-soluble vitamin malabsorption is a problem that occurs with pancreatic insufficiency and cholestatic liver disease. Supplementation at levels exceeding the Recommended Dietary Allowances (RDAs) for normal healthy children is recommended for children with these disorders. The recommended dosage for supplementation of fat-soluble vitamins is presented in Table 17-6.

Liver Transplantation

The most common disease requiring liver transplantation in childhood is biliary atresia (over 50% of cases); other less prominent causes are inherited metabolic disorders (alpha-1-antitrypsin deficiency, glycogen storage disease, Wilson's Disease, tyrosinemia), intrahepatic cholestasis syndromes (i.e., Alagille, Byler), chronic hepatitis with cirrhosis, and fulminant viral or toxic hepatitis. Indications for transplantation include hepatic failure, intractable ascites, recurrent variceal hemorrhage, and hypersplenism.

The patient with end-stage liver disease awaiting transplantation presents a formidable challenge to the medical team. The particular liver disease involved, the magnitude of liver dysfunction, the presence of complications, and the transplantation procedure itself combine to present a complex treatment process including meeting nutritional needs for healing and growth. Pretransplant nutritional care involve both assessment of current status and development of a therapeutic diet

---

Table 17-6 Vitamin Supplementation in Cystic Fibrosis and Hepatic Disorders

Vitamin Needed	Dose
Cystic fibrosis	
Vitamin A	1–2 × RDA
Vitamin D	1–2 × RDA
Hepatic disorders	
Vitamin A (Aquasol A)	5000 IU/d
Vitamin D	2000–10,000 IU/d
or	
25-Hydroxycholecalciferol	50 µg/d
Vitamin E	50–400 IU/d
Vitamin K	2.5–5 mg/d

Source: Adapted with permission from Merritt RJ and Hack S, Infant feeding and enteral nutrition, in *Nutrition in Clinical Practice* (1988;3:47–64), Copyright © 1988, American Society for Parenteral and Enteral Nutrition.

tailored to the liver disease and degree of debilitation. Assessment parameters the dietitian should follow include:

1. *anthropometrics:* height/length, weight, triceps skinfolds, mid-arm circumference, abdominal girth
2. *laboratory studies:* complete blood count with differential; platelet count; prothrombin and partial thromboplastin times; serum levels of total and direct bilirubin, alanine aminotransferase, aspartate aminotransferase, alkaline phosphatase, total protein, prealbumin, albumin, ammonia, electrolytes, calcium, inorganic phosphorous, blood urea nitrogen, creatinine, serum bile salts, and vitamins A, D, and E; serologic testing for titers of hepatitis A and B, Epstein-Barr virus, cytomegalovirus, herpes virus, human immunodeficiency virus
3. *radiology:* ultrasound (to check for patency of vascular structures)

Generally, the pretransplant diet should be as follows. Calories should be provided at 140% of the RDA for age. Adding glucose polymers or medium-chain triglyceride oil to feedings can help boost energy intake to these levels. Enteral drip feedings (intermittent or 24-hour long) may be necessary to ensure intake (however, enteral drip feedings may be contraindicated if the prothrombin time is prolonged or the platelet count is low). Protein should be provided at 2.0 to 2.5 g/kg of dry weight if parenteral nutrition is being employed or at 2.5 to 3.0 g/kg of dry weight if enteral feeding is used. The parenteral nutrition solution used should contain a balanced amino acid mixture; the enteral solution should be low in sodium. If the patient is encephalopathic, the protein intake should be reduced to 1.0 to 1.5 g/kg of dry weight. Branched-chain amino acid solutions may also be considered in this setting. Water-miscible fat soluble vitamins should be used. Zinc and iron are provided as needed, and sodium is restricted to 0.5 to 1.0 mEq/kg to help control ascites.

Immediately after transplantation, total parenteral nutrition (TPN) is begun using a balanced amino acid solution with dextrose and an appropriate intravenous lipid source. Pediatric multivitamins and trace elements are added to the solution based on age. It is suggested the formula provide nutrients at the following specified levels:[1]

> *protein:* 2.0 to 2.5 g/kg of dry weight
> *lipid:* 2 to 3 g/kg of dry weight
> *nonprotein calories:* 80 to 100 kcal/kg of dry weight
> *sodium, potassium, calcium, phosphorous:* based on serum levels

Routine post-transplant care includes monitoring fluid balance closely, which requires strict intake and output measurements and daily weights. The following laboratory tests should be monitored daily: complete blood count and differential and levels of blood and urine glucose, triglycerides, electrolytes, calcium, phosphorous, magnesium, albumin, and liver enzymes. When bowel movements resume, stools should be checked for pH, reducing substances, and occult blood.

Enteral feedings may begin when the postoperative ileus has resolved (exhibited by stooling). Enteral feeds are increased as the patient is gradually weaned from TPN. For the younger child, employ continuous nasogastric feeding using MCT-predominant formula. Advance feedings as tolerated to oral regular formula, as the stooling pattern normalizes. For the older child, employ either continuous nasogastric feedings or oral defined diets, as indicated. Advance the diet to soft low-residue, and then to a regular diet, as tolerated. All children should routinely receive multivitamin supplements, but each child's need for zinc, iron, and vitamin E will depend on his or her serum levels. A mild sodium restriction should be used in all children to prevent fluid retention caused by steroid use.

Possible problems in resumption of oral feeding include oral defensiveness due to prolonged use of TPN and developmental delay in sucking and chewing skills in infants. The appropriate professionals should be consulted to devise an interdisciplinary treatment plan for these problems.

The postdischarge follow-up of liver transplant recipients includes assessment of anthropometric values and the patient's diet log at each clinic visit. Long term, the transplant patient should receive the dietary supplements only if indicated.

Problems the dietitian should be alert for in this population include fat malabsorption, metabolic bone disease, dental caries, hypertension, and anemia. Again, if found, the appropriate professionals should be consulted to provide treatment.

REFERENCES

1. Sutton M. Nutritional support in pediatric liver transplantation. *Diet Nutr Support.* 1989; March/April:1-9.
2. Pennington JAT. Bowes and Church's Food Values of Portions Commonly Used. 15th ed. Philadelphia, Pa: JB Lippincott; 1989.
3. United States Department of Agriculture. USDA Provisional Table on the Dietary Fiber Content of Selected Foods; HNIS/PT-106; 1988.

SUGGESTED READING

Armistead J, Kelly D, Walker-Smith J. Evaluation of infant feeding in acute gastroenteritis. *J Pediatr Gastroenterol Nutr.* 1989;8:240–244.

Byers S, Wood RP, Kaufman S, Williams L, Antonson D, Vanderhoof J. Liver transplantation therapy for children: Part I. *J Pediatr Gastroenterol Nutr.* 1988;7:157–166.

Conway S, Ireson A. Acute gastroenteritis in well nourished infants: comparison of four feeding regimens. *Arch Dis Child.* 1989;64:87–91.

Goulet OJ, deGoyet JDV, Ricour C. Preoperative nutritional evaluation and support for liver transplantation in children. *Transplant Proc.* 1987;14:3249–3255.

Heitlinger L, Lebenthal E. Disorders of carbohydrate digestion and absorption. *Pediatr Clin North Am.* 1988;35:239–255.

Hendricks K. Nutrition aspects of chronic liver disease. *Pediatr G-I Nutr News. (Massachusetts General Hospital)* 1988;2.

Khazal P, Freese D, Sharp H. A pediatric perspective on liver transplantation. *Pediatr Clin North Am.* 1988;35:409–433.

Kleinman RE, Balistreri W, Heyman M, et al. Nutritional support for pediatric patients with inflammatory bowel disease. *J Pediatr Gastroenterol Nutr.* 1989;8:8–12.

Lebenthal E. *Textbook of Gastroenterology and Nutrition in Infancy.* 2nd ed. New York, NY: Raven Press; 1990.

Lin CH, Rossi T, Heitlinger L, Lerner A, Riddlesberger M, Lebenthal E. Nutritional assessment of children with short bowel syndrome receiving home parenteral nutrition. *Am J Dis Child.* 1987; 141:1093–1098.

Rattan J, Levin N, Graff H, Weizer N, Gilat T. A high-fiber diet does not cause mineral and nutrient deficiencies. *J Clin Gastroenterol.* 1981;3:389–393.

Weisdorf S, Lysne J, Cerra F. Total parenteral nutrition in hepatic failure and transplantation. In: Lebenthal E, ed. *Total Parenteral Nutrition: Indications, Utilization, Complications, and Pathophysiological Considerations.* New York, NY: Raven Press; 1986.

PARENT ASSISTANCE

Martens RA, Martens Sherlyn. *The Milk Sugar Dilemma: Living with Lactose Intolerance.* East Lansing, Mich: Medi-Ed Press.

National Foundation for Ileitis and Colitis, Inc. 444 Park Avenue South, New York, NY 10016. (212) 685-3440. Support Group

Chapter 18

Chronic Renal Disease

Nancy S. Spinozzi

Infants and children with chronic renal disease, regardless of etiology, face multiple and frequent dietary manipulations throughout their course of treatment. This occurs at a time when growth and development are at their most dynamic stages and behavioral adaptations to eating and making food choices are so greatly influenced. Dietary modifications, along with the physical and emotional effects of chronic illness, can result in outcomes counterproductive to these activities, so vital to the normal maturation of the child. However, with better understanding of the particular disease and its nutritional management, it is possible to overcome what not too long ago were negative, though tolerated, outcomes: growth retardation and metabolic bone disease.

Chronic renal failure (CRF) in infants and children is almost equally represented by acquired and congenital etiologies.[1] Table 18-1 lists the predominant diagnoses in children with CRF less than 16 years of age. Acquired diseases such as chronic glomerulonephritis fortunately have less impact on growth, due to their more insidious onset. Congenital diseases, however, can result in early and severe growth retardation. Therefore, infants presenting with chronic renal insufficiency (CRI) must be aggressively nourished in order to promote at least a normal growth rate, preferably greater than the fifth percentile of length for age.[2,3] The earlier the age of onset of renal failure (GFR < 30% of normal), the more potentially severe its impact on growth will be.[4-6]

The most current information on the incidence of end-stage renal disease (ESRD) in infants and children comes from the United States Renal Data System, *1991 Annual Data Report* (National Institutes of Health). There were 781 new cases of ESRD in children in 1989. Children under the age of 4 represented 13% of all new cases. The number of adults (greater than 19 years of age) who presented with ESRD in 1988 was 30 times greater than that of children; however, unlike children, many adults develop renal failure secondary to diabetes and hypertension.

Table 18-1 Common Etiologies of Chronic Renal Failure in Children Less Than 16 Years

	Predominant Diagnosis
Congenital/hereditary	Hypoplasia/dysplasia Obstructive uropathy
Acquired	Chronic glomerulonephritis (GN) Membranoproliferative GN Focal segmental sclerosing GN

The consequences of chronic renal failure and its treatments for children all potentially influence growth (see Table 18-2). If any of these conditions are left inadequately managed (and each of them *is* successfully manageable), linear growth of the child will be delayed.[7,8] If properly treated, growth retardation can be arrested; however, catch-up growth is difficult to achieve.

The characteristic symptoms of CRF in children signaling increasing uremia are noted in Table 18-3. Several of those listed, including nausea, growth retardation, swelling, and shortness of breath, may respond favorably to some dietary modification(s).

To summarize, the impact of CRF on growth in children depends upon the severity and duration of the renal insufficiency, the diagnosis, and the age of onset. The treatments of CRF themselves, dialysis and transplantation, will affect growth as well.

CONSERVATIVE MANAGEMENT

Treating children with CRF without dialysis requires judicious and frequent monitoring of diet intake, biochemical parameters, and growth.[9] It has long been recognized that renal osteodystrophy and now aluminum osteopathy contribute significantly to growth retardation in children with renal insufficiency.[10]

Table 18-2 Consequences of Chronic Renal Failure

Water/electrolyte imbalance
Accumulation of endogenous/exogenous toxins
Hypertension
Acidosis
Anemia
Renal osteodystrophy
Anorexia/undernutrition
Need for steroid therapy

Table 18-3 Symptoms of Uremia in Children

> Nausea
> Weakness
> Fatigue
> Decreased school performance
> Loss of attention span
> Growth retardation
> Changes in urine output
> Shortness of breath
> Swelling of face/extremities/abdomen
> Amenorrhea in adolescent girls

Calcium and Phosphorus

Early on in the course of renal disease, synthesis of 1,25-dihydroxycholecalciferol (1.25 (OH)$_2$D$_3$) and the excretion of excessive dietary phosphate become decreased, leading to the development of renal osteodystrophy and secondary hyperparathyroidism if left untreated. Hyperphosphatemia is considered a late indicator of bone deformities. Current therapy may include any or all of the following: dietary restriction of high-phosphorus foods and fluids, supplementation of vitamin D (1.25 (OH)$_2$D$_3$) and calcium, and the prescription of nonaluminum-, nonmagnesium-containing phosphate binders (calcium carbonate, acetate, citrate), to be taken with meals.[11–13]

In infants, PM 60/40 by Ross Laboratories is the formula of choice, given its preferred calcium:phosphorus ratio of 2:1.[3] However, this formula does contain lactose and may not be tolerated by all infants. In that case, a soy-based formula would be indicated.

Sodium, Potassium, and Fluid

Sodium and fluid restriction might well be necessary to prevent or control the incidence of hypertension and edema not uncommonly associated with CRI. Usually, a no-added-salt diet for height age is sufficient. Limitation of fluid should be based on the child's urine output and insensible losses. Hyperkalemia is rarely a problem as long as kidney function is greater than 5% of normal. However, should potassium restriction become necessary, limiting high-potassium foods in the diet is generally adequate.

For infants requiring sodium and/or potassium restriction, formulas such as PM 60/40 or SMA (Wyeth-Ayerst Laboratories) are appropriate. Furthermore, if the volume of formula must be restricted, it is unlikely that any significant contribution of sodium or potassium will come from formula. To the contrary, infants with increased urine losses of sodium will need some sodium supplementation.

Protein/Energy

Energy needs are at least 80% of the Recommended Dietary Allowance (RDA) for height age[14] and may be greater than 100%. It is generally accepted that protein restriction much below the RDA for height age is contraindicated in growing children. With dietary phosphate restriction alone, a considerable limitation of protein intake could occur without restriction of protein per se. Routine nutritional assessment including anthropometric measurements and dietary intake will indicate whether the prescribed protein and calorie levels are adequate.[9]

Infants with CRI without dialysis intervention have been studied at Children's Hospital, Boston, Massachusetts, where it was found that the most efficient nitrogen retention occurs when calorie intake ranges between 8 and 11.9 kcal/cm of height and protein intake is maintained at or below 0.15 g/cm of height. This protein intake represented 5% to 7% of the total calories ingested.[2]

Accomplishing these nutritional goals, particularly in the presence of limited fluid intake (voluntary or involuntary), is possible only by caloric supplementation of the formula to as much as 60 kcal/oz. Increasing caloric density by three times normal dilution requires a methodical approach (Figure 18-1). Attempts should be made to maintain caloric distribution as follows, with the lower intakes of fat calories recommended for children over the age of 2 years:

Carbohydrate	35% to 65%
Protein	5% to 16%
Fat	30% to 55%

Carbohydrate sources such as Polycose (Ross Laboratories, Columbus, Ohio) and Moducal (Mead Johnson) are coupled with an oil (common vegetable or corn oil, or medium-chain triglyceride [MCT] oil for premature infants), as illustrated in Figure 18-2. Concentration of the formula with or without the addition of a protein supplement such as Promod (Ross Laboratories) or Propac (Sherwood Medical, St. Louis, Missouri) increases protein content. Caloric density can be advanced 2 to 4 cal/d as tolerated.

Ensuring the consistent daily intake of a sufficient volume of formula to meet an infant's nutritional goals for growth most often can be achieved only after the initiation of tube feedings. The presence of gastroesophageal reflux in infants with CRI is considered a major factor contributing to feeding problems in this age group.[15] However, continuous nighttime infusions of formula via feeding pump allows maximum tolerance of formula.

Once nutritional goals are realized and a feeding regimen established, additional oral stimulation through non-nutritive sucking can begin.[16] In the author's experience, once children are successfully transplanted they eventually will return to normal feeding practices.

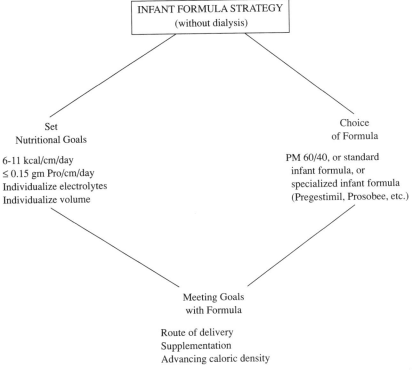

Figure 18-1 Infant formula strategy

Vitamins and Minerals

Since few children with CRI have consistently adequate diets, it is suggested that a multivitamin be routinely recommended. Additionally, 1 mg folic acid should be included. Iron supplementation may be indicated as well, especially if the child is receiving erythropoietin and ferritin and/or transferrin saturation levels are depressed.[17,18]

Lipids

Hypertriglyceridemia secondary to decreased hepatic lipase activity is common in CRI. Management with carbohydrate restriction is controversial given the limited caloric intake of many infants and children.[19,20] Most practitioners currently choose not to restrict carbohydrate at the expense of compromised growth.

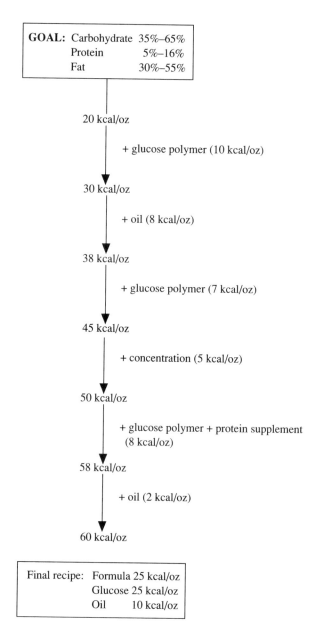

Figure 18-2 Increasing caloric density of formula: an example. (*Editors' note:* Very low fat intake in children less than 2 years of age may compromise development of the brain and central nervous system.)

DIALYSIS

Dialysis is indicated once a child experiences symptoms that significantly interfere with activities of daily living. Peritoneal dialysis (continuous cycling or continuous ambulatory) is the preferred choice of dialytic care for infants and small children. Both hemodialysis and peritoneal dialysis are options for bigger children. Nutritional management is dictated by the type of dialytic therapy chosen; however, the principles are similar to those described for conservative management.

Calcium and Phosphorus

Management of calcium and phosphorus balance continues to be necessary even while on dialysis and is the same as that stated previously.

Sodium, Potassium, and Fluid

A child's recommended intake for sodium and potassium is directly related to his or her residual renal function and the type and effectiveness of dialysis. Likewise, the degree of ultrafiltration possible and the child's urine output will dictate an advisable fluid intake. If restriction of sodium and potassium is necessary, which it usually is, the elimination or limitation of the foods containing especially large amounts of sodium and potassium is generally sufficient. Severely restricted diets often encourage noncompliance and dull a child's interest in food. Individualization of diet, taking into consideration the child's food preferences, is essential to successful control of sodium, potassium, and fluid intake.[21]

Protein/Energy

The nutritional requirements for protein and energy for patients undergoing peritoneal dialysis are not clear.[22] It is known that some protein is lost to the dialysate, while glucose is absorbed from the dialysate.[23] The degree to which these changes occur can only be determined through measurement of individual patients. Periodic calculations of urinary and dialysate urea nitrogen, dialysate protein and amino acids, and miscellaneous nitrogen losses are necessary.[24] Diets can then be developed and altered when measurements indicate the need, promoting growth while preventing obesity. During periods of peritonitis, there is an increased loss of protein to the dialysate, and the child usually feels ill. Careful attention to dietary intake is important to prevent a potentially significant loss of lean body weight during this time of infection.

Protein and energy requirements for children on hemodialysis have been studied using urea kinetic modeling as well as actual nitrogen balance techniques.[25] It was concluded that a protein intake of 0.3 g/cm/d and an energy intake of 10 kcal/cm/d produced positive nitrogen balance. The protein catabolic and urea generation rates of the children in positive balance were uniformly lower; therefore, there was no increase necessary in dialysis requirements with these levels of intake.

The routine use of urea kinetic modeling is especially helpful in determining dialysis and nutritional adequacy in children.[26,27] Monthly monitoring of protein catabolic rates and urea generation provide insight into subtle changes in dialysis treatment and/or diet intake that otherwise might go unnoticed. Kinetic modeling, usually conducted by the dietitian, allows the dietitian access to the fundamental parameters and concepts of dialysis prescription, ensuring maximum confidence in the nutrition counseling of patients.

Lipids

Hyperlipidemia remains a problem in children on dialysis.[28] Treatment with carbohydrate restriction or carnitine supplementation remains controversial.

Vitamins

It is advisable that children on both hemodialysis and peritoneal dialysis be provided water-soluble vitamins and folate, which are lost to dialysate. Although studies have not been conducted in children, it is current practice to provide 1 mg folate, 5 to 10 mg vitamin B6, and up to 100 mg ascorbic acid per day. Additional water-soluble vitamins should be given according to the RDAs for height age.[9] There are specially formulated dialysis vitamin preparations on the market (Nephro-Vite Rx by R&D Laboratories, Marina del Rey, California, and Nephrocaps by Fleming & Co., Fenton, Missouri) that fulfill most patients' needs. Infants can be given a standard liquid multivitamin such as Polyvisol by Mead Johnson, and young children can take a flavored chewable multivitamin; however, both should be accompanied by folate.

TRANSPLANTATION

The ultimate goal of all pediatric end-stage renal disease programs is transplantation. This is the only treatment option thus far that provides children with the opportunity for normal growth and potentially for catch-up growth.[29] Clinicians must be constantly vigilant for signs of rejection and infection, especially in the first postoperative year. Immunosuppression and antibiotic therapy result in side effects related to inefficient digestion and metabolism of nutrients as well as to growth retardation. Alternate-day steroid therapy has been shown to promote normal and, at times, catch-up growth. The medical course of the patient and the individual transplant program's protocol for immunosuppression will dictate just how quickly a patient can begin alternate-day dosing. The usual immunosuppressive medications prescribed today include azathiaprine, prednisone, and cyclosporine. OKT[3] and antilymphocyte globulin are used as short-term therapies.

For small children receiving adult kidneys, it is advisable that parenteral nutrition be considered immediately postoperatively due to the likelihood of ileus developing from the manipulation of bowel necessary to accommodate an adult kidney into a small body cavity.

Once feedings are resumed, the dietary recommendations are once again individualized. If kidney function is not normal, attention to sodium, potassium, phosphorus, and fluid will be necessary. A rise in blood urea nitrogen (BUN) level and a slow recovery to normal is usual even with normal kidney function due to the catabolic stress of surgery. If it is possible, aggressive nutritional support of the patient should resume soon after transplant.[30]

With the attainment of normal kidney function, a no-added-salt diet is still advisable.[31] Hypertension, now a potential result of high-dose steroid therapy, is frequently seen after transplantation, and sodium restriction, at least during the acute phase (first 6 to 8 months after transplant), is helpful. Also, tubular loss of phosphate is often present, requiring phosphorus supplementation. Dietary phosphorus intake usually is not adequate to maintain blood levels above 3.0 mg/dL.

Finally, children may develop steroid-induced hypoglycemia, requiring a no-concentrated-sweets diet. Occasionally, insulin is indicated. However, because hyperglycemia in the transplanted patient is due to insulin resistance and is usually a temporary situation while steroids are at their highest dosage, it is current practice not to attempt tight control of blood sugar. Rather, fasting sugars within the 200 to 300 range are acceptable. At this point a diabetic diet (e.g., one with a designated caloric level using commercially recognized exchanges of food groups and portion size) should begin (see Chapter 19).

Perhaps the most important aspect of the diet at this time is instruction in appropriate portion sizes. Most children have never heard the principles of "the basic four" or learned to eat nutritionally balanced meals. Additionally, the increased appetite accompanying prednisone therapy should be manipulated in a positive, healthy fashion, before a taste develops for high-carbohydrate, high-fat foods. It is common to hear parents describe the mealtimes of their newly transplanted children as lasting all day—one meal overlapping another.

Once steroids are tapered to levels where hypertension and hyperglycemia are no longer problematic, a diet appropriate for height age is indicated. Continued assessment of nutritional adequacy of the diet is necessary even with normal kidney function.

Table 18-4 Major Nutritional Considerations

Nutrient	Indication for Treatment	Modification
Phosphorus	CRI, elevated parathormone level, elevated alkaline phosphatase level, with or without hyperphosphatemia	Phosphate binders; low-phosphate diet; calcium and vitamin D supplement
	Post-transplant tubular loss; hypophosphatemia	Add supplement
Sodium	Hypertension; fluid retention	↓
	Daily steroid therapy	↓
	Increased urine losses	↑
	Increased peritoneal dialysate losses	↑
Potassium	< 5% GFR; hyperkalemia	↓
	Diuretic therapy; hypokalemia (peritoneal dialysis or post-transplant losses; diarrhea)	↑
Protein	Infants with CRI (no dialysis)	0.15 g/cm/d
	Children with CRI (no dialysis)	Limit to RDA for height age
	Children on hemodialysis	0.30 g/cm/d
	Infants/children on peritoneal dialysis	Usually ↑
	Post-transplant	RDA for height age
Energy	Undernutrition/anorexia	80% RDA for height age
	Infants with CRI (no dialysis)	6–11.9 kcal/cm/d
	Children on hemodialysis	10 kcal/cm/d
	Dextrose absorption from peritoneal dialysate	Varies depending on absorption
	Post-transplant steroid therapy	Varies depending on dose
	Steroid-induced hyperglycemia	No concentrated sweets

CONCLUSION

The nutritional intake of the child is especially important in order to ensure optimal growth and development during all stages of renal disease. The diet must be adequate and consistent. This is no easy task in light of the symptomatology accompanying the disease. Anorexia and taste changes commonly associated with CRF[32,33] constantly challenge the dietitian's attempts to promote optimal nutritional care. Additionally, dietary modification (see Table 18-4) and implementation must be individualized for all age groups, taking into account developmental levels, growth potentials, and renal functional limitations. Input from the entire renal team at all times is critical to ensuring successful nutritional management of this population. Frequent evaluation of food intake, growth, kidney function, and developmental stages is essential to adequate care.

REFERENCES

1. Fine RN. Growth in children with renal insufficiency. In: Nissenson A, Fine RN, Gentile D, eds. *Clinical Dialysis*. New York, NY: Appleton-Century Crofts;1984:661.

2. Spinozzi NS, Grupe WE, Harmon WE. Nutritional management of infants with chronic renal insufficiency (CRI) without dialysis. Presented at the American Dietetic Association, 70th Annual Meeting; October 1987; Atlanta, GA.

3. Wassner SJ, Abitol C, Alexander S, et al. Nutritional requirements for infants with renal failure. *Am J Kidney Dis*. 1986;7:300–305.

4. Betts PR, White RHR. Growth potential and skeletal maturity in children with chronic renal insufficiency. *Nephron*. 1976;16:325–332.

5. Broyer M. Growth in children with renal insufficiency. *Pediatr Clin North Am*. 1982;29:991–1003.

6. Rizzoni G, Broyer M, Guest G, et al. Growth retardation in children with chronic renal disease: scope of the problem. *Am J Kidney Dis*. 1986;7:256–261.

7. Rizzoni G, Basso T, Setari M. Growth in children with chronic renal failure on conservative treatment. *Kidney Int*. 1984;26:52–58.

8. Kleinknecht C, Broyer M, Hout D, et al. Growth and development of nondialyzed children with chronic renal failure. *Kidney Int*. 1983;24(S15):40–47.

9. Hellerstein S, Holliday MA, Grupe WE, et al. Nutritional management of children with chronic renal failure. *Pediatr Nephrol*. 1987;1:195–211.

10. Mehls O, Salusky IB. Recent advances and controversies in childhood renal osteodystrophy. *Pediatr Nephrol*. 1987;1:212–223.

11. Tamanah K, Mak RH, Rigden SP, Turner C, et al. Long-term suppression of hyperparathyroidism by phosphate binders in uremic children. *Pediatr Nephrol*. 1987;1:145–149.

12. Schiller LR, Santa Ana CA, Sheikh MS, et al. Effect of the time of administration of calcium acetate on phosphorus binding. *New Engl J Med*. 1989; 320:1110–1113.

13. Schmitt, J. Selecting an appropriate phosphate binder. *J Renal Nutr*. 1990;1:38-40.

14. Betts PR, Macgrath G. Growth pattern and dietary intake of children with chronic renal insufficiency. *Br Med J*. 1974;2:189.

15. Ruley EJ, Boch GH, Kerzner B, Abbott AW. Feeding disorders and gastroesophageal reflux in infants with chronic renal failure. *Pediatr Nephrol*. 1989;3:424–429.

16. Bebaum JC, Pererra GR, Watkins JB, et al. Non-nutritive sucking during gavage feeding enhances growth and maturation in premature infants. *Pediatrics*. 1983;71:41–45.

17. Eschbach MD, Egrie JC, Downing MR, et al. Correction of the anemia of end-stage renal disease with recombinant human erythropoietin. *N Engl J Med*. 1987;310:73–78.

18. Van Wyck DB, Stivelman JC, Ruiz J. Iron status in patients receiving erythropoietin for dialysis-associated anemia. *Kidney Int.* 1989;35:712–716.

19. Arnold WC, Danford D, Holliday MC. Effects of calorie supplementation on growth in children with uremia. *Kidney Int.* 1983;24:205.

20. Betts PR, Magrath G, White RHR. Role of dietary energy supplementation in growth of children with chronic renal insufficiency. *Br Med J.* 1977;1:416.

21. Spinozzi NS, Grupe WE. Nutritional implications of renal disease. *J Am Diet Assoc.* 1977;70:493–497.

22. Stover J, Nelson P. Nutritional recommendations for infants, children and adolescents with ESRD. In: Gillit D, Stover J, Spinozzi NS, eds. *A Clinical Guide to Nutritional Care in ESRD.* Chicago, Ill: American Dietetic Association; 1987:71–94.

23. Salusky IB, Kopple JD, Fine RN. Continuous ambulatory peritoneal dialysis—a 20 month's experience. *Kidney Int.* 1983;23(S15):S101-S105.

24. Geehan BP, Brown JM, Schleifer CR. Kinetic modeling in peritoneal dialysis. In: Nissenson AR, Fine RN, Gentile DE, eds. *Clinical Dialysis.* 2nd ed. Norwalk, Conn: Appleton and Lange; 1990:319–329.

25. Grupe WE, Harmon WE, Spinozzi NS. Protein and energy requirements in children receiving chronic hemodialysis. *Kidney Int.* 1983;24:S6–S10.

26. Harmon WE, Spinozzi NS, Meyer A, Grupe WE. The use of protein catabolic rate to monitor pediatric hemodialysis. *Dial Transplant.* 1981;10:324.

27. Grupe WE, Spinozzi NS, Harmon WE. Nutritional assessment of hemodialysis in children using urea kinetics. In: Brodehl J, Ehrich JHH, eds. *Pediatric Nephrology: Proceedings of the Sixth International Symposium of Paediatric Nephrology.* Berlin, Germany: Springer-Verlag; 1984:86–91.

28. Querfeld U, Salusky IB, Nelson P, et al. Hyperlipidemia in pediatric patients undergoing peritoneal dialysis. *Pediatr Nephrol.* 1988;2:447–452.

29. Inglefinger JR, Grupe WE, Harmon WE, et al. Growth acceleration following renal transplantation in children less than 7 years of age. *Pediatrics.* 1981;68:255–259.

30. Seagraves A, Moore EE, Moore FA, et al. Net protein catabolic rate after kidney transplantation: impact of corticosteroid immunosuppression. *J Parenter Enter Nutr.* 1986;10:453–455.

31. Gammarino M. Renal transplant diet: recommendations for the acute phase. *Dial Transplant.* 1987;16:497.

32. Spinozzi NS, Murray CL, Grupe WE. Altered taste acuity in children with ESRD. *Pediatr Res.* 1978;12:442. Abstract.

33. Shapera MR, Moel DI, Kamath SK, et al. Taste perception of children with chronic renal failure. *J Am Diet Assoc.* 1986;86:1359–1365.

Chapter 19

Diabetes

Lyllis Ling and Joyce Mosiman

NUTRITION MANAGEMENT OF THE CHILD WITH DIABETES

Successful control of diabetes entails achieving a balance among food, insulin, and exercise, as depicted in Figure 19-1. Meeting the nutritional needs of children and adolescents with diabetes while providing foods that children will eat is often identified by parents as the most difficult element of diabetes management. Families already faced with altering their lifestyle to include insulin injections often experience the attempt to follow a meal plan as a never-ending task. The challenge to the dietitian on the diabetes team is to support the family's efforts and to help promote healthy eating habits by using information gained from current research coupled with insight into family dynamics. To be successful, the meal plan must not only meet nutritional requirements but also facilitate adherence by both child and parents. Flexibility is an important key to success.

The goals for nutrition management are listed in Table 19-1. Every attempt should be made to establish a meal plan that reflects the child's food preferences and the family's usual diet. The dietitian should avoid recommending radical change except when clearly needed. Graduated goal setting increases the chances of the child's adhering to the meal plan, achieving normoglycemia, and decreasing the development of complications.

GUIDELINES FOR NUTRITION MANAGEMENT

In 1986, the Committee on Food and Nutrition of the American Diabetes Association (ADA) updated its recommendations for macronutrient distribution in the diabetic diet. The currently recommended goals are 55% to 60% of calories from carbohydrate, 30% or less from fat, and 0.8 g protein per kilogram of body weight or the Recommended Dietary Allowance (RDA) for adults. However, some adaptations of these must usually be made for children with diabetes (Table 19-2).[1]

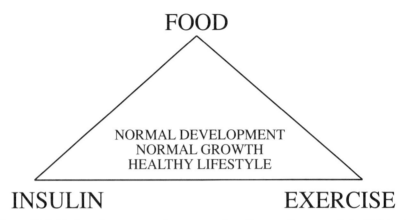

MAKING DIABETES LIVE WITH YOU

FOOD

NORMAL DEVELOPMENT
NORMAL GROWTH
HEALTHY LIFESTYLE

INSULIN   EXERCISE

Figure 19-1 Tools and outcomes of treatment plan. *Source:* Courtesy of the Children's Diabetes Center, The Children's Mercy Hospital, Kansas City, MO.

Calories

Including enough calories (cal) in the meal plan to maintain a consistent growth curve and to achieve and/or maintain a desirable body weight is of major importance. Comparing energy needs based on height, ideal body weight (IBW), and average energy allowance per day (see Table 19-2) will provide the best method to estimate energy needs for an individual.[2] Mahan and Rosebrough recommend adapting the RDA figures and basing the estimate of calorie and protein needs on height for adolescents.[3] From age 11 to 22, the estimate ranges from 16 to 17 cal/cm for boys and from 13 to 14 cal/cm for girls.[3] Other guidelines for determining calorie needs of children are found in Chapters 2 and 5.

Table 19-1 Goals for Nutrition Management

1. To develop a meal plan that is nutritionally adequate to maintain normal growth and development and that is based on the child's appetite, food preferences, and family lifestyle.
2. To encourage consistency in the times of meals, snacks, and amounts of food to maintain normoglycemia, in order to prevent or delay long-term complications of diabetes.
3. To provide the level of information that meets the family's interest and ability so they can be flexible in meeting changing growth and activity needs of the child.
4. To provide information on current research to help the family make appropriate decisions regarding healthy eating habits.

Table 19-2 Recommended Energy and Protein Intake for Weight, Height, and per Day

Category	Age (years)	Weight (kg)	(lb)	Height (cm)	(in)	Average Energy Allowance (kcal) Per day[a]	Per kg[a]	Per cm[a]	Average Protein Allowance (g) Per day[a]	Per kg[a]	Per cm[a]
Infants	0.0–0.5	6	13	60	24	650	108		13	2.2	0.3
	0.5–1.0	9	20	71	28	850	98		14	1.6	0.3
Children	1–3	13	29	90	35	1300	102		16	1.2	0.3
	4–6	20	44	112	44	1800	90		24	1.1	0.3
	7–10	28	62	132	52	2000	70		28	1.0	0.3
Males	11–14	45	99	157	62	2500	55	16	45	1.0	0.3
	15–18	66	145	176	69	3000	45	17	59	0.9	0.3
	19–24	72	160	177	70	2900	40	16	58	0.8	0.3
Females	11–14	46	101	157	62	2200	47	14	46	1.0	0.3
	15–18	55	120	163	64	2200	40	13	44	0.8	0.3
	19–24	58	128	164	65	2200	38	13	46	0.8	0.3

[a]Figure is rounded.

Source: Adapted with permission from *Recommended Dietary Allowances*, 10th edition, © 1989 by the National Academy of Sciences. Published by National Academy Press.

Carbohydrate

The current recommendation to increase the level of calories from carbohydrates to 55% to 60% of total calories is linked to a secondary recommendation to substitute complex and unrefined carbohydrates for simple carbohydrates. However, achieving both with children can be difficult because of the relatively greater bulk of the complex carbohydrate foods and the small stomachs of children.

The glycemic index, which categorizes foods according to their effect on blood glucose level, provides the basis for the statement by the ADA that persons with diabetes in good control may tolerate the addition of small amounts of sucrose to their diet.[1,4] Table 19-3 summarizes the glycemic index of selected foods. Flexibility in allowing some sucrose in the diet may lead to better adherence to the meal plan. To moderate the impact of sucrose on the blood glucose level, it is better to include foods containing sucrose in a mixed meal or to use them when extra activity is planned.

Protein

Questions raised by research concerning the role of protein versus glycemic control in the development of kidney damage have encouraged the current trend to consider decreasing the amount of protein in the diet.[5-7] Family acceptance of a child's diet limited in protein is often poor because of food preferences and lifestyle. In addition, it may be difficult to meet requirements for calories, calcium and other minerals within the limitations of this recommendation in conjunction with the recommendation to reduce fat in the diet. The strict limitation of protein foods may result in an increase in the frequency of snacks to provide carbohydrates for maintenance of normoglycemia. A level of 12% to 17% of total calories from protein seems to be a realistic starting point for children. Protein needs can also be estimated based on the RDA data in Table 19-2.

Recent research done in young adults by Chase et al. links kidney and eye changes to extended poor glycemic control (above 9% glycohemoglobin) rather than high protein intake.[5] The protein issue will remain controversial until more studies are done in children.

Fat

Diabetes is a risk factor for the development of cardiovascular heart disease (CHD). The American Diabetes, Heart, and Cancer Associations recommend that all adults decrease fat intake to no more than 30% of calories, with 10% saturated fat, 10% monounsaturated fat, and 10% polyunsaturated fat. An intake of less than 300 mg of cholesterol daily is also recommended.[1] These goals are being sug-

Table 19-3 Glycemic Index of Foods*[†‡]

100%	60%–69%	40%–49%	20%–29%
Glucose	Bread (white)	Spaghetti (whole	Kidney beans
	Rice (brown)	meal)	Lentils
80%–90%	Muesli	Porridge oats	Fructose
Corn flakes	Shredded Wheat	Potato (sweet)	
Carrots	"Ryvita"	Beans (canned	**10%–19%**
Parsnips	Water biscuits	navy)	Soya beans
Potatoes (instant	Beetroot	Peas (dried)	Soya beans
mashed)	Bananas	Oranges	(canned)
Maltose	Raisins	Orange juice	Peanuts
Honey	Mars bar		
		30%–39%	
70%–79%	**50%–59%**	Butter beans	
Bread (whole	Buckwheat	Haricot beans	
meal)	Spaghetti (white)	Blackeye peas	
Millet	Sweet corn	Chick peas	
Rice (white)	All-Bran	Apples (Golden	
Weetabix	Digestive biscuits	Delicious)	
Broad beans	Oatmeal biscuits	Ice cream	
(fresh)	"Rich Tea"	Milk (skim)	
Potato (new)	biscuits	Milk (whole)	
Swede	Peas (frozen)	Yogurt	
	Yam	Tomato soup	
	Sucrose		
	Potato chips		

* The glycemic index is defined as the area under the blood glucose response curve for each food, expressed as a percentage of the area after taking the same amount of carbohydrate as glucose.

† Data from normal individuals.

‡ 25-g carbohydrate portions tested.

Source: Reprinted with permission from Jenkins DJA, Lente carbohydrate: a newer approach to dietary management of diabetes, in *Diabetes Care* (1982;5:634), Copyright © 1982, American Diabetes Association.

gested as appropriate for all children at risk for CHD.[7,8] Maintaining a fat limitation for children and adolescents is one of the more challenging goals to achieve. A fat content of 30% to 35% of calories may be a more realistic initial goal. If the family history reveals the presence of family members below age 55 with CHD, the limitation of fat and cholesterol should be approached more vigorously.[8] Careful consideration should be given to strict fat restriction for children less than 2 years of age, as the development of the brain and central nervous system are dependent in part on adequate intake of fats.

Fiber

Some fiber appears to slow the absorption of glucose in the body.[4] In addition, research indicates that soluble fiber from legumes, oat bran, and some fruits and vegetables containing pectin may be helpful in lowering cholesterol.[1,9] Adding a specific amount of fiber to a young child's diet is somewhat controversial since fiber may cause a decrease in the child's capacity to eat other foods necessary for growth and blood glucose maintenance.[10] In addition, fiber may produce flatulence and distention. Nevertheless, children should be encouraged to consume fiber-containing foods. If constipation or elevated cholesterol is a problem, more fiber may need to be introduced into the diet. Fiber is discussed in more detail in Chapters 17 and 19.

Sodium, Vitamins, and Minerals

A prudent intake of sodium is recommended for all people.[1] Hypertension is a risk factor associated with diabetic glomerulonephropathy. Therefore, routine monitoring of blood pressure is necessary and will help identify children who need to reduce sodium intake.[11] If a child's normal eating habits exclude or severely limit foods or food groups, it may be necessary to consider supplementation with vitamins and minerals that provide only the RDAs.[7] Nutrient adequacies should be evaluated periodically as children's food preferences change.

ESTABLISHING THE MEAL PLAN

Establishing the meal plan for a child who has been recently diagnosed with insulin-dependent diabetes mellitus is done in stages (Table 19-4).

Table 19-4 Steps in Developing a Meal Plan

1. Identify typical food intake prior to symptoms.
2. Plot current height and weight on National Center for Health Statistics growth chart, determine percentile, and estimate ideal body weight.
3. Estimate calorie and protein needs.
4. Allow child to eat amounts of food to satisfy appetite at meals and snacks for 2 to 3 days to determine current calorie need. Even though intake is unrestricted, an effort should be made to establish consistency as soon as possible.
5. Develop a meal pattern, including snacks, based on past and current intake.
6. Verify appropriateness of meal plan by asking parent to write menus based on tentative meal plan.
7. Adjust meal plan for usual activities.

Home History

The kinds and amounts of food the child ate just before the development of symptoms of diabetes may not be indicative of what the child needs. Some children eat unusually large amounts of food, while others, especially younger children, show little interest in food but drink large quantities of fluids.

In addition to the food intake, information is needed on recent weight loss, food allergies and preferences, school menus and schedules, and normal activities. Information on vitamin/mineral supplements, medications, and any other chronic diseases should be noted in addition to the family's eating behaviors, food beliefs, and lifestyle.

Anthropometric Evaluation

An accurate measurement of weight and height (or length), information on recent weight loss, and calculation of IBW are needed to estimate the child's current nutrient needs. Determining the percentile of the height (length), weight, weight for height, and the range for IBW will identify the child's initial nutrition status and help guide the development of the meal plan.

Hospital Intake

At the time of diagnosis, the parent and/or child is asked to keep a record of what is eaten at each meal and snack. This helps establish the amount of food that is currently needed to satisfy the child's appetite. It is important to respond to the child's appetite so that hunger is not associated with having diabetes. For a child who was at an appropriate weight for height prior to the onset of symptoms, appetite can be a good indicator of current calorie needs.[12]

The appetite of most children will usually stabilize by the third to fifth day of hospitalization. At that time, the calories consumed are at approximately the recommended level for IBW rather than current body weight. The increased calorie intake may continue until the child reaches presymptom weight or IBW.

The Exchange System

At this point, the amounts and kind of foods consumed in the hospital are compared with those previously eaten at home. Based on this comparison, a judgment is made about how much the child is likely to eat, and a meal plan is drafted with the parent and/or child. This information is translated into exchanges using the exchange lists developed by the American Dietetic Association and the American Diabetes Association (see Exhibit 19-1).[13] Table 19-5 shows the specific amount

Exhibit 19-1 Exchange Lists for Meal Planning*

Starch/Bread List			Meat/Meat Substitute List	
Cooked cereal	1/2 cup		Lean	
Bran cereal, flaked	1/2 cup		Lean beef (round, flank)	1 oz
Frankfurter or			Chicken (without skin)	1 oz
hamburger bun	1/2 (1 oz)		Cottage cheese	1/4 cup
Bread (white or whole			Medium-Fat	
wheat)	1 slice (1 oz)		Ground beef	1 oz
Peas, green	1/2 cup		Pork chop	1 oz
Potato, mashed	1/2 cup		86% fat-free luncheon meat	1 oz
Popcorn, popped			High-fat	
(no fat added)	3 cups		Frankfurter (turkey or	
			chicken) (10/lb)	1 frank
Vegetable List			Cheese (American,	
			Cheddar or Swiss)	1 oz

Vegetable List				
1/2 cup cooked or 1 cup raw vegetable:			Fat List	
Beans (green)				
Broccoli			Margarine	1 tsp
Carrots			Mayonnaise	1 tsp
Cauliflower			Mayonnaise (reduced calorie)	1 Tbsp
Peppers (green)			Salad dressing	1 Tbsp
Spinach (cooked)			Salad dressing (reduced calorie)	2 Tbsp
Summer Squash				
Tomato (1 large)			Free Food List	

Fruit List			Carbonated drinks (sugar free)	
Apple (raw, 2" across)	1		Cocoa powder (unsweetened)	1 Tbsp
Applesauce (unsweetened)	1/2 cup		Celery	1 cup
Banana (9" long)	1/2		Cucumbers	1 cup
Orange (2 1/2" across)	1		Lettuce	
Strawberries (raw, whole)	1 1/4 cups		Gelatin (sugar free)	
Apple juice/cider	1/2 cup		Catsup	1 Tbsp
Grape juice	1/3 cup		Taco Sauce	1 Tbsp
Orange juice	1/2 cup		Pickle, dill	

Milk List	
Skim/very low fat, low fat and whole	8 oz

* Partial listing; shows amounts to equal one exchange.

Source: The Exchange Lists are the basis of a meal planning system designed by a committee of the American Diabetes Association and the American Dietetic Association. While designed primarily for people with diabetes and others who must follow special diets, the Exchange Lists are based on principles of good nutrition that apply to everyone. © 1986 American Diabetes Association, Inc., American Dietetic Association.

Table 19-5 Nutrient Content of Exchanges

Exchange List	Carbohydrate (grams)	Protein (grams)	Fat (grams)	Calories
Starch/bread	15	3	trace	80
Meat				
Lean	—	7	3	55
Medium fat	—	7	5	75
High fat	—	7	8	100
Vegetable	5	2	—	25
Fruit	15	—	—	60
Milk				
Skim	12	8	trace	90
Low fat	12	8	5	120
Whole	12	8	8	150
Fat	—	—	5	45

Source: Reprinted from Exchange Lists for Meal Planning, with permission of American Diabetes Association, Inc. and the American Dietetic Association, © 1986.

of carbohydrate, protein, fat, or combination of these nutrients in each food group. The exchange system is the most commonly used method to achieve a consistent intake of carbohydrate, protein, and fat.

Stipulating a specific fractional division of calories among meals and snacks is sometimes thought to be beneficial. However, it is often more realistic and effective to provide meals and snacks that are of an acceptable size to the child. The child's normal activities, during school and on weekends, and the insulin regimen should always be considered in establishing the meal plan.

Insulin

Most newly diagnosed children can be managed on two injections of mixed insulin daily. A combination of intermediate acting and fast acting insulins or a premixed insulin or an intermediate acting insulin alone may be the initial choice of treatment. Ideally, injections are given approximately 30 minutes before the morning and the evening meals.[14] The onset, peak, and duration of four common types of insulins are listed in Table 19-6. Snacks and meals should be planned for times of peak action of insulins. For instance, a child on NPH and regular insulins who is taking an injection at 7:30 AM should be eating breakfast 30 minutes after the injection, a morning snack approximately 2 hours after breakfast to accommodate for the peak of the morning regular insulin, lunch about 12:00, and an afternoon snack at approximately 3:30 PM to accommodate for the peak of the morning NPH insulin. The evening injection, given at approximately 6:00 PM, would pre-

Table 19-6 Onset, Peak, and Duration of Four Common Types of Insulin*

	Onset	Peak	Duration
Regular (fast acting)	30 minutes	2–4 hours	4–6 hours
NPH (intermediate acting)	1–2 hours	6–10 hours	16–24 hours
Ultra Lente (slow acting)	4–8 hours	18–24 hours	36+ hours
Mixed insulins			
70% Intermediate acting	30 minutes–	3–4 hours	16–24 hours
30% Fast acting	1 hour	& 4–8 hours	

* Human insulin may have a quicker peak and shorter duration of action than the times listed.

Source: Courtesy of the Children's Diabetes Center, The Children's Mercy Hospital, Kansas City, MO.

cede dinner at 6:30, and a bedtime snack approximately 2 to 3 hours after the injection is needed to cover the long-acting insulin at night.

Multiple-injection regimens allow more freedom in the scheduling of meals and may entirely eliminate the need for snacks. If, for example, a child takes regular insulin before meals (in addition to a long-acting insulin such as Ultra Lente), the amount will be based on the size of the meal to be eaten. Ultra Lente does not have a dramatic peak and usually does not require a snack. It serves as a basal dose of insulin to cover periods between regular injections.

Influence of Food on Insulin Dose

Insulin therapy is frequently based on 0.75 to 1 unit (u) of insulin per kilogram (kg) of IBW. As a child grows and food intake increases, the insulin dose also increases. During brief periods of illness or times of stress or decreased activity, insulin needs may increase. When the problem is resolved, the insulin dose should usually be reduced. If insulin is not reduced, the child may eat more in response to the higher insulin level, and inappropriate weight gain may result. A change in the child's level of activity, which may be especially dramatic at the beginning and ending of the school year, usually requires an adjustment in the insulin dosage.

Normal Activity

The times of recess and physical education (PE) classes and the type and length of after-school activities will influence the kind and amount of food needed for snacks. If PE is offered only on Monday and Wednesday at 10:00 AM, for example, the child may need a larger snack than on days without PE. For inactive children, whose main activity is not likely to increase beyond watching television and studying, total calorie needs may be lower than the levels recommended in Table 19-2.

Age-Specific Considerations

Food intake, activities, and problems vary with age as discussed in the following section.

Birth to 12 Months

Most infants consume 50% to 80% of their calories as formula or milk, and most of them eat every 3 to 4 hours. An infant with diabetes will do well following this same schedule and including cereal, vegetables, and/or vegetable-meat dinners with the formula. See Exhibit 19-2 for a food list for infants containing approximately 8 g of carbohydrate.[15,16]

Juice and fruit tend to cause an elevated blood glucose level in most infants, so these may be limited or omitted in the diet until the child is eating more protein

---

Exhibit 19-2 Food List for Infants Containing Approximately 8 Grams of Carbohydrates*

Cereal	
Dry cereal except high protein	3 Tbsp
High protein cereal	5 Tbsp
Strained vegetables—4 1/2 oz jar	
Beets, mixed vegetables, peas	3/4 jar
Carrots, creamed spinach, garden vegetables, green beans, squash	1 jar
Sweet potatoes	1/2 jar
Strained dinners—4 1/2 oz jar	
All Gerber varieties	3/4 jar
Strained lean meat dinners—4 1/2 oz jar	
All Gerber varieties	1 jar
Junior vegetables—6 oz jar	
Carrots, squash	3/4 jar
Peas, creamed green beans	1/2 jar
Sweet potatoes	1/3 jar
Junior dinners—6 oz jar	
All Gerber varieties	1/2 jar
Saltines	4 squares

* Heinz products are frequently a little lower in carbohydrate. The same serving sizes can be used successfully.

Source: Gerber Product Company, *Nutrient Values*, 1988, Fremont, MI.

and fiber. Until one fourth of a jar of meat (which contains about 20 to 25 cal and 2 to 3 g of protein) is consumed regularly, it doesn't need to be counted in the meal plan.

When the infant begins eating 2 to 3 T of table food other than low-calorie vegetables, the regular exchange system can be introduced. Many infants will eat a combination of strained food and table food for several months. Saltine crackers are included in the infant exchanges since these can be substituted for strained foods or formula to meet the child's need for finger foods. Two crackers contain the same amount of carbohydrate as 2 oz of formula.

1 to 4 Years of Age

When the infant starts drinking milk from a cup (usually between 12 and 15 months of age), the milk intake usually decreases and solid food intake increases. A total revision of the meal plan is needed at that time. A better acceptance of meat and cheese also occurs, which makes it possible to include the meat group in the meal plan. Fruits can usually be included in the meal plan at this time, although fruit juice may continue to be limited.

As the toddler develops more mobility and interest in the environment increases, interest in food wanes. In some instances, getting the toddler to eat anything at a meal is an accomplishment. Insulin therapy needs to be closely monitored when this occurs. In extreme cases, insulin is given after it is known whether and how much the toddler has eaten so that the dose of insulin can be based on the amount of food consumed.

School-Age Children

Adjusting diabetes around the school schedule rather than changing PE classes or lunch periods to accommodate an insulin regimen communicates to the child that the child is more important than the diabetes. It is possible to arrange snacks and injections around most school schedules. School-age children will ordinarily need three meals and three snacks a day, spaced according to their insulin regimen. However, some children can omit the morning snack without creating a problem on a two-injection regimen. Children should be instructed to carry a fast-acting carbohydrate (e.g., glucose tablets, Lifesavers, or raisins) with them at all times in case of emergency. The use of chocolate candy bars or other dessert items is discouraged as a treatment for a reaction due to the fat content of the foods, which may slow the absorption of sugar.

Most schools will substitute lunch items appropriate to meet the needs of children following a diabetic meal plan. School personnel should be made aware of the child's food requirements and preferences. Everyone must realize that omitting lunch is not a choice. If school personnel are unwilling to cooperate, reference can be made to Section 504 of the Rehabilitation Act of 1973 or to the Education for All Handicapped Children Act of 1975, commonly referred to as Public Law No. 94-142, which mandates that handicapped students, including children with diabetes, have access to all services necessary to assist in full participation in school.

Snacks frequently need to be adjusted when the child has no daily PE or when recess is used for purposes other than active play. It generally works well to add an extra snack when the activity is increased. It is usually better not to omit a snack when the activity level is decreased unless the blood glucose level is consistently above 150 mg/dL at the next regular blood glucose check.

Omitting foods from the meal plan because of a single high blood glucose reading may not be advisable. An elevated blood glucose level caused by stress may decrease rapidly when the stress is reduced, and hypoglycemia may occur if food is omitted.[17]

Adolescents

The advent of adolescence may bring a great deal of conflict into the lives of families. Adolescents strive for independence and expect parents to trust them to manage on their own. The importance of controlling blood glucose levels during this period increases since complications of diabetes are thought to begin at the onset of puberty.[18]

The key to working successfully with adolescents is finding a way for them to feel they are in control of their diabetes. The health care team should make every effort to make the teen feel capable of and responsible for diabetes control. More flexibility in food choices for occasional use may be appropriate. Food choices may improve if the dietitian provides a nonjudgmental atmosphere. Suggestions for improvement can be made without using the words "must," "ought," and "should."

Weight Control. Weight control can become an important issue when children enter adolescence. Some weight gain is usually seen prior to growth spurts. The sex maturity ratings (SMRs) developed by JM Tanner are a useful guide for identifying appropriate weight loss recommendations. Weight loss before SMR 3 in girls and SMR 4 in boys is not recommended because of the need for calories for continued growth.[19] Age is not necessarily an indicator of SMR (see also Chapters 1 and 2).

Teens who are overly concerned about losing weight but who find it hard to reduce intake may skip insulin injections to promote quick weight loss. When significant weight loss occurs, etiology should be explored to eliminate the presence of eating disorders, which are becoming prevalent in this age group.[20]

Alcohol. Alcohol use and abuse should be discussed with the teenager in an objective manner. Although the use of alcohol is not legal and is always discouraged for teens, facts about how alcohol affects the blood glucose level should be available to teens who express an interest in drinking. It should be made clear that alcohol lowers the blood glucose level and blocks gluconeogenesis and that seizures may occur if carbohydrates are not consumed with the alcohol.[21] Alcohol should only be used when diabetes is under good control. Pointing out that alcohol alters the ability to think clearly may help the teen to use alcohol with caution or avoid its use entirely. Wearing identification is especially important for individuals who choose to drink, as intoxication and diabetic reactions can often be confused. Drinking alone should always be discouraged.

EDUCATING THE FAMILY

Education is the key to enabling families to understand and manage diabetes.[22] Nutrition education in the hospital should be based on the family's ability, interest, and readiness to learn. Exhibits 19-3 and 19-4 list the concepts and skills necessary for successful nutrition management. The length of time required to achieve educational goals varies considerably. Actual teaching may require 3 to 10 hours, with additional time for menu writing and selection by the caretakers. Initial instruction in groups is usually not successful but may be useful after hospitalization. Attempts to present all concepts upon initial diagnosis may result in confusion and the family's loss of confidence in themselves as caretakers. Routine follow-up by phone and on clinic visits is necessary as many questions arise when

---

Exhibit 19-3 Nutrition Education Concepts Presented Initially

Minimal nutrition education concepts to provide before dismissal:
1. Explanation of the relationship between food, blood glucose level, and insulin.
2. Introduction of the six food groups in the exchange system and identification of foods in each group.
3. Introduction of the importance of following the meal pattern.
4. Discussion of treatment to counteract a mild to moderate insulin reaction.

Nutrition education concepts to present if family is ready:
1. Discussion of basic good nutrition principles for normal growth and development.
2. Adjustment of meal plan and schedule for special occasions, changes in schedule, and eating out.
3. Discussion of foods that may be eaten without raising blood glucose level.
4. Explanation of increasing food for extra activity.
5. Explanation of adjustment of schedule for taking insulin and eating meals and snacks for weekdays and weekends.
6. Identification of sugar sources in food labels.

Exhibit 19-4 Desirable Skills for Good Nutritional Management

Minimal skills to be demonstrated by parent/child prior to dismissal:
1. Write menu for meals and snacks for 3 days using the meal plan and listing appropriate amounts of foods.

Intermediate skills if parent/child is ready:
1. Plan a menu for eating out and for a special occasion.
2. Demonstrate ability to evaluate and compensate for school menu.

Advanced skills (often taught after dismissal):
1. Identify nutritive and non-nutritive sweeteners.
2. Convert recipes into exchanges.
3. Evaluate food labels for nutrient information and ingredient content.

normal activity resumes. Continued nutrition follow-up and education are required as the child grows and develops and as the family works to gain expertise in the nutrition management of diabetes.

EVALUATING DIABETES MANAGEMENT

Using available technology, the health care team is able to tailor treatment regimens to individual needs. Guidelines to aid families and health professionals in evaluating diabetes control appear in Exhibit 19-5.

Growth Maintenance

Routine charting of a child's height, weight, and weight-for-height is an excellent way to monitor the growth pattern. Deviation from the child's normal growth channel (except for increased height or decreasing weight in a child who has reached full height potential) needs close monitoring.

Some children have a cyclical weight curve: They gain weight faster in the winter and less rapidly in the summer. This pattern does not appear to affect normal height progression.

In a child who is poorly controlled, weight percentile will often remain stationary or decrease. After about 6 months of little or no weight gain, height velocity also begins to slow. Achieving optimal height potential can be used to motivate boys and some girls to strive for better control. Teenagers are more likely to be interested in improved self-care when they understand the relationship between good control, appropriate weight gain, consistent height increase, and/or normal menses.

Exhibit 19-5 Patient Guidelines for Attaining and Maintaining Good Diabetes Control

1. Maintains glycosylated hemoglobin of less than 9.0% (normal 4.5–7.0).
2. Maintains fasting blood glucose levels between 70–150 mg/dL, 75% of the time.
3. Tests and records blood glucose:
   a. Two injections per day—a minimum of 2 tests per day, varying the times of day
   b. Three or more injections per day—a minimum of three tests per day
   c. Four injections per day or insulin pump—a minimum of four tests per day.
4. Tests urine for ketones when ill or when blood glucose is above 240 mg/dL.
5. Maintains absence of protein in urine (based on quarterly check in clinic), except girls who are menstruating and those who are weight-lifting or engaged in strenuous physical activity.
6. Participates in regular activities.
7. Accommodates appropriately for exercise and special occasions to avoid hypo- and hyperglycemia.
8. Manages brief illness at home and knows when to call for help.
9. Maintains weight/height percentile between the 10th and the 75th percentile with exceptions for children with large or small frames or those who participate in activities to develop muscle vs. fat.
10. Maintains blood pressure below the 90th percentile for age.
11. Maintains cholesterol and other lipid values below the 95th percentile for age.
12. Maintains normal peer and family relationships.
13. Exhibits adequate knowledge, attitudes and skills for controlling diabetes appropriate for age.

Source: Courtesy of The Children's Diabetes Center, The Children's Mercy Hospital, Kansas City, MO.

Monitoring Tools

The test for glycosylated hemoglobin measures the average amount of glucose in the blood over a 2- to 3-month period. Used in conjunction with regularly monitored blood glucose results, glycosylated hemoglobin levels can help evaluate the level of control. However, the glycosylated hemoglobin level reflects an average amount of glucose in the blood and can be the result of very high and low blood glucose levels, which is not indicative of good control. See Table 19-7 for levels of control associated with glycosylated hemoglobin values.

Home glucose monitoring provides the child and family with readily available feedback on the effects of food, exercise, insulin, and stress on blood glucose level. More flexibility in lifestyle can be achieved with blood glucose monitoring.[23,24]

Table 19-8 shows the rationale for tests that are performed annually.

Table 19-7 Levels of Control Associated with Glycosylated Hemoglobin Value

Normal	4.5–7.0%
Excellent	7.0% and under
Good	7.1–9.0%
Fair	9.1–12.0%
Poor	> 12.0%

Source: Courtesy of CP Howard, The Children's Diabetes Center, The Children's Mercy Hospital, Kansas City, MO.

OTHER CONSIDERATIONS

There are many other topics that a family needs to understand to manage diabetes successfully. These topics can be dealt with whenever the family asks questions about them. Many can be dealt with in a group setting and on follow-up visits.

Table 19-8 Screening Tests Completed at Diagnosis and Annually for Children with Diabetes

Test	Group Tested	Reason
Lipid profile	All children	Provides early detection of increased cholesterol and other lipid disorders.
Thyroid function studies	All children	Screens for thyroid disease, provides information helpful in assessing inappropriate weight gain and/or growth problems.
24-hour urine for micro-albumin C-peptides glucose	All children	Helps with early detection of renal problems, provides estimation of endogenous insulin production, provides information on time and amount of glucose spillage.
Eye exam	At diagnosis: All children 5 and older Every 3 years: Ages 5–12 Annually: Ages 12 and older	Provides early detection of eye changes.

Source: Courtesy of The Children's Diabetes Center, The Children's Mercy Hospital, Kansas City, MO.

"Honeymoon" Period

In 50% to 60% of children with diabetes, the insulin dose begins to decrease immediately after hospitalization because residual beta cells continue to produce endogenous insulin for several weeks, months, or even years.[25] Frequently during this "honeymoon" period, sucrose consumption does not cause an elevation in blood glucose level because of the presence of the endogenous insulin. However, overconsumption of sweets may bring this period of good metabolic control to an earlier end. The amount of endogenous insulin being produced can be determined by the laboratory test for C-peptides.

Appetite Variations

Many factors influence a child's natural appetite. Growth spurts are generally preceded by an increase in appetite and sometimes by an increase in weight. Since growth spurts are not predictable, the parent is encouraged to respect the child's requests for more food.

Boredom and stress can also affect the desire for food. The child may want to eat for diversion when bored. Stress may either increase or decrease the interest in food. In the case of either boredom or stress, identifying the problem and working to change the situation is preferred over changing the food intake.

Honest Communication

A child with diabetes has many responsibilities for self-care. Checking and recording the blood glucose level may be one of the most irksome because it must be done so often and because others may inappropriately evaluate and judge the results. Blood glucose results are not totally reliable as a monitor of compliance with meal plans. If, by reporting a high blood glucose reading, a child risks accusations of sneaking food or overeating, the child may choose to record more acceptable but false levels. This practice may result in poor care but may also foster dishonesty in the child. Establishing a nonjudgmental and honest atmosphere for the exchange of information is imperative for the parent, the dietitian, and other health care providers.

High or low blood glucose levels will occur in most children even when insulin and exercise schedules and the meal plan are followed closely. When a high or low level occurs, it is useful to review the day's activities to see if there is an obvious explanation for the level. If the child acknowledges eating a candy bar after school, a reprimand is not likely to encourage the child to be honest in the future.

Letting the Child Make Appropriate Decisions

Children should be allowed to help with decision making. As early as 2 or 3 years of age, a child knows if a cheese or peanut butter sandwich is preferred for lunch. Grade-school children may feel very strongly that they don't want to be different from their peers and may prefer eating a slightly larger breakfast in order to eliminate a morning snack. This adjustment can sometimes be made while maintaining a noon blood glucose level within the desired range.

On clinic visits, the child should be routinely asked if a change in the meal plan is desired. Even if no change is made, the child will enjoy having some control over the meal plan.

Exercise

Regular exercise is an important element in controlling the blood glucose level, lowering the cholesterol level, and maintaining appropriate body weight. Aerobic exercise is necessary to maintain a healthy cardiovascular system as well as to improve glucose control. With evidence mounting that obesity in children is increasing partly because of decreased activity, emphasis should be placed on the importance of routinely scheduled aerobic exercise. An optimum of 30 minutes of daily exercise is a reasonable goal. However, exercising when ketones are present, which may occur when the blood glucose level is above 250 mg/dL, is not recommended.[26,27]

For prevention of hypoglycemia during exercise, an increase in food or decrease in insulin dose usually needs to be made. Generally, increasing food is the treatment of choice unless the exercise is a continuing, daily routine. Food adjustments will depend on the duration and intensity of the exercise and on the blood glucose level prior to exercise (Exhibit 19-6). A general rule is to add 10 to 15 g of carbohydrate for every hour of extra activity.[28]

Prolonged activity may utilize a majority of the glucose stores in the muscle. The body replaces these stores when blood glucose becomes available. It is very important for the child to realize that an adequate snack, probably containing protein as well as complex carbohydrate, may need to be eaten after prolonged exercise to avoid a low blood glucose level which may occur up to 48 hours after the activity.[27]

If possible, it is wise to avoid exercise during the peak activity of an insulin. Often sports events and practices are scheduled when the insulin peaks. In this instance, a larger snack, which includes simple and complex carbohydrates as well as protein, may be needed. However, some find it difficult to eat a large volume of food prior to prolonged activity. For lengthy events, consuming 8 oz of a sugar-

Exhibit 19-6 Guidelines for Food Adjustments for Exercise

Type of Exercise and Examples	If Blood Sugar Is	Increase Food Intake By	Suggested Food
Exercise of short duration or of moderate intensity	Less than 80 to 100 mg/dL	10 to 15 gms of carbohydrate	1 fruit or 1 starch/ bread exchange
	100 mg/dL or above	Not necessary to increase foods	
Examples: walking a half mile or leisurely biking for one mile			
Exercise of moderate intensity	Less than 80 to 100 mg/dL	25 to 50 gms of carbohydrate before exercise, then 10 to 15 gms per hour of exercise, if necessary	1/2 meat sandwich with milk or fruit exchange
Examples: tennis, swimming, jogging, leisure cycling, gardening, golfing or vacuuming for one hour	80 to 170 mg/dL	10 to 15 gms of carbohydrate	1 fruit or 1 starch/ bread exchange
	180–300 mg/dL	Not necessary to increase food	
	300 mg/dL or greater	Don't begin exercise until blood sugar is under better control	
Strenuous activity or exercise	Less than 80 to 100 mg/dL	50 gms of carbohydrate, monitor blood sugars carefully	1 meat sandwich (2 slices of bread) with milk and fruit exchange
Examples: football, hockey, racquetball or basketball games; strenuous cycling or swimming; shoveling heavy snow for one hour	180 to 300 mg/dL	10 to 15 gms of carbohydrate per hour of exercise	1 fruit or 1 starch/ bread exchange
	300 mg/dL or greater	Don't begin exercise until blood sugar is under better control	

Source: Reprinted from *Exchanges for All Occasions* (p 121) by MJ Franz with permission of Diabetes Center, Inc. Publishing and International Diabetes Center, © Revised 1987.

containing liquid, such as Gatorade or diluted juice, every 30 to 45 minutes may be helpful in keeping the blood glucose level in the normal range.[29] Modifications in meal schedules may need to be made to accommodate for early or late insulin injections because of scheduled events.

Table 19-9 Symptoms of Hypoglycemia

Mild
  Weakness, tiredness
  Shakiness, tremors, anxiety
  Increased hunger
Moderate (above symptoms, plus)
  Altered consciousness (sleepy, lethargic)
  Change in personality (inappropriate behaviors)
  Increased pulse rate
  Pale, cold skin
  Feels either hot or cold
  Inappropriate sweating
Severe (above symptoms, plus)
  Unconsciousness (coma)
  Convulsions

Source: Reprinted from *Diabetes Mellitus in Children and Adolescents* (p 98) by LB Travis with permission of WB Saunders, © 1987.

Hypoglycemia

The most common emergency of insulin-dependent diabetes is hypoglycemia. The exact blood glucose level that produces symptoms of hypoglycemia is an individual response and also differs with level of glucose control. Symptoms may occur when the blood glucose level is 60 mg/dL or below. A rapidly dropping blood glucose level may cause symptoms of hypoglycemia even when the level is in the normal range.[30] Table 19-9 describes symptoms of hypoglycemia, and Table 19-10 lists suggestions for treatment of hypoglycemia.[31]

Medical Identification. Children with diabetes should be instructed to wear medical alert identification at all times to ensure proper treatment of insulin reactions, which may render the child unable to communicate.

Sick Days. Illness in the child with diabetes always presents a challenge. During brief illness, the meal plan should be maintained when possible, using foods that can be tolerated. Exhibit 19-7 lists eating guidelines for brief illness. If the child cannot tolerate food, it is important to replace the usual amount of carbohydrate consumed with readily absorbed sugar-containing liquids that can be easily used by the body for energy. Liquids also help to prevent dehydration. Table 19-11 lists amounts of some easily tolerated liquids that contain 15 g of carbohydrate. Consuming room temperature liquids in small sips at a rate of about 15 g of carbohydrate per hour is recommended. Insulin must always be given and may need to be increased during illness. Parents need to know when to call the doctor for assistance in managing illness because prolonged vomiting as well as fever can lead to rapid dehydration and diabetic ketoacidosis.

Table 19-10 Treatment of Symptomatic Hypoglycemia

Mild
  Usually treated by individual
  1 or 2 fruit exchanges (2 to 4 sugar cubes, 3 to 6 oz Coke)
  Rest for 15 minutes after symptoms leave
  1 starch exchange before restarting activity (e.g., 2 peanut butter or cheese crackers)
Moderate
  Diabetic may need help in management
  Same as for "mild"
  May need to repeat "mild" treatment
Severe
  Diabetic will need help in management
  Sips of regular soft drink, if swallowing
  Tube or dispenser of concentrated sugar
    Squeeze entire container into side of mouth
    Assist in swallowing
  Glucagon: 1 cc (1 mg) given by injection (at site)
    Should be supplied by physician/parent
  Secure help from one competent in care
  Transport if does not respond immediately

Source: Reprinted from *Diabetes Mellitus in Children and Adolescents* (p 98) by LB Travis with permission of WB Saunders, © 1987.

Eating Out

Eating out for the under-18 age group usually includes pizza or hamburger and fries. Most children have two to three meat exchanges for dinner plus three to five starch/bread exchanges. Many favorite fast food items (see Exhibit 19-8) when combined with French fries and/or fruit and/or milk fit the evening meal pattern.[28]

As the child grows older, eating out becomes more frequent and may be independent of parents. Peer pressure often takes precedence over the established meal plan. Teaching the child how to be flexible (e.g., exchanging a fruit for a starch/bread or a milk for a meat plus a fruit) is important. Some regard varying the meal plan as cheating. It is not cheating to vary the meal plan using educated choices; it is flexibility. Cheating is a negative message and does not promote an open discussion of meal-planning options.

Special Occasions

Because of excitement and increased activity, most children can enjoy special treats at a birthday party or holiday dinner without elevating their blood glucose level. Unfrosted birthday cake or ice cream may be exchanged for the starch/bread or fruit in the meal plan. A low blood glucose level is not unusual following spe-

Exhibit 19-7 Eating Guidelines for Brief Illness

---

1. If possible, follow regular meal plan.
   - Substitute soft protein foods for regular meat servings.
   - Use liquid sources for starch/bread servings (i.e., soups).
2. If the regular meal plan cannot be followed:
   - Determine the total amount of carbohydrate for each meal and snacks.
   - Replace the number of grams of carbohydrate with liquids or soft foods. Give small amounts frequently.
   - Give about 50 g of carbohydrate every 3–4 hours during the day as a guideline for school-age children.
3. If nausea and/or vomiting are present:
   - Replace the carbohydrate of meals with liquids containing *sugar*.
   - Give small sips every 10 or 15 minutes. A total of 15 g of carbohydrate every hour is a good goal.
   - Fluids are especially important when diarrhea, fever, or vomiting are present.
4. Remember, it is necessary to give some foods *with sugar* even if the blood glucose level is high.

---

cial occasions because of increased activity, so parents need to be sure that the child's food intake is adequate. Giving children a choice of which occasion they want to honor may help build a feeling of being in control.

Craving Sweets

Most children go through periods of craving sweets. It is frequently more realistic to include a sweet in the meal plan than to ignore these cravings. In a controlled study, Loghmani et al. found that replacing isocalorically complex carbo-

---

Table 19-11 Food Sources Containing 15 Grams of Carbohydrate Useful for Illness

Food	Amount to Equal 15 g Carbohydrate
Carbonated beverage (with sugar)	5 oz
Gatorade	8 oz
Gelatin, regular	1/2 cup
Apple juice, regular	1/2 cup
Popsicle	1 bar (2 oz)
Tang	1/2 cup
Ice cream, regular	1/2 cup
Jello Gelatin Pops	2 bars
Jello Fruit Bar	1 bar
Soup, canned	
noodle with meat or cream of vegetable	1 cup, prepared

Exhibit 19-8 Fast Food Exchanges

Food	Quantity	Calories	Exchanges
Burger King, Burger Chef, McDonalds, Hardees			
Quarter pounder	1	430	2 starch/bread 3 med. fat meat 1 fat
French fries	Regular	230	1 1/2 starch/bread 2 fat
Wendy's			
Hamburger	1	350	2 starch/bread 3 med. fat meat
Arby's or Rax			
Regular roast beef	1	350–370	2 starch/bread 2 med. fat meat 1 fat
Kentucky Fried Chicken Original Recipe			
Center breast	1	260	1/2 starch/bread 3 med. fat meat
Drumstick	1	150	2 med. fat meat
Wing	1	180	1/2 starch/bread 1 1/2 med. fat meat 1 fat
Mashed potato with gravy	1	60	1 starch/bread
Cole slaw	1	105	2 vegetable or 1 starch/bread 1 fat
Domino's Pizza			
Cheese pizza, 12" pie	2 slices	340	3 starch/bread 1 med. fat meat 1 vegetable
Pepperoni, 12" pie	2 slices	380	3 starch/bread 2 med. fat meat 1 vegetable
Taco Bell, Zantigo			
Beef burrito	1	415–460	2 1/2 starch/ bread 2 med. fat meat 1 fat

Source: Reprinted from *Exchanges for All Occasions* (pp 96–99) by MJ Franz with permission from Diabetes Center, Inc. Publishing and International Diabetes Center, © Revised 1987.

hydrate with sucrose (at 10% of total calories) at three meals and the afternoon snack for 10 children (age 7 to 12) for two days did not change the glycemic response.[32] A child who has dance practice or basketball practice may be able to eat a sweet during the activity and still keep the blood glucose level within range. Some children go bike riding for an hour in order to be able to indulge in a favorite sweet. Monitoring of the blood glucose level after sweets have been eaten is a good way to objectively evaluate the effect of the sweet.

Other Methods of Consistent Blood Glucose Maintenance

For some individuals who are maintaining glucose levels on multiple injections of regular insulin, using a carbohydrate-counting system in addition to the exchange system is helpful. In this system, only the carbohydrate value of the food is counted. This may be accomplished simply by adding the total number of starch/bread, fruit, and milk servings to be eaten and multiplying by the number of grams of carbohydrate contained in each serving.[33] The general rule is that approximately 1 u of regular insulin will be needed for every 10 g of carbohydrate.[17] Care must be taken not to overeat as increased availability of insulin may promote unwanted weight gain. Older teenagers may be interested in this system because of the flexibility it allows in meal scheduling and in amounts eaten. A good understanding of foods is necessary for the appropriate use of carbohydrate counting. Reinforcement of healthy eating habits is advisable as some teens tend to omit food groups as well as meals to accommodate busy schedules or to control weight.

Alternative Sweeteners

A variety of nutritive and non-nutritive sweeteners are currently available. Fructose, a sugar found in fruits and other plants, is a nutritive sweetener commonly used in sucrose-free products. It may be sweeter than sucrose under some conditions and contains 4 cal/g. It is absorbed more slowly from the intestinal tract and, in individuals with well-controlled diabetes, may not cause a significant elevation in blood glucose level. However, those in poor control may experience an increase in blood glucose level. Fructose tends to lose some sweetness when heated or added to alkaline foods.[34,35] See Exhibit 19-9 for a list of other commonly used nutritive sweeteners.

Non-nutritive sweeteners (sugar alcohols) found in prepared products include sorbitol, xylitol, and mannitol. Sorbitol is the most commonly used sugar alcohol. Sorbitol and mannitol are 50% as sweet as sucrose. Heat may cause a reduction of sweetness in all sugar alcohols. The incomplete absorption of these products from the gastrointestinal tract accounts for their minimal effect on the blood glucose level; however, as little as 15 g of these products may cause osmotic diarrhea.

Exhibit 19-9 Nutritive Sweeteners Commonly Found on Food Labels

> Dextrose, dextrin, or malto-dextrin
> Sucrose
> Lactose
> Glucose
> Corn syrup, corn syrup solids
> Corn sweeteners
> High-fructose corn syrup
> Sugar
> Brown sugar
> Honey
> Molasses

Xylitol is still approved by the Food and Drug Administration (FDA), but currently it is seldom used in the United States. It is 50% sweeter than sugar.[34]

Aspartame (NutraSweet and Equal, G. D. Searle, Deerfield, IL) is made from the naturally occurring amino acid, L-phenylalanine and L-aspartic acid. It is about 180 times sweeter than sucrose. Although it contains 4 cal/g, the amount needed to sweeten products is so small that it is considered non-nutritive. Heat destroys the sweetness of aspartame thus, adding it at the end of the cooking process helps retain the sweetness. Aspartame is found in many products and is widely accepted by consumers.[35–37]

Since its introduction, the safety of aspartame has been questioned. In its role of safeguarding consumers, the FDA has developed a guideline called Acceptable Daily Intake (ADI). The ADI indicates a daily intake level that provides a wide

Table 19-12 Number of Servings of Aspartame-Sweetened Products To Reach ADI

50-lb. Child	150-lb. Teenager	
7	20	12-oz. containers of carbonated soft drink
		or
11	34	8-oz. servings of powdered soft drink
		or
14	42	4-oz. servings of gelatin dessert
		or
32	97	Packets of table top sweetener

Note: The chart shows the number of servings of typical foods sweetened completely with aspartame that individuals would have to consume every day to reach the ADI.

Source: Reprinted from *What You Should Know About . . . Aspartame* with permission of the International Food Information Council, Copyright © 1989.

margin of safety for specific substances. The current ADI for aspartame is 50 mg/ kg of IBW.[38] The aspartame content of NutraSweet-containing products is approximately 150 mg for a 12-oz beverage, 55 mg for 1 cup of cereal or 4 oz of pudding, and 35 mg for one package of Equal. Hypothetical combinations of various products that might be consumed by children 2 to 16 years of age projected that it would be unlikely for most children to consume 50 mg/kg/d.[39] See Table 19-12 for the delineation of safe levels.[38]

Saccharin has been controversial since 1971 because of its association with bladder cancer in laboratory animals.[35] It has been allowed to remain on the market because the studies on animals have been inconclusive. Although it is calorie-free, many individuals report a bitter aftertaste.

Acesulfame potassium or acesulfame-K (Sunette and Sweet-One, Hoechst Celanese Corporation, Somerville, NJ), the latest addition to artificial sweeteners to win FDA approval, is approximately 200 times sweeter than sucrose. It is a derivative of acetoacetic acid and is not metabolized by the body, therefore it contributes no calories. It remains stable under high temperature and reportedly has no aftertaste, does not contribute to tooth decay, and is stable in acidic products.[35] ADI for acesulfame-K is 15 mg/kg of body weight. In the United States, acesulfame-K is approved for use in chewing gum, dry mixes for beverages, instant coffee, tea, gelatins, puddings, nondairy creamers, and tabletop sweeteners.[36]

ORGANIZATIONS AND PUBLICATIONS

There are several national organizations that help families dealing with diabetes adapt to their new lifestyles. The American Diabetes Association (ADA) and the Juvenile Diabetes Foundation (JDF) are organizations founded to provide services to persons with diabetes and to fund research in diabetes. Both organizations provide publications for people with diabetes. ADA members receive monthly issues of the magazine *Diabetes Forecast*, which contains informative articles on all aspects of diabetes care including information on new products and the latest research. Summer camps for children with diabetes are sponsored by the ADA in many states.

Numerous cookbooks are available in regular bookstores and libraries containing recipes with information on how to include them in the exchange system. Several cookbooks have been compiled by the American Dietetic Association and the ADA. These books help families as they learn to modify and incorporate their own recipes into the meal plan.

CONCLUSION

Nutrition management of the child with diabetes is one of the most important factors in attaining and maintaining good metabolic control. Devising meal plans that provide flexibility while conforming to guidelines based on current research is a challenge to the dietitian. A thorough understanding of all the components of diabetes management will help the family adapt diabetes to their lifestyle and will provide the foundation for long-term maintenance of good control.

REFERENCES

1. American Diabetes Association. Nutritional recommendations and principles for individuals with diabetes mellitus: 1986. *Diabetes Care.* 1987;10:126.
2. Food and Nutrition Board. *Recommended Dietary Allowances.* 10th ed. Washington, DC: National Academy of Sciences; 1989.
3. Mahan LK, Rosebrough RH. Nutritional requirements and nutrition status assessment in adolescence. In: Mahan LK, Rees JM, eds. *Nutrition in Adolescence.* St Louis, Mo: Times Mirror/Mosby College Publishing; 1984.
4. Jenkins DJA. Lente carbohydrate: a newer approach to the dietary management of diabetes. *Diabetes Care.* 1982;5:634.
5. Chase HP, Jackson WE, Hoops SL, Cockerham RS, Archer PG, O'Brien D. Glucose control and the renal and retinal complications of insulin dependent diabetes. *JAMA.* 1989;261:1155.
6. Hostetter TH, Rinnke HG, Brenner BM. The case for intrarenal hypertension in the initiation and progression of diabetic and other glomerulopathies. *Am J Med.* 1982;72:375.
7. Reynolds JW. Nutritional management with insulin-dependent diabetes mellitus. *Pediatr Rev.* 1987;9:155.
8. Kafonek SD, Kwiterovich PO. Detection and management of hyperlipidemias in children and young adults. *Compr Ther.* 1989;15:54.
9. Anderson JW, Ward K. Long-term effects of high carbohydrate, high fiber diets on glucose and lipid metabolism: a preliminary report on patients with diabetes. *Diabetes Care.* 1978;1:77.
10. Committee on Nutrition, American Academy of Pediatrics. Plant fiber intake in the pediatric diet. *Pediatrics.* 1981;67:572.
11. Report of the Second Task Force on Blood Pressure Control in Children—1987. *Pediatrics.* 1987;79:1.
12. Drash AL, Becker DJ, Kenien AG, Steranchak L. Nutritional considerations in the treatment of the child with diabetes mellitus. In: Suskind RM, ed. *Textbook of Pediatric Nutrition.* New York: Raven Press; 1981.
13. American Diabetes Association and the American Dietetic Association. *Exchange Lists for Meal Planning.* New York: American Diabetes Association; 1986.
14. Travis LB, Johnson TA. Normal glucose-insulin dynamics: an overview. In: Travis LB, Brouhard BH, Schreiner BJ. *Diabetes Mellitus in Children and Adolescents.* Philadelphia: WB Saunders; 1987.
15. *Nutritive Values—1988.* Fremont, Mich: Gerber Products Co.; 1988.
16. Heinz USA. *Nutrition Information for Heinz Baby Food per 100 Grams.* Pittsburgh, Pa: Heinz USA; 1986.
17. Schade DS, Santiago JV, Skyler JS, Rizza RA. *Intensive Insulin Therapy.* Princeton, NJ: Excerpta Medica; 1983.
18. Mann NP, Johnston DI. Improvement in metabolic control in diabetic adolescents by the use of increased insulin dose. *Diabetes Care.* 1984;7:460.
19. Behrman RE, Vaughan VC. *Nelson Textbook of Pediatrics.* 12th ed. Philadelphia: WB Saunders; 1983:43.
20. Birk R, Spencer ML. The prevalence of anorexia nervosa, bulimia, and induced glycosuria in IDDM females. *Diabetes Educator.* 1989;15:336.

21. Gaudini L, Feingold KR. Alcohol and diabetes: mix with caution. *Clinical Diabetes.* 1984;2:122.
22. Arky RA. Nutrition therapy for the child and adolescent with type 1 diabetes mellitus. *Pediatr Clin North Am.* 1984;31:711.
23. Brouhard BH. Monitoring results of management. In: Travis LB, Brouhard BH, Schreiner BJ, eds. *Diabetes Mellitus in Children and Adolescents.* Philadelphia: WB Saunders; 1987.
24. Mann NP, Noronha JL, Johnston DI. A prospective study to evaluate the benefits of long-term self-monitoring of blood glucose in diabetic children. *Diabetes Care.* 1984;7:322.
25. Travis LB. The clinical disease. In: Travis LB, Brouhard BH, Schreiner BJ, eds. *Diabetes Mellitus in Children and Adolescents.* Philadelphia: WB Saunders; 1987.
26. Skyler JS. Diabetes and exercise: clinical implications. *Diabetes Care.* 1979;2:307.
27. Maynard T. Exercise: Part I. Physiological response to exercise in diabetes mellitus. *Diabetes Educator.* 1991;17:196.
28. Franz MJ. *Exchanges for All Occasions.* Minneapolis, Minn: Diabetes Center, Inc.; 1983.
29. Brown SP, Thompson WR. The therapeutic role of exercise in diabetes mellitus. *Diabetes Educator.* 1988;14:202.
30. Brouhard BH. Hypoglycemia. In: Travis LB, Brouhard BH, Schreiner BJ, eds. *Diabetes Mellitus in Children and Adolescents.* Philadelphia: WB Saunders; 1987.
31. Travis LB. Exercise. In: Travis LB, Brouhard BH, Schreiner BJ. *Diabetes Mellitus in Children and Adolescents.* Philadelphia: WB Saunders; 1987.
32. Loghmani E, Rickard K, Washburne L, Vandagriff J, Fineberg N, Golden M. Glycemic response to sucrose-containing mixed meals in diets of children with insulin-dependent diabetes mellitus. *J Pediatr.* 1991;119:531.
33. McMahon P, Travis LB. Dietary management. In: Travis LB, Brouhard BH, Schreiner BJ. *Diabetes Mellitus in Children and Adolescents.* Philadelphia: WB Saunders; 1987.
34. Olefsky JM, Crapo P. Fructose, xylitol and sorbitol. *Diabetes Care.* 1980;3:390.
35. Crapo PA, Powers MA. Alias sugar. *Diabetes Forecast.* 1990;43:59.
36. American Diabetes Association. Use of noncaloric sweeteners. *Diabetes Care.* 1987;10:526.
37. Bertorelli SM, Czarnowski-Hill JV. Review of present and future use of non-nutritive sweeteners. *Diabetes Educator.* 1990;16:415.
38. *What You Should Know About Aspartame.* Washington, DC: International Food Information Council; 1989.
39. Thompson-Dobersen D. Calculation of aspartame intake in children. *J Am Diet Assoc.* 1989;89:831.

SUGGESTED READING

Chase P. *Understanding Insulin Dependent Diabetes.* Barbara Davis Center for Childhood Diabetes, Department of Pediatrics, University of Colorado Health Sciences Center, Denver, CO; 1983.
Etzwiler DD, Franz M, Hollander P, Joynes J. *Learning to Live Well with Diabetes.* Minneapolis, MN: International Diabetes Center, Park Nicollet Medical Foundation; 1985.
Hollerworth H. *A Guide for Parents of Children and Youth with Diabetes.* Boston: Joslin Diabetes Center; 1987.
Moynihan P, Balik B, Eliason S, Haig B. *Diabetes Youth Curriculum—A Toolbox for Educators.* Wayzata, MN: International Diabetes Center, Inc.; 1988.
National Diabetes Advisory Board. National standards for care. *Diabetes Care.* 1984;7:XXXI–XXXV.
Travis, L. *An International Aid on Insulin Dependent Diabetes Mellitus.* Fort Worth, TX: Stafford-Lowdon; 1985.

Chapter 20

Oncology and Marrow Transplantation

Karen V. Barale

Childhood cancer is the second most common cause of death in children older than 6 weeks of age.[1] The incidence of malignancies in children under the age of 15 is 12 per 100,000 population among whites and 9 per 100,000 among blacks.[2] Table 20-1 lists the common childhood tumors with their standard treatment. Approximately 50% of the cases are leukemia and lymphomas.

Prognosis depends upon tumor histology, tumor stage, age of patient, and certain laboratory indexes. Treatment may include surgery, irradiation, chemotherapy, and marrow transplantation. In many instances, initial treatment is curative because of excellent response to multimodal therapy. Advances in nutrition support have paralleled improvements in treatment, making optimum care of these patients possible. Pediatric nutrition support goals in oncology are to prevent or reverse nutritional deficits, promote normal growth and development, minimize morbidity and mortality, and maximize quality of life.[3] The disease, its therapy, and any complications will affect the nutritional status of the child.

NUTRITIONAL EFFECTS OF CANCER

Protein-Energy Malnutrition

Protein-energy malnutrition (PEM) is a common secondary diagnosis in pediatric patients with cancer.[4] At diagnosis the incidence ranges from 6% in children with newly diagnosed leukemia to as high as 50% in children with stage IV neuroblastoma.[1] Certain populations of children with neoplastic disease are at high risk of developing PEM. In general, patients with advanced disease during initial intense treatment and those who relapse or do not respond to treatment are most

Note: This work was supported in part by Grant Number HL36444 awarded by National Cancer and Heart, Lung and Blood Institute, DHHS.

Table 20-1 Cancers in Childhood

Malignancy	% of Cases	Standard Treatment	Comment
Hematologic			
Leukemia			
Acute lymphoblastic leukemia (ALL)	42	Induction chemo Consolidation chemo CNS prophylaxis (RT or IT chemo) Oral maintenance chemo with intermittent IV Rx lasts about 3 years BMT for persistent relapse or second remission	60% 5-year disease-free survival
Acute nonlymphoblastic leukemia (ANL)		Remission induction with intensive chemo Continuation therapy up to 18 mos. CNS prophylaxis BMT for persistent relapse or first remission	30%–50% 3-year continuous complete remission
Chronic myelocytic leukemia (CML)		Chronic phase: oral chemo for symptomatic relief, BMT Length of Rx based on symptoms & phase Blast crisis: aggressive chemo, BMT	<5% incidence in children Blast crisis <20% survival
Juvenile chronic myelocytic leukemia (JCML)		Oral chemo BMT	Usually diagnosed before 2 years of age Median survival <9 mo.
Hodgkin's disease and lymphoma	13.2		
Hodgkin's disease Stages I–IV, with involvement ranging from single node region to diffuse or disseminated		IA, IIA: Subtotal nodal RT IB, IIB: Subtotal nodal RT or combination chemo if no symptoms; chemo for others IIIA: Chemotherapy; RT only for minimal disease	In children <10 years, male incidence higher Chemo preferred for stages II & IIIA to avoid high-dose radiation to the growing spine and improve cure. *continues*

Table 20-1 continued

Malignancy	% of Cases	Standard Treatment	Comment
involvement to extralymphatic organs Symptoms: A. No symptoms B. Fevers > 38°C, night sweats, or 10% weight loss within 6 mos. prior to diagnosis		Bulky mediastinal disease: chemo + RT IIIB/IV Combination chemo Autologous BMT for failure to achieve remission or relapse	70%–96% survival
Nonlymphoblastic lymphoma		Chemo with/without RT for 6–18 mos.	Therapy depends on extent of disease Cure rate 10%–40% with bone marrow involvement; to 90% with limited disease
Lymphoblastic lymphoma		Aggressive chemo, autologous or allogeneic BMT during early remission, plus whole-brain RT, IT chemo	Adverse prognostic factors: extensive marrow or CNS involvement
Brain tumors Astrocytoma (33% of all cases) Medulloblastoma Brainstem glioma Ependymomas	24	Surgical removal/debulking Chemo and RT	Survival based on tumor type & location 5-year survival 15%–70% Brainstem gliomas lead to CNS dysfunction and swallowing problems Can have cranial nerve palsies or paresis

Tumor		Treatment	Notes
Neuroblastoma Stages I–IV, with involvement ranging from localized disease to metastatic disease	8	Surgical resection of local disease Palliative RT to shrink tumor size Chemo BMT, allogeneic or autologous, for advanced disease	2 years = median age at diagnosis 50%–90% survival, depending on stage & location Most common primary site is adrenal gland, which produces an abdominal mass, metastatic disease Most common extracranial solid tumor in childhood; comprises up to 50% of malignancies in infants
Wilms' tumor Stages I–V, with involvement ranging from well-encapsulated tumor to bilateral disease	7.8	All stages: surgery for staging and tumor removal Chemo—preferred therapy Stage II or metastatic disease to bone, liver, or lung: RT	Usually seen between ages 1 and 5 years 59%–90% survival, stages I–III Survival dependent on stage at presentation
Bone tumors Rhabdomyosarcoma Stages I–IV, with involvement ranging from localized disease to distant metastasis	8.4	Surgery—total excision if possible Chemo RT 5000–6000 cGy to primary tumor with wide ports	Most common soft tissue sarcoma in children 28%–71% survival, depending on stage
Osteogenic sarcoma		Surgery: amputation or limb salvage Chemo to prevent metastasis	Resistant to RT Common sites: around knee joint and below shoulder Primary malignant tumor of bone Peak incidence during adolescent growing spurt 60% survival

continues

Table 20-1 continued

Malignancy	% of Cases	Standard Treatment	Comment
Ewing's sarcoma	5.6	RT, based on leg length growth: if length discrepancy won't be excessive, 6000–7000 cGy; if it will be excessive, amputation and chemo	Males predominate 2:1 Peak age of incidence: 11–12 years, female; 15–16 years, male Small-cell bone tumor 2-year disease-free survival 70%
Retinoblastoma Stages I–V, based on number and size of lesions	3.4	Surgery RT Chemo for advanced disease	90% < 5 years of age; average age is 18 months Increased risk for other sarcoma, secondary to therapy 90% survival

Note: BMT, bone marrow transplant; chemo, chemotherapy; CNS, central nervous system; IV, intravenous; IT, intrathecal; RT, radiation therapy; Rx, treatment.

Source: Data from references 2 and 6.

likely to develop PEM.[5] Additionally, certain types of treatment promote the development of PEM: major abdominal surgery; irradiation of the head, neck, esophagus, abdomen, or pelvis; or intense, frequent courses of chemotherapy (3-week intervals or less) in the absence of corticosteroids. Finally, complications such as pain, fever, and frequent or severe infections decrease appetite and may increase energy requirements.

PEM ultimately results from decreased energy intake, increased energy requirements, and malabsorption.[5] The organ systems most readily affected by PEM—hematopoietic, gastrointestinal, and immunological—are also the most sensitive to oncologic treatment. Thus the prevention or reversal of PEM to maximize the function of these organ systems seems prudent in childhood cancer.[5]

Cachexia

Cancer cachexia is a poorly understood syndrome that includes tissue wasting, anorexia, weakness, anemia, hypoalbuminemia, hypoglycemia, lactic acidosis, hyperlipidemia, impaired liver function, glucose intolerance, accelerated gluconeogenesis, skeletal muscle atrophy, visceral organ atrophy, and anergy.[6] The particular combination of features varies with tumor type and patient (Table 20-2). It is one of the major sources of morbidity for young cancer patients and requires aggressive treatment.[7] Children with progressive and metastatic disease have an incidence of cachexia as high as 40%.[8]

In the pediatric patient, tumor growth raises metabolic demand, amplifying the problem of cachexia.[7] Additionally, poor utilization of nutrients, either absorbed or infused, can contribute to cachexia.[6]

Alterations in Taste and Smell

Abnormalities of the sensations of taste and smell have been observed in patients with cancer. Changes in taste thresholds and aversions for specific foods can develop. DeWys suggests that aversion to meat products in adult populations may be a result of decreased threshold for bitter taste.[9]

Table 20-2 Major Contributors to Cachexia in Young Cancer Patients

Abnormal host metabolism of macronutrients
Tumor consumption of nutrients for tumor growth
Host requirement of adequate nutrients for normal growth
Anticancer therapy
Inadequate intake of nutrients to meet expenditures

Source: Data from references 1, 5, 6, 7, and 8.

NUTRITIONAL EFFECTS OF CANCER THERAPY

Multimodal treatments can have an additional adverse effect on nutritional status.[10] Antitumor therapies may produce only mild, transient nutritional disturbances or may lead to severe, permanent problems.

Chemotherapy

The nutritional consequences of chemotherapeutic agents are shown in Table 20-3. These drugs affect normal as well as malignant cells and are typically most active on rapidly dividing cells such as the epithelial cells of the gastrointestinal tract. The degree to which gastrointestinal functions are altered depends on the particular drug, dosage, duration of the treatment, rates of metabolism, and the child's susceptibility.

Nausea and vomiting are the most common problems interfering with adequate oral intake.[5] These occur as a result of a direct central nervous system effect as drugs are administered. In addition, alterations in taste and smell as a result of chemotherapy may persist well beyond periods of nausea and vomiting and result in prolonged anorexia. Mucositis is a major gastrointestinal complication and may be worsened when radiation therapy is given concurrently. Mucositis can affect any part of the gastrointestinal tract and lead to ulceration, bleeding, and malabsorption. Chemotherapy-induced neutropenia accentuates these complications. Rigorous mouth care prevents additional oral breakdown.[5] Fortunately, the renewal rate of the gastrointestinal tract mucosa is rapid, so that mucositis from chemotherapy is usually short-lived.

Malabsorption, with associated weight loss and intractable diarrhea, can be directly caused by certain chemotherapy agents as well as by antibiotic-induced alterations in the gut flora.[5] Constipation related to use of vincristine or narcotics or inactivity may result in significant abdominal discomfort and loss of appetite.

Surgery

Surgical removal of a tumor may lead to insufficient oral intake over several days during a time of increased requirements. Radical surgery of the head and neck can lead to chewing and swallowing problems. Massive intestinal resection may cause malabsorption of vitamin B_{12} or bile acids.[11]

Radiation

Complications of radiation (Table 20-4) may develop acutely or become chronic and progress after completion of therapy.[11] Side effects and their intensity

Table 20-3 Chemotherapeutic Agents and Toxicities Affecting Nutritional Status

Drug	Synonyms	Antitumor Spectrum	Toxicities
Alkylating agents			
Cyclophosphamide	Cytoxan, CTX	Lymphomas, leukemias, sarcomas, neuroblastoma	N&V, cystitis, water retention; cardiac (HD)
Ifosfamide	IFOS	Sarcomas	N&V, cystitis, NT, renal
Cisplatin	Platinol, CDDP	Testicular and other germ cell, osteosarcoma, brain tumors, neuroblastoma	N&V, renal, NT
Dacarbazine	DTIC	Neuroblastoma, sarcomas	N&V, flulike syndrome, hepatic
Melphalan	Akeran, L-PAM	Rhabdomyosarcoma, sarcomas, neuroblastoma, and leukemias	N&V, mucositis & diarrhea (HD)
Mechlorethamine	Mustargen, HN₂, nitrogen mustard	Hodgkin's, brain tumors	N&V, mucositis; NT (HD)
Procarbazine	Matulan, PCZ	Hodgkin's, brain tumors	N&V, NT, rash, mucositis
Lomustine	CCNU	Brain tumors, lymphomas	N&V, renal & pulmonary toxicity
Antimetabolites			
Methotrexate	MTX	Leukemia, lymphoma, osteosarcoma	Mucositis, rash, hepatic; renal (HD), NT
6-Mercaptopurine	Purinethal, 6-MP	Leukemia (ALL, CML)	Hepatic, mucositis
6-Thioguanine	6-TG	Leukemia (ANL)	N&V, mucositis, hepatic
Cytarabine	Cytosine arabinoside, Cytosar, Ara-C	Leukemia, lymphoma	N&V, mucositis, GI; NT, ocular, skin (HD)
Antibiotics			
Adriamycin	Doxorubicin, ADR	Leukemia (ALL, ANL), lymphoma, most solid tumors	Mucositis, N&V, cardiac (acute and chronic)
Daunomycin	Daunorubicin, DNR	Leukemia (ALL, ANL)	Same as adriamycin
Bleomycin	Blenoxane, BLEO	Lymphoma, testicular cancer	Lung, skin, hypersensitivity; Raynaud's
Dactinomycin	Cosmegen, ACT-D, actinomycin D	Wilms' tumor, sarcomas	N&V, mucositis

continues

Table 20-3 continued

Drug	Synonyms	Antitumor Spectrum	Toxicities
Plant alkaloids			
Vincristine	Oncovin, VCR	Leukemia (ALL), lymphomas, most solid tumors	NT, SIADH, hypotension, constipation
Vinblastine	Velban, VLB	Histiocytosis, Hodgkin's, testicular	Mucositis, mild NT
Etoposide	VePesid, VP-16, VP-16-213	Leukemias (ALL, ANL), lymphomas, neuroblastoma, sarcomas, brain tumors	N&V, mucositis, mild NT, hypotension, allergic
Miscellaneous			
Prednisone (po) Prednisolone (IV)	Deltasone, PRED	Leukemia, lymphoma	Increased appetite, centripetal obesity, myopathy, osteoporosis, aseptic necrosis of
Dexamethasone	Decadron, DEX	Leukemia, lymphoma, brain tumors	hip, peptic ulceration, pancreatitis, hyperactivity, hypertension, diabetes, growth failure, amenorrhea, impaired wound healing, atrophy of subcutaneous tissue
L-Asparaginase	Elspar, L-ASP	Leukemia (ALL), lymphoma	N&V, acute pancreatitis, decreased serum albumin, insulin & lipoproteins

Note: ALL, acute lymphoblastic leukemia; ANL, acute nonlymphoblastic leukemia; CML, chronic myelogenous leukemia; GI, gastrointestinal toxicity; HD, high-dose; IV, intravenous; N&V, nausea and vomiting; NT, neurotoxicity.

Source: Adapted from Norton JA and Peter J, Nutritional supportive care, in *Principles and Practice of Pediatric Oncology* (pp 874–875) by PH Pizzo and DG Poplack (eds) with permission of JB Lippincott, © 1989.

Table 20-4 Radiation Effects in Pediatric Patients

Head and neck
  Nausea, anorexia
  Mucositis, esophagitis
  Decreased taste and smell
  Damage to developing teeth
  Decreased salivation→thick, viscous mucus
  Decreased jaw mobility
Thoracic
  Pharyngeal and esophageal inflammation and cell damage
  Sore throat, dysphagia
Abdominal or pelvic
  Nausea, vomiting, diarrhea
  Ulceration
  Colitis
  Malabsorption
  Fluid, electrolyte imbalance
Total body
  Nausea, vomiting, diarrhea
  Mucositis, esophagitis
  Decreased taste and salivation
  Anorexia

Source: Data from references 1, 5, and 11.

vary according to the (1) region of the body irradiated; (2) dose, fractionation, length of time, and field size of the radiation administered; (3) concurrent use of other antitumor therapy such as surgery or chemotherapy; and (4) the child's initial nutritional status.[11]

Other Complications

Bacterial sepsis and fever secondary to neutropenia are other problems that increase metabolic demands in the child. Secondary complications such as neutropenic enterocolitis can further impair ability to absorb nutrients. Chronic pain may also decrease the child's interest in eating.

Marrow Transplantation

Marrow transplantation has become an established treatment modality for a number of pediatric hematologic and oncologic disorders.[12] Marrow transplantation is used to restore normal marrow function following high-dose chemoradiotherapy directed at eradicating the malignancy. The source of marrow may be the patient (autologous), an identical twin (syngeneic), or a family member or suitably matched unrelated donor (allogeneic). Bone marrow is obtained from the donor under general anesthesia in the operating room and infused directly into the patient through an indwelling venous catheter. If the marrow is obtained from the patient (autologous), it is usually aspirated and stored frozen until the patient is prepared for transplantation.

Preconditioning Regimen

Bone marrow infusion is preceded by multimodal chemotherapy or high-dose chemoradiotherapy administered over a 4- to 10-day period. This intense conditioning regimen is designed to eliminate malignant cells as well as to facilitate immunosuppression of the patient to allow acceptance of the marrow graft.

Post-transplantation Course

Severe pancytopenia and frequent infections occur following the conditioning regimen and last from 2 to 6 weeks post-transplantation, until the marrow engrafts. Patients are protected in isolation rooms or, in some institutions, in laminar airflow rooms. Supportive care includes frequent red blood cell and platelet transfusions and systemic antibiotic therapy as well as aggressive parenteral nutrition support.

Nutritional effects of marrow transplantation are due to conditioning therapy, infections, graft-versus-host disease (GVHD), and medications, including anti-infectious and immunosuppressive agents.[13–15] Complications interfering with nutrient intake include mucositis, esophagitis, altered taste, xerostomia, viscous saliva, nausea, vomiting, diarrhea, anorexia, diarrhea, steatorrhea, and multiple-organ dysfunction.[12,16–20] The duration and intensity of symptoms as well as the stress of treatment preclude oral intake for a period of 1 to 7 weeks post-transplantation and necessitate the use of parenteral nutrition support.

Oral intake is encouraged as soon as tolerated. Protein and calorie goals are defined for the patient and family. When oral feeding is possible, a general diet as tolerated is encouraged. Some hospitals restrict raw, fresh fruits and vegetables or provide a low-microbial diet for neutropenic patients.[21] No other restrictions are needed unless gastrointestinal symptoms occur. At discharge, many patients are still unable to eat an adequate amount of nutrients, and partial parenteral nutrition may be prescribed.[22] Follow-up nutritional counseling and assessment are imperative to prevent PEM.[23]

Graft-versus-Host Disease

Patients who receive allogeneic marrow are at risk for the development of GVHD once the marrow engrafts. GVHD is an immunologic reaction in which the newly engrafted marrow recognizes the host's cells as foreign; the ensuing immunologic response can cause multiple-organ damage.[12] It may occur as an acute reaction early post-transplantation or progress to a chronic condition. Because of its potentially devastating effects, efforts are directed at prevention of GVHD. Methotrexate, cyclosporine A, steroids, and antithymocyte globulin are most frequently used as treatment for GVHD.

Acute GVHD can affect the skin, liver, or gastrointestinal tract. Clinical symptoms include maculopapular rash, cholestatic liver dysfunction, or diarrhea. Gastrointestinal GVHD can involve either upper or lower gastrointestinal tract.[17] Upper gastrointestinal GVHD symptoms include anorexia, dyspepsia and inability to eat. In lower gastrointestinal GVHD, diarrhea may be severe and, at its worst, associated with bleeding. In addition, it is often associated with crampy abdominal pain, nausea or vomiting, and requires a period of bowel rest with total parenteral nutrition support. Empiric guidelines have been developed to reinitiate oral feeding as patients are recovering from severe gut GVHD.[18]

NUTRITIONAL ASSESSMENT

Nutritional status at diagnosis has been associated with treatment outcome in children with cancer.[24,25] Nutrition assessment should begin at diagnosis and continue through and following treatment.[3] Techniques for the newly diagnosed patient do not differ from normal assessment recommendations as presented in Chapter 2. Table 20-5 provides guidelines for ongoing assessment in the pediatric cancer patient.

Anthropometry

Initial measurements should include age, height, weight, and, in children younger than 3 years of age, head circumference. Any measurement below the 10th percentile should be investigated as a sign of growth impairment due to inadequate nutrition. Weight-height percentile is believed to be the most reliable anthropometric indicator of nutritional status in the child with cancer.[26] It can be used to reliably predict nutritional status because of its high direct correlation with triceps skinfold and mid-arm muscle circumference measurements. In the pediatric cancer patient, current or previous chemoradiotherapy may depress growth. Catch-up growth has been observed in these patients.[27] However, patients who receive cranial irradiation may develop long-term growth disturbances.[28]

Evaluation of Nutrient Intake

For a thorough evaluation of intake, daily food intake records provide a basis for decisions regarding supplemental or nonvolitional feeding. Parenteral or en-

Table 20-5 Ongoing Nutrition Assessment Measurements That Identify Real or Impending Nutritional Depletion in Children with Cancer

Measurements	Risk Criteria and Interpretation	Comments
Nutrient intakes		
Energy (kcal/kg) % of healthy children	<80% of median intake: low intake	Energy intakes calculated from records kept by trained parents or personnel and reviewed by a dietitian for completeness, explicitness, and use of acceptable measures.
		Adjust for emesis: emesis within half hour—do not include in calculations; emesis 1 to 2 hours after eating—calculate as half intake; emesis 3 to 4 hours later—calculate as all intake.
		Energy intakes >80% of medium intake may be low when diarrhea occurs.
Anthropometric		
Height		
Height for age	<5th percentile: growth stunting which may be due to chronic PEM*	
Weight		
% change	>5% loss: acute PEM (with adequate hydration state)	Percentage weight loss derived from highest previous weight. Weight is inaccurate when child has edema, large tumor masses and organs extensively infiltrated with tumor, effusions or organ congestion, solid mass or excess fluid administration (twice maintenance) for chemotherapy.
Weight for age	<5th percentile: acute or chronic PEM	Weight losses of >2% a day suggest dehydration.
Weight for height	<5th percentile: acute PEM when height for age is <10th percentile	
Skinfold thickness measurements		Steroid therapy may increase fat deposition. Measurements are inaccurate when child has edema.
Triceps	<10th percentile: depleted body fat stores	

continues

Table 20-5 continued

Measurements	Risk Criteria and Interpretation	Comments
Subscapular	>0.3 mm decrease: subclinical PEM[†]	
Biochemical		
Albumin % change	<3.2 gm/dl:[‡] acute or chronic PEM >10% decrease:[§] subclinical PEM	Biological half life of 14 days. May be decreased in presence of overhydration, severe liver dysfunction, or zinc deficiency.
Transferrin % change	<200 mg/dl: subclinical PEM >20% decrease:[§] subclinical PEM	Biological half life of 8 days. May be decreased in the presence of liver dysfunction; may be elevated in the presence of infection or iron deficiency.
Prealbumin % change	<20 mg/dl: subclinical PEM >20% decrease:[§] subclinical PEM	Biological half life of 2 days. May be decreased in the presence of severe liver dysfunction, vitamin A deficiency, or zinc deficiency; can be useful in assessing adequacy of nutrition support regimens.
Retinol-binding protein % change	<4 mg/dl: subclinical PEM >20% decrease:[§] subclinical PEM	Biological half life of 12 hours. May be elevated in the presence of renal failure; can be useful in assessing adequacy of nutrition support regimens.

* PEM, protein-energy malnutrition.

† More than twice coefficient of variation (method error) determined from 265 data sets of measurements obtained by two trained examiners.

‡ Lowest percentile of healthy children.

§ More than twice coefficient of variation.

Source: From Rickard KA, Grosfeld JL, Coates TD, Weetman R and Baehner RL, Advances in nutrition care of children with neoplastic disease: a review of treatment, research and application. Copyright The American Dietetic Association. Reprinted by permission from *Journal of The American Dietetic Association* (1986;86:1666).

teral nutrient solutions, other intravenous fluids, and oral intake must all be included when evaluating intake. Patients and family members may assist with record keeping and provide valuable intake information.

Determination of feeding skills in the young child will facilitate choices for self-feeding. Many children's feeding skills will regress during acute illness.[29]

Biochemistry

Laboratory data used for nutritional assessment may be affected by the disease or treatment. Hemoglobin and hematocrit values in children with leukemia, lymphoma, and Hodgkin's disease reflect the disease state rather than nutritional status.[4] Many chemotherapeutic agents cause bone marrow suppression and decreased total lymphocyte count. The complete blood count must also be interpreted cautiously in patients with solid tumors, because once therapy begins, complete blood counts primarily reflect treatment effects.

A concentration of serum albumin of less than 3 g/dl may reflect protein-calorie malnutrition; however, infection, impaired liver function, certain chemotherapy agents, and overhydration can all depress serum albumin level. Furthermore, serum albumin level does not clearly reflect weight-height percentiles, calorie intake, or dietary protein intake in pediatric cancer patients.[30]

NUTRIENT REQUIREMENTS

Energy and Protein

The Recommended Dietary Allowances (RDAs) of the National Academy of Sciences, categorized by age, gender, and body weight, can serve as an initial estimation of calorie and protein needs. Although the RDAs include factors for activity that may not apply to hospitalized children, the factor increase may approximate the additional calorie levels required by a child with cancer due to fever, active tumor metabolism, or host metabolism demands. Nitrogen balance and actual energy balance can be measured to ensure that desired results have been achieved. The best long-term indicator of adequate nutrient intake is growth (refer to Chapter 1 for additional information).

The Harris-Benedict formula and other equations have been used to estimate calorie needs in adults and may be appropriate for children who have completed their growth. Estimates of basal metabolic rate in children have been published by Altman[31] and the Mayo Clinic.[4] When these figures are used as a basis to determine energy needs, factors must be added for growth, infection, and stress. Multiplying basal metabolic rate by a factor of 1.8 to 1.9 will allow for growth, stress, and light activity.[3]

Vitamin and Mineral Requirements

Marginal nutrient deficiencies can occur in the pediatric patient with cancer. Patients who (1) are receiving total parenteral nutrition (TPN) who have no gastrointestinal function for an extended period, (2) have sustained radiation or surgical damage to an area of the intestine, or (3) are receiving antibiotics for chronic infections are especially susceptible to nutrient deficiencies due to malabsorption or inadequate supplementation.[6] Specific nutrient deficiencies can be masked by therapy effects and are difficult to identify. For example, thiamin deficiency has been noted in children treated with long-term TPN. The peripheral neuropathy that can accompany this deficiency mimics chemotherapy toxicity.[6]

NUTRITIONAL SUPPORT

Suboptimal oral intake of short duration during treatment is of less concern if the child is initially well nourished and can compensate when feeling well. These children may benefit from high-density foods that increase energy and other nutrient levels of the diet. Table 20-6 suggests appropriate foods to recommend during and following therapy.

Supplementation

The greatest limitation of supplements in the pediatric population is patient acceptance.[6] Milkshakes made with familiar products, supplemented by glucose polymers or other nondetectable modular components, are usually best tolerated. Supplements are often acceptable if offered in an unobtrusive manner as part of the regular meal or snack pattern. For the lactose-intolerant child, lactose-reduced or soy-based products can be useful. Oral and esophageal lesions may limit tolerance for oral supplements. Diarrhea may be aggravated by hyperosmolar or lactose-containing products. Encouragement from staff, patient education, and cooking classes can help improve acceptance of supplements.

Tube Feeding

Children who cannot or will not eat may benefit from tube feeding (TF). Enteral nutrition has numerous practical and psychologic advantages over parenteral nutrition, including lower risk of infection or other catheter-related complications, more normal play activities, a lifestyle that provides a positive way for parent and child to become involved in the child's care, and decreased cost.[6] Despite these advantages, TF is underutilized by many health care professionals. Patients must be carefully selected so that they have minimal gastrointestinal complaints, an adequate platelet level, family education, and continuing support. Nasogastric TF may not be appropriate in the older infant, toddler, and preschool-age groups because of psychologic trauma associated with insertion and maintenance of tubes. In addition, nausea and vomiting as well as decreased intestinal motility and absorption secondary to oncologic therapy make TF less favorable and less effective. Some children do well with a gastric button for long-term gastric TF.

The most common complications of TF are diarrhea and delayed gastric emptying.[32] In determining the cause of diarrhea, it is important to decide whether the problem occurred prior to initiation of the feeding, as the diarrhea may be related

Table 20-6 Potential Nutrition Problems, with Suggested Approaches

Problem	Frequent Small Meals	High Protein High Kcal Supplements	Avoid Strong Odors	Cool or Room Temperature Foods	Increase kcal Content of Foods	Increase Fluid Intake	Decrease Fiber Intake and Roughage	Limit High Fat Foods	Avoid Gas Forming Foods	Regular Exercise if Tolerated	Avoid Liquids at Mealtime	Avoid Highly Seasoned Foods	Comments
Loss of appetite and early satiety	X	X	X	X	X					X	X		Pleasant mealtime atmosphere. Set meal times. Avoid forcing food.
Diarrhea	X			X		X	X	X	X		X	X	Clear fluids helpful. Limit beverages containing caffeine and lactose.
Nausea and vomiting	X		X	X	X	X		X			X	X	Clear, cool beverages recommended. Eat and drink slowly. Activity after a meal can stimulate vomiting.
Heartburn (reflux)								X				X	Avoid caffeine, chocolate, peppermint.
Chewing and swallowing difficulties (sore mouth or throat)	X	X		X	X	X	X					X	Citrus fruits and juices, tomatoes and other acid c foods may aggravate a sore throat or mouth. Cooked or canned vegetables and fruits may be easier to eat than raw or fresh ones. Moist, soft foods may help.
Constipation						X				X			Balanced diet with additional servings of fruits, vegetable, and whole grain products.
Abdominal gas							X	X	X	X			Avoid eating rapidly, "gulping" beverages, "drawing" on straws, or sipping beverages frequently. It may be necessary to avoid lactose and the artificial sweeteners sorbitol and mannitol.
Dry mouth	X	X				X							Hard candy, preferably sugar-free, may be used throughout the day to keep the mouth moist. Sip liquids with meals or use artificial saliva Soft, moist foods.

Source: From Pemberton CM, Moxness KE, German MJ, Nelson JK, Gastineau CF, eds. *Mayo Clinic Diet Manual.* 6th ed. Toronto: BC Decker, 1988:202–203.

to an underlying infection or medications. Constipation can occur with long-term use of a low-residue product but is rarely a problem.

Total Parenteral Nutrition

For the patient who cannot ingest, digest, or absorb food via the gastrointestinal tract, TPN serves as a reliable source of nutrients.[6] TPN does not appear to improve survival or response to standard therapy, except in marrow transplantation.[33] Parenteral nutrition can be used to maintain normal body composition in a growing patient to prevent starvation.[6]

The decision to use central or peripheral TPN is based on nutritional status, expected duration of nutrition therapy, and availability of peripheral veins. Central venous catheters are often placed for chemotherapy, making central TPN the logical choice.[6] Multiple-lumen catheters help simplify the delivery of medications, blood products, and nutrient solutions (see also Chapter 11).

The percentage of calories from each of the major nutrients should approach the percentage recommended for an oral diet: 25% to 30% fat, 50% to 60% carbohydrate, and 10% to 20% protein. Excessive administration of carbohydrate is avoided to reduce the risk of glucose intolerance and fatty liver. Serum triglycerides should be checked weekly to verify normal lipid clearance, which may be impaired in sepsis or cachexia.[34]

Home TPN can be used to reverse malnutrition while allowing the patient time out of the hospital. A home health care agency can work with the family to provide TPN solutions, education, and monitoring.

SPECIAL CONSIDERATIONS

Low-Microbial Diets

Prevention or treatment of infections in the pediatric cancer population is a major medical focus. Prevention strategies center on protective isolation, antibiotics, and, in neutropenic patients, the use of a low-microbial diet.[22] A diet low in microbial content, also known as a "cooked food" or "low-bacteria" diet, consists of food items that contain few gram-negative bacilli or no pathogenic microorganisms. This diet consists of thoroughly cooked foods and some commercially prepared items packaged by the manufacturer. Raw fruits and vegetables are eliminated. Table 20-7 provides guidelines for a microbiologically tested diet developed for marrow transplant patients in laminar airflow environments. It should be remembered that the microbial content of foods varies between manufacturers and lots.

Table 20-7 Foods Listed by Food Group According to Microbiologic Testing*

Food Group	Acceptable Growth	Not Acceptable Growth
Beverages	Coffee, instant coffee Tea, instant tea Fruit-flavored powdered drink mix Carbonated beverages Canned fruit ades Pasteurized beer Bottled seltzer waters Sterile water and ice	Nonpasteurized beer Wine Bottled, distilled water
Milk and dairy products	Ultra heat-treated milk Instant hot cocoa mix Commercially sterile milkshake product Canned milk Half and half creamer American cheese Cream cheese in individual packets Processed, pasteurized cheese spread and cheese food spread Canned puddings	Whipped cream Nondairy whipped topping Pasteurized milk Yogurt Cheese, except American Buttermilk Ice cream, all varieties Sherbet Cottage cheese Sour cream Powdered instant breakfast drinks Homemade and commercially prepared refrigerated puddings
Fruits and fruit juices	Canned fruit Canned and bottled fruit juices Baked apples	Fresh fruits and juices Raisins, all other dried fruits
Vegetables and vegetable juices	All canned vegetables and vegetable juices Canned bean salad Frozen vegetables, well-cooked Baked fresh squash	Fresh vegetables Onion rings
Potato and substitutes	Cooked white or sweet potatoes, yams, french fries, hash brown potatoes Instant mashed potatoes Rice, pasta, noodles cooked in sterile water Chow mein noodles	Raw potato Au gratin potatoes Rice, pasta, potato cooked in nonsterile water Potato salad Macaroni salad
Breads and cereals	All breads, English muffins, bagels (except onion), hamburger and hot dog buns, dinner rolls Tortillas	All raisin and nut-containing cereals and breads Cinnamon rolls

continues

Table 20-7 continued

Food Group	Acceptable Growth	Not Acceptable Growth
Breads and cereals (continued)	Hot and cold cereals except as noted Pancakes Waffles French toast Blueberry and plain muffins Crackers	Sweet rolls Donuts Onion bagels
Meat, meat substitutes and mixed entrees	All hot, well-cooked beef, pork, poultry, and fish Canned meats, fish, and shellfish Hot dogs, well-cooked Spaghetti sauce Frozen commercial mixed entrees, heated thoroughly: chicken and beef pot pies, macaroni and cheese, beef stroganoff, spaghetti with meat sauce Peanut butter, smooth Canned beans, legumes, refried beans Baby food in jars	Deli meats Processed luncheon meats Raw eggs Dried meats (beef jerky) Rare- and medium-cooked meats, seafood Lasagna Pizza
Soups	All hot canned and dehydrated packaged soups, broths, and bouillons	Homemade soups Commercial refrigerated and frozen soups Cold soups
Fats and oils	Margarine Vegetable oil Fat for deep-fat frying Shortening Mayonnaise, tartar sauce from individual packets Canned gravy, sauces	Butter Homemade gravy Hollandaise sauce Tartar sauce, mayonnaise from multi-serving containers
Condiments and spices	Individually packaged mustard, ketchup, taco sauce, lemon juice, salad dressings, jam, jelly, cranberry sauce, honey, and syrup Sugars Salt Canned chocolate syrup Dill pickle Canned black olives Seasonings, spices, and pepper added before cooking	Condiments from multiserving containers Green olives Sweet pickle relish Seasonings, spices, and pepper added after cooking
Desserts and snacks	Pound and angel food cakes Commercial cookies: gingersnap, frosting-filled sandwich cookie, shortbread, vanilla wafer	All other cakes All other cookies Cracker Jacks Pies

Table 20-7 continued

Food Group	Acceptable Growth	Not Acceptable Growth
Desserts and snacks (continued)	Corn and tortilla chips Crackers Popcorn Dips, canned Cupcakes, individually packaged Fruit pies, individually packaged Popsicles off the stick Jello Custard, homemade Candy: hard candies, jelly beans, gum drops, orange slices, gummi bears, lemon drops, marshmallows, peanut butter cups, plain chocolate disc candies Chewing gum	Nuts, all varieties Potato chips Pretzels Ice cream bars Candy made with nuts or dried fruits Candy bars
Nutritional supplements	Glucose polymers Powdered supplements reconstituted with sterile water All canned supplements	

* Acceptability criteria: $<10^3$ colony-forming units/mL of coagulase-negative staphylococci or *Viridans streptococcus* and $<10^4$ colony-forming units/mL of *Bacillus* spp., diphtheroids, or *Micrococcus*.

Source: Reprinted from *Nutrition Management of the Cancer Patient* (pp 130–131) by AS Bloch (ed), Aspen Publishers, Inc, © 1990.

Feeding Strategies

Food Service

The main hospital kitchen in most institutions provides food service for oncology patients. But a separate kitchen equipped with laminar airflow hoods for aseptic food preparation is ideal to prepare a low-microbial diet. When this is not possible, the main kitchen should employ specific handling techniques to reduce the possibility of contamination after preparation, such as using the first serving immediately after opening a package and serving from the trayline before other trays.[35]

The food service for oncology patients must be designed to provide a variety of foods served at frequent intervals to meet patient tolerance. A review of food items ordered by marrow transplant patients the 2 weeks prior to discharge showed nonacidic beverages were ordered most frequently, followed by bread products and cooked fruits.[36] A well-stocked floor pantry facilitates off-hour food service of similar items for patients when the main kitchen is closed.

Promoting Oral Intake during Hospitalization

Encouraging oral intake in the pediatric cancer patient can be a challenge.[3] Anxious, scared, or depressed children do not feel like eating. Providing a calm, relaxed hospital atmosphere for eating, with uninterrupted time for feeding (door closed, sign posted) may improve intake. Small children require secure feeding positions (highchair or toddler feeding table), a bib, towel, and covered floor area to limit anxiety over spills.

Children should not be forced to eat; a maximum meal time of 20 to 30 minutes should be adequate. Provide food texture and portion size appropriate for age. For patients refusing to eat, behavior modification techniques may be necessary.[37] Older children may benefit from group eating situations, such as a playroom area, or participatory food preparation times, as well as knowing their oral intake goals for hospital discharge.

AREAS FOR FURTHER RESEARCH

Even though food can serve as a vehicle for colonization by pathogenic organisms in immunosuppressed patients, its contribution to the incidence of infection in the granulocytopenic patient or marrow transplant recipient has not been well studied. Further research is needed to determine the most cost-effective way to prepare a palatable, low-microbial diet without special facilities and to document the effectiveness and safety of the diet.

REFERENCES

1. Rickard KA, Grosfeld JL, Coates TD, et al. Advances in nutrition care of children with neoplastic diseases: a review of treatment, research and application. *J Am Diet Assoc.* 1986;86:1666–1676.

2. Young JL Jr, Reis LG, Silverberg E, et al. Cancer incidence, survival, and mortality for children younger than age 15 years. *Cancer.* 1986;58:598–602.

3. Sherry ME, Aker SN, Cheney CL. Nutrition assessment and management of the pediatric cancer patient. *Top Clin Nutr.* 1987;2:38–48.

4. Pemberton CM, Moxness KE, German MJ, Nelson JK, Gastineau CF. *Mayo Clinical Diet Manual, A Handbook of Dietary Practices.* Burlington, Ontario: BC Decker, Inc; 1988.

5. Coates TD, Rickard KA, Grosfeld JL, et al. Nutritional support of children with neoplastic diseases. *Surg Clin North Am.* 1986;66:1197–1212.

6. Norton JA, Peter J. Nutritional supportive care. In: Pizzo PA, Poplack DG, eds. *Principles and Practice of Pediatric Oncology.* Philadelphia: JB Lippincott; 1989.

7. Kern KA, Norton JA. Cancer cachexia. *J Parenter Enter Nutr.* 1988;12:286–298.

8. Van Eys J. Nutrition and cancer: physiological interrelationships. *Annu Rev Nutr.* 1985;5:435–461.

9. DeWys WD. Taste and feeding behavior in patients with cancer. *Curr Concepts Nutr.* 1977;6:131–134.

10. Shils ME. Nutrition and neoplasia. In: Shils ME, Young VR, eds. *Modern Nutrition in Health and Disease.* 7th ed. Philadelphia: Lea and Febiger; 1988:1380–1422.

11. Donaldson SS, Lenon RA. Alterations of nutritional status. Impact of chemotherapy and radiotherapy. *Cancer.* 1979;43:2036–2052.

12. Ramsay NKC. Bone marrow transplantation in pediatric oncology. In: Pizzo PA, Poplack DG, eds. *Principles and Practice of Pediatric Oncology.* Philadelphia: JB Lippincott; 1989.

13. McDonald GB, Sale GE. The human gastrointestinal tract after allogeneic marrow transplantation. In: Sale GE, Shulman HM, eds. *The Pathology of Bone Marrow Transplantation.* New York: Masson Publishing Co; 1984:77–103.

14. McDonald GB, Sharma P, Hackman RD, et al. Esophageal infections in immunosuppressed patients after marrow transplantation. *Gastroenterology.* 1985;88:1111–1117.

15. McDonald GB, Shulman HM, Sullivan KM, Spencer GD. Intestinal and hepatic complications of human bone marrow transplantation, part I. *Gastroenterology.* 1986;90:460–477.

16. McDonald GB, Shulman HM, Sullivan KM, Spencer GD. Intestinal and hepatic complications of human bone marrow transplantation, part II. *Gastroenterology.* 1986;90:770–784.

17. Weisdorf DJ, Snover DC, Haake R, et al. Acute upper gastrointestinal graft-versus-host-disease: clinical significance and response to immunosuppressive therapy. *Blood.* 1990;76:624–629.

18. Darbinian J, Schubert MM. Special Management Problems. In: Lenssen P, Aker SN, eds. *Nutritional Assessment and Management during Marrow Transplantation: A Resource Manual.* Seattle, Wash: Fred Hutchinson Cancer Research Center; 1985:63–80.

19. Carson JA, Gormican A. Disease-medication relationships in altered taste sensitivity. *J Am Diet Assoc.* 1976;68:550–553.

20. Shubert MM, Sullivan KM, Truelove EL. Head and neck complications of bone marrow transplantation. In: Peterson DE, Sonis ST, eds. *Head and Neck Management of the Cancer Patient.* The Hague: Martinus Nijhoff Publishing; 1986:92–112.

21. Moe GL. The low microbial diets for patients with granulocytopenia. In: Bloch A, ed. *Nutritional Management of the Cancer Patient.* Gaithersburg, Md: Aspen Publishers; 1990:125–134.

22. Lenssen P, Moe GL, Cheney CL, et al. Parenteral nutrition in marrow transplant recipients after discharge from the hospital. *Exp Hematol.* 1983;11:974–981.

23. Aker SN. Oral feedings in the cancer patient. *Cancer.* 1979;43:2103–2107.

24. Donaldson SS, Wesley MN, DeWys WD, et al. A study of the nutritional status of pediatric cancer patients. *Am J Dis Child.* 1981;135:1107–1112.

25. Rickard KA, Detamore CM, Coates TD, et al. Effect of nutrition staging on treatment delays and outcome in stage IV neuroblastoma. *Cancer.* 1983;52:587–598.

26. Carter P, Carr D, Van Eys J, Coddy D. Nutritional parameters in children with cancer. *J Am Diet Assoc.* 1983;82:616–622.

27. Katz JA, Chambers B, Everhart C, et al. Linear growth in children with acute lymphoblastic leukemia treated without cranial irradiation. *J Pediatr.* 1991;118:575–578.

28. Meadows AT, Silber J. Delayed consequences of therapy for childhood cancer. *CA—A Cancer Journal for Clinicians.* 1985;35:271–281.

29. Pipes P. *Nutrition in Childhood.* St Louis, Mo: CV Mosby; 1977.

30. Merritt RJ, Kalsch M, Roux LD, et al. Significance of hypoalbuminemia in pediatric oncology patients—malnutrition or infections? *J Parenter Enter Nutr.* 1983;9:303–306.

31. Altman PL, DS Dittmer. *Metabolism.* Bethesda, Md: Federation of American Societies for Experimental Biology; 1968:344.

32. Bernard M, Forlaw L. Complications and their prevention. In: Rombeau JL, Caldwell MD, eds. *Enteral and Tube Feeding.* Philadelphia, Pa: WB Saunders; 1984:542–569.

33. Weisdorf SA, Lysne J, Wind D. Positive effect of prophylactic total parenteral nutrition on long-term outcome of bone marrow transplantation. *Transplantation.* 1987;43:833–838.

34. Seashore JH. Nutritional support of children in the intensive care unit. *Yale J Biol Med.* 1984;57:111–134.

35. Aker SN, Cheney CL. The use of sterile and low microbial diets in ultraisolation environments. *J Parenter Enter Nutr.* 1983;7:390–397.

36. Gauvreau-Stern J, Cheney CL, Aker SN, Lenssen P. Food intake patterns and foodservice requirements on a marrow transplant unit. *J Am Diet Assoc.* 1989;89:367–372.

37. Handen BL, Mandell F, Russo DC. Feeding induction in children who refuse to eat. *Am J Dis Child.* 1986;140:52–54.

Chapter 21

Nutrition in the Burned Pediatric Patient

Michele M. Gottschlich

Trauma is a major cause of mortality in children, and a significant number of these deaths are from burns. Burn injury poses a complex metabolic challenge that is directly related to subsequent morbidity and mortality. As such, an important determinant of outcome is adequacy of energy and nutrient provision. If nutriture becomes impaired, wound healing and organ function will suffer. In addition, malnutrition will induce deterioration of immune defenses and profound catabolism.

The purpose of this chapter is to point out special metabolic changes in and physiologic deficiencies and nutritional requirements of burned infants and children. Because the common denominator to which all nutrients are related is adequacy of energy intake, methods for evaluating caloric requirements will be emphasized. The basis for selecting the safest and most efficacious route of support and ratio of nutrients will be addressed. This section will also review enteral and parenteral hyperalimentation techniques as well as present options available for assessing and monitoring the nutrition rehabilitation program.

ANATOMIC AND PHYSIOLOGIC CONSIDERATIONS

Pediatric burn injury has a high mortality rate compared to that of adults with equivalent burns,[1,2] although outcome has clearly improved with advancements in burn care.[3] The higher incidence of complications in pediatric burn patients is partially attributable to the fact that the unique physical and metabolic features of infants and children are frequently overlooked. It is important to recognize that the burned youngster in need of medical and nutritional therapy presents a separate and often much more complex therapeutic problem than his or her adult counterpart.

Although the older child rapidly approaches the adult and responds to injury and treatment in a corresponding fashion, specialized nutrition care is required by younger age groups owing to their anatomic and physiologic immaturity (Table 21-1). All burned children, however, pose a special challenge to meet obligatory growth needs; burn injuries represent a particular threat to growth through imposition of a catabolic state. A burned child, with both more limited reserves and greater caloric and protein requirements than an adult, quickly reaches negative nitrogen balance with a smaller area of burn than an adult. Furthermore, the functional immaturity of infants' gastrointestinal tract and renal system[4–6] poses a unique challenge to their ability to tolerate nonvolitional feeding regimens and nutrient-dense products. They are extremely susceptible to diarrhea, dehydration, and malnutrition, which only worsens the degree of catabolism.

METABOLIC MANIFESTATIONS OF THERMAL INJURY

In addition to developmental immaturities, the burned child must respond to the metabolic challenges associated with thermal injury. Extensive burn injury ini-

---

Table 21-1 Anatomic and Physiologic Immaturities of Children of Various Ages

System	Deficit	Clinical Implications	Age Maturation
Temperature regulation	Labile system Surface area-body weight ratio greatly increased	Increased radiant and evaporative heat loss Increased metabolic rate in an attempt to maintain core temperature	10–12 years
Integument	Thin skin	Heat penetrates more rapidly with resultant deeper burn	16–18 years
Gastrointestinal	Immature tract Limited surface area of the small intestinal mucosa Decreased gastric volume capacity	Limited capacity to digest or assimilate some nutrients Prone to antigen absorption High incidence of diarrhea	1–2 years
Renal	Glomerular immaturity Young kidneys inefficient in excretion of sodium chloride and other ions as well as in water reabsorption	Renal concentrating ability low, therefore, more water required to excrete the renal solute load produced by the metabolism of protein and electrolytes Susceptible to dehydration	1–2 years

tiates the most marked alterations in body metabolism that can be associated with any illness. The pattern of physiologic events following thermal injury falls into two phases, the ebb and the flow responses.[7,8] The initial or ebb response of the burn syndrome is short, lasting 3 to 5 days postinjury. This phase is characterized by general hypometabolism and is manifested by reductions in oxygen consumption, cardiac output, blood pressure, and body temperature (Table 21-2). Fluid resuscitation is conducted during this time in response to the tremendous fluid losses that occur during the early postburn period.

With the resuscitative restoration of circulatory blood volume, the body advances to a prolonged state of hypermetabolism and increased nutrient turnover, termed the flow phase. This second phase is influenced by elevations in circulat-

Table 21-2 Metabolic Alterations Following Burns

| | | Flow Response | |
	Ebb Response	Acute Phase	Adaptive Phase
Dominant factors	Loss of plasma volume Shock Low plasma insulin levels	Elevated catecholamines Elevated glucagon Elevated glucocorticoids Normal or elevated insulin High glucagon to insulin ratio	Stress hormone response subsiding
Symptoms	Hyperglycemia Decreased oxygen consumption Depressed resting energy expenditure Decreased blood pressure Reduced cardiac output Decreased body temperature	Catabolism Hyperglycemia Increased respiratory rate Increased oxygen consumption Hypermetabolism Increased body temperature Increased cardiac output Redistribution of polyvalent cations such as zinc and iron Mobilization of metabolic reserves Increased urinary excretion of nitrogen, sulphur, magnesium, phosphorus and potassium Accelerated gluconeogenesis	Anabolism Normoglycemia Energy turnover diminished Convalescence

Source: Adapted from Gottschlich MM, Alexander JW, Bower RH, Enteral nutrition in patients with burns or trauma, in *Enteral and Tube Feeding,* JL Rombeau and MD Caldwell, (eds) with permission of WB Saunders Co, 1990.

ing levels of catecholamines,[9,10] glucocorticoids,[11-13] and glucagon.[14-17] Insulin levels are usually in the normal range or even elevated. But the rise in the glucagon:insulin ratio,[17,18] in combination with the other hormonal derangements, initiates gluconeogenesis, lipolysis, and protein degradation. Hypermetabolism and hypercatabolism also vary with the time postburn. Wilmore's classic studies show that following the ebb phase, catabolic hormone production and oxygen consumption increase dramatically, peaking between the 6th and 10th day following burns.[10,19] Thereafter, metabolic rate slowly begins to decrease, and a gradual recession of catabolism occurs. These metabolic and hormonal sequelae have important implications from a nutritional perspective.

FLUID REQUIREMENTS

Water is the most critical of all nutrients. It is an essential component of all cellular structures and is the medium in which all chemical reactions of the host take place. The body composition of the infant is 70% to 75% water, compared with that of an adult, which is 60% to 65% water. The extracellular fluids of the infant constitute approximately 50% of the total body weight, compared to 20% to 25% in the adult. Excesses or deficits in water of more than 5% of the optimal value produce measurable effects, and large deviations may lead to death.

Immediately after burns, altered capillary permeability results in the escape of fluid, electrolytes, and protein from the vascular compartment to the interstitial area surrounding the burn wound. The injured area also loses its ability to act as a barrier to water evaporation. In children, with their relatively larger surface area per weight, the insensible water loss is of critical magnitude. Infants and young children are particularly susceptible to a lack of sufficient water intake because of their considerably higher obligatory urinary and insensible water losses, compared to those of adults. Hemodynamic dysfunction as a consequence of fluid shifts necessitates prompt provision of intravenous fluid resuscitation to restore tissue blood flow and prevent shock following burns, keeping in mind that children will require more fluid per square meter of body surface area than adults with burns.[20]

The most popular pediatric fluid replacement formula in use is the Parkland formula,[21] modified for children (Exhibit 21-1). The modified Parkland formula includes a factor for basal fluid needs in addition to compensation for losses from the burn wound. Lactated Ringer's solution is currently the fluid of choice in resuscitation regimens since its concentration of electrolytes most closely resembles that of extracellular fluid. Fluid replacement formulas serve as guidelines. The patient's vital signs, blood pressure, and urinary output should be constantly evaluated to determine adequacy of replacement.

Exhibit 21-1 Pediatric Fluid Calculations for Resuscitation and Maintenance

Modified Parkland Formula

Total resuscitation fluids = [4 ml × % burn × weight (kg)] + [basal fluid
   (ml/24 hours)   requirements (1500 × m²)]
                          1/2 of calculated fluid volume given in the first 8 hours
                          1/2 of calculated fluid volume given in the next 16 hours

Maintenance Fluid Calculation

Total maintenance fluids = Basal fluids + evaporative losses
(ml/hour)

$$= \frac{1500 \text{ ml} \times m^2}{24 \text{ hours}} + (35 + \% \text{ burn}) \times m^2$$

Source: Courtesy of the Shriner Hospitals Burn Institute, Cincinnati, Ohio.

CALORIC NEEDS

Increases in energy expenditure accompany burn injury. The degree of hypermetabolism is generally related to the size of the burn,[19] with burns of approximately 50% body surface area encountering a peak in energy expenditure, generally twice that of preinjury. It was once thought that the increase in metabolic rate was a response to the tremendous evaporative heat loss from the wound,[22,23] supported by the finding that raising ambient temperature partially reduced the hypermetabolic response. However, even in very warm environments, burn patients remained hypermetabolic, and their core and skin temperatures persisted. Other causes of hypermetabolism were sought after Zawacki and associates demonstrated that blocking evaporation by application of impermeable dressings to the burn wound produced only a modest reduction in metabolic rate.[24] The root cause of hypermetabolism continues to be an active area of investigation; it presently appears to be primarily driven by catecholamines.[10,25,26] Metabolic rate slows with wound healing and convalescence, although reactivation of hypermetabolism can occur with complications such as infection or organ failure.

The substantial energy demands imposed by rapid growth and development during infancy and childhood are well documented. The caloric requirements of pediatric patients may be two to three times as great as those of adults in terms of body weight. Furthermore, youngsters' caloric reserves are usually small, particularly during infancy, and deficiencies develop more rapidly as a consequence. Every effort should be made to minimize energy demands by reducing external stresses such as pain, anxiety, and fear. The pediatric burn patient also has a major problem with temperature control. Therefore, when operative procedures, tubbings, and dressing changes are warranted, attention should be given to maintaining a warm environment.

The provision of sufficient calories to meet the increased metabolic expenditure is a critical factor in the management of the burned child. Energy needs may be estimated or measured. Numerous formulas exist for estimating the daily metabolic expenditure of burn patients; however, most of the popular equations have been predicated on data obtained from adults.[27,28] Recently, various equations that specifically address metabolic differences in children have appeared in the literature.[29–35] The pediatric formula proposed by Hildreth and colleagues[31,32] estimates maintenance caloric requirement obtained from the Recommended Dietary Allowances (RDAs) for normal children, expressed in terms of body surface area rather than age or weight. The formula also considers energy needs relative to burns by taking into account the heat loss associated with the predicted fluid losses occurring as a result of evaporation and exudation of the burn wound:

Caloric Requirements = (1800 kcal/m^2 body surface area) + (2200 kcal/m^2 body surface area burned)

Long's modification[35] of the Harris-Benedict equation[36] has also been used to estimate energy expenditure of burned children. Developed in 1919, the Harris-Benedict equation estimates basal metabolic rate (BMR) with reasonable accuracy. The Harris-Benedict equation for BMR was derived by multiple-regression analysis using indirect calorimetry measurements performed on healthy volunteers and includes a factor for age. Long proposed that BMR be adjusted for hospitalized patients by taking into account activity and injury factors. An injury factor of 2.1 was recommended for burns:

Men

$$BMR = (66.47 + 13.75\,W + 5.0\,H - 6.76\,A) \times (\text{activity factor}) \times (\text{injury factor})$$

Women

$$BMR = (655.10 + 9.56\,W + 1.85\,H - 4.68\,A) \times (\text{activity factor}) \times (\text{injury factor})$$

$$W = \text{weight in kg};\ H = \text{height in cm};\ A = \text{age in years}$$

Activity Factor	**Injury Factor**
a. Confined to bed = 1.2	a. Severe thermal burn = 2.1
b. Out of bed = 1.3	

Curreri et al.[27] proposed calculating caloric needs of the burned adult on the basis of 25 cal/kg of body weight plus 40 cal per percent of total body surface area burned. This formula has subsequently been modified for pediatrics,[30] using balance studies of weight in burned children:

Ages 0 to 1: Basal calories + 15 calories per percent burn
Ages 1 to 3: Basal calories + 25 calories per percent burn
Ages 3 to 15: Basal calories + 40 calories per percent burn

The aforementioned Curreri junior formula is designed for burns of less than 50% total body surface area. It typically overestimates caloric requirements in burns exceeding 50%.[31]

Studies in burned children at the Shriners Burns Institute, Boston Unit, show that energy intake approximates the RDAs with generous protein intake and aggressive early excision and grafting procedures. Their data suggest that the elevated energy needs due to burns (without sepsis) are offset by reduced physical activity; hence energy needs approximate those for healthy children of the same age.[37] The contribution of physical activity to total energy expenditure becomes more pronounced after the burn is healed and activity is resumed.

The wide range of formulas for calculating energy needs is an indication of the uncertainties of this approach. Most mathematical derivations utilize body weight, age, and burn size as the only determinants of caloric requirements. Although these three factors represent significant effectors of metabolic rate, energy expenditure is also influenced by surgery, pain, anxiety, sepsis, body composition, sex, thermic effect of food, and physical activity. Therefore, mathematical formulas could derive fairly inaccurate caloric goals, considering the variability among individuals. If caloric needs are underestimated, some tissues as well as exogenous substrates will be consumed for energy. Although it is important to provide pediatric burn patients with the energy needed to compensate for hypermetabolism as well as for growth and development, reports also caution against the delivery of an overabundance of calories.[38] Administering a surfeit of calories has been associated with increased metabolic rate, hyperglycemia, and liver abnormalities and can cause an increase in carbon dioxide production.[39,40]

Portable indirect calorimetry represents a recent technological advance in terms of energy assessment of the pediatric burn patient. The use of indirect calorimetry in burn care has been extensively reviewed elsewhere.[41,42] In general, the patient's caloric goal should be calculated at 120% to 130% of the measured resting energy expenditure (REE).[41,43] Although there is some degree of error possible with this extrapolation, it is more accurate than estimates based solely on weight, age, burn size, sex, and/or height. To ensure the clinical validity of this goal, one needs to repeat tests regularly. Since hypermetabolism undergoes transient variation during the recovery phase, it is recommended that indirect calorimetry be conducted twice weekly at minimum (Table 21-3) for proper adjustment of the nutritional support regimen.

CARBOHYDRATE NEEDS

Metabolic changes that occur following thermal injury include deranged carbohydrate metabolism. Early in the response to burns, glycosuria and hyperglycemia frequently occur. A similar response is observed in patients with supervening sepsis.

Predisposition to glucose intolerance is correlated with the severity of the burn injury. Elevated blood glucose is also modulated by the phase of injury. During

Table 21-3 Nutritional Assessment Protocol

Parameter	Frequency	Comments
Diet history	On admission	Obtain usual food intake history. Look for evidence of preinjury malnutrition, food allergies, intolerances, and chewing or swallowing difficulties.
Indirect calorimetry	Biweekly	Valuable indicator of severity of hypermetabolism as well as the progression of convalescence. Nutrition support is inadequate when REE × 1.3 exceeds caloric intake or when RQ is less than 0.83.
Weight	Daily	Admission weight and height measurements should be compared to NCHS percentiles. In addition, daily weight monitoring can provide a means of assessing the adequacy of nutrition support. However, a weight change greater than 1 lb/d indicates fluid imbalances and will skew interpretation of visceral proteins. Corrections must be made for amputations, occlusive dressings, and major escharotomies.
Nitrogen balance	Daily	Amount of urine urea nitrogen excreted per 24 hours is a valuable index of severity of hypercatabolism. Nitrogen balance indicates whether nitrogen intake is exceeding body mass breakdown. Nutrition support is considered inadequate if nitrogen balance is negative.
Serum albumin, transferrin, prealbumin, retinol-binding protein levels	Weekly	Deficits of serum protein levels occur rapidly as a result of protein losses through the wound and altered protein metabolism. Repletion of visceral proteins occurs when adequate nutrients are provided. These parameters also are helpful in identifying burn patients at risk of infection.
Serum glucose level	Daily	Some patients with previously normal glucose tolerance may require sliding scale insulin therapy during aggressive nutritional support following burns.
BUN and serum creatinine levels	Daily until stable, then twice weekly	If azotemia develops, increase the delivery of free water and/or decrease protein content of nutrient substrate.
Calorie and protein intake	Daily	Daily monitoring of oral, tube feeding, and parenteral intake can identify nutritional deficits or excesses before weight and laboratory values reveal an imbalance. Modification in nutrition support should be made if deviation of actual intake from goal is detected.
Delayed hypersensitivity skin testing, total lymphocyte count, C_3 and IgG levels	Optional	Suboptimal nutritional status can cause deficits in immune function.

Note: BUN, blood urea nitrogen; NCHS, National Center for Health Statistics; RQ, respiratory quotient.

Source: Data from references 92 to 95.

the shock phase, hyperglycemia is primarily caused by decreased peripheral tissue utilization in lieu of impaired tissue perfusion and low insulin levels.[44–46] Glucose intolerance typically persists during the flow phase, but at this point it appears to be the result of enhanced hepatic glucose production and gluconeogenesis.[25,47]

Carbohydrate plays an important role in the nutritional support of the burned child. It appears to be the most important nonprotein calorie source in terms of nitrogen retention in burned patients,[48–51] although a limit exists to its effectiveness as an energy source.[39] Excessive glucose loads, which can increase carbon dioxide production, heighten glucose intolerance, and induce hepatic fat deposition, should be avoided.[37,40,49,52,53] Therefore, all burn patients should be monitored for hypercapnia and hyperglycemia. When these symptoms are present, the intake of total calories or carbohydrate may need to be reduced. Exogenous insulin administration is often necessary to improve blood glucose levels and achieve maximal glucose utilization.

PROTEIN NEEDS

Thermal injury also brings about momentous changes in protein metabolism. For one thing, there is increased proteolysis as energy needs are met by deamination of amino acids in the generation of carbon skeletons for glucose.[44,47] Transamination of amino acids likewise occurs as an intermediary step in the formation of nonessential amino acids and priority proteins associated with host defense, wound healing, and survival.[54] Reservoirs of amino acids that are mobilized to the liver include skeletal muscle, connective tissue, and gastrointestinal mucosa. The degree of amino acid mobilization is related to the size of the burn and adequacy of protein intake.

The protein requirements of the burned infant and child are elevated because of accelerated tissue breakdown and exudative losses during a period of rapid repair and growth. Failure to meet heightened protein needs can be expected to yield suboptimal clinical results in terms of wound healing and resistance to infection. The infant and child further adapt to inadequate protein intake by curtailing growth of cells, conceivably sacrificing genetic potential.

Studies have shown that enteral fortification using large quantities of protein can accelerate the synthesis of visceral proteins and promote positive nitrogen balance and host defense factors.[43,55–60] For example, Alexander et al.[55] demonstrated that severely burned children on enteral diets containing approximately 22% of calories as protein had higher levels of total serum protein, retinol-binding protein, prealbumin, transferrin, C_3, and IgG and better nitrogen balance compared to patients receiving 15% of calories as protein. In addition, the high-protein group had improved survival and fewer episodes of bacteremia. Therefore, in planning a nutritional intervention strategy for a burned youngster, an important goal is the provision of a sufficient quantity of protein. It is recommended that 20% to 23% of calories be delivered as protein,[7,55,61] which translates to 2.5 to 4.0 g/kg for a nonprotein calorie:nitrogen ratio of 80:1. Other factors that influence protein repletion, assuming an adequate intake of energy, include the quality of dietary protein and the source of nonprotein energy that the patient receives.

Of the 20 amino acids, 8 are essential in healthy adults, 9 are considered essential in infants, and several others are conditionally essential in the presence of stressors such as burns, prematurity, and extremely rapid growth (Table 21-4). Such changes in amino acid metabolism are illustrated by the alterations in plasma amino acids following burns.[43,55,62–64] It appears that many reparative and immunologic functions are dependent on the availability of specific amino acids. Improvements in aminograms and outcome in burned patients receiving supplemental arginine, histidine, and cysteine suggest that the percentage of nitrogen needed for semi-essential amino acids may be significantly increased.[43]

Close monitoring of protein intake is necessary as excessive protein loads or amino acid imbalances may result in azotemia, hyperammonemia, or acidosis. Particular care must be taken when administering high-protein feedings to children under 12 months of age, as excessive amounts can have adverse effects on immature or compromised kidneys. Ongoing assessment of fluid status, blood urea nitrogen (BUN) level, levels of plasma proteins, and nitrogen balance is recommended for individual evaluation of tolerance and adequacy. However, when fluid intake is not restricted, renal or hepatic dysfunction does not exist, and path-

Table 21-4 Essential and Conditionally Essential Amino Acids

Amino Acid	Condition
Threonine	Adult and infant
Leucine	Adult and infant
Isoleucine	Adult and infant
Valine	Adult and infant
Lysine	Adult and infant
Methionine	Adult and infant
Phenylalanine	Adult and infant
Tryptophan	Adult and infant
Histidine	Infants, burn patients
Cystine/cysteine	Premature infants, burns
Arginine	Premature infants, burns
Tyrosine	Premature infants
Glutamine	Catabolic states

Source: Data from references 43, 58, 96, and 97.

ways of intermediary metabolism are relatively mature, a high-protein diet is usually well tolerated.

FAT NEEDS

During the flow phase, burn-mediated increases in catecholamine and glucagon levels stimulate an accelerated rate of fat mobilization and oxidation. It is recognized, however, that lipid is important to the diet of the burned child because of its high caloric density, its role in myelination of nerve cells and brain development, the palatability it imparts to food, and its role as a carrier for the fat-soluble vitamins. In addition, fat in the form of the essential fatty acid linoleate provides vital components for cellular membranes and is a precursor for dienoic prostaglandin synthesis.

The minimum requirement for linoleic acid needed to prevent omega-6 fatty acid deficiency is considered to be approximately 2% to 3% of the calories consumed. This requirement is usually not difficult to accomplish as most enteral feeding supplements and intravenous fat emulsions contain high levels of fat and linoleic acid.[43,61,65] An overabundance of dietary lipid, however, can be detrimental to recovery from burns.[66] Complications ascribed to excessive fat intake have been reported. These include lipemia, fatty liver, diarrhea, and decreased resistance to infection.[65–67] Furthermore, lipid appears to represent an inefficient source of calories for the maintenance of nitrogen equilibrium and lean body mass following major injury.[49,51,68] Therefore, conservative administration of fat, particularly linoleic acid, is recommended.[67]

MICRONUTRIENT NEEDS

The functions of vitamins and trace elements pertinent to burn injury have been summarized elsewhere.[61] Optimal vitamin and mineral intake of the burned child remains to be determined, as few satisfactory data are available in this area of nutrition. Nevertheless, several facts are indisputable and bring to mind the importance of micronutrient supplementation. First, vitamin and mineral requirements increase with severity of thermal injury, related to heightened protein synthesis, enhanced caloric expenditure, and increased micronutrient losses. Second, individual vitamin and mineral needs are also dependent on preburn status. Finally, micronutrient stores are low in the young.

Undoubtedly, a deficiency of vitamins and minerals would compromise reparative processes. However, oral, tube feeding, and intravenous hyperalimentation regimens frequently do not meet the needs for certain micronutrients in a burned patient. Thus it is recommended that additional supplementation be provided,[61,65,69–72] especially of those vitamins and trace elements associated with energy expenditure, wound healing, and immune function, and those likely to have enhanced urinary and wound losses. Thiamine, riboflavin, niacin, folate, biotin, vitamin K, magnesium, phosphorus, chromium, and manganese are all cofactors for energy-dependent processes. The requirement for pyridoxine is closely related to dietary protein intake and protein metabolism. Vitamin B_{12}, folate, and zinc are cofactors necessary for collagen synthesis. Furthermore, inadequacy of many micronutrients, particularly vitamins A, C, E, and pyridoxine, as well as zinc, copper, and iron inadequacies, can adversely affect immune function. Iron supplementation, however, remains controversial,[43] as excessive iron also appears to enhance susceptibility to infection.[73]

Daily intake of a multivitamin and supplemental vitamin A, vitamin C, and zinc (Table 21-5) are usually suggested. Many centers administer folate and vitamin E as well, although there is much less information on which to base levels of intake at this time. While select vitamin and mineral replacement in excess of RDAs appears to be justified in burned children, some micronutrients, particularly fat-soluble vitamins, are toxic in large amounts. Hence, all micronutrients should be administered judiciously.

NUTRITIONAL INTERVENTION STRATEGIES

Nowhere is the importance of specialized nutritional support more important than in the rehabilitation of the infant and child who has sustained a burn injury. A

Table 21-5 Vitamin and Trace Mineral Recommendations

Children and adolescents (3 years or older)
1. Major burn
   - One multivitamin daily
   - 500 mg ascorbic acid twice daily*
   - 10,000 IU vitamin A daily
   - 220 mg zinc sulfate daily*
2. Minor burn (<20%) or reconstructive patient
   - One multivitamin daily

Children (<3 years of age)
1. Major burn
   - One children's multivitamin daily
   - 250 mg ascorbic acid twice daily*
   - 5000 IU vitamin A daily
   - 100 mg zinc sulfate daily*
2. Minor burn (<10%) or reconstructive patient
   - One multivitamin daily

*Recommended delivery in suspension for tube feeding, as oral vitamin C and zinc in large doses may precipitate nausea or vomiting.

decade ago, many children with thermal injuries died from malnutrition and sepsis because nutritional support was not possible or was inadequate. More recently, there have been exceptional clinical advances in applied nutrition support, with the marketing of oral supplements and improvements in enteral and parenteral hyperalimentation techniques. This technological progress has had a significant positive impact on the survival of extensively burned victims.

The goal of nutritional support for the pediatric burn patient is to provide adequate calories and nutrients to offset the increased metabolic demands induced by injury and growth. Ideally, nutrition intervention should be aimed at facilitating wound healing, maximizing immunocompetence, maintaining or improving organ function, and preventing loss of lean body mass. Specific objectives vary, however, according to the underlying metabolic and nutritional status of each patient. Special consideration is indicated whenever fluid restriction, organ failure, septicemia, mechanical ventilation, or any other presenting condition limits the ability to obtain vital nutrients.

Small burns (<20% surface area) not complicated by facial injury, psychologic problems, inhalation injury, or preburn malnutrition can usually be supported by an oral high-protein, high-calorie diet if time is allocated for individual menu selection. Experience has shown that common food preferences among pediatric burn patients include hamburgers, hot dogs, spaghetti, chicken, and beef barbeque.[74] Vitamins and mineral supplements should be provided for the pediatric burn victim as noted in Table 21-5. Between-meal snacks should be encouraged. Commercial meal replacement beverages or the addition of nutrient modules to menu selections may be helpful in boosting a marginal intake of calories or protein.

At our unit, collaboration between the departments of child life and nutrition has led to the implementation of various creative, nutritious food-related activities, including group dining, family picnics, edible adventures with new and unique foods, cooking and food preparation activities, restaurant meals, nutrition lessons, and skits, to name a few (Figure 21-1). The programs have proven useful in terms of promoting hospital adjustment for the child, encouraging patient/family unit development, and improving dietary intake. Additional suggestions for improving food consumption are listed in Exhibit 21-2.

Children with burns covering a larger surface area (20%) generally cannot meet their nutrient requirements by oral intake alone. In these cases, alternative forms of feeding must be implemented. Nutrients should be provided to the burned youngster by the enteral route whenever possible. The enteral route is preferred over the intravenous because it is safer, gastrointestinal function is preserved, and the integrity of the small intestinal mucosal surface is better maintained,[65,75,76] thus possibly minimizing bacterial translocation from the gastrointestinal tract.[75,77]

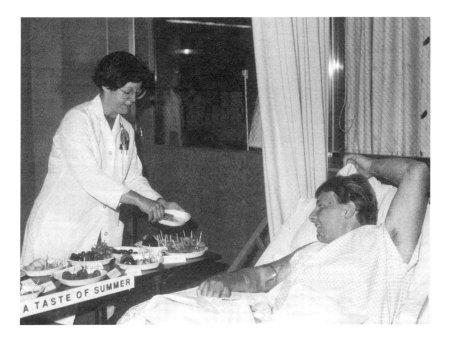

Figure 21-1 An edible adventure taking place at bedside.

Ordinarily, patients with thermal injuries can be successfully fed enterally.[7,61,78–80] The most common tube feeding routes are nasogastric and nasoenteric. Burn severity and projected frequency of surgeries are factors that can be used to gauge which enteral route is clinically indicated. In general, the stomach is the more traditional area of placement. It is appropriate in alert patients with an intact gag reflex who are presenting with a mild injury. A functional gastrointestinal tract is a prerequisite for nasogastric feedings. Continuous infusions using a tube feeding pump are recommended, with hourly monitoring of gastric residuals.

Exhibit 21-2 Dietary Interventions Frequently Helpful in Improving Appetite

- Provide small, frequent meals and snacks
- Serve food in an attractive or creative manner
- Incorporate variety into the meals
- Avoid scheduling painful procedures shortly before mealtimes
- Hold tube feedings 1 to 2 hours before meals

Aspirates in excess of the previous hour's feeding are considered significant and warrant holding the tube feeding for 1 hour. Other tube feeding problems and solutions are reviewed in Exhibit 21-3.

In the more critically injured burn patient, stomach motility is diminished, resulting in acute gastric dilation and paralytic ileus, which limits the usefulness of the stomach for nutritional support. Other contraindications for nasogastric tube feedings include intractable vomiting as well as required preoperative, perioperative, and postoperative periods of fasting.

Owing to the grave concern for possible aspiration, enteral alimentation that bypasses the stomach and uses the functional small intestine is desirable. Fluoroscopically or endoscopically placing feeding tubes into the third portion of the duodenum can be a safe means of enteral nutritional support, even during critical periods such as resuscitation, surgery, anesthesia for major dressing changes, or septic ileus. Care must be taken that the duodenal tube remains in the small bowel. This can be accomplished by measuring the portion of the feeding tube that is left outside, from the nares to the end of the tube, once enteric placement is verified and then repeating this measurement at frequent intervals. Securing the feeding tube with staples or suture can be utilized as a safeguard against accidental displacement. Gastric decompression can be simultaneously maintained using a nasogastric tube connected to intermittent suction. Once bowel sounds are present, the nasogastric tube can be removed.

The question regarding the correct time for initiating a tube feeding program requires consideration. In general, enteral nutritional support should commence as

---

Exhibit 21-3 Common Tube Feeding Problems and Solutions

Diarrhea	May develop upon initiation of enteral alimentation following a period of parenteral support, which is associated with gut mucosal atrophy. Diarrhea may also result from lactose or fat intolerance, as well as altered gut flora secondary to antibiotic therapy. Enteric feeding tubes positioned significantly beyond the ligament of Treitz can bring about malabsorption due to diminished absorptive surface area. Early enteral administration of moderate fat regimens, vitamin A supplementation, and proper positioning of feeding tubes can help decrease the incidence of diarrhea.
Gastric ileus	Is an indicator for nasoduodenal or nasojejunal tube feedings. Enteric feeding can be a safe means of alimentation during surgical, postburn, or septic ileus. Gastric decompression is essential.
Poor appetite	Can be minimized if tube feeding is held at mealtime. As appetite improves, nocturnal tube feeding may be sufficient.

Source: Data from reference 65.

soon as possible. The obvious reasons include the fact that a significant nutrient deficit can develop when alimentation is delayed following thermal injury, which has a direct bearing on morbidity and mortality. In addition, aggressive enteral support has been associated with improved tube feeding tolerance and sustained bowel mucosal integrity.[65,76,81] Furthermore, when tube feeding is initiated within the first few hours postburn, the hypermetabolic response can be partially suppressed, as evidenced by decreased energy expenditure and improvements in measurements of nitrogen balance, visceral proteins, and catabolic hormones.[56,76,79,80]

Since burn patients usually have unscathed digestive and absorptive capabilities, products containing intact nutrients should be used. Elemental or dipeptide formulations are unnecessary unless dictated by concomitant disease or anatomic anomalies[82] and appear to yield less favorable results in burns.[83] Most tube feedings can be started at full strength. The initial hourly infusion rate should begin at approximately half of the final desired volume and be increased by 5 mL/h in the child and 10 mL/h in the adolescent as tolerated until the final hourly rate is achieved. As oral intake improves and nutrient needs decrease, the child can be gradually weaned from the tube feeding regimen. Initially, tube feedings can be held at mealtime to stimulate appetite. Once the patient demonstrates the ability to consume 25% to 50% of caloric needs by mouth, the tube feeding program may only be necessary at night. Eventually, when the patient is able to meet approximately 90% or greater of his or her caloric needs orally, tube feedings can be discontinued.

The composition of the enteral infusate should take into account the unique metabolic and age-related alterations in nutrient utilization that accompany an extensive burn injury. Suggested tube feeding regimens for pediatric burn patients can be divided into two major categories: those appropriate for children less than 12 months of age and those for patients 1 year of age or older.

To date, no one has examined in a randomized, controlled study the unique nutritional needs of the burned infant. Consequently, enteral protocols for infants up to 1 year old are generally conservative, relying on commercial infant formulas. The normal dilution of infant formula is 20 cal/oz (0.66 kcal/mL). Gradually advancing the concentration to 24 cal/oz is routinely safe. Further progression to 27 to 30 cal/oz to meet the infant's energy needs must be monitored carefully due to the resulting increased renal solute load.

The protein content of infant formulas ranges from 9% to 12% of total calories. This level is sometimes insufficient in those with large surface area burns. The addition of a protein module to the infant formula may be indicated in such cases if, once again, the patient is carefully monitored. Infant formulas derived from soy protein should not be used unless casein or whey intolerances have been confirmed, because the biologic value of soy protein is less than that of animal protein. Nutrition support regimens containing significantly reduced fat content are likewise not routinely recommended during infancy, since fat is an extremely important nutrient during the period of central nervous system maturation.

Tube feeding products for children over 12 months of age can generally be selected from formularies established for adults. The coincident fluid needs and energy requirements normally result in utilizing a tube feeding concentration of 30 cal/oz or 1 cal/mL. Since most tube feeding products on the market are low in protein according to the guidelines established for burn patients,[7,55,61,84] products can be enriched with protein modules to yield 20% to 23% of their energy content as protein, using recipes such as that illustrated in Exhibit 21-4.

To date, there are no commercially manufactured tube feeding formulas specifically designed for the burn patient. However, it is clear from recent studies that this patient population has atypical nutritional needs that transcend traditional recommendations for a high-calorie, high-protein solution. Modular tube feeding recipes have evolved, which not only take into consideration energy and quantitative protein guidelines but also offer the only means of currently incorporating findings regarding their unique fat, amino acid, vitamin, and mineral requirements.[43,65,80,85,86] Employment of modular tube feeding prescriptions has been correlated with statistically significant reductions in infection rates and length of hospital stay.[12] However, since complex recipes are not feasible at many institutions due to the laborious, complicated preparation procedures involved, protein enrichment of commercial substrates is recommended as a practical alternative.

PARENTERAL HYPERALIMENTATION

During the late 1960s it became possible to provide nutritional support to virtually any child, when intravenous feeding was shown to permit growth and development.[87] This technique has subsequently been incorporated into the care plans of many burned children.[88,89] While the gastrointestinal tract is the preferred route of nutritional support, under certain circumstances intravenous feeding can become a necessary and even lifesaving part of burn management.

Appropriate indications for intravenous feeding in burns are listed in Exhibit 21-5. There are two general categories of pediatric patients for whom parenteral nutrition is indicated. The first major category includes youngsters with protracted diarrhea or serious tube feeding intolerances resulting in caloric insufficiency. If at all possible, however, at least some nutrients should be administered enterally during episodes of diarrhea. Children with gastrointestinal disease or injury form a second group who frequently require total parenteral nutrition (TPN).

In general, peripheral parenteral support does not provide adequate calories and nitrogen in and of itself, and the delivery of intravenous nutrients via a central line is necessary to promote anabolism in the presence of burns.[90] Standard central

Exhibit 21-4 Recipe Card for Modular Protein Enrichment of Commercial Tube Feeding Product

No.: Formula 1	Equipment: Waring Blender, Gram Scale, Graduated Cylinder	Date: 1/87	Note:
		Rev.:	(1) Wash and sanitize all utensils and equipment prior to preparation
			(2) Discard after 24 hours.
			(3) Label contains—Item, Amount, Patient's Name, Date and Initials of Preparer.

Diet: Osmolite/Promix Tube Feeding

Ingredients	*1000ml*	*2000ml*	*3000ml*	*4000ml*		*Method*
Sterile Water	175 ml	350 ml	525 ml	700 ml	1.	Measure Sterile Water and pour into Waring Blender.
Osmolite*	3 bottles plus 105 ml Osmolite	6 bottles plus 210 ml Osmolite	10 bottles plus 75 ml Osmolite	13 bottles plus 180 ml Osmolite	2.	Measure Osmolite using graduated cylinder.
					3.	Weigh Promix. Add to liquids in blender.
Promix RDP+	34 g	68 g	102	136	4.	Measure Centrum Liquid using graduated cylinder. Add to blender.
Centrum Liquid#	30 ml	60 ml	90 ml	120 ml	5.	Add Aquasol-A preparation. (note: Aquasol-A contains 5000 USP units of vitamin A/0.1 ml)
Vitamin A¶	0.1 ml	0.2 ml	0.3 ml	0.4 ml		Mix all ingredients in blender on low speed for 30 seconds. Do not overmix. Pour into one liter paper cartons. DO NOT WAIT for foam to settle. The foam will create additional volume so you may end up with an additional carton. (Example—recipe for 4000 cc = 5 cartons). Label each container. Deliver to Nursing Unit. Refrigerate immediately.

Key: *Ross Laboratories, Columbus, OH
+Corpak, Inc., Wheeling, IL
#Lederle Laboratories, Pearl River, NY
¶Astra Pharmaceuticals, Westborough, MA

Source: Courtesy of Shriner Hospitals Burn Institute, Cincinnati, Ohio.

Exhibit 21-5 Indications for Total Parenteral Nutrition in Burns

- Gastrointestinal trauma
- Curling's ulcer
- Severe pancreatitis
- Superior mesenteric artery syndrome
- Obstructions of the gastrointestinal tract
- Severe vomiting or abdominal distention
- Intractable diarrhea
- Adjunct to insufficient enteral support

venous regimens for the thermally injured patient usually consist of a final concentration of 25% dextrose and 5% crystalline amino acids, although individualized balancing is often warranted. Patients receiving 100% of their energy needs via the parenteral route will also require the administration of modest amounts of intravenous fat. Five hundred milliliters of 10% lipid emulsion infused two to three times weekly will suffice in meeting essential fatty acid requirements.

The application of parenteral nutrition has undoubtedly contributed to improved outcome in pediatric burn victims unable to be supported enterally. No longer does the thermally injured patient need to deteriorate when enteral feeding is insufficient or contraindicated. However, the metabolic and mechanical complications of parenteral hyperalimentation and the high incidence of septic complications in burns speak for reserving TPN for those whose nutritional needs cannot be met by the enteral route. Adherence to strict protocols of infection control, along with continuous monitoring of tolerance, will most often promote a successful intravenous feeding program in burns.[90]

NUTRITIONAL ASSESSMENT

Nutritional assessment is the process of identifying an individual's energy and nutrient requirements and evaluating the adequacy of enteral or parenteral nutrition support programs in meeting these needs. Since there is little specific information regarding the precise nutritional requirements of the burned child, assessment and monitoring patient response to diet therapy are especially important so that the clinician can react to alterations in metabolism that occur over time and reduce the opportunity for complications. At a minimum, this should include plotting of growth charts, daily evaluation of caloric and protein intake, clinical inspection of feeding lines, records of bowel function, determination of changes in body weight, and laboratory monitoring of serum albumin, glucose, BUN, and creatinine levels. Table 21-3 outlines parameters that can aid in the evaluation of nutritional status in burns. Interpretation of these data has been extensively reviewed elsewhere.[28,41,91]

CONCLUSION

Burn injury in pediatrics has important ramifications for nutrition. Decisions regarding what and how to feed patients continue to pose perplexing problems. Prompt provision of individually tailored diet therapy is of paramount importance in preventing malnutrition in burned children. This nutritional challenge is complicated by the fact that our knowledge of these patients' precise nutrient requirements remains incomplete. Burned infants and children represent separate and much more complex diet therapy problems compared to their adult counterparts, since requirements for growth and development must be considered as well as increased nutrient needs imposed by burns. It is obvious that we have much to learn regarding optimal feeding practices in pediatric burn patients. Further research is needed to establish more definitive guidelines for nutritional intervention in burned children.

REFERENCES

1. Curreri PW, Luterman A, Braun DW, et al. Burn injury: analysis of survival and hospitalization time for 937 patients. *Ann Surg.* 1980;192:472–478.
2. Feller I, Jones CA. The national burn information exchange. *Surg Clin North Am.* 1987;67:167–189.
3. Tompkins RG, Remensnyder JP, Burke JF, et al. Significant reductions in mortality for children with burn injuries through the use of prompt eschar excision. *Ann Surg* 1988;208:577–585.
4. Grybowski JD. Gastrointestinal function in the infant and young child. *Clin Gastroenterol.* 1977;6:253–265.
5. Lebenthal E, Lee PC. Development of functional response in human exocrine pancreas. *Pediatrics.* 1980;66:556–560.
6. Spitzer A. The role of the kidney in sodium homeostasis during maturation. *Kidney Int.* 1982;21:539–545.
7. Gottschlich M, Alexander JW, Bower RH. Enteral nutrition in patients with burns or trauma. In: Rombeau JL, Caldwell MD, eds. *Enteral and Tube Feeding.* 2nd ed. Philadelphia: WB Saunders; 1990:306–324.
8. Cuthbertson DP, Zagreb H. The metabolic response to injury and its nutritional implications: retrospect and prospect. *J Parenter Enter Nutr.* 1979;3:108–130.
9. Aikawa N, Caulfield JB, Thomas RJS, et al. Postburn hypermetabolism: relation to evaporative heat loss and catecholamine level. *Surg Forum.* 1975;26:74–76.
10. Wilmore DW, Long JM, Mason AD, et al. Catecholamines: mediators of the hypermetabolic response to thermal injury. *Ann Surg.* 1974;180:653–669.
11. Bane JW, McCaa RE, McCaa CS. The pattern of aldosterone and cortisone blood levels in thermal burn patients. *J Trauma.* 1974;14:605–611.
12. Dolocek R, Adamkova M, Sotornikova T. Endocrine response after burn. *Scand J Plast Reconstr Surg.* 1979;13:9–16.
13. Vaughn GM, Becker RA, Allen JP, et al. Cortisol and corticotrophin in burned patients. *J Trauma.* 1982;22:263–273.

14. Wilmore DW, Lindsey CA, Moylan JA, et al. Hyperglucagonemia after burns. *Lancet.* 1974;1:73–75.

15. Johoor F, Herndon DH, and Wolfe RR. Role of insulin and glucagon in the response of glucose and alanine kinetics in burn-injured patients. *J Clin Invest.* 1986;78:807–814.

16. Orton CI, Segal AW, Bloom SR, et al. Hypersecretion of glucagon and gastrin in severely burned patients. *Br Med J.* 1975;2:170–172.

17. Shuck JM, Eaton RP, Shuck LW, et al. Dynamics of insulin and glucagon secretions in severely burned patients. *J Trauma.* 1977;17:706–713.

18. Shuck JM. Insulin-glucagon ratios and catabolic state. *J Trauma.* 1979;19:909–910.

19. Wilmore DW. Nutrition and metabolism following thermal injury. *Clin Plast Surg.* 1974;1:603–619.

20. Merrell SW, Saffle JR, Sullivan JJ, et al. Fluid resuscitation in thermally-injured children. *Am J Surg.* 1986;152:664–669.

21. Baxter CR, Shires T. Physiological response to crystalloid resuscitation of severe burns. *Ann NY Acad Sci.* 1968;150:874–894.

22. Caldwell FT. Energy metabolism following thermal burns. *Arch Surg.* 1976;111:181–185.

23. Caldwell FT, Bowser BH, Crabtree JH. The effect of occlusive dressings on the energy metabolism of severely burned children. *Ann Surg.* 1981;193:579–591.

24. Zawacki BE, Spitzer KW, Mason AD, et al. Does increased evaporative water loss cause hypermetabolism in burn patients? *Ann Surg.* 1970;171:236–240.

25. Wilmore DW, Orcutt TW, Mason AD, et al. Alterations in hypothalamic function following thermal injury. *J Trauma.* 1975;15:697–703.

26. Harrison TS, Seaton JF, Feller I. Relationship of increased oxygen consumption to catecholamine excretion in thermal burns. *Ann Surg.* 1967;165:169–172.

27. Curreri PW, Richmond D, Marvin J, et al. Dietary requirements of patients with major burns. *J Am Diet Assoc.* 1974;65:415–417.

28. Morath MA, Miller SF, Finley RK, et al. Interpretation of nutritional parameters in burn patients. *J Burn Care Rehabil.* 1983;4:361–366.

29. Solomon JR. Nutrition in the severely burned child. *Prog Pediatr Surg.* 1981;14:63–79.

30. Day T, Dean P, Adams MC, et al. Nutritional requirements of the burned child: the Curreri junior formula. *Proc Burn Assoc.* 1986;18:86.

31. Hildreth MA, Herndon DN, Desai MH, et al. Reassessing caloric needs in pediatric burn patients. *J Burn Care Rehabil.* 1988;9:616–618.

32. Hildreth MA, Carvajal HF. Caloric requirements in burned children: a simple formula to estimate daily caloric requirements. *J Burn Care Rehabil.* 1982;3:78–80.

33. Sutherland AB, Batchelor ADR. Nitrogen balance in burned children. *Ann NY Acad Sci.* 1968;150:700–710.

34. Pleban WE. Nutritional support of burn patients. *Conn Med.* 1979;43:767–768.

35. Long CL, Schaffel N, Geiger JW, et al. Metabolic response to injury and illness: estimation of energy and protein needs from indirect calorimetry and nitrogen balance. *J Parenter Enter Nutr.* 1979;3:452–456.

36. Harris JA, Benedict FG. Biometric studies of basal metabolism in man. *Carnegie Institute of Washington*, publication no. 279, 1919.

37. Young VR, Motil KJ, Burke JF. Energy and protein metabolism in relation to requirements of the burned pediatric patient. In: Suskind RM, ed. *Textbook of Pediatric Nutrition.* New York: Raven Press; 1981:309–340.

38. Wolfe RR. Burn injury and increased glucose production. *J Trauma.* 1979;19:898–899.

39. Burke JF, Wolfe RR, Mullany CJ, et al. Glucose requirements following the burn injury: parameters of optimal glucose infusion and possible hepatic and respiratory abnormalities following excessive glucose intake. *Ann Surg.* 1979;190:274–283.

40. Askanazi J, Elwyn DH, Silverberg PA, et al. Respiratory distress secondary to high carbohydrate load. *Surgery.* 1980;87:596–598.

41. Saffle JR, Medina E, Raymond J, et al. Use of indirect calorimetry in the nutritional management of burned patients. *J Trauma.* 1985;25:32–39.

42. Ireton-Jones CS. Use of indirect calorimetry in burn care. *J Burn Care Rehabil.* 1988;9:526–529.

43. Gottschlich MM, Jenkins M, Warden GD, et al. Differential effects of three enteral regimens on selected outcome parameters. *J Parenter Enter Nutr.* 1990;14:225–236.

44. Wilmore DW, Goodwin CW, Aulick LH, et al. Effect of injury and infection on visceral metabolism and circulation. *Ann Surg.* 1980;192:491–500.

45. Wilmore DW, Mason AD, Pruitt BA. Insulin response to glucose in hypermetabolic burn patients. *Ann Surg.* 1976;183:314–320.

46. Wolfe RR, Burke JF. Effect of burn trauma on glucose turnover, oxidation and recycling in guinea pigs. *Am J Physiol.* 1977;223:80–85.

47. Wolfe RR, Durkot MJ, Allsop JR, et al. Glucose metabolism in severely burned patients. *Metabolism.* 1979;28:1031–1039.

48. McDougal WS, Wilmore DW, Pruitt BA. Effect of intravenous near isosmotic nutrient infusions on nitrogen balance in critically ill injured patients. *Surg Gynecol Obstet.* 1977;145:408–414.

49. Long JM, Wilmore DW, Mason AD, et al. Effect of carbohydrate and fat intake on nitrogen excretion during total intravenous feeding. *Ann Surg.* 1977;185:417–422.

50. Pearson E, Soroff HS. Burns. In: Schneider HA, Anderson CE, Coursin DB, eds. *Nutritional Support of Medical Practice.* New York, NY: Harper and Row; 1977:222–235.

51. Souba WW, Long JM, Dudrick SJ. Energy intake and stress as determinants of nitrogen excretion in rats. *Surg Forum.* 1978;29:76–77.

52. Barrocas A, Tretola R, and Alonso A. Nutrition and the critically ill pulmonary patient. *Respir Care.* 1983;28:50–61.

53. Askanazi J, Rosenbaum SH, Hyman AI, et al. Respiratory changes induced by large glucose loads of total parenteral nutrition. *JAMA.* 1980;243:1444–1447.

54. Blackburn GL, Bistrian BR. Protein metabolism and nutritional support. *J Trauma.* 1981;21:707–711.

55. Alexander JW, MacMillan BG, Stinnett JD, et al. Beneficial effects of aggressive protein feeding in severely burned children. *Ann Surg.* 1980;192:505–517.

56. Dominioni L, Trocki O, Mochizuki H, et al. Prevention of severe postburn hypermetabolism and catabolism by immediate intragastric feeding. *J Burn Care Rehabil.* 1984;5:106–112.

57. Serog P, Baigts F, Apfelbaum M, et al. Energy and nitrogen balances in 24 severely burned patients receiving 4 isocaloric diets of about 10 MJ/m²/day (2392 Kcalories/m²/day). *Burns.* 1983;9:422–427.

58. Saito H, Trocki O, Wang S, et al. Metabolic and immune effects of dietary arginine supplementation after burn. *Arch Surg.* 1987;122:784–789.

59. Dominioni L, Trocki O, Fang CH, et al. Nitrogen balance and liver changes in burned guinea pigs undergoing prolonged high-protein enteral feeding. *Surg Forum.* 1983;34:99–101.

60. Dominioni L, Trocki O, Fang CH, et al. Enteral feeding in burn hypermetabolism: nutritional and metabolic effects of different levels of calorie and protein intake. *J Parenter Enter Nutr.* 1985;9:269–279.

61. Gottschlich MM. Acute thermal injury. In: Lang CE, ed. *Nutritional Support in Critical Care.* Gaithersburg, Md: Aspen Publishers; 1987;159–181.

62. Cynober L, Nguyen Dinh F, Blonde F, et al. Plasma and urinary amino acid pattern in severe burn patients—evolution throughout the healing period. *Am J Clin Nutr.* 1982;36:416–425.

63. Groves AC, Moore JP, Woolf LI, et al. Arterial plasma amino acids in patients with severe burns. *Surgery.* 1978;83:138–143.

64. Herndon DN, Wilmore DW, Mason AD, et al. Abnormalities in phenylalanine and tyrosine kinetics: significance in septic and nonseptic burned patients. *Arch Surg.* 1978;113:133–135.

65. Gottschlich MM, Warden GD, Michel MA, et al. Diarrhea in tube-fed burn patients: incidence, etiology, nutritional impact and prevention. *J Parenter Enter Nutr.* 1988;12:338–345.

66. Mochizuki H, Trocki O, Dominioni L, et al. Optimal lipid content for enteral diets following thermal injury. *J Parenter Enter Nutr.* 1984;8:638–646.

67. Gottschlich MM, Alexander JW. Fat kinetics and recommended dietary intake in burns. *J Parenter Enter Nutr.* 1987;11:85–89.

68. Freund H, Yoshimura N, Fischer JE. Does intravenous fat spare nitrogen in the injured rat? *Am J Surg.* 1980;140:377–383.

69. Pochon JP. Zinc and copper replacement therapy—a must in burns and scalds in children? *Prog Pediatr Surg.* 1981;14:151–172.

70. King N, Goodwin CW. Use of vitamin supplements for burned patients: a national survey. *J Am Diet Assoc.* 1984;84:923–925.

71. Council on Scientific Affairs. Vitamin preparations as dietary supplements and as therapeutic agents. *JAMA.* 1987;257:1929–1936.

72. Shippee RL, Wilson SW, King N. Trace mineral supplementation of burn patients: a national survey. *J Am Diet Assoc.* 1987;87:300–303.

73. Weinberg ED. Iron and susceptibility to infectious disease. *Science.* 1974;184:952–956.

74. Holli BB, Oakes JB. Feeding the burned child. *J Am Diet Assoc.* 1975;67:240–242.

75. Saito H, Trocki O, Alexander JW, et al. The effect of route of nutrient administration on the nutritional state, catabolic hormone secretion, and gut mucosal integrity after burn injury. *J Parenter Enter Nutr.* 1987;11:1–7.

76. Saito H, Trocki O, Alexander JW. Comparison of immediate postburn enteral versus parenteral nutrition. *J Parenter Enter Nutr.* 1985;9:115.

77. Deitch EA, Maejima K, Berg R. Effect of oral antibiotics and bacterial overgrowth on the translocation of the gastrointestinal tract microflora in burned rats. *J Trauma.* 1985;25:385–392.

78. Kravitz M, Woodruff J, Petersen S, et al. The use of the Dobhoff tube to provide additional nutritional support in thermally injured patients. *J Burn Care Rehabil.* 1982;3:226–228.

79. Jenkins M, Gottschlich M, Waymack JP, et al. An evaluation of the effect of immediate enteral feeding on the hypermetabolic response following severe burn injury. *Proc Am Burn Assoc.* 1988;20.

80. Jenkins M, Gottschlich MM, Alexander JW, et al. Enteral alimentation in the early postburn phase. In: Blackburn GL, Bell SJ, Mullen JL, eds. *Nutritional Medicine: A Case Management Approach.* Philadelphia: WB Saunders; 1989:1–5.

81. Mochizuki H, Trocki O, Dominioni L, et al. Mechanism of prevention of postburn hypermetabolism and catabolism by early enteral feeding. *Ann Surg.* 1984;200:297–310.

82. Gottschlich MM. Managing chylothorax in a pediatric burn patient. *RD.* 1987;7:10–12.

83. Trocki O, Mochizuki H, Dominioni L, et al. Intact protein versus free amino acids in the nutritional support of thermally injured animals. *J Parenter Enter Nutr.* 1986;10:139–145.

84. Gottschlich MM, Alexander JW, Jenkins M, et al. Burns. In: Blackburn GL, Bell SJ, Mullen JL, eds. *Nutritional Medicine: A Case Management Approach.* Philadelphia: WB Saunders; 1989: 6–9.

85. Bell SJ, Molnar JA, Carey M, et al. Adequacy of a modular tube feeding diet for burned patients. *J Am Diet Assoc.* 1986;86:1386–1391.

86. Gottschlich MM, Stone M, Havens P, et al. Therapeutic effects of a modular tube feeding recipe in pediatric burn patients. *Proc Am Burn Assoc.* 1986;18:84.

87. Dudrick SJ, Wilmore DW, Vars HM, et al. Can intravenous feeding as the sole means of nutrition support growth in the child and restore weight loss in an adult? *Ann Surg.* 1969;169:974–984.

88. Derganc M. Parenteral nutrition in severely burned children. *Scand J Plast Reconstr Surg.* 1979;13:195–200.

89. Popp MB, Law EJ, MacMillan BG. Parenteral nutrition in the burned child: a study of twenty-six patients. *Ann Surg.* 1974;179:219–225.

90. Gottschlich MM, Warden GD. Parenteral nutrition in the burned patient. In: Fischer JE, ed. *Total Parenteral Nutrition.* Boston: Little, Brown and Co; 1991:270–298.

91. Bell SJ, Molnar JA, Krasker WS, et al. Prediction of total urinary nitrogen from urea nitrogen for burned patients. *J Am Diet Assoc.* 1985;85:1100–1104.

92. Kagan RJ, Matsuda T, Hanumadass M, et al. The effect of burn wound size on ureagenesis and nitrogen balance. *Ann Surg.* 1982;195:70–74.

93. Jensen TG, Long JM, Dudrick SJ, et al. Nutritional assessment indications of postburn complications. *J Am Diet Assoc.* 1985;85:68–72.

94. Morath MA, Miller SF, Finley RK. Nutritional indicators of postburn bacteremic sepsis. *J Parenter Enter Nutr.* 1981;5:488–491.

95. Ogle CK, Alexander JW. The relationship of bacteremia to levels of transferrin, albumin and total serum protein in burn patients. *Burns.* 1981;8:32–38.

96. Snyderman SE, Boyer A, Roitman E, et al. The histidine requirement of the infant. *Pediatrics.* 1963;31:786–801.

97. Pohland F. Cystine: a semi-essential amino acid in the newborn infant. *Acta Pediatr Scand.* 1974;63:801–804.

Chapter 22

Childhood Obesity

Ruth W. Crocker

Obesity is an excess accumulation of adipose tissue containing stored fat in the form of triglycerides. This chapter describes obesity among children and adolescents and offers suggestions for its assessment, diagnosis, and treatment.

DESCRIPTION OF THE PROBLEM

Obesity is a proliferating health problem among children in the United States, affecting as many as 25% of grade-school children and 15% of adolescents, depending on the standards used to define obesity.[1,2] The prevalence rate has been rising steadily, increasing since 1965 by 54% in children aged 6 to 11 years and 39% in adolescents.[2] Children are also becoming obese at younger ages, and obesity that occurs earlier and persists throughout childhood is more difficult to treat. The older the child, the less likely it is that he or she will outgrow obesity due to slowed weight gain, weight maintenance, or weight loss.[1,3,4]

RISKS ASSOCIATED WITH CHILDHOOD OBESITY

Obesity in childhood also presents health risks. Chronically obese children have a tendency to develop hypertension, and within 7 years as many as 25% of obese hypertensive adolescents will develop evidence of cardio- or cerebrovascular disease.[5] However, there is general agreement that morbidity related to obesity is considerably less for children and adolescents than for adults, but there is concern that obesity that persists through adolescence into adulthood leads to chronic diseases such as hypertension, diabetes, and heart disease.[6]

The greatest risk accompanying chronic childhood obesity is the emotional distress and loss of self-esteem caused by the stigma of being too fat.[7] In the United States children are regarded as responsible for their weight, with failure to be thin being regarded as a sign of weakness and lack of will power.[8] Among adolescents, obesity and an intense preoccupation with appearance may lead to a poor self-image, social isolation, and difficult interactions with family and peers.

DEFINITION AND MEASUREMENT

There are three commonly used methods for measuring obesity in children: body mass index (weight in kilograms divided by height in square meters), triceps skinfold thickness, and weight-for-height by age and sex. There is no single level of fatness in children that demarcates a higher or lower mortality rate.[9] For this reason we must rely on purely statistical definitions of obesity.

Standards Used and Measurement Techniques

The National Institutes of Health Consensus Development Panel on the Health Implication of Obesity[10] finds that the body mass index as a single measurement is highly correlated with other estimates of fatness. Obesity is most commonly measured by triceps skinfold thickness and/or weight-for-height using established procedures and standardized reference charts. In children, the recommended standard is the National Center for Health Statistics (NCHS) percentile curves for assessing physical growth of children in the United States.[11] Using the NCHS growth charts, obesity in children is defined as a state in which the triceps skinfold exceeds the 85th percentile and/or body weight-for-height is greater than 20% above "ideal" body weight-for-height, controlling for age and sex.[1]

Problems with Identifying Obesity in a Specific Child

While it is true that skinfold thicknesses are highly correlated with total body fat, it is very difficult to get an accurate measurement on an individual with a large skinfold thickness, using a skinfold caliper.[12] The use of weight-for-height is preferable but presents problems as well because of the increase in lean body mass that accompanies obesity.[13] However, the use of a standardized growth chart is the best rough estimate because of the close relationship between a child's ideal body weight percentile and his or her height percentile.[12] According to Dietz, "If the diagnosis of obesity is questionable, measurements of the triceps skinfold should be made. Because of the extreme anxiety and attention given to obesity, and the absence of distinct morbid effects in patients less than 130 percent IBW (ideal body weight), underdiagnosis is preferable to overdiagnosis."[14] Dietz is describing children at their ideal body weight as being 100% of ideal body weight. This should not be confused with being 100% *over* ideal body weight. Thus, 130% IBW represents 30% above ideal body weight for height.

ETIOLOGY

Ultimately, obesity is caused by an imbalance between energy intake and expenditure. The factors controlling the growth, development, and metabolism of adipose tissue are complex and are related to both genetics and the environment. Some evidence has suggested that thermogenesis may be impaired in human obesity.[15] However, there is no direct evidence that the defect is related to brown fat. As more information is obtained about the mechanisms that regulate thermogenesis, the role of brown fat in regulating obesity may become more clear.[16]

While a genetic susceptibility may be present, if is difficult to separate its effect from social and environmental factors.[17,18] Obesity varies with population density, season, and geographic region[19] as well as with socioeconomic status, parental education,[20] ethnicity,[21] and parent marital status.[21] Parent marital status has been associated with the incidence of obesity as well as with rate of weight loss in children in a treatment program.[21] The family environment clearly plays a significant role in the etiology and maintenance of childhood obesity.

LONGITUDINAL PERSPECTIVE ON CHILD AND ADOLESCENT OBESITY

In order to understand the relationships of early and later fatness, it is useful to have a longitudinal overview. With this kind of information we can more precisely determine the relative risk of obesity at a particular age and focus prevention and treatment efforts on those children who are at the greatest risk for chronic obesity. Table 22-1 highlights the ages of children in which obesity is associated with an increased risk of continuing to be obese.

Infant Fatness and Later Obesity

High birth weights and fatness in early infancy have been examined as a potential cause of later obesity because of the possibility of excess fat cell proliferation.[22] However, there appears to be no simple causal relationship between obesity in infancy and later obesity. While larger maternal weight gains may result in heavier-for-date babies, these babies are not necessarily more likely to be obese

---

Table 22-1 Relationship between Early and Later Obesity

Obesity at 0–1 years of age and adult obesity . . . . Weak
Obesity at 3–5 years of age and adult obesity . . . . Stronger
Obesity in adolescence and adult obesity . . . . Strongest

later in life.[23] In regard to infant feeding methods, obesity is related to a greater energy intake but not to type of milk feeding or timing of introduction of solids. However, infant obesity in the first year is not significantly related to fatness in early childhood.[24] In regard to infancy, it is important to consider the magnitude of the expected and required growth during the first year; the accumulation of fat tissue is normal. The Committee on Nutrition of the American Academy of Pediatrics[25] states that the correlation between obesity in late childhood, adolescence, and adulthood are considerably stronger than that between obesity in infancy and in adulthood.

Fatness in Preschool and School-Age Children

In children who are close to their ideal body weight-for-height, percent body fat increases in both boys and girls to about age 4. However, excess fatness during the later preschool years predicts later childhood obesity.[26] For example, there is some relationship between fatness in the second year of life and later fatness, but excess fatness at around age 5 is a strong predictor of adolescent obesity.

Between the ages of 4 and 11 the amount of body fat is stable in children close to their ideal body weight.[26] A small but continuous intake of calories beyond what is needed for growth may result in a gradual increase in excess body fat. Conversely, as long as a child has a potential for linear growth, simply slowing the child's rate of weight gain over a period of months or years can limit the potential for obesity in adolescence and adulthood.

Adolescent Fatness and Later Obesity

Adolescence is also a vulnerable time for the development of obesity. Early adolescence is frequently characterized by transient fatness in both boys and girls. Among females, percent body fat increases to approximately age 16 and then plateaus for a period of time before it begins to increase again. Among males, percent body fat increases until age 16 and then decreases.[26] Children should be evaluated as to their stage of physical maturation so that an estimate of potential for linear growth can be made. With this information parents and children can be informed as to whether an overweight child will need to lose weight, maintain weight, or gain slowly. In our clinic we have found that using the growth chart as an educational tool with both parents and children at each session is very useful. Parents and children frequently have unrealistic notions about weight control goals for children. A thorough understanding of why the child needs to merely maintain his or her weight for a period of time is reassuring for parents and children.

ASSESSMENT AND DIAGNOSIS

The assessment of the obese child is critical in the treatment of childhood obesity. Persistence of the condition is based on a wide variety of factors including age, sex, family history of obesity, developmental stage, ethnicity, and the social environment. Each of these factors will influence the treatment goal, the selection of type of treatment, and the course of therapy. Obesity is a complex disease, and even with excellent adherence to treatment recommendations, progress is necessarily slow. Because of the extended period that children often need to be in treatment, the assessment must include a careful review of family lifestyle patterns and the child's social environment. The first step, however, is the physical assessment. This will establish whether the obesity is accompanied by any other disorder and whether the child has any physical limitations that will be affected by an exercise program.

Physical Assessment

Each child should be given a complete physical examination by a pediatrician or a pediatric nurse practitioner. The physical should begin with the child's neonatal and birth history, looking for the possibility of an undiagnosed developmental disability. For example, a history of congenital hypotonia followed by failure to thrive in the first few months of life may suggest a rare condition such as Prader-Willi syndrome. Other symptoms associated with various developmental disabilities include cold intolerance and constipation associated with hypothyroidism and headaches or vision changes related to Cushing's syndrome.

Height may be increased above expected and should be measured carefully. Surges in height are frequently seen in children and adolescents who have experienced rapid and excessive weight gain. A child with less than expected height with respect to average parental height or expected linear growth must be evaluated for endocrine disorders or one of the rare congenital syndromes. The skin may show white stretch marks (striae), which are not unexpected even in moderately obese children. Purplish striae may indicate Cushing's syndrome. One may also find acanthosis nigricans, a blackish pigmentation around the neck that suggests hormonal imbalance or insulin resistance.[14,27]

The child's rate and pattern of weight gain should also be carefully assessed. A rapid and excessive weight gain in recent months may be due to a lifestyle change or an emotional reaction to a significant event. If the events paralleling the weight gain have not been resolved, these children and their families may need psychologic counseling before weight control is initiated in order to prevent failure in a weight control program.

Physical Problems That May Result from Obesity

Obese children may experience orthopaedic problems such as a slipped capital femoral epiphysis, Blount's disease, or bowed femurs. They may also develop such respiratory problems as increased incidence of infection and sleep apnea. Obstructive sleep apnea is an obstruction of the airway during sleep caused by an increase in peripharnygeal fat and large tonsils. It should be suspected in obese children who snore at night and are sleepy during the day. This condition is thought to be the major cause of Pickwickian syndrome, a condition rarely found in children but having a mortality rate of 25% if it is found in children.[14]

All obese children should be assessed for hyperlipidemia and abnormal glucose metabolism. Hypertension is also more prevalent among obese children than in normal-weight children.[5,28] While the cause of hypertension in obese children is not clear, there is frequently an immediate reduction in blood pressure following the initiation of a hypocaloric diet.[14] Finally, the risk of persistence of obesity into adulthood is substantial, with 80% of obese adolescents becoming obese adults.[29]

Social Assessment

Behavioral and social factors predominate in both the etiology and the maintenance of obesity.[3] A detailed social assessment, including a family interview, at the onset of treatment is a key component of a weight control program for children. Parents, grandparents, siblings, and any others who are involved in caring for the child should attend. The purpose of the family interview is to gather as much information as possible about daily life in the family and to explore attitudes and beliefs about obesity and obesity treatment. Exhibit 22-1 lists sample questions that might be asked by the interviewer during the family interview. Questions such as how much weight the child should lose are aimed at exploring disagreements and conflicts between parents. Parents who agree on child-rearing practices and have a better marital relationship have children who are more successful in a weight control program.[30]

Another goal of the family interview is to open communication among family members and establish a collaborative atmosphere. The interview may provide the family with their first experience discussing the problem as a family unit. The tone of the interview must be exploratory and nonjudgmental. Some family members may have strong feelings that weight loss should be immediate and dramatic even when this is not necessary or appropriate. Such beliefs should be addressed and corrected, but only after all of the family members have responded and shared their views. Emphasis should stay on the family by encouraging them to respond to one another. This will yield the greatest amount of information about parenting style, lifestyle patterns, achievement of family developmental tasks, and social and economic resources.

Exhibit 22-1 Sample Questions for Family Interview

Who prepares food in the family?
Who shops, organizes meals?
Are special foods prepared on holidays, at family events?
How often does the family eat together?
What does the family do for recreation?
Who else in the family has a weight problem?
Do parents feel that the obese child has a weight problem, or that he will "grow out of it"?
How much weight should the child lose?
What if the child doesn't lose weight?
Have there been previous attempts to lose weight?
Who makes the rules about child behavior in the family?
Who enforces them?
What caused the child to become obese?
Is there obesity elsewhere in your family (other relatives)?
How close do you live to grandparents and other relatives?
Who is the most independent member of your family?
Who is the most dependent member of your family?
Which words best describe your family?

Dietary and Physical Activity Assessment

Food intake in childhood obesity has been a subject of controversy. While it is widely believed that obesity is caused by excessive calorie intake, several investigators have reported that they could find no difference between the food intakes of lean and obese children.[31-34] There is more conclusive evidence that adults who regain lost weight are likely to snack more frequently than adults who maintain weight loss.[35] Adults may be more accurate in keeping food records than children, but it has also been found that even when parents kept records of their child's food intake, no differences could be found in the food intake of lean and obese children.[36] Variations in food selection are related to patterns of physical and social activities and degree of stability in timing of eating. The season of the year alters availability and choice of foods, and individuals also vary intake in response to changes in appetite.[37]

A detailed dietary history will yield important information about diet content, eating patterns, and who the child eats with and where. Who shops for family food and how often are also important questions. Some children eat meals with several different family members at different times of the day, for various reasons. It is very useful to begin the dietary assessment by asking the child what time he or she awakes and what is the first thing he or she has to eat or drink, and then to proceed through the day. After the basic framework of the child's eating pattern is established, information about nonschool days, weekends, and seasonal differences can be gathered. All dietary information should be collected in as neutral a manner as possible, reserving any suggestions for modifications until a complete picture of the child's food habits has developed. The use of humor and a positive tone is beneficial, especially when parents attempt to make a child "confess" to overeating or consuming particular food. Parents are often uncomfortable around discussions of food and their overweight child. Every effort should be made to help parents save face and to support them as capable and competent parents.

It is also effective to collect information about activity patterns of both the child and family while gathering dietary information. Usually children's food and activity patterns are intertwined, such as stopping at a convenience store while bike riding or having pizza after a sports event. In any case, the interviewer is listening for places where the simplest changes can be made when it is time to give treatment recommendations.

Developing a Hypothesis

The development of a working hypothesis about the treatment needs of the child and family is a crucial step in therapy. In some cases the treatment team in our clinic has hypothesized that dietary intervention, although necessary, is not appropriate at this time. This is often the case when there is severe parental conflict or when children have attended several weight control programs without success. We may refer patients for family counseling if the family is in the midst of a crisis. We have found that an obese child in a poorly functioning family is often willing to be identified as the family problem as a distraction from more painful family issues. Obese children of divorced or separated parents may find that weight control attempts act like glue to hold their parents together. In both of these cases children are more likely to fail at weight control.

Exhibit 22-2 lists five fundamental interactional factors that have been associated with chronic obesity in children.[38] Chronic unresolved marital discord, exclusion of one parent from an overinvolved parent-child relationship, an overprotective orientation by one or both parents, and parental reinforcement of overeating

---

Exhibit 22-2 Family Factors Associated with Chronic Obesity in Children

- Chronic, unresolved marital discord
- Exclusion of one parent from an overinvolved parent-child relationship
- Overprotection by one or both parents
- Encouragement to overeat and not exercise
- Overinvolvement of child in parental problems

and decreased physical activity have also been associated with failure of a pediatric weight control program.[39]

TREATMENT

A conservative approach to treatment is recommended for all ages of obese children. Appetite depressants and other substances of this nature should never be used by children and adolescents. In younger children emphasis is placed on modifying the behavior of parents and other caretakers. Children are more successful when weight control involves lifestyle changes for the whole family. The family must be considered not only as a transmitter of health maintenance practices but also as a psychologic milieu that can support and sustain or inhibit childhood obesity.[39]

Dietary modification is essential in the treatment of childhood obesity. In young children a balanced diet with a calorie deficit of 20% to 30% below usual is recommended.[14] A calorie deficit can usually be achieved by reducing dietary fat and/or limiting consumption of high-calorie liquids such as regular soft drinks, whole milk, full-strength juices and flavored, sweetened beverages. Simply modifying a child's beverage intake can result in substantial savings in calories. High-fat foods can be replaced with lower-fat foods, foods containing more fiber, and complex carbohydrates. Such changes are well accepted by children when changes are made throughout the household.

The use of the American Dietetic Association exchange lists (Chapter 19, Exhibit 19-1) for meal planning[40] is also an effective method of teaching families about the nutrient content of foods and the calorie content of various portion sizes of foods grouped according to similar nutrient content. The plan has recently been revised to emphasize a high-carbohydrate, high-fiber diet, as well as to better reflect the order of foods in menu planning.

Careful attention must be paid to monitoring linear growth if calories are reduced, and protein intake must be adequate to protect lean body mass. The goal of treatment is twofold. First, weight gain should be stopped or slowed until the child "grows into" an appropriate weight for height and age. If the patient is a severely obese adolescent, then weight loss may be necessary. Weight loss or weight maintenance should be monitored carefully to ensure that fat is being lost while linear growth is continuing normally and lean body mass is maintained. Second, interventions should be directed toward the development of a healthy, active lifestyle with little or no emphasis on dieting.

There are two groups, however, in which a stricter approach to diet modification may be indicated. The protein-sparing modified fast (PSMF), a low-calorie, low-carbohydrate, high-protein diet, has been used with success in children with

Prader-Willi syndrome and with adolescents whose obesity is not associated with a syndrome.[41,42] Close medical supervision is necessary if this diet is used, and recent studies have shown that mineral supplementation with potassium, magnesium, and calcium may be essential to achieve positive mineral balance.[43]

The modification of physical activity may also contribute to successful weight control. In general, reduced physical activity among children appears to be related to both the etiology and maintenance of childhood obesity.[7] Hours of television viewing have been positively associated with increased obesity in children.[44] The remedy, however, does not appear to be the institution of structured exercise programs but rather encouraging children to participate in a variety of common daily games and activities. Children who simply increase the amount of time they spend playing active games with other children make more lasting lifestyle changes.[45] Obese adolescents may be reluctant and self-conscious about joining their peers in physical activities. They should be encouraged to come up with emotionally comfortable ways for themselves to get regular aerobic exercise.

Behavior modification has been very successfully adapted for use in child weight control programs. In most child treatment studies utilizing behavior modification there is some form of self and/or parent monitoring.[46] Stimulus control techniques typically include, but are not limited to, sitting in only one place when eating, not engaging in other activities while eating, eating from smaller plates, storing food out of sight, and removing particular foods from the household.[47] Positive reinforcement with an appropriate reward system by members of the child's social network is extremely important.[48] Daily record keeping of weight, exercise, and/or food intake is also very effective with some children and adolescents.

Educational methods must be appropriate to the child's level of cognitive development. For example, rewarding a child for choosing one color-coded group of foods more frequently than another is very effective. With this method children do not have to understand abstract concepts concerning the chemistry of food in order to be successful at weight control.[49] Parents are sometimes surprised at the ease with which children will make dietary changes. Parents often imagine that the child feels deprived because they (the parents) cannot adapt as readily to dietary substitutions. Reassuring and supporting parents is an essential part of anticipating factors that may contribute to the maintenance of obesity.

Older children and adolescents need treatment strategies that are appropriate for their developmental stage. Obese adolescents frequently experience rejection and disdain by both peers and adults at a time when increased involvement with people outside the family is normal and necessary. Adolescent weight control groups and camp settings offer opportunities for socialization and individualization in a supportive, nonjudgmental environment.

CONCLUSION

The relationship between childhood obesity and adult obesity increases as children grow older. The younger the child is when he or she becomes obese, the more likely there will be a spontaneous remission. However, the longer the child continues to be obese, the more likely it is that the obesity will persist into adolescence. Children who enter adolescence with obesity are likely to become even more obese, and to become obese adults.

Environmental and social factors predominate in both the etiology and the maintenance of obesity. Treatment should be preceded by a thorough physical and social assessment. The treatment of all obese children should be age-appropriate, and management of the obese child and family must be approached with sensitivity and awareness of the tremendous complexity of the disease.

REFERENCES

1. Dietz WH. Obesity in infants, children and adolescents in the United States. I. Identification, natural history, and after effects. *Nutr Res.* 1983;3:43–50.
2. Gortmaker SL, Dietz WH, Sobol AM, et al. Increasing pediatric obesity in the United States. *Am J Dis Child.* 1987;141:535–540.
3. Weil WB. Current controversies in childhood obesity. *J Pediatr.* 1977;91:175.
4. Zack P, Harlan WR, Leaverton PE, Cornoni-Huntley J. A longitudinal study of body fatness in childhood obesity. *J Pediatr.* 1979;95:126.
5. Rames LK, Clarke WR, Connor WE. Normal blood pressures and the evaluation of sustained blood pressure elevation in childhood: the Muscatine study. *Pediatrics.* 1978;61:245.
6. Dietz WH. Childhood and adolescent obesity. In: Frankle RT, Yang M, eds. *Obesity and Weight Control.* Gaithersburg, Md: Aspen Publishers; 1988.
7. Lloyd JK, Wolff OH. Overnutrition and obesity. In: Falkner F, ed. *Prevention in Childhood of Health Problems in Adult Life.* Geneva: World Health Organization; 1980.
8. Striegel-Moore R, Rodin J. Prevention of obesity. In: Rosen JC, Solomon LJ, eds. *Prevention in Health Psychology.* London: University Press of New England; 1985.
9. Garn SM. *Continuities and Changes in Fatness from Infancy Through Adulthood.* Chicago, Ill: Year Book Medical Publishers; 1985.
10. NIH Consensus Development Panel. Health implications of obesity. *Ann Intern Med.* 1985;103:1073.
11. Hamill PV, Drizd TA, Johnson CL, et al. Physical growth: National Center for Health Statistics percentiles. *Am J Clin Nutr.* 1979;32:607.
12. Durnin J, Rahaman M. The assessment of the amount of fat in the human body from measurement of skinfold thickness. *Br J Nutr.* 1967;21:681.
13. Forbes GB. Lean body mass and fat in obese children. *Pediatrics.* 1964;34:308.
14. Dietz WH. Nutrition and obesity. In: Grand RJ, Sutphen JL, Dietz WH, eds. *Pediatric Nutrition: Theory and Practice.* Boston, Mass: Butterworths; 1987.

15. Garn SM, Clark DC. Trends in fatness and origins of obesity. *Pediatrics.* 1975;57:443.

16. Garn SM, Higgins ITT. Effects of socio-economic status, family line and living together on fatness and obesity. In: Shekelle SA, ed. *Proceedings of the International Symposium on Primary Prevention in Childhood Atherosclerosis and Hypertensive Diseases.* New York, NY: Raven Press; 1979.

17. Dietz WH, Gortmaker SL. Factors within the physical environment associated with childhood obesity. *Am J Clin Nutr.* 1984;39:619.

18. Garn SM, Bailey SM, Cole PE, et al. Level of education, level of income, and level of fatness in adults. *Am J Clin Nutr.* 1977;30:721.

19. Dietz WH. Family characteristics affect rate of weight loss in obese children. *Nutr Res.* 1983;3:43.

20. Knittle JL, Timmers K, Ginsberg-Fellner F. The growth of adipose tissue in children and adolescents. *J Clin Invest.* 1979;63:239.

21. Davies DP. Size at birth and growth in the first year of life of babies who are overweight and underweight at birth. *Proc Nutr Soc.* 1980;39:25.

22. Yeung D. Obesity in infancy and early childhood—any relationship? Presented at the Fourth International Congress on Obesity; October 5–8, 1983; New York City, NY.

23. Committee on Nutrition. Nutritional aspects of obesity in infancy and childhood. *Pediatrics.* 1981;68:880.

24. Garn SM, Clark DC. Nutrition, growth, development, and maturation—findings from the Ten-State Nutrition Survey of 1968–1970. *Pediatrics.* 1975;56:306.

25. Wharton RH, Crocker RW. Childhood obesity. In: Jellinek MS, Herzog DB, eds. *Massachusetts General Hospital: Psychiatric Aspects of General Hospital Pediatrics.* Chicago, Ill: Year Book Medical Publishers; 1990.

26. Engle MA. Hypertension. In: Hoekelman RA, ed. *Primary Pediatric Care.* St Louis, Mo: CV Mosby; 1987.

27. Rimm I, Rimm AA. Association between juvenile onset obesity and severe adult obesity in 73,532 women. *Am J Public Health.* 1976;66:479.

28. Crocker RW. Correlates of success in the treatment of childhood obesity. Ann Arbor, MI: University Microfilms International; vol 50-02B, p 500, No. 8902358.

29. Johnson ML, Burke BS, Mayer J. The prevalence and incidence of obesity in a cross section of elementary and secondary school children. *Am J Clin Nutr.* 1956;4:231.

30. Huenemann R. Environmental factors associated with preschool obesity. *J Am Diet Assoc.* 1974;64:480.

31. Huenemann RL, Shapiro LR, Hampton MC, et al. Food and eating practices of teen-agers. *J Am Diet Assoc.* 1968;53:17.

32. Mayer J. *Overweight.* Englewood Cliffs, NJ: Prentice-Hall; 1968.

33. Leon GR, Chamberlain K. Comparison of daily eating habits and emotional state of overweight persons successful or unsuccessful in maintaining a weight loss. *J Consult Clin Psychol.* 1973;41:108.

34. Cohen E, Gelfand DM, Dodd DK, et al. Self-control practices associated with weight loss maintenance in children and adolescents. *Behav Ther.* 1980;11:26.

35. Beal V. Traditional approaches to dietary data collection. In: Beal VA, Laus MJ, eds. *Proceedings of the Symposium on Dietary Data Collection, Analysis, and Significance.* Amherst, Mass: Massachusetts Agricultural Experiment Station; 1982.

36. Bruch H. Family transactions in eating disorders. *Compr Psychiatry.* 1971;12:238.

37. Frankle RT. Obesity a family matter: creating new behavior. *J Am Diet Assoc.* 1985;85:597.

38. Dietz WH, Gortmaker SL. Do we fatten our children at the television set? Obesity and television viewing in children and adolescents. *Pediatrics*. 1985;75:807.

39. Epstein LH, Wing RR, Kowske R, et al. A comparison of lifestyle change and programmed aerobic exercise on weight and fitness changes in obese children. *Behav Ther*. 1982;13:651.

40. Wells KC, Copeland BC. Childhood and adolescent obesity: progress in behavioral assessment and treatment. *Prog Behav Modif*. 1985;19:145.

41. Buckmaster L, Brownell KD. Behavior modification: the state of the art. In: Frankle R, Yang M, eds. *Obesity and Weight Control*. Gaithersburg, Md: Aspen Publishers; 1988.

42. Brownell KD, Stunkard AJ. Behavioral treatment of obesity in children. *Am J Dis Child*. 1978;132:403.

43. Epstein LH, Masek BJ, Marshall WR. A nutritionally based school program for control of eating in obese children. *Behav Ther*. 1978;9:766.

44. James WPT, Trayhurn P. Thermogenesis and obesity. *Med Bull* 1981;37:43.

45. Schulz LO. Brown adipose tissue: regulation of thermogenesis and implications for obesity. *J Am Diet Assoc*. 1987;87:761.

46. Franz MJ, Barr P, Holler H, Powers MA, Wheeler ML, Wylie-Rosett J. Exchange lists: revised 1986. *J Am Diet Assoc*. 1987;87:28.

47. Bistrian BR, Blackburn GA, Stanbury JB. Metabolic aspects of a protein sparing modified fast in the dietary management of Prader-Willi syndrome. *N Engl J Med*. 1977;296:774.

48. Merritt RJ, Bistrian BR, Blackburn GA, Suskind RM. Consequences of modified fasting in obese pediatric and adolescent patients. I. Protein-sparing modified fast. *J Pediatr*. 1980;96:13.

49. Stallings VA, Archibald EH, Pencharz PB. Potassium, magnesium, and calcium balance in obese adolescents on a protein-sparing modified fast. *Am J Clin Nutr*. 1988;47:220.

Chapter 23

Eating Disorders

Andrea Bull-McDonough

Eating disorders can start as early as age 9, or before puberty.[1] Girls are predominantly affected, but approximately 5% of all cases are males.[1] Anorexia nervosa and bulimia nervosa are complex, multidimensional disorders having psychologic, medical, sociocultural, and nutritional components.[2] An interdisciplinary team approach with clinicians experienced in these varied areas is the treatment model of choice. It is critical for dietitians to define their role on the team. The dietitian will assess nutritional status, implement a nutrition care plan, coordinate his or her treatment goals with those of other team members, and monitor progress of the treatment.[3] Most often, these clinical activities are pursued in the context of a long-term counseling relationship. It should be borne in mind that owing to the psychological disturbances frequently at work in eating disorders, the conduct of the therapeutic relationship is no less important for treatment success than is monitoring concrete data, such as height, weight, kilocalories eaten, or energy expenditure.

Apart from actual involvement with eating-disordered patients, the dietitian has a role to play in the prevention of eating disorders. With an alarming 34% of 9-year-old girls reporting a fear of fatness, restrictive eating patterns, and binge eating, and an even higher incidence of these symptoms being reported by 13- and 18-year-old girls,[4] dietitians need to consider intervening before an eating disorder appears. The genesis of disordered eating behaviors typically includes the use of unsafe diets and unproven diet products and obsession with arbitrary standards of ideal weight.[3] Dietitians counseling patients for weight loss need to recognize the warning signs of unsafe eating practices[5] and assess both the short- and long-term impact of restrictive dieting on patients' psychologic and physical health.

Note: Because anorexia nervosa and bulimia nervosa patients are primarily girls, such patients are referred to as female throughout this chapter.

This chapter presents information about the etiology, incidence, and prognosis of anorexia nervosa and bulimia nervosa and their clinical treatment guidelines relevant to the dietitian's role.

DEFINITIONS

Exhibit 23-1 gives the definitions of anorexia nervosa and bulimia nervosa according to the third edition, revised, of *The Diagnostic and Statistical Manual of Mental Disorders.*[6] For a diagnosis to be made, all features of the eating disorder must be met.

Although the eating disorders are defined separately, common characteristics are shared by both:

1. a fear of becoming fat and a drive to be or become thin
2. an obsession with food, weight, calories, and dieting
3. the use and abuse of eating or not eating to cope with emotional discomfort, stressful life events, and developmental challenges

---

Exhibit 23-1 Diagnostic Criteria for Eating Disorders

Anorexia Nervosa (Diagnostic Code 307.10)

A. Refusal to maintain body weight over a minimal normal weight for age and height, e.g., weight loss leading to maintenance of body weight 15% below that expected; or failure to make expected weight gain during period of growth, leading to body weight 15% below that expected.

B. Intense fear of gaining weight or becoming fat, even though underweight.

C. Disturbance in the way in which one's body weight, size, or shape is experienced, e.g., the person claims to feel fat even when emaciated, believes that one area of the body is "too fat" even when obviously underweight.

D. In females, absence of at least three consecutive menstrual cycles when otherwise expected to occur (primary or secondary amenorrhea).

Bulimia Nervosa (Diagnostic Code 307.51)

A. Recurrent episodes of binge eating (rapid consumption of a large amount of food in a discrete period of time).

B. A feeling of lack of control over eating behavior during the eating binges.

C. The person regularly engages in self-induced vomiting, use of laxatives or diuretics, strict dieting or fasting or vigorous exercise in order to prevent weight gain.

D. A minimum average of two binge eating episodes a week for at least three months.

E. Persistent overconcern with body shape and weight.

Source: Reprinted from American Psychiatric Association, *Diagnostic and Statistical Manual of Mental Disorders,* 4th ed; 1987.

4. an increased incidence of depression, obesity, substance abuse, and eating disorders in the families of the sufferers
5. a world view valuing external appearance over personal integrity

ETIOLOGY

Anorexia Nervosa

It is believed that underlying developmental disturbances are the primary antecedents of anorexia nervosa.[2] Some time before the illness manifests itself, girls have felt helpless and ineffective in conducting their own lives, and severe discipline over their bodies represents their paramount effort to ward off panic about being completely powerless. This serious illness occurs in individuals who, according to family and school reports, have been unusually good, successful, and gratifying children. With the onset of the disorder, marked changes in behavior appear. A previously compliant girl becomes negativistic, angry, and distrustful. Help and care is stubbornly rejected by the girl, who claims not to need it and insists on the right to be as thin as she wants to be.[2]

Bulimia Nervosa

Bulimia nervosa often begins after a restrictive diet has failed and the person moves from not eating to overeating. The overeating creates shame and fear making her vulnerable to purging. Also, a distressing life event (loss of a close relationship), a challenge (making the soccer team) or any other situation that encourages the person to think about body weight and shape as a way to achieve control, popularity and success overemphasizes external appearance over internal self worth setting up a similar struggle with diet, binging, and purging. Body weight and shape become the primary focus to help make life's discomfort feel comfortable. Three major factors are believed to interact to encourage development of bulimia.[7] The first is a biologic vulnerability or predisposition, which supports the etiologic role of genetics, physiology, the endocrine system, and biochemical mechanisms. Next are psychologic predispositions such as early negative experiences and family interactions that result in psychodevelopmental problems. Lastly, sociocultural influences are involved, such as the cultural bias toward thinness and conflicting messages of female success that seem to counterpose independence and intimate relationships.

INCIDENCE AND PREVALENCE

A conservative estimate is that 4% of girls 13 to 18 years old have symptoms of anorexia nervosa, and approximately 8% of young women between the ages of 13 and 24 have symptoms of bulimia nervosa.[1,7] Further studies are needed to verify the prevalence of these eating disorders.[8] Girls are at least nine times more likely to develop any sort of eating disorder than are boys.

The peak ages of onset for anorexia are 14 and 18, coinciding with the beginning and end of high school.[1] The average age of onset for bulimia is 23.9 years, and 86% of this population falls between 15 and 30 years.[7] Some researchers believe the incidence of eating disorders is on the rise while the age of onset continues to decline.[9]

Eating disorders have been described as a "wealthy person's disease," implying that only families from the upper income brackets are susceptible to them. Today, patients from all socioeconomic backgrounds are being diagnosed and treated, although the middle to upper income brackets are most represented.[2]

MEDICAL, PSYCHOLOGIC, AND BEHAVIORAL CHANGES

People with eating disorders are at medical risk (see Table 23-1). The complications of anorexia nervosa are primarily a result of starvation. In bulimia, it is the purging behavior that places the person at greatest medical risk. The psychologic and behavioral changes associated with anorexia nervosa are similar to those caused by starvation. In a study on the long-term effects of a semi-starvation diet on 36 male volunteers, none of the men had an eating disorder prior to joining the study, and they were healthy and psychologically well adjusted. The following parallel features were noticed with these men as it relates to starvation: 1) obsessions about food and weight, 2) unusual eating and drinking habits, 3) emotional disturbance, 4) social withdrawal, and 5) binge eating. The same features are evident in patients with food restrictive bulimia nervosa.

PROGNOSIS

Reports on the prognosis for anorexia nervosa are varied. A review of these reports finds that younger patients represent a higher percentage of recovered patients and have reduced mortality, in comparison to older patients.[10] The general consensus of outcome studies is as follows: 40% of all patients totally recover, 30% are improved, and 30% either die as a result of the illness or are chronically afflicted. Approximately 5% of all patients with anorexia nervosa will die as a result of the illness.

The prognosis for bulimia nervosa has not been investigated as thoroughly. Outcome studies show that 85% of patients recover in 5 years or less.[7] Overall, the effects of different treatment approaches on long-term outcome have not been studied. Given that a longer duration of illness is associated with a lesser chance of recovery, earlier intervention may boost the chances of a better outcome. Therefore, the earlier the intervention, the better the prognosis.[10]

Table 23-1 Medical Risks Associated with Eating Disorders

Cardiovascular Complications
- Sudden death
- Arrhythmias
- Congestive heart failure
- Cardiac tamponade

Fluid and Electrolyte Disturbances
- Dehydration
- Overhydration
- Hypokalemia
- Hypernatremia

Gastrointestinal Problems
- Esophageal tear (from vomiting)
- Delayed gastric emptying
- Constipation
- Altered bowel function

Reproductive Problems
- Amenorrhea

Musculoskeletal Problems
- Osteoporosis

Endocrine
- Hypothyroidism

Dental and Salivary Abnormalities
- Loss of tooth enamel (vomiting)

TREATMENT

The Initial Interview

The initial interview provides the dietitian with his or her first opportunity to develop a therapeutic alliance with the patient, while gathering information critical to the assessment. The interview process can be quite difficult for patients, especially those who have never shared their story. Developing an alliance with the patient is important in building a trusting relationship. Ensuring an atmosphere of acceptance during the interview allows the patient to feel comfortable and share openly.

The dietitian should start the interview with a question about the patient's understanding of why she is hospitalized or why she is seeing a dietitian. The responses may range from "my parents made me" to "I want to stop binging and purging." The response helps clarify what level of acceptance or denial the patient is in. The responses of the patient in denial might be more concrete and less revealing of self as compared to the responses from the patient acknowledging her illness and voluntarily seeking treatment.

Exhibit 23-2 lists the topics to cover during the initial interview. An initial interview takes approximately 1 hour to complete.

Exhibit 23-2 Important Topics for Initial Interviews

1. *Background information*
   - Diagnosis
   - Age and age of onset
   - Treatment history: treaters, time in treatment
   - Weight: premorbid and current
   - Height
   - Menstruation history: last menstrual period, typical cycle
2. *Food/dieting/exercise history*
   - "Usual" intake prior to diagnosis
   - Typical day's intake or food frequency or 24-hour recall
   - Safe and forbidden foods
   - Food likes and dislikes
   - Weight loss techniques employed
   - Exercise and activity level: current and premorbid
3. *Weight history*
   - History of weight conflicts
   - Weight high/low
   - Patient's goal weight
4. *Binge/purge activity*
   - Frequency of binges
   - Method of purging
   - Frequency of purging
   - Subjective report on severity of binging/purging
5. *Family history*
   - Family members at home
   - Food/dieting/exercise/weight conflicts among other members
   - Heights and weights of family members
   - History of psychiatric illness, especially affective illness
   - General health status of family members
6. *Social history*
   - School and grade
   - Overall school performance: current and premorbid
   - Peer interactions: current and premorbid
7. *Physical status*
   - General observations: hair loss; dry, flaking skin; swollen parotid glands; calluses on knuckles
   - Reported clinical effects of starvation: decreased tolerance to cold, poor sleep habits, increased moodiness
8. *Medication and substance use*
   - Prescription medication
   - Over-the-counter medication, including laxatives, diuretics, and vomiting agents such as ipecac
   - Alcohol use
   - Other substance use

Exhibit 23-3 Additional Data Needed for the Initial Assessment

---

1. Growth data
- Frame size
- Height
- Weight
- Weight-for-length (when appropriate for age)
- Ideal body weight range for height (using National Center for Health Statistics tables or the Metropolitan Life Insurance tables)
- Percent ideal body weight for height

2. Energy
- Basal energy expenditure for ideal body weight for height
- Requirement for weight gain (BEE × 1.5)

3. Body composition data (if available)
- Triceps skinfold measurement
- Electrical impedance calibration

4. Biochemical data with nutritional implications
- Electrolyte balance
- Calcium status (bone scan when indicated)
- Lipid status (cholesterol level elevated with starvation)
- Phosphorus status
- Thiamin status
- Urine specific gravity

Additional Assessment

In addition to the information gathered from the initial interview, a nutrition assessment should include at a minimum the data listed in Exhibit 23-3.

Treatment Goals and the Counseling Relationship

At the end of the interview, it is important to clarify goals of the treatment and what type of therapeutic relationship the dietitian will have with the patient. Goals are generally cognitive-behavioral in nature, addressing the issues of food and weight and how one thinks about these two concerns. The dietitian treating eating-disordered patients will find that helping patients meet these goals requires a degree of psychotherapeutic sophistication. Eating-disordered patients have underlying psychological disturbances that can range from mild depression to severe personality disorders.[11] Finding ways of developing the necessary counseling skills is challenging but necessary to treat patients with eating disorders. The nutrition counseling model for dietitians provides useful guidelines for developing a treatment strategy for long-term counseling relationships.[12] Counseling skills can also be developed through additional coursework and supervision from a psychologist, psychiatrist, or social worker.

The success of outpatient nutrition counseling depends in part on establishing a long-term collaborative relationship between the patient and the dietitian.[3] However, some patients will require hospitalization. The decision to hospitalize a patient is based on team findings of signs of medical and/or psychologic crisis. These may include a drop in weight (e.g., >40% loss of premorbid weight or >30% loss within a 3-month period), severe metabolic disturbances, severe depression or suicide risk, severe binging and purging, psychosis, or family crisis.[2,13]

There are no universally accepted formulas the dietitian can apply to set goals. The treatment goals for the anorexic patient weighing 70% ideal body weight (IBW) will be different from those for a recovering patient maintaining 90% IBW. The bulimic patient binging and purging 10 times a day will need treatment goals different from those of the patient binging and purging 2 times a week. Understanding where the patient is in terms of the recovery process (e.g., is there complete denial of illness? sincere interest in getting help?) helps clarify where treatment should start. It is generally helpful to frame goals in terms of small incremental changes that are realistically achievable for a given patient. Unrealistic expectations and all-or-nothing thinking may result in failure to achieve treatment goals and patient discouragement.[14]

One important initial goal is to determine the rules concerning communication between the clinician, the patient under 18, and her parent(s). As parents are responsible for the health of their child, they need to be privy to certain information. Deciding what information from the patient gets shared with parents needs to be determined at the onset of treatment. Without these guidelines, it may be difficult to establish an alliance, which depends on trust and confidentiality. Consulting with other team members may help in establishing these guidelines.

Treatment Strategies

This section will include treatment options for patients needing weight rehabilitation (anorexia nervosa and low-weight bulimia) and management of the binge/purge cycle (bulimia nervosa). Three key areas of nutrition intervention will be discussed:

1. weight status and nutritional rehabilitation
2. normalization of eating patterns
3. education: nutrition and psychoeducation

A case study for anorexia nervosa and bulimia nervosa will be reviewed to illustrate a nutrition intervention.

Weight Status and Nutritional Rehabilitation

The physical, behavioral and psychologic effects of starvation on humans were studied by Keys et al. in the 1940s.[15] It was determined that weight loss and malnutrition due to food deprivation promote unusual eating behaviors (prolongation of meals, increased use of seasonings and spices, secretive and ritualized eating, food hoarding and obsessive thoughts).[16] Additional effects secondary to starvation were social isolation, impaired concentration, apathy, and mood swings.[16] Improving nutritional status reversed these consequences, although for some binging behavior erupted.[15] Nutrition intervention to relieve the effects of starvation is accepted as a necessary prerequisite to successful psychiatric intervention in the anorexia nervosa patient.[16]

Determining the calorie amount necessary for weight gain in patients with anorexia nervosa is a primary concern of the dietitian. Great variation is found in this population when the caloric cost of weight gain is quantified. In a study conducted by Dempsey, the excess calories necessary to gain 1 kg of body weight ranged from 5569 to 15,619 kcal; the mean was 9768 kcal/week.[17] In a different study, the average energy cost of weight gain was 5.3 kcal/g.[18] Another study found 34 cal/lb of current body weight is a beginning estimate for weight restoration in anorexia nervosa.[19] It is important to note that long-term weight changes during nutritional rehabilitation in anorexia nervosa are meaningful indicators of caloric balance, but short-term weight changes (daily, weekly) are not.[17] On any given day, body weight in young women can fluctuate by 0.5 to 1 kg.[20] When a patient first starts on a nutritional rehabilitation program, rapid weight gain can occur. This is a result of increased retention of water through expansion of the extracellular compartment, retention of electrolytes, and restoration of liver and muscle glycogen.[21]

Studies looking at the metabolic effects of the "refeeding" process show that physiologic disturbances contribute to the maintenance of weight after patients complete a weight restoration program.[22] Kaye looked at weight gain in nonbulimic and bulimic anorexics. Nonbulimic anorexics require 30% to 50% more calories than bulimic anorexics to maintain a stable weight. This finding was noted at low weights and at intervals after weight restoration.[22]

Body composition changes after weight restoration were studied in twelve anorexic patients. During the refeeding period, one group had 10% total dietary protein and the other group had 20% total dietary protein. For both groups, weight gain occurred, and two thirds of the weight gain was lean tissue.[18]

Normalization of Eating Patterns: Refeeding and Rethinking

The refeeding period often marks the beginning of normalized eating patterns. Patients with severe cachexia and electrolyte imbalance may receive peripheral hyperalimentation or nasogastric tube feedings.[3,19] Because of the increased medical and psychologic risks associated with these refeeding methods, they are recommended for acute interventions only. Refeeding with food is the treatment of choice. Meals should consist of adequate amounts of carbohydrate, protein, and fat. The dietitian helps the patient select acceptable food, thereby starting the process of relearning how to eat normally. A critical balance exists between allowing gradual, small changes in a patient with very restricted eating patterns and ensuring adequate nutrition and weight gain. Reminding the patient that the treatment team does not want her fat and that her weight gain is not out of control but reflective of physiologic changes may soothe fears about adding new foods and increasing the amount of calories consumed.

Specific principles for nutritional intervention for anorexia nervosa were developed by Rock:[16]

1. Diets should be nutritionally balanced but may be varied according to patient preferences (e.g., vegetarian).
2. Provide multivitamin-mineral supplements at Recommended Dietary Allowance (RDA) levels.
3. Provide dietary fiber from grain sources to enhance elimination.
4. Whenever possible, permit small frequent feedings, to reduce sensation of bloating.
5. Liquid supplements may be used when the patient cannot achieve goal intake via foods.
6. Satiety sensations may be reduced by providing cold or room temperature food.
7. Reduce caffeine intake if appropriate.

Bulimic patients of normal or excess body weight often present with a history of attempts to control weight through severe caloric restriction.[16] Foods become categorized as "good" and "bad" or "safe" and "forbidden." Low-fat foods (e.g., fruits, vegetables, rice cakes, nonfat yogurt) become the staples at meals, leading to decreased satiety at meals and an increased vulnerability to binging. Food intake patterns are usually quite rigid, and the patient often believes this seemingly controlled intake is healthy and the only way to eat to lose or maintain weight. These unrealistic diet restrictions need to be met with clear guidelines that promote satiety, thereby reducing the risk of bingeing. Specific recommendations for nutrition intervention are as follows:[16]

1. Provide well-balanced diets and meals, to increase satiety.
2. Increase the variety of foods consumed.
3. Include warm foods rather than cold or room temperature foods, to increase meal satiety.
4. Choose high-fiber foods to increase satiety and aid in digestion.
5. Plan meals and snacks.

Additionally, other areas need to be addressed:

1. attitudes about "good" and "bad" choices
2. anticipating difficult eating situations
3. reinforcing health as the goal, not weight

Self-monitoring tools can be helpful in revealing to the patient her food beliefs and eating patterns. Through recognition of certain harmful or self-defeating behaviors, choices can be made about finding alternative healthy behaviors. Food records often include

1. type and amount of food eaten
2. time of day
3. degree of hunger and fullness
4. binge/purge activity
5. affective changes (feelings, thoughts, concerns)

Reviewing these records with a patient can help quantify progress, identify problems, and help patients gain back some control over their eating patterns.[3]

Education: Psychoeducation and Nutrition

It is commonly believed that patients with eating disorders know more about nutrition than the average person. Although this may be true, the manner in which they practice their knowledge is not keeping them healthy. Nutrition education is a critical component of treatment. Using nutrition visits as the forum in which to discuss weight and food frees up the therapy sessions to focus on the psychologic aspects of the illness.

For the hospitalized patient, specialized nutrition classes may be implemented to address concerns. Group classes create an environment in which patients may feel freer to discuss difficult emotional issues related to weight and food issues, and information regarding nutrition facts and fallacies may be efficiently imparted. The dietitian should instruct outpatients in the same information in individual counseling sessions. Topics to cover in such a group include the following:

1. sociocultural influences on weight and body image
2. the effects of dieting
3. facts about metabolism, weight gain, and body composition
4. food and eating beliefs
5. body image

The psychoeducational component of patient education expands on nutrition topics by including how cultural factors and emotional responses to weight regulation and dieting affect one's thinking about self and self-worth. An excellent review of psychoeducational factors can be found in Garfinkle and Garner's *Handbook of Psychotherapy for Anorexia Nervosa and Bulimia.*[2] A more specific reference for dietitians is Reiff and Reiff's *Eating Disorders: Nutrition Therapy in the Recovery Process.*[23]

CASE STUDY: ANOREXIA NERVOSA

Sarah is a 153/12-year-old female presenting with rapid weight loss over the past 4 months. She meets all criteria for anorexia nervosa. She denies any laxative or diuretic use or vomiting. This is her second hospitalization. Nutrition intervention during the first hospitalization consisted of 1500 kcal of liquid supplement per day and bed rest. When discharged, she continued to lose weight. At the time of admission, Sarah had not received any psychiatric intervention.

When Sarah is asked about her understanding of why she is in the hospital, she acknowledges it is because of her low weight, although she sees nothing wrong with it: "I know I would look and feel better if I could lose more weight." Four months earlier, a girl on the track team introduced Sarah to the benefits of eating a low-fat diet. Sarah took the information to heart and vehemently began a rigid diet of "no fat." Her usual weight was 122 lb (height 5 feet, 4 inches), and she had never before gone on a diet to lose weight. She could not remember growing up feeling fat but did remember her father commenting after her returning from a physical, "How could you weigh that much?"

Sarah's current daily intake is less than 1000 kcal/d. During the day, she runs 4 miles, completes a 1-hour aerobic tape, and walks whenever she gets the chance. She will not allow herself any fat and eats the same thing every day. Before the anorexia, Sarah was interested in every type of food and was known to "chow sometimes" (eat large quantities of food).

Sarah's last menstrual period was 3 months ago at a weight of 109 pounds. She reports an increased intolerance to cold, difficulty sleeping, irritability, and some hair loss. Sarah's parents want her to get it together and get better: "She's so smart, why can't she beat this thing?" "You will be missing out on so much if you stay sick." Neither parent can understand why their daughter is starving herself.

Clinical Parameters

- Height: 5 feet, 4 inches
- Weight: 96 lb
- Frame size: medium
- Ideal body weight range: 113 to 128 lb[24]

- Premorbid body weight: 122 lb
- Calories required for weight gain: 96×34 cal/lb = 3264 and/or basal energy expenditure (BEE) $\times$ 1.5 and take the average kcal/d as a goal

Recommendations for Refeeding

Start calorie level at 1250 kcal/d (composition: calories 55%, protein 20%, fat 25%). Provide a multivitamin with minerals. Increase calories in a stepwise fashion up to caloric requirement for weight restoration, to within 5% of ideal body weight range for height. For each day weight does not increase 0.2 kg/d, 500-calorie supplements will be given. The weekly weight gain goal is 1.2 kg; if it is not reached, the daily calorie ration is to increase by 500 cal.

Meals should consist of a variety of foods from all food groups. Develop meal plans reflecting a variety of calorie levels, use American Diabetic Association exchange lists to develop meals. Have the patient choose meals, emphasizing a variety of foods; limit patient dislikes to three foods. Time parameters must be set for completion of meals; for example, 30 minutes per meal. When calories are increased, the dietitian may choose to add snacks (250 or 500-cal snacks at 10 AM, 2 PM, or 8 PM).

Review nutritional guidelines for addressing delayed gastric emptying: provide dietary fiber from grain sources and small frequent feedings when possible. Providing cold or room temperature foods may decrease satiety sensations.

Activity

Exercise should be limited; specific recommendations need to be made. For example, the patient may be allowed to stretch 30 min/d for first week, add 30-minute walks per day during second week (depending on weight gain and mental status), and increase exercise up to a healthy "normalized" level with progress in treatment.

Education

See recommendations in "Education: Nutrition and Psychoeducation" section.

Family Work

Meetings with the family members, especially parents, are an important component of treatment. These meetings can be a place to discuss anorexia nervosa, the varied effects of starvation, and calorie and nutrient needs. Meetings with parents should be arranged to review changes, progress with treatment, and plans for outpatient work. Parents need to understand the food plan even though they are not often responsible for monitoring intake. The medical doctor should be responsible for patient's weight status, informing the dietitian of the need for increasing caloric intake when there is weight loss. Ultimately, patients need to be responsible for their own food intake and their overall health.

CASE STUDY: BULIMIA NERVOSA

Jen is a 146/12-year-old presenting with bulimia nervosa. The binging and purging started 1 year ago and then ended for 3 months. Jen was symptom-free until the fall, when she started at a new school and her parents had separated. She started dieting and lost 15% of her usual weight. At this point, her mother took her to a therapist, and she stopped dieting. The bulimic symptoms returned when she started gaining back the weight she had lost.

Jen has never been hospitalized. Jen is the youngest of three children; she has two sisters aged 19 and 21. Her oldest sister is somewhat overweight, and the middle sister exercises excessively and has shown signs of bulimia. Jen's father is a successful businessman and has always been a bit overweight but relies on exercise to keep in shape. Jen's mother is starting her own food business, has a "perfect" body, and follows a low-fat meal plan to keep her shape.

Jen's peer relations have varied over the years due to school changes. She talks about being lonely for friends but at the same time puts down the kids at her school. Jen is an average student, maintaining a high C average. Her parents deemphasize grades and emphasize interpersonal relationships.

Although part of her wants to stop the bulimia, she believes the only way she can control her weight is to throw up. Her daily intake is as follows: no breakfast, no lunch, snack food before tennis practice, a big dinner, and bingeing all night. Jen throws up once before she goes to bed. Bulimia is her biggest secret, and at one point she said, "If you only knew how bad it was."

Clinical Parameters

- height: 5 feet, 7 inches
- weight: 143 lb
- frame size: medium
- ideal body weight range: 125 to 140 lb
- percent body fat: 17% (quite muscular due to sports and inherited body type from father)
- BEE: 1386 requirement; for maintenance, multiply BEE × 30% to get 1800 cal

Treatment Plan

- weekly visits with a psychiatrist
- weekly visits with dietitian
- periodic meetings with parents and dietitian
- family therapy
- medical follow-up

Recommendations for Normalization of Eating Patterns

Establish patient goals for "normal" eating. Set the calorie level for weight maintenance, to reduce the risk of increased hunger and increased vulnerability to binging and to model weight control. Develop a meal plan with the following in mind: The patient should develop a list of "safe" and "forbidden" foods. Most often, the "safe" foods are not adequate for meeting nutrient needs and creating satiety, therefore, (1) find out why certain foods are forbidden and dispel any myths and (2) slowly negotiate adding foods from forbidden list to meal plan. Ensure patient eats at least 3 regular meals per day. Consider implementing small, frequent meals, if that would help. Use food records to monitor eating patterns and follow changes. (However, for a variety of reasons some patients are not able to complete food records; therapeutically, it is best to work with what the patient feels comfortable doing.) Help the patient recognize internal and external cues for binging and purging behavior and develop alternative behaviors when cues occur.

Activity

Develop exercise guidelines that support moderation and are achievable.

Education

The patient needs to learn how to eat in a way that promotes emotional and physical health. Dispelling diet myths, eliminating food rules, and letting go of value judgments associated with eating or not eating certain foods are crucial for recovery. Strict meal plans and weekly weigh-ins are counterproductive for this process. The patient needs to be reminded people are not good or bad because of the food they eat. Food has such power over the patient that it becomes the barometer for her self-esteem. Helping the patient feel she has choices and can make them gives her back a sense of control. (See recommendations in "Education: Nutrition and Psychoeducation" section.)

REFERENCES

1. Levine M. *How Schools Can Combat Student Eating Disorders: Anorexia Nervosa and Bulimia.* Washington, DC: National Education Association; 1987.

2. Garner D, Garfinkle P. *Handbook of Psychotherapy for Anorexia Nervosa and Bulimia Nervosa.* New York: Guilford Press; 1985.

3. American Dietetic Association. Position of the American Dietetic Association: nutrition intervention in the treatment of anorexia nervosa and bulimia nervosa. *J Am Diet Assoc.* 1988;88:68.

4. Mellin L. Responding to disordered eating in children and adolescents. *Nutrition News.* 1988;Summer:5–6.

5. Satter E. *How to Get Your Kid to Eat . . . But Not Too Much.* Palo Alto, Calif: Bull Publishing; 1987:341–343.

6. American Psychiatric Association. *Diagnostic and Statistical Manual of Mental Disorders.* 3rd ed, rev. Washington, DC: American Psychiatric Association; 1980.

7. Johnson C, Connors M. *The Etiology and Treatment of Bulimia Nervosa.* New York: Basic Books; 1987.

8. Clark K, Parr R, Castelli W. *Evaluation and Management of Eating Disorders, Anorexia, Bulimia and Obesity.* Chicago, Ill: Life Enhancement Publications; 1988:189–190.

9. Casper RC. The pathophysiology of anorexia nervosa and bulimia nervosa. *Ann Rev Nutr.* 1986;6:299–316.

10. Garfinkle P, Garner D. *Anorexia Nervosa: A Multidimensional Perspective.* New York: Brunner Mazel; 1982.

11. Swift W, Andrews D, Barklage NE. The relationship between affective disorder and eating disorders: a review of the literature. *Am J Psychiatry.* 1989;149:290–299.

12. Snetselaar L. *Nutrition Counseling Skills.* 2nd ed. Gaithersburg, Md: Aspen Publishers; 1989.

13. Herzog D, Copeland P. Eating disorders. *New Engl J Med.* 1985;313:295–303.

14. Reiff D. Nutrition therapy in the treatment of anorexia nervosa and bulimia nervosa. Presented at Anorexia/Bulimia Nervosa Symposium on Theories of Treatment, February 1984; Bergen, Norway.

15. Keys A, Brozek J, Henshel A, et al. *The Biology of Human Starvation.* Minneapolis, Minn: University of Minnesota Press; 1950.

16. Rock CL, Yager J. Nutrition and eating disorders: a primer for clinicians. *Int J Eating Disord.* 1987;6:267–279.

17. Dempsey DT, Crosby LO, Pertschuk MJ, et al. Weight gain and nutritional efficacy in anorexia nervosa. *Am J Clin Nutr.* 1984;39:236–242.

18. Forbes GB, Kriepe AE, Lipinski BA. Body composition changes during recovery from anorexia nervosa: comparison of two dietary regimens. *Am J Clin Nutr.* 1984;40:1137–1145.

19. Walker J, Roberts SL, Halmik, et al. Caloric requirements for weight gain in anorexia nervosa. *Am J Clin Nutr.* 1979;32:1396–1400.

20. Robinson M, Watson P. Day-to-day variations in body weight of young women. *Br J Nutr.* 1965;19:225–235.

21. Huse D, Lucas A. Dietary treatment of anorexia nervosa. *Am J Clin Nutr.* 1983;40:687–690.

22. Kaye WH, Gwirtsman HE, Obarzanek E, et al. Caloric intake necessary for weight maintenance in anorexia nervosa: nonbulemics require greater caloric intake than bulemics. *Am J Clin Nutr.* 1986;44:435–443.

23. Reiff DW, Reiff K Lampson. *Eating Disorders: Nutrition Therapy in the Recovery Process.* Gaithersburg, Md: Aspen Publishers; 1992.
24. National Dairy Council. *YOU: A Guide to Food, Exercise, and Nutrition for Teens.* Rosemont, Ill: National Dairy Council; 1987.

RECOMMENDED READINGS

American Dietetic Association. Nutrition intervention in the treatment of anorexia nervosa and bulimia nervosa—technical support paper. *J Am Diet Assoc.* 1988;88:69–71.

Bo-Linn GW, Santa CA, Morawski SG, et al. Purging and calorie absorption in bulimic patients and normal women. *Ann Intern Med.* 1983;99:14–17.

Boskind-White M, White WC. *Bulimarexia—The Binge/Purge Cycle.* New York, NY: WW Norton; 1983.

Brownell KD, Foreyt JP. *Handbook of Eating Disorders—Physiology, Psychology and Treatment of Obesity, Anorexia and Bulimia.* New York, NY: Basic Books; 1986.

Bruch H. *Eating Disorders: Obesity, Anorexia Nervosa and the Person Within.* New York: Basic Books; 1973.

Fernstrom MH, Epstein LH, Spiker DG, et al. Resting metabolic rate is reduced in patients treated with antidepressants. *Biol Psychiatry.* 1985;20:688.

Frisch RE. Food intake, fatness, and reproductive ability in anorexia nervosa. In: Vigersky R, ed. *Anorexia Nervosa.* New York, NY: Raven Press; 1977:149–161.

Frisch RE, McArthur JW. Menstrual cycles. Fatness as a determinant of minimum weight for height necessary for their maintenance or onset. *Science.* 1974;85:949–951.

Gwirtsman HE, Kaye WH, Curtis SR, et al. Energy intake and dietary macronutrient content in women with anorexia nervosa and normal volunteers. *J Am Diet Assoc.* 1989;88:54–57.

Halmi KA. Treatment of anorexia nervosa. *J Adolesc Health Care.* 1983;4:47–50.

Health and Public Policy Committee, American College of Physicians. Position paper on eating disorders: anorexia nervosa and bulimia. *Ann Intern Med.* 1986;105:5.

Kagan DM, Squires RL. Dieting, compulsive eating and feelings of failure among adolescents. *Int J Eating Disord.* 1983;3:15–26.

Keesey RE. A set-point analysis of the regulation of body weight. In: Stunkard AJ, ed. *Obesity.* Philadelphia, Pa: WB Saunders; 1980:144–165.

Krey SH, Palmer K, Porcelli KA. Eating disorders: the clinical dietitian's changing role. *J Am Diet Assoc.* 1989;88:41–43.

Lacey JH, Gibson E. Does laxative abuse control body weight? A comparative study of purging and vomiting bulimics. *Hum Nutr Appl Nutr.* 1985;39A:36–42.

Lowe M. The role of anticipated deprivation in overeating. *Addict Behav.* 1982;7:103–112.

Mitchell JE, Pyle RL, Eckert ED, et al. Electrolyte and other physiological abnormalities in patients with bulimia. *Psychiatr Med.* 1983;13:273–278.

Mitchell JE, Boutacoff LI. Laxative abuse complicating bulimia: medical and treatment implications. *Int J Eating Disord.* 1986;5:323–334.

National Center for Health Statistics. *Height and Weight of Youths 12–17 Years.* 1973.

O'Connor M, Touyz S, Beaumont P. Nutritional management and dietary counseling in bulimia nervosa: some preliminary observations. *Int J Eating Disord.* 1988;7:657–662.

Omizo SA. Anorexia nervosa: psychological considerations for nutritional counseling. *J Am Diet Assoc.* 1988;88:49–51.

Peterson DS, Barkmeier WW. Oral signs of frequent vomiting in anorexia. *Am Fam Physician.* 1983;27:199–200.

Reinke J. Counseling techniques: nutrition intervention. In: Clark KL, Parr RB, Castelli WP, eds. *Evaluation and Management of Eating Disorders.* Champaign, Ill: Life Enhancement Publications; 1988.

Rigotti NA, Nussbaum SR, Herzog DB, et al. Osteoporosis in women with anorexia nervosa. *N Engl J Med.* 1984;311:1601–1606.

Russell GFM, Mezey AG. An analysis of weight gain in patients with anorexia nervosa treated with high calorie diets. *Clin Sci.* 1962;23:449–461.

Schwartz DM, Thompson MG, Johnson CL. Anorexia nervosa and bulimia: the socio-cultural context. *Int J Eating Disord.* 1986;1:20–36.

Sedlet KL, Ireton-Jones CS. Energy expenditure and the abnormal eating pattern of a bulimic: a case report. *J Am Diet Assoc.* 1989;88:74–77.

Taylor ME, Lawrence RW, Allen KG. Nutritional assessment of college age women with bulimia. *Int J Eating Disord.* 1986;5:59–71.

Warren MP, Vande Wiele RL. Clinical and metabolic features of anorexia nervosa. *Am J Obstet Gynecol.* 1973;117:435–449.

Worsley A. Teenagers' perceptions of fat and slim people. *Int J Obesity.* 1981b;5:15–24.

ASSOCIATIONS

National Anorexic Aid Society
5796 Karl Road
Columbus, OH 43229
(614) 436-1112

National Association of Anorexia Nervosa and Associated Disorders
Box 7
Highland Park, IL 60035
(312) 831-3438

Anorexia Bulimia Care
PO Box 213
Lincoln Center, MA 01773
(617) 259-9767

American Anorexia/Bulimia Association
133 Cedar Lane
Teaneck, NJ 07666
(201) 836-1800

Anorexia Nervosa and Related Eating Disorders, Inc.
PO Box 5102
Eugene, OR 97405
(503) 344-1144

Maryland Anorexia Nervosa and Bulimia Nervosa Association
Sheppard Pratt Hospital
6501 North Charles Street
Baltimore, MD 21204
(410) 938-3000, ext. 2199

EDUCATIONAL MATERIALS

Eating Disorders: Nutrition Therapy in Recovery Process, Dan W. Reiff, MPH, RD, and Kathleen Kim Lampson Reiff, PhD, 1992; Aspen Publishers, Inc., Gaithersburg, MD.

A Five Day Lesson Plan Book on Eating Disorders: Grades 7–12, Michael Levine, PhD, Laura Hill, PhD, 1991; The National Anorexic Aid Society of Harding Hospital, Columbus, OH.

How Schools Can Help Combat Student Eating Disorders: Anorexia Nervosa and Bulimia. Michael P. Levine, PhD, 1987; National Education Association, Washington, DC.

Index

A

Abetalipoproteinemia, 342
  acute illness nutrition support, 357
  medication–nutrient interaction, 357
  nutrition assessment parameters, 357
Acquired immunodeficiency syndrome.
  See AIDS
Acrodermatitis enteropathica, 343
  acute illness nutrition support, 358
  medication–nutrient interaction, 358
  nutrition assessment parameters, 358
  recommended nutrient intake, 350
Activity category, energy expenditure, 44
Activity energy expenditure, 34, 39
Acute diarrhea, 137–138
  therapeutic diet, 463–464
Acute infantile diarrhea, 137–138
Adipose tissue, growth, 9
Adolescent
  body image, 151
  diabetes, 495–496
    alcohol, 495–496
    weight control, 495
  food intake, 156–157
  growth, 6–7
  obesity, 563
  substance abuse, 164–165
  vegetarianism
    iron, 178, 182
    risks, 178, 182

Adolescent pregnancy
  diet, 163–164
  nutritional status, 163
  risk factors, 163–164
Adverse food reaction
  categories, 206, 207
  differential diagnosis, 209–210
  incidence, 206–208
Age, exercise, 188–191
AIDS
  clinical manifestations, 388–389
  definitions for surveillance of children,
    385, 386
  diagnosis, 385–387
  energy requirements, 392
  enzyme-linked immunosorbent assay,
    385
  epidemiology, 387
  formula selection, 392–397
  hypometabolism, 391
  infection control, 389–390
  meal selection, 392–397
  nutritional management, 390–392
  polymerase chain reaction, 385–387
  protein-calorie malnutrition, 391
  resting energy expenditure, 391
  risk factors, 388
Albumin, 61–64
Alcohol, substance abuse, 164–165
Amenorrhea, sports nutrition, 201
Amino acid. *See also* Specific type
  burned patient, 545